THE FORM.
IDENTIFICATI(
CUSTOMARY INT:
IN INTER:
INVESTM...

CW00816433

Rules of customary international law provide basic legal protections to foreign investors doing business abroad. These rules remain of fundamental importance today despite the growing number of investment treaties containing substantive investment protection. In this book Patrick Dumberry provides a comprehensive analysis of the phenomenon of custom in the field of international investment law. He analyses two fundamental questions: how customary rules are created in this field and how they can be identified. The book examines the types of manifestation of State practice which should be considered as relevant evidence for the formation of customary rules and to what extent they are different from those existing under general international law. The book also analyses the concept of States' *opinio juris* in investment arbitration. Offering guidance to actors called upon to apply customary rules in concrete cases, this book will be of significant importance to those involved in investment arbitration.

PATRICK DUMBERRY is an associate professor at the University of Ottawa, Faculty of Law (Civil Law Section), Canada.

Established in 1946, this series produces high quality scholarship in the fields of public and private international law and comparative law. Although these are distinct legal sub-disciplines, developments since 1946 confirm their interrelations.

Comparative law is increasingly used as a tool in the making of law at national, regional and international levels. Private international law is now often affected by international conventions, and the issues faced by classical conflict rules are frequently dealt with by substantive harmonization of law under international auspices. Mixed international arbitrations, especially those involving state economic activity, raise mixed questions of public and private international law, while in many fields (such as the protection of human rights and democratic standards, investment guarantees and international criminal law) international and national systems interact. National constitutional arrangements relating to 'foreign affairs', and to the implementation of international norms, are a focus of attention.

The series welcomes works of a theoretical or interdisciplinary character, and those focusing on the new approaches to international or comparative law or conflicts of law. Studies of particular institutions or problems are equally welcome, as are translations of the best work published in other languages.

General Editors

James Crawford SC FBA
Whewell Professor of International Law, Faculty of Law,
University of Cambridge

John S. Bell FBA
Professor of Law, Faculty of Law, University of Cambridge

A list of books in the series can be found at the end of this volume.

THE FORMATION AND IDENTIFICATION OF RULES OF CUSTOMARY INTERNATIONAL LAW IN INTERNATIONAL INVESTMENT LAW

PATRICK DUMBERRY

Associate professor at the University of Ottawa
Faculty of Law (Civil Law Section), Canada

CAMBRIDGE
UNIVERSITY PRESS

CAMBRIDGE
UNIVERSITY PRESS

University Printing House, Cambridge CB2 8BS, United Kingdom

One Liberty Plaza, 20th Floor, New York, NY 10006, USA

477 Williamstown Road, Port Melbourne, VIC 3207, Australia

314-321, 3rd Floor, Plot 3, Splendor Forum, Jasola District Centre, New Delhi - 110025, India

79 Anson Road, #06-04/06, Singapore 079906

Cambridge University Press is part of the University of Cambridge.

It furthers the University's mission by disseminating knowledge in the pursuit of education, learning and research at the highest international levels of excellence.

www.cambridge.org
Information on this title: www.cambridge.org/9781316503072

© Patrick Dumberry 2016

First published 2016
First paperback edition 2018

A catalogue record for this publication is available from the British Library

Library of Congress Cataloging in Publication data
Dumberry, Patrick, author.
The formation and identification of rules of customary international law in international investment law / Patrick Dumberry.
Cambridge, United Kingdom : Cambridge University Press, 2016. | Series: Cambridge studies in international and comparative law ; 119 | Includes bibliographical references and index.
LCCN 2015049712 | ISBN 9781107138520 (hardback)
LCSH: Investments, Foreign – Law and legislation. | Customary law, International |
BISAC: LAW / Arbitration, Negotiation, Mediation.
LCC K3830 .D86 2016 | DDC 346/.092–dc23
LC record available at http://lccn.loc.gov/2015049712

ISBN 978-1-107-13852-0 Hardback
ISBN 978-1-316-50307-2 Paperback

À mes enfants Ophélie et Florent

CONTENTS

FOREWORD

MICHAEL WOOD[1]

Customary international law remains the bedrock of international law. Its merits and demerits as compared with that other great source of the law, treaties, have often been discussed. It used to be thought in some quarters that custom would cease to be important as treaties multiplied. In recent years, a number of writers have expressed the view that custom had become irrelevant in modern international law[2] But that was never a realistic view. As noted by Dinstein, 'every once in a while, custom has a tendency to leap to the fore even within special fields of international law where it seemed to have ceded primacy to treaties long ago, thereby reminding the international legal profession that it is not just barely alive but is still pulsating with some intensity'.[3] Even when whole areas of international law are codified in widely accepted international conventions, customary international law continues to play a vital role, as can be seen from the recent case-law of international and national courts and tribunals.

This book addresses the question of customary international law in the specific field of international investment law, and does so in a largely practical manner. It should be of great assistance to all those practising in this field, but it is equally of interest to those looking more generally at the formation and identification of rules of customary international law. As noted by d'Aspremont, 'the scholarship on international investment law has remained bereft of theoretical reflection on the sources of investment

---

[1] Barrister, 20 Essex Street, London; Member of the International Law Commission and Special Rapporteur for the topic 'Identification of customary international law'.

[2] See, inter alia: N.C.H. Dunbar, 'The Myth of Customary International Law', Australian YIL 8 (1983), p. 1; J. Patrick Kelly, 'The Twilight of Customary International Law', Virginia JIL 40 (2000), p. 449; J.L. Goldsmith and E.A. Posner, The Limits of International Law (Oxford: Oxford University Press, 2005).

[3] Y. Dinstein, 'The Interaction between Customary International Law and Treaties', Rec. des cours 322 (2006), p. 262.

law'.[4] He says that 'international investment law has now reached a stage of its development where the doctrine of sources can no longer be left in limbo and needs to be critically explored' in order for this field of law to 'rest on solid bases in terms of sources'.[5] This is the aim of the present book.

One of the most notable features of international investment law is the overwhelming importance of treaties. Thus, more than 3,000 treaties containing provisions on investment protection have been signed by States. Treaties have become the dominant source of international law in this area. Why should one bother then with custom in this context? In my First Report as the International Law Commission (ILC) Special Rapporteur, I explained the basic reasons why custom remains important in contemporary international law:

> Even in fields where there are widely accepted 'codification' conventions, the rules of customary international law continue to govern questions not regulated by the conventions and continue to apply in relations with and between non-parties. Rules of customary international law may also fill possible lacunae in treaties, and assist in their interpretation.[6]

The present book shows that this is the case in the field of international investment law. Customary rules remain important in contemporary international investment law despite the fact that existing investment protection rules are now overwhelmingly found in bilateral and multi-lateral treaties.

This book concerns the *formation* and the *identification* of rules of customary international law. The International Law Association (ILA) examined this question in 2000 (focusing on the issue of formation), in the context of public international law as a whole.[7] More recently, the ILC

---

[4] Jean d'Aspremont, 'International Customary Investment Law: Story of a Paradox', in T. Gazzini and E. de Brabandere (eds.), *International Investment Law: The Sources of Rights and Obligations* (Leiden; Boston: Martinus Nijhoff, 2012), p. 8.

[5] *Id.*

[6] International Law Commission, 'First Report on Formation and Evidence of Customary International Law', by Michael Wood, Special Rapporteur, Sixty-fifth session, Geneva, 6 May-7 June and 8 July-9 August 2013, UN doc. A/CN.4/663, 17 May 2013, p. 20 [hereinafter referred to as ILC, First Report, 2013], p. 15. See also O. Sender and M. Wood, 'Custom's Bright Future: The Continuing Importance of Customary International Law', in C.A. Bradley (ed.), *Custom's Future: International Law in a Changing World* (Cambridge University Press, forthcoming 2016).

[7] International Law Association, 'Statement of Principles Applicable to the Formation of General Customary International Law', Final Report of the Committee on the Formation of Customary Law, Conference Report London (2000).

decided in 2012 to include the topic 'Formation and Evidence of Customary International Law' in its programme of work.[8] As ILC Special Rapporteur, I have so far produced three reports (2013, 2014 and 2015).[9] These have been debated by the Commission, and the Drafting Committee has provisionally adopted a set of 16 draft conclusions.[10] It is expected that the Commission itself will consider these draft conclusions, together with commentaries, at its session in 2016.

Why is it important to study the methodology for the determination of rules of customary international law? In the First Report, I noted that 'in order to determine whether a rule of customary international law exists, it is necessary to consider both the requirements for the formation of a rule of customary international law, and the types of evidence that establish the fulfilment of those requirements'.[11] In other words, the basic questions at the centre of any analysis regarding the existence of a customary norm are (1) how these rules are actually created and (2) how they can be identified. The present book provides a first attempt to answer these fundamental questions in the field of investment arbitration. The book will provide all those involved in investor-State arbitration (arbitrators, investors, States) guidance for assessing the validity and soundness of claims regarding the customary status of any given rule.

This book is in many ways complementary to the work of the ILC on the topic 'Identification of customary international law'. In the Second Report, I raised the question whether 'there are different approaches to the formation and evidence of customary international law in different

---

[8] The Commission later changed the title of the topic to 'Identification of customary international law', since it was felt that to enter directly into questions of formation would lead the Commission into areas beyond the intended scope of the topic, which is what Article 38.1(*d*) of the ICJ Statute refers to as the 'determination' of rules of law.

[9] ILC, First Report, 2013; International Law Commission, 'Second Report on Identification of Customary International Law', by Michael Wood, Special Rapporteur, Sixty-sixth session, Geneva, 5 May–6 June and 7 July–8 August 2014, A/CN.4/672, p. 13 [hereinafter referred to as ILC, Second Report, 2014]; International Law Commission, 'Third Report on Identification of Customary International Law', by Michael Wood, Special Rapporteur, Sixty-seventh session, Geneva, 4 May-5 June and 6 July-7 August 2014, A/CN.4/682 [hereinafter referred to as ILC, Third Report, 2015].

[10] International Law Commission, 'Text of the Draft Conclusions Provisionally adopted by the Drafting Committee, Sixty-seventh session, Geneva, 4 May-5 June and 6 July-7 August 2014, 14 July 2015, A/CN.4/L.869 [hereinafter referred to as ILC, Draft Conclusions, 2015]. See also the 2014 and 2015 reports of the Chairman of the Drafting Committee, available on the Commission's website http://legal.un.org/ilc/.

[11] ILC, First Report, 2013, p. 6.

fields of international law' and 'to what degree, different weight may be given to different materials depending on the field in question'.[12] This book undertakes an analysis of this question in respect of international investment law. It considers whether the elements evidencing State practice in international investment law are different from those in other fields of international law. It shows that there may indeed be a number of noteworthy matters that may be peculiar to the formation and evidence of customary international law in international investment law.

On the one hand, the basic approach to the formation of customary rules in the field of international investment law is the same as the basic approach in other fields. Thus, the existence of any customary rule in international investment law requires evidence of *both* State practice and *opinio juris*. On the other hand, the author's conclusion is that some aspects related to the identification of customary rules are in fact different. Thus, some elements of practice have had a much more limited role in the field of investment arbitration compared to their role elsewhere. Also, the types of statements that are considered as evidence of State practice in this field are not always the same as those in other areas of international law. In fact, some statements examined in this book have a unique importance to the field of investment arbitration.

This is an important book that is likely to have a significant impact on existing scholarship regarding customary international law. It will have a long-lasting influence in the field of international investment law.

Sir Michael Wood
London,
October 2015

---

[12] ILC, Second Report, 2014, pp. 7–8. See also: ILC, Third Report, 2015, p. 7.

PREFACE

Why write a book on custom? To this day I can still remember one of my first international law classes at the Université de Montréal in 1993 when Professor Jacques-Yvan Morin explained the mysterious way that customary rules emerge. He brilliantly told us that these rules emerge in the same way that footsteps through a field eventually transform into a pathway followed by all. It was only many years later that I discovered that the analogy was actually introduced by Professor Cobbett and later refined by Professor de Visscher:

> On a pu comparer la lente constitution de la coutume internationale à la formation graduelle d'un chemin à travers un terrain vague. À l'origine on y relève des pistes multiples et incertaines, à peine visibles au sol. Puis, la majorité des usagers, pour quelque raison d'utilité commune, adopte un même parcours; un sentier unique se dégage qui, à son tour, fait place à un chemin reconnu désormais comme la seule voie régulière, sans que l'on puisse dire à quel moment précis cette dernière transformation s'est accomplie.[1]

Ever since these early law school days I have remained fascinated by the phenomenon of the formation of customary rules. Back then, however, it never crossed my mind that some 20 years later I would actually write a book on the topic.

The idea of writing a book on custom emerged from my own experience as a lawyer. Before becoming a professor at the University of Ottawa in 2009, I practised law for about ten years in the field of international arbitration in Geneva (at Lalive and at Lenz & Steahelin), in Montreal (at Ogilvy Renault, now known as Norton Rose Fulbright) and in Ottawa (at Canada's Ministry of Foreign Affairs and International Trade, 'Trade Law Bureau'). For the first time, in the context of these arbitration

---

[1] Charles de Visscher, *Théories et réalités en droit international public* (Paris: Pedone, 1953), pp. 182–184, referring to Pitt Cobbett, *Leading Cases on International Law* (London: Sweet and Maxwell, 5th edn., vol. 1, 1931–1937), p. 5.

proceedings, I had to concretely apply the theoretical concept of customary international law that I had learned in law school to real facts in real cases. This is when I truly discovered the multifaceted complexity of the principle. At the time, I desperately looked for scholarly works examining the application of custom in the specific field of international investment law. No such work existed.

The situation is not entirely different today. No book on international investment law has ever specifically focused on custom. In fact, only a limited number of books and articles have been published on the more general issue regarding the sources of international investment law.[2] While a number of articles have examined some aspects of the phenomenon of custom in investment arbitration,[3] none have systematically and thoroughly investigated the important preliminary issue of identifying the different types of relevant manifestations (or evidence) of State practice and *opinio juris*.

---

[2] T. Gazzini and E. de Brabandere (eds), *International Investment Law: The Sources of Rights and Obligations* (Leiden: Martinus Nijhoff, 2012); Patrick Juillard, 'L'évolution des sources du droit des investissements', *Rec. des cours* 250 (1994), pp. 9–216; M. Hirsch, 'Sources of International Investment Law', ILA Study Group on the Role of Soft Law Instruments in International Investment Law (2011) (also in: Andrea K. Bjorklund and August Reinisch (eds.), *International Investment Law and Soft Law* (Cheltenham: Elgar, 2012); Florian Grisel, 'The Sources of Foreign Investment Law', in: Z. Douglas, J. Pauwelyn and J.E. Viñuales (eds.), *The Foundations of International Investment Law: Bringing Theory into Practice* (Oxford: Oxford University Press, 2014), pp. 213–233; Claire Crépet Daigremont, 'Les sources du droit international des investissements', in: C. Leben (ed.) *Droit international des investissements et l'arbitrage transnational* (Paris: Pedone, 2015).

[3] Stephen M. Schwebel, 'Investor-State Disputes and the Development of International Law: The Influence of Bilateral Investment Treaties on Customary International Law', *ASIL Proc.* 98 (2004), pp. 27–30; Steffen Hindelang, 'Bilateral Investment Treaties, Custom and a Healthy Investment Climate – The Question of whether BITs Influence Customary International Law Revisited', *J. World Invest. & Trade* 5 (2004), pp. 789–809; Andreas F. Lowenfeld, 'Investment Agreements and International Law', *Columbia JTL* 42 (2003), p. 123–130; Bernard Kishoiyian, 'The Utility of Bilateral Investment Treaties in the Formulation of Customary International Law', *Northwestern J. Int'l L.* 14(2) (1993), pp. 327–375; Cai Congyan, 'International Investment Treaties and the Formation, Application a Transformation of Customary International Law Rules', *Chinese JIL* 7 (2008), pp. 659–679; Abdullah Al Faruque, 'Creating Customary International Law through Bilateral Investment Treaties: a Critical Appraisal', *Indian JIL* 44 (2004), p. 292–318; Tarcisio Gazzini, 'The Role of Customary International Law in the Field of Foreign Investment', *J. World Invest. & Trade* 8 (2007), pp. 691–715; Jean d'Aspremont, 'International Customary Investment Law: Story of a Paradox', in T. Gazzini and E. de Brabandere (eds), *International Investment Law: The Sources of Rights and Obligations* (Leiden: Martinus Nijhoff, 2012), pp. 5–47; José Enrique Alvarez, 'A BIT on Custom', *N.Y. U. J. Int'l L. & Pol* 42 (2009), pp. 17–80.

In 2011, when I started thinking about these questions I realized that even *before* examining the question of which specific rules of custom should be recognized in investment arbitration, one should first consider two very basic *preliminary* questions: (1) how these customary rules are actually created, and (2) how they can be identified. No comprehensive study has analysed these fundamental questions in the field of investment arbitration. The objective of this book is to fill this void.

My belief in the contemporary relevance of these questions was reinforced by the fact that the International Law Commission (ILC) decided in 2012 to include the topic of the 'Formation and Evidence of Customary International Law' in its programme of work and appointed Sir Michael Wood as its Special Rapporteur. While I was writing this book, the ILC Special Rapporteur published his first (2013[4]), second (2014[5]), and third (2015[6]) reports. The ILC Drafting Committee adopted its draft conclusions in 2015.[7] As noted by ILC Special Rapporteur Wood, 'in order to determine whether a rule of customary international law exists, it is necessary to consider both the requirements for the formation of a rule of customary international law, and the types of evidence that establish the fulfilment of those requirements'.[8] In his Second Report, ILC Special Rapporteur Wood also noted the importance of determining whether or not 'there are different approaches to the formation and evidence of customary international law in different fields of international law' and 'to what degree, different weight may be given to different materials depending on the field in question'.[9] The purpose of this book is to

---

[4] International Law Commission, 'First Report on Formation and Evidence of Customary International Law', by Michael Wood, Special Rapporteur, Sixty-fifth session, Geneva, 6 May–7 June and 8 July–9 August 2013, UN doc. A/CN.4/663, 17 May 2013, p. 8 [hereinafter referred to as ILC, First Report, 2013].

[5] International Law Commission, 'Second Report on Identification of Customary International Law', by Michael Wood, Special Rapporteur, Sixty-sixth session, Geneva, 5 May–6 June and 7 July–8 August 2014, A/CN.4/672, p. 13 [hereinafter referred to as ILC, Second Report, 2014].

[6] International Law Commission, 'Third Report on Identification of Customary International Law', by Michael Wood, Special Rapporteur, Sixty-seventh session, Geneva, 4 May–5 June and 6 July–7 August 2014, A/CN.4/682 [hereinafter referred to as ILC, Third Report, 2015].

[7] International Law Commission, 'Text of the Draft Conclusions Provisionally adopted by the Drafting Committee', Sixty-seventh session, Geneva, 4 May–5 June and 6 July–7 August 2014, 14 July 2015, A/CN.4/L.869 [hereinafter referred to as ILC, Draft Conclusions, 2015].

[8] ILC, First Report, 2013, p. 6.   [9] ILC, Second Report, 2014, pp. 7–8.

provide the answer to these questions in the field of investment arbitration.

Specifically, this book aims to offer guidance to actors on how to identify rules of customary international law in the field of investor-State arbitration. It will therefore provide arbitrators with indispensable (yet currently scarcely available) tools to enhance their ability to solve disputes between foreign investors and States. Above all, this book intends to show that customary rules remain fundamentally important in contemporary international investment law despite the fact that existing investment protection rules are now overwhelmingly found in bilateral and multilateral investment treaties.

Patrick Dumberry
Montreal
May 2015

ACKNOWLEDGMENTS

This book is the result of more than three years of research. I would like to thank the Faculty of Law (Civil Law Section) of the University of Ottawa, my colleagues and members of the administrative staff (including Martine Saint-Louis and Lorraine DeVanthey) for their support throughout the years. I am grateful to the Government of Canada for having provided me with generous funding through the 'Standard Research Grants Program' of the Social Sciences and Humanities Research Council of Canada (SSHRC) to complete this work. I am especially indebted to several bright and talented students from the University of Ottawa who have assisted me over the last three years with research and editing. Their assistance was invaluable to the completion of this book. I want to sincerely thank Lila Amara, Micha Benjamin, Eugenia Bouras, Melissa Tara Bramson, Sébastien Cusson, Noushin Dewan, Gabrielle Dumas-Aubin, Evelyne Gauvin, Alexandre Genest, Christina Georgaklis, Constantina Georgaklis, Amélie B. Goudreau, Alexandra Hébert, Emily Kissel, Geneviève Martin-Lafleur, Jonathan Nadler, Franck Marvel Ngandui, Ivana Nenadic, Shunghyo Kim, Isaac Benjamin Martin, Lou Janssen Dangzalan, Marilynn Rubayika, Laura Miles, Lara Hammound and Rouba Wehbe. All of them have done an amazing job.

Special thanks go to Sir Michael Wood for having written the foreword to this book. Sir Michael was the principal Legal Adviser to the United Kingdom Foreign and Commonwealth Office between 1999 and 2006. He was also appointed as the International Law Commission's Special Rapporteur on the 'Identification of Customary International Law'.

Many thanks to all the people at Cambridge University Press (Elizabeth Spicer, Karthik Orukaimani, Mary Bongiovi, Emma Collison, Fleur Jones) for their patience and support in the revision process for the publication of this book.

Most importantly, I would like to dedicate this book to my parents and my children. I would like to first express my gratitude to my parents for their unconditional support throughout my life. I also wish to thank my beautiful, funny and bright young children, Ophélie and Florent. Your love and affection have given me the strength to write this book during a rather turbulent period of my personal life. I hope that one day you will read this book and fully understand the extent to which this whole odyssey would have simply been impossible (and really pointless) without your constant love and support. My daughter (who is now 7 years old) once told me 'Daddy, I personally don't really care what your books are all about, what I am happy about is that you like to write them so much'. That is exactly the kind of support that I needed when I wrote this book. Florent (now 5 years old), I promise you that one day I will write an international law book involving Pirates and (less likely) Ninja Turtles!

Patrick Dumberry
Montreal
May 2015

ABBREVIATIONS

ABAJ	American Bar Association Journal
AFDI	Annuaire français de droit international
AJIL	American Journal of International Law
Alabama L.Rev	Alabama Law Review
American Rev. Int'l Arb	American Review of International Arbitration
American University ILR	American University International Law Review
American University LR	American University Law Review
Arb. Int'l	Arbitration International
Arbitration & ADR	Arbitration & Alternative Dispute Resolution
ASA Bull.	Bulletin of the Association Suisse de l'Arbitrage
ASDI	Annuaire Suisse de droit international
ASIL Proc.	American Society of International Law Proceedings
Australian YIL	Australian Yearbook of International Law
Austrian RIEL	Austrian Review of International & European Law
BITs	Bilateral investment treaties
British IICL	British Institute of International and Comparative Law
British YIL	British Yearbook of International Law
Brook. J. Int'l L	Brooklyn Journal of International Law
Brooklyn L.R	Brooklyn Law Review
Cal. L. Rev	California Law Review
Cal. W.Int'l.J	California Western International Law Journal
Cambridge J Intl Comp L	Cambridge Journal of International and Comparative Law
Canadian YIL	Canadian Yearbook of International Law
Chicago L.Rev.	Chicago Law Review
Chinese JIL	Chinese Journal of International Law
Columbia JTL	Columbia Journal of Transnational Law
Duke L.J.	Duke Law Journal
Duke J Comp & IL	Duke Journal of Comparative & International Law
EJIL	European Journal of International Law
EJIL Talks!	European Journal of International Law: Talks!
FET	Fair and equitable treatment

FTA	Free Trade Agreement
FTC	Free Trade Commission
FTC Note	Free Trade Commission Notes of Interpretation of 31 July 2001
Ga. J. Int'l & Comp L.	Georgia Journal of International and Comparative Law
GEO. L.J.,	Georgetown Law Journal
Geo. Wash. Int'l L. Rev	George Washington International Law Review
German YIL	German Yearbook of International Law
Harvard ILJ	Harvard International Law Journal
Hofstra L Rev	Hofstra Law Review
Howard L.J	Howard Law Journal
I.L.S.A. J.I.L	International Law Students Association Journal of International Law
ICJ	International Court of Justice
ICJ Rep.	International Court of Justice Reports of Judgments, Advisory Opinions and Orders
ICJ Statute	Statute of the International Court of Justice
ICLQ	International and Comparative Law Quarterly
ICSID Rev	International Centre for Settlement of Investment Disputes Review – Foreign Investment Law Journal
ICSID	International Centre for Settlement of Investment Disputes
ICRC	International Committee of the Red Cross
ICTR	International Criminal Tribunal for Rwanda
ICTY	International Tribunal for the Former Yugoslavia
IISD	International Institute for Sustainable Development
ILA	International Law Association
ILA, Final Report	International Law Association, 'Statement of Principles Applicable to the Formation of General Customary International Law', Final Report of the Committee on the Formation of Customary Law, Conference Report London (2000)
ILC	International Law Commission
ILC, First Report, 2013	International Law Commission, 'First Report on Formation and Evidence of Customary International Law', by Michael Wood, Special Rapporteur, Sixty-fifth session, Geneva, 6 May-7 June and 8 July-9 August 2013, UN doc. A/CN.4/ 663, 17 May 2013
ILC, Second Report, 2014	International Law Commission, 'Second Report on Identification of Customary International Law', by

<table>
<tr><td></td><td>Michael Wood, Special Rapporteur, Sixty-sixth session, Geneva, 5 May-6 June and 7 July-8 August 2014, UN doc. A/CN.4/672</td></tr>
<tr><td>ILC, Memorandum, 2013</td><td>International Law Commission, 'Formation and Evidence of Customary International Law, Elements in the Previous Work of the ILC that Could be Particularly Relevant to the Topic', Memorandum by the Secretariat, Sixty-fifth session Geneva, 5 May-7 June and 8 July-9 August 2013, UN doc. A/CN.4/659, p. 17</td></tr>
<tr><td>ILC, Third Report, 2015</td><td>International Law Commission, 'Third Report on Identification of Customary International Law', by Michael Wood, Special Rapporteur, Sixty-seventh session, Geneva, 4 May-5 June and 6 July-7 August 2014, A/CN.4/682</td></tr>
<tr><td>ILC, Articles on State Responsibility</td><td>Titles and Texts of the Draft Articles on Responsibility of States for Internationally Wrongful Acts Adopted by the Drafting Committee on Second Reading, 26 July 2001</td></tr>
<tr><td>ILC, Commentaries</td><td>Commentaries to the Draft Articles on Responsibility of States for Internationally Wrongful Acts Adopted by the International Law Commission at its Fifty-Third Session (2001), November 2001</td></tr>
<tr><td>ILM</td><td>International Legal Materials</td></tr>
<tr><td>ILR</td><td>International Legal Reports</td></tr>
<tr><td>Ind. J. Global Legal Stud</td><td>Indiana Journal of Global Legal Studies</td></tr>
<tr><td>Indian J Int'l L</td><td>Indian Journal of International Law</td></tr>
<tr><td>Int'l L</td><td>International Lawyer</td></tr>
<tr><td>Int Rev Red Cross</td><td>International Review of the Red Cross</td></tr>
<tr><td>Israel L.Rev</td><td>Israel Law Review</td></tr>
<tr><td>Italian YIL</td><td>Italian Yearbook of International Law</td></tr>
<tr><td>J. Int'l Arb.</td><td>Journal of International Arbitration</td></tr>
<tr><td>J. Int Disp Settl</td><td>Journal of International Dispute Settlement</td></tr>
<tr><td>J. Int'l Econ. L</td><td>Journal of International Economic Law</td></tr>
<tr><td>J. World Invest. & Trade</td><td>Journal of World Investment & Trade</td></tr>
<tr><td>J. World Trade</td><td>Journal of World Trade</td></tr>
<tr><td>Journal CEPMLP</td><td>Journal of the Centre of Energy, Petroleum and Mineral Law and Policy</td></tr>
<tr><td>J.P.L.</td><td>Journal of Public Law</td></tr>
<tr><td>L. & Bus. Rev. Am.</td><td>Law and Business Review of the Americas</td></tr>
<tr><td>Law & Pol'y Int'l Bus</td><td>Law and Policy in International Business</td></tr>
</table>

Law & Prac Int'l Cts & Tribunals	Law and Practice of International Courts and Tribunals
Leiden J. Int'l L.	Leiden Journal of International Law
Max Planck Yrbk. UNL	Max Planck Yearbook of United Nations Law
McGill LJ	McGill Law Journal
Mealey's Int'l Arb. Rep	Mealey's International Arbitration Report
Melbourne JIL	Melbourne Journal of International Law
Michigan JIL	Michigan Journal of International Law
Michigan State JIL	Michigan State Journal of International Law
Michigan LR	Michigan Law Review
Minnesota JIL	Minnesota Journal of International Law
MFN	Most-Favored-Nation
MST	Minimum standard of treatment
NAFTA	North American Free Trade Agreement
N.Y.U. J. Int'l L. & Pol	New York University Journal of International Law and Politics
Nordic JIL	Nordic Journal of International Law
North Carolina JIL & Comm Reg	North Carolina Journal of International Law & Commercial Regulation
Northwestern J. Int'l L & Bus	Northwestern Journal of International Law & Business
Netherlands ILR	Netherlands International Law Review
NYBIL	Netherlands Yearbook of International Law
OECD	Organisation for Economic Co-operation and Development
OJLS	Oxford Journal of Legal Studies
P.C.I.J.	Permanent Court of International Justice
Penn State ILR	Penn State International Law Review
Rec. des cours	Collected Courses of the Hague Academy of International Law
RBDI	Revue belge de droit international
RGDIP	Revue générale de droit international public
RQDI	Revue québécoise de droit international
Santa Clara J. Int'l L	Santa Clara Journal of International Law
Singapore YB Int'L	Singapore Yearbook of International Law
Sri Lanka J. Int'l L	Sri Lanka Journal of International Law
SSRN	Social Science Research Network
Stanford JIL	Stanford Journal of International Law
Suffolk Transnat'l L. Rev.	Suffolk Transnational Law Review
Sw. J. Int'l L.	Southwestern Journal of International Law
TDM	Transnational Dispute Management Journal
Texas ILJ	Texas International Law Journal

U. Cin. L. Rev	University of Cincinnati Law Review
U.N.	United Nations
UNCTAD	United Nations Conference on Trade and Development
UNTS	United Nations Treaty Series
UNRIAA	United Nations Reports of International Arbitral Awards
U. Pa. J. Int'l Econ. L	University of Pennsylvania International Economic Law
Univ. Pennsylvania LR	Univ. Pennsylvania Law Review
UCLA L. Rev	*UCLA Law Review*
US	United States
Vand. J. Transnat'l L.	Vanderbilt Journal Transnational Law
Virginia JIL	Virginia Journal of International Law
Washington L.R.	Washington Law Review
W. Arb & Med Rev	World Arbitration and Mediation Review
Yale Human Rights & Dev.	Yale Human Rights & Development Law Journal
Yale JIL	Yale Journal of International Law
Yale LJ	Yale Law Journal
Yb Int'l Invest. L. & Pol.	Yearbook of International Investment Law and Policy
Yearbook ILC	Yearbook of the International Law Commission
ZaöRV	Zeitschrift für ausländisches öffentliches Recht und Völkerrecht

~

Introduction

I.1   The scope of this book

Rules of customary international law are binding on all States. They gradually develop over time based on the uniform and consistent practice of a large number of representative States, which have the conviction (or the belief) that such practice is required by law (*opinio juris*). The general aim of this book is to provide a comprehensive analysis of the phenomenon of custom in the context of international investment law (also known as investor-State arbitration).[1] No book on international investment law has ever focused specifically on custom. In fact, only a limited number of books and articles have been published on the fundamental question of the sources of international investment law.[2] As noted by d'Aspremont, 'the scholarship on international investment law has

---

[1] Throughout this book the terms 'international investment law', 'investor-State arbitration' or 'investment arbitration' will be used interchangeably. Similarly, I have decided to use different expressions to refer to the same concept of 'custom': 'customary international law', 'customary law'. These terms will be used interchangeably in this book.

[2] T. Gazzini and E. de Brabandere (eds.), *International Investment Law: The Sources of Rights and Obligations* (Leiden; Boston: Martinus Nijhoff, 2012); Patrick Juillard, 'L'évolution des sources du droit des investissements', *Rec. des Cours*, 250 (1994), pp. 9–216; M. Hirsch, 'Sources of International Investment Law', ILA Study Group on the Role of Soft Law Instruments in International Investment Law (2011) (also in Andrea K. Bjorklund and August Reinisch [eds.], *International Investment Law and Soft Law* [Elgar, 2012]); Martins Paparinskis, 'Investment Protection Law and Sources of Law: A Critical Look', *ASIL Proc.*, 103 (2009), pp. 76–79; C.J. Tams, 'The Sources of International Investment Law', in T. Gazzini and E. de Brabandere (eds.), *International Investment Law: The Sources of Rights and Obligations* (Leiden; Boston: Martinus Nijhoff, 2012), pp. 319–332; F. Grisel, 'The Sources of Foreign Investment Law', in: Z. Douglas, J. Pauwelyn and J.E. Viñuales (eds.), *The Foundations of International Investment Law: Bringing Theory into Practice*, (Oxford: Oxford University Press, 2014). See also, more generally, S. Zamora, 'Is there Customary International Economic Law?', *German YIL* 32 (1989), pp. 9–52; Claire Crepet Daigremont, 'Les sources du droit international des investissements', in C. Leben (ed.) *Droit international des investissements et l'arbitrage transnational* (Paris: Pedone, 2015).

1

remained bereft of theoretical reflection on the sources of investment law'.[3] He believes that 'international investment law has now reached a stage of its development where the doctrine of sources can no longer be left in limbo and needs to be critically explored' so that this field of law 'rests on solid bases in terms of sources'.[4] He is right.[5]

But why should one enquire about customary rules in today's international investment law when foreign investors, in fact, obtain sufficient protection under the numerous investment treaties that have been entered into by States in recent decades? As noted by one writer, 'for all practical purposes, treaties have become the fundamental sources of international law in the area of foreign investment'.[6] The basic reasons for the remaining importance of custom have been identified by the Iran–US Claims Tribunal in the *Amoco* case: 'the rules of customary law may be useful in order to fill in possible *lacunae* of the treaty, to ascertain the meaning of undefined terms in the text or, more generally, to aid the interpretation and implementation of its provision'.[7]

The first reason for the continuing importance of custom in today's investment arbitration is because these rules represent the applicable legal regime of protection in the absence of any BIT. However numerous BITs have become, they still do not cover the whole spectrum of possible bilateral treaty relationships between States. This necessarily results in gaps in the legal protection of foreign investments. Therefore, a foreign investor originating from a State that has not entered into a BIT with the

[3] Jean d'Aspremont, 'International Customary Investment Law: Story of a Paradox', in T. Gazzini and E. de Brabandere (eds.), *International Investment Law: The Sources of Rights and Obligations* (Leiden; Boston: Martinus Nijhoff, 2012), p. 8, further explaining that 'Any investigation in the foundations of the sources of investment law may have seemed overly arcane to such practitioners, to whom the doctrine of sources of investment law may seem to work properly and an invitation to explore its theoretical foundations a purely academic whim'.
[4] *Id.*
[5] See also, the same assessment made in 1989 by Zamora, 'Is there Customary International Economic Law?', pp. 10–11, in the field of international economic law.
[6] Jeswald W. Salacuse, 'The Treatification of International Investment Law: a Victory of Form Over Life? A Crossroads Crossed?' *TDM* 3(3) (2006), p. 5. See also: ILA, 'Sources of International Investment Law', report by M. Hirsch, ILA Study Group on the Role of Soft Law Instruments in International Investment Law (2011), p. 7; Christoph H. Schreuer, Loretta Malintoppi, August Reinisch and Anthony Sinclair, *The ICSID Convention; A Commentary* (2nd edn., Cambridge: Cambridge University Press, 2009), p. 605 ('The large and rapidly growing number of BITs and multilateral treaties dealing with investment makes them the most important source of international law for ICSID tribunals'); Grisel, 'The Sources of Foreign Investment Law', p. 219.
[7] *Amoco Int'l Fin. Corp.* v. *Iran*, Iran-US CT, 14 July 1987, in *ILR* 83 (1990), para. 112.

State where the investment is made will not be given the legal protection which would have otherwise been typically offered under such a treaty. Customary rules will apply to that investor. So, even in light of the proliferation of BITs, these rules continue to play an important role in investment protection. Another fundamental reason for the remaining importance of custom is the fact that several BITs make explicit reference to the application of 'customary international law'. An arbitral tribunal must necessarily determine the content of a customary rule when faced with such a specific provision. While the number of investment treaties expressly referring to custom is rapidly increasing, it remains that such reference is still only found in a small *minority* of treaties. Custom also plays a gap-filling role whenever a treaty, a contract or domestic legislation is silent on a given issue. Tribunals have had to frequently apply customary rules as the ultimate reservoir of investment protection norms. In any event, I will argue in this book that arbitral tribunals should *always* take into account relevant rules of customary international law.

Specifically, this book addresses the question of the *formation* and the *identification* of rules of customary international law in the field of international investment law. The International Law Association (ILA), in the more general context of public international law, examined this question in 2000.[8] More recently, the International Law Commission (ILC) decided in 2012 to include the topic of the 'Formation and Evidence of Customary International Law' in its programme of work and appointed Sir Michael Wood as its Special Rapporteur.[9] In his First Report (of 2013), ILC Special Rapporteur Wood indicated that the objective of the ILC's work on this question was to 'offer some guidance to those called upon to apply rules of customary international law on how to identify such rules in concrete cases'.[10] He further added that 'the terms "formation" and "evidence" were intended to indicate that, in order to determine whether a rule of customary international law exists,

[8] International Law Association, 'Statement of Principles Applicable to the Formation of General Customary International Law', Final Report of the Committee on the Formation of Customary Law, Conference Report London (2000).
[9] Report of the International Law Commission on the work of its sixty-fourth session, 7 May to 1 June and 2 July to 3 August 2012, UN Doc. A/67/10, 2012, chp.VIII, paras. 156–202, p. 108.
[10] International Law Commission, 'First Report on Formation and Evidence of Customary International Law', by Michael Wood, Special Rapporteur, Sixty-fifth session, Geneva, 6 May-7 June and 8 July-9 August 2013, UN doc. A/CN.4/663, 17 May 2013, at p. 6 [hereinafter referred to as ILC, First Report, 2013].

INTRODUCTION

it is necessary to consider both the requirements for the formation of a rule of customary international law, and the types of evidence that establish the fulfilment of those requirements'.[11] The ILC later decided to change and simplify the title of the topic to 'The Identification of Customary International Law', with the general goal remaining the same.[12] The ILC Special Rapporteur Wood published three reports from 2013 to 2015.[13] The ILC Drafting Committee adopted its 'Draft conclusions' in 2015.[14]

The aim of this book is to provide the different actors involved in investor-State arbitration (arbitral tribunals, investors, States) as well as other stakeholders (international organizations, NGOs, civil society) with the first sets of comprehensive guidelines regarding the formation and identification of rules of customary international law in the field of international investment law. It is important to highlight from the outset the type of issues that will *not* be specifically addressed in this book. In general, my goal is not to examine whether any specific rule contained in investment treaties should (or should not) be considered as custom. In other words, the present book does not contain a 'shopping list' of *all existing* customary rules in investment arbitration. Yet, I will explain that these rules *do exist*. Thus, the principle of the 'minimum standard of treatment' (MST) and the general prohibition against expropriation without compensation will be analysed in this context at Chapter 2. I also decided to use throughout this book the example of the fair and equitable treatment (FET) standard found in numerous investment

---

[11] *Id.*

[12] International Law Commission, 'Second Report on Identification of Customary International Law', by Michael Wood, Special Rapporteur, Sixty-sixth session, Geneva, 5 May-6 June and 7 July-8 August 2014, A/CN.4/672, p. 2 [hereinafter referred to as ILC, Second Report, 2014]. The abandonment by the ILC of the term 'evidence' in favour of 'identification' has been praised by some insofar as 'proof of customary law is not a matter of fact' and thus 'the term "evidence" is inapposite': James Crawford, 'The Identification and Development of Customary International Law', ILA British Branch Conference (2014), p. 3.

[13] ILC, First Report, 2013; ILC, Second Report, 2014; International Law Commission, 'Third Report on Identification of Customary International Law', by Michael Wood, Special Rapporteur, Sixty-seventh session, Geneva, 4 May-5 June and 6 July-7 August 2014, A/CN.4/682 [hereinafter referred to as ILC, Third Report, 2015].

[14] International Law Commission, 'Text of the Draft Conclusions Provisionally adopted by the Drafting Committee, Sixty-seventh session, Geneva, 4 May-5 June and 6 July-7 August 2014, 14 July 2015, A/CN.4/L.869 [hereinafter referred to as ILC, Draft Conclusions, 2015].

treaties as an illustration of the strict conditions under which a treaty-based norm can transform into a customary rule.[15]

Another important point to mention is that my book does not address the question of how provisions in investment treaties can (or should) be *interpreted* with the use of rule of custom. Thus, it does not specifically examine the question of the proper application of Article 31(3)(c) of the *Vienna Convention on the Law of Treaties*, whereby a tribunal shall take into account, together with the context of the treaty, 'any relevant rules of international law applicable in the relations between the parties', which includes any 'relevant' rules of customary international law.[16] This issue will only be briefly addressed in Chapter 5.[17]

The goal of this book is to provide guidance to those faced with a claim that a standard of protection is a rule of custom. In the words of ILC Special Rapporteur Wood, it is 'a practical guide for assisting practitioners in the task of identifying customary international law'.[18] This book will provide the essential tools to allow different actors to identify customary rules based on the essential requirements for the formation and the identification of custom. In this sense, this book is following in the footsteps of the work of the ILC. In his First Report, Special Rapporteur Wood thus mentioned that '[t]he topic is not concerned with determining the substance of particular rules'; instead it is aimed at providing

---

[15] It should be noted in 2011, the ILC inscribed the subject of 'fair and equitable treatment' in its long-term work plan: Report of the ILC, 63d Sess., Apr. 26–June 3, July 4–Aug. 12, 2011, para. 362, U.N. Doc. A/66/10; GAOR, 66th Sess., Supp. No. 10 (2011), para. 365. At Annex D it is indicated that the ILC will examine a number of questions, including whether the FET standard now represents customary international law. The question is examined in J. Harrison, 'The International Law Commission and the Development of International Investment Law', *Geo. Wash. Int'l L. Rev*, 45 (2013), p. 439. The question is further examined in Patrick Dumberry, 'Has the Fair and Equitable Treatment Standard become a Rule of Customary international Law? An Empirical Study of the Practice of States (forthcoming, 2016).

[16] On this question, see M. Paparinskis, 'Investment Treaty Interpretation and Customary Investment Law, Preliminary Remarks', in C. Brown and K. Miles (eds.), *Evolution in Investment Treaty Law and Arbitration* (Cambridge: Cambridge University Press, 2011); E. Milano, 'The Investment Arbitration between Italy and Cuba: The Application of Customary International Law under Scrutiny', *Law & Prac Int'l Cts & Tribunals* 11 (2012), pp. 499–524. Suffice it to note that Ole Kristian Fauchald, 'The Legal Reasoning of ICSID Tribunals – An Empirical Analysis', *EJIL* 19 (2008), p. 310, in his study of decisions rendered by tribunals between 1998 and 2006, concluded that 'tribunals used customary international law as a separate legal basis in 34 of the 98 decisions'. He further indicated that customary law was discussed in relation to a broad range of jurisdictional, procedural and substantive issues as well as questions dealing with secondary rules of international law.

[17] See, discussion in Chapter 5, Section 5.2.3.   [18] ILC, Third Report, 2015, p. 2.

'guidance on how to identify a rule of customary international law at a given moment, not to address the question of which particular rules have achieved such status'.[19]

No wide-range study has ever been conducted on this topic. It is true that a number of articles have been published in recent years regarding customary rules in investor-State arbitration.[20] Yet, most of them have only addressed one specific issue: whether the content of the rules contained in bilateral investment treaties for the protection and promotion of investments (BITs) can be said to have 'transformed' into 'new' customary international law (this question will be fully examined in Chapter 3[21]). It is also not uncommon for scholars to proclaim that one rule or another found in these BITs is of customary nature. Yet, typically they do so without providing much analysis as to why this is the case. They rarely examine in much detail the basic elements that are necessary for the formation of customary rules. With a few exceptions, they almost never go through the exercise of actually examining the practice of States and their *opinio juris* (i.e. the belief of States that such practice is *required by law*). The present book will critically assess the claim by some writers that the FET standard is of customary nature and highlight the flawed methodology they have used.[22]

In any event, the existing literature typically does not systematically and thoroughly investigate the important preliminary question of what

---

[19] ILC, First Report, 2013, p. 9. See also: ILC, Second Report, 2014, p. 5.

[20] Stephen M. Schwebel, 'Investor-State Disputes and the Development of International Law: The Influence of Bilateral Investment Treaties on Customary International Law', *ASIL Proc.*, 98 (2004), pp. 27–30; Steffen Hindelang, 'Bilateral Investment Treaties, Custom and a Healthy Investment Climate – The Question of whether BITs Influence Customary International Law Revisited', *J. World Invest. & Trade*, 5 (2004), pp. 789–809; Andreas F. Lowenfeld, 'Investment Agreements and International Law', *Columbia JTL* 42 (2003), pp. 127–130; Bernard Kishoiyian, 'The Utility of Bilateral Investment Treaties in the Formulation of Customary International Law', *Northwestern J. Int'l L.* 14(2) (1993), pp. 327–375; Cai Congyan, 'International Investment Treaties and the Formation, Application and Transformation of Customary International Law Rules', *Chinese JIL* 7 (2008), pp. 659–679; Abdullah Al Faruque, 'Creating Customary International Law through Bilateral Investment Treaties: a Critical Appraisal', *Indian J Int'l L* 44 (2004), p. 295; Tarcisio Gazzini, 'The Role of Customary International Law in the Field of Foreign Investment', *J. World Invest. & Trade*, 8 (2007), p. 692; d'Aspremont, 'International Customary Investment Law'; José Enrique Alvarez, 'A BIT on Custom', *N.Y.U. J. Int'l L. & Pol*, 42 (2009), p. 17.

[21] See, Chapter 3, Section 3.3.3.2.2. On this issue: P. Dumberry, 'Are BITs Representing the "New" Customary International Law in International Investment Law?', *Penn State ILR* 28(4) (2010), pp. 675–701.

[22] See, discussion in Chapter 3, Sections 3.2.4 and 3.3.3.2.1.3.

are the different types of manifestations (or evidence) of State practice relevant in the context of the creation of customary rules in the specific field of investor-State arbitration. These shortcomings are no doubt the result of the typical space constraint that scholars face when publishing articles in law journals. Such an investigation can indeed only be properly undertaken in the format of a book. In fact, the question as to whether one standard of investment protection should (or should not) be considered as a customary rule can, in my view, only be fully addressed once a number of *preliminary* questions have been tackled. These basic questions, which will be explored in this book, include the following:

– What is the nature of custom and how is it created?
– Does the creation of custom require both State practice and *opinio juris* in the field of investor-State arbitration?
– Does the practice of non-State actors matter for the formation of customary rules?
– Does State practice need to be uniform, consistent, extensive and representative during a certain period of time for a customary rule to emerge in the field of investor-State arbitration?
– What are the manifestations of State practice (in other words, where can one concretely find such practice)?
– Can rules contained in BITs transform into customary rules, and if so, under which circumstances and conditions? Should these numerous BITs, taken together, be considered as the 'new' custom?
– Can statements made by States be considered as relevant evidence of State practice? What are the types of statements that matter in the field of investor-State arbitration and which ones are less relevant? How much weight should actually be given to these different types of statements?
– What is the role of arbitral awards (if any) in the formation and development of customary rules?
– Does the internal practice of States (i.e. the conduct of the executive, legislative and the judiciary branches of a government) play any meaningful role as evidence of State practice? What about the practice of States within international organizations?
– Is it really necessary to demonstrate States' *opinio juris* to prove the existence of a customary rule in the field of investor-State arbitration? Where does one find such *opinio juris* anyway? Do States have any *opinio juris* when signing BITs or when including certain types of protection in these instruments?

Another fundamental question, addressed in Chapter 5 of this book, is determining what is the actual role and relevance of customary rules in an era significantly marked by the phenomenon of 'treatification', whereby investment protections are overwhelmingly found in treaties. In other words, what practical purpose do these rules serve for the different actors involved in arbitration proceedings?

Although my book and the work of the ILC both address the same issue of the formation and identification of custom, they are in fact complementary to each other because of their different scope. In his First Report, Special Rapporteur Wood mentioned a long list of the range of materials that would be consulted in the course of the Commission's work on the topic,[23] including a brief reference to 'tribunals in the field of investment protection'.[24] The Second Report refers to a few arbitration awards.[25] However, the focus of the ILC's work is clearly on general international law, not on investment arbitration.

There is another reason why the present book is complementary to the work of the ILC. ILC Special Rapporteur Wood noted in his Second Report the importance of determining whether 'there are different approaches to the formation and evidence of customary international law in different fields of international law' and 'to what degree, different weight may be given to different materials depending on the field in question'.[26] He specifically referred to the fields of international human rights law, international criminal law and international humanitarian law. Investor-State arbitration is absent from the list.

This book will show that there are indeed a number of specific elements which are noteworthy regarding the formation and evidence of customary international law in the field of international investment law. For instance, some of the most important elements of State practice under general international law only have a limited practical impact in investment arbitration. Conversely, I will show that some manifestations of State practice (such as specific types of statements by States) have a unique importance in this field compared to their limited prevalence and

---

[23] ILC, First Report, 2013, p. 19.   [24] *Id.*, p. 36.

[25] See, for instance, *Mondev International Ltd.* v. *United States*, ICSID No. ARB(AF)/99/2, Award, 2 October 2002 (referred to in: ILC, Second Report, 2014, pp. 34, 53); *Camuzzi International S.A.* v. *Argentina*, ICSID Case No. ARB/03/2, Decision on Objections to Jurisdiction, 11 May 2005 (referred to in: *Id.*, p. 54); *United Parcel Service of America Inc* v. *Canada*, UNCITRAL, Award on Jurisdiction, 22 November 2002 (referred to in: *Id.*, p. 48).

[26] ILC, Second Report, 2014, pp. 7–8. See also: ILC, Third Report, 2015, p. 7.

usefulness in general public international law. In sum, this book will explain that the *identification* of the different manifestations of State practice necessary for the formation of custom is *not* the same in investor-State arbitration as in international law. The other question of whether or not a different approach to the *creation* and *formation* of custom in investment arbitration exists is controversial. A number of writers have indeed claimed in recent years that the traditional requirements of uniform, consistent and representative State practice should be relaxed, or applied differently, in investment arbitration. Some scholars also believe that the traditional requirement of *opinio juris* should be applied differently in this field of law. Some of them have actually come up with their own theories as to the meaning and relevance of the *opinio juris* requirement. This book will examine in detail whether these approaches are sound.

In sum, this book is the natural continuation of the ILC's work insofar as its general tenets are applied specifically to one area of international law. In fact, one writer has recently suggested that the ILC should undertake the analysis of the identification of relevant State practice and *opinio juris* in the field of international investment law.[27] The aim of this book is precisely to undertake such an analysis.

Finally, a few words should be dedicated to methodology. The present author has comprehensively surveyed a significant number of articles and books dealing with customary international law in general. I have also surveyed all major textbooks on investor-State arbitration as well as relevant legal journals to find and read (almost) everything that has ever been written (in English or French) on the phenomenon of custom in international investment law and, more generally, on the sources of law in that field. Importantly, my investigation has *not* been limited to

---

[27] Harrison, 'The International Law Commission', p. 439 ('given the fact that tribunals are increasingly faced with having to identify and apply rules of customary international law in relation to the protection of foreign investors, there would appear to be an urgent need for action on this point. Moreover, despite many statements about the evolution of customary international law, particularly in relation to the minimum standard of treatment, there has been little substantive and comprehensive analysis of state practice and *opinio juris* in this area'), see also at p. 440 ('The ILC could make a substantial contribution to this question by identifying relevant state practice and *opinio juris*. Not only can it assist tribunals in identifying relevant material evidence of customary international law, but the ILC can also suggest, in accordance with the understanding of codification discussed above, how to fill gaps in a manner that may contribute to the development of law in this area').

scholarly work. This is an important point. In a recent posting on *EJIL Talks*, Roberts made the following comment:

> Even when people say that they are finding custom, they are usually relying on short cuts, such as referring to case law that says something is custom, General Assembly resolutions that declare something to be custom, or academic articles that opine that something is custom. Almost no one actually "finds" custom. Instead, arbitrators, academics and counsel typically refer to other sources that supposedly have already "found" custom.[28]

This book is an attempt to (at least partially) address some of these legitimate criticisms. Thus, I have not simply reviewed the work of international law scholars to find out what *they believe* are the relevant types of evidence of State practice for the formation of customary rules. My book investigates numerous awards as well as a number of different government sources to concretely determine which manifestations of State practice are specifically relevant in the field of international investment law. In other words, this book is the first attempt to actually 'find' 'real life' examples of such relevant State practice and also to explain how they can concretely influence the creation of customary rules in investor-State arbitration. I will also provide several examples of specific situations showing States' *opinio juris*. The following is a (non-exhaustive) list of the different types of material that I have used to find concrete examples of State practice and *opinio juris* relevant to the creation of custom in the field of international investment law:

- Websites specializing in investment arbitration, including 'Investment Claims', 'Investor-State LawGuide', 'Kluwer Arbitration', 'Investment Law Digest' (International Investment Law Centre Cologne), 'Investment Treaty Arbitration 'Investment Treaty News' and 'NAFTA Claims';
- Websites of a number of international organizations (ICSID, UNCITRAL, ILC) and other groups (e.g. ILA);
- Official websites of a number of States where case law can be found;
- Sections on State practice of more than 15 national yearbooks of international law (e.g. *Canadian Yearbook of International law*) published in English and French;

---

[28] A. Roberts, 'Custom, Public Law and the Human Rights Analogy', *EJIL Talks*, 14 August 2013.

– A number of books examining the practice of specific States (e.g. *Digest of United States Practice in International Law*).

I.2   The structure of this book

Chapter 1 examines the concept of custom under general international law. One of the issues addressed is the complex nature of custom and how it is created. Another question that will be examined is whether States' consent is necessary for the development of customary rules. This chapter analyses the 'double requirement' of State practice and *opinio juris* that has been adopted by international tribunals to determine the existence of customary rules. I will examine specifically whether or not this 'double requirement' has been endorsed by investor-State arbitration tribunals. Finally, I will analyse the role played by judges and courts in 'revealing' the existence of a customary rule and the question as to whether their role is in fact broader than that. Specifically, the actual role played by arbitral tribunals regarding customary rules in investment arbitration will be investigated.

Chapter 2 examines the evolution of the importance and relevance of the different sources of international law in the field of international investment law. This is a fascinating odyssey in which the main relevant sources of law in this field (custom and treaties) have played different roles in different eras. The story is best told by specifically examining the evolution of two principles which are now generally considered to be rules of customary international law in investor-State arbitration: the 'minimum standard of treatment' and the general prohibition against expropriation without compensation. The existence of these two rules was seriously challenged in the 1960s and 1970s by a large segment of States, including those that emerged from colonialism. As a result, the foundation of these two rules as the basic set of legal investment protection for investors doing business abroad has been severely weakened. For this reason, Western States have increasingly started to adopt a bilateral approach to secure legal protection with capital-importing States on an *ad hoc* basis. The 1990s were also marked by developing States dramatically changing their historical position regarding basic legal protections for foreign investors. They started signing BITs *en masse*. In light of the present day proliferation of BITs (a phenomenon known as 'treatification'), one might naturally question what remains of the historical importance of custom as a source of investment protection (this question is also examined in detail in Chapter 5).

Chapter 3 examines the first requirement for the existence of any customary rule: State practice. Before doing so, I will first briefly discuss whether the practice of non-State actors is relevant to the phenomenon of the formation of custom in both general international law and investor-State arbitration. This chapter will then examine the extent to which State practice needs to be uniform, consistent, extensive and representative during a certain period of time for a customary rule to emerge. This chapter will mainly focus on examining the different 'manifestations' of practice, that is, the type of evidence of State Practice that is relevant to the creation of custom in both general international law and investor-State arbitration. Specifically, four manifestations of said practice will be examined.

First, the role of treaties will be assessed. I will observe that treaties can contribute to the formation of new rules of customary international law and that they can also codify existing customary rules. In the context of arbitration, I will examine the strict conditions under which rules contained in BITs can transform into customary rules and the reason why said transformation is very rare in practice. The controversial question of whether BITs taken together represent a 'new' custom will also be fully explored. Second, the role of statements under general international law will be examined. Different types of statements (some of them unique to the field of investor-State arbitration) will then be assessed: State pleadings in arbitration proceedings, interventions by non-disputing treaty parties during arbitration proceedings, official statements made by parties to a treaty, and Model BITs adopted by States. Third, this chapter will explore the conduct of States within international organizations as evidence of their practice in both general international law and investor-State arbitration. Another question that will be examined is the impact of the practice of international organizations on the formation of customary rules. Fourth, the internal national practice of States will be analysed. I will examine to what extent the conduct of the executive, legislative and judiciary branches of government can be considered as the practice of that State. I will also examine the actual weight that should be given to such conduct in the process of custom formation. Finally, I will address the question of the role and relevance (if any) of arbitral awards in the formation of custom.

Chapter 4 examines the second requirement for the existence of any customary rule: *opinio juris*. I will first analyse the contours of the *opinio juris* requirement under international law. Some of the issues addressed include explaining the reasons why it is necessary to demonstrate *opinio juris* and determining its concrete manifestations. The requirement will then be specifically assessed in the context of investment arbitration. One question examined is the role played by *opinio juris* in the process of transforming a similarly drafted provision, contained in numerous BITs, into a customary rule. Another question is whether or not States have any *opinio juris* when signing BITs. Finally, I will explore the soundness of some of the theories that have been put forward by writers to explain why it is (in their view) not necessary to specifically show States' *opinio juris* in the context of investor-State arbitration.

Chapter 5 examines the fundamental importance that customary rules continue to play in international investment law *despite* the impressive number of investment treaties that States have entered into in the last few decades. I will examine in some detail a number of situations where custom remains significant, including its gap-filling role and the fact that it is the applicable legal regime in the absence of any BIT. Investment treaties are also increasingly referring to the concept of custom (even though such references are still only found in a small *minority* of treaties). I will further argue that, in any event, arbitral tribunals always have to apply custom. Another question examined will be that of the limits of custom. I will therefore discuss the soundness of the argument advanced by some writers that a 'rule' of customary international law has now emerged providing investors with an automatic procedural 'right' to bring arbitration claims against the State where they make an investment, even in the absence of any BIT. Finally, I will examine the question of whether a State can claim the status of 'persistent objector' in arbitration proceedings in order to prevent the application of an established rule of customary law.

1

The concept of customary international law

Introduction

This first chapter focuses on defining the contours of the concept of customary international law in both general international law and international investment law. We will therefore not examine the different notions of custom that have been put forward by scholars and tribunals in other sub-fields of international law, such as international human rights law, international criminal law or international humanitarian law (Section 1.1). The following five questions will be addressed in this chapter.

First, we will begin with an analysis of the complex nature of custom as one of the formal sources of international law (Section 1.2). Any book dealing with the sources of law in investor-State arbitration must be solidly grounded on general public international law. The following basic (yet fundamental) questions will be examined in this section:

- Where does custom fit amongst the formal sources of international law?
- How do customary rules emerge?
- Why are customary rules obligatory?
- What is the role of the consent of States in the development of customary rules?

Second, another basic question that must be assessed at the outset of this book is the so-called double requirement of State practice and *opinio juris* which has been adopted by international tribunals to draw conclusions on the existence of customary rules (Section 1.3). We will briefly explore the so-called traditional and modern approaches, which have been adopted by scholars, regarding the necessity to demonstrate both requirements. This will bring us to the next issue, which is how this double requirement has been applied by investor-State arbitration tribunals. Moreover, I will examine the position that States have adopted in their pleadings and treaties regarding the necessity to demonstrate the two requirements of State practice and *opinio juris*.

Third, I will address the basic requirement that the party who is alleging the existence of a customary rule must demonstrate that the norm has acquired such status by presenting relevant evidence of State practice and *opinio juris* (Section 1.4). I will observe that this basic principle has been adopted by all investment tribunals.

Fourth, I will analyse the role played by judges and courts, including arbitral tribunals, in the formation and identification of customary rules in both general international law and investment arbitration (Section 1.5). Finally, I will examine the question of the actual role played by scholars in the identification of customary rules (Section 1.6).

1.1 Introductory remarks: this book examines custom in the context of general international law

The present book only examines the concept of custom under *general* international law. I will therefore not analyse the question of the status and the formation of custom in the specific context of sub-fields of international law, such as international human rights law,[1] international criminal law or international humanitarian law.[2] As noted by the ILC Special Rapporteur Wood in his First Report, 'different weight may be given to different materials depending on the field in question'.[3]

A number of scholars have pointed out that the jurisprudence of international criminal tribunals such as the International Tribunal for

---

[1] For an analysis of custom in international human rights law, see *inter alia*, the following writers: B. Simma and P. Alston, 'The Sources of Human Rights Law: Custom, *Jus Cogens*, and General Principles', *Australian YIL*, 12 (1988–1989), p. 82; R.B. Lillich, 'The Growing Importance of Customary International Human Rights Law', *Ga. J. Int'l & COMP. L.*, 25 (1995/6), p. 1–30.

[2] For an analysis of custom in humanitarian law, see *inter alia*, the following writers: J.M. Henckaerts, 'International Humanitarian Law as Customary International Law', *Refugee Survey Quarterly*, 21(3) (2002), pp. 190–192; T. Meron, *Human Rights and Humanitarian Norms as Customary Law* (Oxford: Oxford: Clarendon Press, 1991); T. Meron, 'The Continuing Role of Custom in the Formation of International Humanitarian Law', *AJIL* 90 (1996); N. Arajärvi, *The Changing Nature of Customary International Law: Methods of Interpreting the Concept of Custom in International Criminal Tribunals* (London; New York: Routledge, 2014); T. Meron, 'Revival of Customary Humanitarian Law', *AJIL* 99 (2005), pp. 817–834; M. Swart, 'Judicial Lawmaking at the ad hoc Tribunals: The Creative Use of the Sources of International Law and "Adventurous Interpretation"', *ZaöRV* 70 (2010), p. 459.

[3] International Law Commission, 'First Report on Formation and Evidence of Customary International Law', by Michael Wood, Special Rapporteur, Sixty-fifth session, Geneva, 6 May–7 June and 8 July–9 August 2013, UN doc. A/CN.4/663, 17 May 2013, p. 8 [hereinafter referred to as ILC, First Report, 2013].

the Former Yugoslavia (ICTY) and the International Criminal Tribunal for Rwanda (ICTR) has in recent years distanced itself from the traditional conception of custom.[4] For many writers, 'customary international law in the context of international criminal law means something different than customary international law in the context of traditional international law'.[5] For instance, scholars are increasingly speaking of 'signs of a fragmentation of the theory of customary international law'.[6] Thus, while the so-called double requirement of State practice and *opinio juris* (a question further discussed below at Section 1.3) has been recognized by a number of ICTY decisions,[7] a number of other cases from the chambers of the Tribunal have found custom to exist mainly based on *opinio juris* without requiring evidence of substantive State practice.[8] A good example of such approach is the position adopted by the Trial Chamber of the ICTY in the *Kupreskić* case:

> Admittedly, there does not seem to have emerged recently a body of State practice consistently supporting the proposition that one of the elements of custom, namely *usus* or *diuturnitas* has taken shape. This is however an area where *opinio iuris sive necessitatis* may play a much greater role than *usus*, as a result of the aforementioned Martens Clause. In the light of the way States and courts have implemented it, this Clause shows that principles of international humanitarian law may emerge through a

---

[4] R.B. Baker, 'Customary International Law in the 21st Century: Old Challenges and New Debates' *EJIL* 21(1) 2010, p. 184; N. Arajärvi, 'Changing Customary International Law and the Fluid Nature of Opinio Juris', paper presented at the conference 'The Role of *Opinio Juris* in Customary International Law', Duke-Geneva Institute in Transnational Law, Geneva, 2013, p. 5 ff; Jean d'Aspremont, 'An Autonomous Regime of Identification of Customary International Humanitarian Law: Do not Say What you do or do not do What you Say?' in R. van Steenberghe (ed.), *Droit international humanitaire: un régime spécial de droit international?* (Brussels: Bruylant, 2013).

[5] W. Schabas, 'Customary Law or 'Judge-Made' Law: Judicial Creativity at the UN Criminal Tribunals', in J. Doria *et al.* (eds.), *The Legal Regime of the International Criminal Court: Essays in Honour of Professor Igor Blishchenko* (Leiden: Martinus Nijhoff, 2009), p. 101. See also: ILC, First Report, 2013, p. 29, referring to the works of a number of scholars.

[6] Jean d'Aspremont, 'Customary International Law as a Dance Floor: Part II', *EJIL Talks!*, 15 April 2014.

[7] ILC, First Report, 2013, p. 29 ff.

[8] Arajärvi, 'Changing Customary International Law', p. 3; J. Wouters and C. Ryngaert, 'Impact on the Process of the Formation of Customary International Law', in M. Kamminga and M. Scheinin (eds.), *The Impact of Human Rights Law on General International Law* (Oxford: Oxford University Press, 2009), p. 112 ('the more important the common interests of the states or humanity are, the greater the weight that might be attached to *opinio juris* as opposed to state practice. If the stakes are high, inconsistent state practice may be glossed over, and a high premium may be put on states' statements and declarations, *inter alia* in multilateral for a, in identifying customary law combined with general principles of law').

customary process under the pressure of the demands of humanity or the dictates of public conscience, even where State practice is scant or inconsistent. The other element, in the form of *opinio necessitatis*, crystallising as a result of the imperatives of humanity or public conscience, may turn out to be the decisive element heralding the emergence of a general rule or principle of humanitarian law.[9]

The question remains open as to whether or not the method of customary law formation is fundamentally different in the fields of human rights and international humanitarian law because these areas are 'closely touching upon fundamental moral issues'.[10] In his Second Report, ILC Special Rapporteur Wood emphasized that *both elements* of State practice and *opinio juris* are in fact required in all areas of international law since 'any other approach risks artificially dividing international law into separate fields, which would run counter to the systemic nature of international law'.[11] However, he added that there may be 'a difference in application of the two-element approach in different fields'.[12]

[9] *Prosecutor v. Kupreškić*, ICTY Case No. IT-95-16-T (ICTY Trial Chamber), 14 January 2000, para. 527. See also: *Prosecutor v. Tadić*, ICTY Case No. IT-94-1, Decision on the Defence Motion for Interlocutory Appeal on Jurisdiction (ICTY Appeals Chamber), 2 October 1995, para. 99 ('Before pointing to some principles and rules of customary law that have emerged in the international community for the purpose of regulating civil strife, a word of caution on the law-making process in the law of armed conflict is necessary. When attempting to ascertain State practice with a view to establishing the existence of a customary rule or a general principle, it is difficult, if not impossible, to pinpoint the actual behaviour of the troops in the field for the purpose of establishing whether they in fact comply with, or disregard, certain standards of behaviour. This examination is rendered extremely difficult by the fact that not only is access to the theatre of military operations normally refused to independent observers [often even to the ICRC] but information on the actual conduct of hostilities is withheld by the parties to the conflict; what is worse, often recourse is had to misinformation with a view to misleading the enemy as well as public opinion and foreign Governments. In appraising the formation of customary rules or general principles one should therefore be aware that, on account of the inherent nature of this subject-matter, reliance must primarily be placed on such elements as official pronouncements of States, military manuals and judicial decisions'). See also: Appeal Judgment of the Extraordinary Chambers in the Courts of Cambodia (Supreme Court Chamber), Case number 001/18-07-2007-ECCC/SC, 3 February 2012, para. 93.
[10] Arajärvi, 'Changing Customary International Law', p. 9.
[11] International Law Commission, 'Second Report on Identification of Customary International Law', by Michael Wood, Special Rapporteur, Sixty-sixth session, Geneva, 5 May-6 June and 7 July-8 August 2014, A/CN.4/672, p. 13 [hereinafter referred to as ILC, Second Report, 2014].
[12] *Id.*, p. 12. See also: International Law Commission, 'Third Report on Identification of Customary International Law', by Michael Wood, Special Rapporteur, Sixty-seventh session, Geneva, 4 May-5 June and 6 July-7 August 2015, A/CN.4/682 [hereinafter referred to as ILC, Third Report, 2015], p. 3 adding, 'Delegations fully supported the

The world of international investment law is quite different from humanitarian law. To paraphrase the ICTY's *Kupreskić* case, questions pertaining to 'the pressure of the demands of humanity or the dictates of public conscience' are rather unlikely to arise in the context of investor-State arbitration. For this reason, I will not examine the work of scholars that have developed alternative theories on custom in the sub-fields of international humanitarian law or human rights.[13]

1.2   The nature of custom

This section briefly examines the basic features of the phenomenon of custom in international law as one of the formal sources[14] of international law to be applied by international courts and tribunals (Section 1.2.1). Some of the other issues addressed in this section include a description of the informal (and quite mysterious) way by which customary rules emerge (Section 1.2.2). Another controversial question examined in this section is the actual role played by the consent of States in the development of such customary rules (Section 1.2.3).

1.2.1   *Custom is one of the sources of international law*

Although it has been criticized for being unsatisfactory,[15] the starting point of any analysis on custom is Article 38(1) of the Statute of the

---

two-element approach, with several adding that the view according to which, in some fields, one constituent element alone would be sufficient to establish a rule of customary international law was not supported by international practice and in the jurisprudence'.

[13] J. Kammerhofer, 'Orthodox Generalists and Political Activists in International Legal Scholarship', in M. Happold (ed.), *International Law in a Multipolar World* (London: Routledge, 2012), p. 147 ('Because of the perceived incommensurability of what is regarded as traditional or orthodox methods of customary international lawmaking with the humanist goals espoused by the activist scholars, an influential part of human rights and humanitarian legal scholarship has developed a new approach to customary international law for these areas of international law over the past decade').

[14] Nguyen Quoc Dinh, Patrick Dallier, Mathias Forteau and Alain Pellet, *Droit International Public* (8th edn., Paris: LGDJ, 2007), p. 353.

[15] See, the observations in: Karol Wolfke, *Custom in Present International Law* (2nd edn., Dordrecht: Nijhoff, 1993), pp. 5–8; Maurice H. Mendelson, 'The Formation of Customary International Law', *Rec. des Cours* 192 (1985), p. 187; G. Abi-Saab, 'La coutume dans tous ses états', in *Le droit international à l'heure de sa codification – Etudes en l'honneur de Roberto Ago* (Milan: Giuffrè, 1987, t. 1), p. 58; James Crawford, *Brownlie's Principles of Public International Law* (8th edn., Cambridge: Cambridge University Press, 2012) p. 23; G.J.H. Van Hoof, *Rethinking the Sources of International Law* (Deventer: Kluwer, 1983), p. 87.

International Court of Justice (ICJ).[16] The provision enumerates a (non-exhaustive) list of the formal 'sources of international law',[17] one of which is 'international custom'.[18] Article 38 uses the following (rather awkward) wording: 'international custom, as evidence of a general practice accepted as law'. The shortcomings of this formulation are readily apparent. As rightly noted by Villiger, 'the Court cannot apply a custom, [but] only customary law',[19] and it is in fact the 'general practice accepted as law which constitutes evidence of a customary rule' not the other way around.[20] In the words of Crawford, 'the existence of a custom is not to be confused with the evidence adduced in its favor'.[21] A better definition of custom is the one adopted by ILC Special Rapporteur Wood in his Second Report: customary international law 'means those rules of international law that derive from and reflect a general practice accepted as law'.[22]

Yet, however flawed its language may be, it remains that the sources of international law defined in Article 38 are generally regarded as valid and applicable not only in ICJ cases, but also before other international courts and tribunals (subject to any specific rules contained in such court's statutes).[23] Investor-State arbitration tribunals frequently refer to this provision as an authoritative statement of the sources of international

[16] *Statute of the I.C.J.*, reprinted in International Court of Justice, Charter of the United Nations, Statute and Rules of Court and other Documents 61 (No. 4 1978).

[17] For a recent study on the question, see: A. Pellet, 'Article 38', in A. Zimmermann *et al.* (eds.), *The Statute of the International Court of Justice: A Commentary* (2nd edn., Oxford: Oxford University Press, 2012), pp. 812–832. *Contra*: J.A. Barberis, 'Réflexions sur la coutume internationale', *AFDI*, 36 (1990), p. 17 (for whom 'le procédé coutumier n'est pas une source de droit précisément parce qu'il n'est pas réglé par le droit').

[18] Treaties and general principles of law are the two other formal sources of international law mentioned at Article 38 whereas 'judicial decisions and the teachings of the most highly qualified publicists of the various nations' are considered as 'subsidiary means for the determination of rules of law'.

[19] Mark E. Villiger, *Customary International law and Treaties: A Manual on the Theory and Practice of the Interrelation of Sources* (2nd edn., The Hague: Kluwer, 1997), p. 15.

[20] *Id.*, p. 15; R. Jennings and A. Watts, *Oppenheim's International Law* (9th edn., London: Longman, 1996, vol. 1(1)), p. 26.

[21] Crawford, *Brownlie's Principles of Public International Law*, p. 23. See also: James Crawford, 'The Identification and Development of Customary International Law', ILA British Branch Conference (2014), p. 2 ('this definition is defective in that it puts the elements of customary international law in the wrong order. Evidence is not a constitutive element of customary international law. Rather, evidence is adduced to "prove" its existence').

[22] ILC, Second Report, 2014, p. 7, Draft Conclusion 2 of the ILC 'Proposed draft conclusions on the identification of customary international law'.

[23] ILC, First Report, 2013, p. 14. See also: ILC, Second Report, 2014, p. 6.

law.[24] They have also consistently held that they must apply custom as one of the sources of international law. To the best of the present author's knowledge, no arbitral tribunal has ever rejected the relevance of Article 38(1) of the ICJ Statute in the field of international investment law.

In the present author's view, any enquiry into the sources of international investment law must be based on the recognized sources of general international law listed under Article 38(1) of the ICJ Statute. This is because investment arbitration is part of public international law.[25] It is not a self-contained regime.[26] However, as mentioned by Tams, reference to Article 38 can only be the *starting point* of any enquiry about the sources of international *investment* law.[27] According to d'Aspremont, 'Article 38 has never been more than a provision that modestly aims to define the law applicable by the ICJ' and it has 'never purported to provide an exhaustive list of the sources of international law'.[28] The sources mentioned in Article 38 are not the only sources of international law. Similarly, relying on Article 38 *does not* mean that the sources of investment arbitration are the *same* as those under general international law.[29] A recent book on the sources of rights and obligations in international investment law includes chapters on sources other than those mentioned at Article 38, including State contracts and national laws.[30]

---

[24] One recent example is *Merrill & Ring Forestry L.P.* v. *Canada*, UNCITRAL, Award, 31 March 2010, para. 184 [hereinafter *Merrill & Ring* v. *Canada*]. See also: *Methanex Corporation* v. *United States*, UNCITRAL, Award, 3 August 2005, Part II-Chap. B, para. 3.

[25] C. Tams, 'The Sources of International Investment Law' in T. Gazzini and E. de Brabandere (eds.), *International Investment Law: The Sources of Rights and Obligations* (Leiden; Boston: Martinus Nijhoff, 2012), p. 320; M. Forteau, 'La contribution au développement du droit international général de la jurisprudence arbitrale relative aux investissements étrangers', *Anuário Brasileiro de Direito Internacional*, 4(1) (2009), p. 14; Jose E. Alvarez, 'A Bit on Custom', *N.Y.U. J. Int'l L. & Pol.* 42 (2009–2010), p. 76; C. McLachlan, L. Shore and M. Weiniger, *International Investment Arbitration: Substantive Principles* (Oxford: Oxford University Press, 2007), p. 15; Claire Crépet Daigremont, 'Les sources du droit international des investissements', in C. Leben (ed.) *Droit international des investissements et l'arbitrage transnational* (Paris: Pedone, 2015), p. 84.

[26] *Archer Daniels Midland Company and Tate and Lyle Ingredients Americas, Inc.,* v. *Mexico*, ICSID Case No. ARB(AF)/04/05, Award, 21 November 2007, para. 195.

[27] Tams, 'The Sources of International Investment Law', p. 319.

[28] J. d'Aspremont, *Formalism and the Sources of International Law* (Oxford: Oxford University Press, 2011), p. 149.

[29] The question is examined in Tams, 'The Sources of International Investment Law', pp. 319–321.

[30] See, for instance, P. Dumberry, 'International Investment Contracts' in T. Gazzini and E. de Brabandere (eds.), *International Investment Law: The Sources of Rights and Obligations*.

In other words, by relying on Article 38 as the place to find the formal sources of international law applicable in investor-State arbitration, the present author does not intend to deny the hybrid nature of this field of law.[31]

1.2.2   The informal (and mysterious) way by which customary rules emerge

The major difference between the two most important sources of international law, that is, treaties and custom, is well known. A treaty is a *formal* process leading to the creation of written norms binding only on the parties to the instrument. On the contrary, custom is by 'its very nature the result of an *informal* process of rule-creation, so that the degree of precision found in more formal processes of law-making is not to be expected here'.[32] In other words, customary rules are 'unwritten' (and often imprecise) rules that develop over time. Customary international law was clearly 'intended to add flexibility to the rigidity of treaties as a source of international law'.[33] However, d'Aspremont recently raised the question as to whether the interpretation given by some scholars to custom has become *too* flexible and not rigid enough: 'the intellectual prison of custom seems to be gradually transformed into a large dance floor where (almost) every step and movement is allowed or, at least, tolerated'.[34]

The first notable aspect of 'imprecision' is the fact that customary rules have no 'birth certificates'. The formation of a customary rule is indeed a

---

[31]   Z. Douglas, 'The Hybrid Foundations of Investment Treaty Arbitration', British YIL 74 (2003), pp. 152–153. See also: Florian Grisel, 'The Sources of Foreign Investment Law', in: Z. Douglas, J. Pauwelyn and J.E. Viñuales (eds.), *The Foundations of International Investment Law: Bringing Theory into Practice* (Oxford: Oxford University Press, 2014), p. 216 ('Unfortunately, the analysis of sources of foreign investment law has not followed this evolution. When identifying sources of foreign investment law, most authors use the categories set out under Article 38(1) of the Statute of the International Court of Justice (ICJ), thus signalling the conceptual influence of public international law on the study of investment arbitration. This focus on public international law seems to derive from the qualification of investment tribunals as public international tribunals, and therefore disregards the hybrid nature of investment tribunals').

[32]   International Law Association, 'Statement of Principles Applicable to the Formation of General Customary International Law', Final Report of the Committee on the Formation of Customary Law, Conference Report London (2000), p. 2 (emphasis in the original) [hereinafter ILA, Final Report, 2000]; Mendelson, 'The Formation of Customary International Law', pp. 172–176.

[33]   Crawford, 'The Identification and Development of Customary International Law', p. 10.

[34]   d'Aspremont, 'Customary International Law as a Dance Floor: Part I'.

continuous process, which often takes decades to crystallize.[35] There is therefore no precise date at which point one can state that a rule has fully emerged and therefore become obligatory for all States.[36] This is because there is no agreed-upon and ready-to-be-used general formula that identifies how many States are needed (and how long it takes) for a rule of customary international law to emerge. In the *Nuclear Weapons Advisory Opinion*, the Court itself speaks of 'the nascent *opinio juris*' of States on the prohibition of the use of nuclear weapons.[37] In the words of one writer, such a reference clearly 'implies that custom does not spring into existence fully formed, but it must undergo a period of maturation'.[38] This specific feature of the emergence of custom has led Abi-Saab to affirm that 'le *modus operandi* de la coutume dans l'accomplissement de [sa fonction de source formelle du droit] reste (…) un processus mystérieux et une des énigmes permanentes du droit international'.[39]

Yet, however mysterious and puzzling the process of maturation of customary rules may be, it remains that at some point in time an independent observer (a State, a judge, a scholar, etc.) will be able to assess whether or not a given rule has indeed emerged and crystallized. But this is an *a posteriori* revelation. Therefore, while the observer may not be able to determine precisely *when* the rule has actually crystallized, he/she may still be able to conclude (based on evidence of State practice and *opinio juris*) that the rule *now* exists and is therefore binding on all States.[40] Mendelson provides the following useful analogy with the building of a house:

> It is often not easy or even possible to say exactly when a house has been created. Clearly, it is not when the first foundation stone is laid. But it is not when the last lick of paint has been added either. It is problematic at exactly what point we could say "This is a house." Do we have to wait for

---

[35] Wolfke, *Custom in Present International Law*, p. 54.

[36] *Id.*; Villiger, *Customary International law and Treaties*, p. 54; Crawford, 'The Identification and Development of Customary International Law', p. 11.

[37] *Nuclear Weapons*, Advisory Opinion, ICJ Rep. 1996, paras. 67, 73.

[38] Crawford, 'The Identification and Development of Customary International Law', p. 11.

[39] Abi-Saab, 'La coutume dans tous ses états', p. 58, see also, at 59: ' [e]n attendant, le processus [coutumier] lui-même reste toujours insaisissable. Car il s'agit en effet d'un *processus exogène*, autonome, d'une dynamique émanant directement du corps social, en dehors de tout cadre spécifique, qui n'est ni réglementé, centralisé, ou canalisé'.

[40] Crawford, *Brownlie's Principles of Public International Law*, p. 23 ('the existence of a custom … is the conclusion drawn by someone (a legal adviser, a court, a government, a commentator) as to two related questions: (a) is there a general practice; (b) is it accepted as international law?').

the roof to go on, for the windows to be put in, or for all of the utilities to be installed? So it is with customary law.

Moreover, even when the house is "finished", that is not the end of the matter. It may be substantially altered, for example by the addition of a new wing or a new storey, while still remaining the "same" house. Furthermore, the house has to be kept constantly under repair. If a tile slips off the roof and it is not replaced, the rain will get in and rot the timbers. If that is not rectified, the roof will fall in, and eventually the walls and so on. On the other hand, repairs to the house may actually strengthen it. So it is with customary law. Even after the rule has "emerged", every act of compliance will strengthen it, and every violation, if acquiesced in, will help to undermine it.[41]

Perhaps the most famous explanation is Pitt Cobbett's path analogy described as follows by de Visscher:

> On a pu comparer la lente constitution de la coutume internationale à la formation graduelle d'un chemin à travers un terrain vague. À l'origine on y relève des pistes multiples et incertaines, à peine visibles au sol. Puis, la majorité des usagers, pour quelque raison d'utilité commune, adopte un même parcours; un sentier unique se dégage qui, à son tour, fait place à un chemin reconnu désormais comme la seule voie régulière, sans que l'on puisse dire à quel moment précis cette dernière transformation s'est accomplie.[42]

Ultimately, what really matters is to be able to determine 'at the moment the appreciation is being made' whether or not 'practice has matured into a rule of law'.[43] As aptly put by one author, 'it is not often that we need to know precisely at what moment the fruit became ripe: we are more

[41] Mendelson, 'The Formation of Customary International Law', p. 175.
[42] Charles de Visscher, *Théories et réalités en droit international public* (Paris: Pedone, 1953), pp. 182–184, referring to Pitt Cobbett, *Leading Cases on International Law* (London: Sweet and Maxwell, 5th edn., vol. 1, 1931–1937), p. 5 (translation: 'The growth of usage and its development into custom may be likened to the formation of a path across a common. At first each wayfarer pursues his own course; gradually, by reason either of its directness or on some other ground of apparent utility, some particular route is followed by the majority; this route next assumes the character of a track, discernible but not as yet well defined, from which deviation, however, now becomes more rare; whilst in its final stage the route assumes the shape of a well-defined path, habitually followed by all who pass that way. And yet it would be difficult to point out at what precise moment this route acquired the character of an acknowledged path. The growth of usage and formation of custom, both as between a community of individuals and the community of nations, proceeds much on the same lines').
[43] Mendelson, 'The Formation of Customary International Law', p. 176. See also: Y. Dinstein, 'The Interaction between Customary International Law and Treaties', *Rec. des cours* 322 (2006), p. 292.

interested in knowing, when we bite it, if it is *now* ripe or still too hard or sour'.[44]

1.2.3   The role of consent in the development of customary rules

A rule that has already crystallized into customary law is binding upon *all* States of the international community. A State is not allowed to opt out unilaterally.[45] Thus, for the ICJ, 'by their very nature, [customary rules] must have equal force for all members of the international community, and cannot therefore be the subject of any right of unilateral exclusion exercisable at will by any one of them in its favour'.[46] In fact, allowing a State to dissent on the ground that an already existing rule is contrary to its own interests would amount to a complete denial of the very existence of any customary rules in international law.[47] This is why States generally argue that a rule has *not* yet crystallized into custom rather than flatly rejecting its application. One controversial question is whether a State should be permitted not to be bound by such a rule in the event that it objected to it in the early stage of its formation and did so constantly thereafter. This is the theory of the 'persistent objector' (a question addressed below[48]).

The most interesting question is *why* customary law is binding upon all States. Different views have been put forward. The voluntarist theory of international law is based on the assumption that the sovereign State's will is at the foundation of international law. Accordingly, a State is bound only by the rules to which it has itself consented. The Permanent Court of International Justice (PCIJ), in the *Lotus* case, set out the classic formulation of this theory.[49] As a matter of principle, supporters of the theory believe that each and every State needs to give its actual consent to

---

[44] *Id.* (emphasis in the original).

[45] M. Akehurst, 'Custom as a Source of International Law', *British YIL*, 47 (1974–1975), pp. 24–26. See, however the critical analysis in: Curtis A. Bradley and Mitu Gulati, 'Withdrawing from International Custom', *Yale LJ* 120 (2010), p. 202.

[46] *North Sea Continental Shelf Cases (Federal Republic of Germany v. Denmark / Federal Republic of Germany v. Netherlands)*, ICJ Rep.1969, para. 63.

[47] O. Schachter, 'International Law in Theory and Practice: General Course in Public International Law', *Rec. des Cours* 178 (1982), p. 38.

[48] See, Chapter 5, Section 5.4.

[49] *Lotus Case (France v. Turkey)*, PCIJ Rep Series A No 10, at 18 ('The rules of law binding upon states . . . emanate from their own free will as expressed in conventions or by usages generally accepted as expressing principles of law'). See, the critical analysis of this case in: Nguyen *et al.*, *Droit International Public*, p. 354.

a customary rule before it can be considered bound by it. Opponents of the theory have correctly objected that such requirement is 'inconsistent with reality' insofar as 'it is simply impossible to show that each and every State positively consented to the emergence' of all customary rules.[50]

The vast majority of scholars believe that it is not necessary to show the actual and specific consent of a State in the formation and development of a customary norm.[51] This is the position adopted by the ILA in its 2000 Report: 'Where a rule of general customary international law exists, for any particular State to be bound by that rule it is not necessary to prove either that State's consent to it or its belief in the rule's obligatory or (as the case may be) permissive character'.[52] The ILA Report added that 'no international court or tribunal has ever refused to hold that a State was bound by a rule of alleged general customary international merely because it had not itself actively participated in the practice in question or deliberately acquiesced in it'.[53]

While actual State consent is not necessary for *general* custom, it should be added that the situation is clearly different in the context of *regional custom*.[54] Since regional custom is (by definition) in derogation from a more *general* rule, a State's specific acceptance of the 'special' rule is naturally required for such a rule to be binding on it.[55] Consequently, a State should be given the opportunity to claim the status of the 'persistent

[50] Mendelson, 'The Formation of Customary International Law', p. 255.
[51] For instance, see: L. Henkin, 'International Law: Politics, Values and Function: General Course on Public International Law', *Rec. des cours* 216 (1989), p. 57 (for whom, custom is 'not a product of the will of States but a "systemic creation", reflecting the "consent" of the international system, not the consent of individual States'); E. Jimenez de Arechaga, 'International Law in the Past Third of a Century', *Rec. des cours* 159 (1978), p. 29 (Custom is 'the product of general consensus, not of individual State consent, express or implied'); Akehurst, 'Custom as a Source of International Law', p. 23 ('A State can be bound by a rule of customary international law even if it has never consented to that rule').
[52] ILA, Final Report, p. 8, see also, at p. 39 ('it is not necessary for any particular State to have consented to a rule of general international law to be bound by it'). The ILA (*Id.* p. 27), however, makes an exception for the 'persistent objector' ('If whilst a practice is developing into a rule of general law, a State persistently and openly dissents from the rule, it will not be bound by it'). A point further discussed at Chapter 5, Section 5.4.
[53] *Id.*, p. 24.
[54] A. D'Amato, 'The Concept of Special Custom in International Law', *AJIL* 63 (1969) p. 211; G. Cohen-Jonathan, 'La coutume locale', *AFDI*, 7 (1961), pp. 119–140; Nguyen *et al.*, *Droit International Public*, p. 354.
[55] H. Waldock, 'General Course on Public International Law', *Rec. des cours* 106 (1962), p. 50; Schachter, 'International Law in Theory and Practice', p. 36.

objector' from a regional custom.[56] Indeed, this was the conclusion reached by the ICJ in the *Asylum* case.[57]

1.2.4   Is there such a thing as 'tacit' consent?

In the context of *general* customary law, voluntarist writers have put forward the concept of a State's 'tacit' or 'implied' consent to explain the development of such rules.[58] Most writers reject this interpretation, revealing that it is a mere fiction that does not represent the actual practice of States.[59] For example, according to Guzman, 'a state may fail to object for any number of reasons having nothing to do with consent'.[60] Nevertheless, the tacit consent theory could (at best) only apply to *some* States, *not all* of them. The theory is simply irrelevant for three groups of States: (1) the ones who did not know at the time that a new rule was emerging, (2) new States which simply did not exist at that time and, finally, (3) States which were not in a position to contribute to the formation of a new customary rule when it emerged.

First, the tacit theory can only be justified for States who knew at the time that a norm was emerging. This is because 'only affected states which knew, or might have been expected to know, of the practice can be said to have acquiesced to it'.[61] Thus, as explained by Byers, 'if a State is

---

[56] B. Conforti, 'Cours général de droit international public', *Rec. des cours* 212 (1988), p. 76; D'Amato, 'The Concept of Special Custom', pp. 233–234, 248–249, 252–254, 261; G. Abi-Saab, 'Cours général de droit international public', *Rec. des cours* 207 (1987), p. 181.

[57] *Asylum Case (Colombia v. Peru)*, ICJ Rep.1950, p. 276. In this case, Colombia was relying on the existence of a so-called Latin-American regional custom giving the right to a unilateral and definitive qualification of the status of an individual by a State when granting diplomatic asylum, and maintaining that such special rule was binding on Peru. The Court rejected Colombia's contention of the existence of a regional custom and added in an *obiter dictum* that 'even if it could be supposed that such a custom existed between certain Latin-American States only, it could not be invoked against Peru which, far from having by its attitude adhered to it, has, on the contrary, repudiated it (. . .)' (*Id.*, pp. 277–278).

[58] Dionisio Anzilotti, *Cours de droit international* (Paris: Sirey, 1929), pp. 73–74.

[59] L. Condorelli, 'Custom', in M. Bedjaoui, *International Law: Achievement and Prospects* (Unesco, 1991), p. 203; de Visscher, *Théories et réalités en droit international public*, p. 182; Nguyen *et al.*, *Droit International Public*, p. 354.

[60] Andrew T. Guzman, 'Saving Customary International Law', *Michigan JIL* 27 (2006), p. 143 ('It may prefer to avoid objecting for political reasons, it may not feel that the norm is changing into custom—making objection unnecessary—or it may simply not be sufficiently affected by the rule to make objection a priority').

[61] Jörg Kammerhofer, 'Uncertainty in the Formal Sources of International Law: Customary International Law and Some of Its Problems', *EJIL* 15(3) (2004), p. 533.

aware that a customary rule is developing or changing, and chooses not to object to nor actively oppose that development or change, then the failure to object or oppose is regarded as demonstrating support for the new rule'.[62] The tacit consent theory simply does not apply to the other States which did not know (and could not have known) that a new norm was emerging. A State that does *not* know that a norm is emerging, and therefore (quite logically) does nothing, cannot be said in any plausible way to have tacitly 'agreed' to the emergence of such a rule.

Nevertheless, once the rule has crystallized it will ultimately apply to *all States*, including those who knew nothing about it at the time of its formation.[63] This is the main reason why the 'tacit' consent theory has been rightly qualified as 'superficially an attractive explanation, but in fact "a mere fiction" which does not describe what actually happens'[64]:

> [i]t is simply not true that, whilst the rule is in the course of emerging, *all* States consent in one way or another to it. Obviously, those who initiate the practice *do* consent to the rule. This applies also to those who imitate the practice. Similarly for those who, being specially affected by a claim, fail to protest against it (. . .) But there may well be a significant number of States who do nothing and who are not so directly affected by a claimed new rule that a response on their part seems called for. (Especially when it is borne in mind that even a protest is often regarded as a relatively unfriendly act.) If the practice nevertheless eventually achieves the requisite level of generality and representativeness, those States will find one day that a rule binding on them has come into being without their having consented to it in any real sense of the term. So, once again, to presume their consent is a mere fiction.[65]

Second, the tacit theory is unfit for new States.[66] Thus, a State that did not exist when a new rule emerged cannot be said to have tacitly agreed to its development. The tacit theory simply cannot explain why those rules are nevertheless binding on new States despite the fact that they did not (and could not have) consent to them.

It is generally recognized that new States are automatically bound by rules of customary international law.[67] Thus, allowing new States to

---

[62] M. Byers, *Custom, Power and the Power of Rules: International Relations and Customary International Law* (Cambridge: Cambridge University Press, 1999), p. 143.

[63] Nguyen *et al., Droit International Public*, p. 354.

[64] Mendelson, 'The Formation of Customary International Law', pp. 255–256.

[65] ILA, Final Report, p. 39 (emphasis in the original).

[66] Mendelson, 'The Formation of Customary International Law', p. 260; Dinstein, 'The Interaction between Customary International Law and Treaties', p. 283.

[67] ILA, Final Report, p. 24.

simply reject rules which enjoy broad community support would amount to 'deny[ing] the existence of a general international legal order'[68] and would 'create unacceptable disorder'.[69] Writers believe that by freely entering the international community new States are acquiring rights and obligations, which are attached to the status of an independent State.[70] While the ICJ has never had the opportunity to deal with this issue directly,[71] a passage taken from the *Case Concerning the Frontier Dispute* suggests that the Court supports the automatic application of custom to new States.[72] The opposite view only seems to be maintained by a small minority of (voluntarist) writers.[73] One ICJ Judge in the *North Sea Continental Shelf* Cases expressly endorsed a similar position in his separate opinion.[74]

Third, the tacit theory does not explain why customary rules also apply to States that did nothing when the rule emerged because, at that time, they were not in a position to contribute in any way to the formation of the law.[75] The classic example is that of a landlocked country which did not (and could not) participate in the formation of rules regarding coastlines.[76] In the event that this State eventually gains access to the

---

[68] Waldock, 'General Course on Public International Law', p. 52.

[69] Henkin, 'International Law: Politics, Values and Function', p. 57; G.M. Danilenko, *Law-Making in the International Community* (Dordrecht: Martinus Nijhoff, 1993), p. 115.

[70] Schachter, 'International Law in Theory and Practice', p. 34; T.M. Franck, 'Fairness in the International Legal and Institutional System: General Course on Public International Law', *Rec. des cours* 240 (1993), p. 60.

[71] The United Kingdom in the *Fisheries Jurisdiction case (United Kingdom v. Iceland)*, ICJ Rep. 1974, *Pleadings*, vol. II (Reply submitted by the Government of the United Kingdom) took the view that 'there is universal agreement that a new state has no option but to adhere to generally accepted customary law'.

[72] *Case Concerning the Frontier Dispute (Burkina Faso v. Mali)*, Judgment, ICJ Rep. 1986, p. 568, where the Chamber decided that customary law (in this case the principle of *uti possidetis*) would apply to new States 'immediately and from that moment onwards'. On this case, see Danilenko, *Law-Making in the International Community*, pp. 116–118.

[73] H. Thierry, J. Combacau, S. Sur and C. Vallee, *Droit international public* (Montchrestien, 1985), p. 119; Villiger, *Customary International Law and Treaties*, p. 36; Van Hoof, *Rethinking the Sources of International Law*, pp. 77–78; Danilenko, *Law-Making in the International Community*, pp. 113–118.

[74] *North Sea Continental Shelf Cases*, p. 48, Judge Ammoun for whom a rule of customary law 'does not require the consent of all States, (...) but at least the consent of those who were aware of this general practice and, being in a position to oppose it, have not done so. (...) Thus the right of countries becoming independent, which have not participated in the formation of rules which they consider incompatible with the new state of affairs, is preserved' (p. 130).

[75] Dinstein, 'The Interaction between Customary International Law and Treaties', p. 283.

[76] *Id.*, p. 283; Mendelson, 'The Formation of Customary International Law', p. 261.

sea, it would be bound by existing rules that have already been consolidated. Clearly, that State cannot be said to have 'consented' (tacitly or otherwise) in any way to the creation of such rules.

For all these reasons, the 'tacit' theory explaining the nature of custom is *not* convincing.[77] However, this does not mean that consent is altogether irrelevant to the phenomenon of custom creation. It is undeniable that *some States* have necessarily consented along the way for any rule of law to have developed.[78] According to the ILA, 'if it can be shown that a particular State *has in fact* assented to an alleged rule of customary international law, that will usually be enough to bind it'.[79] For this reason, the ILA concluded that '[t]he consent of a State is therefore a *sufficient*, but it is not a *necessary*, condition of its being bound by a rule of customary international law'.[80]

Why then are customary rules binding upon all States if it is not based on State consent?[81] According to some writers, 'the obligation to conform to rules of international law is not derived from the voluntary decision of a State to accept or reject the binding force of a rule of law'; it is instead 'the societal context which motivates States to have an international law and obligates them to conform to its norms'.[82] Some scholars speak of the 'social necessity'[83] or the 'moral necessity which underlies observance of all law'.[84] According to de Visscher, all customary norms are found to be morally and sociably acceptable by a sufficient number of States and well-adapted to the ultimate need for order within the international society.[85] This is indeed the conclusion reached by the

---

[77] Mendelson, 'The Formation of Customary International Law', p. 261; Nguyen *et al.*, *Droit International Public*, p. 354.

[78] *Id.*, p. 264, mentioning that this is the case for 'the State or States initiating the practice, and the State or States imitating or genuinely acquiescing in it'.

[79] ILA, Final Report, pp. 39–40 (emphasis in the original).

[80] *Id.* p. 40 (emphasis in the original)

[81] C. Tomuschat, 'Obligations Arising for States Without or Against Their Will', *Rec. des cours* 241 (1993), p. 209 ('consent alone cannot explain the binding force of international law').

[82] J. Charney, 'The Persistent Objector Rule and the Development of Customary International Law', *British YIL* (1985), pp. 16, 18.

[83] Nguyen *et al.*, *Droit International Public*, p. 355; Pierre-Marie Dupuy and Yann Kerbrat, *Droit international public* (12th edn., Paris: Dalloz, 2014), p. 364 ('l'expression d'une nécessité sociale ressentie par les membres de la collectivité internationale et les incitant les uns et les autres à agir d'une certaine manière'). See also: Pierre-Marie Dupuy, 'L'unité de l'ordre juridique international', *Rec. des cours* 297 (2002), p. 163.

[84] D.P. O'Connell, *International Law* (London: Stevens and Sons, 1970), p. 16.

[85] de Visscher, *Théories et réalités en droit international public*, pp. 182–184: 'les précédents, qui souvent sont des dérogations conscientes au droit en vigueur, qui tout au moins sont presque toujours des actes autonomes et incoordonnés, ne rallient l'adhésion générale constitutive de la coutume qu'après qu'ils sont apparus sous l'aspect d'une pratique

Chamber of the ICJ in the *Gulf of Maine* case wherein it referred to customary international law as 'comprises a limited set of norms for ensuring the coexistence and vital cooperation of the members of the international community'.[86]

Having examined the complex nature of custom and the way by which customary rules emerge, the next section will address the question of the two basic requirements (State practice and *opinio juris*), which are necessary to conclude to the existence of a customary rule. Specifically, I will examine how investment tribunals have applied this so-called double requirement.

1.3 The double requirement of State practice and *opinio juris*

This section examines the two basic requirements (State practice and *opinio juris*), which are necessary to conclude to the existence of a customary rule. I will begin by briefly exploring the so-called traditional and modern approaches adopted by scholars regarding the necessity to demonstrate both requirements (Section 1.3.1). I will then examine the position adopted by international tribunals regarding this 'double requirement'. Lastly, this section will provide an analysis of investor-State arbitration awards and the position adopted by States in these proceedings (Section 1.3.2).

1.3.1 The traditional and modern approaches regarding the relevance of these two elements

Under Article 38(1)b of the ICJ Statute, 'international custom' has two constitutive elements: a 'general practice' that is 'accepted as law'.[87] The

cohérente portant en elle les éléments d'un ordre moralement et socialement acceptable, parce que soutenu par des forces suffisantes et adapté à des besoins généralement ressentis (. . .) C'est que l'ordre reste le besoin primordial des rapports internationaux; c'est aussi parce que, si l'ordre postule le pouvoir, celui-ci ne s'assure la durée que s'il rallie à lui un certain assentiment morale. (. . .) En définitive, sans s'opposer l'une à l'autre, la perspective juridique, qui est celle des réalisations historiques. Le juriste à la recherche d'un principe de légitimisation, justifie ex post facto la coutume établie par sa correspondance avec les exigences de l'ordre: l'historien découvre le jeu des forces politiques qui ont présidé à son élaboration. Les deux ponts de vue ne s'excluent pas. La coutume internationale nous met en présence de l'une des manifestations les plus importantes de l'action conjuguée de la force et du droit'.

[86] *Delimitation of the Maritime Boundary in the Gulf of Maine Area (Canada v. United States)*, Judgment, ICJ Rep. 1984, para. 111.

[87] Art. 38, Statute of the I.C.J., reprinted in International Court of Justice, Charter of the United Nations, Statute and Rules of Court and other Documents 61 (No. 4 1978).

former is generally referred to as the 'material' (or 'objective') requirement.[88] The question of how extensive, uniform and consistent such a general practice should be will be discussed in Chapter 3.[89] The second constitutive element is the State's belief that such practice is *required* by law (*opinio juris sive necessitatis*). It is generally referred to as *opinio juris* or as the 'psychological' (or 'subjective') requirement.[90]

This so-called double requirement is one of the best-established principles of international law.[91] Thus, as explained by ILC Special Rapporteur Wood, the 'double requirement' is 'generally adopted in the practice of States and the decisions of international courts and tribunals, including the [ICJ]' and it is 'widely endorsed in the literature'.[92] The double requirement has in fact been recognized by most scholars.[93] It is often referred to as the 'traditional' approach. In a recent article, Roberts notably described this approach as one 'focus[ing] primarily on state practice in the form of interstate interaction and acquiescence', with *opinio juris* being 'a secondary consideration invoked to distinguish between legal and nonlegal obligations'.[94]

A number of scholars have contested the strict delimitation between these two elements.[95] Some have also used different concepts,[96] while

---

[88] State practice is examined in Chapter 3.   [89] See, Chapter 3, Section 3.2.
[90] This requirement is examined in Chapter 4.   [91] ILC, First Report, 2013, p. 22.
[92] ILC, Second Report, 2014, p. 8. See also: ILC, Third Report, 2015, p. 3, 7. See, International Law Commission, 'Text of the Draft Conclusions Provisionally adopted by the Drafting Committee, Sixty-seventh session, Geneva, 4 May-5 June and 6 July-7 August 2014, 14 July 2015, A/CN.4/L.869 [hereinafter referred to as ILC, Draft Conclusions, 2015], conclusion no. 2 ('To determine the existence and content of a rule of customary international law, it is necessary to ascertain whether there is a general practice that is accepted as law (*opinion juris*)').
[93] For a long list of authors, see, *Id.*, pp. 10–11.
[94] A.E. Roberts, 'Traditional and Modern Approaches to Customary International Law: A Reconciliation', *AJIL* 95 (2001), p. 758. See also: Philip Moremen, 'National Court Decisions as State Practice: A Transnational Judicial Dialogue?', *North Carolina JIL & Comm Reg* 32 (2006), p. 268 ('A "traditional" view of custom, associated primarily with legal positivism, tends to regard state practice as the most important element. Thus, the existence of a customary rule is determined inductively, based on an accumulation of instances of state practice. *Opinio juris* is of lesser significance, invoked as a secondary step in custom formation [...]').
[95] P. Haggenmacher, 'La doctrine des deux éléments du droit coutumier dans la pratique de la Cour internationale', *RGDIP*, 90 (1986), pp. 113–114 ('Les deux prétendus éléments n'ont en réalité aucune individualité propre; ils se trouvent inextricablement mêlés au sein d'une "pratique" unitaire. Cette pratique forme pour ainsi dire un *seul* "élément" complexe, fait d'aspects "matériels" et "psychologiques"').
[96] A. D'Amato, *The Concept of Custom in International Law* (Ithaca: Cornell University Press, 1971), p. 88, using the concepts of 'articulation' and 'act'.

others have argued for the existence of elements in addition to them.[97] In his First Report, ILC Special Rapporteur Wood summarized the reasons often invoked by these writers for rejecting the 'traditional' approach:

> Some, however, have challenged the "traditional" approach, arguing that it is doctrinally incoherent and riddled with "inner mysteries" that make it difficult, if not impossible, to apply in practice. Other critics have stressed that customary international law so constructed "is of too slow growth to keep pace with the changing relations of the states which it endeavors to regulate", as well as fundamentally inefficient in doing so. It is further claimed that the "traditional" doctrine embodies a severe democratic deficit, that its positivistic nature does not allow the identification of customary international law to have due regard to the values of the international community, and, moreover, that it might make customary international law incommensurable with basic human rights. Finally, some writers have gone as far as to claim that the 'traditional' theory is mere fiction.[98]

A number of scholars have thus developed alternative theories on how custom is created. These theories are generally referred to collectively as 'modern custom'. Some of these theories focus on the prevalence of *opinio juris* rather than actual State practice,[99] while others support the view that State practice is in fact irrelevant. The ILC Special Rapporteur has described the distinctive features of the approach generally adopted by supporters of 'modern custom':

> [This approach] ultimately turns the ascertainment of "new customary international law" into a normative exercise rather than a strictly empirical one. Employing a deductive methodology, it attempts to make

---

[97] Michael P. Scharf, *Customary International Law in Times of Fundamental Change: Recognizing Grotian Moments* (Cambridge: Cambridge University Press, 2013), p. 211, for whom a 'third ingredient' of custom is the 'context of fundamental change' which serve as an 'accelerating agent, enabling customary international law to form much more rapidly and with less state practice than is normally the case' (see also, at pp. 60–61). See also: Baker, 'Customary International Law in the 21st Century', p. 175 ('The jurisprudence of these international criminal tribunals, on a wide range of international legal questions, has slowly begun to be elevated into norms of customary international law. Given this fact, then, the debate over whether consistent state practice and *opinio juris* are the only building blocks of customary international law is over, because clearly, for better or for worse, they no longer are').

[98] ILC, First Report, 2013, p. 47.

[99] Moremen, 'National Court Decisions as State Practice', p. 269 ('In contrast, the "modern" view, influenced by a normative, natural law perspective sees *opinio juris* as more significant, to the extent that state practice may have little or no role in the formation of customary law. In the modern view, *opinio juris* is derived more from what states say than from what states do').

customary international law a more rapid and flexible source of international law, one that is able to fulfil a "utopian potential" and "compensate for the rigidity of treaty law", particularly in the fields of human rights and humanitarian and environmental law." (...) Such "conceptual stretching", celebrated as the "new vitality of custom", has also encouraged calls for opening the process of customary law creation to non-State actors, namely, international organizations and their agencies, as well as individuals.[100]

So-called modern custom is based on a *deductive* methodology. As a result, it has been argued that the process of customary law-making is 'turned into a self-contained exercise in rhetoric'.[101] As explained by Roberts, 'modern custom derives norms primarily from abstract statements of *opinio juris* – working from theory to practice'.[102] As a result, one writer has noted that 'the criterion of the deductive method is an abstract affair' insofar as it 'deduces the rules from more general propositions' which is based 'from logic or another normative order (natural law or morals)' using 'extra-legal, non-factual "authorities"'.[103]

While some of these alternative theories will be discussed in Chapter 4,[104] one should be cautious and reflect on their 'real-world' impact. As explained by ILC Special Rapporteur Wood, 'such writings are always interesting and provocative, and have been (and should be) duly taken into account, it remains the case that they do not seem to have greatly influenced the approach of States or courts'.[105] Therefore, as further explained in the next section, international courts and tribunals applying general international law have adopted the 'traditional' double requirement approach. This is also the case for investor-State arbitral tribunals.

In fact, it has been suggested that some of the 'novel' approaches have become so detached from how custom is generally understood that they should no longer qualify as custom.[106] A good example is the 'modern' theory of custom based on game theory and rational choice

---

[100] ILC, First Report, 2013, pp. 51–52.
[101] Simma and Alston, 'The Sources of Human Rights Law', p. 89.
[102] Roberts, 'Traditional and Modern Approaches to Customary International Law', p. 763.
[103] Kammerhofer, 'Uncertainty in the Formal Sources of International Law', p. 537.
[104] See, Chapter 4, Section 4.1.2.   [105] ILC, Second Report, 2014, p. 11.
[106] R. Jennings, 'What is International Law and How Do We Tell It When We See It', *The Cambridge Tilburg Lectures* (Kluwer, 1983), p. 11 ('Perhaps it is time to face squarely the fact that the orthodox tests of custom – practice and *opinio juris* – are often not only inadequate but even irrelevant for the identification of much new law today. And the reason is not far to seek: much of this new law is not custom at all, and does not even resemble custom. It is recent, it is innovatory, it involves topical policy decisions, and it is often the focus of contention. Anything less like custom in the ordinary meaning of that

of States.[107] For instance, Guzman put forward 'a firm and modern theoretical foundation for the analysis of custom' based on rational States.[108] He defines a rule of custom as 'a legal rule that, by virtue of its status, affects the payoffs of states'.[109] He rejects the requirements of *opinio juris* and State practice because such definition 'tells us nothing about state behavior' and 'in a world of rational states, [custom] is relevant only when it has some impact on payoffs'.[110] While I do not question the validity of the assumption used by these writers, nor the conclusion they reached, I simply note that such an approach is not particularly helpful in the context of international investment law.

term would be difficult to imagine'). G. Abi-Saab, 'Custom and Treaties', in A. Cassese and J.H.H. Weiler (eds.), *Change and Stability in International Law-Making* (Berlin: Walter de Gruyter, 1988), p. 10 ('We are calling different things custom, we are keeping the name but *expanding the phenomenon* . . . In fact we have a new wine, but we are trying to put it in the old bottle of custom. At some point this qualitative change will have to be taken into consideration, and we will have to recognize that we are no longer speaking of the same source, but that we are in the presence of a very new type of law-making', emphasis in the original).

[107] *See*, for instance: Jack L. Goldsmith and Eric A. Posner, *The Limits of International Law* (New York: Oxford University Press, 2005), p. 43; Jack L. Goldsmith and Eric A. Posner, 'A Theory of Customary International Law', *Chicago L.Rev.* 66 (1999), p. 1113; Jack L. Goldsmith and Eric A. Posner, 'Understanding the Resemblance Between Modern and Traditional Customary International Law', *Virginia JIL* 40 (2000), pp. 639–640; Andrew T. Guzman, 'A Compliance-Based Theory of International Law', *Cal. L. Rev.* 90 (2002), p. 1823; Pierre-Hugues Verdier, 'Cooperative States: International Relations, State Responsibility and the Problem of Custom', *Virginia JIL* 42 (2002), p. 839; George Norman and Joel Trachtman, 'The Customary International Law Game', *AJIL* 99 (2005), p. 541; Edward T. Swaine, 'Rational Custom', *Duke L.J.* 52 (2002), p. 559.

[108] Guzman, 'Saving Customary International Law', pp. 116–117.   [109] *Id.*, p. 133.

[110] *Id.* He explains right at the outset of his article (p. 122) why State practice is not relevant to his analysis: 'A rational choice approach, however, looks to compliance and incentives affecting state behavior. This, it turns out, leaves no room for a practice requirement. Because the consequences of violating a legal rule depend only on the attitudes of other states, state practice plays no direct role. Practice may affect the attitudes of states, of course, but it does not directly contribute to the existence of a rule of CIL'. See also, at p. 153 ('CIL is really about the *opinio juris* requirement and not the practice requirement. This is so because, as already discussed, what matters for the presence of reputational sanctions is the perspective of other states. If states as a group believe there is a legal obligation, this is enough to generate reputational (and perhaps direct) sanctions. The question of practice is not directly relevant to the issue. Thus, for example, if there is a general perception that torture is a violation of international legal norms, it can be a rule of CIL notwithstanding the fact that its use is widespread. A rational choice approach, then, leaves no room for a state practice requirement other than as an evidentiary touchstone to reveal *opinio juris*. Practice can shed light on whether a particular norm is regarded as obligatory, but it does not by itself make it so'.). See also, at p. 146 ff.

Arbitral tribunals have never used these theories and are very unlikely to do so in the future.

Both the deductive and the inductive approaches certainly have strengths and weaknesses.[111] It is clearly beyond the scope of this book to examine this question in great detail. In fact, it is sufficient to state that the present book adopts the 'traditional' approach whereby both State practice and *opinio juris* must be demonstrated. As will be further explained in the next section, this is indeed the approach which has been adopted by international tribunals and by investor-State arbitration tribunals.

1.3.2 The position adopted by investor-State arbitration tribunals and States

The PCIJ and the ICJ have consistently held that a customary rule requires the presence of both State practice and *opinio juris*.[112] For instance, in the *Continental Shelf* case, the Court stated that 'it is of course axiomatic that the material of customary international law is to be looked for primarily in the actual practice and *opinio juris* of States'.[113] This double requirement has also been recognized by other international tribunals, such as the International Tribunal for the Law of the Sea,[114] the ICTY and the ICTR as well as a number of 'internationalized courts' (including the Special Court for Sierra Leone, the Courts of Cambodia and the Special Tribunal for Lebanon).[115] The same is true for Panels and

[111] Kammerhofer, 'Uncertainty in the Formal Sources of International Law', p. 537: 'Both approaches have strengths and weaknesses. Induction's results immediately resemble provable facts, an empirical correspondence. Deduction has the benefit of internal logical consistency. The first approach, however, violates the duality of norm and fact: law is precisely not facts, it is not (necessarily) a description of reality – unless everybody obeys the law – but a prescription for future behaviour. The second approach, on the other hand, is improvable. Its arguments are based on anything but the law (or things the law says determine the relevant law) and it must remain a fiction'.

[112] *S.S. Lotus Case (France v. Turkey)*, Merits, 1927 P.C.I.J. (ser. A) No. 9, at pp. 18, 28; *Asylum Case*, p. 276-7; *Right of Passage Case (Portugal v. India)*, ICJ Rep. 1960, pp. 42–43; *North Sea Continental Shelf*, p. 44, para. 77; *Military and Paramilitary Activities in and around Nicaragua (Nicaragua v. United States)*, Merits, Judgment, ICJ Rep. 1986, p. 97, para. 183; *Delimitation of the Maritime Boundary in the Gulf of Maine Area (Canada v. United States)*, Judgment, ICJ Rep. 1984, p. 299, para. 111; *Jurisdictional Immunities of the State (Germany v. Italy: Greece intervening)*, Judgment, ICJ Rep. 2012, p. 122, para. 55.

[113] *Continental Shelf Case (Libya v. Malta)*, Judgment, ICJ Rep. 1985, p. 13, para. 27.

[114] *M/V "SAIGA" (No. 2) (Saint Vincent and the Grenadines v. Guinea)*, Judgment, ITLOS Reports 1999, p. 10, paras. 133-134.

[115] See, the analysis in: ILC, First Report, 2013, p. 29 ff.

the Appellate Body of the World Trade Organization (WTO) as well as a number of regional courts, including the Inter-American Court of Human Rights, the Court of Justice of the European Union and the European Court of Human Rights.[116] Domestic courts have also recognized this double requirement.[117]

The double requirement has also been recognized by a number of investor-State arbitration tribunals. It should be added that while a number of tribunals refer to the concept of customary international law without specifying its content,[118] those that do explain the concept always refer to these two elements.[119] For instance, the *UPS* Tribunal stated that 'to establish a rule of customary international law, two requirements must be met: consistent state practice and an understanding that the practice is required by law'.[120]

Another important point to mention is that States have often recognized in their pleadings in arbitration proceedings that custom requires

[116] *Id.*, p. 34 ff.
[117] A number of examples are cited in: *Id.*, p. 38 ff. One example is *R. v. Hape*, Supreme Court of Canada, 292, 2007 SCC 26, para. 46.
[118] See, for instance, *Enron Corporation and Ponderosa Assets LP* v. *Argentina*, ICSID Case No. ARB/01/3, Award, 15 May 2007, para. 258.
[119] *Cambodia Power Company* v. *Cambodia and Electricité du Cambodge LLC*, ICSID Case No. ARB/09/18, Decision on Jurisdiction, 22 March 2011, para. 333 ('general practices of states followed by them from a sense of legal obligation'); *Daimler Financial Servcies AG* v. *Argentina*, ICSID Case No ARB/05/1, Award, 22 August 2012, paras. 622, 310 ('combination of a sufficiently broad, lasting and consistent state practice and supported by *opinio juris*'); *Glamis Gold Ltd* v. *United States*, UNCITRAL, Award, 14 May 2009, para. 602 ('(1) "a concordant practice of a number of States acquiesced in by others," and (2) "a conception that the practice is required by or consistent with the prevailing law (opinio juris)"'.); *MCI Power Group LC and New Turbine Incorporated* v. *Ecuador*, ICSID Case No. ARB/03/6, Award, 26 July 2007, para. 369 ('the repeated, general, and constant practice of States, which they observe because they are aware that it is obligatory'); *Mobil Investments Canada Inc. and Murphy Oil Corporation* v. *Canada*, ICSID Case No. ARB(AF)/07/4, Decision on Liability and on Principles of Quantum, 22 May 2012, para. 127 ('The Tribunal posed the following question to the parties during the hearing: "What evidence of "state practice" and *opinio juris* is available, if any, to support the conclusion that "fair and equitable treatment" encompasses a substantive obligation to protect the legitimate expectation of the parties?'); El Paso Energy International Company v. Argentina, ICSID Case No. ARB/03/15, Award, 31 October 2011, para. 622 ('general practice and *opinio juris*'); *Merrill & Ring* v. *Canada*, Award, 31 March 2010, paras. 193, 204, 201; *Railroad Development Corporation (RDC)* v. *Guatemala*, ICSID Case No ARB/07/23, Award, 29 June 2012, para. 216 ('State practice followed because of a sense of obligation'); *Apotex Holdings Inc & Apotex Inc.* v. *United States*, ICSID Case No. ARB(AF)/12/1, Award, 25 August 2014, para. 9.25.
[120] *United Parcel Service of America Inc.* v. *Canada*, UNCITRAL, Award on Jurisdiction, 22 November 2002, para. 84 [hereinafter *UPS v. Canada*].

both State practice and *opinio juris*. This is indeed the position which has been expressly adopted by, *inter alia*, the United States,[121] El Salvador,[122] Canada,[123] and Mexico.[124] The present author has in fact found no examples of State practice, such as pleadings, where a State rejected the necessity to demonstrate both elements of custom. It should be added that there are also many examples of States recognizing the importance of these two requirements outside the field of investment arbitration.[125]

---

[121] *ADF Group Inc.* v. *United States*, ICSID Case No. ARB(AF)/00/1, Award, 6 January 2003, para. 112 (referring to the position of the United States: 'The Pope and Talbot Tribunal did not examine the mass of existing BITs to determine whether those treaties represent concordant state practice and whether they constitute evidence of the opinio juris constituent of customary international law'.); *Railroad Development Corporation (RDC)* v. *Guatemala*, ICSID Case No. ARB/07/23, Award, 29 June 2012, para. 207 (referring to the position of the United States: 'customary international law, *i.e.*, the law that develops from the practice and *opinio juris* of States themselves'); *Teco Guatemala Holdings, LLC* v. *Guatemala*, ICSID Case No. ARB/10/23, Submission of the United States, 23 November 2012, para. 4; *Glamis Gold, Ltd.* v. *United States*, US Rejoinder, 15 March 2007, p. 141; *Spence International Investments et al.* v. *Costa Rica*, UNCITRAL (ICSID Case No. UNCT/13/2), Non-Disputing Party Submission by the United States, 17 April 2015, paras. 15–16.

[122] *Railroad Development Corporation (RDC)* v. *Guatemala, Ibid.*, para. 207 (referring to the position of El Salvador: 'general and consistent State practice resulting from a sense of legal obligation'); *Spence International Investments et al.* v. *Costa Rica*, UNCITRAL (ICSID Case No. UNCT/13/2), Non-Disputing Party Submission by El Salvador, 17 April 2015, para. 6.

[123] *Chemtura Corporation* v. *Canada*, UNCITRAL, Award, 2 August 2010, para. 114 ('the Respondent argues that the Claimant bears the burden of proving the content of the minimum standard of treatment through evidence of both State practice and *opinio juris*'); *Loewen Group, Inc. and Raymond L. Loewen* v. *United States*, ICSID Case No. ARB(AF)/98/3, Second Submission of Canada pursuant to NAFTA Article 1128, 27 June 2002, paras. 12, 19, 23; *Mobil Investments Canada Inc. and Murphy Oil Corporation* v. *Canada*, ICSID Case No. ARB(AF)/07/4, Decision on Liability and on Principles of Quantum, 22 May 2012, para. 123, referring to the position of Canada: '[t]he Claimants [have submitted] no evidence of state practice or *opinio juris* to support their assertion that the minimum standard of treatment afforded to foreign investors by customary international law includes a protection of legitimate expectations or the obligations to provide a stable regulatory environment for foreign investments' (see also, at para. 132).

[124] *Loewen Group, Inc. and Raymond L. Loewen* v. *United States, Ibid.*, Mexico's Submission, 2 July 2002, paras. 33, 36, 37.

[125] See, *inter alia*: J.B. Bellinger and W.J. Haynes, 'A US Government Response to the International Committee of the Red Cross Study on Customary International Humanitarian Law', *Int Rev Red Cross* 89 (866) (2007), p. 444; United Kingdom, 'Legal Adviser of the Foreign and Commonwealth Office, statement at the Meeting of National Committees on International Humanitarian Law of Commonwealth States, Nairobi, 20 July 2005', *British YIL* 76 (2005), pp. 694–695; *Updated European Union Guidelines on promoting compliance with international humanitarian law* (2009/C 303/06), section 7.

States also recognize the double requirement in their investment treaties. For instance, in recent separate BITs entered into by the United States, on the one hand, and Rwanda and Uruguay, on the other hand, the parties explain their 'shared understanding, that customary international law . . . results from a general and consistent practice of States that they follow from a sense of legal obligation'.[126] The same 'understanding' is likely to be found in many future US BITs given the fact that it is found in the 2012 US Model BIT.[127] The Canada-China BIT also expressly refers to the two elements of the definition of custom ('evidenced by general State practice accepted as law'), without, however, expressly using the term.[128]

Finally, it should be added that the double requirement has been recognized by many writers that have focused on the specific nature of customary rules in the context of international investment law.[129] As further examined in another chapter,[130] a number of writers have nonetheless been critical regarding the application of such two requirements.[131] For instance, Lowenfeld recently argued that 'perhaps the traditional definition of customary law is wrong, or at least in this area, incomplete'.[132]

---

[126] US-Rwanda BIT, 2008, Annex A; US-Uruguay BIT, 2005, Annex A. See also, US-Singapore FTA (2004), Article 15.5, referring to the 'customary international law minimum standard of treatment of aliens' and Article 15.6 on expropriation where in two footnotes it is indicated that these provisions need to be interpreted in accordance with a letter exchanged between the two countries. The letter (dated 6 May 2013) mentions that the use of the words 'customary international law' refers to customary law that results from a 'general and consistent practice of States that they follow from a sense of legal obligation'.

[127] US Model BIT, 2012, Annex A.   [128] Canada-China BIT, 2014, Article 4.

[129] See, Cai Congyan, 'International Investment Treaties and the Formation, Application and Transformation of Customary International Law Rules', *Chinese JIL* 7 (2008), p. 660; Ionna Tudor, *The Fair and Equitable Treatment Standard in International Foreign Investment Law* (Oxford: Oxford University Press, 2008), p. 60; Steffen Hindelang, 'Bilateral Investment Treaties, Custom and a Healthy Investment Climate – The Question of whether BITs Influence Customary International Law Revisited', *J. World Invest. & Trade*, 5 (2004), p. 790; Matthew C. Porterfield, 'State Practice and the (Purported) Obligation under Customary International Law to Provide Compensation for Regulatory Expropriations', *North Carolina JIL & Comm Reg*, 37 (2011), p. 171; Abdullah Al Faruque, 'Creating Customary International Law through Bilateral Investment Treaties: a Critical Appraisal', *Indian J Int'l* 44 (2004), p. 295.

[130] See Chapter 4, Section 4.2.3.3.

[131] Tudor, *The Fair and Equitable Treatment Standard*, p. 69.

[132] Andreas F. Lowenfeld, 'Investment Agreements and International Law', *Columbia JTL* 42 (2003), pp. 129–130.

1.4 A customary rule needs to be proven by the party that alleges it

One of the basic principles of international law is that the burden of proving the existence of a rule of customary international law rests on the party that alleges it. Many international tribunals, including the ICJ, have upheld the principle.[133] It has also been well recognized by scholars[134] and by States in arbitration proceedings.[135]

Investor-State arbitration tribunals have also held that a customary rule needs to be proven by the party that alleges it.[136] NAFTA tribunals have so far provided the most interesting illustration of such a pattern. For example, the *Cargill* Tribunal stated that 'it is for the party asserting the custom to establish the content of that custom'.[137] The *UPS* Tribunal has effectively explained how this principle should be applied in practice. The Tribunal first stated that the 'relevant [State] practice and the related understandings must still be assembled in support of a claimed rule of

---

[133] *Case Concerning Rights of Nationals of the United States of America in Morocco (France. v. U.S.)*, ICJ Rep. 1952, p. 176 (quoting *Asylum (Colombia v. Peru)*, ICJ Rep. 1950, p. 266) ('The Party which relies on a custom of this kind [i.e. in the specific context of *regional* custom] must prove that this custom is established in such a manner that it has become binding on the other Party').

[134] Nguyen *et al.*, *Droit International Public*, p. 365; UNCTAD, 'Fair and Equitable Treatment', UNCTAD Series on Issues in International Investment Agreements II, United Nations (2012), p. 45 [hereinafter referred to as UNCTAD, 'Fair and Equitable Treatment', 2012].

[135] See, for instance: *Railroad Development Corporation (RDC) v. Guatemala*, Award, 29 June 2012, para. 207 (referring to the position of the United States: 'The burden is on the claimant to establish the existence and applicability of a relevant obligation under customary international that meets these requirements'); *Teco Guatemala Holdings, LLC v. Guatemala*, Submission of the United States, 23 November 2012, para. 4; *Spence International Investments et al. v. Costa Rica*, Non-disputing party submission by El Salvador, 17 April 2015, para. 7.

[136] *Mihaly International Corporation v. Sri Lanka*, ICSID Case No. ARB/00/2, Award, 15 March 2002, para. 60, noting that 'The Tribunal is of the view that *de lege ferenda* the sources of international law on the extended meaning or definition of investment will have to be found in conventional law or in customary law. The Claimant has not succeeded in furnishing any evidence of treaty interpretation or practice of States, let alone that of developing countries or Sri Lanka for that matter, to the effect that pre-investment and development expenditures in the circumstances of the present case could automatically be admitted as "investment" in the absence of the consent of the host State to the implementation of the project'.

[137] *Cargill, Inc. v. Mexico*, ICSID Case No. ARB(AF)/05/02, Award, 18 September 2009, para. 271. Another example is the reasoning of the Tribunal in: *ADF Group Inc. v. United States*, Award, 9 January 2003, paras. 183, 185.

customary international law'.[138] The Tribunal rejected UPS's claim specifically on the ground that the investor 'did not attempt to establish (. . .) the practice element of a customary international law rule requiring the prohibiting or regulating of anticompetitive behaviour'[139] and that any such state practice 'reflects an understanding of the existence of a generally owed international legal obligation'.[140] The *UPS* Tribunal therefore concluded that there exists 'no rule of customary international law prohibiting or regulating anticompetitive behaviour'.[141]

What then are the *kinds* of rules of customary international law that must be proven? In the *ADF* case, the Tribunal rejected the argument put forward by the United States that a claimant 'must show a violation of a *specific rule* of customary international law relating to foreign investors and their investments'.[142] Therefore, the Tribunal indicated that there is no need to prove that 'current customary international law concerning standards of treatment consists only of discrete, specific rules applicable to limited contexts'.[143] The *ADF* Tribunal refers instead to 'a *general* customary international law standard of treatment'.[144]

Tribunals have also recognized the obvious fact that 'the obligations imposed by customary international law may and do evolve'.[145] Nevertheless, as pointed out again by the *UPS* Tribunal, 'relevant practice and the related understandings must still be assembled' in support of such a claim of a new rule of customary international law.[146] A party therefore has the burden to prove any subsequent changes in the evolution of custom. In other words, any allegation that custom has changed over time must be demonstrated based on actual State practice and *opinio juris*. As explained by the *Glamis* Tribunal:

> If, as Claimant argues, the customary international law minimum standard of treatment has indeed moved to require something less than the "egregious," "outrageous," or "shocking" standard as elucidated in *Neer*,

---

[138] *UPS v. Canada*, Award on Jurisdiction, 22 November 2002, para. 84.
[139] *Id.*, para. 85.   [140] *Id.*, para. 86.   [141] *Id.*, para. 92.
[142] *ADF Group Inc. v. United States*, Award, 9 January 2003, para. 182 (emphasis added).
[143] *Id.*, para. 185.   [144] *Id.*, para. 186 (emphasis in the original).
[145] *UPS v. Canada*, Award on Jurisdiction, 22 November 2002, para. 84. See also: *ADF Group Inc. v. United States*, Award, 9 January 2003, para. 179 (custom is 'constantly in a process of development'); *Pope & Talbot Inc. v. Canada*, UNCITRAL, Award in Respect of Damages, 31 May 2002, para. 59 ('it is a facet of international law that customary international law evolves through state practice'); *Mondev International Ltd. v. United States*, ICSID Case No. ARB(AF)/99/2, Award, 2 October 2002, para. 117.
[146] *UPS v. Canada*, Award on Jurisdiction, 22 November 2002, para. 84.

then the burden of establishing what the standard now requires is upon Claimant.[147]

The same position was later supported by the *Cargill* Tribunal:

> The Parties disagree, however, as to how that customary standard has in fact, if at all, evolved since that time. The burden of establishing any new elements of this custom is on Claimant. The Tribunal acknowledges that the proof of change in a custom is not an easy matter to establish. However, the burden of doing so falls clearly on Claimant. If Claimant does not provide the Tribunal with the proof of such evolution, it is not the place of the Tribunal to assume this task. Rather the Tribunal, in such an instance, should hold that Claimant fails to establish the particular standard asserted.[148]

There is no doubt that establishing the content of customary international law 'is methodologically difficult and puts a heavy burden on the claimants'.[149] In fact, according to Weiler, 'the very notion that an individual claimant could assemble proof for the proposition of any specific rule of customary international law, suited to fit the particular facts of his case, verges on hallucination'.[150] The conclusion reached by the *Cargill* Tribunal emphasizes how ascertaining State practice was a difficult task, especially in the context of the FET standard:

> The Tribunal acknowledges, however, that surveys of State practice are difficult to undertake and particularly difficult in the case of norms such as "fair and equitable treatment" where developed examples of State practice may not be many or readily accessible. Claimant has not provided the Tribunal with such a survey of recent State practice, nor is the Tribunal aware of such a survey.[151]

[147] *Glamis Gold Ltd* v. *United States*, Award, 14 May 2009, para. 601. See also, at para. 603 where the Tribunal added that it was 'necessarily Claimant's place to establish a change in custom'. See, Margaret Clare Ryan, 'Glamis Gold, Ltd. v. The United States and the Fair and Equitable Treatment Standard,' *McGill LJ* 56(4) (2011), pp. 952–953, criticizing the award's reasoning on this question.
[148] *Cargill, Inc.* v. *Mexico*, Award, 18 September 2009, para. 273.
[149] UNCTAD, 'Fair and Equitable Treatment', 2012, pp. 28–29. See also: Tudor, *The Fair and Equitable Treatment Standard*, p. 73.
[150] Todd Weiler, *The Interpretation of International Investment Law: Equality, Discrimination, and Minimum Standards of Treatment in Historical Context* (Martinus Nijhoff, 2013), p. 279.
[151] *Cargill, Inc.* v. *Mexico*, Award, 18 September 2009, para. 274. The award in *Glamis Gold Ltd* v. *United States*, Award, 14 May 2009, para. 603, suggests, however, that '[a]lthough one can readily identify the practice of States, it is usually very difficult to determine the intent behind those actions'. The Tribunal added that '[l]ooking to a claimant to

Finally, one last remark should be made about timing. According to the *Mondev* Tribunal, the customary rules, which must be taken into account, are those existing 'no earlier than the time at which NAFTA came into force'.[152] In other words, the rules that matter are those which existed at the time of the conclusion of the treaty (1994), and not before. This is a sound solution. It was especially reasonable in the context of the *Mondev* claim, where the alleged breach took place shortly after the entry into force of the NAFTA in 1994 and where the award was rendered in 2002. However, this solution may not be the most appropriate in other situations where a long period of time elapses between the entry into force of a treaty and the moment when the allegations are brought before a tribunal. This is because customary rules will necessarily evolve over time. A tribunal would not be able to take into account such an evolution if it were to adopt a strict view that only applies those customary rules that existed when the treaty came into force. This is why it is preferable that a tribunal considers the customary rules which existed at the time when the alleged violation of the treaty was committed rather than the ones existing when the treaty came into force.[153]

1.5   The role of judges in the formation and identification of customary rules

What is the actual role played by tribunals in the creation of custom? Under Article 38 of the ICJ Statute, 'judicial decisions' are considered along with the 'writings of eminent publicists' as a 'subsidiary means for the determination of rules of law'. Therefore, judicial decisions and arbitral awards are not a *formal* source of international law (unlike treaties, custom and general principles of law). Judicial decisions do not *create* law and judges are *not law-makers*.[154] In other words, international

---

ascertain custom requires it to ascertain such intent, a complicated and particularly difficult task'.

[152] *Mondev v. United States*, Award, 11 October 2002, para. 125, later approved by *Waste Management, Inc.* v. *Mexico ("Number 2")*, ICSID Case No. ARB(AF)/00/3, Award, 30 April 2004, para. 91 (indicating that the FTC Note 'incorporates current international customary law, at least as it stood at the time that NAFTA came into force in 1994, rather than any earlier version of the standard of treatment').

[153] Tarcisio Gazzini, 'The Role of Customary International Law in the Field of Foreign Investment', *J. World Invest. & Trade*, 8 (2007), p. 711.

[154] E. de Brabandere, 'Judicial and Arbitral Decisions as a Source of Rights and Obligations', in: T. Gazzini and E. de Brabandere (eds), *International Investment Law: The Sources of Rights and Obligations* (Leiden: Martinus Nijhoff, 2012), p. 248.

judges or arbitrators have no *formal* role in the *creation* of customary rules. States create these rules, not judges. In Chapter 3, I will further examine the question of whether or not arbitral awards can be considered as evidence of relevant State practice for the creation of custom.[155] The present section deals with the other question of the actual role played by an international judge or an arbitrator in the formation and identification of customary rules.

This section will demonstrate that even if judges and arbitrators are clearly not law-makers (and have no formal role in the creation of customary rules), it is undeniable that they do in fact play an important role regarding the evolution of such rules. They not only play an essential role in 'revealing' the existence of customary rules (Section 1.5.1), but they also play an important role in the development of such rules (Section 1.5.2). Finally, I will specifically examine the concrete role played by arbitral tribunals regarding the formation and identification of customary rules in investment arbitration (Section 1.5.3).

1.5.1   A role in revealing the existence of customary rules

In the context of settling international disputes, a court or a tribunal will sometimes identify rules of customary international law. In this respect, the role of the judge is very important insofar as it will 'reveal' *a posteriori* whether any given customary rule exists. D'Aspremont speaks of a process of 'formalization of the evidence of customary international law'.[156] In fact, as noted by Gazzini, the judge not only *confirms* the existence of customary rules, but also contributes to *clarify* its content.[157] According to him, the 'final assessment' of both State practice and *opinio juris* rests with a court or a tribunal.[158] The role of revealing the existence of customary rules is indeed an important one. Thus, although unable to formally create customary rules by its own conduct, the judge is nevertheless entrusted by States with the fundamental task of determining whether such rules exist. A decision by a tribunal identifying a given rule of custom is, of course, not per se conclusive as to the existence of such a rule. The actual weight to be given to such a decision will depend on the

---

[155] See, Chapter 3, Section 3.4.
[156] d'Aspremont, *Formalism and the Sources of International Law*, p. 152.
[157] Gazzini, 'The Role of Customary International Law', pp. 692–693; C.J. Tams and A. Tzanakopoulos, '*Barcelona Traction*: the ICJ as an Agent of Legal Development', *Leiden JIL* 23 (2010), p. 784.
[158] Gazzini, 'The Role of Customary International Law', p. 695.

authoritative stature of the court which has rendered the decision as well as the quality of the reasoning.[159]

The existence of such an influential function has led some writers to speak of the creative and quasi-legislative role that is actually played by judges in the context of the formation of custom.[160] As further explained in the next section, the role of the judge goes beyond merely 'revealing' or confirming the existence of customary norms.

1.5.2   A role in the development of customary rules

A statement by a tribunal on whether or not a rule exists may have a decisive influence on the very development of such a rule.[161] Such an influence can be exercised in two ways.

First, a well-reasoned and well-researched pronouncement by a court that one given State conduct is *not* part of custom can be fatal to its evolution and effectively stop it from ever becoming custom.[162] A good illustration is found in the ICJ's decision that it 'has been unable to deduce from' State practice 'that there exists under customary international law any form of exception to the rule according immunity from criminal jurisdiction and inviolability to incumbent Ministers for Foreign Affairs, where they are suspected of having committed war

---

[159] ILC, Third Report, 2015, p. 43.

[160] Haggenmacher, 'La doctrine des deux éléments', pp. 113–114 ('L'établissement d'une norme coutumière ne se réduit pas à vérifier objectivement la réalisation du pseudo-processus de formation suggéré par la doctrine classique et à en constater passivement le résultat: le juge ne se borne pas à cueillir un fruit mûri sur l'arbre de la pratique au soleil de l'*opinio juris*. Son rôle est au contraire créateur, quasi-législatif, et il demande à être saisi comme tel'); Stern, 'Custom at the Heart of International Law', p. 101 ('It is always the case that controversy as to the existence of a customary rule, referring to the element of *opinio juris*, undeniably gives the judge a very wide margin in which to maneuver. And there is a great deal of truth in that which Kelsen affirmed in his early writings where he considered that *opinio juris* simply masks the role of the judge in the creation of law'); Wolfke, *Custom in Present International Law*, p. 73 ('Courts and tribunals participate in the creation of international law primarily by way of their decisions and opinions'), pp. 72–73 ('A decision of the court on what is the law is always based, to a greater or lesser degree, on free evaluation. Hence it is a truism to say that a judicial organ ascertaining customs to some extent creates them. (. . . .) A statement by the court that a certain rule applies in settling a dispute involves a law-creating factor').

[161] A.E. Roberts, 'Power and Persuasion in Investment Treaty Interpretation: The Dual Role of States', *AJIL* 104 (2010), p. 188 ('In practice, however, international courts play a critical role in the development of international law because the distinction between interpreting and creating the law is a fiction').

[162] Wolfke, *Custom in Present International Law*, pp. 72–73 ('a case in which a declaration is made by the court that there is no sufficient evidence for admission of the existence of a custom may for a long time paralyse the development of such a custom').

crimes or crimes against humanity'.[163] Such a finding analysing a number of different sources of State practice may have the effect of stopping the evolution of custom on this issue.

Second, the opposite situation is also possible. As noted by Henckaerts and Doswald-Beck, 'a finding by an international court that a rule of customary international law exists constitutes persuasive evidence to that effect'.[164] In other words, when a court convincingly enunciates (based on a comprehensive and detailed analysis of both State practice and *opinio juris*) that a rule *is* custom, this will often provide sufficient 'proof *in itself* to others that it is indeed the case. Therefore, according to one writer, 'After *Nicaragua*, the customary character of common Articles 1 and 3 of the 1949 Geneva Conventions is "now taken for granted and almost never questioned"'.[165] In fact, 'by drawing attention to a certain practice, the court may considerably accelerate its ripening into custom'.[166] Put differently, by 'revealing' the existence of a customary rule, the judge will firmly crystallize such status. Such crystallization may thus take place *even* when, using the above-mentioned illustrative analogy by Mendelson,[167] the 'fruit' of the evolution of a customary norm is *not* yet ripe.[168]

In sum, it seems undeniable that a judicial decision may have a 'formative effect on custom by crystallizing emerging rules'.[169] In fact, as further explained in the next paragraphs, a judicial finding on custom will influence not only international courts and tribunals, which will apply its reasoning in the future, but also State practice in response to a court's decisions regarding that rule.[170]

First, any decision containing a comprehensive and persuasive analysis of whether a customary rule exists will be considered as an inestimable

---

[163] *Case Concerning the Arrest Warrant of 11 April 2000 (Democratic Republic of the Congo v. Belgium)*, Judgment, ICJ Rep. 2002, para. 58 (examining 'State practice, including national legislation and those decisions of national higher courts, such as the House of Lords or the French Court of Cassation').

[164] Jean-Marie Henckaerts and Louise Doswald-Beck, *Customary International Humanitarian Law*, Vol. 1–2: Rules, p. xxxviii.

[165] Crawford, 'The Identification and Development of Customary International Law', p. 5 (quoting from Theodor Meron, *The Humanization of International Law* (Brill, 2006) p. 403).

[166] Wolfke, *Custom in Present International Law*, pp. 72–73.

[167] See, Chapter 1, Section 1.2.2.

[168] Mendelson, 'The Formation of Customary International Law', p. 176.

[169] Roberts, 'Traditional and Modern Approaches to Customary International Law', p. 775.

[170] Alberto Alvarez-Jimenez, 'Methods for the Identification of Customary International Law in the International Court of Justice's Jurisprudence: 2000–2009', *ICLQ*, 60 (2011), pp. 683–684; Roberts, 'Power and Persuasion in Investment Treaty Interpretation', p. 188 (judicial decisions are 'routinely looked to—by states, other courts, and academics—as evidence of the content of international law').

guide for future tribunals having to address the same issue.[171] This is indeed the situation prevailing at the ICJ.[172] According to Alvarez-Jimenez, 'the ICJ has recognized the existence of customary law not only on the basis of State practice and *opinio juris*, but also on the basis of previous international judicial decisions'.[173] Thus, the Court 'relies on its own past judicial decisions or on others' as part of the justification for the declaration of existence or absence of a customary role'.[174] Moreover, once the ICJ has ruled on the custom status of a given rule, its findings will have a long-lasting influence by its use and application by *other* international courts and tribunals.[175] There are indeed many examples of international tribunals simply referring to an ICJ decision to demonstrate the customary nature of one rule.[176] They include the European Court of Justice,[177] the WTO Appellate Body,[178] and the International Tribunal for the Law of the Sea Tribunal.[179]

[171] Gazzini, 'The Role of Customary International Law', pp. 692–693.

[172] On the question of custom at the ICJ, see: Luigi Fumagalli, 'Evidence before the International Court of Justice: Issues of Fact and Questions of Law in the Determination of International Custom', in Nerina Boschiero *et al.* (eds.), *International Courts and the Development of International Law: Essays in Honour of Tullio Treves* (The Hague: Asser Press, 2013); Peter Tomka, 'Custom and the International Court of Justice', *Law & Prac Int'l Cts & Tribunals*, 12(2) (2013), pp. 195–216; Yeghishe Kirakosyan, 'Finding Custom: the ICJ and the International Criminal Courts and Tribunals compared', in Larissa van den Herik and Carsten Stahn (eds.) *The Diversification and Fragmentation of International Criminal Law* (Leiden: Brill & Nijhoff, 2012); J.P. Kelly, 'The Twilight of Customary International of Custom and the Hague Court', *ZaöRV*, 31 (1971), p. 853; R.H. Geiger, 'Customary International Law in the Jurisprudence of the International Court of Justice: A Critical Appraisal', in U. Fastenrath *et al.* (eds.), *From Bilateralism to Community Interest: Essays in Honour of Judge Bruno Simma* (Oxford: Oxford University Press, 2011), p. 692; A. D'Amato, 'Trashing Customary International Law', *AJIL* 81 (1987), p. 101; G.L. Scott and C.L. Carr, 'The International Court of Justice and the Treaty/Custom Dichotomy', *Texas ILJ*, 16 (1981), p. 353.

[173] Alvarez-Jimenez, 'Methods for the Identification of Customary International Law', p. 698.

[174] *Id.*, p. 698. See also: Arthur Mark Weisburd, 'The International Court of Justice and the Concept of State Practice', UNC Legal Studies Research Paper No. 1282684, pp. 1, 25 ff, 67, 70, indicating that the Court rarely relies on actual State practice to determine the content of customary rules, but instead frequently bases its conclusions on non-binding resolutions of international bodies (such as the ILC) and *its own decisions*.

[175] Alvarez-Jimenez, 'Methods for the Identification of Customary International Law', pp. 683–684.

[176] Crawford, 'The Identification and Development of Customary International Law', p. 14.

[177] Many examples are discussed in: R. Higgins, 'The ICJ, the ECJ, and the Integrity of International Law', *ICLQ* 52 (2003), p. 8–9.

[178] WTO Appellate Body Report, *United States – Standards for Reformulated and Conventional Gasoline*, WT/DS2/AB/R, adopted on 20 May 1996, p. 17, referring to *Territorial Dispute Case (Libyan Arab Jamahiriya v. Chad)*, Judgment, ICJ Rep. 1994, para. 41, p. 21, to determine the customary status of Article 31(1) of the *Vienna Convention on the Law of Treaties*, signed in 1969 and entered into force on 27 January 1980, *UNTS* 1155 (1969), p. 331.

[179] *The M/V "SAIGA" (No. 2) Case (Saint Vincent and the Grenadines v. Guinea)*, Merits, Judgment, ITLOS Case No 2, ICGJ 336 (ITLOS 1999), 1 July 1999, International

Second, any convincingly argued decision on the existence of a custom rule will also influence the subsequent practice of States.[180] States will thus refer to such a decision in their internal legal analysis as well as in their correspondence with other States and in their pleadings before international tribunals. Thus, according to Alvarez-Jimenez, ICJ 'decisions stating that certain treaty provisions have the status of customary international law have sometimes led States, even those not party to the treaty, to regard themselves bound to comply with the obligations provided therein'.[181] In fact, when a tribunal declares the existence of a customary norm, States will start invoking such norm in international litigation. Courts and tribunals will then begin applying them, both relying on the ICJ's statements.[182] As suggested by one writer, 'the overall process ends up reinforcing the customary nature of the given norm so declared by the International Court'.[183]

1.5.3 The practice of investment tribunals

The previous two sections have shown that judges not only play an essential role in 'revealing' the existence of customary rules, but also in the development of such rules. This section examines the role that arbitral tribunals have played regarding customary rules in investment arbitration.

Investment tribunals have generally failed in their task of properly revealing the existence of customary rules. According to one writer, 'an examination of most decisions rendered by investment tribunals during 2009 (awards on the merit) indicates that tribunals that pronounce various customary rules are inclined *not* to discuss the existence (or lack of) of general practice; and that they frequently rely on decisions of international courts and tribunals as well as decisions of international bodies'.[184] This is also the conclusion reached by Fauchald in his study

---

Tribunal for the Law of the Sea, paras. 133–134, relying on *Case Concerning the Gabčíkovo-Nagymaros Project (Hungary v. Slovakia)*, Judgment, *ICJ Rep.* 1997, pp. 40–41, paras. 51–52 when examining the status of the 'State of necessity'.

[180] Gazzini, 'The Role of Customary International Law', pp. 692–693; Roberts, 'Traditional and Modern Approaches to Customary International Law', p. 775.

[181] Alvarez-Jimenez, 'Methods for the Identification of Customary International Law', pp. 683–684, giving the example of common articles 1 and 3 of the Geneva Conventions, which were declared customary norms by the ICJ in the *Nicaragua case*.

[182] *Id.*, p. 685.   [183] *Id.*

[184] ILA, 'Sources of International Investment Law', report by M. Hirsch, ILA Study Group on the Role of Soft Law Instruments in International Investment Law (2011), p. 12

of ninety-eight decisions rendered by tribunals from 1998 to 2006. While his analysis shows that 'tribunals used customary international law as a separate legal basis in 34 of the 98 decisions',[185] he also notes that not one single tribunal had conducted its *own* analysis and enquiry to establish the existence of a custom rule. He further explains that tribunals have instead consistently relied on the findings of the ICJ[186] or on the reasoning of *other tribunals* when 'revealing' the customary nature of rules:

> ICSID tribunals generally based their findings with regard to the existence and content of rules of customary international law on references to case law from the ICJ, the Permanent Court of International Justice, and arbitral tribunals, references to treaties, in particular the VCLT, references to documents adopted by the International Law Commission, and references to the legal doctrine. No tribunal made its own assessment of whether a rule of customary international law existed, and only exceptionally did tribunals explicitly address questions concerning *opinio juris*. Some tribunals analysed the content of rules of customary international law based on several sources.[187]

Other writers,[188] as well as my own survey of NAFTA case law,[189] have confirmed this phenomenon, which can be observed more generally in

[185] (emphasis in the original). See also, at p. 27 (also in: Andrea K. Bjorklund and August Reinisch (eds.), *International Investment Law and Soft Law* (Cheltenham: Elgar, 2012)). Ole Kristian Fauchald, 'The Legal Reasoning of ICSID Tribunals – An Empirical Analysis', *EJIL*, 19 (2008), p. 310.
[186] *Id.*, p. 341 ('References to decisions of the ICJ and its predecessor, the Permanent Court of International Justice, were found in 46 decisions. (. . .) ICJ case law was often used to determine rules of customary international law'). The issue is discussed in: Forteau, 'La contribution au développement du droit international général', p. 15.
[187] Fauchald, 'The Legal Reasoning of ICSID Tribunals', p. 311. He further explains (at p. 325) that tribunals have also resorted to customary international law as an *interpretive argument* in twenty-four cases: 'The tribunals based their arguments on a thorough analysis of the status or content of the customary international law in only seven decisions. They made a summary analysis of the rules in eight decisions, and included no analysis of the rules in 13 decisions. Customary international law was used as a general starting point for the subsequent reasoning in six decisions, it was used as an essential argument in 14 decisions, and as a non-essential argument in 11 decisions'.
[188] Hirsch, 'Sources of International Investment Law', p. 12: 'The examination of most investment awards rendered in 2009 reveals that investment tribunals often cite decisions of the ICJ as a proof of the existence of international customary law. Investment arbitrators also often infer the existence of customary rules from the awards of other investments tribunals, and sometimes from rules adopted by the International Law Commission or expert's publications'.
[189] Patrick Dumberry, *The Fair and Equitable Treatment Standard: A Guide to NAFTA Case Law on Article 1105* (Alphen aan den Rijn: Wolters Kluwer, 2013).

investor-State case law.[190] A good illustration is found in the reasoning of the *Glamis* Tribunal, which examined the prohibition against arbitrary conduct under the FET standard.[191] The Tribunal first made the general observation that '[a]scertaining custom is necessarily a *factual inquiry*, looking to the actions of States and the motives for and consistency of these actions'.[192] However, the Tribunal did not do such 'factual enquiry'; it did not examine State practice and *opinio juris*. Following its statement that 'previous [NAFTA] tribunals have indeed found a certain level of arbitrariness to violate the obligations of a State under the fair and equitable treatment standard',[193] the Tribunal concluded that 'claimant has sufficiently substantiated its arguments that a duty to protect investors from arbitrary measures exists in the customary international law minimum standard of treatment of aliens'.[194] Thus, the *Glamis* Tribunal entirely relied on the findings of previous NAFTA tribunals to 'reveal' the existence of the prohibition of arbitrary conduct as a customary rule.

This example is not isolated. A number of other NAFTA tribunals (*Thunderbird*,[195] *Waste Management*[196] and *Mobil*[197]) have also come to the same conclusion about the customary nature of the prohibition against arbitrary conduct as part of the minimum standard of treatment (MST). However, none of these tribunals have actually gone through the process of examining State practice and *opinio juris* on the matter. Just like the *Glamis*

---

[190] See, for instance, the remarks by Paraguay in *Bureau Veritas, Inspection, Valuation, Assessment and Control, BIVAC BV v. Paraguay*, ICSID Case No. ARB/07/9, Further Decision on Objections to Jurisdiction, 9 October 2012, paras. 156, 160.

[191] See, more generally, P. Dumberry, 'The Prohibition Against Arbitrary Conduct and the Fair and Equitable Treatment Standard under NAFTA Article 1105', *J. World Invest. & Trade* 15 (2014) pp. 117–151.

[192] *Glamis Gold Ltd v. United States*, Award, 14 May 2009, para. 607 (emphasis added).

[193] *Ibid.*, para. 625.   [194] *Ibid.*, para. 626.

[195] *International Thunderbird Gaming Corporation v. Mexico*, UNCITRAL, Award, 26 January 2006, para. 194 [hereinafter *Thunderbird v. Mexico*]: 'acts that would give rise to a breach of the minimum standard of treatment prescribed by the NAFTA and customary international law as those that, weighed against the given factual context, amount to a gross denial of justice or manifest arbitrariness falling below acceptable international standards'.

[196] *Waste Management, Inc. v. Mexico ("Number 2")*, ICSID Case No. ARB(AF)/00/3, Award, 30 April 2004, para. 98: 'minimum standard of treatment of fair and equitable treatment is infringed by conduct attributable to the State and harmful to the claimant if the conduct is arbitrary (...)'.

[197] *Mobil Investments Canada Inc. and Murphy Oil Corporation v. Canada*, Decision on Liability and on Principles of Quantum, 22 May 2012, para. 152: 'the fair and equitable treatment standard in customary international law will be infringed by conduct (...) that is arbitrary'.

Tribunal, these NAFTA tribunals have based their support for this affirmation on the previous findings of other tribunals.[198] Tribunals have typically
referred to the reasoning of the ICJ in the *ELSI* case.[199]

A good example of this phenomenon is found in the reasoning of the
Merrill & Ring Tribunal. The Tribunal observed that custom has evolved
since the 1920s: 'today's minimum standard is broader than that defined
in the *Neer* case and its progeny'.[200] Earlier in the award, the Tribunal
stated that 'in spite of arguments to the contrary, there appears to be a
shared view that customary international law has not been frozen in time
and that it continues to evolve in accordance with the realities of the
international community'.[201] For the Tribunal, the MST 'provides for the
fair and equitable treatment of alien investors within the confines of
reasonableness'.[202] In other words, the minimum standard has evolved
to the point where it protects all foreigners against State conduct that is
'unreasonable'. Thus, any 'unreasonable' act would (apparently) now be
considered as a violation of international law. The *Merrill & Ring*
Tribunal also noted that 'in the end, the name assigned to the standard
does not really matter'.[203] Therefore, the minimum standard under
custom and an unqualified stand-alone FET clause offer the *same* level
of protection to foreign investors. According to the Tribunal, '[w]hat
matters is that the standard protects against all such acts or behavior that
might infringe a sense of fairness, equity and reasonableness'.[204] These
are very controversial findings. The present author has explained elsewhere why the Tribunal's conclusion is inconsistent with the specific
features of NAFTA Article 1105 on the FET standard.[205]

It is more relevant, for the purposes of the present discussion, to
examine *how* the *Merrill & Ring* Tribunal came to this controversial
conclusion. Earlier in the award, the Tribunal mentioned that the important issue consisted of 'establish[ing] in which direction customary law
has evolved' and added that 'State practice and *opinio juris* will be the
guiding beacons of this evolution'.[206] However, the Tribunal omitted

---

[198] For instance, the tribunal in *Thunderbird* v. *Mexico*, Award, 26 January 2006,
referred to in footnotes (at paras. 193–194) to several NAFTA awards (*S.D. Myers,
Mondev, ADF, Azinian, Loewen*), one non-NAFTA award (*Genin*) and one ICJ case
(*ELSI*). See also: *Waste Management, Inc.* v. *Mexico* ("Number 2"), Award, 30 April
2004, para. 98.
[199] *Sicula S.p.A. (ELSI) (US v. Italy)*, Judgment, ICJ Rep. 1989.
[200] *Merrill & Ring* v. *Canada*, Award, 31 March 2010, para. 213.   [201] *Ibid.*, para. 193.
[202] *Ibid.*, para. 213 (emphasis added).   [203] *Ibid.*, para. 210.   [204] *Ibid.*
[205] Dumberry, *The Fair and Equitable Treatment Standard*, p. 115 ff.
[206] *Merrill & Ring* v. *Canada*, Award, 31 March 2010, para. 193.

citing *a single* example of State practice in support of the so-called 'convergence thesis' whereby custom is said to have apparently evolved so rapidly in recent years that it now has the same content as an unqualified FET clause (i.e., not linked to international law).[207] No arbitral decision is mentioned to support its proposition that custom had evolved so rapidly in recent years. The old arbitration cases from the 1920s, which the Tribunal refers to[208] in support of its claim of the existence of a so-called 'second track' of the evolution of the MST, do not demonstrate such an evolution. In sum, the *Merrill & Ring* Tribunal completely failed to examine State practice and *opinio juris* to support its proposition about the evolution of custom.[209] As correctly pointed out by a recent UNCTAD report, 'the *Merrill & Ring* tribunal failed to give cogent reasons for its conclusion that the MST made such a leap in its evolution'.[210]

One exception to this line of disappointing awards is found in the reasoning of the *UPS* Tribunal. While the *UPS* Tribunal ultimately concluded that there was 'no rule of customary international law prohibiting or regulating anticompetitive behaviour',[211] it did, however, examine whether any State practice supported such a claim. The Tribunal surveyed the content of different competition laws adopted by States and concluded that they were not consistent and uniform:

> Many states do not have competition laws – only 13 out of the 34 Western Hemisphere nations and about 80 of the WTO members do; more than half of the laws have been enacted in the past 10 years. Further, national legislation, for instance that of the three NAFTA Parties, differs markedly, reflecting their unique economic, social and political environment.[212]

---

[207] On the 'convergence thesis', see Dumberry, *The Fair and Equitable Treatment Standard*, p. 113 ff.

[208] *Merrill & Ring* v. *Canada*, Award, 31 March 2010, para. 206, referring to the following cases: *Case Concerning Certain German Interests in Polish Upper Silesia* (Merits), PCIJ, Series A. No. 7, at p. 19 (1926); *German Settlers in Poland*, PCIJ, Series B., No. 6, pp. 19–20, 35–38 (1923); *Aboilard Case* (Haiti, France), 9 *UNRIAA*, 1925, p. 71, pp. 79–81; *Robert E. Brown Case* (United Kingdom, United States), 6 *UNRIAA*, 1923, p. 120, pp. 129–130; *George W. Cook Case* (Mexico, United States), 4 *UNRIAA*, 1927, pp. 214–215; *Hopkins Case* (Mexico, United States), 4 *UNRIAA*, 1926, p. 41, at pp. 46–47; *Lalanne and Ledoux Case* (France, Venezuela), 10 *UNRIAA*, 1902, p. 18.

[209] In any event, it should be noted that these controversial findings have had no *practical effect* on the host State's liability. The Tribunal ruled that Canada did not breach the FET standard (Article 1105).

[210] UNCTAD, 'Fair and Equitable Treatment', 2012, p. 57.

[211] *UPS* v. *Canada*, Award on Jurisdiction, 22 November 2002, para. 92.

[212] *Id.*, para. 85.

According to the Tribunal, the claimant 'did not attempt to establish that aspect or the practice element of a customary international law rule requiring the prohibiting or regulating of anticompetitive behaviour'.[213] Moreover, there was 'no indication in any material before the Tribunal that any of that legislation was enacted out of a sense of general international legal obligation'.[214] The Tribunal came to the conclusion that there was an 'absence of current general obligations as indicated by state practice in national legislation'.[215] The Tribunal then referred to some BITs that have been cited by the claimant, but concluded that it had 'not attempted to establish that that state practice reflects an understanding of the existence of a generally owed international legal obligation which, moreover, has to relate to the specific matter of requiring controls over anticompetitive behaviour'.[216]

According to the Tribunal, 'the absence of any such [customary] rule is also demonstrated by multilateral treaty making and codification processes'.[217] For example, the GATT and WTO treaties do not contain any general set of provisions prohibiting or controlling anticompetitive behaviour. Moreover, the 'WTO Ministerial Declaration of 14 November 2001 (the Doha Declaration) shows that WTO Members are only now beginning to address the possibility of negotiating competition rules on a multilateral basis'.[218] Finally, the Tribunal provided additional proof of the absence of any customary rule, by mentioning that the draft articles prepared by the ILC's Special Rapporteur, F.V. Garcia Amador in 1961 on State responsibility 'said nothing at all about regulating anticompetitive behaviour'.[219] The Tribunal came to the same conclusion regarding the 'Draft Convention on the International responsibility of States for injuries to Aliens'[220] and added that the claimant 'did not refer us to material subsequent to the Harvard draft to demonstrate that general international law had moved in the direction of requiring states to prohibit or regulate anticompetitive behaviour'.[221] For all of these reasons, the Tribunal concluded that 'there is no rule of customary international law prohibiting or regulating anticompetitive behaviour'.[222]

[213] Id.   [214] Id.   [215] Id., para. 88.   [216] Id., para. 86.   [217] Id., para. 87.   [218] Id.
[219] Id. para. 88.
[220] 'Draft Convention on the International responsibility of States for injuries to Aliens', prepared for the International Law Commission by Sohn and Baxter of the Harvard Law School in 1961, in: AJIL 55 (1961), pp. 545, 553.
[221] UPS v. Canada, Award on Jurisdiction, 22 November 2002, paras. 89–90.
[222] Id., para. 91.

In sum, what almost all investment tribunals typically do is simply refer to the findings of other investment tribunals instead of examining whether there is consistent and uniform State practice and *opinio juris*. This technique of *renvoi* is not necessarily condemnable per se in situations where the awards referred to *do* contain a comprehensive and convincing analysis of State practice and *opinio juris*. Therefore, nothing should prevent future tribunals from referring to the reasoning of the *UPS* award on the customary status of a rule prohibiting or regulating anticompetitive behaviour. However, what is more problematic and regrettable is the systematic reference to awards which have *not* undertaken the difficult exercise of actually assessing the two elements of custom. Perhaps, as noted by one writer, tribunals should not be blamed for such failure insofar as their decisions are 'largely a response to the evidence that parties have placed before them' and that it may not be 'reasonable to expect litigants to comprehensively collect and present evidence of state practice and *opinio juris*'.[223] Yet, in my view, it is ultimately the task of a tribunal to convincingly demonstrate that a rule of custom is truly based on uniform, consistent and representative State practice. As further discussed at Chapter 5,[224] most investment disputes have to be decided by tribunals based on international law. The pronouncement by a tribunal of the customary status of a given norm cannot be taken lightly. It is a fundamental aspect of adjudication which will have long-lasting consequences.

Finally, it should be mentioned that the lack of proper investigation of State practice and *opinio juris* is not a phenomenon limited to the world of investment arbitration.[225] Scholars have long identified similar shortcomings in the decisions of the ICJ.[226] While the Court openly

---

[223] J. Harrison, 'The International Law Commission and the Development of International Investment Law', *Geo. Wash. Int'l L. Rev*, 45 (2013), p. 435.

[224] See, at Chapter 5, Section 5.2.

[225] Dinstein, 'The Interaction between Customary International Law and Treaties', p. 318; J.I. Charney, 'Universal International Law', *AJIL* 87 (1993), p. 537. See also: S. Zamora, 'Is there Customary International Economic Law?', *German YIL* 32 (1989), p. 25, coming to the same conclusion regarding how courts and tribunals assess the customary nature of any prohibition of expropriation.

[226] Crawford, 'The Identification and Development of Customary International Law', p. 8 ('the ICJ is not systematic in its approach to identifying customary international law, particularly with regards to *opinio juris*. It often affirms that a particular rule is declaratory of customary international law without detailed analysis'); A. Pellet, 'Shaping the Future of International Law: The Role of the World Court in Law-Making', in M.H. Arsanjani *et al.* (eds.), *Looking to the Future: Essays on International Law in Honor of W. Michael Reisman* (Leiden: Martinus Nijhoff, 2011), p. 1076; F. Orrego Vicuña,

acknowledges that it must itself investigate whether a rule can be con-sidered as custom,[227] recent empirical studies have shown that 'in some cases the Court finds that a rule of customary international law exists (or does not exist) without detailed analysis'.[228] In fact, the President of the ICJ, Peter Tomka, recently admitted that 'the Court has never found it necessary to undertake such an inquiry [about existing State practice and *opinio juris*] for every rule claimed to be customary in a particular case and instead has made use of the best and most expedient evidence available to determine whether a customary rule of this sort exists', including the work of codification by the International Law Commission.[229] This assessment is confirmed by recent empirical studies of ICJ decisions.[230]

'Customary International Law in a Global Community: Tailor Made?', *Estudios Internacionales*, 148 (2005), pp. 25–26; Geiger, 'Customary International Law in the Jurisprudence of the International Court of Justice', pp. 673, 674; O. Yasuaki, 'Is the International Court of Justice an Emperor Without Clothes?', *International Legal Theory*, 81 (2002), p. 16.

[227] See, *Military and Paramilitary Activities in and against Nicaragua (Nicaragua v. United States)*, Merits, Judgment, ICJ Rep. 1986, p. 14, para. 184.

[228] ILC, First Report, 2013, p. 24, also noting that 'In other cases the Court engages in a more detailed analysis of State practice and *opinio juris* in order to determine the existence or otherwise of a rule of customary international law'.

[229] Tomka, 'Custom and the International Court of Justice', p. 197, adding that 'Sometimes this entails a direct review of the material elements of custom on their own, while more often it will be sufficient to look to the considered views expressed by States and bodies like the International Law Commission as to whether a rule of customary law exists and what its content is, or at least to use rules that are clearly formulated in a written expression as a focal point to frame and guide an inquiry into the material elements of custom'. See also, at p. 202.

[230] Mitu Gulati, 'How the Courts Find International Custom?', paper presented at the conference 'The Role of *Opinio Juris* in Customary International Law', Duke-Geneva Institute in Transnational Law, Geneva, 2013, examined all ICJ decisions to determine the type of evidence which had been used by the Court in applying custom. The author concluded that while treaties were the most cited material, decisions of international tribunals were also very often mentioned. By contrast, actual State practice and state-ments of States indicating *opinio juris* were barely mentioned by the Court. See also: Weisburd, 'The International Court of Justice and the Concept of State Practice', p. 67 ('It is clear then that what the Court has not been doing in CIL cases is basing its judgments on carefully described state practice. What it has been doing instead is also significant: it has been relying on international bodies, the governing legal instruments of which confer on them no authority to create general obligations in international law. More precisely, the Court has relied, 1) on actions by the General Assembly and by states meeting in international conferences; 2) on determinations by bodies composed of individual experts; and 3) on its own precedents and policy determinations).

1.6 The role of scholars in the identification of custom

As mentioned earlier in this chapter, under Article 38(1) of the ICJ Statute, along with the formal sources of international law (treaties, custom and general principles of law), reference is made to 'the teachings of the most highly qualified publicists of the various nations'. Doctrine is considered as a 'subsidiary means for the determination of rules of law'. In other words, the writings of scholars cannot 'create' international law.[231] As stated by Kammerhofer, 'it may seem obvious that scholars cannot make law, just as little as lepidopterologists cannot "make" butterflies (...) If they do so (we may instinctively feel), they cease to be scholars and become legislators'.[232]

In fact, things used to be quite different. Scholars have historically played an important role in making statements about what the law is (or should be). Such statements have often been at the origin of emerging patterns of State practice, and have eventually crystallized into customary rules.[233] Their historical role is well-summarized by Dinstein:

> When the "fathers" of international law – most prominently, Hugo Grotius published the first tractates setting out in a systematic fashion the norms that States have to observe in the international arena, they frequently started off almost from scratch in terms of earlier general practice of States. There being scarcely any custom or treaties that they could rely upon in a given field, the "fathers" of international law filled the vacuum by borrowing from Roman law, canon law, etc., and were

---

[231] Pellet, 'Article 38', p. 791. See also: Michael Wood, 'Teachings of the Most Highly Qualified Publicists (Art. 38(1) ICJ Statute)' in Rüdiger Wolfrum (ed.), *Max Planck Encyclopedia of Public International Law* (Oxford: Oxford University Press, vol. 9, 2012), pp. 783–787.

[232] Jörg Kammerhofer, 'Law-making by Scholars', in Catherine Brölmann and Yannick Radi (eds.), *Research Handbook on the Theory and Practice of International Law-Making* (Cheltenham: Elgar 2013), p. 1 (of the paper version).

[233] J. Patrick Kelly, 'Opinio Juris in Historical Context', paper presented at the conference 'The Role of *Opinio Juris* in Customary International Law', Duke-Geneva Institute in Transnational Law, Geneva, 2013, p. 11: 'Much of CIL doctrine was deduced from other sources not from an examination of either the general acceptance of a norm by states or state practice. (...) Treatise writers created a narrative of customary law based on little state practice or diplomatic correspondence, but great reliance on arbitration panels and general natural law principles. It is striking that both the writings of publicists and arbitration decisions which are formally only subsidiary means for discovering rules of law are treated as of greater importance than the practices and views of states. The centuries long encounter between the nations of Europe and non-Europeans distorted the concept of custom in order justify the exercise of power. What was Natural law in one era became customary law in another era with little state practice or general acceptance by states'.

occasionally prone to creating new law under one guise or another. The practice of States ultimately either confirmed or revised the scholarly statements of the law, but the trail was initially blazed by Grotius or by other eminent scholars. At the present time, the position has undergone a profound alteration compared to the era of Grotius *et al.* No contemporary scholar can create international law.[234]

In contemporary international law, scholars are clearly no longer capable of international law-making. The best they can do is 'attest (on the basis of their research) that a specific custom can be inferred from the general practice of States and the communal *opinio juris*'.[235] Thus, scholarly works remain for States and courts 'a useful source of information and analysis for application to the identification of rules of customary international law'.[236] Scholars are indeed 'expected to undertake the painstaking research into the raw materials of the conduct and statements of States, panning the gravel for nuggets of customary law'.[237] In a recent Memorandum, the ILC Secretariat observed that '[t]he writings and opinions of jurists have often been considered by the Commission in the identification of rules of customary international law'.[238] Today, such work is undertaken not only by scholars, but also by NGOs, international organizations and the ILC. A number of international law scientific societies of great reputation (including the Institut de droit international and the ILA) also undertake codifications of various questions related to international law.

Nevertheless, there remain significant practical difficulties with finding relevant State practice in international law. As noted by Wood, obtaining access to the practice of many of the world's 190 States remains difficult (except for their practice within international organizations): '[w]hile some States systematically publish a good deal of material relating to

---

[234] Dinstein, 'The Interaction between Customary International Law and Treaties', pp. 313–314.

[235] *Id.*, p. 315.

[236] ILC, Third Report, 2015, p. 44. See also: ILC, Draft Conclusions, 2015, conclusion no. 14: 'Teachings of the most highly qualified publicists of the various nations may serve as a subsidiary means for the determination of rules of customary international law'.

[237] Dinstein, 'The Interaction between Customary International Law and Treaties', p. 314. See also: Hirsch, 'Sources of International Investment Law', pp. 21–22.

[238] International Law Commission, 'Formation and Evidence of Customary International Law, Elements in the Previous Work of the ILC that Could be Particularly Relevant to the Topic', Memorandum by the Secretariat, Sixty-fifth session Geneva, 5 May–7 June and 8 July–9 August 2013, UN Doc., A/CN.4/659, paras. 30–33.

their practice in the field of international law, most do not'.[239] The paradox is that when such State practice is actually available, 'the quantity of available material is daunting'.[240] Moreover, even when State practice is available, it is often difficult to ascertain such practice. This is because 'governments do not always act openly or consistently, and do not always indicate publicly, clearly, or at all, the legal basis for each and every act that they do or refrain from doing'.[241]

In a recent article, Gulati made an interesting observation. He discussed whether international law governing governmental succession to debts contains an exception for 'odious debts' and whether such exception can be considered as a rule of custom. He described one of his frustrations with assembling evidence of State practice as requiring 'superhuman research skills'.[242] Similarly, in a recent posting on *EJIL Talks*, Roberts summarized the many problems facing anyone undertaking such a task:

> But practice can be hard to find and cumbersome or difficult to collect. (...) Even when we can find smatterings of practice, it is almost impossible to collect real evidence of (1) general and consistent state practice followed out of (2) a sense of legal obligation. Even when people say that they are finding custom, they are usually relying on short cuts, such as referring to case law that says something is custom, General Assembly resolutions that declare something to be custom, or academic articles that opine that something is custom. Almost no one actually "finds" custom. Instead, arbitrators, academics and counsel typically refer to other sources that supposedly have already "found" custom. The rules for determining

[239] Michael Wood and Omri Sender, 'State Practice', in Rüdiger Wolfrum (ed.), *Max Planck Encyclopedia of Public International Law* (Oxford: Oxford University Press, 2013), para. 4. The other question of where to find such State practice is examined in: *Id.*, paras. 21 ff.

[240] *Id.*, para. 34 quoting the work of C. Parry, *The Sources and Evidences of International Law* (Manchester UP, 1965), p. 67: '[t]here are two obstacles in the way of a thorough-going comparative enquiry into the practice of States. They are the question of access to the materials and the enormous bulk of the latter'.

[241] Wood and Sender, 'State Practice', para. 8.

[242] Gulati, 'How do Courts Find International Custom?', p. 6: 'At the end of a couple of years of research on odious debts, the conclusion that many of us reached was that it was impossible to collect the kind of evidence that the definition required for even a small subset of these states. Not only was the type of evidence being requested unlikely to exist as a logical matter as discussed above (over fifty states engaging in a practice for multiple decades, all the while believing that they were acting consistent with the law, even though they were wrong about the law?), but it struck many of us as impossible to collect unless one somehow assembled an extraordinary team of anthropologists, economists, historians, political scientists, and lawyers that would then be able to spend decades excavating the historical record. Again, implausible'.

custom are not a good description of what any of us actually do. Instead, they are largely used to critique the work of others. For instance, "you say that X is custom" but "you have only referred to the practice of a handful of states" or "you have not proved that those states acted out of a sense of legal obligation." The bar is so high that everyone fails. Is it possible to reformulate the rules for establishing custom in a way that is theoretically defensible and yet could actually be satisfied as a matter of practice? Could the bar be set at a level that encouraged us to stretch and yet was not clearly out of reach? What sort of evidence could we look for and how much of it would we need? Could the test for custom ever be realistic instead of idealistic?[243]

One related question is whether the role of writers is only limited to the *identification* of custom, which is similar to the role of a lepidopterologist in the collection and study of butterflies. According to Wolfke, 'by attracting attention to international practice and appraising it, the writers indirectly influence its further evolution, that is, the development of custom'.[244] D'Aspremont explains that writers have a certain *indirect influence* on the evolution and development of custom:

> It is argued here that international legal scholars, although they are not at the origin of a practice of law ascertainment generative of communitarian semantics, undoubtedly participate in the fine-tuning and streamlining of the formal criteria of law-ascertainment which, in turn, are picked up by the social actors involved in the application of international legal rules. In other words, it is submitted here that legal scholars come to play the role of grammarians of formal law-ascertainment who systematize the standards of distinction between law and non-law. It is undeniable that scholars may occasionally be conducive to the progressive development of primary norms. Indeed, while they certainly are not law-makers, international legal scholars often play a public role or participate in public affairs. Although international legal scholars themselves may be tempted to see their offerings as more influential than they really are, and even though their contribution is more modest today than it used to be a century ago—for States have grown weary of the influence that scholars can have—their writings, their opinions, and their decisions also influence law-making and international legal adjudication. (. . .) International law would not have reached its current level of systemic development without the input of international legal scholarship. One of the paramount tasks undertaken as grammarians has been the systematization and the streamlining of the criteria for the distinction between law and non-law. While

---

[243] A. Roberts, 'Custom, Public Law and the Human Rights Analogy', *EJIL Talks*, 14 August 2013. See also: Zamora, 'Is there Customary International Economic Law?', pp. 38–39.

[244] Wolfke, *Custom in Present International Law*, p. 77. See also: Zamora, 'Is there Customary International Economic Law?', p. 38.

their work in this respect does not constitute, strictly speaking, the practice of law-applying authorities, the law ascertainment criteria carved out and polished by legal scholars have been very conducive to shaping the practice of law-applying authorities. That means that international legal scholars do not themselves yield social practice.[245]

International tribunals often refer to the work of scholars concerning custom.[246] This is certainly the case in investor-State arbitration.[247] This situation contrasts with the practice of the ICJ, which very rarely refers to doctrine (except in the individual opinions of judges).[248] Fauchald recently examined the actual influence of scholars in arbitral awards. He concluded that their work had been used as an interpretive argument in seventy-three of the ninety-eight decisions he surveyed, making it 'the second most frequently used interpretive argument, second only to ICSID case law'.[249] Moreover, he mentioned that their work 'was used extensively in relation to specific questions of treaty interpretation and questions concerning rules of customary international law'.[250] However, a survey conducted by Weeramantry led him to conclude that while older awards frequently referred to doctrine, recent awards refer more to past awards than to the work of scholars.[251]

---

[245] d'Aspremont, *Formalism and the Sources of International Law*, pp. 210–211; J. Kammerhofer, 'Law-Making by Scholarship? The Dark Side of 21st Century International Legal "Methodology"', in J. Crawford *et al.* (eds.), *Selected Proceedings of the European Society of International Law* (Oxford: Hart, vol. 3, 2011).

[246] Hirsch, 'Sources of International Investment Law', pp. 21–22: 'scholarly writings are an important source for organizing and analyzing the structure and content of international law; and of elucidating the nature, history and practice of the rules of law, and they certainly influence tribunals' decisions'.

[247] *Id.*, p. 21; Christoph H. Schreuer, Loretta Malintoppi, August Reinisch and Anthony Sinclair, *The ICSID Convention; A Commentary* (2nd edn., Cambridge: Cambridge University Press, 2009), p. 612.

[248] Pellet, 'Article 38', p. 792; J. Romesh Weeramantry, *Treaty Interpretation in Investment Arbitration* (Oxford: Oxford University Press, 2012), pp. 136–137, explaining the reasons why investment arbitration is different.

[249] Fauchald, 'The Legal Reasoning of ICSID Tribunals', p. 351.   [250] *Id.*, p. 352.

[251] Weeramantry, *Treaty Interpretation in Investment Arbitration*, p. 137.

Dancing with the sources: the fascinating story of the relative importance of custom and treaties at different times in the evolution of international investment law

Introduction

After examining the basic features of the concept of custom in Chapter 1, the present chapter looks at the relative importance of different sources of international law in the evolution of the field of international investment law. This is a fascinating story in which the main sources relevant in this field (custom and treaties) have each played important roles in different eras. The story is best told by examining the development of two principles that are now generally considered to be rules of customary international law in investor-State arbitration.

I will first examine the origin and the development of the concept of the 'minimum standard of treatment' (MST) and the emergence of a general prohibition against expropriation without compensation (Section 2.1). This analysis will be followed by a look into the developments that occurred in the 1960s and 1970s, which were characterized by serious and continuing challenges to the very existence of these two rules by a large segment of States, including those which emerged from colonialism (Section 2.2). These events marked a defining moment in the history of investment law. Until then, custom had been the prevalent source of international law obligations for States. Yet, as this chapter shows, this predominance will prove to rest on fragile grounds. At different phases in the evolution of international investment law, non-Western States have rejected to be bound by any MST and contested to have to provide compensation for unlawful expropriation. As a result, the foundations of these two rules as the basic sets of legal investment protection for investors doing business abroad have been severely weakened.

It is in this context of uncertainties that Western States have increasingly adopted a bilateral approach to secure legal protection with capital-importing States on an *ad hoc* basis. Section 2.3 explains that by the early 1990s everything had changed. Developing States dramatically changed their historical position regarding basic legal protections for foreign investors and started to sign BITs *en masse* with (mostly) Western States. In light of the present-day proliferation of BITs (a phenomenon referred to as 'treatification'), one might naturally question what remains of the historical importance of custom? In other words, while existing legal rules in the field of investment arbitration are overwhelmingly found in bilateral and multilateral investment treaties, should custom still be considered relevant today? As further explained below, custom does in fact continue to play an important role in this age of 'treatification' (Section 2.4). Some authors have in fact argued that the present period is marked by the 'return' of custom as an important source of law (Section 2.5). Finally, this chapter will offer readers a brief outline of the existing customary rules of international investment law, including the MST and a general prohibition against expropriation without compensation (Section 2.6).

2.1 The origin and the development of basic investment protections under custom

This section will examine the historical development of two customary rules providing basic legal protection to foreign investors which emerged in the twentieth century:

- The 'minimum standard of treatment' (MST) (Section 2.1.1); and
- The prohibition of expropriation without compensation (Section 2.1.2).

2.1.1 The historical foundation of the minimum standard of treatment

The historical aspects of the emergence of the MST have already been the subject of substantial scholarship.[1] Moreover, a number of recent

---

[1] *See*, for instance, Edwin Borchard, 'The "Minimum Standard" of the Treatment of Aliens', *ASIL Proc.* 33 (1939), p. 55; Edwin Borchard, *The Diplomatic Protection of Citizen Abroad* (New York: Bank Law Publishing Co., 1915); Edwin Borchard, 'The "Minimum Standard" of the Treatment of Aliens', *Mich. L. Rev.* 38 (1940), p. 445; Elihu Root, 'The Basis of Protection to Citizens Residing Abroad', *AJIL* 4 (1910), p. 521; Clyde Eagleton, *The Responsibility of States in International Law* (New York: New York University Press,

articles[2] and books[3] have also made a significant contribution to the understanding of the concept of the MST.

The origin of the MST is grounded in the international law doctrine of State responsibility for injuries to aliens.[4] It is rooted in a due diligence obligation for States to respect the rights of foreigners within their country. Before the twentieth century, the prevailing view was that individuals conducting business in another State should be subject to the law of that State.[5] One reason for the emphasis on local law was that, in many circumstances, Western States simply felt that there was no need for any international rules protecting their nationals abroad. Such was the case in the context of investments made by imperial States in their colonies (in Africa and parts of Asia for instance).[6] There was also no need for any 'international law' protection in the different context of the 'extraterritoriality' system that was imposed by powerful European States upon independent (yet weaker) States in Asia (the best-known example being that of the legations in Chinese cities).[7] Thus, under these 'unequal treaties'[8] of capitulation, foreigners were not subject to local laws and

---

1928), p. 103; Andreas Hans Roth, *The Minimum Standard of International Law Applied to Aliens* (The Hague: A.W. Sijthoff, 1949).

[2] *See, inter alia*: M.A. Orellana, 'International Law on Investment: The Minimum Standard of Treatment (MST)', *TDM* 3 (2004), pp. 1–2; Todd Weiler, 'An Historical Analysis of the Function of the Minimum Standard of Treatment in International Investment Law', in Todd Weiler and Freya Baetens (eds.), *New Directions in International Economic Law: In Memoriam Thomas Wälde* (Leiden: Martinus Nijhoff, 2011); Alireza Falsafi, 'The International Minimum Standard of Treatment of Foreign Investors' Property: A Contingent Standard', *Suffolk Transnat'l L. Rev.* 30 (2006–2007), p. 317; Hussein Haeri, 'A Tale of Two Standards: 'Fair and Equitable Treatment' and the Minimum Standard in International Law', *Arb. Int'l* 27 (2011), pp. 31–32.

[3] Martins Paparinskis, *The International Minimum Standard and Fair and Equitable Treatment* (Oxford: Oxford University Press, 2013), pp. 39–83; T. Weiler, *The Interpretation of International Investment Law: Equality, Discrimination and Minimum Standards of Treatment in Historical Context* (Leiden: Martinus Nijhoff, 2013).

[4] Hollin Dickerson, 'Minimum Standards', in Rüdiger Wolfrum (ed.) *Max Planck Encyclopedia of Public International Law* (Oxford: Oxford University Press, vol. 9, 2013), para. 2.

[5] C. Schreuer and R. Dolzer, *Principles of International Investment Law* (Oxford: Oxford University Press, 2008); pp. 11–12; Ionna Tudor, *The Fair and Equitable Treatment Standard in International Foreign Investment Law* (Oxford: Oxford University Press, 2008), p. 60. This period is examined in detail in: Weiler, 'An Historical Analysis of the Function of the Minimum Standard of Treatment', p. 337 ff.

[6] M. Sornarajah, *The International Law on Foreign Investment* (2nd edn., Cambridge: Cambridge University Press, 2004), pp. 19–20.

[7] *Ibid.*

[8] Dong Wang, *China's Unequal Treaties: Narrating National History* (Rowman and Littlefield, 2005).

representatives of their States adjudicated their disputes under their own laws.[9]

Another reason for the prevalence of the host State's laws was the strong opposition from many States, especially in Latin America, to any other solution. At the time, the Argentinian scholar Carlos Calvo developed a theory whereby foreigners receive a treatment that was not more favourable than that accorded to nationals of the host State.[10] The Calvo doctrine also required foreigners to give up their right to receive diplomatic protection from their home State and prohibited access to international arbitration for dispute resolution. This view was based on the fundamental international law principle of the sovereign equality of States.[11] Latin American States adopted this position to counter the so-called 'gunboat diplomacy' and other interference in their internal affairs by Western States.[12] Such interferences by Western States have often been made under the pretext of protecting the interests of their nationals abroad.[13] In this context, many States rejected the idea of the existence of any obligation under international law to accord a 'minimum' level of protection to foreigners.[14]

Despite strong opposition from many States, the early twentieth century nevertheless saw the gradual emergence of the MST.[15] The development of this standard of treatment grew out of a concern by capital-exporting States that governments of the territories receiving the investments lacked the basic measures of protection for aliens and their property.[16] At the time, the minimum standard focused almost

---

[9] Weiler, 'An Historical Analysis of the Function of the Minimum Standard of Treatment', p. 346.

[10] It is noteworthy that the *Montevideo Convention on the Rights and Duties of States*, 26 Dec. 1933, entered into force 26 Dec. 1934, 165 *L.N.T.S.* 19, indicated that aliens and nationals were on the same footing and that 'foreigners may not claim rights other or more extensive than those of nationals'. These issues are discussed in: Falsafi, 'The International Minimum Standard', p. 326 ff.

[11] Jeswald W. Salacuse, *The Law of Investment Treaties* (Oxford: Oxford University Press, 2010), p. 47.

[12] Orellana, 'International Law on Investment', pp. 1–2.

[13] Weiler, 'An Historical Analysis of the Function of the Minimum Standard of Treatment', p. 345, providing a number of examples of such interventions and referring to 'no fewer than one hundred instances of "protection by force" between 1813 and 1927 by the United States alone, including two dozen in the 20th century'.

[14] S. Schill, *The Multilateralization of International Investment Law* (Cambridge: Cambridge University Press, 2009), pp. 26–27. This issue is discussed in: Falsafi, 'The International Minimum Standard', p. 324 ff.

[15] Weiler, 'An Historical Analysis of the Function of the Minimum Standard of Treatment', p. 351.

[16] Orellana, 'International Law on Investment', p. 1.

exclusively on the non-discriminatory aspects of the treatment of aliens and in preventing the denial of justice.[17] These concerns were legitimate and warranted due to the numerous acts of expropriation without compensation that took place in Russia during the Revolution of 1917 and in Mexico in the turmuttuous events of the 1930s.[18] Western States argued that all governments were bound under international law to treat foreigners with at least a minimum standard of protection.[19] Such MST was said to be required precisely because the existing standard of protection in many countries was considered to be too low.[20] As explained by US Secretary of State, Mr. Elihu Root, in an article published in 1910, States sought to establish a threshold which would render certain treatments unacceptable and contrary to international law:

> Each country is bound to give to the nationals of another country in its territory the benefit of the same laws, the same administration, the same protection, and the same redress for injury which it gives to its own citizens, and neither more nor less: *provided the protection which the country gives to its own citizens conforms to the established standard of civilization.* There is [however] a standard of justice very simple, very fundamental, and of such general acceptance by all civilized countries as to form a part of the international law of the world. The . . . system of law and administration shall conform to this general standard. If any country's system of law and administration does not conform to that standard, although the people of the country may be content to live under it, no other country can be compelled to accept it as furnishing a satisfactory measure of treatment of its citizens.[21]

Several decades later, the NAFTA *S.D. Myers* Tribunal would explain why such an 'absolute' (non-contingent)[22] standard of treatment was necessary in modern investment treaty practice:

---

[17] Paparinskis, *The International Minimum Standard*, p. 64.
[18] Alexandra Diehl, *The Core Standard of International Investment Protection: Fair and Equitable Treatment* (Alphen aan den Rijn: Wolters Kluwer, 2012), pp. 146–147.
[19] Schreuer and Dolzer, *Principles of International Investment Law*, pp. 12–13.
[20] Salacuse, *The Law of Investment Treaties*, p. 47; J.C. Thomas, 'Reflections on Article 1105 of NAFTA: History, State Practice and the Influence of Commentators', *ICSID Rev.* 17(1) (2002), p. 26.
[21] Root, 'The Basis of Protection to Citizens Residing Abroad', p. 521 (emphasis added). On this question, *see* Paparinskis, *The International Minimum Standard*, pp. 39–46.
[22] J. Roman Picherack, 'The Expanding Scope of the Fair and Equitable Treatment Standard: Have Recent Tribunals Gone Too Far?', *J. World Invest. & Trade*, 9(4) (2008), p. 265. *Contra*: Falsafi, 'The International Minimum Standard', p. 354 (for whom the MST is a contingent standard).

The inclusion of a 'minimum standard' provision is necessary to avoid what might otherwise be a gap. A government might treat an investor in a harsh, injurious and unjust manner, but do so in a way that is no different than the treatment inflicted on its own nationals. The 'minimum standard' is a floor below which treatment of foreign investors must not fall, even if a government were not acting in a discriminatory manner.[23]

International jurisprudence slowly developed the concept of a minimum standard of protection.[24] While a number of cases have had a significant impact on the emergence of that standard,[25] the best known is certainly the *Neer* case of 1926. This case was decided by the US-Mexico Claims Commission, established in the 1920s to adjudicate claims arising out of widespread unrest in Mexico, which caused harm to US nationals.[26] The case involved a claim for compensation for the death of an American citizen, Mr. Paul Neer. It was alleged that 'the Mexican authorities showed an unwarrantable lack of diligence or an unwarrantable lack of intelligent investigation in prosecuting the culprits'.[27] While the Commission dismissed the claim, it nevertheless provided for an explanation of the minimum standard:

> The propriety of governmental acts should be put to the test of international standards, and ... the treatment of an alien, in order to constitute an international delinquency, should amounts to an outrage, to bad faith, to wilful neglect of duty, or to an insufficiency of governmental action so far short of international standards that every reasonable and impartial man would readily recognize its insufficiency.[28]

The *Neer* case had and continues to have considerable influence on the emergence of the concept of the MST.[29] In fact, international law casebooks

---

[23] *S.D. Myers Inc.* v. *Canada*, UNCITRAL, First Partial Award, 13 November 2000, para. 259.

[24] M. Kinnear, A. Biorklund and J.F.G. Hannaford, *Investment Disputes under NAFTA: An Annotated Guide to NAFTA Chapter 11* (Alphen aan den Rijn: Kluwer Law International, 2006), section on Art. 1105, pp. 11–12; Schill, *The Multilateralization of International Investment Law*, pp. 26–28 (noting however, the 'shaky foundations of the standards of customary international law with regard to the protection of aliens and their property'); Orellana, 'International Law on Investment', p. 2.

[25] See, *inter alia*: *Roberts* v. *Mexico*, Award, 2 November 1926, 4 *UNRIAA*, p. 77; *Chevreau* v. *United Kingdom*, Award, 9 June 1931, 2 *UNRIAA*, p. 1113; *George W. Hopkins* v. *Mexico*, Award, 31 March 1926, 4 *UNRIAA*, pp. 41, 50.

[26] *USA (LF Neer)* v. *Mexico*, Award, 15 October 1926, 4 *UNRIAA*, p. 60.   [27] *Ibid.*, p. 61.

[28] *Ibid.*, pp. 61–62.

[29] Roth, *The Minimum Standard of International Law*, p. 95. The case is discussed in detail in: Thomas, 'Reflections on Article 1105 of NAFTA', p. 29 ff; Paparinskis, *The International Minimum Standard*, pp. 48–54.

typically refer to *Neer* as evidence of the existence of such a standard.[30] This conclusion has recently been contested by a number of tribunals[31] and several writers who argue that little weight should be given to a three-page award which only makes a general statement not substantiated by State practice.[32] It is sufficient to conclude (in the context of the present book[33]) that the *Neer* case offers little value in determining the *actual* content of the MST in contemporary international investment law because the standard has evolved substantially since the 1920s. This position has been adopted by several tribunals[34] as well as by many scholars.[35]

According to Paparinskis, the evolution of the minimum standard up until the 1940s can be summarized as follows:

> The creation of the international minimum standard (. . .) passed through a number of stages. The first stage is reflected in the nineteenth-century state practice, (almost) exclusively focusing on the non-discriminatory aspects of the treatment of aliens and denial of justice. Elihu Root's speech of 1910 illustrates the second stage of development, simultaneously explicit about the non-exhaustive nature of the non-discriminatory aspect of the international standard, and uncertain and contradictory about the source and content of this exception that could go further and apply to

[30] For instance, Ian Brownlie, *Principles of Public International Law* (5th edn., Oxford: Oxford University Press, 1998), pp. 527–528; J.L. Brierly, *The Law of Nations* (6th edn., Oxford: Clarendon Press, 1963), p. 280; G. Schwartzenberger, *International Law as Applied by International Courts and Tribunals* (London: Stevens and Sons, 1949), p. 201.

[31] *Railroad Development Corporation v. Guatemala*, ICSID Case No. ARB/07/23, Award, 29 June 2012, para. 216; *Mondev International Ltd. v. United States*, ICSID Case No. ARB(AF)/99/2, Award, 2 October 2002, para. 115 [hereinafter *Mondev v. United States*]. See also: *Merrill & Ring Forestry L.P. v. Canada*, UNCITRAL, Award, 31 March 2010, paras. 197, 204.

[32] Stephen M. Schwebel, 'Is Neer far from Fair and Equitable?', *Arb. Int'l* 27(4) (2011), pp. 555–561; Jan Paulsson, 'Neer-ly Misled?', *Miami Law Research Paper*, p. 247 (*see also*: J. Paulsson and G. Petrochilos, 'Neer-ly Misled?', *ICSID Rev.* 22(2) (2007), pp. 242–257).

[33] The question is examined in: Patrick Dumberry, *The Fair and Equitable Treatment Standard: A Guide to NAFTA Case Law on Article 1105* (Alphen aan den Rijn: Wolters Kluwer, 2013), pp. 16–19.

[34] *ADF Group Inc. v. United States*, ICSID Case No. ARB(AF)/00/1, Award, 6 January 2003, para. 181; *Mondev v. United States*, Award, 2 October 2002, paras. 116, 117; *Loewen Group, Inc. and Raymond L. Loewen v. United States*, ICSID Case No. ARB(AF)/98/3, Award on Merits, 26 June 2003, para. 132 [hereinafter *Loewen v. United States*].

[35] Andrew Newcombe and Luis Paradell, *Law and Practice of Investment Treaties: Standards of Treatment* (Alphen aan den Rijn: Kluwer, 2009), p. 237; Tudor, *The Fair and Equitable Treatment Standard*, p. 64; Roland Kläger, *Fair and Equitable Treatment in International Investment Law* (Cambridge: Cambridge University Press, 2011), p. 53; Paulsson, 'Neer-ly Misled?', p. 257. For Paparinskis, *The International Minimum Standard*, p. 216, the *Neer* case 'operates as the default rule', to be 'replaced by more specific and detailed rules on the issue when they exist or are developed' (p. 53).

outrageous cases. The third stage is exemplified by the 1926 award of the US-Mexico General Claims Commission in the LFH Neer and Pauline Neer (Neer) case. The Commission attempted to define the international standard by means of analogy, deriving criteria of procedural outrage from the better-established rules of denial of justice and then applying these more generally. Neer was a relative improvement, attempting to give some juridical certainty to the previously indefinable exception (. . .). However and simultaneously, the focus on procedural outrage made it more complicated to develop rules that fell outside this paradigm (. . .). Despite the implicit consensus of the nineteenth century and the first decades of the twentieth century on the existence of such a rule and the explicit confirmation by the PCIJ in the 1920s, State practice in the 1930s Hague Conference during the 1930s raised questions about the continuing correctness of this view.[36]

Following the Second World War, Eastern Europe was marked by large-scale expropriations.[37] During this time, the concepts of denial of justice and the minimum standard were considered unsatisfactory to address such wrongful acts. Arbitration practice began focusing instead on the issue of compensation.[38] In fact, the question of adequate compensation accorded to a foreign investor as a result of expropriation and nationalization acts stood as the most controversial issue at the time. It shifted attention away from the older and prevalent debate on the MST.[39] The question of adequate compensation, which in itself has a long history and has been the object of significant controversy under international law, will be explained further in the next section.

2.1.2   The emergence of a general prohibition against expropriation without compensation

In the 1920s and 1930s, international jurisprudence started developing the requirement for States to provide compensation in the event of expropriation.[40] The *Chorzów Factory* case, decided by the PCIJ in 1928, was undoubtedly the most important. The Court held that

[36] Paparinskis, *The International Minimum Standard*, p. 64.
[37] Andrew T. Guzman, 'Why LDCs Sign Treaties That Hurt Them: Explaining the Popularity of Bilateral Investment Treaties', *Virginia JIL* 38(4) (1998), pp. 646–647.
[38] Paparinskis, *The International Minimum Standard*, pp. 67–73, 83.
[39] *Ibid.*, pp. 68–69.
[40] K.J. Vandevelde, *Bilateral Investment Treaties: History, Policy and Interpretation* (Oxford: Oxford University Press, 2010), p. 283; R. Dolzer, 'Indirect Expropriation of Alien Property', *ICSID Rev.* (1987), p. 44 ff.

'reparation must, as far as possible, wipe out all the consequences of the illegal act and re-establish the situation which would, in all probability, have existed if that act has not been committed'.[41] This statement represents today the prevailing basic requirement for compensation in the event of unlawful expropriation.[42] A series of expropriations of foreign companies in Mexico in the 1930s led to a famous exchange of letters between the governments of Mexico and the United States. In one note to his Mexican counterpart, US Secretary of State, Mr. Cordell Hull, argued that international law required 'prompt, adequate and effective' compensation for the expropriation of foreign investments:

> The Government of the United States merely adverts to a self-evident fact when it notes that the applicable precedents and recognized authorities on international law support its declaration that, under every rule of law and equity, no government is entitled to expropriate private property, for whatever purpose, without provision for prompt, adequate, and effective payment therefor.[43]

While Mexico strongly objected to what would become known as the Hull formula,[44] it has nevertheless been argued as representing the state of custom at the time.[45] The Hull formula was soon incorporated by the United States in its treaty practice.[46] US 'Friendship, Commerce, and Navigation' (FCN) treaties of the time also began to include a series of conditions for expropriation to be considered legal (respect of due process, for public purpose, not discriminatory, and effective

[41] *Case Concerning the Factory at Chorzów (Indemnity)*, 13 September 1928, P.C.I.J. Ser. A. No. 17, p. 47.

[42] Vandevelde, *Bilateral Investment Treaties*, p. 283.

[43] Letter of 22 August 1938, in Green H. Hackworth, *Digest of International Law* (1942, vol. 3, Washington DC: Department of State), p. 228.

[44] See, note dated 3 August 1938 whereby the Mexican Minister of Foreign Affairs stated '[m]y Government maintains (. . .) that there is in international law no rule universally accepted in theory nor carried out in practice, which makes obligatory the payment of immediate compensation nor even of deferred compensation, for expropriations of a general and impersonal character', in *ibid.*, p. 657.

[45] R. Dolzer 'New Foundations of the Law of Expropriation of Alien Property', *AJIL* (1981), p. 558 ('It is assumed here that United States Secretary of State Hull accurately presented the then current position in international law in 1938 when he wrote his famous letter to the Mexican Government asking Mexico for "prompt, adequate and effective" compensation. Even though the Soviet Union and Latin American countries had challenged the rule before that time, it appears that the overwhelming practice and the prevailing legal opinion supported Hull's position. Judgments such as in the *Norwegian Shipowners* case and the *Spanish-Moroccan Claims*" arbitration, and the famous dictum of the Permanent Court of International Justice in the *Chorzów Factory* case support this view').

[46] Vandevelde, *Bilateral Investment Treaties*, p. 283.

compensation). Slowly other BITs started to impose the same conditions.[47] According to one writer, 'the classic elements of a BIT expropriation provision all had been identified by the end of the 1950s and had become prevalent in BIT practice by the mid 1960s'.[48]

2.2 Challenges to existing customary rules on investment protection

The question of whether or not any customary rule had firmly crystallized after the Second World War in the field of investment arbitration has solicited plenty of controversy.[49] It is safe to say that the MST was an established rule of custom at the time.[50] While many believe that a general prohibition of expropriation without compensation also existed,[51] others denied this affirmation.[52] There are reasons to believe

---

[47] *Ibid.*, p. 285.   [48] *Ibid.*, p. 287.

[49] Weiler, *The Interpretation of International Investment Law*, p. 228, fn 646 ('To be fair to both sides, the CIL consensus of the time could not have extended any further than agreement that: (1) discriminatory takings were prohibited; (2) sovereign authority could not be exercised in bad faith; and (3) host States were obliged to accord protection and security to aliens both in their person and in the exercise of their property rights').

[50] This is indeed the position taken by these writers *in the 1950s*: Robert R. Wilson, *The International Law Standard in Treaties of the United States* (Cambridge, Mass., Harvard UP, 1953), pp. 103–104; G. Schwarzenberger, *International Law* (3rd edn., vol. 1, London: Stevens and Sons, 1957), pp. 206–207. See also: Paparinskis, *The International Minimum Standard*, pp. 64–67, 83 ff.; Jose E. Alvarez, 'A Bit on Custom', *N.Y.U. J. Int'l L. & Pol.* 42 (2009–2010), p. 39; José E. Alvarez, 'The Public International Law Regime Governing International Investment', *Rec. des cours* 344 (2009), p. 292.

[51] Guzman, 'Why LDCs Sign Treaties That Hurt Them', pp. 641, 651; A. Ruzza 'Expropriation and Nationalization', in Rüdiger Wolfrum (ed.), *Max Planck Encyclopedia of Public International Law* (Oxford: Oxford University Press, vol. 9, 2013), para. 3.

[52] Patrick Juillard, 'L'évolution des sources du droit des investissements', *Rec. des cours* 250 (1994), p. 76: 'Est-il exact que, dès avant la seconde guerre mondiale, s'était formée une coutume générale en matière de protection des investissements, et, plus particulièrement, en matière d'expropriation ou de nationalisation de ces investissements? Les pays développés l'ont constamment soutenu. Leur position, à cet égard, semble fragile: s'il a existé une coutume générale, c'est en matière de protection des biens, et non en matière de protection des investissements'. See also, at p. 83 ('A supposer qu'il ait bien existé une pratique étatique en matière de protection des biens étrangers dès avant la seconde guerre mondiale et que cette pratique ait été transposée du domaine de la protection des biens étrangers au domaine de la protection des investissements internationaux, présentait-elle des caractères de clarté, de stabilité et de généralité tels que l'on puisse y dicter les fondements d'une coutume internationale? On peut en douter. Mais, même si l'on prend pour hypothèse qu'il ait existé une coutume générale en cette matière, il n'en faut pas moins se demander si celle-ci a survécu aux attaques dont elle a été l'objet de la part, notamment, des pays en développement – attaques qui ont trouvé pour véhicule juridique les résolutions des organisations internationales intergouvernementales').

as well that the Hull formula represented the state of custom at the time.[53]

The next sections will examine a number of dramatic developments that took place in the decades following the Second World War. First, I will examine the strong opposition led by Newly Independent States in the 1960s and 1970s against these basic customary norms (Section 2.2.1). Second, I will analyse the impact that this contestation had on existing customary rules (Section 2.2.2), including the Hull formula (Section 2.2.3).

2.2.1   A concerted attack led by newly independent States in the 1960s and 1970s

In the 1960s and 1970s, a group of States revived the opposition towards the existence of any custom rules in the field of investment law. This era was fundamentally marked by the arrival on the international scene of a growing number of 'Newly Independent States' emerging from colonialism in Asia and Africa.[54] They openly contested the *legitimacy* of existing

---

[53] Dolzer, 'New Foundations of the Law of Expropriation of Alien Property', p. 558; Jean d'Aspremont, 'International Customary Investment Law: Story of a Paradox', in T. Gazzini and E. de Brabandere (eds.), *International Investment Law: The Sources of Rights and Obligations* (Leiden; Boston: Martinus Nijhoff, 2012), p. 13.

[54] The *Vienna Convention on Succession of States in Respect of Treaties*, signed on 23 August 1978 and entered into force on 6 November 1996, 1946 *UNTS* 3 (*I.L.M.*, 17 (1978), p. 1488), defines the expression 'Newly Independent State', as 'a successor State the territory of which immediately before the date of the succession of States was a dependent territory for the international relations of which the predecessor State was responsible' (Art. 2). The Vienna Convention adopted different rules for them because of their unique historical and political characteristics in the context of decolonization. It is generally admitted that the territory of a colony should not be considered as part of the territory of the colonial State administrating it. See: *Declaration of Principles of International Law Concerning Friendly Relations and Co- Operation Among States in Accordance with the Charter of the United Nations*, adopted by U.N. General Assembly Res. 2625 (XXV), of 24 October 1970. In that sense, a Newly Independent State is a new State which, however, cannot be said to have 'seceded' from the colonial power to the extent that its territory was never formally part of it. It is generally recognized that different rules of State succession should apply to these States in order for them to freely exercise their right to self-determination and to break the vicious circle of economic domination. On this question, see: Yilma Makonnen, 'State Succession in Africa: Selected Problems', *Rec. des cours* 200 (1986-V), pp. 130–131; Mohammed Bedjaoui, 'Problèmes récents de succession d'États dans les États nouveaux', *Rec. des cours* 130 (1970-II), pp. 468–469, 530; Zidane Meriboute, *La codification de la succession d'États aux traités: décolonisation, sécession, unification* (Paris: PUF, 1984), pp. 29–30, 49, 56, 63.

customary international law.[55] As mentioned in Chapter 1,[56] a settled principle of international law is that new States are bound by *existing* principles of custom. These principles are therefore binding on States which did not (and could not since they did not exist) participate in their development. Newly Independent States demanded a revision of these 'outdated' rules that did not take into account the fundamental changes that had occurred in the international community since the end of the colonization period.[57] According to one prominent scholar, these States '[did] not easily forget that the same body of international law that they [were] now asked to abide by, sanctioned their previous subjugation and exploitation and stood as a bar to their emancipation'.[58] In sum, as a matter of principle, these new States rejected to be bound by existing customary rules.[59]

Specifically, these new developing States rejected having to provide any minimum standard of protection to foreign investors under customary international law.[60] They also contested the existence of any international

---

[55] Guzman, 'Why LDCs Sign Treaties That Hurt Them', p. 646 ('As former colonies became sovereign states, however, these newly minted countries were able to voice their own views, and those views became relevant to the formulation of customary international law. As their numbers grew, these states carried greater weight in the international arena, and as they questioned existing international norms, including the Hull Rule, the status of those norms was threatened').

[56] Chapter 1, Section 1.2.4.

[57] Georges Abi-Saab, 'The Newly Independent States and the Rules of International Law: An Outline', *Howard L.J.*, 8 (1962), p. 118.

[58] *Ibid.* p. 100. Accordingly, a revision of the existing rules of customary international law was needed in order 'to redress the balance of centuries of domination and exploitation by these big power of the newly independent states' (p. 119). *See also*: S.N. Guha-Roy, 'Is the Law of Responsibility of States for Injuries to Aliens A Part of Universal International Law?', *AJIL* 55 (1961), p. 866: 'The history of the establishment and consolidation of empires overseas by some of the members of the old international community and of the acquisition therein of vast economic interests by their nationals teems with instances of a total disregard of all ethical considerations. A strange irony of fate now compels those very members of the community of nations on the ebb tide of their imperial power to hold up principles of morality as shields against the liquidation of interests acquired and held by an abuse of international intercourse. Rights and interests acquired and consolidated during periods of such abuse cannot for obvious reasons carry with them in the mind of the victims of that abuse anything like the sanctity the holders of those rights and interests may and do attach to them. To the extent to which the law of responsibility of states for injuries to aliens favours such rights and interests, it protects an unjustified status quo or, to put it more bluntly, makes itself a handmaid of power in the preservation of its spoils'.

[59] Juillard, 'L'évolution des sources du droit des investissements', p. 76.

[60] Sornarajah, *The International Law on Foreign Investment*, p. 140 ff.; OECD, 'International Investment Law: A Changing Landscape: A Companion Volume to International Investment Perspectives' (2005), p. 82. See, for instance: 'Report of the Fourth Session

law norms requiring compensation for expropriated foreign properties. Moreover, they supported a less stringent compensation requirement than the Hull formula.[61] The conflicting ideologies of the time are summarized as follows by Schwebel:

> Capital-exporting States generally maintained that host States were bound under international law to treat foreign investment at least in accordance with the 'minimum standard of international law'; and where the host State expropriated foreign property, it could lawfully do so only for a public purpose, without discrimination against foreign interests, and upon payment of prompt, adequate and effective compensation. Capital importing States maintained that host States were not in matters of the treatment and taking of foreign property bound under international law at all; that the minimum standard did not exist; and that States were bound to accord the foreign investor only national treatment, only what their domestic law provided or was revised to provide. The foreign investor whose property was taken was entitled to no more than the taking State's law afforded.[62]

At the time, developing States took the debate to the United Nations General Assembly, where they were now representing the majority of States.[63] They used their status within the international body to advance their interests by way of resolutions and declarations at the General Assembly.[64] The States held the view that said resolutions were evidence of State practice and *opinio juris* necessary for the creation of new custom norms.[65] These new States believed that customary rules should develop

of the Asian African Legal Consultative Committee', 2 *Yearbook ILC*, (1961), pp. 78, 82–84.

[61] Guzman, 'Why LDCs Sign Treaties That Hurt Them', p. 647 ('The lines of disagreement were clear: capital importers supported a less stringent rule and capital exporters supported the Hull Rule. In the battle for international legitimacy, both sides of the debate claimed that customary international law was on their side to the support it had received both in practice and in writings by commentators. In response, LDCs pointed out that practice had not always accorded with the Hull Rule and that, in any event, the rule simply lacked the broad international support that customary international law requires. Although the developed world denied the point, it seemed that the debate itself was undermining the claim that the rule retained its status as customary international law'). See also: UNCTAD, 'Bilateral Investment Treaties 1995–2006: Trends in Investment Rulemaking' (2007), p. 48.

[62] S.M. Schwebel, 'The United States 2004 Model Bilateral Investment Treaty: An Exercise in the Regressive Development of International Law', *TDM* 3(2) (2006), p. 3.

[63] Juillard, 'L'évolution des sources du droit des investissements', p. 84 ff.

[64] M. Byers, *Custom, Power and the Power of Rules: International Relations and Customary International Law* (Cambridge: Cambridge University Press, 1999), p. 41.

[65] *Ibid.*

at a more rapid pace in order to replace the old existing rules, to which they had not participated and which were contrary to their own interests. These arguments were rejected at the time by Western States who feared that their influence on the evolution and the formulation of rules of international law was eroding in light of these important changes.[66] These developments have led to notable doctrinal controversies amongst writers. While some authors have embraced the new phenomenon,[67] others have been more critical, characterizing it as 'coutume sauvage'.[68]

The 1960s and 1970s were marked by a series of resolutions passed at the General Assembly which emphasized the sovereignty of nations with respect to foreign investments.[69] A compromise was reached in 1962 with the General Assembly's *Resolution on Permanent Sovereignty over Natural Resources*. While this resolution affirmed the right for host States to nationalize foreign-owned property, it nevertheless required 'appropriate compensation in accordance with the rules in force in the State taking such measures in the exercise of its sovereignty and in accordance with international law'.[70] The resolution was adopted with eighty-seven votes in favour, two against, and twelve abstentions. It should be noted that while the US representative voted in favour of the resolution, he also explained that he was 'confident' that the terms 'appropriate compensation' would be 'interpreted as meaning prompt, adequate and effective compensation'.[71]

What 'appropriate compensation' was supposed to mean was clarified in the subsequent Resolution 3171, adopted in 1973, which indicated that 'each State is entitled to determine the amount of possible compensation and the mode of payment' and that any dispute on the issue 'should be settled in accordance with the national legislation of each State carrying

---

[66] T.L. Stein, 'The Approach of the Different Drummer: The Principle of the Persistent Objector in International Law', *Harvard ILJ* (1985), p. 466.

[67] Georges Abi-Saab, 'La coutume dans tous ses États ou le dilemme du développement du droit international général dans un monde éclaté', in Roberto Ago (dir.), *Le droit international à l'heure de sa codification : études en l'honneur de Roberto Ago* (Giuffrè, 1987), p. 53.

[68] R.J. Dupuy, 'Coutume sage et coutume sauvage', in *Mélanges Rousseau* (Paris: Pedone, 1974), p. 75. See also: P Weil, 'Toward Relative Normativity in International Law', *AJIL* 77 (1983), pp. 433–434.

[69] Guzman, 'Why LDCs Sign Treaties That Hurt Them', pp. 648–649.

[70] G.A. Res. 1803, 14 December 1962, U.N. GAOR, 17th Sess., Supp. No. 17, p. 15, U.N. Doc. A/5217 (1962), in *I.L.M.* 2 (1963), p. 223. In doctrine, see: Stephen M. Schwebel, 'The Story of the U.N.'s Declaration on Permanent Sovereignty over Natural Resources', *ABAJ* 49 (1963), p. 463.

[71] Schwebel, *ibid.*, pp. 463–466.

out such measures'.[72] In other words, the so-called Hull formula, which provided for 'prompt, adequate and effective' compensation in the event of expropriation was clearly rejected. This was also clear when the General Assembly adopted in 1974 the *Charter of Economic Rights and Duties of States*.[73] Under this 'New International Economic Order' the requirement to provide 'appropriate compensation' for expropriation still existed, but any related disputes (or 'controversy') had to be 'settled under the domestic law of the nationalizing State and by its tribunals', and not by an international tribunal under international law.[74] One hundred and four States voted in favour of that resolution, sixteen against, with six abstaining. As noted by one writer, this resolution in fact 'opère un double clivage, entre, d'une part, pays capitalistes et pays socialistes, et entre, d'autre part, pays développés et pays en développement'.[75]

2.2.2   *An impact assessment of the attack on existing rules*

What has been the impact of such contestation on custom? One thing is clear: considering the opposition between developing and developed States, the *Charter of Economic Rights and Duties of States* could hardly be considered as a reflection of existing international law at the time.[76] In other words, the Charter did *not* create a new rule of customary international law.[77]

---

[72] G.A. Res. 3171, U.N. GAOR, 28th Sess., Supp. No. 30, p. 52, U.N. Doc. A/9030 (1974), in *ILM* 13 (1974), p. 238.

[73] G.A. Res. 3281, U.N. GAOR, 29th Sess., Supp. No. 31, p. 50–55, U.N. Doc. A/9631 (1974), in *ILM* 14 (1975), p. 251.

[74] The resolution adds that disputes could be settled by 'other peaceful means' than domestic courts if it is 'freely and mutually agreed by all States concerned' on 'the basis the sovereign equality of States and in accordance with the principle of free choice of means'.

[75] Juillard, 'L'évolution des sources du droit des investissements', p. 90.

[76] Stephen M. Schwebel, 'Investor-State Disputes and the Development of International Law: The Influence of Bilateral Investment Treaties on Customary International Law', *ASIL Proc.*, 98 (2004), p. 28 ('As a General Assembly resolution not adopted as declaratory of international law, which plainly was not declaratory of international law, and terms of which were vigorously contested, the charter could neither make nor reflect international law'); Schwebel, 'The United States 2004 Model Bilateral Investment Treaty', p. 1; C. Brower and John B. Tepe, 'Charter of Economic Rights and Duties of States-A Reflection or Rejection of International Law?', *Int'l Law* 9 (1975), p. 295.

[77] D. Carreau and P. Juillard, *Droit international économique* (Paris: L.G.D.J., 1998), p. 464; Salacuse, *The Law of Investment Treaties*, p. 75.

Another question raised is whether or not the effect of the attack by new States had been to *destroy* the few rules of custom which existed after the Second World War. A number of writers believe this is the case.[78] Without specifically taking a position on the impact that the contestation may have had on custom, the International Court of Justice (ICJ) in the famous *Barcelona Traction* case of 1970 simply noted that no rules of customary international law existed in the field of international investment law:

> Considering the important developments of the last half-century, the growth of foreign investments and the expansion of international activities of corporations, in particular of holding companies, which are often multinational, and considering the way in which the economic interests of states have proliferated, it may at first sight appear surprising that the evolution of the law has not gone further and that no generally accepted rules in the matter have crystallized on the international plane.[79]

The more established position, as mentioned previously, is that some customary rules *already existed* at the time when developing States started opposing them. Thus, while contested by many States, it remains that the MST had long been established as a basic rule of custom.[80] In the 1990 *ELSI* case, the ICJ indeed referred explicitly to

---

[78] Carreau and Juillard, *ibid.*, pp. 464–465; Sornarajah, *The International Law on Foreign Investment*, pp. 19–20, 89–93, 213; A. Akinsanya, 'International Protection of Direct Foreign Investments in the Third World', *ICLQ*, 36 (1987), p. 58; Abdullah Al Faruque, 'Creating Customary International Law through Bilateral Investment Treaties: a Critical Appraisal', *Indian J Int'l* 44 (2004), pp. 312–313; d'Aspremont, 'International Customary Investment Law', p. 14 ('It is not at all unreasonable to claim that there was a very strong opposition that lingered in the 1960s and 1970s to developing (and socialist countries continued to bar) the emergence of a minimal consensus necessary for a customary international regime of protection of investment. And even if there could have been customary international rules back then, the uncompromising 1974 UN General Assembly resolutions must be read as having ditched the little customary international law existing at that time. It is surely not the very evasive and non-normative 1962 resolution that could be said to contain the seeds of a customary international investment protection regime').

[79] *Barcelona Traction, Light and Power Company, Limited, (Belgium v. Spain)*, Judgment, ICJ Rep. 1970, p. 3, pp. 46–47.

[80] See, Paparinskis, *The International Minimum Standard*, p. 83 ff. But see, Schwebel, 'The United States 2004 Model Bilateral Investment Treaty', p. 4, for whom 'There was, and is, no agreement within the international community on the content of "the customary international law minimum standard of treatment of aliens", or even on whether such a minimum standard existed or exists'.

the existence of a 'minimum international standard'.[81] Similarly, the conditions for lawful expropriation and the requirement for States to provide investors with *some sort* of 'adequate' compensation had acquired customary status (a question examined further in this chapter).

These few rules have generally survived the attack launched by Newly Independent States in the 1960s and 1970s.[82] Nevertheless, it is undeniable that the challenge posed by the strong contestation of a large segment of States has 'served to undermine the solidity of the traditional international legal framework for foreign investment'.[83] In other words, the traditional rules of customary law survived the assault, but with some casualties (the question is further discussed in this chapter[84]).[85] The next section will specifically examine one such casualty of war: the fate of the so-called Hull formula.

---

[81] *Sicula S.p.A. (ELSI) (US v. Italy)*, Judgment, ICJ Rep. 1989, p. 115, para. 111 ('The primary standard laid down by Article V is "the full protection and security required by international law", in short the "protection and security" must conform to the minimum international standard').

[82] J.A. Westberg, 'Compensation in Cases of Expropriation and Nationalization: Awards of the Iran-United States Claims Tribunal', *ICSID Rev.* 5 (1990), p. 269; Alvarez, 'A Bit on Custom', p. 39 (referring to 'numerous arbitral decisions that have, consistent with considerable scholarship questioning the normative impact of the relevant General Assembly resolutions, concluded that the traditional customary rules of state responsibility, including the international minimum standard, were not displaced by some LDCs' efforts to establish the NIEO'); Alvarez, 'The Public International Law Regime Governing International Investment', p. 292.

[83] Salacuse, *The Law of Investment Treaties*, pp. 45–46 ('Where there is significant disagreement among states or significant differences in practice, finding a rule of customary international law may be next to impossible. As will be seen, the field of international investment law has generated significant disagreement among nations as to the nature and content of applicable international rules. As a result, in many forums the very existence of customary international investment law has been questioned, if not challenged outright, over the years'). See also, at p. 75, adding that this 'led both investors and their home countries to search for means to strengthen it in order to protect their economic interests in a new era'.

[84] See, Chapter 2, Section 2.3.1.

[85] Juillard, 'L'évolution des sources du droit des investissements', p. 90 ('si les pays en développement ont ouvert une phase de réévaluation et de réélaboration de la coutume en matière d'expropriation et de nationalisation, ils n'ont pu mener leur démarche à son point d'aboutissement. Mais il paraît tout aussi évident que, ce faisant, les pays en développement, compte tenu des circonstances, n'en ont pas moins affaibli considérablement le consensus qui, vaille que vaille, s'était établi sur la teneur que l'on avait présenté comme coutume générale en matière d'expropriation ou de nationalisation des investissements').

2.2.3 One war casualty: the Hull formula

As mentioned in the previous section, in spite of the strong opposition by Newly Independent States there are good reasons to believe that the requirement for States to provide investors with 'adequate' compensation had become custom.[86] Thus, in the 1977 *Texaco* case, the sole arbitrator Dupuy concluded that the conditions for expropriation contained in the 1962 General Assembly *Resolution on Permanent Sovereignty over Natural Resources*, which included the requirement to provide 'appropriate compensation' in accordance with international law, represented the state of custom at the time.[87] This position was also held in the work of Dolzer in 1987:

> The radical efforts against international legal rules covering foreign investment as embodied in Article 2(2)(c) of the Charter of Economic Rights and Duties of States:' which were typical of the 1970's must by now be deemed to have failed for ideological, economic and legal reasons. In other words, the international law of expropriation has, in principle, remained intact *even though certain adaptations and modifications have occurred* in the past decades.[88]

The question, then, is what are these 'adaptations and modifications' which have occurred in the past decades? In other words, what happened to the Hull formula (providing for 'prompt, adequate and effective compensation')? Dolzer, writing in 1981, came to the conclusion that 'as far as currently applicable law is concerned, close examination lends little support to the Hull rule: recent practice, prevailing legal opinion, and the development of national property orders all speak against it'.[89] He further concluded that:

---

[86] Baxter, 'Treaties and Custom', *Rec. des cours* 129 (1970), p. 88. *Contra*: S. Zamora, 'Is there Customary International Economic Law?', *German YIL* 32 (1989), p. 25.

[87] *Texaco Overseas Petroleum Co. & California Asiatic Oil Co. v. Libyan Arab Republic*, Award, 19 January 1977, *I.L.R.*, 53 (1977), p. 459, para. 87 ('En fonction des conditions de vote précédemment évoquées et traduisant une *opinio juris communis*, la résolution 1803 (XVII) paraît au tribunal de céans refléter *l'état du droit coutumier existant en la matière*. En effet, à partir du vote d'une résolution constatant *l'existence d'une règle coutumière*, les États expriment clairement leur opinion. L'acquiescement en l'espèce d'une majorité d'États appartenant aux différents groupes représentatifs indique sans ambiguïté la reconnaissance universelle des règles incorporées, à savoir, en ce qui concerne les nationalisations et l'indemnisation, l'utilisation des règles en vigueur dans l'État nationalisant, mais cela en conformité avec le droit international', emphasis added).

[88] Dolzer, 'Indirect Expropriation of Alien Property', p. 42 (emphasis added).

[89] *Ibid.*, p. 570.

> To summarize the practice of the past decades [i.e. 1945 to 1980] from the
> viewpoint of the Hull rule, it is easy to conclude that only one part of
> Hull's concept is confirmed, *i.e.*, that compensation must be paid for
> expropriated alien property as a matter of international law; as for the
> second part, concerning the mode and the amount of compensation, the
> evidence for the Hull rule's continuing validity falls short of the mark that
> an international court would require to be convinced that state practice
> confirms the existence of the old rule. Not surprisingly, an analysis of the
> second traditional element governing the status of all customary law, *i.e.*,
> the necessary *opinio juris*, does not reveal a very different picture.[90]

According to Guzman, the 'challenge to the Hull Rule proved successful
and, by the mid 1970s (and perhaps sooner), the Hull Rule had ceased to
be a rule of customary international law'.[91] A number of writers also
held at the time that the Hull formula was not a rule of custom.[92] For
instance, in an article written by Schacter in 1984, he critically reviewed
the 1982 American Law Institute's *Restatement of the Foreign Relations
Law of the United States (Revised)*, which referred to 'just compensation' as a shorthand for prompt, adequate and effective compensation.[93]
He concluded that 'the Hull formula cannot be considered as existing
international law applicable to all cases of expropriation of alien
property'.[94]

[90] *Ibid.*, pp. 561–562, see also, pp. 564–565.
[91] Guzman, 'Why LDCs Sign Treaties That Hurt Them', pp. 641, 651 ('because a large
majority of countries made it clear that they felt no legal obligation to follow the Hull
Rule, the resolutions demonstrated that "prompt, adequate, and effective" was no longer a
rule of customary international law'). See also: Salacuse, *The Law of Investment Treaties*,
p. 76 ('Thus, although there was strong evidence that customary international law
required the payment of compensation upon nationalization of an investor's property,
no specific principles had crystallized as to how that compensation was to be calculated');
A. Reinisch, 'Legality of Expropriations', in A. Reinisch (ed.), *Standards of Investment
Protection* (Oxford: Oxford University Press, 2008) p. 194.
[92] See the list of writers in: Bernard Kishoiyian, 'The Utility of Bilateral Investment Treaties
in the Formulation of Customary International Law', *Northwestern J. Int'l L. & Bus* 14(2)
(1993), p. 360. A different position was taken by R. Robinson, 'Expropriation in the
Restatement (Revised)', *AJIL* 78 (1984), pp. 176–177: '[s]tates have shown their real
practice by establishing a network of international treaties. (. . .) They contain provisions
calling for compensation in terms equivalent to the traditional standard, although there
are slight drafting variations. The history of these agreements indicates that the parties
recognized that they were thereby making the customary rule of international law explicit
in the treaty language and reaffirming its effect'.
[93] Oscar Schachter, 'Compensation for Expropriation', *AJIL* 78 (1986), p. 121, referring to
the *Restatement of the Foreign Relations Law of the United States (Revised)*, §712 (Tent.
Draft No. 3, 1982).
[94] *Ibid.*, p. 122, see also at p. 125 ('the fact that no international judicial or arbitral decision on
compensation has adopted the "prompt, adequate and effective" rule is in itself striking

In sum, while it can be safely assumed that some customary rules continued to exist despite opposition from developing States in the 1970s, this was certainly not the case for the Hull formula.

2.3 From a lack of consensus on existing custom to the proliferation of BITs

In the previous section, I concluded that while the two traditional customary rules existing in investment law have generally survived the concerted attack led by Newly Independent States, the Hull formula could no longer be considered as a firm rule of custom by the 1980s. The attack also had another subtler consequence: both developing and developed States now perceived these rules as ineffective in providing basic legal protection to foreign investors.

It is in this historical context that States began signing BITs providing clearer rules on investment protection (Section 2.3.1). This phenomenon was accentuated by the climate of the early 1990s, a period marked by globalization. A newly found consensus emerged regarding the necessity to offer better legal protection to foreign investments in order to accelerate economic development. This period was characterized by the new phenomenon of the proliferation of BITs (also known as 'treatification') (Section 2.3.2). A remarkable feature of this era was how developing States fundamentally changed their position on the benefit of foreign direct investments. They suddenly embraced treaties that provided the very basic legal protection that they had rejected for decades (Section 2.3.3).

2.3.1 Combat fatigue or the sorry state of custom after the attacks

In the 1980s, many developing (and socialist) States believed that the absence of consensus on existing basic legal protection had in effect prevented the development and crystallization of rules of customary international law in the field of international investment law.[95] Other

---

evidence that it has not attained the status of a customary rule through state practice'). He referred to: *Texaco Overseas Petroleum Co. & California Asiatic Oil Co.* v. *Libyan Arab Republic, ILM* 17 (1978), p. 29, paras. 143–144; *Kuwait* v. *American Independent Oil Company (Aminoil)*, Award, 24 March 1982, *ILM* 21 (1982), p. 976; *Banco National de Cuba* v. *Chase Manhattan Bank*, Court of Appeals for the Second Circuit, 658F, 2nd 875 (2nd Cir. 1981).

[95] Al Faruque, 'Creating Customary International Law through Bilateral Investment Treaties', pp. 294–295.

(mainly developed) States held the view that while such customary rules existed, their effectiveness was limited as a result of the vehement opposition of a large number of States.[96] In any event, what all States could agree on was the obvious fact that the (very) few rules that were said to exist provided no solid legal protection for investors doing business abroad. Thus, as explained by one writer, 'the principles that did exist were often vague and subject to varying interpretations'.[97] For instance, the same writer noted that 'although there was strong evidence that customary international law required the payment of compensation upon nationalization of an investor's property, no specific principles had crystallized as to how that compensation was to be calculated'.[98] Most importantly, the same author noted the existence of 'no effective enforcement mechanism to pursue claims against host countries that seized their investments or refused to respect their contractual obligations'.[99] The situation prevailing at the time is well-explained by d'Aspremont:

> Despite international investment lawyers perpetuating the myth of a customary international law protection of investment, international actors and policy-makers grew wary of the inconclusiveness and indefiniteness of the foreign investment protection regime. First, the absence of consensus on the world plane as to the type and level of investment protection spawned a lot of uncertainty and undermined the authority of the international regime of investment protection. Second, the standards that had allegedly emerged fell short of providing sufficient substantive guidance and were beset by lack of normativity – a finding which in itself traditionally sufficed to bar the emergence of customary international law. At best, the standards offered, provided that there were any, were growingly deemed too minimalistic, especially since interferences with property rights have grown more intricate and indirect. All-in-all, the customary international law of investment protection which investment lawyers strove to devise before the 1st World War gradually proved

---

[96] The member States of the OECD certainly believed at the time that these customary rules existed. Thus, the OECD, *Draft Convention on the Protection of Foreign Property*, adopted on 12 October 1967, *ILM* 7 (1967), p. 117, Article 1 cmt., explicitly used the expression 'minimum standard which forms part of customary international law'. It should be noted that the OECD used a different expression ('general principles of international law') in its 1984 study: OECD Committee on International Investment and Multinational Enterprise, *Inter-Governmental Agreements Relating to Investment in Developing Countries*, Doc. No. 84/14, 27 May 1984, p. 12, para. 36. On this question, see OECD, 'International Investment Law', p. 97.

[97] Salacuse, *The Law of Investment Treaties*, p. 76. See also: Jeswald W. Salacuse, *The Three Laws of International Investment. National, Contractual, and International Frameworks for Foreign Capital* (Oxford: Oxford University Press, 2013), pp. 329–330.

[98] *Ibid.* [99] *Ibid.*

incapable of meeting the needs of the multinational companies and the business sector.[100]

It is in this historical context that bilateral investment treaties emerged.[101] An UNCTAD Report explains why States turned to BITs to solve the uncertainties regarding the conditions for lawful expropriation:

> The international debate on the law on expropriation originally focused on the prerequisites for lawful expropriation (Sornarajah, 2004). Some countries – mostly capital-exporting economies – argued that under customary international law, countries were allowed to expropriate foreign investors provided that the expropriation measure met four conditions: it had to be taken for a public purpose, on a non-discriminatory basis, under due process of law and based upon the payment of prompt, adequate and effective compensation. As a number of developing countries denied that such conditions were part of customary international law, capital-exporting economies turned to conventional international instruments – mostly BITs – to specifically provide for investment protection against unlawful expropriations.[102]

The next section examines this new phenomenon which rapidly developed in the 1990s.

2.3.2   The roaring 1990s or the 'treatification' of international investment law

The 1990s were marked by a new era of globalization wherein private foreign investments were (almost) universally deemed by States as an essential tool for their economic development.[103] Yet great uncertainty still remained about the types of legal protection existing for foreign investors under custom. Not surprisingly, efforts by the OECD in 1995 to

---

[100] d'Aspremont, 'International Customary Investment Law', p. 16.

[101] Chester Brown, 'The Evolution of the Regime of International Investment Agreements: History, Economics and Politics', in M. Bungenberg, J. Griebel, S. Hobe and A. Reinisch (eds.), *International Investment Law: A Handbook* (Munich *et al*: C.H. Beck, Hart, Nomos, 2015), pp. 158–160; Stephan Hobe, 'The Development of the Law of Aliens and the Emergence of General Principles of Protection under Public International Law', in *Ibid.*, p. 13.

[102] UNCTAD, 'Bilateral Investment Treaties 1995–2006', p. 47.

[103] Thus, the 1992 World Bank *Guidelines on the Treatment of Foreign Direct Investment* explained in its preamble that it 'recognizes' that 'a greater flow of foreign direct investment brings substantial benefits to bear on the world economy and on the economies of developing countries in particular'.

negotiate a comprehensive Multilateral Agreement on Investment (MAI) were unsuccessful.[104] As explained by two scholars, it is because 'customary law was deemed be too amorphous and not be able to provide sufficient guidance and protection' to foreign investors that capital-exporting and developing States started to frenetically conclude *ad hoc* BITs.[105] The same conclusion is reached by many writers,[106] including Kläger:

> Many states felt that an international minimum standard – whatever concrete contours it had – existed, but also that it had been challenged every now and again. Due to the failure to establish a multilateral framework for foreign investments, states pursued the reaffirmation and clarification of the legal status of foreign investments through the conclusion of bilateral treaties. In this way, states tried to overcome the uncertainty pertaining to the customary law in this field and to establish a firmer set of rules that applied at least *inter partes*.[107]

[104] *The Multilateral Agreement on Investment*, Draft Consolidated Text, DAFFE/MAI(98)7/REV1 (22 April 1998).

[105] R. Dolzer and A. von Walter, 'Fair and Equitable Treatment – Lines of Jurisprudence on Customary Law', in F. Ortino (ed.), *Investment Treaty Law, Current Issues ii* (2007), p. 99.

[106] Orellana, 'International Law on Investment', p. 3; Jean-Pierre Laviec, *Protection et promotion des investissements, étude de droit international économique* (Paris: PUF, 1985), pp. 87–88; Campbell McLachlan, 'Investment Treaties and General International Law', *ICLQ* 57 (2008), p. 365; Jeswald W. Salacuse, 'BIT by BIT: The Growth of Bilateral Investment Treaties and Their Impact on Foreign Investment in Developing Countries' *Int'l L.* 24 (1990), p. 659; Kishoiyian, 'The Utility of Bilateral Investment Treaties', pp. 332, 372 ('The main objective of the treaties is to create a separate legal regime of investment protection quite apart from the "customary" international law on foreign investment protection which though not fully agreed upon, it is also not sufficiently developed to afford protection to the new forms of foreign investment. Faced with the need for certitude in the legal regime of foreign investment protection more suited to modern conditions, states have seen in the making of BITs an acceptable way of achieving this objective'); Al Faruque, 'Creating Customary International Law through Bilateral Investment Treaties', p. 293; d'Aspremont, 'International Customary Investment Law', pp. 16–18.

[107] Kläger, *Fair and Equitable Treatment*, pp. 263–264. See also: Jeswald W. Salacuse, 'Towards a Global Treaty on Foreign Investment: the Search for a Grand Bargain' in N. Horn and S. Kröll (eds.), *Arbitrating Foreign Investment Disputes: Procedural and Substantive Legal Aspects* (The Hague: Kluwer International Law, 2004), p. 58 ('The lack of consensus on the customary international law applicable to foreign investments also created uncertainty in the minds of investors as to the degree of legal protection they might expect under international law. To gain such certainty and to counter the threat of national law and regulation, the host countries of these investors undertook to conclude a series of bilateral investment treaties that would provide clear rules and effective enforcement mechanisms, at least with regard to their treaty partners'); Salacuse, *The Law of Investment Treaties*, p. 77; C. McLachlan, L. Shore and M. Weiniger, *International*

According to both Schreuer and Dolzer, as a result of the new climate of international economic relations of the 1990s, 'the fight of previous decades against customary rules protecting foreign investment had abruptly become anachronistic and obsolete'.[108] Consequently, by the 1990s 'the tide had turned' and developing States were no longer opposed to the application of a minimum standard of protection under custom. Instead, they granted 'more protection to foreign investment than traditional customary law did, now on the basis of treaties negotiated to attract additional foreign investment'.[109]

It is now estimated that over 2,923 BITs have been concluded worldwide.[110] Moreover, by 2008 there were 345 international agreements (other than BITs and double taxation treaties) which also included provisions on investment protection.[111] The 2014 *World Investment Report* mentions the existence of a grand total of 3,268 treaties providing investment protection.[112] The substantive rules for the protection of foreign investments are mostly found in these bilateral and multilateral investment treaties.[113]

Investment treaties regulate the treatment of foreign investors and their investments in the host State. They provide foreign investors with an unprecedented level of substantive legal protection. Investment treaties typically contain detailed definitions of who qualifies as an 'investor' and what constitutes a protected 'investment'. They normally provide for equal treatment of domestic and foreign investors (the so-called national treatment and most-favoured-nation treatment clauses), the obligation for the host State to provide a fair and equitable treatment, and compensation in the case of expropriation of an investment by the host State.[114] BITs also offer ground-breaking procedural benefits to foreign investors,

---

Investment Arbitration: Substantive Principles (Oxford: Oxford University Press, 2007), p. 17.

[108] Schreuer and Dolzer, *Principles of International Investment Law*, p. 16.

[109] *Ibid.* See also: Schwebel, 'Investor-State Disputes and the Development of International Law', p. 28 ('BITs specify in terms more explicit, detailed, and far-reaching than was ever advanced under what was customary international law in the time of Cordell Hull what may be described as an ideal law of international investment').

[110] UNCTAD, *Recent Trends, in IIAs and ISDS*, IIA Issues Note, no. 1, Feb. 2015, p. 2.

[111] *Ibid.*   [112] World Bank, *World Investment Report* (2014), p. xxiii.

[113] Protection is also often found in *contracts* entered into directly between foreign investors and States (or State-owned entities) or in the legislation of the host State of the investment.

[114] W. Salacuse, 'The Treatification of International Investment Law?', *Law & Bus. Rev. Am.* 13 (2007), p. 155.

such as the ability to resolve investment disputes by bringing arbitration claims directly against the States in which they invest. This aspect has rightly been described as 'one of the most important progressive developments in the procedure of international law of the twentieth century'.[115] It offers foreign investors significant legal protection that is over and above than that which is otherwise available to them. Thus, under these treaties, a foreign investor is generally no longer required to go before local courts or to have its claim 'espoused' by its State of origin under the traditional mechanism of diplomatic protection.[116] In the 2007 *Diallo* case, the ICJ recognised that in 'contemporary international law' the question of the protection of the rights of investors and shareholders is 'essentially governed' by investment treaties and that 'the role of diplomatic protection somewhat faded'.[117]

As a result of these developments, the number of arbitration cases between investors and States is booming.[118]

2.3.3 Change of heart: the paradox of why developing States started signing BITs

What is also remarkable about the 1990s is that developing States which had long-rejected the Hull formula providing for 'prompt, adequate and effective' compensation were now concluding hundreds of BITs

---

[115] Schwebel, 'The United States 2004 Model Bilateral Investment Treaty', p. 2.

[116] ILC's *Draft Articles on Diplomatic Protection with commentaries*, Text adopted by the International Law Commission at its fifty-eighth session, in 2006, and submitted to the General Assembly as a part of the Commission's report covering the work of that session (UN Doc. A/61/10), pp. 89–90: 'The dispute settlement procedures provided for in BITs and ICSID offer greater advantages to the foreign investor than the customary international law system of diplomatic protection, as they give the investor direct access to international arbitration, avoid the political uncertainty inherent in the discretionary nature of diplomatic protection and dispense with the conditions for the exercise of diplomatic protection'.

[117] *Case Concerning Ahmadou Sadio Diallo (Rep. Guinea v. Dem. Rep. Congo)*, ICJ Rep. 2007, p. 103, para. 88.

[118] According to the most recent UNCTAD Report (UNCTAD, 'Recent Trends, in IIAs and ISDS', IIA Issues Note, no. 1, Feb. 2015, p. 5), at the end of 2014, 101 different States had been respondents in a total of 608 known treaty-based cases. By the end of 2014, 356 cases had been concluded. Thirty-seven per cent of these cases were decided in favour of the respondent State and 25% in favour of the investor (28% were settled and 8% were discontinued for other reasons). It should be noted that there are also a number of investor-State disputes currently being settled by arbitration about which information is not publicly available (for instance, some proceedings conducted under the UNCITRAL Arbitration Rules as well as those other *ad hoc* arbitration).

containing that exact same formula.[119] As stated by Guzman, this is quite a paradox.[120] In 1981, Mann asked the following question: 'is it possible for a State to reject the rule according to which alien property may be expropriated only on certain terms long believed to be required by customary international law [i.e. the Hull formula], yet to accept it for the purpose of these treaties?'[121] He answered the question in the negative: 'where these treaties express a duty which customary international law imposes or is widely believed to impose, they give very strong support to the existence of such a duty and preclude the Contracting States from denying its existence. (. . .) The cold print of these treaties is a more reliable source of law than rhetorics in the United Nations'.[122]

Yet, one should not exaggerate the importance of this so-called paradox.[123] For instance, Alvarez argues that developing States have simply not rejected and embraced the Hull formula *at the same time*.[124] In any event, by the 1990s they were prepared to accept this formula in the hope

---

[119] Guzman, 'Why LDCs Sign Treaties That Hurt Them', p. 642.

[120] *Ibid.*, pp. 642, 666 ('On the one hand, they have repeatedly sought to establish a norm that leaves significant power in the hands of the sovereign state in its relations with investors, makes it difficult for states to enter into binding contracts with foreign investors and, therefore, leaves the dynamic inconsistency problem unresolved. On the other hand, developing countries have willingly and, indeed, enthusiastically, signed BITs with developed countries. These bilateral treaties undermine precisely the independence and control that the countries have fought so hard to protect').

[121] F.A. Mann, 'British Treaties for the Promotion and Protection of Investment', *British YIL* 52 (1981), pp. 241, 249.

[122] *Ibid.*, pp. 249–250. A similar argument had already been raised in 1967 by R. Jennings, 'General Course on Principles of International Law', *Rec. des cours* 121 (1967-II), p. 491.

[123] See, for instance, the following explanation given by Dolzer, 'New Foundations of the Law of Expropriation of Alien Property', p. 567, in 1981 about the position adopted by developing States: 'Thus, a contradiction cannot be observed today between the conduct and the attitudes of countries that voted for Article 2(2)(c) of the Charter and that previously or subsequently concluded investment treaties with property protection clauses. The apparent contradiction can be easily explained in the light of the special benefits that developing countries enjoy under such treaties. From a policy viewpoint, such treaties signify that the countries concerned do not view the Hull rule as undesirable per se; the inference is warranted that these countries assume that the Hull rule should apply only under conditions of mutually intensified cooperation and that these conditions are not secured by the general norms of present customary international law'.

[124] Alvarez, 'A Bit on Custom', p. 40: 'The era of using BITs as credible commitment devices (especially through recourse to effective investor-state dispute settlement) came *after* the NIEO was dead, namely with the end of the Cold War' (emphasis in the original). In other words, for him, 'Most LDCs turned to BITs *after* attempting (and failing) to change the traditional rules protecting foreign investors (and aliens generally), at a time when the world was turning, collectively, towards market-based approaches consistent with BITs and FTAs' (*ibid.*, emphasis in the original).

of attracting more foreign investments and boost their economic development.[125] Lowenfeld provides three reasons for this change of position:

> Three phenomena in the last quarter of the twentieth century could have contributed to the conversion of those who supported the Charter of the Economic Rights and Duties of States in 1974. First, the most striking phenomenon was the decline and fall of the Soviet Union and its satellites. Second, the economic stagnation of virtually all of Africa and much of Latin America became apparent, compared to the rapid economic development of the countries in East Asia, such as South Korea, Taiwan, Singapore, Hong Kong, and to a lesser extent Thailand, that had welcomed foreign investment and free or freer markets. Third, countries that had not quite rejected foreign direct investment but had not encouraged it came to realize that an attractive investment climate would be needed if they were to advance up the economic ladder through inflow of foreign capital.[126]

Finally, it should be added that not everyone has endorsed this convincing explanation. For instance, Guzman rejects the 'possibility that developing countries have simply changed their views on the subject'.[127] He explains that this change of attitude is based on the prisoner's dilemma: 'LDCs face a prisoner's dilemma in which it is optimal for them, as a group, to reject the Hull Rule, but in which each individual LDC is better off "defecting" from the group by signing a BIT that gives it

---

[125] *Ibid.*, p. 40; Alvarez, 'The Public International Law Regime Governing International Investment', p. 289 ('Guzman ignores, in short, the possibility that LDCs, *both as a group and as individual States,* had more than sufficient reasons to abandon any lingering hostilities to traditional customary protections for foreign investment and more than enough reasons to adopt (or to resume) policies, including concluding investment agreements with investors and investment treaties with States, intended to create a generally favourable environment for capital flows (and not merely for investors from specific BIT parties', emphasis in the original); Steffen Hindelang, 'Bilateral Investment Treaties, Custom and a Healthy Investment Climate – The Question of whether BITs Influence Customary International Law Revisited', *J. World Invest. & Trade*, 5 (2004), pp. 801–802. See also, the analysis of Asha Kaushal, 'Revisiting History: How the Past Matters for the Present Backlash Against the Foreign Investment Regime', *Harvard ILJ* 50(2) (2009), pp. 501–507, examining a number of different explanations.

[126] Andreas F. Lowenfeld, 'Investment Agreements and International Law', *Columbia JTL* 42 (2003), pp. 126–127.

[127] Guzman, 'Why LDCs Sign Treaties That Hurt Them', p. 667, further explaining that 'the period in which BITs have been signed has overlapped considerably with the period in which LDCs sought to discredit the Hull Rule (...). In other words, during the very period when the General Assembly was denouncing the Hull Rule, large numbers of developing countries were signing bilateral treaties'. For a critical analysis of this argument, see, Hindelang, 'Bilateral Investment Treaties, Custom and a Healthy Investment Climate', p. 799 ff.

an advantage over other LDCs in the competition to attract foreign investors'.[128] The theory put forward by Guzman has been contested by many.[129] At the end of the day, one cannot deny the remarkable fact that by the 1990s developing States now agreed to provide foreign investors with investment protection that they had long before rejected.

2.4 Does custom still matter today in this age of treatification?

As mentioned above, States have concluded thousands of BITs as a result of the perceived lack of established customary principles. As noted by one writer, 'for all practical purposes, treaties have become the fundamental source of international law in the area of foreign investment'.[130] The fact that international investment law is largely based on bilateral treaties is clearly its most distinctive feature when compared to other sub-fields of

---

[128] Guzman, 'Why LDCs Sign Treaties That Hurt Them', pp. 679–680. The theory is further explained as follows: 'The General Assembly, therefore, has provided capital-importing countries with an excellent forum to advocate for the dismantling of the Hull Rule and the "adoption" of much more lenient rules of investor protection. (. . .) BITs, however, provide a mechanism through which individual countries can easily "cheat" on this "cartel" of capital importers. (. . .) Any single capital-importing country has an incentive to sign a BIT because such a treaty helps that country attract foreign investment. On the other hand, the treaties are harmful to capital importers as a group because they lead to a world in which contracts between firms and host states are binding. (. . .) the analysis here explains why investments treaties are almost exclusively bilateral rather than multi-lateral. The incentive to sign a BIT comes from the ability to get an advantage over one's rival host countries'.

[129] See, Alvarez, 'A Bit on Custom', p. 39: 'Guzman's description of the rise and spread of BITs, an excellent example of a classic Prisoner's Dilemma, remains just that: an elegant academic exercise bearing little resemblance to the real world'. See also: José E. Alvarez, 'The Once and Future Investment Regime', in Mahnoush Arsanjani *et al.* (eds.), *Looking to the Future: Essays on International Law in Honor of W. Michael Reisman* (Leiden: Martinus Nijhoff, 2010); Alvarez, 'The Public International Law Regime Governing International Investment', p. 261 ff.

[130] Salacuse, 'The Treatification of International Investment Law?', p. 5; ILA, 'Sources of International Investment Law', report by M. Hirsch, ILA Study Group on the Role of Soft Law Instruments in International Investment Law (2011), p. 7; Christoph H. Schreuer, Loretta Malintoppi, August Reinisch and Anthony Sinclair, *The ICSID Convention; A Commentary* (2nd edn., Cambridge: Cambridge University Press, 2009), p. 605 ('The large and rapidly growing number of BITs and multilateral treaties dealing with invest-ment makes them the most important source of international law for ICSID tribunals'); Florian Grisel, 'The Sources of Foreign Investment Law', in: Z. Douglas, J. Pauwelyn and J.E. Viñuales (eds.), *The Foundations of International Investment Law: Bringing Theory into Practice* (Oxford: Oxford University Press, 2014), p. 219.

international law.[131] Yet, Tams also accurately observes that the relative importance of various sources of law unavoidably evolve over time.[132] Therefore, the current pre-eminence of BITs would have been surprising to any arbitration specialist examining the issue 50 years ago. In any event, as noted by one writer, custom has been the obvious 'victim' of the success of treaties.[133] Schill goes further and argues that since custom plays only a limited role in investment arbitration, its historical function as a source of international law has been somehow 'replaced' by the jurisprudence of arbitral tribunals.[134]

In this context, why should one enquire about the importance of custom today when foreign investors in fact obtain sufficient protection under these numerous BITs? In other words, why is custom relevant today when so many BITs exist?

The question of the relevance of custom is part of a larger discussion currently ongoing in contemporary international law. Custom has historically had a dominant role as a source of international law, but the last century has been marked by the growing importance of treaties in numerous spheres of activity on the international plane. Writers often speak of the superiority of treaties over custom for the development of international rules.[135] In recent years, a number of writers have expressed the view that custom had become irrelevant in modern international

---

[131] C.J. Tams, 'The Sources of International Investment Law', in Gazzini and de Brabandere (eds.), *International Investment Law: The Sources of Rights and Obligations*, p. 323.

[132] *Ibid.*, pp. 327–328.

[133] Juillard, 'L'évolution des sources du droit des investissements', p. 208: 'L'autre victime, c'est la coutume internationale, victime, certes, et comme on l'a dit, de la suspicion qu'elle a provoquée auprès de certains pays en développement, mais victime, aussi, de la mise en question qu'elle a subie du côté des pays développés. Car, dès lors que, par le truchement des instruments bilatéraux, pays développés et pays en développement découvraient qu'ils pouvaient s'accorder sur des règles traduisant un niveau élevé de protection, la coutume, source rudimentaire, et dont la teneur cryptique n'offrait jamais qu'un niveau moins élevé de protection, perdait beaucoup des attraits dont certains l'avaient parée *in toto vacuo juris*'.

[134] Stephan W. Schill, 'From Sources to Discourse: Investment Treaty Jurisprudence as the New Custom?', in *Is There an Evolving Customary International Law on Investment?* (London: BIICL, 2011), pp. 1–2, asking the question 'whether investment jurisprudence, and the application thereof by investment treaty tribunals, do not bring about a new customary international law of foreign investment protection?'. For him, 'reference to precedent increasingly replaces customary international law as a source of a multilateral order in the absence of a multilateral treaty'.

[135] Baxter, 'Treaties and Custom', p. 36: 'What is the case for saying that such an imaginary treaty can be taken as powerful or even conclusive proof of customary international law binding even on a non-party and perhaps even overriding other evidence of the state of customary international law? The most telling argument for giving the treaty that effect

law.[136] Yet, to paraphrase Mark Twain, reports of the death of customary international law are greatly exaggerated.[137] As noted by Dinstein, 'every once in a while, custom has a tendency to leap to the fore even within special fields of international law where it seemed to have ceded primacy to treaties long ago, thereby reminding the international legal profession that it is not just barely alive but is still pulsating with some intensity'.[138] Custom is indeed resilient and continues to play a crucial role in today's international relations.[139] Guzman provides five reasons for the importance of custom in contemporary international law:

> First, there remain important areas of international relations governed primarily by customary rules. To pick one example, the law of state responsibility remains largely the domain of custom. Second, even in areas where one or more treaties exist, CIL often plays an important role. For example, in the human rights area there are a number of important treaties, but there remains the question of which human rights rules have the status of CIL and therefore apply to all states, including non-signatories. CIL can also serve to influence treaty regimes. Treaties,

is that it is superior to all other forms of evidence of the law. In the first place, the treaty is clear evidence of the will of States, free of the ambiguities and inconsistencies characteristic of the patchwork of evidence of State practice that is normally employed in proving the state of international law'. See also: Joel P. Trachtman, 'The Obsolescence of Customary International Law', SSRN Working Paper (2014), p. 1 ('At a time when the world needs more, and more complex, international legal rules and institutions to address major cooperation problems, customary international law ("CIL") has several important limitations: (i) it cannot be made in a coordinated manner in advance of events, (ii) it cannot be made with sufficient detail, (iii) it cannot be made with sufficiently heterogeneous reciprocity between states, (iv) it cannot be made with specifically-designed organizational support, (v) it is generally not subject to national parliamentary control, (vi) it purports to bind states that did not consent but failed to object to its formation, and (vii) it provides excessive space for auto-interpretation by states, or for sometimes insufficiently disciplined interpretation by judges').

[136] See, *inter alia*: N.C.H. Dunbar, 'The Myth of Customary International Law', *Australian YIL* 8 (1983), p. 1; J. Patrick Kelly, 'The Twilight of Customary International Law', *Virginia JIL* 40 (2000), p. 449; J.L. Goldsmith and E.A. Posner, *The Limits of International Law* (Oxford: Oxford University Press, 2005), p. 43; Jack L. Goldsmith and Eric A. Posner, 'Understanding the Resemblance Between Modern and Traditional Customary International Law', *Virginia JIL* 40 (2000), pp. 639–640.

[137] Michael P. Scharf, *Customary International Law in Times of Fundamental Change: Recognizing Grotian Moments* (Cambridge: Cambridge University Press, 2013), p. 29, referring to Mark Twain, 'Cable from London to the Associated Press' (1897), *Bartlett's Familiar Quotations* (15th edn., 1980), p. 625.

[138] Y. Dinstein, 'The Interaction between Customary International Law and Treaties', *Rec. des cours* 322 (2006), p. 262.

[139] Nguyen Quoc Dinh, Patrick Dallier, Mathias Forteau and Alain Pellet, *Droit International Public* (8th edn., Paris: LGDJ, 2007), p. 373.

for instance, sometimes refer to rules of customary international law, making such rules relevant to the interpretation of the treaty. Additionally, CIL provides rules of treaty interpretation that are important to treaties, especially in the context of dispute resolution. Third, CIL is sometimes relevant to or a part of domestic law. (...) Fourth, custom remains an integral part of the rhetoric used in the international legal landscape. Countries routinely reference CIL to support their actions and those of their allies, or to condemn behavior by other states. (...) Fifth, CIL is one of the recognized sources of international law. One could hardly claim to understand international law without an understanding of CIL, how it works, and its relevance. Even if one seeks to dismiss the relevance of CIL as a source of law, it is necessary to have some understanding of what CIL is.[140]

A palpable sign of the persisting relevance of custom today is the recent decision (2012) by the International Law Commission (ILC) to include the topic of 'Formation and Evidence of Customary International Law' in its programme of work. ILC Special Rapporteur, Sir Michael Wood, succinctly explained why custom is still relevant today:

> Even in fields where there are widely accepted 'codification' conventions, the rules of customary international law continue to govern questions not regulated by the conventions and continue to apply in relations with and between non-parties. Rules of customary international law may also fill possible lacunae in treaties, and assist in their interpretation.[141]

These are the same three basic reasons which had been identified by the Iran-US Claims Tribunal in the *Amoco* case: 'the rules of customary law may be useful in order to fill in possible *lacunae* of the treaty, to ascertain the meaning of undefined terms in the text or, more generally, to aid the interpretation and implementation of its provision'.[142]

These observations are perfectly applicable in the area of international investment law, where customary rules continue to play a fundamental role.[143] These rules constitute the 'indispensable background for any

---

[140] Andrew T. Guzman, 'Saving Customary International Law', *Michigan JIL* 27 (2006), pp. 119–212.
[141] International Law Commission, 'First Report on Formation and Evidence of Customary International Law', by Michael Wood, Special Rapporteur, Sixty-fifth session, Geneva, 6 May-7 June and 8 July-9 August 2013, UN doc. A/CN.4/663, 17 May 2013, p. 15.
[142] *Amoco Int'l Fin. Corp.* v. *Iran*, Iran-US CT, 14 July 1987, in *ILR* 83 (1990), para. 112.
[143] Schreuer *et al.*, *The ICSID Convention*, p. 606; Schreuer and Dolzer, *Principles of International Investment Law*, pp. 16–17, asking rhetorically the question whether 'the elucidation of the state of customary law is no longer a central concern of academic commentators' and concluding that 'the issue certainly remains alive'; Hirsch, 'Sources of International Investment Law', pp. 7–8; Tarcisio Gazzini, 'The Role of Customary

consideration of international legal rules and instruments'.[144] The question of the importance of customary rules in contemporary international investment law will be fully examined in Chapter 5 of this book.

2.5 The 'return' of custom?

Finally, reference should be made to the position of several writers arguing in favour of the 'return' of custom *precisely because* of the proliferation of BITs. One controversial issue currently being debated in academia and amongst arbitrators is whether BITs represent the 'new' custom in this field. According to some writers, the content of custom would now simply be the *same* as that of thousands of BITs. However, the present author has explained elsewhere why custom *does not* correspond to the *total sum* of 2500 BITs.[145] This question will be examined in detail in Chapter 3.[146]

In my view, one should not talk about the 'return' of custom since it had *never gone* in the first place. As mentioned above, a limited number of customary rules have emerged in the twentieth century and have *continued to exist* in spite of contestation in the early part of the century and in the 1960s and 1970s (the question is further examined in the next section). In any event, the very idea of a so-called return of custom is not without irony considering the turbulent history of the evaluation of the sources of investment arbitration:

> [I]t could have been reasonably anticipated that the BITs-based treatification of investment protection would come as tolling the knell for the need for (and the interest in) customary international law in international investment protection. With a few thousand BITs in force, the quest for customary international law that had dominated the century seemed doomed to become anachronistic and solely of academic interest. Yet, it is the exact opposite which occurred. As soon as treatification of investment protection neared completion, the need felt by investment lawyers for a return to customary law abruptly came back to the fore. It is as if the

International Law in the Field of Foreign Investment', *J. World Invest. & Trade*, 8 (2007), p. 691; Alvarez, 'A Bit on Custom', p. 74 ('the move to investment treaties does not displace resort to CIL or general principles' and treatification does not 'demonstrate the "twilight of customary international law". Indeed, debates over the content of customary international law are now livelier than ever before, despite treatification').

[144] UNCTAD, 'Trends in International Investment Agreements: An Overview' (1999), p. 39.
[145] P. Dumberry, 'Are BITs Representing the "New" Customary International Law in International Investment Law?' *Penn State ILR* 28(4) (2010), pp. 675–701.
[146] See, Chapter 3, Section 3.3.3.2.2.

proliferation of BITs spawned a new crave for customary international law. Said differently, the story of the sources of investment law in the last quarter of the 20th century is the ironical story of treatification, originally conceived as a move away from to custom, generating its antithesis, that is, a return to custom.[147]

2.6   A brief outline of existing customary rules of international investment law

As discussed above,[148] the aim of the present book is *not* to provide a comprehensive analysis of all existing customary rules in the field of international investment law. This book focuses instead on a different question: how customary rules are *created* in the field of investor-State arbitration and how they can be *identified*. In other words, I want to determine what types of manifestation of State practice and *opinio juris* are relevant for the formation of customary rules. Yet, I am also aware that the whole exercise would be rather futile without at least presenting some basic evidence as to the existence of *some* customary rules. To use the example of the lepidopterologists and the butterflies already mentioned,[149] what would be the point of theoretically studying how butterflies are created and how they should be categorized without first firmly establishing their existence?

This last section will therefore briefly examine two existing customary rules in the field of international investment law: the MST (Section 2.6.2) and the general prohibition against expropriation without compensation (Section 2.6.3). It should be added that the question of the customary status of the fair and equitable treatment (FET) standard will also be discussed (in Chapter 3) to concretely illustrate how treaty-based norms can transform into customary rules. Before doing so, a few words should be devoted to the ongoing doctrinal debate regarding whether or not any such rules exist today (Section 2.6.1).

2.6.1   *Scholarship on the existence of any such customary rules*

The vast majority of writers believe that some principles in the field of international investment law should be considered as customary

---

[147] d'Aspremont, 'International Customary Investment Law', pp. 19–20. One reason why he speaks of the 'return' of custom is because he believes that customary rules no longer existed as a result of their rejection by developing States in the 1970s (see, p. 14).
[148] See Introduction, Section I.1.   [149] See, Chapter 1, Section 1.6.

rules.[150] Only a few writers have adopted a different position.[151] For instance, Sornarajah denies the existence of any rule of customary law since 'it would be difficult to show that there was free consent on the part of all the developing states to the creation of any customary international law' in international investment law.[152] According to him, any such rules of custom would have been imposed on developing States which have always rejected them:

> The formation of customary principles has been associated with power. The role of power in this area is evident. Powerful States sought to construct rules of investment protection largely aimed at developing States by espousing them in their practice and passing them off as customary principles. They were always resisted . . . Nevertheless, the norms that were supported by the developed states were maintained on the basis that they were accepted as custom though that was never the case. The significance of the General Assembly resolutions associated with the New International Economic Order is that they demonstrated that there were a large number, indeed a majority, of states of the world, which did not subscribe to the norms maintained by the developed world. After that, it was no longer credible to maintain that there was in fact an international law on foreign investment, though the claim continues to be made simply because of the need to conserve the gains made for investment protection by developed States.[153]

Nevertheless, Sornarajah also admits that there are 'few' rules of custom in the field of international investment law.[154] For instance, he believes, like many other scholars,[155] that the right of the host State to

---

[150] See, for instance, Grisel, 'The Sources of Foreign Investment Law', p 222; Charles Leben, 'L'évolution du droit international des investissements' *Journal CEPMLP*, 7(12) (2000); Cai Congyan, 'International Investment Treaties and the Formation, Application and Transformation of Customary International Law Rules', *Chinese JIL* 7 (2008), p. 670. The position of these different writers on specific rules will be examined in this section.

[151] See, for instance: Kishoiyian, 'The Utility of Bilateral Investment Treaties', p. 372 ('No definite universally accepted and consistently applied rules have crystallized in the intervening period since the Barcelona Case. (. . .) Effectively, the BITs have contributed not to the creation of universal customary international law as such, but to the creation of special custom between contracting parties'). The controversial question of the existence of any such 'special custom' will be examined in Chapter 3, Section 3.3.3.2.1.1. See also the assessment made in 1989 by Zamora, 'Is there Customary International Economic Law?', pp. 23–25, 34–35.

[152] Sornarajah, *The International Law on Foreign Investment*, p. 213.

[153] *Ibid.*, pp. 92–93.   [154] *Ibid.*, p. 89.

[155] Hindelang, 'Bilateral Investment Treaties, Custom and a Healthy Investment Climate', p. 804; Vandevelde, *Bilateral Investment Treaties*, pp. 405, 422; Kishoiyian, 'The Utility of Bilateral Investment Treaties', p. 346; Dickerson, 'Minimum Standards', para. 3; Salacuse, *The Three Laws of International Investment*, pp. 308–309.

refuse entry to any foreign investor is customary international law.[156] Yet, Sornarajah also adds that even 'if there was such customary international law, many developing States would regard themselves as persistent objectors who were not bound by the customary law'.[157] The question regarding whether or not the controversial concept of 'persistent objector' should apply in investor-State arbitration will be further examined in Chapter 5.[158]

Although the present section deals specifically with two rules (MST and expropriation), a few words shall be devoted to the customary status of other principles which have also been discussed by scholars and tribunals. A number of them have stated that there is no principle of customary international law preventing host States from providing different treatment to foreign investors, compared to that offered to their own nationals.[159] Consequently, almost all writers believe that the

---

[156] Sornarajah, *The International Law on Foreign Investment*, p. 117. His position on whether or not there exist any customary rules on the MST or the prohibition of expropriation will be further discussed in this section.

[157] *Ibid.* He also argues elsewhere (p. 151) that 'it is difficult to establish that state responsibility for economic injuries to alien investors was recognized as a principle of customary international law. Latin American states as well as African and Asian States must be taken to be persistent objectors to the formation of such customary international law'. See also: M. Sornarajah, 'Power and Justice in Foreign Investment Arbitration', *J. Int'l Arb.* 14(3) (1997), p. 118; Stephen Vasciannie, 'The Fair and Equitable Treatment Standard in International Investment Law and Practice', *British YIL*, 70 (1999), p. 99, at footnote 305.

[158] See, Chapter 5, Section 5.4.

[159] *Methanex Corp. v. United States*, UNCITRAL, Award, 3 August 2005, Part IV, Ch. C, para. 25: 'As to the question of whether a rule of customary international law prohibits a State, in the absence of a treaty obligation, from differentiating in its treatment of nationals and aliens, international law is clear. In the absence of a contrary rule of international law binding on the States parties, whether of conventional or customary origin, a State may differentiate in its treatment of nationals and aliens'. See, the authorities referred to by the United States in these pleadings: *Grand River Enterprises Six Nations, Ltd., et al. v. United States*, UNCITRAL, 'US Counter-Memorial', 22 December 2008, paras. 472, 473, 475; *Methanex v. United States*, 'US Amended Statement of Defense', 5 December 2003, para. 367. See also: Newcombe and Paradell, *Law and Practice of Investment Treaties*, p. 251; Andrea Bjorklund, 'Reconciling State Sovereignty and Investor Protection in Denial of Justice Claims', *Virginia JIL* 45 (2005), p. 836; Thomas, 'Reflections on Article 1105 of NAFTA', p. 24. See, however, R. Doak Bishop; James Crawford and W. Michael Reisman, *Foreign Investment Disputes: Cases, Materials and Commentary* (The Hague: Kluwer Law International, 2005), p. 949 ('The principle of non-discrimination is recognized in international customary practice, as part of general international law, judicial decisions, and treaty law. Furthermore, a great majority of jurists have supported the principle as a yardstick of the legality of various state actions. Thus, no one doubts that in customary international law the principle is now firmly established').

'national treatment' clause and the 'most-favoured-nation' clause, which are found in many BITs, are treaty-based obligations which cannot be considered as part of custom.[160] Also, reference is often made in doctrine to the absence of any rule of customary international law requiring the continuous nationality of the claimant investor, from the date of the injury until the date of the award (the *Loewen* Tribunal adopted a different view).[161] A number of tribunals have also concluded that there

---

[160] Newcombe and Paradell, *Law and Practice of Investment Treaties*, p. 149 ('In international investment law, national treatment is a treaty-based obligation. Although the prevalence of national treatment provisions in international investment agreements (IIAs) might suggest consistent and general state practice sufficient for the formation of a customary international law obligation, the scope and content of the provisions vary widely and the obligations are subject to myriad exceptions. Even if sufficient state practice existed to satisfy the requirements for establishing a customary international law obligation, there is little evidence that national treatment in IIAs is accorded out of a sense of legal obligation (*opinio juris*). At present, the more persuasive view is that national treatment obligations with respect to the treatment of foreign investment arise only on the basis of an express treaty obligation'), p. 194 ('Although some commentators have suggested that MFN treatment is required under customary international law based on the principle of the sovereign equality of states, there is little state practice or *opinio juris* to support this contention. Although the prevalence of MFN provisions in IIAs might suggest consistent and general state practice sufficient for the formation of a customary international law obligation, the scope and content of the provisions varies widely and the obligations are subject to myriad exceptions. Even if sufficient state practice existed to satisfy the requirements for establishing a customary international law obligation, there is little evidence that MFN treatment in IIAs is accorded out of a sense of legal obligation [*opinio juris*]'). See also: International Law Commission, 'Report of the ILC on the Work of its 30th Session', in *ILC Yearbook* (1978), vol 2, part. 2, p. 25; Zamora, 'Is there Customary International Economic Law?', pp. 28–29; C. MacLachlan, L. Shore and M. Weiniger, *International Investment Arbitration: Substantive Principles* (Oxford: Oxford University Press, 2007), pp. 17, 212–213, 251, 262–263; C. McLachlan, 'Investment Treaties and General International Law', *ICLQ* 57 (2008), p. 400; Barton Legum, 'Dallas Workshop 2001: Commentary Scene III: ICSID Proceedings in the Absence of a Bilateral Investment Treaty', *Arb. Int'l* 18(3) (2002), p. 306; Al Faruque, 'Creating Customary International Law through Bilateral Investment Treaties', p. 304; N. Stephan Kinsella and Noah D. Rubins, *International Investment, Political Risk, and Dispute Resolution* (Dobbs Ferry: Oceana, 2005), p. 185; Thomas, 'Reflections on Article 1105 of NAFTA', p. 69; UNCTAD, 'Most-Favoured-nation Treatment', UNCTAD Series on Issues in International Investment Agreements II (2010), p. 22.

[161] *Loewen v. United States*, Award, 26 June 2003, para. 225, which held that the rule of continuous nationally requires that a person have the relevant nationality until the 'resolution of the claim'. ILC Special Rapporteur, John R. Dugard, is of the view that '[t]he traditional "rule" of continuous nationality has outlived its usefulness' and 'has no place in a world in which individual rights are recognized by international law and in which nationality is not easily changed' ('Addendum to First Report on Diplomatic Protection', by Mr John R. Dugard, ILC Special Rapporteur, 20 April 2000, U.N. Doc. A/CN.4/506/Add.1, para. 24). He makes reference to the 'dubious status of the requirement of continuity of nationality as a customary rule' (in: *ibid.*, para. 12) which is

is an absence of any customary rule 'prohibiting or regulating antic-ompetitive behaviour'.[162]

The following sections examine two undeniable rules of custom: the MST (Section 2.6.2) and the general prohibition against expropriation without compensation (Section 2.6.3). The question as to whether or not the FET standard is a rule of custom is controversial. The present author believes that it is not (a question discussed in Chapter 3[163]).

2.6.2   Minimum standard of treatment

Despite some disagreement between States on the existence of the MST in the last few decades, the concept is now predominantly recognized as a rule of customary international law. This means in practical terms that this obligation applies to *all States*, including those that have not entered into any BITs. Moreover, it means that the standard of protection can be invoked by *any foreign investor* irrespective of whether or not its State of origin has entered into a BIT with the country where it makes its investment.[164]

'emphasized by the uncertainties surrounding the content of the alleged rule' and in particular the question of the 'date until which continuous nationality of the claim is required' (*ibid.,* para. 16). The *Loewen* dictum was also criticised in doctrine: M.S. Duchesne, 'The Continuous Nationality of Claims Principle: Its Historical Development and Current Relevance to Investor-State Investment Disputes', *Geo. Wash. Int'l L. Rev.* 36 (2004), pp. 801–802; P. Acconci, 'The Requirement of Continuous Corporate Nationality and Customary International Rules on Foreign Investment: the Loewen Case', *Italian YIL* 14 (2004), pp. 195–223; M. Mendelson, 'The Runaway Train: the Continuous Nationality Rule from the Panevezys-Saldutiskis Railway Case to Loewen', in T. Weiler (ed.) *International Investment Law and Arbitration: Leading Cases from the ICSID, NAFTA, Bilateral Treaties and Customary International Law* (London: Cameron May, 2005), pp. 97–149; F. Orrego Vicuña, 'Changing Approaches to the Nationality of Claims in the Context of Diplomatic Protection and International Dispute Settlement', in S. Schlemmer-Schulte and K.-Y. Tung (eds.) *Liber amicorum Ibrahim F.I. Shihata: International Finance and Development Law* (Kluwer Law International, 2001), pp. 503–525: R. Wisner and N. Gallus, 'Nationality Requirements in Investor-State Arbitration', *J. World Invest. & Trade* 5 (2004), pp. 927–945; N. Rubins, 'Loewen v. United States: the Burial of an Investor-State Arbitration Claim', *Arb. Int'l* 21 (2005), pp. 1–36; Gazzini, 'The Role of Customary International Law', p. 697.

[162] *United Parcel Service of America Inc.* v. *Canada*, UNCITRAL, Award on Jurisdiction, 22 November 2002, para. 93 [hereinafter *UPS v. Canada*]. See, discussion in Chapter 1, Section 1.5.3.

[163] See, discussion in Chapter 3, Sections 3.2.4 and 3.3.3.2.1.3.

[164] A different question is whether or not a tribunal has jurisdiction to enforce the minimum standard of treatment. On this point, *see*: UNCTAD, 'Fair and Equitable Treatment',

This section will begin by examining all evidence suggesting that the MST is clearly part of customary international law (Section 2.6.2.1). I will then examine the more controversial and contested question regarding the actual content of the umbrella concept of the MST (Section 2.6.2.2).

2.6.2.1 A firmly established rule

A number of States have explicitly affirmed that the MST is part of customary international law. Paparinskis refers to the pleadings of many States made before the PCIJ and the ICJ where explicit reference is made to the MST.[165] A number of States have also explicitly recognized the customary status of the MST in their pleadings in the context of investment arbitration proceedings.[166] In fact, to the best of the present

---

UNCTAD Series on Issues in International Investment Agreements II (2012), p. 19: 'The question is whether an investor would be able to enforce the minimum standard of treatment of aliens through an IIA's investor-State dispute settlement (ISDS) mechanism. This will depend on the breadth of the treaty's ISDS clause. For instance, the ISDS clause in the India Singapore Comprehensive Economic Cooperation Agreement applies only to disputes 'concerning an alleged breach of an obligation of the former under this Chapter' (Article 6.21); therefore, given the absence of the FET clause in the treaty, claims alleging breaches of the minimum standard of treatment of aliens will fall outside the tribunal's jurisdiction. In contrast, the New Zealand-Thailand Closer Economic Partnership Agreement's arbitration clause encompasses all disputes 'with respect to a covered investment' (Article 9.16) – there is no requirement that relevant claims arise from a violation of the Agreement itself. Such a clause is broad enough to include, among others, claims of violation of the minimum standard of treatment of aliens under customary international law'.

[165] Paparinskis, *The International Minimum Standard*, pp. 14–15.

[166] See, for instance, the following (non-exhaustive) list of cases: *Azurix Corp* v. *Argentina*, ICSID Case No. ARB/01/12, Award, 14 July 2006, paras. 332–333; *Bayindir Insaat Turizm Ticaret ve Sanayi A Ş* v. *Pakistan*, ICSID Case No. ARB/03/29, Award, 27 August 2009, para. 164, 173; *Bureau Veritas, Inspection, Valuation, Assessment and Control, BIVAC BV* v. *Paraguay*, ICSID Case no ARB/07/9, Further Decision on Objections to Jurisdiction, 9 October 2012, paras. 105, 152–153; *Biwater Gauff (Tanzania) Ltd* v. *Tanzania*, ICSID Case No. ARB/05/22, Award and Concurring and Dissenting Opinion, 24 July 2008, para. 587; *Chevron Corporation and Texaco Petroleum Corporation* v. *Ecuador*, UNCITRAL, Partial Award on Merits, 30 March 2010, para. 227; *CMS Gas Transmission Company* v. *Argentina*, ICSID Case No. ARB/01/8, Award, 25 April 2005, paras. 270–271, 282; *Compañía de Aguas del Aconquija SA and Vivendi Universal SA* v. *Argentina*, ICSID Case No. ARB/97/3, Award, 20 August 2007, paras. 5.2.2., 6.6.2; *Continental Casualty Company* v. *Argentina*, ICSID Case No. ARB/03/9, Award, 5 September 2008, paras. 56, 248, 253; *Duke Energy Electroquil Partners and Electroquil SA* v. *Ecuador*, ICSID Case No. ARB/04/19, Award, 18 August 2008, para. 331; *EDF International SA and ors* v. *Argentina*, ICSID Case No. ARB/03/23, Final Award, 11 June 2012, para. 343; *Electrabel SA* v. *Hungary*, ICSID Case No. ARB/07/19, Decision on Jurisdiction, Applicable Law and Liability, 30 November 2012, para. 7.157;

author's knowledge, only Mongolia seems to have adopted the opposite view in one recent case.[167]

The member States of the Organization for Economic Co-operation and Development (OECD) have also acknowledged that the MST is part of customary international law in the context of the 1967 OECD Draft Convention,[168] and in a more recent report in 2005.[169] As will be further discussed in Chapter 5,[170] an increasing number of States have explicitly

El Paso Energy International Company v. Argentina, ICSID Case No. ARB/03/15, Award, 31 October 2011, para. 329; *Enron Corporation and Ponderosa Assets, LP v. Argentina*, ICSID Case No. ARB/01/3, Award, 22 May 2007, para. 253; *Kardassopoulos v. Georgia and joined case*, ICSID Case Nos. ARB/05/18 and ARB/07/15, Award, 3 March 2010, paras. 409, 417; *LG&E Energy Corp., LG&E Capital Corp. and LG&E International Inc. v. Argentina*, ICSID Case No. ARB/02/1, Decision on Liability, 3 October 2006, para. 113; *MCI Power Group LC and New Turbine Inc v. Ecuador*, ICSID Case No. ARB/03/6, Award, 31 July 2007, para. 250; *Metalpar S.A. and Buen Aire S.A. v. Argentina*, ICSID Case No. ARB/03/5, Award on the Merits, 6 June 2008, para. 117; *National Grid PLC v. Argentina*, UNCITRAL, Award, 3 November 2008, para. 161; *Railroad Development Corporation (RDC) v. Guatemala*, ICSID case No. ARB/07/23, Award, 29 June 2012, paras. 159, 207–211 (referring also to the same position adopted by El Salvador and Honduras); *Rumeli Telekom AS and Telsim Mobil Telekomikasyon Hizmetleri AS v. Kazakhstan*, ICSID Case no ARB/05/16, Award, 29 July 2008, para. 611; *Saluka Investments BV v. Czech Republic*, UNCITRAL, Partial Award, 17 March 2006, para. 289; *SAUR International SA v. Argentina*, ICSID Case No. ARB/04/4, Decision on Jurisdiction and Liability, 6 June 2012, para. 472; *Sempra Energy International v. Argentina*, ICSID Case No. ARB/02/16, Award, 28 September 2007, paras. 292, 294; *Suez, Sociedad General de Aguas de Barcelona S.A., and Vivendi Universal S.A. v. Argentina*, ICSID No. ARB/03/19, Decision on Liability, 30 July 2010, para. 183; *Ulysseas, Inc. v. Ecuador*, UNCITRAL, Final Award, 12 June 2012, paras. 206–207; *Unglaube and Unglaube v. Costa Rica*, ICSID Case Nos. ARB/08/1 and ARB/09/20, Award, 16 May 2012, para. 242; *Spence International Investments et al. v. Costa Rica*, UNCITRAL (ICSID Case No. UNCT/13/2), Non-Disputing Party Submission by the United States, 17 April 2015, paras. 12–13, see also, Non-Disputing Party Submission by El Salvador, 17 April 2015, para. 4.

[167] In *Paushok and ors v. Mongolia*, UNCITRAL, Award on Jurisdiction and Liability, 28 April 2011, Mongolia argued that 'the lack of reference to customary international law' in the stand-alone FET clause contained in the Russia-Mongolia BIT was 'indicative of the very limited scope of the protections granted, which protections [were] *below* the customary international law standard' (paras. 272, 403, emphasis added). Mongolia also 'contest[ed]' that the minimum international standard of treatment is part of customary international law' (para. 277).

[168] OECD, *Draft Convention on the Protection of Foreign Property*, commentary on Article 1 indicating that the FET standard 'conforms in effect to the "minimum standard", which forms part of customary international law'.

[169] OECD, 'International Investment Law', p. 82 ('The international minimum standard is a norm of customary international law which governs the treatment of aliens, by providing for a minimum set of principles which States, regardless of their domestic legislation and practices, must respect when dealing with foreign nationals and their property').

[170] See Chapter 5, Section 5.1.2.

recognized the customary nature of the MST in the context of FET standard clauses.[171] This is the case, for instance, of the US[172] and Canadian[173] Model BITs as well as a number of other BITs,[174] including several ones entered into by Mexico,[175] the United States,[176] and Canada.[177] The same recognition of the customary nature of the MST can also be found in several so-called Letters of Submittal sent by the US State Department to the US President requesting approval of BITs by the US Senate.[178]

The customary nature of the MST has also been recognized by several NAFTA awards, including *Mondev*,[179] *Waste Management*,[180] *Glamis*,[181] and others.[182] It has also been recognized by the three

---

[171] This is, for instance, the position adopted by Norway in its commentary to Article 5 of its 2015 Model BIT ('Each Party shall accord to investors of the other Party, and their investments treatment in accordance with customary international law, including fair and equitable treatment and full protection and security'): 'Comments on the Individual Provisions of the Model Agreement' (2015), p. 8, available at: www.regjeringen.no/ contentassets/e47326b61f424d4c9c3d470896492623/comments-on-the-model-for-future-investment-agreements-english-translation.pdf ('The right of investors to fair and equitable treatment and full protection and security is based on the international minimum standard under customary international law, which specifies the minimum threshold for the treatment of foreign nationals').

[172] US Model BIT (2004), Annex 1.   [173] Canada Model BIT (2004), art. 5.

[174] Japan-Laos BIT (2008), art. 5; Model BIT of Colombia (2008), art. 3.

[175] Czech Republic-Mexico BIT (2002), art. 2, protocol; Iceland-Mexico BIT (2005), art. 3, protocol; India-Mexico BIT (2007), art. 5; United Kingdom-Mexico BIT (2006), art. 3; Trinidad and Tobago-Mexico BIT (2006), art. 5; Australia-Mexico BIT (2005), art. 41; China-Mexico BIT (2008).

[176] US-Rwanda BIT (2012), art. 5(2), Annex A; US-Uruguay BIT (2005), art. 5(2), Annex A; US-Chile FTA (2004), art. 10.4, Annex 10.4.

[177] Canada-Czech Republic BIT (2009), art. 3; Canada-Jordan BIT (2009), art. 5; Canada-Latvia BIT (2009), art. 5; Canada-Peru BIT (2007), art. 5; Canada-Romania BIT (2009), art. 2; Canada-Slovakia BIT (2010), art. 3.

[178] This is the case of five 'Letters of Submittal' sent in 1993 as well as all subsequent letters sent after 1994. A number of examples are referred to at Chapters 3 (Section 3.3.4.2.4.2) and 5 (Section 5.1.2).

[179] *Mondev v. United States*, Award, 2 October 2002, para. 121 ('the phrase "minimum standard of treatment" has historically been understood as a reference to a minimum standard under customary international law').

[180] *Waste Management, Inc. v. Mexico ("Number 2")*, ICSID Case No. ARB(AF)/00/3, Award, 30 April 2004, para. 91, where the tribunal endorsed the position taken by the *Mondev* tribunal: 'the *Mondev* tribunal found that the FTC interpretation . . . resolves any dispute about whether there was such a thing as a minimum standard of treatment of investment in international law in the affirmative'.

[181] *Glamis Gold Ltd v. United States*, UNCITRAL, Award, 14 May 2009, para. 627, referring to 'the customary international law minimum standard of treatment, as codified in Article 1105 of the NAFTA'.

[182] *Apotex Holdings Inc & Apotex Inc. v. United States*, ICSID Case No. ARB(AF)/12/1, Award, 25 August 2014, paras. 2.64, 9.15, 9.27 [hereinafter *Apotex v. United States*]

NAFTA Parties themselves in their respective pleadings,[183] by the Free Trade Commission's 2001 Notes of Interpretation,[184] and by Canada in its *Statement on Implementation of NAFTA*.[185] It should be noted, however, that this theoretical controversy is of limited importance in the specific context of NAFTA, where the title of Article 1105 on the FET standard refers specifically to the MST.[186] As established by the *ADF* Tribunal, in the context of NAFTA, 'the long-standing debate as to whether there exists such a thing as a minimum standard of treatment of non-nationals and their property prescribed in customary international law, is closed'.[187]

(speaking of the 'customary international law minimum standard of treatment'); *ADF Group Inc.* v. *United States*, ICSID Case No. ARB(AF)/00/1, Award, 6 January 2003, para. 179 (referring to 'customary international law and the minimum standard of treatment of aliens it incorporates'); *Cargill, Inc.* v. *Mexico*, ICSID Case No. ARB(AF)/05/02, Award, 18 September 2009, para. 278 (referring to the 'customary international law standard'); *Merrill & Ring Forestry L.P.* v. *Canada*, UNCITRAL, Award, 31 March 2010, para. 190 (referring to the 'customary international law minimum standard of treatment of aliens'); *William Ralph Clayton, William Richard Clayton, Douglas Clayton, Daniel Clayton and Bilcon of Delaware, Inc.* v. *Canada*, UNCITRAL, Award on Jurisdiction and Liability, 17 March 2015, paras. 431, 436 [hereinafter *Bilcon* v. *Canada*] (speaking of the 'minimum standard of international law' and the 'international minimum standard under customary international law').

[183] See, for instance, *ADF Group Inc.* v. *United States*, Award, 6 January 2003, para. 112; *Glamis Gold Ltd* v. *United States*, Award, 14 May 2009, para. 543; *Apotex* v. *United States*, Award, 25 August 2014, para. 2.64; *Mondev* v. *United States*, Award, 11 October 2002, para. 111; *Bilcon* v. *Canada*, UNCITRAL, Award on Jurisdiction and Liability, 17 March 2015, paras. 398, 400.

[184] 'Note of Interpretation of Certain Chapter 11 Provisions', 31 July 2001, indicating, *inter alia,* that: 'Article 1105(1) prescribes the customary international law minimum standard of treatment of aliens as the minimum standard of treatment to be afforded to investments of investors of another Party'.

[185] Canada, 'Statement on Implementation of NAFTA', in *Canada Gazette*, 1 January 1994, p. 68, 149, stating that Article 1105(1) 'provides for a minimum absolute standard of treatment, based on longstanding principles of customary international law'.

[186] On this question, see: P. Dumberry, *The Fair and Equitable Treatment Standard*, p. 13 ff.

[187] *ADF* v. *United States*, Award, 9 January 2003, para. 178. See also: *Mondev* v. *United States*, Award, 2 October 2002, para. 120 ('[I]t is clear that Article 1105 was intended to put at rest for NAFTA purposes a long-standing and divisive debate about whether any such thing as a minimum standard of treatment of investment in international law actually exists. Article 1105 resolves this issue in the affirmative for NAFTA Parties').

A number of other awards (outside NAFTA) have also explicitly (or implicitly) recognized (with a few exceptions[188]) the customary nature of the MST.[189]

[188] *Compañía de Aguas del Aconquija SA and Vivendi Universal SA* v. *Argentina*, ICSID Case No. ARB/97/3, Award, 20 August 2007, paras. 5.2.2., 6.6.2., 7.4.5. (referring to the 'so–called minimum standard of treatment under international law'), 7.4.6. ('Article 3 refers to fair and equitable treatment in conformity with the principles of international law, and not to the minimum standard of treatment'), 7.4.7. ('The Tribunal sees no basis for equating principles of international law with the minimum standard of treatment. First, the reference to principles of international law supports a broader reading that invites consideration of a wider range of international law principles than the minimum standard alone').

[189] See, for instance: *Impregilo S.p.A.* v. *Argentina*, ICSID Case No. ARB/07/17, Award, 21 June 21, 2001, para. 285 ('The term "fair and equitable treatment" appears in many BITs. It cannot be easily defined, and it is generally believed to require at least respect for the international minimum standard of protection which, according to *international customary law*, any State is obliged to afford to foreign property in its territory', emphasis added); *Bayindir Insaat Turizm Ticaret ve Sanayi A Ş* v. *Pakistan*, ICSID Case No. ARB/03/29, Award, 27 August 2009, paras. 164 ('At the outset, the Tribunal notes that the basis for importing an FET obligation into the Treaty is provided by its MFN clause, from which it follows that the applicable FET standard is a self-standing treaty obligation as opposed to the *customary international minimum standard* to which the Respondent referred. That being so, whether international customary law and the observations of other tribunals in applying the minimum standard may be relevant here will depend upon the terms of the applicable FET standard', emphasis added); *Biwater Gauff (Tanzania) Ltd* v. *Tanzania*, ICSID Case No. ARB/05/22, Award and Concurring and Dissenting Opinion, 24 July 2008, para. 592 ('the Arbitral Tribunal also accepts, as found by a number of previous arbitral tribunals and commentators, that the actual content of the treaty standard of fair and equitable treatment is not materially different from the content of the *minimum standard of treatment in customary international law*', emphasis added); *CMS Gas Transmission Company* v. *Argentina*, ICSID Case No. ARB/01/8, Award, 25 April 2005, paras. 270–271, 282, 284 (referring to an 'international law minimum standard'); *EDF International SA and ors* v. *Argentina*, ICSID Case No. ARB/03/23, Final Award, 11 June 2012, paras. 343, 999 (referring to the 'customary international minimum standard'); *El Paso Energy International Company* v. *Argentina*, ICSID Case No. ARB/03/15, Award, 31 October 2011, paras. 329, 335–336 (referring to the 'minimum standard of international law' and the international minimum standard); *Enron Corporation and Ponderosa Assets, LP* v. *Argentina*, ICSID Case No. ARB/01/3, Award, 22 May 2007, paras. 253, 258 ('It might well be that in some circumstances where the international minimum standard is sufficiently elaborate and clear, fair and equitable treatment might be equated with it. But in other more vague circumstances, the fair and equitable standard may be more precise than its customary international law forefathers. This is why the Tribunal concludes that the fair and equitable standard, at least in the context of the Treaty applicable to this case, can also require a treatment additional to, or beyond that of, customary law'), see also, Decision on the Application for Annulment of the Argentine Republic, Annulment Committee, 30 July 2010, paras. 302, 304 (using the expression 'customary international law minimum standard'); *Lauder* v. *Czech Republic*, UNCITRAL, Final Award, 3 September 2001, para. 292 ('Fair and equitable treatment is

related to the traditional standard of due diligence and provides a "minimum international standard which forms part of customary international law'"); *Lemire* v. *Ukraine*, ICSID No. ARB/06/18, Decision on Jurisdiction and Liability, 21 January 2010, paras. 250–254 (referring to the expressions 'customary minimum standard' and 'international customary minimum standard'), see also, Award, 28 March 2011, para. 139 (referring to 'the minimum standard of treatment of aliens established under customary international law'); *National Grid PLC* v. *Argentina*, UNCITRAL, Award, 3 November 2008, paras. 167, 169, 170 (referring to the expressions 'standard of treatment under international law' and 'customary minimum standard'); *Occidental Exploration and Production Co* v. *Ecuador*, LCIA Case No. UN3467, Award, 1 July 2004, paras. 188–192 (referring to the expression 'customary international law standard'); *Railroad Development Corporation (RDC)* v. *Guatemala*, ICSID case No. ARB/07/23, Award, 29 June 2012, para. 218 ('Put in slightly different terms, what customary international law projects is not a static photograph of the minimum standard of treatment of aliens as it stood in 1927 when the Award in the Neer case was rendered. For both customary international law and the *minimum standard of treatment of aliens it incorporates*, are constantly in a process of development', emphasis added); *Rumeli Telekom AS and Telsim Mobil Telekomikasyon Hizmetleri AS* v. *Kazakhstan*, ICSID Case No ARB/05/16, Award, 29 July 2008, para. 611 (referring to the expression 'minimum standard of treatment in customary international law'); *Saluka Investments BV* v. *Czech Republic*, UNCITRAL, Partial Award, 17 March 2006, paras. 289, 291–295 (referring to the expression 'customary minimum standard'); *SAUR International SA* v. *Argentina*, ICSID Case No. ARB/04/4, Decision on Jurisdiction and Liability, 6 June 2012, para. 491 (referring to the expression 'le niveau dit "minimal de traitement dû aux étrangers selon le droit international coutumier"'); *Sempra Energy International* v. *Argentina*, ICSID Case No. ARB/02/16, Award, 28 September 2007, para. 302 ('It might well be that in some circumstances in which the international minimum standard is sufficiently elaborate and clear, the standard of fair and equitable treatment might be equated with it. But in other cases, it might as well be the opposite, so that the fair and equitable treatment standard will be more precise than its customary international law forefathers'); *Siemens AG* v. *Argentina*, ICSID No. ARB/02/8, Award, 17 January 2007, paras. 289, 291, 293 (referring to the expression 'minimum standard of treatment of aliens under customary international law'); *Suez, Sociedad General de Aguas de Barcelona S.A., and Vivendi Universal S.A.* v. *Argentina*, ICSID No. ARB/03/19, Decision on Liability, 30 July 2010, para. 184 ('With respect to the Argentina-France BIT, it is to be noted that the text of the treaty refers simply to "the principles of international law," not to "the minimum standard under customary international law." The formulation "minimum standard under customary international law" or simply "minimum international standard" is so well known and so well established in international law that one can assume that if France and Argentina had intended to limit the content of fair and equitable treatment to the minimum international standard they would have used that formulation specifically. In fact, they did not'); *Total SA* v. *Argentina*, ICSID Case No. ARB/04/1, Decision on Liability, 27 December 2010, para. 125 ('the Tribunal is of the opinion that the phrase "fair and equitable in conformity with the principles of international law" cannot be read as "treatment required by the minimum standard of treatment of aliens/investors under international law." This is irrespective of the issue of whether today there really is a difference between this traditional minimum standard and what international law generally requires as to treatment of foreign investors and their investments'); *Ulysseas, Inc* v. *Ecuador*, UNCITRAL, Final Award, 12 June 2012, paras. 206–207, 245 (referring to the expression 'minimum standard of treatment required by international law').

The majority of writers have also accepted the customary status of the MST.[190] In fact, only a few of them have rejected the claim.[191] For instance, Porterfield argues that the assumption that customary international law includes an MST has 'never been supported by any comprehensive empirical study of the actual practice of nations with regard to foreign investment'.[192] He is also critical of the role played

[190] J.C. Thomas, 'Fair and Equitable Treatment under NAFTA's Investment Chapter; Remarks', *ASIL Proc.* 96 (2002), p. 14; Rudolf Dolzer and Margrete Stevens, *Bilateral Investment Treaties* (The Hague: Martinus Nijhoff, 1995), p. 58; Sir Robert Jenning and Sir Arthur Watts, *Oppenheim's International Law* (9th edn., Longman, 1996, vol. I, Part 1), p. 931; L. Reed, J. Paulsson and N. Blackaby, *A Guide to ICSID Arbitration* (The Hague: Kluwer Law, 2004), p. 48; Tudor, *The Fair and Equitable Treatment Standard*, pp. 61–62, 67; Newcombe and Paradell, *Law and Practice of Investment Treaties*, p. 234; Diehl, *The Core Standard of International Investment Protection*, p. 145; Gabriel Cavazos Villanueva, *The Fair and Equitable Treatment Standard: The Mexican Experience* (Saarbrücken: VDM Verlag, 2008), pp. 63–64; D. Carreau, 'Investissements', in *Répertoire de droit international* (Paris: Dalloz 1998), para. 135; Dickerson, 'Minimum Standards', para. 1; Marcela Klein Bronfman, 'Fair and Equitable Treatment: An Evolving Standard', *Max Planck Yrbk. UNL*, 10 (2006), p. 624; Thomas, 'Reflections on Article 1105 of NAFTA', pp. 29 ff; Picherack, 'The Expanding Scope of the Fair and Equitable Treatment Standard', p. 265; Graham Mayeda, 'Playing Fair: The Meaning of Fair and Equitable Treatment in Bilateral Investment Treaties', *J. World Trade* 41(2) (2007), pp. 273–291, 280; Mathias Audit and Mathias Forteau, 'Investment Arbitration without BIT: Toward a Foreign Investment Customary Based Arbitration?' *J. Int'l Arb.*, 29 (2012), p. 640; Paparinskis, *The International Minimum Standard*, pp. 16, 163; Gazzini, 'The Role of Customary International Law', p. 699; T. Kill, 'Don't Cross the Streams: Past and Present Overstatement of Customary International Law in Connection with Conventional Fair and Equitable Treatment Obligations', *Michigan LR* 106 (2008), pp. 853, 856; Laviec, *Protection et promotion des investissements*, pp. 86–88; Orellana, 'International Law on Investment', pp. 1–2; Salacuse, *The Three Laws of International Investment*, p. 311; Trachtman, 'The Obsolescence of Customary International Law', pp. 87–88.

[191] See, Stephen Schwebel, 'The United States 2004 Model Bilateral Investment Treaty: An Exercise in the Regressive Development of International Law', in *Global Reflections on International Law, Commerce and Dispute Resolution, Liber Amicorum in honour of Robert Briner* (Paris: ICC Pub. No. 693, 2005), p. 647: 'the profound, and startling, deficiency of the 2004 provision is that there is no agreement within the international community on the content of "customary international law" on which the 2004 Model BIT relies. There was, and is, no agreement within the international community on the content of "the customary international law minimum standard of treatment of aliens", or even on whether such a minimum standard existed or exists'.

[192] M.C. Porterfield, 'An International Common Law of Investor Rights?', *U. Pa. J. Int'l Econ. L.*, 27 (2006), pp. 81–82.

by tribunal decisions 'guiding the evolution of the minimum standard'.[193] Another prominent writer taking a similar position is Sornarajah, who (as mentioned above) denies the existence of any rule of customary law, and is critical about the existence of any such MST.[194] In subsequent writing, Sornarajah admits that an MST may have emerged, but *only* amongst NAFTA Parties in the context of a 'regional' custom.[195]

2.6.2.2 ... with an imprecise content

If there is no doubt that an MST must be respected by States, and that this is a customary norm of international law, then the root of the controversy lies in the actual *content* of that standard.

The MST is an *umbrella concept*, which *itself* incorporates different elements. As pointed out by Roth in 1949, 'the international standard is nothing else but a set of rules, correlated to each other and deriving from one particular norm of general international law, namely that the treatment of an alien is regulated by the law of nations'.[196] Similarly, according to Newcombe and Paradell, the MST 'consists of a series of interconnecting and overlapping elements or standards that apply to both the treatment of foreigners and their property'.[197] A number of NAFTA tribunals have also endorsed this description of the MST as an umbrella concept.[198]

---

[193] *Ibid.*, p. 98. See also, at pp. 103, 113.

[194] Sornarajah, *The International Law on Foreign Investment*, pp. 64, 92–93. At p. 328, he indicates that 'it cannot be said with certainty that there is an international MST of treatment of foreign investment in customary international law, the violation of which result in State responsibility'. In any event, for him the precise extent of the content of an MST 'is difficult to identify'. Thus, 'one knows that there is such a standard but what the standard contains and what its modern limits are, are unclear' (p. 329). He concludes (at p. 329) that 'There are three instances in which the old cases on state responsibility may provide guidance as to the international minimum standard. These relate to compensation for expropriation, responsibility for destruction or violence by non-state actors and denial of justice'.

[195] M. Sornarajah, 'The Fair and Equitable Standard of Treatment: Whose Fairness? Whose Equity?' in Federico Ortino *et al.* (eds.), *Investment Treaty Law: Current Issues II* (London: BIICL, 2007), p. 177.

[196] Roth, *The Minimum Standard of International Law*, p. 127.

[197] Newcombe and Paradell, *Law and Practice of Investment Treaties*, p. 236.

[198] *Glamis* v. *United States*, Award, 8 June 2009, para. 618 ('The international law minimum standard [of treatment] is an umbrella concept incorporating a set of rules that has crystallized over the centuries into customary international law in specific contexts'); *Cargill, Inc.* v. *Mexico*, ICSID Case No. ARB(AF)/05/02, Award, 18 September 2009, para. 268. In its award, the *Mobil* Tribunal endorsed the position taken by *Cargill*

Many writers have emphasized the vagueness of the concept of the MST and its lack of precise content.[199] For instance, in a recent 2012 report, UNCTAD stated that the minimum standard is 'highly indeterminate, lacks a clearly defined content and requires interpretation'.[200] The report suggested that '[t]he MST is a concept that does not offer ready-made solutions for deciding modern investment disputes; at best, it gives a rough idea of a high threshold that the challenged governmental conduct has to meet for a breach to be established'.[201] As a result, it has been argued that the MST lacks the necessary *normative requirement* (as identified by the ICJ in the *North Sea Continental Shelf* case[202]) to be considered a rule of custom.[203]

Tribunal (*Mobil Investments Canada Inc. & Murphy Oil Corporation* v. *Canada*, ICSID Case No. ARB(AF)/07/4, Decision on Liability and on Principles of Quantum, 22 May 2012, para. 135 [hereinafter *Mobil v. Canada*]). The United States has also consistently interpreted the MST as an umbrella concept in NAFTA proceedings: See, for instance: *ADF v. United States*, 'US Post Hearing Submission', 27 June 2002, pp. 2–4; *Glamis v. United States*, 'US Counter-Memorial', 9 September 2006, p. 223; *Loewen v. United States*, 'US Counter-Memorial', 30 March 2001, p. 124; *Methanex Corporation v. United States*, 'US Statement of Defense', 12 May 2004, p. 157; *Ibid.*, 'US Memorial on Jurisdiction and Admissibility', 13 November 2000, pp. 43–44. The same position has also been adopted by Mexico, see: *Glamis v. United States*, Award, 8 June 2009, para. 618, citing *ADF v. United States*, Mexico's Second Article 1128 Submission, 22 July 2002, p. 8.

[199] Sornarajah, 'The Fair and Equitable Standard of Treatment', p. 172; Sornarajah, *The International Law on Foreign Investment*, p. 328; Porterfield, 'An International Common Law of Investor Rights?' p. 80; Gazzini, 'The Role of Customary International Law', p. 699; d'Aspremont, 'International Customary Investment Law', p. 33.

[200] UNCTAD, 'Fair and Equitable Treatment', p. 28, see also, p. 44.

[201] *Ibid.*, pp. 46–47.

[202] *North Sea Continental Shelf Cases (Federal Republic of Germany* v. *Denmark / Federal Republic of Germany* v. *Netherlands)*, ICJ Rep. 1969, p. 42, para. 72, indicating that a provision must be of a 'fundamentally norm-creating character such as could be regarded as forming the basis of a general rule of law'.

[203] d'Aspremont, 'International Customary Investment Law', pp. 33–34: 'Indeed, most authors sympathetic to the idea of customary investment law have failed to realize that many prescriptions which they claim to be customary rules are not sufficiently normative to have the potential to crystallize in customary international law. A wide number of directives or standards which are deemed to have crystalized in customary international law – as is illustrated by the minimum standard of treatment – are highly imprecise and vague. I am of the opinion that many candidates for customary status in investment law which have been mentioned above [he is certainly referring to the MST] do not provide for clear standards of behavior and suffer from strong normative weakness. They fail to meet the minimum threshold in terms of normative content that is necessary for such norms to

Roth's identification of eight rules on the treatment of aliens in 1949 (not dealing specifically with foreign investment) constituted an early attempt to define the *actual content* of the MST.[204] A recent OECD report stated that 'case law points to a number of areas across which the notion of an international minimum standard applies' including 'the administration of justice in cases involving foreign nationals, usually linked to the notion of denial of justice', 'the treatment of aliens under detention', full protection and security, and finally, the 'general right of expulsion by the host State', which 'should be the least injurious to the person affected'.[205] Moreover, a 2012 UNCTAD report indicated that '[t]he MST is often understood as a broad concept intended to encompass the doctrine of denial of justice along with other aspects of the law of State responsibility for

possibly constitute (or give rise to) a customary rule'. See also, discussion on the MST at pp. 10–12, 23–24.

[204] Roth, *The Minimum Standard of International Law*, pp. 185–186, identifying the following eight rules that general international law imposes on States with regards to the treatment of aliens: '(1) An alien, whether a natural person or a corporation, is entitled by international law to have his juridical personality and legal capacity recognized by the receiving state. (2) The alien can demand respect for his life and protection for his body. (3) International law protects the alien's personal and spiritual liberty within socially bearable limits. (4) According to general international law, aliens enjoy no political rights in their State of residence, but have to fulfil such public duties as are not incompatible with allegiance to their home state. (5) General international law gives aliens no right to be economically active allow in foreign States. In cases where national economic policies of foreign States allows aliens to undertake economic activities, however, general international law assures aliens equality of commercial treatment among themselves. (6) According to general international law, the alien's privilege of participation does not go so far as to allow him to acquire private property. The State of residence is free to bar him from ownership of all certain property, whether movables or realty. (7) Where an alien enjoys the privilege of ownership of property, international law protects his rights in so far as his property may not be expropriated under any pretext, except for moral or penal reasons, without adequate compensation. Property rights are to be understood as rights to tangible property which have come into concrete existence according to the municipal law of the alien's State of residence. (8) International law grants the alien procedural rights in his State of residence as primary protection against violation of his substantive rights. These procedural rights amount to freedom of access to court, the right to a fair, non-discriminatory and unbiased hearing, the right to full participation in any form in the procedure, the right to a just decision rendered in full compliance with the laws of the State within a reasonable time'.

[205] OECD, 'International Investment Law', p. 82. This definition is endorsed by Tudor, *The Fair and Equitable Treatment Standard*, p. 62.

injuries to aliens'.[206] The report referred in turn to an earlier 2004 OECD report,[207] concluding that 'the international minimum standard applies in the following areas: (a) the administration of justice, usually linked to the notion of the denial of justice; (b) the treatment of aliens under detention; and (c) full protection and security'.[208] The UNCTAD report concluded that 'there are no other aspects of the MST that have become apparent to date in customary international law'.[209] Other writers have defined the content of the minimum standard more broadly.[210]

In light of the foregoing, there is a large consensus to the effect that the MST encompasses (at the very least):

[206] UNCTAD, 'Fair and Equitable Treatment', p. 44. A very similar approach is adopted by Sornarajah, 'The Fair and Equitable Standard of Treatment', p. 172: '[t]he precise extent of the content of an international minimum standard has yet to be worked out. ... Yet, the international minimum standard, the existence of which is denied collectively by the developing states, has not been fleshed out. Outside the standards applicable to expropriation and to state responsibility for denying protection and security to aliens which are separately provided for in investment treaties, international minimum standard captures the category which involves a denial of justice'. *See also*: Sornarajah, *The International Law on Foreign Investment*, p. 329 ('There are three instances in which the old cases on state responsibility may provide guidance as to the international minimum standard. These relate to compensation for expropriation, responsibility for destruction or violence by non-state actors and denial of justice').

[207] OECD, 'Fair and Equitable Treatment Standard in International Investment Law', Working Papers on International Investment Law, No. 2004/3 (2004).

[208] UNCTAD, 'Fair and Equitable Treatment', p. 44.

[209] *Ibid.*, at p. 45. *See also*, Kläger, *Fair and Equitable Treatment*, p. 53 ('the concept of the international minimum standard, in its classic sense, may have produced rules for the compensation for expropriation, the physical protection of aliens and the enforcement of the pertinent laws. Beyond that, however, it is highly questionable whether it entails any further guidelines relating to the protection of economic interests of foreign corporations or individuals').

[210] Based on the list mentioned by the Tribunal in *Waste Management v. Mexico*, Award, 30 April 2004, para. 98, Newcombe and Paradell, *Law and Practice of Investment Treaties*, p. 238, indicate that a 'number of specific elements of the minimum standard of treatment where state responsibility may arise for mistreatment of foreign investors and investment, including, but not exhaustively: denial of justice, lack of due process, lack of due diligence, and instances of arbitrariness and discrimination'. Paparinskis, *The International Minimum Standard*, pp. 182, 239, 246–247, 256, argues that denial of justice, arbitrariness and non-discrimination are elements of the minimum standard of treatment.

- An obligation for host States to prevent the denial of justice in the administration of justice[211] and to provide due process[212];
- An obligation to prevent arbitrary conduct;[213] and

---

[211] Newcombe and Paradell, *Law and Practice of Investment Treaties*, pp. 236–238; Tudor, *The Fair and Equitable Treatment Standard*, p. 62; Bjorklund, 'Reconciling State Sovereignty and Investor Protection', p. 837 ('The international minimum standard and denial of justice are often conflated, but the requirement not to deny justice is a subset of the international minimum standard'); Paparinskis, *The International Minimum Standard*, pp. 182, 229, 248; Katia Yannaca-Small, 'Fair and Equitable Treatment Standard: Recent Developments, in *Standards of Investment Protection*' in A. Reinisch (ed.) *Standards of Investment Protection* (Oxford: Oxford University Press, 2008), p. 119; F.V. García Amador, Louis B. Sohn and R.R. Baxter, *Recent Codification of the Law of State Responsibility for Injuries to Aliens* (Dobbs Ferry: Oceana Publ., 1974), p. 180; Congyan, 'International Investment Treaties and the Formation', p. 671; Sornarajah, *The International Law on Foreign Investment*, p. 329. See also: *Chevron Corporation (USA) and Texaco Petroleum Company (USA) v. Ecuador*, UNCITRAL, PCA Case No. 34877, Partial Award on Merits, 30 March 2010, para. 244 (referring to 'denial of justice under customary international law'); *Renta 4 S.V.S.A, Ahorro Corporación Emergentes F.I., Ahorro Corporación Eurofondo F.I., Rovime Inversiones SICAV S.A., Quasar de Valors SICAV S.A., Orgor de Valores SICAV S.A., GBI 9000 SICAV S.A. v. Russian Federation*, SCC No. 24/2007, Award on Preliminary Objections, Separate Opinion of Charles N. Brower, 20 March 2009, para. 23 ('the prohibition against denial of justice not only forms part of customary international law but also is an integral part of the fair and equitable treatment standard itself'); *Spence International Investments et al. v. Costa Rica*, Non-Disputing Party Submission by the United States, 17 April 2015, para. 13; OECD, 'International Investment Law', pp. 82, 108, 125; UNCTAD, 'Fair and Equitable Treatment', p. 44. For a recent analysis of denial of justice in the context of NAFTA Article 1105, see: P. Dumberry, 'Denial of Justice under NAFTA Article 1105: A Review of 20 Years of Case Law', *ASA Bull.* 32(2) (2014), pp. 145–163.

[212] Newcombe and Paradell, *Law and Practice of Investment Treaties*, pp. 238, 241, 243–244; Schreuer and Dolzer, *Principles of International Investment Law*, p. 91; *See also: AAPL v. Sri Lanka*, ICSID Case No. ARB/87/3, Final Award, 27 June 1990, dissenting opinion of Judge Asente ('the general obligation of the host state to exercise due diligence in protecting foreign investment in its territories, an obligation that derives from customary international law').

[213] *Glamis v. United States*, Award, 8 June 2009, para. 626 ('a duty to protect investors from arbitrary measures exists in the customary international law minimum standard of treatment of aliens'); *International Thunderbird Gaming Corporation v. Mexico*, UNCITRAL, Award, 26 January 2006, para. 194; *Waste Management v. Mexico*, Award, 30 April 2004, para. 98: *Mobil v. Canada*, Decision on Liability and on Principles of Quantum, 22 May 2012, para. 152; Newcombe and Paradell, *Law and Practice of Investment Treaties*, pp. 237, 249–250; Schreuer and Dolzer, *Principles of International Investment Law*, p. 176; Todd Weiler, 'Methanex Corp. v. U.S.A: Turning the Page on NAFTA Chapter Eleven?' *J. World Invest. & Trade* 6(6) (2005), p. 917; T. Weiler and I. Laird, 'Standards of Treatment', in Peter Muchlinski, Federico Ortino and Christoph Schreuer (eds.), *The Oxford Handbook of International Investment Law* (Oxford: Oxford University Press, 2008), pp. 284–285; Paparinskis, *The International Minimum Standard*, p. 239; Santiago Montt, *State Liability in Investment Treaty Arbitration* (Oxford: Hart Publ., 2009), pp. 295, 310. See, however: Veijo Heiskanen,

- An obligation to provide investors with 'full protection and security'.[214]

This brings us to one of the most controversial questions in the field of investor-State arbitration: whether the FET standard is one of the elements *encompassed* within the larger umbrella concept of the MST or whether it is an autonomous standard. The present author has examined the question in some detail elsewhere.[215] Suffice it to say (in the context of the present book) that the FET standard should be interpreted *in general* as an *independent* treaty standard with an autonomous meaning from the MST. This is certainly the case when an FET clause is *unqualified* and contains *no* reference whatsoever to international law. This is the position that has been adopted by the majority of writers.[216] In fact, some writers have even argued that the FET standard should now be considered as a rule of customary international law.[217] This controversial claim will be addressed further in Chapter 3.[218]

One notable difficulty is the interpretation of FET clauses that *do* refer to international law. Case law seems to be divided on how to properly interpret such clauses. Questions arise as to what the actual intention of the parties was when they made reference to those terms. In the present author's view, any possible ambiguities disappear when there is clear and

'Arbitrary and Unreasonable Measures' in A. Reinisch (ed.), *Standards of Investment Protection* (Oxford: Oxford University Press, 2008), p. 110 (for whom 'non-impairment standard [prohibiting arbitrary and unreasonable acts] imposes a standard of conduct on governments that is arguably substantially higher than that required by customary international law'). For a recent analysis of the obligation to prevent arbitrary conduct in the context of NAFTA Article 1105, see: P. Dumberry, 'The Prohibition Against Arbitrary Conduct and the Fair and Equitable Treatment Standard under NAFTA Article 1105', *J. World Invest. & Trade* 15 (2014) pp. 117–151.

[214] *AAPL v. Sri Lanka*, Final Award, 27 June 1990, para. 67; *Sicula S.p.A. (ELSI) (US v. Italy)*, Judgment, ICJ Rep. 1989, p. 115, para. 111; *Noble Ventures, Inc. v. Romania*, ICSID Case No. ARB/01/11, Award, 12 October 2005, para. 164 ('the general duty to provide for protection and security of foreign nationals found in the customary international law of aliens'); *Rankin v. Iran*, Award No. 326-10913-2, Iran-U.S. Claims. Trib., Award, 3 November 1987, para. 30(c); *Amco Asia Corporation, Pan American Development Limited, PT Amco Indonesia v. Indonesia*, ICSID Case No. ARB/81/1, Award, 20 November 1984, para. 172; Vandevelde, *Bilateral Investment Treaties*, pp. 243, 244, 247; Weiler, *The Interpretation of International Investment Law*, p. 100; Ralph Alexander Lorz, 'Protection and Security (Including the NAFTA Approach)', in M. Bungenberg, J. Griebel, S. Hobe and A. Reinisch (eds.), *International Investment Law: A Handbook* (Munich *et al.*: C.H. Beck, Hart, Nomos, 2015), p. 766.

[215] See, Dumberry, *The Fair and Equitable Treatment Standard*, p. 37 ff.

[216] *Ibid.*, p. 38 for a long list of writers.

[217] See, Tudor, *The Fair and Equitable Treatment Standard*, p. 65–68; Diehl, *The Core Standard of International Investment Protection*, pp. 10–11, 125–153, 175–179.

[218] See, discussion in Chapter 3, Sections 3.2.4 and 3.3.3.2.1.3.

undeniable evidence that the intention of the parties was in fact to have the FET standard be considered as a reference to the MST under custom. This is clearly the case under NAFTA Article 1105.[219] Under Article 1105, the FET standard must be considered as *one of the elements* included in the umbrella concept of the MST.[220] Several NAFTA tribunals have endorsed this approach.[221] Another important element is Article 1105's title referring to the 'Minimum Standard of Treatment' in its heading. Moreover, all evidence (including a subsequent agreement and substantial subsequent practice between the Parties) supports this interpretation that the term 'international law' in NAFTA Article 1105 is a reference to the MST under customary international law.[222]

2.6.3   General prohibition against expropriation without compensation

In the *Generation Ukraine case*, the Tribunal stated that '[i]t is plain that several of the BIT standards, and the prohibition against expropriation in particular, are simply a conventional codification of standards that have long existed in customary international law'.[223] Other tribunals have come to the same conclusion.[224] For instance, in *Glamis* the Tribunal held that:

> The inclusion in [NAFTA] Article 1110 of the term "expropriation" incorporates by reference the customary international law regarding that subject. Under custom, a State is responsible, and therefore must provide compensation, for an expropriation of property when it subjects the property of another State Party's investor to an action that is confiscatory or that "unreasonably interferes with, or unduly delays, effective enjoyment" of the property.[225]

---

[219]   The question is examined in Dumberry, *The Fair and Equitable Treatment Standard*, pp. 44–46. A different position is adopted by Weiler, *The Interpretation of International Investment Law*, pp. 274, 284, 456–457.

[220]   In fact, this is evident because the provision requires NAFTA Parties to provide foreign investors treatment in accordance with 'international law' (a reference to the MST under custom as reaffirmed by the 2001 FTC Note of Interpretation), *including* fair and equitable treatment.

[221]   *See*, for instance, *UPS* v. *Canada*, Award on Jurisdiction, 22 November 2002, para. 97; *Waste Management* v. *Mexico*, Award, 30 April 2004, para. 98; *Cargill, Inc.* v. *Mexico*, Award, 18 September 2009, para. 296.

[222]   See, the analysis in: Dumberry, *The Fair and Equitable Treatment Standard*, p. 49 ff.

[223]   *Generation Ukraine, Inc.* v. *Ukraine*, ICSID Case No. ARB/00/9, Award, 16 September 2003, para. 11.3.

[224]   *Waguih Elie George Siag and Clorinda Vecchi* v. *Egypt*, ICSID Case No. ARB/05/15, Award, 1 June 2009, paras. 203, 428.

[225]   *Glamis* v. *United States*, Award, 8 June 2009, para. 354.

The obligation to provide compensation for expropriation in certain circumstances is generally recognized as a rule of custom.[226] The question, however, of what those circumstances are and what the proper level of compensation is has long been the object of controversy. These two aspects will be examined in the following paragraphs.

First, several writers believe, with respect to the circumstances, that a State cannot under customary law directly or indirectly nationalize or expropriate the investment of a foreign investor, except in the following circumstances: when the measure is for a public purpose, is taken on a non-discriminatory basis, in accordance with due process of law and accompanied by just compensation.[227] According to one OECD Report, 'customary international law does not preclude host states from expropriating foreign investments provided certain conditions are met' (referring to these four conditions).[228] In addition, UNCTAD has maintained that these four conditions have

---

[226] This is even recognized by Sornarajah, *The International Law on Foreign Investment*, pp. 89, 329, who generally rejects the idea that customary rules have emerged in the field of investment arbitration. See also: Grisel, 'The Sources of Foreign Investment Law', p. 222; Salacuse, *The Law of Investment Treaties*, p. 58 ('Generally speaking, almost all of the nations in the world today would claim to recognize the principle that a state which has expropriated the property of a foreign investor has the obligation to pay compensation to that investor'); Schachter, 'Compensation for Expropriation', p. 127 (referring to the 'generally accepted rule that compensation should be paid when property is expropriated'); Newcombe and Paradell, *Law and Practice of Investment Treaties*, p. 332; Trachtman, 'The Obsolescence of Customary International Law', pp. 87–88. *Contra*: Zamora, 'Is there Customary International Economic Law?', pp. 23–25, 34.

[227] Vandevelde, *Bilateral Investment Treaties*, p. 270; Schreuer and Dolzer, *Principles of International Investment Law*, p. 91; Christopher Dugan, Noah D. Rubins, Don Wallace and Borzu Sabahi, *Investor-State Arbitration* (New York: Oxford University Press, 2008), pp. 437, 442; Congyan, 'International Investment Treaties and the Formation', p. 670; MacLachlan, *International Investment Arbitration*, p. 16; W. Michael Reisman and Robert D. Sloane, 'Indirect Expropriation and its Valuation in the BIT Generation', *British YIL* 74 (2003), p. 115; Al Faruque, 'Creating Customary International Law through Bilateral Investment Treaties', p. 305; Doak R. Bishop, James R. Crawford and W. Michael Reisman (eds.), *Foreign Investment Disputes: Cases, Materials and Commentary* (Kluwer Law International, 2014), pp. 588–589; d'Aspremont, 'International Customary Investment Law', pp. 24–25; Ruzza 'Expropriation and Nationalization', para. 6. A different position seems to be taken by Matthew C. Porterfield, 'State Practice and the (Purported) Obligation under Customary International Law to Provide Compensation for Regulatory Expropriations', *North Carolina JIL & Comm Reg*, 37 (2011), pp. 162, 171: 'an examination of relevant domestic law, however, indicates that there is no general and consistent practice in this area' and that 'there does not appear to be support in state practice for a CIL right to compensation for regulatory expropriations based upon their adverse effects on the value of investments and without regard to whether the government has actually acquired ownership or control of the asset'.

[228] OECD, '"Indirect Expropriation" and The "Right To Regulate" in International Investment Law', Working Papers on International Investment, no. 2004/4, (2004), p. 3.

become an established rule of customary law.[229] A number of investment treaties indicate the parties' 'shared understanding' that the clause on expropriation found in the treaty (which refers to these four conditions) 'is intended to reflect customary international law concerning the obligation of States with respect to expropriation'.[230] It has been pointed out that States have accepted these conditions for lawful expropriation as 'legally binding in contexts *not* governed by BITs'.[231]

Although older BITs were less consistent on this question,[232] most recent BITs now contain these four conditions.[233] The present author's own survey of approximately 479 BITs from 28 representative countries from all continents (including both developing and developed States) shows that these four conditions were found in 345 BITs, while the remaining 134 contain only some of these conditions (but not all four of them).[234] Also, almost all of the BITs examined (except for 10)

---

[229] UNCTAD, 'Expropriation', UNCTAD Series on Issues in International Investment Agreements II (2012), p. 27 ('An overwhelming majority of IIAs allow States to expropriate investments as long as the taking is effected according to [these four] criteria (. . .). IIAs may display some difference in formulations (. . .) but in general, these four conditions have not changed or otherwise evolved in recent years (. . .). They have crystallized sufficiently to represent customary international law on Expropriation'). See also UNCTAD, 'International Investment Agreements; Key Issues' (2004), p. 235.

[230] See, US Model BIT (2004), Annex B; Dominican Republic-Central America-United States Free Trade Agreement (2006 to 2009), Annex 10-C; US-Rwanda BIT (2008), Annex A; US-Uruguay BIT (2005), Annex A; US-Chile FTA (2004), Annex 10-A; US-Singapore FTA (2004), Arts. 15.5 and 15.6 (with letter exchange between the two countries, 6 May 2013, using the same expression to define custom).

[231] Reisman and Sloane, 'Indirect Expropriation', p. 150, emphasis added.

[232] See, Mohamed Khalil, 'Treatment of Foreign Investment in BITs', *ICSID Rev.*, 7(2) (1992), p. 350. This study is discussed in: Kishoiyian, 'The Utility of Bilateral Investment Treaties', p. 358, noting that 'of the 335 BITs surveyed in the ICSID study, 309 make the furtherance of public interest a condition precedent for embarking on any measures of expropriation. of these BITs require that the measure should be non-discriminatory and not in breach of any specific commitment not to expropriate. 24 BITs fail to expressly stipulate the furtherance of public interest as a condition for expropriation, but merely provide that the measure should be nondiscriminatory and not inconsistent with a specific commitment not to expropriate'.

[233] UNCTAD, 'Bilateral Investment Treaties 1995–2006', p. 47 ('A survey of the BITs concluded since 1995 reveals a remarkable degree of convergence with respect to the conditions required to make expropriations lawful. Most agreements include the four substantive requirements').

[234] In 2011, the present author received funding from the Canadian Federal Government ('SSHRC') to investigate the existing rules of customary international law in the field of international investment law. This project is hereinafter referred to as 'P. Dumberry, *Rules of Customary International Law in the Field of International Investment Law*, SSHRC Research Project (2012–2014)'.

prohibited both direct and indirect expropriation.[235] Another recent
study of sixty-three BITs signed in the period from 2011 to 2013 has
shown that all of them mentioned these four conditions.[236]

Finally, it should be added that the present author has recently
examined 165 different domestic laws on foreign investment from
some 160 States.[237] The results show that out of these 165 domestic
laws, only 22 of them actually refer explicitly to the four conditions
(public purpose, non-discriminatory, due process of law, compensation)
under which an expropriation is considered legal. A large number of
other laws (66) refer instead to a combination of two or three of these
different conditions (but not all of them). Finally, only a few laws (11)
contain vague reference to compensation. What is striking is that a large
number of the domestic laws examined do not contain any provision
dealing with expropriation (some of them containing no provision on
investment protection at all). In sum, while the four conditions under
which an expropriation is considered legal are systematically contained
in modern BITs, the same is not true regarding host States' own domestic
laws on investments.

Second, with respect to compensation, it has been argued by writers,[238]
and by arbitral tribunals,[239] that the standard of compensation under
customary international law is 'full' compensation. The present author's

---

[235] *Ibid.*

[236] Anna Kuprieieva, 'Regulatory Freedom and Indirect Expropriation: Seeking
Compatibility With Sustainable Development In New Generation of Bilateral
Investment Treaties', Master of Laws Thesis, University of Ottawa, 2015, p. 88
(Disclaimer: the present author acted as an examiner).

[237] P. Dumberry, *Rules of Customary International Law in the Field of International
Investment Law.* In the context of this analysis, a survey was first made of the investment
laws contained in ICSID's *Investment Laws of the World* compilation, which is updated
twice a year. Then, the investment laws of the remaining countries were retrieved online
through official government websites or, alternatively, through general online search
engines.

[238] Gazzini, 'The Role of Customary International Law', p. 714; Newcombe and Paradell,
Law and Practice of Investment Treaties, pp. 332, 378; Kinsella and Rubins, *International
Investment, Political Risk, and Dispute Resolution*, p. 157; Nigel Blackaby, Constantine
Partasides, Alan Redfern and J. Martin H. Hunter, *Redfern and Hunter on International
Arbitration* (Oxford: Oxford University Press, 2009), p. 503; Schill, *The
Multilateralization of International Investment Law*, p. 84; Congyan, 'International
Investment Treaties and the Formation', p. 670; ILA, 'Report', by Andrea K. Bjorklund
and August Reinisch, ILA Study Group on the Role of Soft-Law Instruments in
International Investment Law, ILA Conference, Sofia (2012), p. 2.

[239] *CME Czech Republic B.V.* v. *Czech Republic*, UNCITRAL, Final Award, 14 March 2003,
para. 497.

own survey of 479 BITs shows that the overwhelming majority (452 treaties) specifically refer to 'prompt, adequate and effective' compensation.[240] The vast majority of them (389) also specifically refer to 'fair market value' as the valuation method of compensation.[241] Again, this situation contrasts with older BITs, which show less consistency on this question.[242] In a recent study, UNCTAD noted an 'increasing level of convergence regarding the standard of compensation' included in BITs with 'most of them' incorporating the Hull standard.[243] The report concluded that 'appropriate' compensation (not full compensation) 'may still represent the standard of customary international law'.[244] While other writers have stated that the Hull formula does not represent custom today,[245] an OECD Report concluded that 'nowadays, the Hull formula and its variations are often used and accepted and considered as part of customary international law'.[246]

Whether or not *full* compensation (i.e., the Hull formula) has acquired a customary status remains controversial.[247] Suffice it to say that if it were

---

[240] Dumberry, *Rules of Customary International Law in the Field of International Investment Law*. It should be added that a small number of those BITs (6) did not use the word 'adequate' but instead referred to 'fair market value'.

[241] *Ibid.*

[242] See, Khalil, 'Treatment of Foreign Investment in BITs', p. 350. This study is discussed in: Kishoiyian, 'The Utility of Bilateral Investment Treaties', p. 351, noting that out of the 335 BITs surveyed 167 BITs adopted the Hull formula, 47 used the terms 'just', 'full', 'reasonable' or 'fair and equitable' compensation and the rest referred to 'appropriate' compensation.

[243] UNCTAD, 'Expropriation' (2012), p. 40. See also: UNCTAD, 'Bilateral Investment Treaties 1995–2006', p. 52, indicating that the 'overwhelming majority of BITs' refer to the Hull formula.

[244] UNCTAD, 'Expropriation', p. 41, see also at p. 111. Reaching the same conclusion: Kishoiyian, 'The Utility of Bilateral Investment Treaties', p. 361; Surya P. Subedi, *International Investment Law: Reconciling Policy and Principle* (Hart Publ., 2008), pp. 142–143, arguing that the rules of custom have not changed since the 1962 General Assembly *Resolution on Permanent Sovereignty over Natural Resources*.

[245] See, Sornarajah, *The International Law on Foreign Investment*, pp. 441–443 ('It is safe to conclude that there is no customary practice supporting the norm of full compensation for expropriation'); Al Faruque, 'Creating Customary International Law through Bilateral Investment Treaties', p. 306 ('State practice of BITs widely varies regarding the standard of compensation'); Kishoiyian, 'The Utility of Bilateral Investment Treaties', pp. 358–359, 361; A. Reinisch, 'Legality of Expropriations' in A. Reinisch (ed.), *Standards of Investment Protection* (Oxford: Oxford University Press, 2008), p. 194. Similarly, for Guzman, 'Why LDCs Sign Treaties That Hurt Them', pp. 641, 651, the Hull formula ceased to exist as a rule of custom in the 1970s as a result of the objection by developing States.

[246] OECD, 'Indirect Expropriation', p. 2.

[247] The issue is further discussed below, see Chapter 3, Section 3.3.3.2.2.5.

indeed the case, it would represent quite an astonishing evolution given the fact that the Hull formula had been declared by most writers in the 1980s as no longer representative of custom. It is worth recalling that the United States 'developed its BIT model in reaction to the challenge at the United Nations to traditional norms of State responsibility to aliens'[248] and that it 'believed that a network of treaties embracing this principle [the Hull rule] would be one highly visible way of building state practice in support of that traditional position'.[249] One can deduce that the United States has in fact presently achieved that very goal. One author stated that 'the overwhelming majority of State practice in this field in the last few decades has been through the medium of treaty-making', which resulted in 'starving custom of independent progressive development'.[250] The evolution of the Hull formula would suggest, on the contrary, that BITs practice has not 'starved' custom of any progress, but has in fact *contributed* to its development. In any event, as will be further discussed in the next chapter,[251] for the Hull formula to transform into a customary rule, two conditions must be met.

---

[248] Alvarez, 'The Public International Law Regime Governing International Investment', p. 270. See also: Kenneth J. Vandevelde, 'U.S. Bilateral Investment Treaties: The Second Wave', *Michigan JIL* 14 (1993), p. 625; Thomas, 'Reflections on Article 1105 of NAFTA', p. 48.

[249] Kenneth J. Vandevelde, 'The BIT Program: A Fifteen-Year Appraisal', *ASIL Proc.* 86 (1992), pp. 532, 534. See also: E. Denza and S. Brooks, 'Investment Protection Treaties: United Kingdom Experience', *ICLQ* 36 (1987), p. 912 (examining UK's BITs); Alvarez, 'The Public International Law Regime Governing International Investment', p. 270 ('the US Model BIT of 1987, like many other BITs, is, at least in part, an explicit effort to provide investors with the traditional protections of customary law, including the international minimum standard and protections against denials of justice and assurances of full protection and security').

[250] McLachlan, 'Investment Treaties and General International Law', p. 365.

[251] See, Chapter 3, Section 3.3.3.2.1.

3

State practice

Introduction

As previously mentioned, under Article 38(1)b of the Statute of the International Court of Justice (ICJ) the formation of a rule of 'international custom' requires a 'general practice' by States which is 'accepted as law'.[1] This chapter examines the first requirement necessary to demonstrate the existence of any customary rule: State practice. Before doing so, I will first briefly discuss the preliminary (and yet fundamental) question of *whose* practice actually matters for the creation of customary rules. In other words, I will enquire as to whether or not the practice of non-State actors is relevant to the phenomenon of custom creation in both general international law and investor-State arbitration (Section 3.1). The next section will examine the basic requirements for the practice of States to be considered relevant in the process of creating customary norms. I will show that the practice of States needs to be uniform, consistent, extensive and representative for a rule of custom to emerge (Section 3.2). I will specifically examine whether this is the case regarding the fair and equitable treatment (FET) standard found in the vast majority of BITs.

The objective of this chapter is to analyse the different 'manifestations' of practice, that is, the types of evidence of State practice that are relevant for the creation of custom in both general international law and investor-State arbitration (Section 3.3). I will start by making a number of introductory remarks on the requirement that the practice be public and whether or not omissions should count as practice (Section 3.3.1). I will also examine the variety of forms of State practice and their relative weight (Section 3.3.2). I will then specifically examine four different categories of 'manifestations' of State practice.

First, I will assess the role of treaties (Section 3.3.3). I will observe that treaties can contribute to the formation of new rules of customary

[1] Art. 38, Statute of the I.C.J., reprinted in International Court of Justice, Charter of the United Nations, Statute and Rules of Court and other Documents 61 (No. 4 1978).

international law and that they can also codify existing customary rules. In the context of arbitration, I will examine the strict conditions under which rules contained in BITs can transform into customary rules and the reason why such transformation is very rare in practice. In this context, I will analyse the controversial proposition made by some scholars that all BITs *taken together* represent a 'new' custom.

Second, I will consider the role of statements as evidence of State practice under general international law (Section 3.3.4). I will focus on the different types of statements that are relevant in the field of investor-State arbitration, including State pleadings in arbitration proceedings. I will also examine other types of statements that have a particular importance in this field of law, including interventions by non-disputing treaty parties during arbitration proceedings, official statements made by parties to a treaty, joint statements by States parties to a treaty on matters of interpretation and Model BITs adopted by States. My analysis will not only explore whether these different types of statements should be considered as State practice, but also the actual weight which they should be given, depending on a number of factors and circumstances.

Third, this chapter will explore the issue of State conduct within international organizations as evidence of relevant practice for the creation of custom, in both general international law and in the field of investor-State arbitration (Section 3.3.5). Another question addressed in this section will be the impact of the practice of international organizations on the formation of customary rules.

Fourth, I will investigate the question of internal national practice as being relevant evidence of State practice (Section 3.3.6). In other words, should the conduct of the legislative and the judiciary branches of government be considered as State practice, and if so, what weight should they be given?

Finally, I will briefly address the question of the role and relevance (if any) of arbitral awards in the formation of custom as well as in its development and evolution (Section 3.4).

3.1   Whose practice matters?

International investment law is arguably the sphere of international law in which non-State actors play the greatest role.[2] In fact, as noted by one

---

[2] P. Dumberry and E. Labelle Eastaugh, 'Non-State Actors in International Investment Law: The Legal Personality of Corporations and NGOs in the Context of Investor-State Arbitration', in Jean d'Aspremont (ed.), *Participants in the International Legal System: Multiples Perspectives on Non-State Actors in International Law* (London: Routledge-Cavendish, 2011), p. 360.

writer, 'that regime is itself arguably a product of non-State actors, at least to the extent that the State originators of BITs were responding to demands from private entrepreneurs dissatisfied with diplomatic espousal and seeking increased forms of international protection'.[3] The question addressed in this section is whether or not the practice of *foreign investors* (both corporations and individuals) counts in the formation of customary rules in the field of international investment law.

3.1.1   Non-State actors do not directly participate in the creation of customary rules

As previously mentioned, Article 38(1) of the ICJ Statute uses the expression 'international custom, as evidence of a general practice accepted as law'. While there is no explicit reference to the practice being necessarily that of States, it is generally recognized that 'for practice to be relevant for the formation of customary international law it must be attributable to the State'.[4] There is (almost) unanimous agreement amongst scholars that what matters is indeed the practice of *States*.[5] This is also the conclusion reached by the ICJ.[6] Specifically, State practice means 'the

---

[3] José E. Alvarez, 'The Public International Law Regime Governing International Investment', *Rec. des cours* 344 (2009), p. 483.

[4] International Law Commission, 'Second Report on Identification of Customary International Law', by Michael Wood, Special Rapporteur, Sixty-sixth session, Geneva, 5 May-6 June and 7 July-8 August 2014, UN doc. A/CN.4/672, p. 17 [hereinafter referred to as ILC, Second Report, 2014].

[5] See, for instance: G.J.H. van Hoof, *Rethinking the Sources of International Law* (Deventer, Kluwer, 1983), p. 63; Maurice H. Mendelson, 'The Formation of Customary International Law', *Rec. des cours* 192 (1985), p. 203; Y. Dinstein, 'The Interaction between Customary International Law and Treaties', *Rec. des cours* 322 (2006), p. 266; H.W.A. Thirlway, *International Customary Law and Codification* (Leiden: Sijthoff, 1972), p. 58; Mark E. Villiger, *Customary International Law and Treaties: A Manual on the Theory and Practice of the Interrelation of Sources* (2nd edn., The Hague: Kluwer, 1997), pp. 16–17; A.M. Weisburd, 'Customary International Law: The Problem of Treaties', *Vand. J. Transnat'l L.*, 21 (1988), p. 5; J. d'Aspremont, 'Conclusion: Inclusive Law-Making and Law-Enforcement Processes for an Exclusive International Legal System', in J. d'Aspremont (ed.), *Participants in the International Legal System* (London: Routledge, 2011), p. 430; M. Byers, *Custom, Power and the Power of Rules: International Relations and Customary International Law* (Cambridge: Cambridge University Press, 1999), pp. 78–79, 86; ILC, Second Report, 2014, p. 16; Michael Wood and Omri Sender, 'State Practice', in Rüdiger Wolfrum (ed.), *Max Planck Encyclopedia of Public International Law* (Oxford: Oxford University Press, 2013).

[6] *Jurisdictional Immunities of the State (Germany v. Italy: Greece intervening)*, Judgment, ICJ Rep. 2012, p. 99, p. 143, para. 101. See also, other cases referred to in: ILC, Second Report, 2014, p. 16.

practice of the executive, legislative and judicial organs of the State'[7] (this question is further examined below[8]). In accordance with Article 4 of the ILC *Articles on the Responsibility of States for Internationally Wrongful Acts*,[9] State practice also includes the conduct of entities (and even individuals) who act as *de facto* organs of the State, as well as that of the internal political subdivisions of a State (provinces, States, autonomous regions, etc.)[10]

Although the idea is not new,[11] a number of writers have argued in recent years that the practice of non-governmental organizations (NGOs) and individuals has also contributed to the formation of custom.[12]

---

[7] International Law Association, 'Statement of Principles Applicable to the Formation of General Customary International Law', Final Report of the Committee on the Formation of Customary Law, Conference Report London (2000), p. 17 [hereinafter ILA, Final Report, 2000]; ILC, Second Report, 2014, pp. 17–18.

[8] See, Chapter 3, Section 3.3.6.

[9] *Titles and Texts of the Draft Articles on Responsibility of States for Internationally Wrongful Acts Adopted by the Drafting Committee on Second Reading*, 26 July 2001, U. N. Doc. A/CN.4/L.602/Rev.1.ILC [hereinafter referred to as ILC, *Draft Articles on Responsibility of States*].

[10] See, however, ILA, Final Report, 2000, p. 16, noting that the conduct of such subdivisions 'which do not enjoy separate international legal personality do not as such normally constitute State practice, unless carried out on behalf of the State or adopted ("ratified") by it'.

[11] Lazare Koplemanas, 'Custom as a Means of the Creation of International Law', *British YIL*, 18 (1937), p. 151 ('all the subjects of law which are in close or even distant touch with international relations contribute to the formation of international custom').

[12] See, for instance, the following writers: Isabelle R. Gunning, 'Modernizing Customary International Law: The Challenge of Human Rights', *Virginia JIL* 31 (1991), p. 221; Jordan Paust, 'The Complex Nature, Sources and Evidences of Customary Human Rights', *Ga. J. Int'l & Comp. L.* 25 (1996), p. 155; Christiana Ochoa, 'The Individual and Customary International Law Formation', *Virginia JIL* 48 (2007), p. 140; Till Muller, 'Customary Transnational Law: Attacking the Last Resort of State Sovereignty: Conference on Democracy and the Transnational Private Sector,' *Ind. J. Global Legal Stud.* 15 (2008), pp. 31–47; C. Steer, 'Non-State Actors in International Criminal Law', in J. d'Aspremont (ed.), *Participants in the International Legal System: Multiple Perspectives on Non-State Actors in International Law* (London: Routledge, 2011), pp. 295–310; Jordan J., Paust, 'Non-State Actor Participation in International Law and the Pretense of Exclusion', *Virginia JIL* 51(4) (2011), p. 977; N. Arajärvi, 'From State-Centricism to Where? The Formation of (Customary) International Law and Non-State Actors', SSRN (2010); Robert McCorquodale, 'An Inclusive International Legal System', *Leiden J. Int'l L.* 17 (2004), pp. 479–480, 496. See also, the analysis of Anthea Roberts and Sandesh Sivakumaran, 'Lawmaking by Nonstate Actors: Engaging Armed Groups in the Creation of International Humanitarian Law', *Yale JIL* 37 (2012), p. 107 (outlining a number of justifications for granting non-state actors a role in lawmaking, but concluding that this question depends on the advantages and disadvantages of recognizing such a role for that particular type of actor). For the authors, p. 110, 'recognizing a limited lawmaking role for some armed groups [in the creation of international humanitarian law applicable in non-international armed conflicts] could create significant benefits (such as increasing a sense of ownership and compliance) and that some of the possible costs of doing so have

D'Aspremont calls it the 'illusion of heterogeneity' of the international law-making process.[13] The reality is that non-State actors do not participate *directly* in the creation of customary norms. This proposition is widely endorsed by scholars,[14] the ILC Special Rapporteur Wood,[15] and the ILA's Committee on 'non-State actors' in its Second Report of 2012.[16]

been overplayed (such as inappropriately legitimizing armed groups and affecting their legal status)'. See also, the comment by J. Pauwelyn, 'Treaty Regimes and *opinio juris*', paper presented at the conference 'The Role of *Opinio Juris* in Customary International Law', Duke-Geneva Institute in Transnational Law, Geneva, 2013, p. 4.

[13] J. d'Aspremont, 'The Doctrinal Illusion of Heterogenity of International Lawmaking Processes', in H. Ruiz-Fabri, R. Wolfrum, and J. Gogolin (eds.), *Select Proceedings of the European Society of International Law* (Oxford: Hart, vol. 2, 2010), p. 6 ('There is no doubt that, whatever the influence of these non-State actors may be, States remain the exclusive international lawmakers. The upstream influence wielded by some non-State actors can help ignite new lawmaking initiative or orientate ongoing lawmaking under-takings but this is insufficient to elevate these actors to the status of lawmakers. Indeed, no formal international lawmaking powers have been bestowed upon these actors and States always retain the final word').

[14] van Hoof, *Rethinking the Sources of International Law*, p. 63.; A.C. Arend, *Legal Rules and International Society* (New York: Oxford University Press, 1999), p. 176; J. d'Aspermont, 'Inclusive Law-Making and Law-Enforcement Processes for an Exclusive International Legal System', in J. d'Aspremont (ed.), *Participants in the International Legal System: Multiple Perspectives on Non-State Actors in International Law* (London: Routledge, 2011), pp. 425, 430; Mendelson, 'The Formation of Customary International Law', p. 203.

[15] ILC, Second Report, 2014, p. 30. It should be added that Draft Conclusion 5 of the ILC 'Proposed draft conclusions on the identification of customary international law' initially read as follows: 'The requirement, as an element of customary international law, of a general practice means that it is primarily the practice of States that contributes to the creation, or expression, of rules of customary international law.' It was later decided (International Law Commission, 'Third Report on Identification of Customary International Law', by Michael Wood, Special Rapporteur, Sixty-seventh session, Geneva, 4 May-5 June and 6 July-7 August 2014, A/CN.4/682 [hereinafter referred to as ILC, Third Report, 2015], p. 54) to delete the word 'primarily' and to add this new paragraph: 'Conduct by other non-State actors is not practice for the purposes of forma-tion or identification of customary international law'). It should be added that in International Law Commission, 'Text of the Draft Conclusions Provisionally adopted by the Drafting Committee, Sixty-seventh session, Geneva, 4 May-5 June and 6 July-7 August 2014, 14 July 2015, A/CN.4/L.869 [hereinafter referred to as ILC, Draft Conclusions, 2015], conclusion no. 4 reads as follows: '1. The requirement, as a consti-tuent element of customary international law, of a general practice means that it is primarily the practice of States that contribute to the formation, or expression, of rules of customary international law; 2. In certain cases, the practice of international organiza-tions also contributes to the formation, or expression, of rules of customary international law; 3. Conduct of other actors is not practice that contributes to the formation, or expression, of rules of customary international law, but may be relevant when assessing the practice referred to in paragraphs 1 and 2'.

[16] ILA, 'Second Report of the Committee Non-State Actors in International Law: Lawmaking and Participation Rights', Committee on 'Non State Actors' (2012), p. 5.

The only exception is the International Committee of the Red Cross (ICRC), which has been recognized as having an international legal personality[17] and whose work has been qualified by the International Criminal Tribunal for the former Yugoslavia (ICTY) in the *Tadic* case as 'an element of actual international practice', which 'has been conspicuously instrumental in the emergence or crystallisation of customary rules'.[18] Interestingly, while the ICRC considers its *own* practice (statements) as relevant in the formation of custom in the field of international humanitarian laws,[19] it believes that the practice of armed opposition groups 'does not constitute State practice as such'.[20] It should be added that the US government has criticized the ICRC study on the rules of custom in the field of humanitarian law for giving 'undue weight to statements by non-governmental organizations and the ICRC itself, when those statements do not reflect whether a particular rule constitutes customary international law accepted by States'.[21]

While it is true that non-State actors do not *directly* participate in the *creation* of custom,[22] this does not mean that their conduct and participation in debates is completely *irrelevant* to the phenomenon of custom creation.[23] Thus, as one writer noted, 'nonstate actors such as nongovernmental organizations and corporations often have an impact on

[17] See, *inter alia*: C. Dominicé, 'La personnalité juridique internationale du CICR', in C. Swinarski (ed.), *Studies and Essays on International Humanitarian Law and Red Cross Principles in Honour of Jean Pictet* (The Hague: Nijhoff/Geneva: ICRC, 1984), p. 663; P. Reuter, 'La personnalité juridique internationale du Comité international de la Croix-Rouge', *Ibid.*, p. 783.

[18] *Prosecutor* v. *Tadic*, Decision on the Defence Motion for Interlocutory Appeal on Jurisdiction, 2 October 1995, para. 109.

[19] Jean-Marie Henckaerts and Louise Doswald-Beck (eds.), *Customary International Humanitarian Law* (Cambridge: Cambridge University Press, 2005, vol. I), pp. 40–41.

[20] *Ibid.*, p. vii. On this question, see, Roberts and Sivakumaran, 'Lawmaking by Nonstate Actors'.

[21] J.B. Bellinger and W.J. Haynes, 'A US Government Response to the International Committee of the Red Cross Study on Customary International Humanitarian Law', *Int Rev Red Cross* 89 (866) (2007), p. 445.

[22] Mendelson, 'The Formation of Customary International Law', p. 203; Dinstein, 'The Interaction between Customary International Law and Treaties', p. 267; Karsten Nowrot, 'Legal Consequences of Globalization: The Status of NGO's Under International Law', *Ind. J. Global Legal Stud.* 6 (1999), pp. 591–595; John King Gamble and Charlotte Ku, 'International Law—New Actors and New Technologies: Center Stage for NGOs?', *Law & Pol'y Int'l. Bus.* 31 (2000), p. 243.

[23] Dinstein, 'The Interaction between Customary International Law and Treaties', p. 268 ('behind the corporate veil of the fictitious entity of the State, there are of course human beings (. . .) [who] participate in the process of treaty-making and of shaping customary international law').

custom'.[24] The conduct of non-State actors may contribute to the customary process in its 'extended sense' when it is 'carried out on behalf of the State or adopted' by a State.[25] For instance, Wolfke argues that 'captains of private vessels, fishermen and pearldivers fishing in their own name in certain areas of the sea contribute, by their conduct to the development of international customs concerning open sea, territorial sea, the continental shelf, etc.'.[26] Yet, the ILA explains that such practice should not be considered as constituting a *direct* source in the creation of custom, but rather as its 'material, historical or indirect' source.[27] In other words, the practice of these actors has influenced the development of custom through its endorsement and adoption by States.[28] In that sense, it is undeniable that non-State actors 'can contribute *indirectly* to the formation' of custom.[29] It is true that in the context of State contracts, individuals and companies can directly participate in the elaboration of legal norms, which may over time develop into customary rules. In that sense, non-State actors may have a 'direct' influence on the formation of custom. Yet, even in this context, these rules simply *cannot* develop without the consent of States (the other party to these contracts).[30] It is difficult to imagine how private actors could develop *between themselves* customary rules which would then be *imposed* on States.[31] In any event, this scenario is improbable in the field of investor-State

---

[24] A.E. Roberts, 'Traditional and Modern Approaches to Customary International Law: A Reconciliation', *AJIL* 95(4) (2001), p. 775 ('[NGOs] have an indirect effect by influencing state behavior and statements through actions such as lobbying and calling boycotts. They have assisted in setting the agenda for international conferences and participated in the negotiation and drafting of treaties and resolutions. Nongovernmental organizations help to articulate emerging customs and monitor state compliance with international law by investigating and publicizing breaches of the law in areas such as human rights and environmental protection'). See also: J. Mertus, 'Considering Nonstate Actors in the New Millennium: Toward Expanded Participation in Norm Generation and Norm Application', *International Law and Politics*, 32 (2000), p. 562.

[25] ILA, Final Report, 2000, p. 16; Villiger, *Customary International Law and Treaties*, pp. 16–17. See also: ILC, *Draft Articles on Responsibility of States*, at Article 11, whereby attribution to the State will occur only 'if and to the extent that the State acknowledges and adopts the conduct in question as its own'.

[26] Karol Wolfke, *Custom in Present International Law* (2nd edn., Dordrecht: Nijhoff, 1993), p. 85. See also: K. Wolfke, 'Some Persistent Controversies Regarding Customary International Law', *NYBIL* 24 (1993), p. 4.

[27] ILA, 'Second Report of the Committee Non-State Actors', p. 6.

[28] Dinstein, 'The Interaction between Customary International Law and Treaties', p. 271.

[29] ILA, 'Second Report of the Committee Non-State Actors', p. 6 (emphasis in the original).

[30] Nguyen Quoc Dinh, Patrick Dallier, Mathias Forteau and Alain Pellet, *Droit International Public* (8th edn., Paris: LGDJ, 2007), p. 358.

[31] This is, however, the position adopted by Nguyen, *Ibid.*, p. 363.

arbitration. The issue surrounding the contribution of international organizations to the formation of customary law is a much more complex question which will further be examined separately in Section 3.3.5.[32]

The situation is not any different in investor-State arbitration. Thus, the practice of foreign investors (both corporations and individuals) *does not* count in the formation of customary rules in the field of international investment law.

It is important to mention the idea developed by d'Aspremont, who believes that the practice of non-State actors does *not* contribute directly to the formation of custom.[33] In his opinion, even if one were to adopt the opposite view, the fact remains that the practice of non-State actors could only be taken into account to ascertain norms that govern their *own* behaviour, not that of others.[34] One could certainly envisage, for instance, that the practice of armed groups *directly involved* in conflicts could contribute to the creation of customary norms regulating *their own* conduct.[35] The same logic, however, should not apply to other actors that are *not* directly involved in armed conflicts (such as NGOs).[36]

---

[32] See, Chapter 3, Section 3.3.5.

[33] d'Aspremont, 'Conclusion: Inclusive Law-Making and Law-Enforcement Processes', p. 430.

[34] *Ibid.*, p. 430. See, in support: ILA, 'Second Report of the Committee Non-State Actors', p. 6.

[35] ILA, 'Second Report of the Committee Non-State Actors', p. 6, indicating that the 'Committee has some sympathy for the proposal to give non-State armed groups a role in the formation of "quasi-custom", to "allow armed groups to play *some* role in the creation of customary norms without ceding all, or even equal, control to armed groups"' (emphasis added).

[36] Jean d'Aspremont, 'Customary International Law as a Dance Floor: Part II', *EJIL Talks!*, 15 April 2014 ('international lawyers have been forced to resort to all new sorts of nets and traps to hunt and capture practice where there was none. (. . .) The stratagems and ploys which are being used to "discover" practice are numerous and well-known. (. . .) Another ruse to discover practice involves a move away from the self-generating character of customary international law. According to that stratagem, customary rules are no longer emerging by virtue of the behaviour and beliefs of those actors whom those rules are meant to apply to. This means, for instance, that the practice of international organisations or that of non-state actors is said to be instrumental in the crystallisation of purely inter-state rules. In that sense, third-party practice becomes a source of practice for the sake of customary international law. This is so even if the practice of that third party is purely virtual. In the same vein, non-state actors who are not engaged as belligerent in armed conflicts are sometimes said to generate practice for customary rules prescribing how States should behave as belligerent on the battle field. It is probably here that the newly experienced emancipation from the constraints of customary international law reaches its apex. This is also where the creativity witnessed in the hunt for practice illustrates the best how wild the revelling can go on the dance floor of customary law when it is late night'). See, however, Muller, 'Customary Transnational Law', p. 28, noting

In my opinion, it is difficult to understand how the aforementioned scenario could find application in the world of investment arbitration. Arbitration under BITs basically regulates *the behaviour of host States* towards foreign investors, not the other way around. Under the vast majority of BITs, arbitral tribunals only have jurisdiction to adjudicate claims brought *by investors*, and not those submitted by the host State of the investment. In any event, the investor is not a party to the BITs and has not consented to arbitration. Nonetheless, there are a limited number of BITs that expressly allow a State to institute arbitral proceedings against an investor.[37] Yet, in order to bring a claim under a BIT, the respondent State must show that the investor has breached one of its *rights* contained *in that treaty*. Currently, BITs are asymmetrical (and imbalanced) insofar as investors are accorded substantive rights (without being subject to any specific obligations), while States only have *obligations*.[38] In other words, an investor simply cannot breach any *rights* of the host State under these treaties since no such rights actually exist. This is why no BIT claim has ever been commenced by a host State against an investor under the ICSID Convention.[39] The situation is different under State contracts where both parties have rights and obligations. Yet, it is only in rare situations that corporations are acting as respondents in claims submitted by States (or State-owned entities) alleging violation of their rights under a contract. Only five such claims have been identified under ICSID.[40] In sum, even if one were to consider the conduct of foreign investors as contributing to the formation of customary rules *specifically applicable to them*, it remains that in reality it would have almost no practical impact. This is because investment

---

that the ICTY refers to the practice and statements of non-State actors to assess customary norms.

[37] Helene Bubrowski, 'Counterclaims', in A. De Mestral and C. Lévesque (eds.), *Improving International Investment Treaties: Negotiation, Substantive Obligations and Dispute Resolution* (London: Routledge, 2013), p. 221. These treaties generally contain broadly worded dispute resolution clauses referring, for instance, to 'disputes with respect to investments', 'all disputes', 'any disputes' or 'any legal disputes'.

[38] See, discussion in: Mehmet Toral and Thomas Schultz, 'The State, a Perpetual Respondent in Investment Arbitration? Some Unorthodox Considerations', in Michael Waibel, Asha Kaushal, Kyo-Hwa Liz Chung and Claire Balchin (eds.), *The Backlash Against Investment Arbitration: Perceptions And Reality* (Alphen aan den Rijn: Kluwer Law International, 2010), p. 577.

[39] Gustavo Laborde, 'The Case for Host State Claims in Investment Arbitration', *J. Int Disp Settl*, 1(1) (2010), p. 102.

[40] Toral and Schultz, 'The State, a Perpetual Respondent in Investment Arbitration?', p. 589 (discussing these cases).

tribunals (almost) never have to assess the legality of the conduct of investors in violation of contracts or treaty obligations.

Finally, it is important to note that for a number of writers, the main reason why States are the only actors that can participate directly in the formation of customary rules is because they are the *only* subjects of international law with an international legal personality.[41] This question is further explored in the next section.

3.1.2 The international legal personality of corporations and their international law-making powers

As explained by one writer, 'many opponents of direct non-state actor participation argue that non-state actors are already excluded from any participation because they are mere objects or only partial subjects of international law'.[42] In my view, the international legal personality of non-State actors and their law-making capacity are separate issues.[43] In other words, from the conclusion that the practice of foreign investors is *not* relevant to the formation of customary rules in the field of international investment law, it should *not* necessarily be concluded that corporations do not have an international legal personality.

What does it mean to have an 'international legal personality'? To say that corporations (who represent the vast majority of foreign investors) possess an international legal personality is not to say that they are co-equal with States. As famously stated by the ICJ in the *Reparations* case, 'subjects of law in any legal system are not necessarily identical in their nature or in the extent of their rights, and their nature depends upon the needs of the community'.[44] In other words, not all international legal persons are created equal. States occupy a unique place in the international legal order, serving as both the source and the object of legal norms. It is, after all, appropriate that States should possess certain powers and privileges denied to other entities. However, it has long been recognized that as the primary subjects of international law, States have

---

[41] Byers, *Custom, Power and the Power of Rules*, pp. 78–79.

[42] Muller, 'Customary Transnational Law', p. 31.

[43] See also: d'Aspremont, 'The Doctrinal Illusion of Heterogenity', p. 8; Roberts and Sivakumaran, 'Lawmaking by Nonstate Actors', p. 112; Andrew Clapham, *Human Rights Obligations of Non-State Actors* (Oxford: Oxford University Press, 2006), pp. 28–29.

[44] *Reparations for Injuries Suffered in the Service of the United Nations*, Advisory Opinion, ICJ Rep. 1947, p. 179.

the power to create new non-State legal persons through their mutual consent.[45]

For the ICJ, the international personality of the United Nations means that it is 'a subject of international law', which is 'capable of possessing international rights and duties' and has 'the capacity to maintain its rights by bringing international claims'.[46] In other words, possession of a legal personality gives an entity the right to bring a claim against a State before an international tribunal. The analytical framework developed by the Court in the *Reparations* case has since been endorsed in doctrine.[47] It has also been applied in other contexts in reverse order: the fact that an entity has been granted direct right of action has been used as evidence that it possesses international legal personality. For example, some authors have concluded that private individuals are subjects of international human rights law when, as in the case of the *European Convention on Human Rights*, they are given a direct right of action against a State before an international tribunal.[48]

Corporations possess both substantive rights and the ability to bring claims on the basis of those rights before international tribunals under 'State contracts'[49] and under modern bilateral and multilateral investment treaties. Although this is controversial in doctrine,[50] the present author has argued elsewhere that in both situations corporations should be considered

[45] W.C. Jenks, 'Multinational Entities in the Law of Nations', in *Transnational Law in a Changing Society: Essays in Honor of Philip C. Jessup* (New York: Columbia University Press, 1972), pp. 74–75; G. Schwarzenberger, *International Law* (vol. I, London: Stevens and Sons, 1957), p. 146.

[46] *Reparations for Injuries Suffered in the Service of the United Nations*, p. 179.

[47] C. Berezowski, 'Les problèmes de la subjectivité internationale', in V. Ibler (ed.), *Mélanges offerts à Juraj Andrassy* (The Hague: Martinus Nijhoff Publ., 1968), pp. 33–35; J.A. Barberis, 'Nouvelles questions concernant la personnalité juridique internationale', *Rec. des cours* 179 (1983-I), pp. 168–169.

[48] Article 34, *Convention for the Protection of Human Rights and Fundamental Freedom*, Protocol 11 of 1st November 1998. In doctrine, see: C. Dominicé, 'L'émergence de l'individu en droit international public' *Annales d'études internationales* 16 (1987–1988), p. 8; K.P. Menon, 'The Legal Personality of Individuals', *Sri Lanka J. Int'l L.* 6 (1994), pp. 127–128; Alexander Orakhelashvili, 'The Position of the Individual in International Law', *Cal. W.Int'l.J.* 31 (2001), p. 264; Edwin W. Tucker, 'Has the Individual Become the Subject of International Law?', *U. Cin. L. Rev.* 34 (1965), pp. 341, 345.

[49] P. Dumberry, 'International Investment Contracts', in T. Gazzini and E. de Brabandere (eds.), *International Investment Law. The Sources of Rights and Obligations* (Leiden; Boston: Martinus Nijhoff Publ., 2012), pp. 215–243.

[50] For an overview of the controversy, see: P. Dumberry, 'L'entreprise, sujet de droit international? Retour sur la question à la lumière des développements récents du droit international des investissements', *RGDIP*, 108(1) (2004), pp. 103–122.

as having an international legal personality.[51] The present author, however, does not suggest that corporations should be considered as *full* subjects of international law having equal standing alongside States.

Corporations have a *qualified* legal personality for two reasons. First, it is a *limited* personality, in the sense that corporations under BITs or contracts do not possess the full range of capacity recognized by States under international law. A corporation may only exercise the limited powers and claim the rights that its 'constituent instrument' has granted it. In practice, the extent of an investor's legal personality is determined by the arbitration clause, which will indicate which substantive rights contained in the treaty can form the basis of a claim. Second, the legal personality is *derivative* in the sense that a corporation is a 'secondary' subject of international law. Its personality is not inherent, rather it emanates from the express will of (at least) one State either in a BIT or in a State contract. In the context of BITs, corporations are also *passive* subjects in the sense that they are not direct participants in the negotiation and generation of the legal norms on which their personality rests. Indeed, this personality can be modified or withdrawn without their consent, as treaties may always be modified by the contracting States. However, the situation is somewhat different in the context of State contracts, where a corporation is a direct participant in the *creation* of legal norms (the contractual terms), which must be complied with by the contracting State. In these circumstances, a corporation is not a mere bystander, rather it possesses a law-making power on the international plane.

Yet, as mentioned previously, the fact that corporations have a *limited* international legal personality under these instruments *does not* entail that they are endowed with any formal international law-making powers.[52]

Finally, another question (beyond the scope of this book) is the likely *consequences* of characterizing corporations as *partial and limited* subjects of international law.[53] Subjects of international law do not only have rights, but they also have *obligations* under international law. For

---

[51] Dumberry and Labelle Eastaugh, 'Non-State Actors in International Investment Law', pp. 360–371.

[52] d'Apremont, 'The Doctrinal Illusion of Heterogeneity', pp. 7–8, coming to the same conclusion regarding individuals and NGOs.

[53] Jose E. Alvarez, 'Are Corporations "Subjects" of International Law?', *Santa Clara J. Int'l L.* 9 (2011), pp. 23–24, examines the *different question* of the consequences of recognizing a *full* international law personality to corporations under investor-State arbitration, including their entitlement to a wider panoply of protection under international human rights law.

instance, in contemporary international law individuals have rights (typically contained in human rights treaties) and also have obligations which are directly imposed upon them by rules of international law, such as in the area of international criminal law. Because corporations possess a limited international legal personality in the context of BITs and State contracts, I have argued elsewhere that they should also have obligations, including human rights obligations.[54] There are indeed no theoretical objections preventing imposing obligations on corporations under international law.[55] Yet, in their current form, BITs are asymmetrical insofar as investors are accorded substantive *rights* without being subject to any specific *obligations*. I have shown elsewhere how new BITs could be drafted (and existing ones be amended) in order to impose some direct human rights, labour and environmental obligations on corporations.[56]

3.2   The basic requirements of State practice

This section examines the basic requirements needed for the practice of States to be considered as relevant in the process of creating customary norms. There are three basic requirements: (1) the practice of States needs to be uniform and consistent (Section 3.2.1), (2) it needs to be extensive and representative (Section 3.2.2), and finally, (3) such practice must have taken place for a certain period of time (Section 3.2.3). This section will specifically examine whether or not these requirements have been met regarding the FET standard, which is found in the vast majority of BITs (Section 3.2.4).

---

[54] This question is addressed in: P. Dumberry, 'Corporate Investors' International Legal Personality and their Accountability for Human Rights Violations under Investment Treaties', in A. De Mestral and C. Lévesque (eds.), *Improving International Investment Agreements Negotiation, Substantive Obligations and Dispute Resolution* (London: Routledge, 2012) pp. 179–194. See also: Toral and Schultz, 'The State, a Perpetual Respondent in Investment Arbitration?', p. 602.

[55] 'Interim Report of the Special Representative of the Secretary-General of the United Nations on the Issue of Human Rights and Transnational Corporations and other Business Enterprises,' John Ruggie, E/CN.4/2006/97, 22 February 2006, para. 65.

[56] P. Dumberry and G. Dumas-Aubin, 'How to Impose Human Rights Obligations on Corporations under Investment Treaties?', *Yb Int'l Invest. L. & Pol.* 4 (2011–2012), pp. 569–600; P. Dumberry and G. Dumas-Aubin, 'When and How Allegations of Human Rights Violations can be Raised in Investor-State Arbitration', *J. World Invest. & Trade* 13(3) (2012), pp. 349–372.

3.2.1   Uniform and consistent practice

The first requirement is that the practice of States must be 'uniform' and consistent.[57] In the *Asylum* case, the ICJ stated that a State 'must prove that the rule invoked by it is in accordance with a constant and uniform usage practiced by the States in question'.[58] In the *Nicaragua* case, the Court indicated that it is 'sufficient that the conduct of States should, in general, be consistent with such rules' to consider it as custom.[59] In another case, the Court declared that State practice must be 'common, consistent and concordant'.[60] The ILA speaks of the requirement of 'virtual uniformity',[61] both 'internally' and 'collectively'.[62] These two points will be examined in the following paragraphs.

First, as explained by the ILA report, 'internal uniformity means that each State whose behaviour is being considered should have acted in the same way on virtually all of the occasions on which it engaged in the practice in question'.[63] In other words, for the practice of one State to count towards the formation of a customary rule, that State must have

---

[57] Cai Congyan, 'International Investment Treaties and the Formation, Application and Transformation of Customary International Law Rules', *Chinese JIL* 7 (2008), p. 660; Abdullah Al Faruque, 'Creating Customary International Law through Bilateral Investment Treaties: a Critical Appraisal', *Indian J Int'l* 44 (2004), pp. 295–296; Matthew C. Porterfield, 'State Practice and the (Purported) Obligation under Customary International Law to Provide Compensation for Regulatory Expropriations', *North Carolina JIL & Comm Reg*, 37 (2011), p. 171; Tarcisio Gazzini, 'The Role of Customary International Law in the Field of Foreign Investment', *J. World Invest. & Trade*, 8 (2007), p. 692. See also: International Law Commission, 'Formation and Evidence of Customary International Law, Elements in the Previous Work of the ILC that Could be Particularly Relevant to the Topic', Memorandum by the Secretariat, Sixty-fifth session Geneva, 5 May-7 June and 8 July-9 August 2013, UN Doc., A/CN.4/659, p. 9 [hereinafter referred to as ILC, Memorandum, 2013]; ILC, Second Report, 2014, pp. 34, 65; ILC, Draft Conclusions, 2015, conclusion no. 8(1).

[58] *Asylum Case (Colombia v. Peru)*, ICJ Rep. 1950, p. 276.

[59] *Military and Paramilitary Activities in and around Nicaragua (Nicaragua v. United States)*, Merits, Judgment, ICJ Rep. 1986, para. 186.

[60] *Fisheries Jurisdiction Case (United Kingdom v. Iceland)*, Merits, ICJ Rep. 1974, p. 50 (Joint Separate Opinion of Judges Forster, Bengzon, Jiménez de Aréchaga, Nagendra Singh and Ruda).

[61] *North Sea Continental Shelf Cases (Federal Republic of Germany v. Denmark / Federal Republic of Germany v. Netherlands)*, ICJ Rep. 1969, para. 74 (referring to the practice which must be 'virtually uniform').

[62] ILA, Final Report, 2000, p. 21. See also: Mendelson, 'The Formation of Customary International Law', p. 212.

[63] ILA, Final Report, 2000, p. 21. See also: Dinstein, 'The Interaction between Customary International Law and Treaties', p. 274; M. Akehurst, 'Custom as a Source of International Law', *British YIL* 47 (1974–1975), p. 22; Nguyen *et al.*, *Droit International Public*, p. 358.

adopted the *same* attitude (almost) every time it has had the occasion to do so in its relations with other States. Yet, perfect 'internal uniformity' is not required. Thus, in the *Fisheries case*, the ICJ considered the practice of Norway regarding the ten-mile closing line as uniform despite evidence of 'few uncertainties or contradictions, real –or apparent'.[64]

But 'internal uniformity' also means something else. As mentioned previously, the practice of the executive, legislative and judicial branches of the State is to be considered, according to the circumstances, as State practice. So-called 'internal uniformity' requires that different State organs do not act inconsistently with each other.[65] Thus, for the practice of one State to count towards the formation of customary rules, the legislative and judicial branches of government should, as a matter of principle, adopt the same position as the executive on issues of international law. As noted by Dinstein, 'Human rights legislation that is disregarded by the executive branch, and amounts to "little more than window-dressing", cannot be relied upon "as significant evidence of practice" of the affected State for purposes of custom-making'.[66] I will examine later in the chapter the question of the actual weight that should be given to domestic court decisions whenever they *contradict* the position held by the government on matters of international law.[67]

Second, the concept of 'collective' uniformity requires that 'different States must not have engaged in substantially different conduct, some doing one thing and some another'.[68] Thus, as noted by the ILA, 'if there is too much inconsistency between States in their practice, there is no

---

[64] *Fisheries case (United Kingdom v. Norway)*, Judgement, ICJ Rep. 1951, p. 138. See, discussion in: Mendelson, 'The Formation of Customary International Law', p. 213.

[65] See, discussion in Chapter 3, Sections 3.3.6.2 and 3.3.6.3. It should be noted that some writers have taken a different position, see: Ingrid Wuerth, 'National Court Decisions and *Opinio Juris*', paper presented at the conference 'The Role of *Opinio Juris* in Customary International Law', Duke-Geneva Institute in Transnational Law, Geneva, 2013, pp. 6–7: 'There is a strong case for abandoning the internal consistency requirement, however, assuming that there is even such a requirement. If customary international law is built on plural forms of state practice and *opinio juris*, with diminished significance for practice itself, it is appropriate to recognize in the formation of customary international law that states may have more than one practice, and indeed may provide conflicting evidence of *opinio juris*'.

[66] Dinstein, 'The Interaction between Customary International Law and Treaties', p. 274 (quoting from: O. Schachter, 'International Law in Theory and Practice: General Course in Public International Law', *Rec. des Cours* 178 [1982], p. 335).

[67] See, Chapter 3, Section 3.3.6.3.1.

[68] ILA, Final Report, 2000, p. 21. See also: Nguyen *et al., Droit International Public*, p. 358.

general custom and hence no general customary rule'.[69] Similarly, isolated acts of only a very few States cannot form the basis of a custom rule. This requirement has been recognized by States in investment arbitration proceedings[70] and by tribunals.[71]

A good illustration[72] of the 'collective' uniformity requirement is provided by the ICJ *Fisheries case*. The Court noted that while the ten-mile closing line for bays had 'been adopted by certain States both in their national law and in their treaties and conventions' (and had also been applied by some arbitral decisions), a different limit had also been adopted by other States.[73] For this reason, the Court came to the conclusion that 'the ten-mile rule ha[d] not acquired the authority of a general rule of international law'.[74] In the *Asylum* case, Columbia was relying on the existence of a so-called Latin-American regional custom giving the right to a unilateral and definitive qualification of the status of an individual by a State when granting diplomatic asylum, and maintained that such special rule was binding on Peru. The Court rejected Colombia's argument towards the existence of a regional custom. The Court explained that there is no uniformity when the practice shows some 'uncertainty and contradiction' as well as 'fluctuation and discrepancy':

---

[69] ILA, *Ibid.*, p. 22 (emphasis in the original). See also: Dinstein, 'The Interaction between Customary International Law and Treaties', p. 284 ('radical variations in solutions offered to the same basic problem are lethal to the emergence of custom').

[70] *Glamis Gold Ltd* v. *United States*, UNCITRAL, Award, 14 May 2009, paras. 567, 602 (referring to the position of the United States: 'a concordant practice of a number of States acquiesced in by others'); *Apotex Holdings Inc & Apotex Inc.* v. *United States*, ICSID Case No. ARB(AF)/12/1, Award, 25 August 2014, para. 2.65 (referring to the position of the United States: 'general and consistent practice of States'); *Mobil Investments Canada Inc. & Murphy Oil Corporation* v. *Canada*, ICSID Case No. ARB(AF)/07/4, Decision on Liability and on Principles of Quantum, 22 May 2012, para. 131 (referring to the position of Canada: 'widespread and consistent practice undertaken out of a sense of legal obligation'); *Spence International Investments et al.* v. *Costa Rica*, UNCITRAL (ICSID Case No. UNCT/13/2), Non-Disputing Party Submission by the United States, 17 April 2015, paras. 15–16, see also, Non-disputing party submission by El Salvador, 17 April 2015, para. 6.

[71] *Glamis Gold Ltd* v. *United States*, Award, 14 May 2009, para. 603 ('The evidence of such "concordant practice" undertaken out of a sense of legal obligation is exhibited in very few authoritative sources: treaty ratification language, statements of governments, treaty practice (e.g., Model BITs), and sometimes pleadings'); *Merrill & Ring Forestry L.P.* v. *Canada*, UNCITRAL, Award, 31 March 2010, para. 204 ('in the absence of a widespread and consistent state practice in support of a rule of customary international law there is no opinio juris').

[72] See, Mendelson, 'The Formation of Customary International Law', p. 212.

[73] *Fisheries case (United Kingdom v. Norway)*, ICJ Rep. 1951, p. 131. [74] *Ibid.*

> The facts brought to the knowledge of the Court disclose so much
> uncertainty and contradiction, so much fluctuation and discrepancy in
> the exercise of diplomatic asylum and in the official views expressed on
> various occasions, there has been so much inconsistency in the rapid
> succession of conventions on asylum, ratified by some States and rejected
> by others, and the practice has been so much influenced by considerations
> of political expediency in the various cases, that it is not possible to discern
> in all this any constant and uniform usage, accepted as law, with regard to
> the alleged rule of unilateral and definitive qualification of the offence. The
> Court cannot therefore find that the Colombian Government has proved
> the existence of such a custom.[75]

Finally, it should be added that, in practical terms, it would be almost
impossible for a rule of custom to ever emerge if *perfect and total*
'collective' consistency and uniformity was required amongst States.[76]
For this reason, Villiger affirms that 'the uniformity need not be complete: a substantial, virtual uniformity or consistency of practice suffices'.[77] In the *Nicaragua* case, the Court explained that for a rule to be
established as customary, practice does not need to be 'in absolutely
rigorous conformity with the rule'.[78] Many ICJ judges have recognized
(in their individual opinions) the fact that custom does not require that

---

[75] *Asylum Case (Colombia v. Peru)*, ICJ Rep. 1950, p. 277.
[76] Congyan, 'International Investment Treaties and the Formation', p. 660; ILC,
Memorandum, 2013, p. 12 ('Where there was a unifying thread or theme underlying
international practice, a certain variability in practice has often not precluded the
Commission from identifying a rule of customary international law'); ILC, Second
Report, 2014, p. 34; Al Faruque, 'Creating Customary International Law', p. 296.
[77] Villiger, *Customary International Law and Treaties*, p. 43. See also: ILC, Second Report,
2014, p. 38; G. Fitzmaurice, 'The Law and Procedure of the International Court of Justice,
1951–54: General Principles and Sources of Law', *British YIL* 30 (1953), p. 45; J. Crawford,
Brownlie's Principles of Public International Law (8th edn., Oxford: Oxford University
Press, 2012), p. 24; Gazzini, 'The Role of Customary International Law', p. 692.
[78] *Military and Paramilitary Activities in and around Nicaragua*, ICJ Rep. 1986, para. 186: 'It
is not to be expected that in the practice of States the application of the rules in question
should have been perfect, in the sense that States should have refrained, with complete
consistency, from the use of force or from intervention in each other's internal affairs. The
Court does not consider that, for a rule to be established as customary, the corresponding
practice must be in absolutely rigorous conformity with the rule. In order to deduce the
existence of customary rules, the Court deems it sufficient that the conduct of States
should, in general, be consistent with such rules, and that instances of State conduct
inconsistent with a given rule should generally have been treated as breaches of that rule,
not as indications of the recognition of a new rule. If a State acts in a way prima facie
incompatible with a recognized rule, but defends its conduct by appealing to exceptions
or justifications contained within the rule itself, then whether or not the State's conduct is
in fact justifiable on that basis, the significance of that attitude is to confirm rather than to
weaken the rule'.

the practice of States be unanimous (or universal).[79] A customary rule can therefore emerge even when some States do not act in conformity with the rule as long as, for instance, they justify their conduct by claiming the application of an exception to the rule.[80]

3.2.2 Extensive and representative practice

The second requirement is that State practice must be general.[81] In order for a rule to emerge, such practice must be shared by a sufficient number of States.[82] However, no 'precise number or percentage of States' is required to demonstrate general practice.[83] Nonetheless, it is clear that universality of practice by States is *not* required.[84]

State practice needs to be, in the words of the ICJ, 'widespread'[85] and 'sufficiently extensive and convincing'.[86] This is, however, a relative requirement.[87] Whether or not a practice is widespread and extensive enough cannot be determined in the abstract; it will always depend on the

---

[79] *North Sea Continental Shelf Cases*, ICJ Rep. 1969, p. 104 (Separate Opinion of Judge Ammoun) and p. 229 (Dissenting Opinion of Judge Lachs); *Nuclear Tests (Australia v. France)*, Judgment, ICJ Rep. 1974, p. 253, p. 435 (Dissenting Opinion of Judge Barwick); *Gabčikovo-Nagymaros Project (Hungary/Slovakia)*, Judgment, ICJ Rep. 1997, p. 7, 95 (Separate Opinion of Judge Weeramantry).

[80] Mendelson, 'The Formation of Customary International Law', p. 214; Villiger, *Customary International Law and Treaties*, p. 44.

[81] ILC, Memorandum, 2013, pp. 10–11 (noting the different expressions used by the ILC); Al Faruque, 'Creating Customary International Law', p. 296. See also: ILC, Second Report, 2014, pp. 34, 65; ILC, Draft Conclusions, 2015, conclusion no. 8(1) ('The relevant practice must be general, meaning that it must be sufficiently widespread and representative, as well as consistent').

[82] Al Faruque, 'Creating Customary International Law', p. 295; Gazzini, 'The Role of Customary International Law', p. 692.

[83] Mendelson, 'The Formation of Customary International Law', pp. 219–224; Porterfield, 'State Practice and the (Purported) Obligation', p. 172; ILC, Second Report, 2014, p. 35.

[84] Congyan, 'International Investment Treaties and the Formation', p. 660; ILA, Final Report, 2000 p. 23; Dinstein, 'The Interaction between Customary International Law and Treaties', p. 282; Nguyen *et al.*, *Droit International Public*, p. 360.

[85] *Maritime Delimitation and Territorial Questions between Qatar and Bahrain*, Merits, Judgment, ICJ Rep. 2001, p. 102, para. 205 (referring to '[a uniform and] widespread State practice'); *Fisheries Jurisdiction Case (United Kingdom v. Iceland)*, ICJ Rep. 1974, pp. 45, 52 (Joint Separate Opinion of Judges Forster, Bengzon, Jiménez de Aréchaga, Nagendra Singh and Ruda, referring to 'sufficiently widespread' practice).

[86] *Delimitation of the Maritime Boundary in the Gulf of Maine Area (Canada v. United States)*, Judgment, ICJ Rep. 1984, p. 299, para. 111. See also: *North Sea Continental Shelf Cases*, ICJ Rep. 1969, para. 74, using the term 'extensive'.

[87] It should be added, however, that the position taken by some writers (for instance: A. D'Amato, *The Concept of Custom in International Law* [Ithaca: Cornell University Press,

specific circumstances of each case. In certain circumstances, not even the practice of a *majority* of States would be required for a rule of custom to emerge. This may be the case, for instance, when the conduct of a significant number of States is met by the majority of others with indifference and inaction.[88] In this situation, what matters is the degree of representativeness of the States actively engaged in that practice.[89]

The *representativeness* of practice is therefore a key aspect. Thus, for the ILA, 'it is not simply a question of how many States participate in the practice, but *which* States'.[90] The ICJ in the *North Sea Continental Shelf* cases also speaks of 'very widespread and *representative* participation' in the development of a rule (in the context of when a rule is alleged to have emerged in a short period of time).[91] Different (but not necessarily conflicting) interpretations as to what representativeness actually means have been put forward. For some, a representative practice means that it includes States from 'all major political and social-economic systems'.[92] This is, for instance, the position taken by Judge Lachs in his dissenting opinion in the *North Sea Continental Shelf* cases:

> This mathematical calculation, which is already so important of itself, must be completed by a spectral analysis, as it were, of the representation of States.... Indeed in today's world, one must take into account an essential factor in the formation of a new rule of general international law, namely the fact that States with different political, economic and legal systems, States from all continents, take part in this process. The time has

1971], pp. 87–98, 91; Wolfke, *Custom in Present International Law*, p. 60) that the practice of *one single* State could suffice to create a rule of custom should be rejected.

[88] ILC, Second Report, 2014, p. 35 ('it very well may be that only a relatively small number of States engage in a practice, and the inaction of others suffices to create a rule of customary international law'); M. Akehurst, 'Custom as a Source of International Law', p. 18 ('A practice followed by a very small number of States can create a rule of customary law if there is no practice which conflicts with the rule').

[89] ILA, Final Report, 2000, p. 25 ('much will depend on circumstances and, in particular, on the degree of representativeness of the practice (...). Provided that participation is sufficiently representative, it is not normally necessary for even a majority of States to have engaged in the practice, provided that there is no significant dissent'), see also, at p. 26. See also: ILC, Second Report, 2014, p. 34.

[90] ILA, Final Report, 2000, p. 25 (emphasis in the original). See also: Mendelson, p. 224; Porterfield, 'State Practice and the (Purported) Obligation', p. 172; Congyan, 'International Investment Treaties and the Formation', p. 660 ('the requirement is met if those States being capable of participating in the general practice or those States having interests in the objects of the general practice actually participate in it').

[91] *North Sea Continental Shelf Cases*, ICJ Rep. 1969, para. 73 (emphasis added).

[92] Villiger, *Customary International Law and Treaties*, p. 29; Brigitte Stern, 'Custom at the Heart of International Law', *Duke J Comp & IL* 11 (2001), p. 105.

passed when a general rule could be established according to the will of a single or small number of States—or even as was once claimed—by the consensus of European States only.[93]

What matters, to quote the ICJ in the *North Sea Continental Shelf* cases,[94] and the reasoning of several ICJ judges in their individual opinions,[95] is the practice of those 'specially affected' States.[96] Which States are 'specially affected' will vary depending on the circumstances.[97] For instance, States with extensive coastal areas (e.g., Canada, United States, Russia, Indonesia, Chile) will be 'specially affected' by all questions related to the law of the sea. It is important to note that the 'specially affected' States will *not* necessarily be those that are the most powerful in the world.[98] For instance, small Island States (such as Seychelles and Mauritius) are clearly 'specially affected' by climate change. Northern African States are also 'specially affected' by the phenomenon of desertification. In the context of armed conflict, the ICRC study concluded that '[w]ith respect to any rule of international humanitarian law, countries that participated in an armed conflict are "specially affected" when their practice examined for a certain rule was relevant to that armed conflict'.[99]

---

[93] *North Sea Continental Shelf Cases*, ICJ Rep. 1969, p. 227 (Dissenting Opinion of Judge Lachs).

[94] *Ibid.*, para. 73.

[95] *Ibid.*, pp. 175–176 (Dissenting Opinion of Judge Tanaka); *Fisheries Jurisdiction Case (United Kingdom v. Iceland)*, ICJ Rep. 1974, p. 90 (Separate Opinion of Judge De Castro), p. 161 (Separate Opinion of Judge Petrén).

[96] *North Sea Continental Shelf Cases*, ICJ Rep. 1969, paras. 73–74. Yet, it should be added that the practice of *every* single 'specially affected' State in one area of activity is not required for a rule of custom to emerge. See: Dinstein, 'The Interaction between Customary International Law and Treaties', p. 289; ILC, Second Report, 2014, pp. 34, 65, Draft Conclusion 9(4) of the ILC 'Proposed draft conclusions on the identification of customary international law' ('In assessing practice, due regard is to be given to the practice of States whose interests are specially affected'). It should be added, however, that the ILC, Draft Conclusions, 2015, conclusion no. 9 does not refer to those 'specially affected' States.

[97] ILA, Final Report, 2000, p. 26; See also: R. Baxter, 'Treaties and Custom', *Rec. des cours* 129 (1970), p. 66; Dinstein, 'The Interaction between Customary International Law and Treaties', p. 289; ILC, Second Report, 2014, p. 36.

[98] ILA, Final Report, 2000, p. 26.

[99] Henckaerts and Doswald-Beck, *Customary International Humanitarian Law*, p. xxxix. This position has been criticized by the United States: Bellinger and Haynes, 'A US Government Response', p. 445: 'This rendering dilutes the rule and, furthermore, makes it unduly provisional. Not every State that has participated in an armed conflict is "specially affected"; such States do generate salient practice, but it is those States that have a distinctive history of participation that merit being regarded as "specially affected". Moreover, those States are not simply "specially affected" when their practice has, in fact,

In the context of international investment law, the 'specially affected' States are those who receive the most foreign investments as well as the States of origin of corporations and individuals making the most investments abroad.[100] The 'specially affected' States are those who have signed the greatest number of investment treaties, investment contracts and have enacted local domestic law on investment. Finally, another factor that can measure the status of a 'specially affected' State is the number of arbitration disputes in which that State or its nationals are involved. North Korea and Somalia are clearly not, by any measure, 'specially affected' States in the field of international investment law.

Based on the basic international law principle of the equality of sovereign States, the same weight *should* be given to the practice of each State no matter its size, population, power, and so on.[101] Yet, in reality not all States are (in practical terms) perfectly equal when it comes to their actual weight *in the formation of international law*.[102] Thus, powerful States have historically played a preeminent role in the practice of States leading to the creation of custom.[103] Thus, as explained by the

been examined and found relevant by the ICRC. Instead, specially affected States generate practice that must be examined in order to reach an informed conclusion regarding the status of a potential rule'.

[100] Porterfield, 'State Practice and the (Purported) Obligation', pp. 172–173 ('in determining the content of CIL with regard to the treatment of foreign investment, it is appropriate to focus on the practices of the major capital importing and exporting countries, which presumably constitute the relevant "specially affected" States'); T. Treves, 'Customary International Law', in Rüdiger Wolfrum (ed.), *Max Planck Encyclopedia of Public International Law* (Oxford: Oxford University Press, vol. 9, 2012), para. 36 ('rules on economic relations, such as those on foreign investment, require practice of the main investor States as well as that of the main States in which investment is made').

[101] Villiger, *Customary International Law and Treaties*, p. 33.

[102] Wolfke, *Custom in Present International Law*, p. 78; Dinstein, 'The Interaction between Customary International Law and Treaties', p. 288.

[103] See, the classic explanation given by Charles de Visscher, *Théories et réalités en droit international public* (Paris: Pedone, 1953), pp. 182–184: 'Parmi les usagers, il en est toujours qui, plus profondément que d'autres, marquent la terre de l'empreinte de leurs pas, soit en raison de leurs poids, c'est-à-dire de leur puissance en ce monde, soit parce que leurs intérêts les appellent plus fréquemment à effectuer le parcours. C'est ainsi qu'après avoir imprimé à l'usage une orientation définie, les grandes Puissances s'en constituent encore les garants et les défenseurs. Leur rôle, qui de tout temps fut décisif dans la formation du droit international coutumier, est de conférer aux usages ce degré d'effectivité sans lequel la conviction juridique, condition de l'assentiment général, ne trouverait pas une base suffisante dans la réalité sociale. Nombre de coutumes ne doivent leur origine qu'à des décisions ou des actes de grandes Puissances, qui du fait de leur répétition ou de leur enchaînement, du fait surtout de l'idée d'ordre qui finalement s'en dégage, ont perdu peu à peu leur caractère personnel, contingent, en un mot politique, pour revêtir les aspects de la coutume en formation. On peut citer en exemple dans cet

ILA, while '[t]here is no rule that major powers have to participate in a practice in order for it to become a rule of general customary law',[104] the fact of the matter is that '[g]iven the scope of their interests, both geographically and *ratione materiae*, [major powers] often will be "specially affected" by a practice; and *to that extent and to that extent alone*, their participation is necessary'.[105] In other words, the practices of major powers weigh more heavily in the custom formation process because they are more often than not 'specially affected' by the development of legal rules.[106]

Finally, it is worth noting the closely related question of what the ILA report calls the 'negative aspect' of representativeness.[107] The opposition of a small but particularly dynamic and influential group of 'specially affected' States to a new rule may in fact prevent the rule from crystallizing into customary law.[108] The same is true in regards to the objection

ordre d'idées l'impulsion considérable donnée par les États-Unis, à partir de la fin du XVIIIe siècle, au développement du droit de la neutralité' (an english translation can be found in: C. de Visscher, *Theory and Reality in Public International Law* [Princeton UP, 1968], p. 155). See also: Byers, *Custom, Power and the Power of Rules*, p. 37 ff.; Roberts, 'Traditional and Modern Approaches to Customary International Law', p. 768; L. Ferrari-Bravo, 'Méthodes de recherche de la coutume internationale dans la pratique des États', *Rec. des cours* 192 (1985), p. 254; Wolfke, *Custom in Present International Law*, p. 78.

[104] ILA, Final Report, 2000, p. 26.   [105] *Ibid.*, (emphasis in the original).

[106] Mendelson, 'The Formation of Customary International Law', pp. 225–226: 'First of all, States which are particularly active in a given area may be more concerned about it than others and devote more resources to thinking about and planning the development of the law. (...) Secondly, the more influential States are in a better position to encourage others to follow their lead, or deter others from obstructing the development they favour. States with worldwide interests also have more opportunities to develop practice: major powers, for example, send and receive more diplomatic legations than others, and have thus had more occasion to influence the development of the customary law on diplomatic relations. Accessibility of the State's practice is another factor: for example, developed countries have been able to influence perceptions of what State practice is considerably, and perhaps even disproportionately, due to the fact that they are the ones who tend to publish their practice in the form of readily accessible digests and so on. The extent and quality of publication by the scholars of the various nations plays a part, too; and the fact that publications from a particular country are in a language widely understood in the international community (such as English) will also help'. See also: Dinstein, 'The Interaction between Customary International Law and Treaties', p. 289; Byers, *Custom, Power and the Power of Rules*, p. 38; ILC, Second Report, 2014, p. 36.

[107] ILA, Final Report, 2000, p. 26.

[108] Villiger, *Customary International Law and Treaties*, pp. 36–37; ILA, Final Report, 2000, p. 27; Mendelson, 'The Formation of Customary International Law', p. 226; J. Charney, 'The Persistent Objector Rule and the Development of Customary International Law', *British YIL*, (1985), p. 23; Dinstein, 'The Interaction between Customary International Law and Treaties', pp. 288–289; Nguyen *et al.*, *Droit International Public*, p. 360.

of one very powerful State. For instance, the United States successfully argued in its pleadings before the ICJ in the context of its advisory opinion on the *Legality of the Threat or Use of Nuclear Weapons* that its opposition (and that of a few other powerful States) blocked the development of a customary norm preventing the threat of the use of nuclear weapons.[109] This question remains controversial, as others have concluded, on the contrary, that the rule had nevertheless emerged as custom and that the United States should be considered as a 'persistent objector'.[110] The question of the so-called persistent objector will be discussed further in Chapter 5.[111]

3.2.3 The time requirement

Lastly, State practice needs to fulfil a time duration requirement.[112] According to the ILA, 'there is no specific time requirement: it is all a question of accumulating a practice of sufficient *density*, in terms of uniformity, extent and representativeness'.[113] The situation is best described in the following passage by Villiger:

> The necessary duration of practice would depend mainly on the generality and consistency of practice. In other words, the less States actively engage

---

[109] *Legality of the Threat or Use of Nuclear Weapons*, Advisory Opinion, ICJ Rep. 1996. In his dissenting opinion, Judge Schwebel, p. 312, stated 'This nuclear practice is not a practice of a lone and secondary persistent objector. This is not a practice of a pariah Government crying out in the wilderness of otherwise adverse international opinion. This is the practice of five of the world's major Powers, of the permanent members of the Security Council, significantly supported for almost 50 years by their allies and other States sheltering under their nuclear umbrellas. That is to say, it is the practice of States— and a practice supported by a large and weighty number of other States—that together represent the bulk of the world's military and economic and financial and technological power and a very large proportion of its population'.

[110] Henckaerts and Doswald-Beck, *Customary International Humanitarian Law*, pp. 201–206, referring to the emergence of a customary rule prohibiting the use of methods or means of warfare that are intended to cause widespread, long-term and severe damage to the environment in the specific context of the use of nuclear weapons. For a critical analysis, see Dinstein, 'The Interaction between Customary International Law and Treaties', p. 289.

[111] See, Chapter 5, Section 5.4.

[112] Congyan, 'International Investment Treaties and the Formation', p. 660.

[113] ILA, Final Report, 2000, p. 20 (emphasis in the original). See also: ILC, Second Report, 2014, pp. 39, 65; ILC, Draft Conclusions, 2015, conclusion no. 8(2) ('Provided that the practice is general, no particular duration is required'); O. Corten, *Métholodologie du droit international public* (Brussels: Ed. Université de Bruxelles, 2009), pp. 150–151; Nguyen *et al.*, *Droit International Public*, p. 359.

in practice, and the more inconsistent the practice, the longer the formation of a customary rule will take. By contrast, active and consistent practice of a comparatively large, "representative" group of States may harden into a customary rule after a comparatively short period of time.[114]

In the *North Sea Continental Shelf* cases, the ICJ explained that in certain circumstances, a rule of law can develop within a relatively short period of time. Thus, in the opinion of the Court, 'even without the passage of any considerable period of time, a very widespread and representative participation in the convention might suffice of itself, provided it included that of States whose interests were specially affected'.[115] Yet, the Court also added that in such a situation the practice of the affected States must be 'both extensive and virtually uniform'.[116] It is clear that 'in the nature of things *some* time will normally need to elapse before a practice matures into a rule'.[117] This is why the very existence of the concept of 'instant custom' is widely rejected in doctrine.[118] However, it is also undeniable that customary rules are created more rapidly these days as a result of the density of practice in modern international relations.[119] As noted by one writer, '[t]he intensification of practice within international organizations and conferences, the adoption of multilateral treaties, and the existence and activity of specialized international tribunals has contributed to the acceleration of the formation of customary rules in these and other fields'.[120]

---

[114] Villiger, *Customary International Law and Treaties*, p. 46.

[115] *North Sea Continental Shelf Cases*, ICJ Rep. 1969, paras. 73–74.

[116] *Ibid.*, para. 74. See also, at p. 124 (Separate Opinion of Judge Ammoun), p. 230 (Dissenting Opinion of Judge Lachs) and p. 244 (Dissenting Opinion of Judge Sørensen).

[117] ILA, Final Report, 2000, p. 20 (emphasis in the original). See also: Mendelson, 'The Formation of Customary International Law', pp. 210, 371; James Crawford, 'The Identification and Development of Customary International Law', ILA British Branch Conference (2014), pp. 1–2 ('custom requires a certain amount of time to develop, even if it is a short time').

[118] In one famous article, B. Cheng, 'United Nations Resolutions on Outer Space: "Instant" International Customary Law?', *Indian J Int'l L* 5 (1965) p. 23, argued that a UN General Assembly resolution could, in theory, create an instant custom. See, discussion and criticisms in: Mendelson, 'The Formation of Customary International Law', p. 371, summarizing Cheng's theory as follows: 'In essence (....), Cheng's proposition is that practice is not an indispensable element in customary law; that whilst it is normally present, the crucial element is *opinio juris*, of which usage is merely the evidence. Time is not an essential element in the creation of customary rules, which can come into existence instantly. General Assembly resolutions, provided that they satisfy the requirements of a general and representative *opinio juris*, can enunciate new rules of international law'.

[119] Nguyen *et al.*, *Droit International Public*, p. 359.

[120] Treves, 'Customary International Law', para. 25.

3.2.4   One illustration: is the fair and equitable treatment standard uniformly and consistently found in BITs?

This section examines whether or not the practice of States to include FET clauses in their BITs is widespread, representative, uniform and consistent.

3.2.4.1   The position adopted by tribunals and scholars on the customary status of the FET standard

A number of scholars have openly endorsed the proposition that the FET standard has a customary status.[121] The basic reason invoked by all of them is the fact that the standard is found in so many BITs.[122] Tudor has developed the most comprehensive theory in support of this position. From the fact that the vast majority of investment treaties contain FET clauses,[123] she concludes that this 'cannot be without consequence to the place occupied by the FET in the body of international law'[124] and has, in fact, 'contributed to creating a norm of customary international law'.[125] Tudor's conclusion is that 'the FET standard became a customary norm of its time: quick in its formation and based essentially on a State practice derived from the treaties signed by an overwhelming number of States, which in the majority contain a FET clause'.[126]

---

[121] Ionna Tudor, *The Fair and Equitable Treatment Standard in International Foreign Investment Law* (Oxford: Oxford University Press, 2008), pp. 65–68; Alexandra Diehl, *The Core Standard of International Investment Protection: Fair and Equitable Treatment* (Alphen aan den Rijn: Wolters Kluwer, 2012), pp. 10–11; Alfred Siwy, 'Investment Arbitration – Indirect Expropriation and the Legitimate Expectations of the Investor', in Christian Klausegger, Peter Klein, *et al.* (eds.), *Austrian Arbitration Yearbook* (Vienna: C.H. Beck, Stämpfli and Manz 2007).

[122] See: Tudor, *Ibid.*, p. 74 ff.; Courtney C. Kirkman, 'Fair and Equitable Treatment: Methanex v. United States and the Narrowing Scope of NAFTA Article 1105', *Law & Pol'y Int'l Bus.* 34 (2002–2003), p. 392; Diehl, *The Core Standard of International Investment Protection*, pp. 10–11, 125–153, 175–179; Todd Weiler, 'NAFTA Investment Arbitration and the Growth of International Economic Law', *Bus. L. Int'l*, 2 (2002), p. 188; I. Laird, 'Betrayal, Shock and Outrage – Recent Developments in NAFTA Article 1105', in T. Weiler (ed.), *NAFTA Investment Law and Arbitration: Past Issues, Current Practice, Future Prospects* (Ardsley: Transnational Publ., 2004), pp. 70, 74; Jan Schokkaert and Yvon Heckscher, *International Investments Protection: Comparative Law Analysis of Bilateral and Multilateral Interstate Conventions, Doctrinal Texts and Arbitral Jurisprudence Concerning Foreign Investments* (Bruylant, 2009), p. 331.

[123] Tudor, *The Fair and Equitable Treatment Standard*, p. 75.   [124] *Id.*   [125] *Id.*

[126] *Ibid.*, p. 85. Yet, in subsequent writing (Ioana Knoll-Tudor, 'The Fair and Equitable Treatment Standard and Human Rights Norms', in P.M. Dupuy, F. Francioni and E.U. Petersmann [eds.], *Human Rights in International Investment Law and Arbitration*

Only a few tribunals have taken the position that the FET standard has become a rule of customary international law in and of itself. To the best of the present author's knowledge, only NAFTA tribunals have so far discussed the issue in their awards. The first tribunal to openly adopt this view was the NAFTA *Pope & Talbot* Tribunal in its second award of 2002. For the Tribunal, the fact that the FET standard was found in so many BITs basically established the element of State practice necessary to prove the existence of a rule of customary international law:

> Canada's views on the appropriate standard of customary international law for today were perhaps shaped by its erroneous belief that only some 70 bilateral investment treaties have been negotiated; however, the true number, now acknowledged by Canada, is in excess of 1800. Therefore, applying the ordinary rules for determining the content of custom in international law, one must conclude that the practice of states is now represented by those treaties.[127]

The Tribunal's reasoning is controversial and questionable on many grounds. First, the Tribunal completely disregarded the requirement to show States' *opinio juris* to establish the existence of a customary rule. Second, the Tribunal did not at all discuss the actual content of these BITs – which is a requirement in international law to prove that State practice is actually consistent. These grounds of criticism were echoed in the subsequent NAFTA *ADF* case where the Tribunal made reference to the United States' view that '[t]he *Pope and Talbot* Tribunal did not examine the mass of existing BITs to determine whether those treaties represent concordant state practice and whether they constitute evidence of the *opinio juris* constituent of customary international law'.[128] For the United States, the *Pope and Talbot* Tribunal was therefore 'not in a position to state whether any particular BIT obligation has crystallized into a rule of customary international law'.[129] In the *Mondev* ruling, the Tribunal also referred to the NAFTA Parties' strong disapproval of the

[Oxford: Oxford University Press, 2009], p. 317) she seems to have changed her mind when stating that 'to justify and bring enough proof as to the Customary character of FET is a challenging operation with few chances of success'.

[127] *Pope & Talbot Inc.* v. *Canada*, UNCITRAL, Award in Respect of Damages, 31 May 2002, para. 62.

[128] *ADF Group Inc.* v. *United States*, ICSID Case No. ARB(AF)/00/1, Award, 9 January 2003, para. 112.

[129] *Ibid.*, see also, the *ADF* Tribunal's reference to Mexico's position (at para. 125) to the effect that 'given the absence of "a careful analysis of state practice and opinion juris", the sheer number of extant BITs today does not suffice to show that conventional international law has become customary international law'.

reasoning of the *Pope & Talbot* award on this issue. This is the relevant passage from the *Mondev* award:

> In their post-hearing submissions, all three NAFTA Parties challenged holdings of the Tribunal in *Pope & Talbot* which find that the content of contemporary international law reflects the concordant provisions of many hundreds of bilateral investment treaties. In particular, attention was drawn to what those three States saw as a failure of the *Pope & Talbot* Tribunal to consider a necessary element of the establishment of a rule of customary international law, namely *opinio juris*. These States appear to question whether the parties to the very large numbers of bilateral investment treaties have acted out of a sense of legal obligation when they include provisions in those treaties such as that for 'fair and equitable' treatment of foreign investment.[130]

The *Mondev* Tribunal mentioned that the question was 'entirely legitimate'.[131] The Tribunal also added that '[i]t is often difficult in international practice to establish at what point obligations accepted in treaties, multilateral or bilateral, come to condition the content of a rule of customary international law binding on States not party to those treaties'.[132] For the Tribunal, the answer was quite simple: the respondent (United States) had apparently contended that 'when adopting provisions for fair and equitable treatment and full protection and security in NAFTA (as well as in other BITs), the intention was to incorporate principles of customary international law'.[133] In other words, these statements represented *opinio juris*. The United States had indeed argued that the FET was a reference to the MST existing under custom. The Tribunal concluded, in the NAFTA context, as follows:

> Thus the question is not that of a failure to show *opinio juris* or to amass sufficient evidence demonstrating it. The question rather is: what is the content of customary international law providing for fair and equitable treatment and full protection and security in investment treaties?[134]

This passage is ambiguous. It is not entirely clear whether the *Mondev* Tribunal endorsed the position adopted by the *Pope & Talbot* Tribunal wherein the FET standard had become a rule of customary international law. However, there are a few passages in the award that seem to suggest that this is indeed the case. Thus, the Tribunal mentions that existing BITs 'almost uniformly' contain an FET clause adding that 'such

---

[130] *Mondev International Ltd. v. United States*, ICSID Case No. ARB(AF)/99/2 [hereinafter referred to as *Mondev v. United States*], Award, 2 October 2002, para. 110.
[131] *Ibid.*, para. 111.   [132] *Ibid.*   [133] *Ibid.*   [134] *Ibid.*, para. 113. See also, at para. 122.

a body of concordant practice will necessarily have influenced the content of rules governing the treatment of foreign investment in current international law'.[135] It also added that the content of 'current international law' was 'shaped by the conclusion of more than two thousand bilateral investment treaties and many treaties of friendship and commerce' and that 'those treaties largely and concordantly' include an FET clause.[136] This position was later endorsed by the *Chemtura* Tribunal, which stated that the determination of NAFTA Article 1105 'cannot overlook the evolution of customary international law, nor the impact of BITs on this evolution'.[137] In sum, the different statements made by the *Mondev* Tribunal suggest that it endorsed the proposition that such a 'uniform' practice of States incorporating FET clauses in their BITs had led to the formation of a rule of custom.[138]

A few months later in 2003, the *ADF* Tribunal stated that while the *Mondev* Tribunal was 'implying that the process was in motion', it had in fact *not* endorsed the position that the FET obligation was a customary rule.[139] In any event, the *ADF* Tribunal expressly *rejected* the contention (made by the investor in the proceedings) that the FET standard had become part of custom:

> We are not convinced that the Investor has shown the existence, in current customary international law, of a general and autonomous requirement (autonomous, that is, from specific rules addressing particular, limited, contexts) to accord fair and equitable treatment and full protection and security to foreign investments. The Investor, for instance, has not shown that such a requirement has been brought into the corpus of present day customary international law by the many hundreds of bilateral investment treaties now extant. It may be that, in their current state, neither concordant state practice nor judicial or arbitral case law provides convincing substantiation (or, for that matter, refutation) of the Investor's position.[140]

Despite the clear language (at least in the *ADF* case), it has been argued in doctrine that both the *Mondev* and the *ADF* cases stand for the proposition of the 'recognition of the existence of a general requirement to accord fair and equitable treatment under customary international law'.[141]

---

[135] *Ibid.*, para. 117.   [136] *Ibid.*, para. 125.

[137] *Chemtura Corporation v. Canada*, UNCITRAL, Award, 2 August 2010, para. 121.

[138] Alexander Orakhelashvili, 'The Normative Basis of "Fair and Equitable Treatment": General International Law on Foreign Investment?', *Archiv des Völkerrechts* 1 (2008), p. 78; Laird, 'Betrayal, Shock and Outrage', pp. 67, 69, 70.

[139] *ADF v. United States*, Award, 9 January 2003, para. 183.   [140] *Ibid.*, paras. 183, 185.

[141] Laird, 'Betrayal, Shock and Outrage', p. 70, see also, pp. 67, 69.

The *Merrill & Ring* Tribunal was of the same view. It held that 'against the backdrop of the evolution of the minimum standard of treatment' it was 'satisfied that fair and equitable treatment has *become a part of customary law*'.[142] The Tribunal gave the following explanation:

> A requirement that aliens be treated fairly and equitably in relation to business, trade and investment is the outcome of this changing reality and as such it has become sufficiently part of widespread and consistent practice so as to demonstrate that it is reflected today in customary international law as *opinio juris*. In the end, the name assigned to the standard does not really matter. What matters is that the standard protects against all such acts or behavior that might infringe a sense of fairness, equity and reasonableness. Of course, the concepts of fairness, equitableness and reasonableness cannot be defined precisely: they require to be applied to the facts of each case. [148] In fact, the concept of fair and equitable treatment has emerged to make possible the consideration of inappropriate behavior of a sort, which while difficult to define, may still be regarded as unfair, inequitable or unreasonable.[143]

This passage is controversial insofar as it suggests that consistent and uniform State practice can be considered as representing the *opinio juris* of States (a point further discussed in Chapter 4). In any event, the *Merrill & Ring* Tribunal did not embark on a concrete analysis of State practice and *opinio juris*.[144]

The *Cargill* Tribunal adopted a much more cautious approach. First, it stated that it is 'widely accepted that extensive adoption of identical treaty language by many States may in and of itself serve – again with care – as evidence of customary international law'.[145] The Tribunal mentioned that FET clauses were widespread in BITs, but also noted that their actual language varies. For this reason, it held that 'significant evidentiary weight should not be afforded to autonomous clauses inasmuch as it could be assumed that such clauses were adopted precisely because they set a standard other than that required by custom'.[146] The Tribunal concluded that it did not 'believe it prudent to accord significant weight

---

[142] *Merrill & Ring Forestry L.P.* v. *Canada*, UNCITRAL, Award, 31 March 2010, para. 211 (emphasis added).

[143] *Ibid.*, para. 210.

[144] For a critical analysis of the award, see Patrick Dumberry, *The Fair and Equitable Treatment Standard: A Guide to NAFTA Case Law on Article 1105* (Alphen aan den Rijn: Wolters Kluwer, 2013), pp. 115–117.

[145] *Cargill, Inc.* v. *Mexico*, ICSID Case No. ARB(AF)/05/02, Award, 18 September 2009, para. 276.

[146] *Ibid.*

to even widespread adoption of such [FET] clauses'.[147] It also added that: 'It may be that widespread adoption of a strict autonomous meaning to "fair and equitable treatment" may in time raise international expectations as to what constitutes good governance, but such a consequence is different than such clauses evidencing directly an evolution of custom'.[148]

The following sections will show that State practice supports the reasoning of the *Cargill* Tribunal.

3.2.4.2   State practice is general, widespread and representative

A detailed analysis, conducted in the early 1990s, of 335 BITs shows that only 28 BITs did not include a reference to FET.[149] From the 1990s onwards, the standard has been included in the vast majority of BITs. Thus, the model BITs adopted by most capital-exporting countries, such as Canada, the United States, Germany, the United Kingdom and France, all incorporate an FET clause.[150] It was estimated at the time that by the year 2000, 'bilateral investment treaties which omit reference to fair and equitable treatment constitute the exception rather than the rule'.[151] This is confirmed by Tudor's book published in 2008 examining 365 BITs, with only 19 of them not containing a reference to FET.[152]

The present author has examined all 1,964 BITs that were available on the UNCTAD website[153] at the time (February 2014) and found that only 50 of them did not include an FET clause at all, while 25 others only referred to the FET in their preamble.[154] Thus, less than 5% of all BITs examined do not include any formal and binding FET obligation for host States. Although a few BITs contain slightly different language than the expression FET,[155] not so much weight should be given to these

[147] *Ibid.*   [148] *Ibid.*
[149] M. Khalil, 'Treatment of Foreign Investment in BITs', *ICSID Rev* 7(2) (1992), pp. 351–355.
[150] Stephen Vasciannie, 'The Fair and Equitable Treatment Standard in International Investment Law and Practice', *British YIL*, 70 (1999), p. 129.
[151] *Ibid.*, p. 114.   [152] Tudor, *The Fair and Equitable Treatment Standard*, p. 23.
[153] http://investmentpolicyhub.unctad.org/IIA. I have examined BITs available in a number of languages including English, French, Spanish, and so on, but not those in Arabic or Russian.
[154] P. Dumberry, 'Rules of Customary International Law in the Field of International Investment Law', SSHRC Research Project, (2012–2014).
[155] Thus, I have found twelve BITs which only refer to 'fair' treatment, including nine BITs entered into by Iran and three by Russia. Also, five BITs referred to the expression 'just and fair' and thirteen only to 'equitable' treatment, including seven entered into by China and four by Malaysia. Finally, eight BITs referred to 'just and equitable' treatment

variations of language.[156] While my findings are fully discussed else-where[157], a few observations can nevertheless be made in this book about those BITs containing no FET obligations.

First, no State has systematically excluded FET clauses from its treaties. The few States which have omitted such clauses more often than others have only done so in a *minority* of their BITs.

Second, one third of all Japanese and Turkish BITs do not include any binding FET clause. These Japanese BITs have all been entered into with developing States. However, Turkey has entered into those BITs (with no FET clause) with both developing and developed States (all from Eastern Europe and the former USSR, except for Japan). These features suggest that both States may have insisted during treaty negotiation on excluding the presence of any FET clause. Not surprisingly, the Japan–Turkey BIT does not include such a clause.

Third, about 10% of all Romanian, Albanian, Greek and Senegalese BITs have no FET clauses. The majority of such Romanian BITs have been entered into with developing States. All those Greek BITs (containing no FET clause) have been signed with States from Eastern Europe and the former USSR. The same is true for most Albanian BITs. Not surprisingly, the BITs entered into between these three States (Albania–Greece BIT, Albania–Romania BIT) also include no FET clause. These patterns suggest that the absence of an FET clause may have been an important aspect for these States during treaty negotiation.

Overall, it seems that BITs with no FET clauses have been more popular in Eastern Europe than elsewhere. In general (with the exception of Japan), this option has not been favoured by developing States. Only Germany has adopted this approach in nine of its 134 BITs, all with developing States (except for the one signed with Romania). Finally, it should be added that I have examined elsewhere the practical impact of the absence of any FET clause in all of these 50 BITs. I have specifically assessed whether these BITs include an MFN clause which would allow for the importation of an FET standard clause contained in other BITs entered into by these States.[158]

(including three by Germany) and twelve others to the term 'equitable and reasonable' (including three by Italy, six by Norway, and three by the Philippines).

[156] See, discussion in: Dumberry, *The Fair and Equitable Treatment Standard*, p. 58.

[157] See, P. Dumberry, 'Has the Fair and Equitable Treatment Standard become a Rule of Customary international Law? An Empirical Study of the Practice of States (forthcoming, 2016).

[158] P. Dumberry, 'The Importation of the Fair and Equitable Treatment Standard Through MFN Clauses: An Empirical Study of BITs', ICSID Rev. (forthcoming, 2016).

As mentioned previously, the representativeness of the practice of States is another key aspect when assessing the customary nature of a provision contained in treaties.

The FET standard has been included in investment treaties signed by both capital-exporting and capital-importing States. The standard was first developed by Western States to provide protection to their companies when investing in developing countries. This is clear from the inclusion of these clauses in early drafting attempts, such as the 1959 *Draft Convention on Investments Abroad*[159] and the 1967 OECD *Draft Convention on the Protection of Foreign Property*,[160] both reflecting the position of developing States. While the Western origin of the concept is undeniable, it remains today that developing states have also embraced the concept.[161] Thus, the standard was included in regional multilateral instruments related to the protection of foreign investments not only in Europe (Energy Charter Treaty) and in North America (NAFTA), but also in Latin America,[162] Asia[163] Africa,[164] and in Model BITs of developing States (including Chile and China).[165] FET clauses have also been included in BITs entered into *between* developing countries,[166] which now represent 26% of the total number of BITs.[167] Empirical studies show that the content of these South–South BITs is similar to those concluded between developed and developing countries.[168] As

---

[159] Hermann Abs and Hartley Shawcross, 'The Proposed Convention to Protect Private Foreign Investment: A Round Table: Comment on the Draft Convention by its Authors', *J.P.L.* 9 (1960), pp. 115–132; G. Schwarzenberger, 'The Abs-Shawcross Draft Convention on Investments Abroad', *Current Legal Problems* 14 (1961), p. 146.

[160] OECD, *Draft Convention on the Protection of Foreign Property*, adopted on 12 October 1967, *ILM* 7 (1967).

[161] OECD, 'International Investment Law: A Changing Landscape: A Companion Volume to International Investment Perspectives' (2005), p. 78; Vasciannie, 'The Fair and Equitable Treatment Standard', pp. 119, 122; UNCTAD, 'Fair and Equitable Treatment', UNCTAD Series on Issues in International Investment Agreements II (United Nations, 2012), p. 4; OECD, 'Fair and Equitable Treatment Standard in International Investment Law', Working Papers on International Investment Law, No. 2004/3 (2004), p. 5; C. McLachlan, L. Shore and M. Weiniger, *International Investment Arbitration: Substantive Principles* (Oxford: Oxford University Press, 2007), p. 220.

[162] Art. 2, *Colonia Protocol* in the context of Mercosur.

[163] *ASEAN Treaty for the Promotion and Protection of Investments* (Article IV).

[164] *Common Market for Eastern and Southern Africa* (COMESA) (Article 159(1)a).

[165] Vasciannie, 'The Fair and Equitable Treatment Standard', p. 129.

[166] *Ibid.*, pp. 129–130.

[167] UNCTAD, 'Recent Developments in International Investment Agreements (2007–June 2008)', IIA Monitor No. 2 (2008), p. 3.

[168] UNCTAD, 'South-South Cooperation in International Investment Arrangements', UNCTAD Series on International Investment Policies for Development (2005), p. 45.

mentioned above, my own investigation also shows no clear pattern of groups of States systematically rejecting the FET clause. The very few States (Japan, Turkey, Romania, Germany, etc.) which have rejected the clause in only a *minority* of their BITs, come from different continents with very little in common.

In sum, it can be concluded that the practice of States to include FET clauses in their BITs is general, widespread and representative. The other question (examined in the next section) is whether or not such a practice is uniform and consistent enough for a new customary rule to be considered to have emerged.

3.2.4.3   State practice is not uniform and consistent

While admitting that 'BITs do not refer to the FET in a uniform manner',[169] Tudor nevertheless argues that there is enough uniformity in State practice for the emergence of a customary rule:

> However, the existant [sic] differences [between FET clauses] do not relate to the content of the FET but to the various levels of its application (a clear minimum is fixed in the case of the NAFTA, more liberal in the case of certain BITs) and to its relationship with the other dispositions of the treaty. (. . .) The differences encountered refer to the level of the treatment to be accorded to the Investors, not to the standard within its content. There is no doubt that the theoretical requirements relative to the uniformity of State practice are met in the case of the FET, mostly on the basis of the BITs. The consistency criterion is also met. Since their emergence in the 1960s, the number of BITs increased exponentially and the existence of a FET clause has almost each time been confirmed.[170]

Another writer, Diehl, has also recently adopted a similar position. She acknowledges that 'the language of the various investment treaties is not uniform in this respect, varying, above all, between plain description of FET and a combination of the standard with an explicit reference to international law, to the IMS or to other standards of treatment'.[171] Nevertheless, she believes that the practice is uniform:

> Does the evaluation that there are three main categories of broad FET clauses and several equally broad subcategories mean that there is no uniform practice? The answer is clearly no. The differences noted above are merely drafting differences and do not touch upon the core of the FET standard. (. . .) The differences mainly concern the relationship of FET to principles of international law and to other standards. This relationship

---

[169] Tudor, *The Fair and Equitable Treatment Standard*, p. 77.   [170] *Id.*
[171] Diehl, *The Core Standard of International Investment Protection*, p. 132.

cannot and should not be clarified in a uniform and ever-congruent way and thus cannot stand in the way of the formation of custom because it is the very nature of standard not to be uniform and specific but to be broad and open for fact-specific analysis. If this particularity of the notion of standard constituted a bar to the formation of custom, then no standard of treatment could ever become part of customary international law. (...) What truly counts is not whether FET is paired with other standards in the requisite clauses but whether there is a uniform practice insofar as a high number of the BITs existing today provide for FET for investments and/or investors. As this is the case, the first element of custom is fulfilled – despite the fact that several categories of FET clauses exist.[172]

Both authors' conclusions on uniformity are controversial insofar as they acknowledge that BIT provisions on FET contain different wordings. The first obvious criticism of the position adopted by these two writers is indeed whether one can truly speak of 'uniformity' when five or six different FET clause models exist.[173] As a matter of principle, the very existence of these different clauses does not support the claim of uniformity and consistency required for any rule of custom to crystallize. This is also the conclusion reached by a number of scholars.[174]

Moreover, one cannot truly speak of a 'virtually uniform' practice of States when FET clauses containing different language actually mean *different things*. Surprisingly, Tudor admits that 'the *level of treatment* and the *exact meaning* of the FET depend on the wording of each clause'.[175]

---

[172] *Ibid.*, pp. 135–136.
[173] For a discussion of the different existing models, see: Dumberry, *The Fair and Equitable Treatment Standard*.
[174] Andrew Newcombe and Luis Paradell, *Law and Practice of Investment Treaties: Standards of Treatment* (Alphen aan den Rijn: Kluwer, 2009), p. 271, fn 188; Congyan, 'International Investment Treaties', pp. 664, 667; Al Faruque, 'Creating Customary International Law', p. 304; Gazzini, 'The Role of Customary International Law', p. 698; Marcela Klein Bronfman, 'Fair and Equitable Treatment: An Evolving Standard', *Max Planck Yrbk. UNL*, 10 (2006), p. 656; Orakhelashvili, 'The Normative Basis of "Fair and Equitable Treatment"', p. 77. *Contra*: Vasciannie, 'The Fair and Equitable Treatment Standard', p. 157 (not refuting the claim of uniformity of FET clauses, but nevertheless concluding that the FET standard is *not* a rule of custom for other reasons). See also: R. Kläger, *Fair and Equitable Treatment in International Investment Law* (Cambridge: Cambridge University Press, 2011), pp. 267–268 (indicating that 'at first glance, due to the almost uniform presence of fair and equitable treatment in the dense network of BITs, there seems to be at least some evidence that new customary international law may have been created. It is indeed widely assumed that the proliferation of almost identical BITs is evidence of a valuable state practice that has influenced customary law', but concluding, at pp. 268–270, that the FET standard has not become a customary rule because of lack of *opinio juris*).
[175] Tudor, 'The Fair and Equitable treatment Standard and Human Rights Norms', p. 316 (emphasis added). On this point, see the critical reasoning of Schill, in his book review of

In my view, the very fact that different drafting actually means different 'levels of treatment' is quite significant. Contrary to the position held by Diehl, these are *not* merely 'drafting differences' that 'do not touch upon the core of the FET standard'.[176] In fact, these drafting differences affect the *very core* of the *actual types* of FET protection which a State must provide to foreign investors.

As explained elsewhere by the present author,[177] arbitral tribunals have given different interpretations to the scope of FET clauses depending on their actual drafting.[178] A 2012 UNCTAD report indicated that the drafting variations in FET clauses have in fact been interpreted as meaning *different content* as well as *different thresholds*.[179] Many arbitral tribunals have thus interpreted an unqualified (or 'stand-alone') FET clause as 'delinked from customary international law' and have therefore 'focused on the plain-meaning of the terms "fair" and "equitable,"' which 'may result in a low liability threshold and brings with it a risk for State regulatory action to be found in breach of it'.[180] This phenomenon has been recognized by many scholars.[181] The vast majority of tribunals have

Tudor's work: *EJIL* 20 (2009), p. 237 ('it would have been more convincing, and also more helpful to Tudor's argument, to conclude that, despite differences in drafting, states referred to the very same and uniform legal principle of international investment law when including formulations relating to FET in their investment treaties' and that 'differences in wording would not translate into differences in legal meaning').

[176] Diehl, *The Core Standard of International Investment Protection*, pp. 135–136.

[177] Dumberry, *The Fair and Equitable Treatment Standard*, p. 40 ff.

[178] OECD, 'Fair and Equitable Treatment Standard in International Investment Law', p. 40; Hussein Haeri, 'A Tale of Two Standards: "Fair and Equitable Treatment" and the Minimum Standard in International Law', *Arb. Int'l* 27 (2011), p. 26; Christopher F. Dugan, Don Wallace, Jr., Noah Rubins and Borzu Sabahi, *Investor-State Arbitration*, (New York: Oxford University Press, 2008), p. 496.

[179] UNCTAD, 'Fair and Equitable Treatment', 2012, p. 8.   [180] *Ibid.*, p. 22.

[181] Haeri, 'A Tale of Two Standards', p. 26; R. Dolzer, 'Fair And Equitable Treatment in International Law, Remarks', *ASIL Proc.* 100 (2006), p. 69; Katia Yannaca-Small, 'Fair and Equitable Treatment Standard: Recent Developments', in A. Reinisch (ed.), *Standards of Investment Protection* (Oxford: Oxford University Press, 2008), p. 115; Dugan *et al.*, *Investor-State Arbitration*, p. 496; C. Schreuer and R. Dolzer, *Principles of International Investment Law* (Oxford: Oxford University Press, 2008), p. 126; Kläger, *Fair and Equitable Treatment*, p. 85. On the contrary, see the position adopted by the following writers: Stephan W. Schill, 'Fair and Equitable Treatment as an Embodiment of the Rule of Law', in R. Hofmann and C. Tams (eds.), *The International Convention on the Settlement of Investment Disputes (ICSID): Taking Stock after 40 Years* (Baden-Baden: Nomos, 2007), p. 33 (stating that it is 'questionable whether substantial differences result from the different framing of the standard with a view to the actual practice of investment tribunals'); Kenneth J. Vandevelde, 'A Unified Theory of Fair and Equitable Treatment', *N.Y.U. J. Int'l L. & Pol.* 43 (2010), p. 47 ('Differences in the contexts in which the standard appears have made little difference to tribunals interpreting the

in fact interpreted a stand-alone FET clause as having an autonomous character, hence providing a higher a level of standard of treatment than under the MST.[182] In fact, only a limited number of tribunals have interpreted a stand-alone FET standard as an implicit reference to international law.[183] This situation contrasts with the rather confusing approach adopted by tribunals faced with an FET clause containing an explicit reference to 'international law'.[184]

These distinctions are also clear from the present author's own analysis of NAFTA Article 1105 case-law: the 'elements' of legal protection which must be accorded under this provision (whereby the FET standard is linked to international law) are simply *not* the same as those under a typical stand-alone FET clause.[185] Thus, whether or not a State has to protect a foreign investor's legitimate expectations (and, most importantly, the actual contours of such an obligation) will essentially depend on the drafting of the FET clause.[186] The same can be said regarding the so-called obligation of transparency.[187] In my view, legitimate expectations and transparency are not stand-alone elements of the FET obligation under Article 1105, but merely 'factors' to be taken into account by a tribunal when assessing whether or not *other* well-established elements of the standard have been breached.[188]

In sum, the practice of States to include FET clauses in their BITs is clearly not uniform enough for the standard to be considered as having emerged as a customary rule.[189]

---

standard. Rather, the awards have yielded a single coherent theory of the standard, although perhaps not consciously so').

[182] See, Newcombe and Paradell, *Law and Practice of Investment Treaties*, pp. 263–264, referring to several cases.

[183] See, for instance, *Siemens AG v. Argentina*, ICSID No. ARB/02/8, Award, 17 January 2007, para. 291.

[184] UNCTAD, 'Fair and Equitable Treatment', 2012, p. 22. While some tribunals have held that the term 'international law' found in an FET clause was a reference to the minimum standard under custom (see, for instance, *M.C.I. Power Group L.C. and New Turbine, Inc. v. Ecuador*, ICSID No. ARB/03/6, Award, 31 July 2007, para. 369) others have interpreted such an express reference in much the same way as an unqualified FET clause (see, for instance, *Compañía de Aguas del Aconquija S.A. and Vivendi Universal S.A. v. Argentina*, ICSID No. ARB/97/3, Award, 20 August 2007, paras. 7.4.5 ff.; *Técnicas Medioambientales Tecmed, S.A. v. Mexico*, ICSID No. ARB(AF)/00/2, Award, 29 May 2003, para. 155).

[185] Dumberry, *The Fair and Equitable Treatment Standard*, pp. 127–174.

[186] *Ibid.*, pp. 138–170. See also: P. Dumberry, 'The Protection of Investors' Legitimate Expectations and the Fair and Equitable Treatment Standard under NAFTA Article 1105', *J. Int'l Arb.* 31(1) (2014), pp. 47–74.

[187] Dumberry, *The Fair and Equitable Treatment Standard*, pp. 171–180.   [188] *Id.*

[189] The question is further examined at Chapter 3, Section 3.3.3.2.1.3.

3.3   Manifestations of State practice

This section examines the different 'manifestations', or types of evidence, of State practice that are relevant for the creation of custom in both general international law and investor-State arbitration. I will start by making a number of introductory remarks on the requirement that the practice be public and on the question as to whether or not omissions should count as practice (Section 3.3.1). I will then examine the various forms of State practice and the relative weight that should be accorded to them (Section 3.3.2). The rest of this section specifically analyses four different categories of 'manifestations' of State practice: international treaties, statements by States, activities within international organizations and internal national practice of States (Section 3.3.3).

3.3.1   Introductory remarks

3.3.1.1   The publicity requirement

According to certain writers, the only types of evidence of State practice that count towards the formation of custom are those which are communicated to another State, or made public to a certain extent.[190] As noted by Henckaerts and Doswald-Beck, acts may not 'contribute to the formation of customary international law if they are never disclosed'.[191] Thus, States should always be given an opportunity to react to the positions taken by others. Similarly, for the ILA the practice of one State needs to be (at least) disclosed to *another* State: '[f]or a verbal act to count as State practice, it must be public – not in the sense that it need necessarily be communicated to all of the world, but that, if it is not publicized generally (e.g. by legislation, press statements, etc.) it must be communicated to at least one other State'.[192] One should therefore not confuse *confidentiality* with *publicity*. When States exchange views among themselves about the existence (or not) of a rule of customary international law, they do so publicly even if their exchanges remain

---

[190] Mendelson, 'The Formation of Customary International Law', p. 204; Henckaerts and Doswald-Beck, *Customary International Humanitarian Law*, p. xxxviii; ILA, Final Report, 2000, p. 15.

[191] Henckaerts and Doswald-Beck, *Customary International Humanitarian Law*, p. xxxviii.

[192] ILA, Final Report, 2000, p. 15. See also: Mendelson, 'The Formation of Customary International Law', p. 204; Ferrari-Bravo, 'Méthodes de recherche de la coutume internationale', p. 269; Dinstein, 'The Interaction between Customary International Law and Treaties', pp. 275, 278.

confidential.[193] Ultimately, what matters is that they communicate their views publicly to *each other*.

As will be discussed further, confidentiality in the field of investor-State arbitration is rather problematic for any scholar interested in assessing State practice. This is because information is not being made available for a large number of investor-State disputes currently being settled by arbitration. This is true for some cases where the *UNCITRAL Arbitration Rules* and other *ad hoc* arbitration rules apply. Tracking actual State practice is virtually impossible for these publicly unknown cases. In any event, even in the context of ICSID arbitration only awards are typically made publicly available. Thus, in most cases, the pleadings of the parties are not available. Yet, as discussed further,[194] arbitration proceedings also act as valuable publicly available sources of State practice in the forms of a variety of statements made by States.

3.3.1.2 Omissions count as practice

As summarized by one writer, what matters for the creation of customary norms is what 'States have done, or abstained from doing'.[195] Thus, both *positive* acts (actions) and *passive* acts (inaction, omission, abstention) are components of State practice.[196] Scholars generally recognize that in *certain circumstances* States' abstentions to take action can give rise to customary rules.[197] What matters is that the abstention is not ambiguous

---

[193] International Law Commission, 'First Report on Formation and Evidence of Customary International Law', by Michael Wood, Special Rapporteur, Sixty-fifth session, Geneva, 6 May-7 June and 8 July-9 August 2013, UN doc. A/CN.4/663, 17 May 2013, p. 20 [hereinafter referred to as ILC, First Report, 2013]; D. Bethlehem, 'The Secret Life of International Law', *Cambridge J Intl Comp L*, 23 (2012), p. 34.

[194] See, at Chapter 3, Section 3.3.4.2.

[195] Thirlway, *International Customary Law and Codification*, p. 58; Jörg Kammerhofer, 'Uncertainty in the Formal Sources of International Law: Customary International Law and Some of Its Problems', *EJIL* 15(3) (2004), p. 525; Tudor, *The Fair and Equitable Treatment Standard*, p. 71.

[196] Kammerhofer, 'Uncertainty in the Formal Sources of International Law', p. 529.

[197] Villiger, *Customary International Law and Treaties*, pp. 16–17, 37; Wolfke, *Custom in Present International Law*, p. 61; Dinstein, 'The Interaction between Customary International Law and Treaties', pp. 269, 283; Mendelson, 'The Formation of Customary International Law', pp. 207–209 (acknowledging that States' abstention from prosecuting foreign diplomats suspected or accused of crimes contributed substantially to the creation of the rules pertaining to diplomatic immunity); S. Séfériadès, 'Aperçu sur la coutume juridique internationale et notamment sur son fondement', *RGDIP*, 43 (1936), pp. 129, 143; G.I. Tunkin, 'Remarks on the Juridical Nature of Customary Norms of International Law', *Cal. L. Rev* 49 (1961), pp. 419, 421; R. Kolb, 'Selected Problems in the Theory of Customary International Law', *Netherlands ILR*, 50

in its context.[198] A so-called ambiguous omission does not count as relevant State practice.[199] One needs to be able to distinguish between a State doing *simply nothing* for no particular reason (including simple lack of interest in an issue), with an abstention that has an *actual meaning* insofar as it implies a tacit agreement.[200] The distinction and the relevant circumstances are further explained as follows by ILC Special Rapporteur Wood:

> As there could be various reasons for a refusal or failure to act, including a lack of capacity to do so or a lack of direct interest, not every instance of inaction will amount to concurrence: only "qualified silence" (. . .) may be construed as concurrence in the relevant practice. (. . .) First, inaction could be relevant only to establishing concurrence where reaction to the relevant practice is called for: As the International Court of Justice (. . .). This implies that the relevant practice ought to be one that affects the interests or rights of the State failing or refusing to act; (. . .) Second, a State whose inaction is sought to be relied upon in identifying whether a rule of customary international law has emerged must have had actual knowledge of the practice in question or the circumstances must have been such that the State concerned is deemed to have had such knowledge. Third, and related to the requirement of knowledge of the practice in question, is the need for the inaction to be maintained over a sufficient period of time.[201]

As discussed further,[202] the only way to distinguish between relevant and 'ambiguous' omissions is through the concept of *opinio juris*. Thus, as noted by the ILC Special Rapporteur, '[i]naction is a form of practice that (when general and *coupled with acceptance as law*) may give rise to a rule

(2003), p. 136; Weisburd, 'Customary International Law', p. 7; ILA, Final Report, 2000, pp. 15, 10 (providing the following example: 'It is often helpful to think of customary rules as emerging, in the typical case, from a process of express or implied claim and response – an insight which comes from Myres S. McDougal and his associates. Thus, if State A expressly claims the right to exclude foreign warships from passing through its territorial sea, and State B sends a warship through without seeking the permission of A, this is an implicit claim on the part of B that A has no right to prohibit the passage. If A fails to protest against this infringement, this omission can, in its turn, constitute a tacit admission of the existence of a right of passage after all'); ILC, Third Report, 2015, p. 9; Akehurst, 'Custom as a Source of International Law', p. 10; *Restatement of the Law Third: The Foreign Relations Law of the United States*, American Law Institute Publ. (1987), vol. 1. §102, comment b ('Inaction may constitute state practice').

[198] Mendelson, 'The Formation of Customary International Law', p. 208; M. Mendelson, 'The Subjective Element in Customary International Law', *British YIL*, 66 (1996), pp. 177, 199.

[199] ILC, Third Report, 2015, p. 10.

[200] Kammerhofer, 'Uncertainty in the Formal Sources of International Law', p. 529.

[201] ILC, Third Report, 2015, pp. 11–14.   [202] See, Chapter 4, Section 4.1.4.

of customary international law'.[203] The same conclusion was also reached by the ICJ: 'The Court has however to be satisfied that there exists in customary international law an *opinio juris* as to the binding character of such abstention'.[204]

Finally, as noted by ILC Special Rapporteur Wood, '[i]naction may also serve as evidence of acceptance as law (*opinio juris*), when it represents concurrence in a certain practice'.[205]

3.3.2 The various forms of State practice and their relative weight

The so-called positive acts of States (i.e. the opposite of omissions and abstentions) can take various forms. The first obvious form is the *actual conduct* of States.[206] For instance, the ICRC study on customary rules in the field of the laws of war indicates that relevant State conduct includes 'battlefield behaviour, the use of certain weapons and the treatment provided to different categories of persons'.[207] The ILC's work on custom formation provides the following (non-exhaustive) list of examples of 'physical' actions taken by States: 'passage of ships in international waterways; passage over territory; impounding of fishing boats; granting of

---

[203] ILC, Third Report, 2015, p. 9 (emphasis added). See also: ILC, Draft Conclusions, 2015, conclusion no. 6(1): 'Practice may take a wide range of forms. It includes both physical and verbal acts. It may, under certain circumstances, include inaction'.

[204] *Military and Paramilitary Activities in and against Nicaragua*, ICJ Rep. 1986, p. 14, at p. 99, para. 188.

[205] ILC, Third Report, 2015, p. 10, adding: 'in essence, we are here concerned with the toleration by a State of a practice of another or other States, in circumstances that attest to the fact that the State choosing not to act considers such practice to be consistent with international law. Such acquiescence, in the words of the Chamber of the International Court of Justice in *Gulf of Maine*, "is equivalent to tacit recognition manifested by unilateral conduct which the other party may interpret as consent"' (quoting from: *Delimitation of the Maritime Boundary in the Gulf of Maine Area*, p. 305, para. 130). See also: ILC, Draft Conclusions, 2015, conclusion no. 10(3): 'Failure to react over time to a practice may serve as evidence of acceptance as law (*opinio juris*), provided that States were in a position to react and the circumstances called for some reaction'.

[206] This is recognized by scholars, see, *inter alia*: Akehurst, 'Custom as a Source of International Law', p. 10; Tudor, *The Fair and Equitable Treatment Standard*, p. 71; Villiger, *Customary International Law and Treaties*, pp. 16–17; Malcolm N. Shaw, *International Law* (6th edn., Cambridge: Cambridge University Press, 2008), pp. 82–83; P. Malanczuk, *Akehurst's Modern Introduction to International Law* (7th ed., New York and London: Routledge, 1997), pp. 39–40; J. Kammerhofer, 'Uncertainty in the Formal Sources of International Law', p. 525; ILA Report, 2000, pp. 15–16.

[207] Henckaerts and Doswald-Beck, *Customary International Humanitarian Law*, p. xxxviii.

diplomatic asylum; battlefield or operational behaviour; or conducting atmospheric nuclear tests or deploying nuclear weapons'.[208]

State conduct matters for the formation of custom because it some-times provides clear evidence of how one State views the law.[209] Accordingly, it is generally recognized that for such conduct to count as relevant practice for the creation of custom it needs to be 'deliberate or, at least, conscious'; therefore excluding 'mistakes, accidents and other inadvertent acts'.[210]

The most obvious examples of 'physical' conduct of States, in the context of investment arbitration, are expropriation acts where the State (or a State-owned entity) takes over the foreign investor's assets, confiscates them or transfers the property rights.[211] Other classic exam-ples of 'physical' conduct attributable to a State include the occupation of its premises by the State's army,[212] the looting of its property by members of said army,[213] the destruction of its plant,[214] or the arrest, imprison-ment, or expulsion of an investor from the country.[215] For instance, the *Desert Line Projects* case involved a number of physical actions, including physical duress and other related measures of coercion, interference or

---

[208] ILC, Second Report, 2014, p. 22.

[209] Wood and Sender, 'State Practice', para. 11 ('For example, in the field of international humanitarian law, the manner in which States actually conduct hostilities may be the best evidence of their view of the law').

[210] Dinstein, 'The Interaction between Customary International Law and Treaties', p. 269, further arguing (at p. 271) that '*ultra vires* conduct of ordinary organs of State – other than the few highranking office-holders (...) – must not be taken into account in appraising that State's contribution to the genesis of custom'. See also: Ferrari-Bravo, 'Méthodes de recherche de la coutume internationale', p. 261, defining State practice as 'tout comportement d'un État qui soit révélateur d'une attitude consciente de celui-ci vis-à-vis d'une règle de droit international ou d'une situation juridique internationale'.

[211] See, for instance, *Victor Pey Casado and President Allende Foundation v. Chile*, ICSID Case No. ARB/98/2, Award, 8 May 2008; *Biwater Gauff (Tanzania) Ltd. v. Tanzania*, ICSID Case No. ARB/05/22, Award, 24 July 2008; *Wena Hotels Ltd. v. Egypt*, ICSID Case No. ARB/98/4, Award, 8 December 2000.

[212] *S.A.R.L. Benvenuti & Bonfant v. People's Republic of the Congo*, ICSID Case No. ARB/77/2, Award, 8 August 1980.

[213] *American Manufacturing & Trading (AMT) v. Zaire*, ICSID Case No. ARB/93/1, Award, 21 February 1997.

[214] *Asian Agricultural Products Ltd (AAPL) v. Sri Lanka*, ICSID Case No. ARB/87/3, Final Award, 27 June 1990.

[215] *Antoine Biloune (Syria) and Marine Drive Complex Ltd. (Ghana) v. Ghana Investment Centre and the Government of Ghana*, UNCITRAL, Award on Jurisdiction and Liability, 27 October 1989; *Biwater Gauff (Tanzania) Ltd. v. Tanzania*, ICSID Case No. ARB/05/22, Award, 24 July 2008.

intimidation conducted by Yemen's army/police forces, along with the arrest and detention of three of the company's executives.[216]

But, of course, relevant forms of State practice for the creation of custom are not limited to a State's 'physical' conduct.[217] Scholars typically enumerate lists of the different relevant elements of State practice. A good example of such a list is found in Crawford's *Brownlie's Principles of Public International Law*:

> [D]iplomatic correspondence, policy statements, press releases, the opinions of government legal advisers, official manuals on legal questions (e. g. manuals of military law), executive decisions and practices, orders to military forces (e.g. rules of engagement), comments by governments on ILC drafts and corresponding commentaries, legislation, international and national judicial decisions, recitals in treaties and other international instruments (especially when in 'all states' form), an extensive pattern of treaties in the same terms, the practice of international organs, and resolutions relating to legal questions in UN organs, notably the General Assembly.[218]

Similarly, a 2013 document prepared by the ILC Secretariat in the context of Special Rapporteur Wood's work on 'Formation and Evidence of Customary International Law' referred to the following non-exhaustive list of materials upon which the ILC had relied as elements of State practice: 'internal law, municipal court decisions, practice of the executive branch, diplomatic practice and treaty practice'.[219] The document added that the ILC had also relied upon 'other materials as secondary sources of information regarding State practice', including 'Government comments, publications of international organizations and non-

---

[216] *Desert Line Projects LLC v. Yemen*, ICSID Case No. ARB/05/17, Award, 6 February 2008.

[217] ILC, Second Report, 2014, p. 20; K. Zemanek, 'What is 'State Practice' and who Makes It?', in U. Beyerlin *et al.* (eds.), *Festschrift für Rudolf Bernhardt* (Berlin: Springer-Verlag, 1995), p. 299.

[218] Crawford, *Brownlie's Principles of Public International Law*, p. 24 (a similar list is found in: Crawford, 'The Identification and Development of Customary International Law', pp. 3–4). There are other examples of such lists, including Congyan, 'International Investment Treaties and the Formation', p. 661 ('According to the United Nations International Law Commission (ILC) and most international lawyers, the evidence of CIL rules can be distilled from three sources: inter-State diplomatic relations, which take the forms of treaties, declarations and other diplomatic documents; international institutional operation, which takes the forms of decisions, judgments, etc.; intra-State actions, which take the forms of law and regulations, judgments and administrative decision, etc.'). See also: Ferrari-Bravo, 'Méthodes de recherche de la coutume internationale', pp. 233, 257–287; Villiger, *Customary International Law and Treaties*, p. 17.

[219] ILC, Memorandum, 2013, p. 14, 65.

governmental organizations, executive branch publications and international judicial decisions and the writings of jurists'.[220] Conclusion 6(2) of the ILC Draft Conclusions reads as follows:

> Forms of State practice include, but are not limited to: diplomatic acts and correspondence; conduct in connection with resolutions adopted by an international organization or at an intergovernmental conference; conduct in connection with treaties; executive conduct, including operational conduct "on the ground"; legislative and administrative acts; and decisions of national courts.[221]

There is no predetermined hierarchy between the different forms of State practice that count as evidence of custom.[222] As explained by the ILC Special Rapporteur Wood, 'no one manifestation of practice is *a priori* more important than the other; its weight depends on the circumstances as well as on the nature of the rule in question'.[223] Thus, as noted by one writer, 'caution and balance are indispensable, not only in determining the right mix of what States say and do, want and believe, but also in being aware of the ambiguities with which many elements of practice are fraught'.[224] A number of related questions will be specifically discussed in this section, including whether States' statements should count as much as 'physical' conduct in terms of manifestation of practice.[225] Another issue that will be examined is the inconsistency between different forms of practice by the *same* State; for instance, when the executive branch of government says the opposite of the judiciary.[226]

It has been correctly observed that 'State practice takes many forms' and that '[w]hat we look for as State practice or what counts as sufficient State practice may vary depending on the rule (and more generally, the area of international law) concerned'.[227] One central theme of this book is indeed to discover whether the elements evidencing State practice in international investment law are *different* from those relevant in general international law. The next sections will show that some of the important manifestations of State practice under general international law have a

---

[220] *Ibid.*, p. 16.   [221] ILC, Draft Conclusions, 2015, conclusion no 6(2).

[222] Akehurst, 'Custom as a Source of International Law', p. 21; Wolfke, *Custom in Present International Law*, p. 157. See also: ILC, Second Report, 2014, p. 65, Draft Conclusion 8(1) of the ILC 'Proposed draft conclusions on the identification of customary international law' ('There is no predetermined hierarchy among the various forms of practice'). See also: ILC, Draft Conclusions, 2015, conclusion no. 6(3).

[223] ILC, Second Report, 2014, p. 32. See also, at p. 14.

[224] Treves, 'Customary International Law', para. 28.

[225] See, Chapter 3, Sections 3.3.4.1.1 and 3.3.4.1.2.   [226] See, Chapter 3, Section 3.3.6.3.1.

[227] Wood and Sender, 'State Practice', para. 3.

limited impact in investment arbitration. A useful illustration is diplomatic statements and correspondence. Conversely, I will also show that a number of specific types of statements have a unique importance in this field. Yet, in many respects, manifestations of State practice are not that different from general international law. Thus, the question of the role of treaties in the formation and development of customary rules is controversial in both international law and investment arbitration.

As discussed further in the next sections, very few tribunals have examined the relevant manifestations of State practice in investment arbitration. One example is the *Glamis* award:

> The evidence of such "concordant practice" undertaken out of a sense of legal obligation is exhibited in very few authoritative sources: treaty ratification language, statements of governments, treaty practice (e.g., Model BITs), and sometimes pleadings. Although one can readily identify the practice of States, it is usually very difficult to determine the intent behind those actions. Looking to a claimant to ascertain custom requires it to ascertain such intent, a complicated and particularly difficult task.[228]

The next four sections will examine the following relevant manifestations of State practice in the context of both general international law and international investment law:

– International treaties (Section 3.3.3);
– Statements by States (Section 3.3.4);
– Activities within international organizations (Section 3.3.5); and
– Internal national practice of States (Section 3.3.6).

3.3.3   International treaties

This section will examine a first source of evidence of State practice: treaties. I have decided not to analyse the role of *travaux préparatoires* because it is generally recognized that draft negotiation documents do *not* constitute relevant State practice (or any *opinio juris*) in the context of custom creation. This is because 'it is more than doubtful that the participating states would agree to be bound in any way by their opinions or statements delivered in the course of negotiations, except possibly in cases when such has been their clear intention'.[229]

---

[228] *Glamis Gold Ltd* v. *United States*, UNCITRAL, Award, 14 May 2009, para. 603.
[229] Wolfke, *Custom in Present International Law*, pp. 71–72. *Travaux préparatoires* are nevertheless relevant in the context of treaty *interpretation*, see Article 32 of the

This section will first examine the role treaties play in the formation of custom in general international law (Section 3.3.3.1). It will then concentrate on the specific situation of investment treaties (Section 3.3.3.2).

3.3.3.1   Interaction between custom and treaties under general international law

The 1969 *Vienna Convention on the Law of Treaties* defines a treaty as 'an international agreement concluded between States in written form and governed by international law, whether embodied in a single instrument or in two or more related instruments and whatever its particular designation'.[230] A treaty is *only* binding on the States which are parties to the instrument, *not* on third party States.[231]

One important point which should be highlighted from the outset is the (obvious) fact that a treaty cannot *by itself* constitute a rule of custom; it can only serve as *evidence* of the *existence* of such a rule.[232] Treaties often represent persuasive and authoritative evidence of State practice necessary for the creation of customary norms.[233]

The vast majority of writers indeed agree that international treaties can be considered as a form of State practice relevant to the formation of customary rules.[234] D'Amato, for instance, asserts that 'a treaty arguably is

---

Vienna Convention on the Law of Treaties, signed in 1969 and entered into force on 27 January 1980, *UNTS* 1155 (1969), p. 331.

[230] *Vienna Convention on the Law of Treaties, Ibid.*, Art. 2(1).   [231] *Ibid.*, Art. 34.

[232] ILC, Third Report, 2015, p. 17 ('The provisions of treaties do not in and of themselves constitute rules of customary international law, but such provisions, as "an explicit expression of the will of states", may offer valuable evidence of the existence (or otherwise) and content of such rules'). See also Villiger, *Customary International Law and Treaties*, p. 132 ('conventional texts may—though not invariably so—*offer evidence of a customary rule*. Like codes and resolutions, such texts merely reflect or declare, but [on account of the independence of sources] do not actually constitute, the underlying customary rule the existence of which depends on other conditions of State practice and *opinio juris*, and which does not require the additional contractual basis for its binding force').

[233] ILC, Third Report, 2015, p. 17; R. Baxter, 'Multilateral Treaties as Evidence of Customary International Law', *British YIL*, 41 (1965–1966), pp. 278, 297 ('since the treaty speaks with one voice rather than [many], it is much clearer and more direct evidence of the state of the law than the conflicting, ambiguous and multi-temporal evidence that might be amassed through an examination of the practice of each of the individual [signatory] States . . . a structure of treaty law is more persuasive and authoritative than a structure constructed of the diverse and jumbled materials of State practice').

[234] Baxter, 'Treaties and Custom', p. 31; Tudor, *The Fair and Equitable Treatment Standard*, p. 76; ILA Report, 2000, p. 661; Bernard Kishoiyian, 'The Utility of Bilateral Investment Treaties in the Formulation of Customary International Law', *Northwestern J. Int'l L. & Bus* 14(2) (1993), p. 335; Jeswald W. Salacuse, *The Law of Investment Treaties* (Oxford:

a clear record of a binding international commitment that constitutes the "practice of states" and hence is as much a record of customary behavior as any other state act or restraint'.[235] There is indeed no doubt that *signing* a treaty is clearly a positive act which counts as State practice in itself.[236] D'Amato, however, further argues that 'what makes the content of a treaty count as an element of custom is the fact that the parties to the treaty have entered into a binding commitment to act in accordance with its terms' and, more controversially, that 'whether or not they subsequently act in conformity with the treaty, the fact remains that they have so committed to act'.[237] In my opinion, the fact that a State does *not* act in accordance with its own treaty obligations must *also* count as relevant State practice. In fact, such non-compliance should have the effect of limiting the weight given to the initial act of signing the treaty. In other words, the treaties that are complied with by States will have more influence in the creation of customary rules than those that are not.

While custom and treaties are two distinct sources of international law, they remain in many ways 'entangled'.[238] It is generally recognized that there are three forms of interaction between custom and treaties[239]:

Oxford University Press, 2010), p. 113; Steffen Hindelang, 'Bilateral Investment Treaties, Custom and a Healthy Investment Climate – The Question of whether BITs Influence Customary International Law Revisited', *J. World Invest. & Trade*, 5 (2004); Jose E. Alvarez, 'A Bit on Custom', *N.Y.U. J. Int'l L. & Pol.* 42 (2009–2010), p. 49; Al Faruque, 'Creating Customary International Law', p. 298; M. Sornarajah, *The International Law on Foreign Investment* (2nd edn., Cambridge: Cambridge University Press, 2004), p. 206; Crawford, *Brownlie's Principles of Public International Law*, p. 24; Shaw, *International Law*, pp. 82–83; Malanczuk, *Akehurst's Modern Introduction to International Law*, pp. 39–40; Villiger, *Customary International Law and Treaties*, p. 26; D'Amato, *The Concept of Custom in International Law*, p. 104; ILC, Second Report, 2014, p. 24 (providing a long list of examples); Gazzini, 'The Role of Customary International Law', p. 692.

[235] D'Amato, *The Concept of Custom in International Law*, p. 104.
[236] Hindelang, 'Bilateral Investment Treaties', p. 793 ('there does not appear to be any convincing argument as to why the conclusion of a treaty should not serve as evidence of State practice').
[237] A. D'Amato, 'Custom and Treaty: A Response to Professor Weisburd', *Vanderbilt Journal of Transnational Law*, 21 (1988), p. 462, adding that 'the commitment itself, then, is the 'state practice' component of custom'.
[238] Oscar Schachter, 'Entangled Treaty and Custom', in Yoram Dinstein (ed.), *International Law at a Time of Perplexity: Essays in Honour of Shabtai Rosenne* (Drodrecht: Martinus Nijhoff, 1989), pp. 717–738; Maurice Mendelson, 'Disentangling Treaty and Customary International Law', *ASIL Proc.* 81 (1987), pp. 157–163.
[239] On this question, see, Villiger, *Customary International Law and Treaties*, p. 195 ff; Baxter, 'Treaties and Custom', p. 25; D'Amato, *The Concept of Custom in International Law*, pp. 103–166; Thirlway, *International Customary Law and Codification*; Schachter, 'Entangled Treaty and Custom', p. 717.

[F]irst, the conventional text may merely restate a pre-existing rule of customary law; second, the adoption of a treaty norm may catalyse the emergence of a customary rule in *statu nascendi*; or third, a treaty may create new rules that, in due course, themselves become accepted as customary law.[240]

In the following sections, I will examine two forms of interaction (the second and third forms of interaction identified in the above quotation will be assessed together): treaties contributing to the formation of *new* rules of customary international law (Section 3.3.3.1.1) and treaties *codifying existing* customary rules (Section 3.3.3.1.2).

I have decided not to examine another rather theoretical form of interaction between custom and treaties. This is the possibility that a treaty ratified by a very large group of States could, *in and of itself*, be evidence of the creation of new customary legal norms.[241] In this scenario, a treaty does not 'codify' existing custom nor does it contribute to the formation of new rules of customary international law. Here, what is envisaged is the possibility that the content of a treaty could be considered *instantaneously* as *new* custom (and therefore binding on all States) simply because it is widely adopted by States. This unlikely scenario has been endorsed by some writers[242] and has been accepted for 'exceptional

---

[240] Kläger, *Fair and Equitable Treatment*, p. 262. See also: ILC, First Report, 2013, p. 15: 'In short, the interplay between these two "entangled" sources of international law may be highly relevant for the present purposes as it is generally recognized that treaties may be reflective of pre-existing rules of customary international law; generate new rules and serve as evidence of their existence; or, through their negotiation processes, have a crystallizing effect for emerging rules of customary international law'. The ILC, Third Report, 2015, p. 19 makes the same point using a slightly different terminology: 'There are at least three ways in which a treaty provision may reflect or come to reflect a rule of customary international law, or, in other words, assist in determining the existence and content of the rule: the provision may (a) codify a rule that exists at the time of the conclusion of the treaty; (b) lead to the crystallization of a rule that may be emerging; or (c) lead to a general practice accepted as law, such that a new rule of customary international law comes into being'. See also: *Ibid.*, Draft Conclusion 12 of the ILC 'Proposed draft conclusions on the identification of customary international law'; ILC, Draft Conclusions, 2015, conclusion no. 11(1).

[241] This question is examined in: Mendelson, 'The Formation of Customary International Law', p. 322 ff.

[242] See, for example, L. Sohn, 'The Law of the Sea: Customary International Law Developments', *American University LR*, 34 (1985), p. 274 (suggesting that the international community might decide that 'consensus at a conference plus a signature by a vast majority of the participants creates a general norm of international law... binding on [states] from the very moment of [the] adoption [of the international agreement]'). See also: L. Sohn, 'The International Law of Human Rights: A Reply to Recent Criticisms',

cases' by the ILA.[243] One passage from the *North Sea Continental Shelf* cases may be viewed as endorsing this possibility.[244] Yet, as noted by Dinstein, while a treaty can slowly generate new custom it 'cannot pull itself by its own metaphorical bootstraps, and turn into custom'.[245] In any event, while this scenario is (at least theoretically) possible for multilateral treaties, it is improbable for *bilateral* treaties, including BITs.[246]

3.3.3.1.1 Treaties can contribute to the formation of new rules of customary international law

The first form of interaction between custom and treaty is the undeniable fact that *patterns of treaties* can contribute to the formation of *new rules* of customary international law in the future. The phenomenon is widely recognized by scholars[247] and by the work of the ILC.[248] The ILA is of the same opinion, indicating that

---

    Hofstra L Rev 9 (1981), p. 347: L. Sohn, '"Generally Accepted" International Rules', *Washington L.R.* 61 (1986), p. 1073.

[243] ILA, Final Report, 2000, p. 50 ff., indicating that 'In exceptional cases, it may be possible for a multilateral treaty to give rise to new customary rules (or to assist in their creation) "of its own impact" if it is widely adopted by States and it is the clear intention of the parties to create new customary law', but also adding that 'such an occurrence will be extremely rare, and is to be presumed not to have occurred'. See also: Mendelson, 'The Formation of Customary International Law', pp. 327–328.

[244] *North Sea Continental Shelf Cases*, ICJ Rep. 1969, para. 73 ('a very widespread and representative participation in the convention might suffice of itself to create new custom).

[245] Dinstein, 'The Interaction between Customary International Law and Treaties', p. 375. See also: B. Simma and P. Alston, 'The Sources of Human Rights Law: Custom, *Jus Cogens*, and General Principles', *Australian YIL*, 12 (1988–1989), pp. 89–90; A. Boyle and C. Chinkin, *The Making of International Law* (Oxford University Press, 2007), p. 236; Schachter, 'Entangled Treaty and Custom', p. 723 ('Certainly there is no support by courts or scholars for concluding that a treaty becomes customary law solely by virtue of its conclusion or entry into force').

[246] Mendelson, 'The Formation of Customary International Law', p. 329: 'It is difficult, at first sight, to see how isolated bilateral or plurilateral treaties could by themselves, "because of their own impact", create new customary rules: the parties are too few for them to generate general law by the mere fact of their conclusion'. Mendelson also rejects such possibility for a *succession* of bilateral treaties because 'each agreement represents, in a very real sense, an isolated bargain' (*Ibid.*). He further argues that even if the terms of BITs 'have often been copied or adapted, one from the other', it remains that their provisions are the result of compromises between States which do *not* count for the purpose of the formation of customary law (*Ibid.*)

[247] Baxter, 'Treaties and Custom', p. 57 ff; Villiger, *Customary International Law and Treaties*, p. 167 ff; Dinstein, 'The Interaction between Customary International Law and Treaties', p. 371 ff; Al Faruque, 'Creating Customary International Law', pp. 298–299.

[248] ILC, Memorandum, 2013, p. 33 ('the Commission has, on several occasions, recognized that treaties may contribute to the crystallization or development of a rule of customary

the conclusion of multilateral treaties may 'provide the impulse or model for the formation of new customary rules through State practice'.[249] The same phenomenon also exists for a *single* multilateral treaty: 'There can be no doubt that, from time to time, the conclusion of a treaty serves as the impetus or inspiration (so to speak) for State practice which becomes sufficiently widespread for customary law to emerge'.[250] In fact, this possibility is recognized in Article 38 of the *Vienna Convention on the Law of Treaties.*[251] In his Third Report,[252] ILC Special Rapporteur Wood refers to a number of contemporary examples of such a phenomenon, including in the field of the law of the sea (the continental shelf, the exclusive economic zone[253]) and a number of provisions found in the *Vienna Convention on the Law of Treaties* (such as those on treaty interpretation).[254]

This phenomenon has long been recognized by many international courts,[255] including the ICJ.[256] In the *North Sea Continental Shelf* cases, the question at stake was whether or not Article 6 of the *1958 Geneva Continental Shelf Convention* had given rise to a new rule of customary law. The Court explained the phenomenon as follows:

> ... a norm-creating provision which has constituted the foundation of, or has generated a rule which, while only conventional or contractual in its origin, has since passed into the general corpus of international law, and is now accepted as such by the *opinio juris*, so as to have become binding even for countries which have never, and do not, become parties to the Convention. There is no doubt that this process is a perfectly possible one and does from time to time occur: it constitutes indeed one of the recognized methods by which new rules of customary international law

international law'). See also: ILC, Third Report, 2015, p. 23; ILC, Draft Conclusions, 2015, conclusion no. 11(1)

[249] ILA, Final Report, 2000, p. 46.

[250] Mendelson, 'The Formation of Customary International Law', p. 312, providing several illustrations.

[251] Art. 38, *Vienna Convention on the Law of Treaties*: 'Nothing in articles 34 to 37 precludes a rule set forth in a treaty from becoming binding upon a third State as a customary rule of international law, recognized as such'. On this provision, see, Villiger, *Customary International Law and Treaties*, p. 169.

[252] ILC, Third Report, 2015, p. 27.

[253] *Ibid.*, referring to: T. Treves, 'Codification du droit international et pratique des Etats dans le droit de la mer', *Rec. des cours* 223 (1990), pp. 9–302; J.A. Roach, 'Today's Customary International Law of the Sea', *Ocean Development and International Law*, 45 (2014), pp. 239–259.

[254] *Ibid.*, referring to: O. Corten and P. Klein, *The Vienna Convention on the Law of Treaties: A Commentary* (2nd edn., Oxford: Oxford University Press, 2011).

[255] ILC, Third Report, 2015, p. 24, referring to many examples.

[256] *North Sea Continental Shelf Cases*, ICJ Rep. 1969, para. 63. See also: *Ibid.*, p. 96 (Separate Opinion of Judge Padilla Nervo), p. 225 (Dissenting Opinion of Judge Lachs), p. 241 (Dissenting Opinion of Judge Sørensen).

may be formed. At the same time this result is not lightly to be regarded as having been attained.[257]

For this new customary rule to emerge, the Court added that the following requirements should be met:

- The provision contained in a treaty (or treaties) must be of a 'fundamentally norm-creating character such as could be regarded as forming the basis of a general rule of law';[258]
- The 'passage of any considerable period of time' is not required for the new rule to emerge.[259] In other words, 'the passage of only a short period of time is not necessarily, or of itself, a bar to the formation of a new rule of customary international law';[260]
- Yet, during that time 'State practice, including that of States whose interests are specially affected, should have been both extensive and virtually uniform in the sense of the provision invoked';[261]
- Also, such practice should 'have occurred in such a way as to show a general recognition that a rule of law or legal obligation is involved'.[262]

While the treaty (or treaties) can be 'the historic (material) source of a customary rule', it nevertheless cannot be considered as its 'formal' source.[263] In other words, it is not the treaty *itself* which leads to the formation of new custom. It is the actual practice of States *after* the entry into force of the treaty that can be the 'formal' source of the development of a customary rule (the question of *which* State's practice actually matters is examined below).[264] The ICJ has recognized this important distinction.[265]

---

[257] *Ibid.*, para. 71.
[258] *Ibid.*, para. 72. On this notion, see, Villiger, *Customary International Law and Treaties*, pp. 177–178.
[259] *North Sea Continental Shelf Cases*, ICJ Rep. 1969, para. 73.   [260] *Ibid.*, para. 74.
[261] *Ibid.* This question was examined above in Chapter 3, Section 3.2.   [262] *Ibid.*
[263] ILA, Final Report, 2000, p. 46.
[264] See, Villiger, *Customary International Law and Treaties*, p. 26: 'For written rules to have any value in the formative process of customary law, further *instances of material practice*, in conjunction with the written rules are required is not the written text which contributes towards customary law, but the instances whereby States apply these rules in a concrete case, or refer to them, or vote upon them, which do so' (emphasis in the original). See also: S. Zamora, 'Is there Customary International Economic Law?', *German YIL* 32 (1989), p. 19; ILC, Third Report, 2015, p. 18 ('Treaty texts alone cannot serve as conclusive evidence of the existence or content of rules of customary international law: whatever the role that a treaty may play vis-à-vis customary international law (see below), in order for the existence in customary international law of a rule found in a written text to be established, the rule must find support in external instances of practice coupled with acceptance as law').
[265] *Continental Shelf (Libyan Arab Jamahiriya/Malta)*, Judgment, ICJ Rep. 1985, p. 13, at pp. 29–30, para. 27: '[i]t is of course axiomatic that the material of customary international

In the scenario envisaged in the previous paragraph, a treaty (or a number of treaties) will be considered as the *starting point* (or the 'historic' source) of the eventual development of a new customary rule. Another closely related phenomenon is the so-called crystallization of custom. For the ILA, multilateral treaties can thus 'assist in the "crystallization" of *emerging* rules of customary international law'.[266] Here, the treaty is *not* the starting point of the eventual formation of a rule. The treaty intervenes later in the process by *boosting* pre-existing State practice and helping the crystallization of a slowly emerging new rule of custom. One example of such a phenomenon is the 'development of the concept of the exclusive economic zone during the Third United Nations Conference on the Law of the Sea (1973–1982), and its acceptance by States as customary international law even before the adoption of the United Nations Convention on the Law of the Sea in 1982 and its entry into force in 1994'.[267] The ICJ has also long-recognized the phenomenon of 'crystallization'.[268]

Once the rule has crystallized, it is binding on *all States*, not only those which are party to the original treaty (or treaties).[269] In practical terms, this means that a State party to the original treaty cannot be absolved from respecting the obligation contained in the treaty by simply denouncing it.[270]

It is important to mention that while treaties *can* contribute to the formation of new rules of custom, there is certainly *no presumption* that a series of treaties will necessarily lead to said transformation.[271] Thus, as pointed out by the ILA report, 'provisions of multilateral treaties *can* be

---

law is to be looked for primarily in the actual practice and *opinio juris* of States, even though multilateral conventions may have an important role to play in recording and defining rules deriving from custom, or indeed in developing them'. See also: *North Sea Continental Shelf Cases*, ICJ Rep. 1969, p. 104, Separate Opinion of Judge Ammoun.

[266] ILA, Final Report, 2000, p. 49 (emphasis added). See also: ILC, Third Report, 2015, pp. 22–23; ILC, Draft Conclusions, 2015, conclusion no. 11(1).

[267] ILC, Third Report, 2015, p. 23.

[268] *Fisheries Jurisdiction Case (United Kingdom v. Iceland)*, ICJ Rep. 1974, paras. 51–52; *Continental Shelf case (Tunisia v. Libya)*, ICJ Rep. 1982, para. 24.

[269] Villiger, *Customary International Law and Treaties*, p. 186; Wolfke, *Custom in Present International Law*, p. 70.

[270] Baxter, 'Multilateral Treaties as Evidence of Customary International Law', p. 300.

[271] ILA, Final Report, 2000, pp. 47, 49; Vasciannie, 'The Fair and Equitable Treatment Standard', p. 158, fn 323 ('in the absence of positive indications as to *opinio juris* in favour of a particular treaty rule, no presumption arises automatically from the existence of a series of bilateral treaties'); Wolfke, *Custom in Present International Law*, p. 69; C. McLachlan, 'Investment Treaties and General International Law', *ICLQ* 57 (2008), p. 392; ILC, Third Report, 2015, p. 29; ILC, Draft Conclusions, 2015, conclusion no. 11(2).

the historic source of a new customary rule, *they do not necessarily do so*.[272] Thus, the phenomenon of crystallization will occur 'only on condition of fulfilment of the requirements of custom formation'.[273] For the ICJ, what is required is that 'State practice, including that of States whose interests are specially affected, should [be] both extensive and virtually uniform in the sense of the provision invoked; —and should moreover [occur] in such a way as to show a general recognition that a rule of law or legal obligation is involved'.[274]

Most importantly, what matters is the existence of a general, uniform and consistent practice of *third States outside* the treaty framework.[275] It must be shown that these States have adopted 'a practice in-line with that prescribed (or authorized) by the treaty, but which is in fact independent of it because of the general rule that treaties neither bind nor benefit third parties'.[276] In fact, the following distinctions should be made about the type of practice that counts towards the formation of a customary rule.[277]

First, the practice of States *parties* to a treaty must be considered as practice *under that treaty* and, therefore, does not count as practice relevant for the creation of a new customary rule.[278] In the *North Sea Continental Shelf* cases, the ICJ mentioned that the fact that a number of States which were delimiting their continental shelf boundaries according to the equidistance principle 'were or shortly became parties to the Geneva Convention, and were therefore presumably, so far as they were concerned, acting actually or potentially in the application of the Convention'.[279] The Court concluded that 'from their action no inference could legitimately be drawn as to the existence of a rule of customary

---

[272] ILA, Final Report, 2000, p. 47 (emphasis in the original). The Report makes the same assessment regarding bilateral treaties (a question further discussed below).
[273] Wolfke, *Custom in Present International Law*, pp. 68–69; ILA, Final Report, 2000, p. 47.
[274] *North Sea Continental Shelf Cases*, ICJ Rep. 1969, p. 43, para. 74. See also: ILC, Third Report, 2015, p. 26.
[275] Dinstein, 'The Interaction between Customary International Law and Treaties', pp. 376–377; Villiger, *Customary International Law and Treaties*, pp. 183–184; Baxter, 'Multilateral Treaties as Evidence of Customary International Law', pp. 296–297.
[276] ILA, Final Report, 2000, p. 46. see also; Villiger, *Customary International Law and Treaties*, p. 182 ('If generation of a new rule is contended, State practice contributing towards the customary rule must coincide with the substance of the conventional rule. In other words, States will, in their practice, invoke, or refer to, a given conventional rule').
[277] ILA, Final Report, 2000, pp. 46–47.
[278] Villiger, *Customary International Law and Treaties*, p. 183; ILA, Final Report, 2000, p. 46 ('[c]onduct which is wholly referable to the treaty itself [should] not count for this purpose as practice'); ILC, Third Report, 2015, p. 28.
[279] *North Sea Continental Shelf Cases*, ICJ Rep. 1969, para. 76.

international law in favour of the equidistance principle'.[280] As a result, it is paradoxically more difficult to assess the customary nature of a given norm found in a treaty when that instrument has been entered into by almost all States.[281]

Second, the practice of States *parties* to a treaty with other *non-party* States is not considered practice under the treaty, and therefore, counts as practice relevant for the creation of a new customary rule.[282] Third, the practice of *non-party* States counts as relevant practice for the creation of a new customary rule.[283]

3.3.3.1.2   A treaty can codify existing customary rules   The second

form of interaction between treaties and custom is codification.[284] As recognized by the ICJ,[285] a treaty may be evidence of a fully-formed custom.[286] Codification, however, is a rare phenomenon.[287] This is *a*

---

[280] *Ibid.*, para. 76. See also, a number of other ICJ decisions mentioned in: ILC, Third Report, 2015, p. 28.

[281] Baxter, 'Treaties and Custom', p. 64 ('the proof of a consistent pattern of conduct by non-parties becomes more difficult as the number of parties to the instrument increases. The number of participants in the process of creating customary law may become so small that the evidence of their practice will be minimal or altogether lacking. Hence the paradox that as the number of parties to a treaty increases, it becomes more difficult to demonstrate what is the state of customary international law dehors the treaty'). See also, ILC, Third Report, 2015, p. 28, referring to *Prosecutor* v. *Delalić*, International Criminal Tribunal for the former Yugoslavia, Case No. IT-96–21-T, Judgment (Trial Chamber), 16 November 1998, para. 302.

[282] Mendelson, 'The Formation of Customary International Law', p. 316; Villiger, *Customary International Law and Treaties*, p. 184; Dinstein, 'The Interaction between Customary International Law and Treaties', pp. 376–377; ILC, Third Report, 2015, p. 28–29; Henckaerts and Doswald-Beck, *Customary International Humanitarian Law*, p. 1.

[283] Villiger, *Customary International Law and Treaties*, p. 184; Dinstein, 'The Interaction between Customary International Law and Treaties', pp. 376–377; ILA, Final Report, 2000, p. 46 ('[h]istory records several examples of specific treaty provisions being replicated in the practice of States outside the treaty and in due course becoming rules of customary international law'); ILC, Third Report, 2015, pp. 28–29; Henckaerts and Doswald-Beck, *Customary International Humanitarian Law*, p. 1.

[284] Baxter, 'Multilateral Treaties as Evidence of Customary International Law', pp. 275–300; Baxter, 'Treaties and Custom', p. 25; Villiger, *Customary International Law and Treaties*, p. 63 ff; Thirlway, *International Customary Law and Codification*, Chaps. 6 and 7; T.L. Meyer, 'Codifying Custom', *Univ. Pennsylvania LR* 60 (2012), p. 379; ILC, Third Report, 2015, p. 20.

[285] *Continental Shelf (Libya* v. *Malta)* case, Judgment, ICJ Rep. 1985, pp. 29–30, para. 27 ('multilateral conventions may have an important role to play in recording and defining rules deriving from custom, or indeed in developing them').

[286] ILA, Final Report, 2000, p. 43; ILC, Memorandum, 2013, p. 33 ('Recognizing that a treaty may codify existing rules of customary international law, the Commission has often referred to treaties as possible evidence of the existence of a customary rule'); Baxter, 'Treaties and Custom', p. 36.

[287] Baxter, 'Treaties and Custom', p. 38.

fortiori the case for *bilateral* treaties.[288] As noted by one writer, '[t]reaties seldom simply codify well-established and uncontroversial rules of customary international law: it would not be worth the parties' effort to do so'.[289] This is because custom always applies to all States. In other words, these rules find application *notwithstanding* any codification efforts. So why should States pursue an apparently meaningless effort of codification? One reason could be their willingness 'to regulate in detail the means of giving effect to the customary rule'.[290] As put by Baxter, '[t]he one advantage to be gained by reference to the treaty is that the law is there set down in one established form, which, *qua* proof of customary international law, is uniform with the obligation of those States that are parties to the treaty and bound by it *qua* treaty'.[291]

In any event, it is important to note that 'there is no legal presumption that a treaty does or does not reflect customary law if it does not give such an indication on its face'.[292] Thus, why do States usually decide to enter into a treaty in the first place? They may do so to *derogate* from *existing* rules of customary law. Another reason may be their desire to *establish* governing rules due to the *absence* of any customary law on a given subject. This is why there is no presumption in favor of codification. To determine whether or not a treaty codifies custom, one must look closely at the language of the treaty, its character, its object and purpose, and the circumstances of its conclusion.[293] The parties' codification intention will be clear in some treaties.[294]

---

[288] The question is further discussed in Chapter 3, Section 3.3.3.2.

[289] ILA, Final Report, 2000, p. 43.

[290] Mendelson, 'The Formation of Customary International Law', p. 297, mentioning that while some of the basic provisions of the Geneva Convention relative to the Treatment of Prisoners of War (1949) reflected pre-existing customary law, the goal of the Convention was to prescribe in considerable detail the modalities of implementation of these rules. See also: Dinstein, 'The Interaction between Customary International Law and Treaties', p. 365.

[291] Baxter, 'Treaties and Custom', pp. 42–43.

[292] Mendelson, 'The Formation of Customary International Law', pp. 296, 301. See also: ILA, Final Report, 2000, p. 43 ('[t]here is no general presumption that a treaty codifies existing customary international law').

[293] Mendelson, 'The Formation of Customary International Law', p. 301; Baxter, 'Treaties and Custom', p. 56 ('The declaratory treaty is most readily identified as such by an express statement to that effect, normally in the preamble of the instrument, but its character may also be ascertained from preparatory work for the treaty and its drafting history'); Baxter, 'Multilateral Treaties as Evidence of Customary International Law', pp. 286–287; Dinstein, 'The Interaction between Customary International Law and Treaties', pp. 360–363.

[294] See, Baxter, 'Treaties and Custom', p. 28; Mendelson, 'The Formation of Customary International Law', p. 289, providing the example of the *Convention on the Prevention and Punishment of the Crime of Genocide*, 1948, entered into force 12 Jan. 1951, 78 *U.N.*

Yet, as mentioned by ILC Special Rapporteur Wood, '[t]reaties purporting to codify rules of customary international law, however, "are not self-verifying on that point"'.[295] This is because such treaties 'may (and often do) contain provisions that develop the law or represent particular arrangements decided on by the negotiating parties' or because 'the assertion in a treaty text regarding the status of customary international law is incorrect, or that customary international law has evolved since the treaty was concluded'.[296] For these reasons, he maintains that it is 'necessary in each case to verify whether the provision in question was indeed intended to codify custom, and whether it reflects existing customary international law'.[297] Such verification must take into account relevant State practice.[298]

Whenever codification takes place, the content of both custom and the treaty provision *may* be identical.[299] It has long been recognized by the ICJ that a rule of customary international law can continue to exist at the same time alongside a treaty rule.[300] Yet, they are separate and independent sources of obligation.[301] In the future, it may be that a custom rule will further develop and, therefore, have a content that is different from the treaty provision.[302] This type of new customary law will modify a pre-existing treaty rule.[303]

T.S. 277 (where Article 1 indicates that 'The Contracting Parties *confirm* that genocide, whether committed in time of peace or in time of war, is a crime under international law which they undertake to prevent and to punish', emphasis added). He also refers to the *Geneva Convention on the High Seas*, 29 April 1958, entered into force 30 September 1962, 450 *U.N.T.S.* 11 (where the preamble refers to the parties' 'desire' to 'codify the rules of international law relating to the high seas').

[295] ILC, Third Report, 2015, p. 21.   [296] *Ibid.*   [297] *Ibid.*

[298] *Ibid.*; Baxter, 'Treaties and Custom', pp. 43–44.

[299] On this question, see: B.B. Jia, 'The Relations between Treaties and Custom', *Chinese JIL* 9(1) (2010), pp. 93–97.

[300] *Military and Paramilitary Activities in and around Nicaragua*, ICJ Rep. 1986, paras. 175–178; Villiger, *Customary International Law and Treaties*, p. 153 ff; ILC, First Report, 2013, p. 15. See, several references in: ILC, Third Report, 2015, p. 20.

[301] *Application of the Convention on the Prevention and Punishment of the Crime of Genocide (Croatia v. Serbia)*, Judgment, ICJ Rep. 2015, para. 88 ('Where a treaty states an obligation which also exists under customary international law, the treaty obligation and the customary law obligation remain separate and distinct'). See also: Villiger, *Customary International Law and Treaties*, pp. 129–130, 286; Jia, 'The Relations between Treaties and Custom', pp. 93–102; Dinstein, 'The Interaction between Customary International Law and Treaties', p. 386.

[302] Dinstein, 'The Interaction between Customary International Law and Treaties', p. 366; Wolfke, *Custom in Present International Law*, p. 54. *Contra*: Baxter, 'Treaties and Custom', p. 96.

[303] On this question, see: Gazzini, 'The Role of Customary International Law', p. 712. See also: Nancy Kontou, *The Termination and Revision of Treaties in the Light of New Customary International Law* (Oxford: Clarendon Press, 1995).

3.3.3.2 Interaction between custom and treaties under international investment law

In the last two sections, I have shown that under general international law there are two well-recognized forms of interaction between treaties and custom. First, treaties can, under certain specific circumstances, contribute to the formation of *new* rules of customary international law in the future. Second, they can also codify *existing* customary rules. This section examines the first of these two phenomena in the specific context of international investment law.

I have decided not to analyse the process of codification in the context of *bilateral* treaties. Thus, although the process of a bilateral treaty codifying existing customary rules *as a whole* is theoretically possible,[304] it remains that there are no known examples of such phenomenon.[305] As explained by Baxter, bilateral treaties 'rarely carry evidence on their face that they are declaratory or constitutive of law'.[306] Most importantly, since these types of treaties are only binding on two States 'it would be even more wasteful than in the case of multilateral instruments to attempt to demonstrate that the bilateral treaty or treaties reflect customary law in order to use the bilateral treaties as evidence of customary international law'.[307] Thus, why would *two States* decide to enter into a BIT in the first place if they believe that its *whole* content represents custom? The very fact of entering into such a treaty would suggest they consider that they would have not been subject to said obligations in the absence of this agreement.[308] In any event, as previously mentioned,[309] the history of BITs' emergence clearly suggests that they cannot be in any way considered as a *global codification* of existing rules of custom in the field of investment arbitration.[310]

Specifically, the next sections will examine two questions:

- Can the content of a similarly-drafted *provision* found in numerous BITs transform into a customary rule? (Section 3.3.3.2.1);

---

[304] Gazzini, 'The Role of Customary International Law', p. 704; Al Faruque, 'Creating Customary International Law', p. 298.

[305] This is a situation clearly different from the other well-known possibility of some *specific provisions* contained in a bilateral treaty being considered as codification of custom.

[306] Baxter, 'Treaties and Custom', p. 83.   [307] *Ibid.*   [308] *Ibid.*, p. 81.

[309] See Chapter 2, Section 2.3.

[310] See, the analysis of Kishoiyian, 'The Utility of Bilateral Investment Treaties', pp. 332, 372. The codification argument is presented by F.A. Mann, 'British treaties for the promotion and protection of investments', *British YIL*, 52 (1981), p. 249.

– Can the content of *all BITs taken together* be considered as representing the 'new' custom in investment arbitration? (Section 3.3.3.2.2).

3.3.3.2.1 Can rules contained in BITs transform into customary rules? The question examined in this section is whether or not the content of a provision contained in a series of BITs can in time become binding on *all States*, including those that have not entered into BITs containing such a clause (and those that have not signed any BITs at all). In other words, can a series of similarly-drafted provisions found in numerous BITs provide the necessary impulse towards the development of subsequent State practice in line with that provision which will gradually crystallize into a rule of custom?

I will first explore the position adopted by tribunals and scholars on the issue (Section 3.3.3.2.1.1). I will then examine what conditions are necessary in order for treaty-based rules to transform into customary rules (Section 3.3.3.2.1.2). Finally, I will examine a concrete example of the application of these different conditions by analysing whether or not the FET standard contained in numerous BITs can be considered to have transformed into a customary rule (Section 3.3.3.2.1.3).

3.3.3.2.1.1 The position of tribunals and scholars A number of arbitral tribunals have considered investment treaties as a relevant form of State practice. Thus, some of these tribunals have analysed the content of BITs that the States involved have entered into before and after the treaty in question.[311] Yet, it should be noted that in these cases the examination of such practice was not done in order to show the existence of a customary rule.

---

[311] *Emilio Agustín Maffezini* v. *Spain*, ICSID Case No. ARB/97/7, Decision of the Tribunal on Objections to Jurisdiction, 25 January 2000, paras. 58–60; *Lanco International Inc.* v. *Argentina*, ICSID Case No. ARB/97/6, Decision on Jurisdiction, 8 December 1998, para. 32; *Daimler Financial Services AG* v. *Argentina*, ICSID Case No ARB/05/1, Award, 22 August 2012, paras. 261, 265, 271; *Siemens A.G.* v. *Argentina*, ICSID Case No. ARB/02/8, Decision on Jurisdiction, 3 August 2004, para. 71; *Aguas del Tunari, S.A.* v. *Bolivia*, ICSID Case No. ARB/02/3, Decision on Respondent's Objections to Jurisdiction, 21 October 2005, paras. 291, 293, 310–314; *Ambiente Ufficio S.p.A. and others* v. *Argentina*, ICSID Case No. ARB/08/9 (formerly *Giordano Alpi and others* v. *Argentina*), Decision on Jurisdiction and Admissibility, 8 February 2013, paras. 464–465; *Mihaly International Corporation* v. *Sri Lanka*, ICSID Case No. ARB/00/2, Award, 15 March 2002, para. 58; *Sempra Energy International* v. *Argentina*, ICSID Case No. ARB/02/16, Decision on Objections to Jurisdiction, 11 May 2005, paras. 144–145.

A few other tribunals have specifically taken the position that rules contained in BITs can transform into customary rules. For instance, the *Pope & Talbot* Tribunal stated that 'international agreements constitute practice of states and contribute to the grounds of customary international law'.[312] The *Cargill* Tribunal also affirmed that it was 'widely accepted that extensive adoption of identical treaty language by many States may in and of itself serve—again with care—as evidence of customary international law'.[313] The *Camuzzi* v. *Argentina* Tribunal also refuted the claim that 'lex specialis cannot be considered as leading to a rule of customary law' and held that 'there is no obstacle in international law to the expression of the will of States through treaties being at the same time an expression of practice and of the *opinio juris* necessary for the birth of a customary rule if the conditions for it are met'.[314] The same sentence is used by the Tribunal in the *Sempra* case.[315] The reasoning of the *Glamis*,[316] *UPS*,[317] *Chemtura*[318] and *ADF* tribunals[319] also suggests (at least implicitly) that such a transformation is possible.

---

[312] *Pope & Talbot Inc.* v. *Canada*, Award on Damages, 31 May 2002, para. 59.

[313] *Cargill, Inc.* v. *Mexico*, Award, 18 September 2009, para. 276.

[314] *Camuzzi International S.A.* v. *Argentina*, ICSID Case No. ARB/03/2, Decision on Jurisdiction, 11 May 2005, para. 144.

[315] *Sempra Energy International* v. *Argentina*, Decision on Jurisdiction, 11 May 2005, para. 156.

[316] *Glamis Gold Ltd* v. *United States*, Award, 14 May 2009, para. 603, mentioning 'treaty ratification language' amongst the 'very few authoritative sources' which can exhibit 'evidence of such "concordant practice" undertaken out of a sense of legal obligation'.

[317] *United Parcel Service of America Inc.* v. *Canada*, UNCITRAL, Award on Jurisdiction, 22 November 2002 [hereinafter *UPS* v. *Canada*], para. 86. The Tribunal mentioned that a number of BITs had been referred to by the claimant to prove the existence of a rule of custom. The Tribunal did not reject that proposition. But it concluded that 'UPS has not attempted to establish that that state practice reflects an understanding of the existence of a generally owed international legal obligation which, moreover, has to relate to the specific matter of requiring controls over anticompetitive behaviour'.

[318] *Chemtura Corporation* v. *Canada*, Award, 2 August 2010, para. 121 (mentioning that the scope of Article 1105 'cannot overlook the evolution of customary international law, nor the impact of BITs on this evolution'), para. 236 ('the Tribunal has taken into account the evolution of international customary law as a result inter alia of the conclusion of numerous BITs providing for fair and equitable treatment').

[319] *ADF Group Inc.* v. *United States*, Award, 9 January 2003, para. 183: 'We are not convinced that the Investor has shown the existence, in current customary international law, of a general and autonomous requirement (autonomous, that is, from specific rules addressing particular, limited, contexts) to accord fair and equitable treatment and full protection and security to foreign investments. The Investor, for instance, has not shown that such a requirement *has been brought into the corpus of present day customary international law by the many hundreds of bilateral investment treaties now extant*' (emphasis added). Thus, the Tribunal did not exclude the possibility that a 'requirement' found in BITs could transform into a customary rule.

It may be added that the ICJ in the *Diallo* case did not reject the possibility that the content of a BIT could be the historical source for the eventual formation of a new customary rule. This case involved a claim brought by Guinea for the arbitrary arrest of Mr Diallo (a Guinean national), his detention for 72 days without due process and his eventual expulsion from the Democratic Republic of Congo (DRC), where he had lived for over 30 years.[320] In this case, Guinea argued for the existence of a rule of customary law allowing a State to exercise diplomatic protection on behalf of a corporation, which was incorporated in the DRC, but whose sole shareholder was a Guinean national (Mr Diallo). In support of its argument, Guinea relied *inter alia* on many multilateral investment treaties and BITs. The Court rejected Guinea's argument, stating that it had examined 'State practice and decisions of international courts and tribunals' but found no exception to the traditional rule of diplomatic protection, which can only be exercised by a State on behalf of its nationals.[321] The Court then added that: '[t]he fact invoked by Guinea that various international agreements, such as agreements for the promotion and protection of foreign investments and the Washington Convention, have established special legal regimes governing investment protection, or that provisions in this regard are commonly included in contracts entered into directly between States and foreign investors, is not sufficient to show that there has been a change in the customary rules of diplomatic protection; it could equally show the contrary'.[322]

Most scholars agree that, in theory, the content of *a series* of bilateral treaties (or even *one single* treaty[323]) may give rise to the development of a new rule of customary international law, if followed by actual uniform and consistent State practice (a point that is further discussed in the

[320] *Case Concerning Ahmadou Sadio Diallo* (*Rep. Guinea* v. *Dem. Rep. Congo*), ICJ Rep. 2007, p. 324.

[321] *Ibid.*, para. 89.   [322] *Ibid.*, para. 90.

[323] Baxter, 'Treaties and Custom', p. 78 ('A treaty begins to play a role of its own when it is the identifiable point of origin for a rule subsequently accepted into customary international law in the same way that any norm passes from the potential to the actual. The rule of the treaty is well received, it is accepted and acted upon by States, and it becomes a general rule binding upon all'). See also: Hindelang, 'Bilateral Investment Treaties', p. 794, adding that 'in order to rely on a single bilateral treaty as evidence of customary international law, one has to prove that the rule of the treaty has been accepted into custom by independent evidence extrinsic to the treaty'.

next section).[324] A number of writers have also taken the same position regarding BITs.[325]

Finally, a few words should be devoted to the rather confusing position taken by Kishoiyian. He argues that BITs have not contributed to the 'creation of universal customary law as such, but to the creation of special custom between contracting parties'.[326] It is true that in the *Right of Passage* case, the ICJ recognized the existence of a *bilateral* custom between two States.[327] Yet, the concept of 'special custom' between two States only makes sense in the context of the *absence* of any treaty.[328] Kishoiyian is surprisingly basing the existence of this alleged 'special custom' on the *very existence* of a BIT between two States: 'The regime

---

[324] Baxter, 'Treaties and Custom', p. 77, explaining that the 'recurrence of identical or similar provisions in a series of bilateral agreements' may 'in the fullness of time, through a multiplication of instances and an absence of contrary practice, become a rule of customary international law'; D'Amato, *The Concept of Custom in International Law*, pp. 105–107; *Restatement of the Law Third*, sect. 102 comment i ('A wide network of similar bilateral arrangements on a subject may constitute practice and also result in customary law'); Thirlway, *International Customary Law and Codification*, p. 59 ('a series of bilateral treaties concluded over a period of time by various States, all consistently adopting the same solution to the same problem of the relationships between them, may give rise to a new rule of customary international law, so the general ratification of a treaty laying down general rules to govern the future relationships of States in a given field has a similar effect'); S. Zamora, 'Is there Customary International Economic Law?', *German YIL* 32 (1989), p. 19.

[325] Gazzini, 'The Role of Customary International Law', pp. 692, 701, 704; Al Faruque, 'Creating Customary International Law', p. 298; Hindelang, 'Bilateral Investment Treaties', pp. 790–791, 793–795; Kläger, *Fair and Equitable Treatment*, pp. 76, 266; Kishoiyian, 'The Utility of Bilateral Investment Treaties', p. 335, 374; Martins Paparinskis, *The International Minimum Standard and Fair and Equitable Treatment* (Oxford: Oxford University Press, 2013), p. 171; Dugan *et al.*, *Investor-State Arbitration*, p. 439; N. Stephan Kinsella and Noah D. Rubins, *International Investment, Political Risk, and Dispute Resolution* (Oxford: Oxford University Press, 2005), p. 171; Vasciannie, 'The Fair and Equitable Treatment Standard', pp. 102, 156 ff; Congyan, 'International Investment Treaties and the Formation', p. 679; J. Harrison, 'The International Law Commission and the Development of International Investment Law', *Geo. Wash. Int'l L. Rev*, 45 (2013), p. 438; R. Dolzer 'New Foundations of the Law of Expropriation of Alien Property', *AJIL* (1981), p. 565. A different position is taken by Sornarajah, *The International Law on Foreign Investment*, p. 159, arguing that BITs 'cannot' and 'do not contribute' to the creation of customary international law (but see, at p. 206, where he indicates that a treaty norm can become a rule of custom 'if there is concordance of standard' in these treaties, which he believes is not the case for BITs).

[326] Kishoiyian, 'The Utility of Bilateral Investment Treaties', pp. 373–374.

[327] *Case Concerning Right of Passage over Indian Territory, (Portugal v. India) (Preliminary Objections)*, ICJ Rep. 1957, p. 125. See also: ILC, Draft Conclusions, 2015, conclusion no. 16.

[328] Villiger, *Customary International Law and Treaties*, p. 57.

of law established between two sovereign nations in each BIT suffices to establish the special custom if they faithfully follow the dictates of their BIT to the letter'.[329] A more appropriate view is that both parties comply with a BIT simply because they have a legal *obligation* to do so under the instrument, *not* as a result of the existence of any special custom. In other words, they follow the rule contained in the treaty rather than the rule allegedly existing under the special custom between them.[330] In any event, what would be the point of proving the existence of a special custom given the fact that it would have the *same content* and would be binding on the *same (two) parties*? The possibility that both States modify the content of the BITs is better captured by the concept of subsequent practice by the parties than that of custom. In reality, the only potential effect of the existence of such a special custom would occur in the event that the BIT would cease to be in force.[331] In sum, at least in the context of BITs, the concept of special custom only adds confusion to the analysis.

The next section examines the necessary conditions in order for treaty norms to transform into custom.

3.3.3.2.1.2 The necessary conditions for such a transformation to occur While investment tribunals and scholars have generally supported the view that a treaty norm can, as matter or principle, be the source of the formation of a new rule of custom, it remains that there are a number of important roadblocks that prevent this phenomenon from frequently occurring in practice.[332] This section examines the conditions that must be fulfilled in order for a treaty-based rule to transform into a new rule of custom. It is only once these conditions have been met that the question of States' *opinio juris* can be investigated (this question will be further discussed in Chapter 4).[333] Before doing so, it is important to briefly examine the reasons why

---

[329] Kishoiyian, 'The Utility of Bilateral Investment Treaties', p. 374.

[330] See also: Vasciannie, 'The Fair and Equitable Treatment Standard', p. 158, examining the question of how could one prove a State's *opinio juris* which is detached from the basic legal obligation existing under the BIT.

[331] Yet, with the extinction of the BIT, the investor-State dispute settlement clause giving investors access to arbitration would also logically disappear (unless one considers such access as a right under custom, a very unlikely proposition as further discussed at Chapter 5, Section 5.3). With no access to international arbitration, the existence of any such special custom would become purely theoretical for foreign investors.

[332] Gazzini, 'The Role of Customary International Law', p. 701, referring to 'rather exceptional circumstances'.

[333] See, Chapter 4, Section 4.2.2.

there is no presumption that a succession of BITs containing the same provision should necessarily lead to the creation of a new customary norm.

The ILA has correctly observed that '[t]here is no *presumption* that a succession of similar treaty provisions gives rise to a new customary rule with the same content'.[334] Interestingly, the ILA's work specifically addressed the question of the impact that BITs have on custom and concluded as follows:

> The question of the legal effect of a succession of similar treaties or treaty provisions arises particularly in relation to bilateral treaties, such as those dealing with extradition or investment protection. (. . .) [T]here seems to be no reason of principle why these agreements, however numerous, should be *presumed* to give rise to new rules of customary law or to constitute the State practice necessary for their emergence. (. . .) Some have argued that provisions of bilateral investment protection treaties (especially the arrangements about compensation or damages for expropriation) are declaratory of, or have come to constitute, customary law. But (. . .) there seems to be no special reason to *assume* that this is the case, unless it can be shown that these provisions demonstrate a widespread acceptance of the rules set out in these treaties *outside the treaty framework*.[335]

The reason why there is an absence of any such presumption is simple.[336] It relates to the fundamental question of *why* States enter into a bilateral treaty in the first place. Thus, how should one interpret the *very fact* that States have entered into numerous treaties governing a given subject matter? As explained by Baxter, there are essentially two possible interpretations:

> The most difficult problem of all must now be approached – the question of whether a *succession* of similar bilateral treaties may legitimately be employed of itself to establish the existence of a rule of customary international law binding on all States. How can it be told whether the treaties speak in affirmation of the law or in derogation from it? On the one hand,

---

[334] ILA, Final Report, 2000, p. 47, Principle no. 25 (emphasis added). See also: ILC, Memorandum, 2013, p. 34 ('the frequent enunciation of a provision in international treaties [does] not necessarily indicate that the provision had developed into a rule of customary international law'); ILC, Third Report, 2015, p. 29; ILC, Draft Conclusions, 2015, conclusion no. 11(2) ('The fact that a rule is set forth in a number of treaties may, but does not necessarily, indicate that the treaty rule reflects a rule of customary international law'); Wolfke, *Custom in Present International Law*, p. 35.

[335] ILA, *Ibid.*, pp. 47–48 (emphasis in the original).

[336] Hindelang, 'Bilateral Investment Treaties', p. 795.

the repetition of instances might be thought to reflect a customary usage, while on the other, the very existence of the treaties may indicate that the parties had assumed duties to which they would not have been subject in the absence of agreement.[337]

As previously mentioned, the ICJ in the *Diallo* case (although in the different context of diplomatic protection) did not take a position as to whether these numerous BITs support one interpretation or the other. It simply mentioned that the existence of these treaties was 'not sufficient to show that there has been a change in the customary rules of diplomatic protection; it could equally show the contrary'.[338]

Generally, the first approach is the most convincing. Thus, the main reason why States ratify bilateral treaties is 'precisely because they believe that no customary rules exist, or will exist, on the matter'.[339] In other words, they sign these treaties because they believe that no customary principle exists covering the *whole content* of the treaty.

This is exactly what happened with BITs. As previously discussed,[340] States started to sign BITs *en masse* in the 1990s because there were strong disagreements regarding whether or not any customary rule existed at the time.[341] Thus, on the one hand, developing (and socialist) States generally believed that no rule of customary international law had crystallized as a result of their opposition to such norms. On the

---

[337] Baxter, 'Treaties and Custom', p. 81. See also: B. Lepard, *Customary International Law: A New Theory with Practical Applications* (Cambridge: Cambridge University Press, 2010), p. 202; Schachter, 'Entangled Treaty and Custom', p. 732. See also: *Government of Kuwait v. American Independent Oil Co (Aminoil), ILR* 66 (1982), p. 518: '[t]he inclusion of a provision in a treaty is not to be connected to the issue of the customary consistency of the norm. The parties to a treaty may want to record a special rule because they agree on its belonging to customary law as because they do not agree, or have no view as to its customary background but merely wish to be clear as to the rule to apply between themselves' (quoted in Tudor, *The Fair and Equitable Treatment Standard*, pp. 75–76).

[338] *Case Concerning Ahmadou Sadio Diallo (Rep. Guinea v. Dem. Rep. Congo)*, ICJ Rep. 2007, para. 90.

[339] Villiger, *Customary International Law and Treaties*, p. 189. See also: Wolfke, *Custom in Present International Law*, p. 71.

[340] See, Chapter 2, Section 2.3.

[341] Haeri, 'A Tale of Two Standards', p. 43; Dolzer 'New Foundations of the Law of Expropriation of Alien Property', p. 566 ('Thus, a close examination of such treaties indicates that the countries involved have established special regimes that would not have come into existence in the absence of the treaties. (. . .) In other words, the existence of these treaties in itself does not support an argument that the relevant clauses are declaratory of the present state of customary law'); Sornarajah, *The International Law on Foreign Investment*, pp. 19–20, 213–214 ('if there was a definitive conviction as to the existence of customary international law in the area, there would have been little need for such frenetic treaty-making activity on investment protection').

other hand, developed States were of the opinion that while such customary rules existed, their effectiveness was limited as a result of the vehement opposition of a large number of States.[342] In any event, States *believed* that the (very) few rules that were said to have existed at the time provided no solid legal protection for investors doing business abroad.

Yet, one cannot simply deduce from the fact that States have entered into a treaty that they *necessarily* consider that no customary rules exist *at all*. There are indeed perfectly good reasons for States to sign a treaty and *at the same time* consider some *specific* provisions contained in that treaty as codifying existing custom. One good reason to sign such a BIT in this context would be to provide parties with a higher degree of security and predictability about the existing customary norm.[343] Another reason would be to provide foreign investors with access to international arbitration.[344] As explained by one writer, 'the inclusion in a treaty of a provision codifying customary law, far from being redundant, has important practical consequences', including 'permit[ing] the contracting parties to resort to the remedies available under the law of treaties in general and under the BIT in particular, and when applicable, the investors to bring a case before an international tribunal'.[345] As will be further discussed,[346] under customary law foreign investors do not have an automatic right to access international arbitration.

In sum, nothing can be deduced about the customary status of specific provisions contained in BITs from the simple fact that States have entered into numerous treaties. There is no presumption that such occurrence leads to the creation of new custom norms.

Whether or not a provision contained in a BIT should be regarded as a new customary norm requires an analysis that takes into account a number of factors and circumstances.[347] Charney has listed the following relevant factors:

---

[342] The member States of the OECD certainly believed at the time that these customary rules existed, see: OECD, *Draft Convention on the Protection of Foreign Property*, adopted on 12 October 1967, *ILM* 7 (1967), p. 117, Article 1 cmt.

[343] Tudor, *The Fair and Equitable Treatment Standard*, pp. 75–76.

[344] Alvarez, 'A Bit on Custom', p. 59.

[345] Gazzini, 'The Role of Customary International Law', p. 705.

[346] See, Chapter 5, Section 5.3.

[347] Baxter, 'Treaties and Custom', pp. 77, 89 '[T]he weight to be given to any particular line of bilateral treaties varies according to the state of customary international law bearing on the subject matter of the treaty, the number of treaties, the presence or absence of other inconsistent agreements or State practice, and like circumstances. At worst, the presence of a provision in a number of bilateral treaties can strengthen the rule of

(1). The nature of the subject matter. An agreement which addresses generalized interests and aspirations of the international community may be more likely to produce new law than an agreement which focuses on specific state interests.

(2). The nature of the negotiations. A particular rule that was the product of compromises across the range of provisions in the agreement may be less appropriate for merger into customary law than a rule that resulted from a more atomized negotiation.

(3). The nature of the obligation. A rule that is interlinked with other provisions in the agreement would be less able to be considered as a customary rule separated from the fabric of the agreement than a rule that is independent of other obligations.

(4). The nature of the rule. A rule that requires highly technical methods of implementation would require the specificity of an international agreement, as contrasted with more generalized obligations that are possible to implement as custom. Furthermore, if international institutions are required to be used or established, customary law is inappropriate.[348]

Before examining the two *conditions* which need to be fulfilled for a treaty-based rule to transform into a rule of custom, a few words should be said about the importance of a *preliminary* question which must be asked whenever assessing the customary status of a BIT provision.

This basic question is whether or not a certain provision can actually be a potential candidate for the transformation of a treaty-based rule into custom.[349] In the words of the ICJ, such a provision must be of a

international law to which it gives expression. At best the series of similar bilateral treaties can of itself establish the state of the law'. See also: Hindelang, 'Bilateral Investment Treaties', p. 797.

[348] J.I. Charney, 'International Agreements and the Development of Customary International Law', *Washington L.R.*, 61 (1986), p. 983.

[349] ILC, Third Report, 2015, p. 25; UNCTAD, 'Fair And Equitable Treatment', UNCTAD Series on Issues in International Investment Agreements (1999), p. 17 ('where a treaty provision is norm-creating in character, this provision may pass into customary law once certain criteria are satisfied'); Jean d'Aspremont, 'International Customary Investment Law: Story of a Paradox', in T. Gazzini and E. de Brabandere (eds.), *International Investment Law: The Sources of Rights and Obligations* (Leiden; Boston: Martinus Nijhoff, 2012), pp. 33–34. See, however, Hindelang, 'Bilateral Investment Treaties', p. 793, who seems to be arguing that this is not a relevant distinction: 'Yet others [writers, referring to D'Amato] require multiple usage of a treaty clause which contains a rule open to "generalization". In theory, every rule is open to generalization. Thus, due to the fact that this opinion fails to give shape and meaning to the term "generalization", it is not suitable for drawing a distinction between treaty rules which evidence and/or create

'fundamentally norm-creating character such as could be regarded as forming the basis of a general rule of law'.[350] This requires that a provision be 'articulated in general terms, so as to potentially be universally binding'.[351] D'Aspremont noted that 'many candidates for customary status' in international investment law 'do not provide for clear standards of behavior and suffer from strong normative weakness', and therefore, 'they fail to meet the minimum threshold in terms of normative content that is necessary for such norms to possibly constitute (or give rise to) a customary rule'.[352]

The following paragraphs will examine the two necessary conditions for a treaty-based norm to transform into a new customary rule.

The first condition is that a large number of States must have entered into numerous BITs containing the *same provision* (or very similarly-drafted clauses).[353] Thus, according to the ILA, it would be 'difficult to imagine that, in normal circumstances' the drafting and conclusion of a *single* bilateral treaty could assist in the 'crystallization' of emerging rules of customary international law.[354] Only a *succession* of bilateral treaties can potentially lead to the crystallization of an emerging norm.[355] Yet, as pointed out by Kläger, 'further requirements than the mere identification of the great number of treaties concluded are to be met in the generation process of new customary international law'.[356] The practice of States of including the same type of clause in their BITs must indeed be 'uniform'

---

custom and those which are merely *lex specialis*'. The same position seems to be taken by Al Faruque, 'Creating Customary International Law', p. 299 ('According to D'Amato, only those bilateral multilateral treaties that contain generalisable rules can give rise to a rule of customary law. But this straightforward view is not tenable because mere generalisable rules do not generate customary international law unless they are observed by the States out of a conviction that they are obligatory').

[350] *North Sea Continental Shelf Cases*, ICJ Rep. 1969, para. 72. On this notion, see, Villiger, *Customary International Law and Treaties*, pp. 177–178.

[351] P.-H. Verdier and E. Voeten, 'Precedent, Compliance, and Change in Customary International Law: An Explanatory Theory', *AJIL* 108 (2014), p. 426. See also: Thirlway, *International Customary Law and Codification*, p. 84; Villiger, *Customary International Law and Treaties*, pp. 177, 179. See, however, the critical analysis of the concept in: Kolb, 'Selected Problems in the Theory of Customary International Law', pp. 147–148.

[352] d'Aspremont, 'International Customary Investment Law', pp. 33–34.

[353] Gazzini, 'The Role of Customary International Law', p. 701, speaking of a 'remarkably high number of similar treaties'.

[354] ILA, Final Report, 2000, p. 50.

[355] *Ibid.*, p. 50; Kläger, *Fair and Equitable Treatment*, p. 76.

[356] Kläger, *Fair and Equitable Treatment*, p. 266.

and 'consistent'.[357] Another requirement is that said practice exists among 'a largely representative number of States'.[358]

The second condition required to demonstrate that a treaty-based norm has transformed into a new customary rule is that States have also adopted in their *own* practice *outside the treaty framework* the type of conduct prescribed in the instruments.[359] As explained by Schachter: 'the repetition of common clauses in bilateral treaties does not create or support an inference that those clauses express customary law' because '[t]o sustain such a claim of custom one would have to show that *apart from the treaty itself*, the rules in the clauses *are considered obligatory*'.[360]

The next section will provide an illustration of the concrete application of these conditions. I will examine whether or not the FET standard clause found in numerous BITs can be considered as having transformed into a rule of custom.

3.3.3.2.1.3   One illustration: has the fair and equitable treatment standard clause transformed into a customary rule?   The present section examines whether or not the two conditions mentioned in the previous section have been fulfilled regarding the FET standard clause contained in numerous BITs.

Before doing so, it should be highlighted from the outset that the question of whether or not the FET standard can be considered as a rule of customary international law is not relevant in all situations. For instance, the question is of no *practical* importance in the situation where a BIT regulating the relationship between a foreign investor and the host State exists and when that treaty contains an FET clause. In such a case, the host State must provide such standard of protection to the investor. Also, a tribunal will have to apply that clause to an eventual dispute between

---

[357]   See, discussion in Chapter 3, Section 3.2.1.

[358]   Gazzini, 'The Role of Customary International Law', p. 701. See, discussion in Chapter 3, Section 3.2.2.

[359]   ILA, Final Report, 2000, p. 48, indicating that it needs to be 'shown that these provisions [found in BITs] demonstrate a widespread acceptance of the rules set out in these treaties *outside the treaty framework*' (emphasis in the original).

[360]   Oscar Schachter, 'Compensation for Expropriation', *AJIL* 78 (1986), p. 126 (emphasis added). See also: van Hoof, *Rethinking the Sources of International Law*, p. 109 ('a treaty is of course binding on the States parties to it. Consequently, the question of being capable of generating a customary rule is relevant only with respect to States which are not party to it'); Dolzer 'New Foundations of the Law of Expropriation of Alien Property', p. 566 ('Necessarily, it must again be asked whether the rules set forth in the treaties were also followed consistently when the states involved were not bound by treaties').

the parties. In other words, for the actors involved (the investor, the State and the arbitrators) what matters is the *conventional* nature of the FET clause; it is not important for them to know whether the FET standard (in parallel) can *also* be considered as representing a customary norm *outside* the BIT framework.[361]

The question of the customary status of the FET standard is, however, relevant in two situations.

First, the question is of great importance whenever *no BIT* governs the relationship between a foreign investor and the host country of the investment. Thus, however numerous BITs may be,[362] it remains that they do not cover the whole spectrum of possible bilateral treaty relationship between States. According to one writer, BITs, in fact, only cover some 13% of the total bilateral relationship between States worldwide.[363] The *majority* of foreign investors doing business abroad are therefore *not* covered by the legal protections contained in this investment treaties framework. Custom is the applicable legal regime in the absence of any BIT. In this context, it matters a great deal to determine whether or not States are bound to provide an FET protection to all foreign investors under custom.

Second, the question of the customary nature of the FET standard is also (to some extent) relevant in cases where a BIT *does* govern the relationship between a foreign investor and the host country, but where that treaty *does not* contain any FET clause. Yet, it should be added that the question of the customary status of the FET standard under this scenario rarely matters in practice for two reasons. First, as already mentioned,[364] only a small minority of modern BITs do not contain an FET clause. Second, even when this is the case, it may be that an investor will be able to invoke the Most-Favoured Nations (MFN) clause contained in a BIT to rely on provisions found in other treaties entered into by the host State that provide for a 'better' treatment. This is because a BIT containing an FET clause arguably provides (at least in theory) foreign investors with a 'better' treatment than a treaty without such a provision. In other words, under this scenario an investor will be able in all likelihood to benefit from the FET protection contained in another treaty via

[361] Kläger, *Fair and Equitable Treatment*, pp. 260–270.
[362] It is now estimated that 3,268 international agreements provide foreign investors with investment protection: UNCTAD, 'Recent Trends, in IIAs and ISDS', IIA Issues Note, no. 1, Feb. 2015, p. 2. See also: World Bank, *World Investment Report*, 2014, p. xxiii.
[363] Gazzini, 'The Role of Customary International Law', p. 691.
[364] See, Chapter 3, Section 3.2.4.2.

the use of the MFN clause.[365] The question of the actual use of the MFN clause in relation to the FET standard clause is beyond the scope of this book and has been examined by the present author elsewhere.[366]

As mentioned previously, one basic question that needs to be asked whenever assessing whether a treaty-based rule can transform into a rule of custom concerns its 'fundamentally norm-creating character'. While a number of writers have argued that the FET standard is a rule of custom as a result of its inclusion in the vast majority of BITs, very few enquired about this basic question. For some writers, the FET standard has the potential to develop as a rule of custom.[367] Others, on the contrary, have pointed out that the FET standard 'is characterized by lack of clarity concerning the principle's normative content and scope' and that it 'does not have a precise content that can easily be applied'.[368]

In fact, this position is, surprisingly, even adopted by those writers who argue that the FET standard is indeed a rule of custom. For instance, Tudor believes that 'given the flexibility of the notion and the ways in which it is adapted and applied to a case, the FET has no stable or fixed content'.[369] In subsequent writing, she mentions that 'the FET standard may be simply a vague standard which the parties feel should be consolidated on each and every occasion, in each and every investment convention'.[370] But, as pointed out by one writer, 'how a norm without fixed content can become a norm of customary international law'?[371]

---

[365] Tudor, *The Fair and Equitable Treatment Standard*, p. 24; Kläger, *Fair and Equitable Treatment*, p. 269.

[366] Dumberry, 'The Importation of the Fair and Equitable Treatment Standard Through MFN Clauses'; P. Dumberry, 'Shopping for a Better Deal: The Use of MFN Clauses to Get 'Better' Fair and Equitable Protection under other Treaties' (forthcoming 2016).

[367] Vasciannie, 'The Fair and Equitable Treatment Standard', p. 154.

[368] ILA, 'General Public International Law and International Investment Law – A Research Sketch on Selected Issues', *The International Law Association German Branch Sub-Committee on Investment Law* (2009) pp. 10–11: 'The standard of fair and equitable treatment does not have a precise content that can easily be applied. Apart from consensus on the fact that fair and equitable treatment constitutes a standard that is independent from the domestic legal order and does not require state conduct in bad faith, it is hardly substantiated by state practice or elucidated by *travaux préparatoires* and difficult to narrow down by traditional means of interpretation'. See also: Gazzini, 'The Role of Customary International Law', p. 698; Al Faruque, 'Creating Customary International Law', p. 304.

[369] Tudor, *The Fair and Equitable Treatment Standard*, p. 133.

[370] Knoll-Tudor, 'The Fair and Equitable Treatment Standard and Human Rights Norms', p. 317.

[371] S.W. Schill, reviewing Tudor's book, *EJIL* 20 (2009), p. 237. In his book, S.W. Schill, *The Multilateralization of International Investment Law* (Cambridge University Press,

Diehl also explains that 'it is the very nature of standard not to be uniform and specific but to be broad and open for fact-specific analysis'.[372] She further argues that '[i]f this particularity of the notion of standard constituted a bar to the formation of custom, then no standard of treatment could ever become part of customary international law'.[373] This is indeed the conclusion that some scholars have reached specifically regarding the FET standard.[374] In any event, the next paragraphs will examine a number of other reasons why the FET standard should not be considered as a customary rule.

The first condition for any treaty-based norm to transform into a customary rule concerns the practice of States that are *parties* to BITs containing FET clauses. As mentioned previously,[375] while the practice of States of including FET clauses in their BITs is general, widespread and representative, it remains that it is not uniform and consistent. Thus, can one truly speak of the 'uniformity' of FET clauses when there are five or six drafting models? Moreover, these FET clauses, which are worded differently, have been given different interpretations by States as well as by arbitral tribunals. In other words, one can hardly speak of uniformity when tribunals have given these differently worded FET clauses *different meanings* and have applied *different thresholds* of liability to them.

The second condition deals with the practice of States outside the treaty framework. The fact that States that are parties to BITs are providing foreign investors with a FET standard of protection is not relevant here. They simply do so to fulfil their treaty obligations. What matters is, for instance, whether States that are *not party* to any such BITs (or States parties to BITs *not* containing any FET clause) are actually providing the FET protection to foreign investors. What also matters is what States

---

2009), p. 283, further explains that 'Fair and equitable treatment does not have a consolidated and conventional core meaning as such nor is there a definition of the standard that can be applied easily. So far it is only settled that fair and equitable treatment constitutes a standard that is independent from national legal order and is not limited to restricting bad faith conduct of host States. Apart from this very minimal concept, however, its exact normative content is contested, hardly substantiated by State practice, and impossible to narrow down by traditional means of interpretative syllogism'.

[372] Diehl, *The Core Standard of International Investment Protection*, p. 135.   [373] *Ibid.*
[374] Orakhelashvili, 'The Normative Basis of "Fair and Equitable Treatment"', p. 104 (FET is 'due its undefined and in-determinate character, inherently ill-suited to make a norm of customary law'); d'Aspremont, 'International Customary Investment Law', pp. 24, 33–34; Gazzini, 'The Role of Customary International Law', p. 698. See also: Paparinskis, *The International Minimum Standard*, p. 172.
[375] See, Chapter 3, Sections 3.2.4.2 and 3.2.4.3.

parties to BITs do outside the obligation imposed by the treaty. Such practice of providing the FET protection could be found, for instance, in the domestic legislation of the host State or in State contracts. Any evidence that a large number of representative States are uniformly and consistently providing foreign investors with the FET protection in their own domestic legislations would provide solid support for the proposition that the standard is more than just a treaty-based obligation.

Diehl refers to the fact that 'prospective BIT signatories reform their local laws and practices in order to live up to treaty standards like the FET standard' as 'surely part of the "state practice" that needs to be examined with respect to relevant customary law principles'.[376] She concludes that such practice 'further speaks in favour of assuming that the FET standard is a customary rule of law'.[377] However, this is really just an assumption. For instance, she refers to an UNCTAD report indicating that 92% of the 2,395 changes in national laws from 1991 to 2005 were 'aimed at making the investment climate more welcoming to FDI'.[378] She simply *assumes* that these States are increasingly providing FET protection in their own domestic laws, without however having undertaken any comparative analysis of these laws to determine whether this is actually the case.[379]

Some writers have suggested that the FET standard is found in the investment laws of most developed and developing States.[380] Yet, none have actually undertaken any comprehensive analysis of such laws. Such a task is clearly beyond the scope of the present book. Suffice it to mention that one study (conducted in 1999) of the domestic legislations of a number of capital-importing States by Vasciannie showed, in fact, that the 'overwhelming majority' of these States do not provide FET protection to foreign investors.[381] Similarly, in another earlier study conducted in 1992 of

---

[376] Diehl, *The Core Standard of International Investment Protection*, p. 136.   [377] *Ibid.*
[378] *Ibid.*   [379] *Ibid.* See also, her analysis at pp. 169–175.
[380] *Ibid.*, p. 174 ('As most developed and developing countries recognize in their domestic law that FET ought to be applied to foreign investments and investors, one has to conclude that FET is a general principle of law in the realm of foreign investment'); Tudor, *The Fair and Equitable Treatment Standard*, p. 104 ('In the case of the FET standard, the situation as it stands today is that most developed and developing countries do recognize in their domestic laws that FET is to be applied to foreign investors. This is the case even though the term FET itself may not be employed as such but the content of FET, namely procedural and substantive guarantees for foreign investors, is found in national provisions').
[381] Vasciannie, 'The Fair and Equitable Treatment Standard', p. 160.

the national legislations of fifty-one developing countries, Parra found that only three of them incorporated the FET standard.[382]

As mentioned previously,[383] the present author has recently examined 165 different domestic laws on foreign investment from some 160 States.[384] A number of these laws (fifty-nine) do not contain any specific provision dealing with substantive investment protection. For those that do, only a few laws (ten) expressly refer to the FET standard. It should be added that a number of other laws (14) contain references to a 'transparency' obligation. In sum, my analysis of *one specific aspect* of States' domestic legal orders (foreign investment laws) shows that States rarely provide FET protection to foreign investors. I have also found no State contract containing an FET clause.[385]

It should be added that one has to be careful in drawing any conclusions from the fact that a specific aspect of a State's domestic legislation does *not* include any FET protection. As put by one writer, such absence is 'not decisive in itself' since 'some States may well believe fairness and equity to be inherently interwoven within the fabric of their legal system, and therefore beyond the need for an explicit statement'.[386] In other words, just because the FET standard (or some elements generally considered to be contained in that standard) is not expressly mentioned in one State's legislation, one cannot automatically conclude that such standard is absent from its domestic legal order. Conversely, the fact that another State's legislation provides for such protection is no guarantee that investors actually receive such FET treatment.

Finally, the present author is unaware of the existence of any arbitration case where the respondent State has accepted, during the course of the proceedings, that it should offer the FET standard of protection to a claimant investor in the absence of such a clause in the BIT. There are also no cases where a tribunal has decided that such an FET obligation must be imposed upon the host States in situations where there exists no BITs at all. It is true that in a handful of cases foreign investors have been allowed to benefit from FET protection in situations where the BIT under which they started the proceedings did *not* contain any FET clause.

[382] A. Parra, 'Principles Governing Foreign Investment, as Reflected in National Investment Codes', *ICSID Rev* 7 (1992), pp. 435–437.
[383] See, discussion in Chapter 2, Section 2.6.3.
[384] P. Dumberry, 'The Practice of States as Evidence of Custom: An Analysis of Fair and Equitable Treatment Standard Clauses in States' Foreign Investment Laws', McGill Journal of Dispute Resolution (forthcoming, 2016).
[385] *Ibid.*   [386] Vasciannie, 'The Fair and Equitable Treatment Standard', p. 160.

Importantly, however, this was made possible through the use of the MFN clause contained in the BIT.[387] In other words, the concrete application of the FET clauses in these cases had nothing to do with the standard being considered as a rule of custom.

In sum, the concrete examination of the above-mentioned two conditions shows that the treaty-based norm of the FET standard has not transformed into a customary rule. The question as to whether or not States have any *opinio juris* when including FET clauses in their BITs will be discussed in the next chapter.[388]

The next section examines a related question that has been debated amongst scholars, concerning the transformation of treaty-based norms into customary rules.

3.3.3.2.2 When taken together do all BITs represent the new custom? The previous section examined the question of *how* (and under which conditions) the content of a similarly drafted *provision* found in numerous BITs could transform into a customary rule. The present section examines another different question also related to the phenomenon of the transformation of treaty-based norms into customary rules. One controversial issue that is currently being debated in academia and amongst arbitrators is the impact that BITs have had on the existence and content of custom.[389] More specifically, when *taken together* do the thousands of BITs represent the 'new' custom in this field?

---

[387] See, *inter alia, Rumeli Telekom AS and Telsim Mobil Telekomikasyon Hizmetleri AS* v. *Kazakhstan*, ICSID Case no ARB/05/16, Award, 29 July 2008, para. 611 (interpreting the Kazakhstan-Turkey BIT); *Bayindir Insaat Turizm Ticaret ve Sanayi A Ş* v. *Pakistan*, ICSID Case No. ARB/03/29, Award, 27 August 2009, paras. 164, 173 (interpreting the Turkey-Pakistan BIT). These cases and others are examined in Dumberry, 'The Importation of the Fair and Equitable Treatment Standard Through MFN Clauses'.

[388] See, Chapter 4, Section 4.2.2.1.

[389] In doctrine: Stephen M. Schwebel, 'Investor-State Disputes and the Development of International Law: The Influence of Bilateral Investment Treaties on Customary International Law', *ASIL Proc.* 98 (2004), pp. 27–30; Hindelang, 'Bilateral Investment Treaties'; Andreas F. Lowenfeld, 'Investment Agreements and International Law', *Columbia JTL* 42 (2003), pp. 123–130; Kishoiyian, 'The Utility of Bilateral Investment Treaties'; Andrew T. Guzman, 'Why LDCs Sign Treaties That Hurt Them: Explaining the Popularity of Bilateral Investment Treaties', *Virginia JIL* 38(4) (1998); Al Faruque, 'Creating Customary International Law', p. 292; Gazzini, 'The Role of Customary International Law', p. 691; McLachlan, 'Investment Treaties and General International Law', pp. 361–401; Congyan, 'International Investment Treaties and the Formation', pp. 659- 679; Alvarez, 'A Bit on Custom'.

The present author has argued elsewhere that this proposition should be rejected.[390] This is also the view of a number of scholars who have addressed the issue in recent years.[391] In the following sections, I will first examine the arguments advanced by the writers who support the controversial proposition that a 'global' 'new' custom in the field of investment law is emerging (Section 3.3.3.2.2.1). I will then put forward a few basic arguments against the proposition equalling custom and BITs (Section 3.3.3.2.2.2) as well as analysing its main weakness, that is, that it does not meet the necessary requirements for the creation of customary rules (Section 3.3.3.2.2.3). Finally, I will examine the positions of States that have rejected the proposition that BITs represent the 'new' custom (Section 3.3.3.2.2.4).

3.3.3.2.2.1 The arguments advanced by those supporting the proposition equalling custom and BITs   The position of Judge Schwebel, former president of the ICJ and a leading arbitrator in investor-State disputes, is a good starting point to examine the issue. He believes that 'customary international law governing the treatment of foreign investment has been *reshaped* to embody the principles of law found in more than two thousand concordant bilateral investment treaties'.[392] The *CME* Tribunal reached the same conclusion by claiming that BITs had 'reshaped the body of customary international law'.[393] The *Eureko*

---

[390] Patrick Dumberry, 'Are BITs Representing the "New" Customary International Law in International Investment Law?', *Penn State ILR* 28 (2010), p. 675.
[391] Al Faruque, 'Creating Customary International Law', pp. 293, 301 ff; Guzman, 'Why LDCs Sign Treaties That Hurt Them', pp. 684–685; Sornarajah, *The International Law on Foreign Investment*, pp. 158–159, 206, 213; Frédéric G. Sourgens, 'Law's Laboratory: Developing International Law on Investment Protection as Common Law', *Northwestern J. Int'l L* 34 (2014), pp. 187–192; D. Carreau and P. Juillard, *Droit international économique* (Paris: LGDJ, 1998), p. 469; Surya P. Subedi, *International Investment Law: Reconciling Policy and Principle* (Oxford: Hart Publ., 2008), p. 142. Stephan W. Schill, 'Multilateralization: An Ordering Paradigm for International Investment Law', in M. Bungenberg, J. Griebel, S. Hobe and A. Reinisch (eds.), *International Investment Law: A Handbook* (Munich et al: C.H. Beck, Hart, Nomos, 2015), p. 1821; Bruno Simma and Dirk Pulkowski, 'Two Worlds, but Not Apart: International Investment Law and General International Law', in M. Bungenberg, J. Griebel, S. Hobe and A. Reinisch (eds.), *International Investment Law: A Handbook* (Munich et al.: C.H. Beck, Hart, Nomos, 2015), p. 368.
[392] Schwebel, 'Investor-State Disputes and the Development of International Law', p. 27 (emphasis added).
[393] *CME Czech Republic B.V. v. Czech Republic*, UNCITRAL, Award, 14 March 2003, para. 498.

Tribunal has also used the same expression.[394] Similarly, the NAFTA
Mondev Tribunal also held that the 'content' of 'current international
law' was '*shaped* by the conclusion of more than two thousand bilateral
investment treaties and many treaties of friendship and commerce'.[395]
What these last three cases have in common is that Schwebel acted as an
arbitrator in each of them. Finally, reference should be made to a similar
conclusion reached by the NAFTA *Chemtura* Tribunal stating not only
that 'the scope of Article 1105 of NAFTA [on the FET standard] must be
determined by reference to customary international law', but also that
'[s]uch determination cannot overlook the evolution of customary international law, nor the impact of BITs on this evolution'.[396]

As will be further discussed,[397] there is no doubt that contemporary
investment law has indeed been 'reshaped' by these numerous BITs. In
fact, these BITs have certainly had an *influence* on customary international law in the field of international investment law.[398] However, it is
quite another thing to simply proclaim that when *taken together* all BITs
now *represent* the *new* custom in international investment law. Yet, this is
the position adopted by some writers. One of the earliest accounts of this
proposition seems to have been adopted by Mann in his seminal 1981
article on British BITs:

> The importance of the British treaties as well as the numerous foreign
> treaties for the promotion and protection of investments (. . .) lies in the
> contribution they make to the development of customary international
> law, in their being a source of law. In general, as the decision of the
> International Court of Justice in the *North Sea Continental Shelf* cases
> has proved, it is very difficult to deduce a rule of public international law
> from a single treaty. But this decision should not be overrated. It dealt
> with a very specific case in which specific arguments militated against
> finding the existence of a customary rule. In the case of the treaties, the
> subject-matter of this discussion [BITs], many other elements combine to
> facilitate such a finding. There is, in the first place, the very large number
> of treaties the scope of which is increased by the operation of the most-
> favoured-nation clause. There is, secondly, the fact that many States which

---

[394] *Eureko B.V.* v. *Poland*, UNCITRAL, Partial Award and Dissenting Opinion, 19 August
2005, para. 258 ('contemporary customary international law (. . .) has been reshaped by
the conclusion of more than 2000 essentially concordant bilateral investment treaties').

[395] *Mondev* v. *United States*, Award, 2 October 2002, para. 125 (emphasis added). The
Tribunal was interpreting NAFTA Article 1105.

[396] *Chemtura Corporation* v. *Canada*, UNCITRAL, Award, 2 August 2010, paras. 120–121.

[397] See, Chapter 3, Section 3.3.3.2.2.5.

[398] See, *Ibid.*, discussing the twofold impact that BITs have had on customary international
law in this field.

have purported to reject the traditional conceptions and standards included in these treaties have accepted them, when (if the colloquial phrase be permitted) it came to the crunch. There is, thirdly, the most important fact that these treaties establish and accept and thus enlarge the force of traditional conceptions. Is it possible for a State to reject the rule according to which alien property may be expropriated only on certain terms long believed to be required by customary international law, yet to accept it for the purpose of these treaties? The paramount duty of States imposed by international law is to observe and act in accordance with the requirements of good faith. From this point of view it follows that, where these treaties express a duty which customary international law imposes or is widely believed to impose, they give very strong support to the existence of such a duty and preclude the Contracting States from denying its existence.[399]

A number of modern writers have explicitly endorsed this theory. For instance, Laird affirms that 'we have reached that point in the development of international investment law where we must seriously consider these instruments [i.e. BITs] as reflective of the development of *new* customary international law'.[400] What is this so-called new custom? Apparently, it simply consists of the more than 2500 BITs that States have entered into. This is Schwebel's position, for whom 'when BITs prescribe treating the foreign investor in accordance with customary international law, they should be understood to mean the standard of international law embodied in the terms of some two thousand concordant BITs'.[401] This also seems to be the position adopted by Lowenfeld:

[399] Mann, 'British treaties for the promotion and protection of investments', p. 249.

[400] Ian A. Laird, 'A Community of Destiny – The Barcelona Traction Case and the Development of Shareholder Rights to Bring Investment Claims', in Todd Weiler (ed.), *International Investment Law and Arbitration: Leading Cases from the ICSID, NAFTA, Bilateral Treaties and Customary International Law* (London: Cameron May, 2005), pp. 95–96 (emphasis added). See also: 'A strong argument can now be made that sufficient constancy does exist in investment instruments and related jurisprudence, and that this particular area of international law has evolved to reflect a new and consistent state of international custom'.

[401] Schwebel, 'Investor-State Disputes and the Development of International Law', pp. 29–30. See also: Dugan *et al.*, *Investor-State Arbitration*, p. 439. See also, this comment by Alvarez, 'A Bit on Custom', p. 77: '[T]he investment regime reflects and affects CIL. That case is made on the basis of the traditional features of CIL, namely state practice and *opinio juris*—on the premise that these two elements of custom are demonstrated by the conclusion of investment treaties by the full diversity of nations, by the enactment of national laws (including many promulgated with the obligations of BITs and FTAs in mind), and by the practice of states in both defending investor-state disputes and generally acquiescing in arbitral outcomes which not infrequently rely on both treaty and non-treaty sources of law'.

'*taken together*, the [BITs] are now evidence of customary international law, applicable even when a given situation or controversy is not explicitly governed by a treaty'.[402] Yet, he admits that such a proposition does not fit with the traditional definition of customary law, which he criticized as being 'incomplete'.[403] In other words, for these writers the content of custom is now simply the same as that of *all* BITs *taken together*.

This also seems to be the conclusion reached by the *Pope & Talbot* Tribunal in its 2002 award. It first affirmed that *only* State practice was necessary to determine the content of custom, completely omitting any reference to *opinio juris* (a point that will be further discussed[404]).[405] Based on this incorrect assumption, the Tribunal held that in 'applying the ordinary rules for determining the content of custom in international law, one must conclude that the practice of states is now represented by those treaties'.[406] It is not entirely clear what the Tribunal meant to say. It may be that it was simply restating what it had already stated, that is, that these BITs represent evidence of State practice.[407] Another possibility is that the Tribunal believed that these BITs now *represented custom*. At any rate, this is how the *Loewen* Tribunal interpreted this passage one year later when it stated that the *Pope & Talbot* Tribunal had concluded that 'the content of custom in international law is now represented by more than 1800 bilateral investment treaties which have been negotiated'.[408]

As will be further explained in the next section, there are several reasons for rejecting the proposition advanced by these writers and tribunals.

3.3.3.2.2.2   A few basic arguments against the proposition   This section examines six arguments against the proposition advanced by some writers that custom is now represented by all BITs taken together.

---

[402] Andreas F. Lowenfeld, *International Economic Law* (2nd edn., Oxford: Oxford University Press, 2008), p 584 (emphasis added); Lowenfeld, 'Investment Agreements and International Law', pp. 123–130.
[403] *Ibid.*   [404] See, Chapter 3, Section 3.3.3.2.2.3.
[405] *Pope & Talbot Inc.* v. *Canada*, Award in Respect of Damages, 31 May 2002, para. 62, footnote 53.
[406] *Ibid.*
[407] *Ibid.*, para. 59 ('It is a facet of international law that customary international law evolves through state practice. International agreements constitute practice of states and contribute to the grounds of customary international law').
[408] *Loewen Group, Inc. and Raymond L. Loewen* v. *United States*, ICSID Case No. ARB(AF)/98/3, Award, 26 June 2003 [hereinafter *Loewen* v. *United States*], para. 131.

First, the quantity of BITs is irrelevant. Thus, the identification of customary rules cannot simply be a 'mechanical exercise based on mere quantitative consideration'.[409] Clearly a conclusion on the existence of any customary rule cannot be reached by simply adding up the number of treaties.[410] As explained by one writer, 'the mere prevalence of similarly worded treaty language, however numerous, will not, without more, give rise to a binding obligation in custom'.[411]

Second, the proposition advanced by these writers is based on the assumption that these BITs can somehow be analysed *as a whole*. Clearly, the mass of all BITs cannot be assessed globally as a single category because these treaties notably vary in form. For instance, the 10-page BIT entered into by Canada with Poland and Hungary in 1990–1991 cannot be compared to the much more comprehensive 104-page BIT Canada concluded 15 years later with Peru. Similarly, recent BITs entered into by Germany cannot be compared with earlier ones providing only State-to-State dispute resolution mechanisms (such as the BIT entered into with Malaysia in 1960). Moreover, modern BITs also substantially vary in content (a point that will be further discussed below[412]). Logically, only *specific* and *individual* substantive obligations contained in BITs (such as, for instance, the FET standard) can be subject to an enquiry as to whether they have crystallized into a customary rule.[413] In other words, one can only investigate the customary nature of *a provision* and not an entire treaty.[414]

---

[409] Gazzini, 'The Role of Customary International Law', p. 704; Kläger, *Fair and Equitable Treatment*, p. 266; Todd Weiler, *The Interpretation of International Investment Law: Equality, Discrimination, and Minimum Standards of Treatment in Historical Context* (Martinus Nijhoff, 2013), p. 237.

[410] Al Faruque, 'Creating Customary International Law', pp. 300–301; Orakhelashvili, 'The Normative Basis of "Fair and Equitable Treatment"', p. 77.

[411] McLachlan, 'Investment Treaties and General International Law', p. 400. See also: Baxter, 'Treaties and Custom', p. 84 ('The multiplicity of treaties of extradition or of air transport agreements does nothing to prove a rule of customary international law').

[412] See, Chapter 3, Section 3.3.3.2.2.3.

[413] Diehl, *The Core Standard of International Investment Protection*, p. 140, arguing that the far-reaching thesis that 'a BIT *as a whole* could have a customary law character' cannot 'be assumed at the outset' since 'the two-elements theory has to be applied to every provision'. She believes that 'only frequently and constantly used BIT provisions have the potential of becoming a rule of customary international law'. See also: Weiler, *The Interpretation of International Investment Law*, p. 237; Kishoiyian, 'The Utility of Bilateral Investment Treaties', p. 341.

[414] Villiger, *Customary International Law and Treaties*, p. 176 ('It is unlikely that State practice and opinio juris will concern whole sets of rules, or entire conventions. Rather, States in their Practice contribute to the formation of [or apply] individual rules.

The third reason for rejecting the proposition advanced by these writers is its inherent circularity. As previously mentioned, for Schwebel, when a BIT 'prescribe[s] treating the foreign investor in accordance with customary international law' what this really means is 'the standard of international law embodied in the terms of some two thousand concordant BITs'.[415] There is something oddly circular about the proposition that in order to find out the exact meaning of a customary rule as referred to in an *individual* BIT, one should simply look at *all* BITs.[416] Under this interpretation, one cannot help but wonder why BITs should refer to custom at all? In any event, such an across-the-board *renvoi* to thousands of treaties is not particularly helpful to practitioners and arbitrators, who have to actually determine the content of custom. As will be further discussed,[417] many modern BITs refer explicitly to custom.

Fourth, the revolutionary practical impact, which would result from endorsing the proposition that BITs are equal to custom, should be emphasized. If one were to consider that custom consists of all existing BITs together, this would mean that the content of *all these instruments* would now be mandatory for *all States*. In other words, all States would now be bound by the content of more than 2500 BITs, including the countries that have decided *not* to sign any such treaties.[418] For example,

Whether or not new customary law has been generated must, therefore, be examined on the basis of single rules').

[415] Schwebel, 'Investor-State Disputes and the Development of International Law', pp. 29–30.

[416] Kläger, *Fair and Equitable Treatment*, p. 264 ('Some arbitral tribunals have at least indicated that the content of the evolved minimum standard is shaped by the conclusion of more than 2000 BITs incorporating a fair and equitable treatment provision. Consequently, the treaty standard of fair and equitable treatment, as stipulated in the BIT network, would provide the necessary state practice for the formation of a standard of customary law, whereas the treaty standard is said to reflect the customary standard. The circularity of this argument is obvious; it would entail that fair and equitable treatment is ultimately reflective of itself. Regardless of whether one thinks of fair and equitable treatment as restating preexisting customary international law or as contributing to the crystallization of an emerging customary norm, it appears impossible for these approaches to escape from the described circularity').

[417] See, Chapter 5, Section 5.1.2.

[418] Chalamish, 'Future of Bilateral Investment Treaties: A De Facto Multilateral Agreement', *Brook. J. Int'l L.* 34 (2008–2009), p. 342, arguing that 'obligations that are widespread throughout the BIT network can be used as a regulatory framework even when no such framework exists'. For him, 'arbitrators may use the general BIT framework as a source of law when there is no BIT signed between the investor's home State and the host State, provided that the host country has signed other BITs or has become a party to an investor-State arbitration convention, like the Washington Convention'. He adds,

a significant country like Brazil that is currently not bound by any BITs (it signed a number of BITs in the 1990s but none of them have entered into force) would suddenly be bound by *all* BITs. There are certainly perfectly respectable reasons for a State not to have entered into any BITs. There are also basic policy reasons for objecting the imposition of BITs' *entire content* on States that have not signed any of these instruments.[419]

Fifth, there are also some very practical reasons for rejecting the proposition that BITs are equal to custom. The concrete application of the proposition would result in a number of unworkable logistical problems. For instance, if the content of *all* BITs taken together is now considered mandatory for *all States*, how is it possible that every State comply with all BITs at the same time? Furthermore, how is this possible given that the content of these BITs varies? There are also a number of other problems. Thus, would an investor simply be allowed to pick and choose any available treaty protection and claim compensation under *any* existing BIT? For example, would that mean that a Canadian investor doing business in Peru could claim benefit not only from the treaty protection found in the Canada–Peru BIT, but also the one found in *all* BITs that Canada and Peru have entered into with *other States*? And why should that investor be limited to those BITs? Could the investor be allowed to claim benefit from other States' BITs, say the Netherlands–Bolivia BIT? Another problematic question would be the tribunal's jurisdiction over any such claim. Thus, how can a tribunal have jurisdiction over a claim filed by a Canadian investor against Peru regarding an allegation of breach of a BIT other than the Canada–Peru BIT? As will be further discussed, a rule of custom that provides investors with automatic access to international arbitration without State consent does

---

however (at p. 343), that the BIT framework cannot be used when the host State has not given consent to the specific arbitration procedure.

[419] Peter Muchlinski, 'Policy Issues', in Peter Muchlinski, Federico Ortino and Christoph Schreuer (eds.), *The Oxford Handbook of International Investment Law* (Oxford: Oxford University Press, 2008), pp. 3, 17: 'Perhaps the key question is what might be gained by elevating treaty-based standards to customary law. In effect, it would bind all countries to what may remain contested international minimum standards of treatment, regardless of whether such countries have signed IIAs [international investment agreements]. This would prevent freedom of choice for countries as to the extent and nature of their commitments. . . .. Given the widespread application of otherwise contested standards as treaty-based obligations, it would appear unnecessary to do so and, in this very sensitive policy area, it could produce an unfavourable political response, retarding economic integration and development'.

not exist.[420] These practical problems show the extent to which the proposition that BITs are equal to custom is simply unworkable.

Finally, there is something quite ironic about the position defended by those writers who support the proposition that BITs are equal to custom.[421] They are basically arguing in favour of the *'return'* of custom *precisely as a result* of the proliferation of BITs.[422] In one writer's words, they are basically arguing that 'the process of creating an international law of investment has seemingly evolved from a situation where the absence of appropriate custom prompted the creation of over 2400 BITs, which in turn has led to the creation of custom'.[423] As pointed out by d'Aspremont, it would be quite a paradox if the process of 'treatification' that emerged *because* of the perceived lack of customary rules in international investment law could have somehow led to the creation of a global 'new' custom.[424]

3.3.3.2.2.3 *BITs do not fulfil the double requirements of uniform and consistent state practice and* opinio juris The main weakness of the proposition that BITs are equal to custom is its basic failure to fulfil the conditions under which customary norms are created. As previously mentioned,[425] two basic requirements (State practice and *opinio juris*) are necessary in order to conclude that a customary rule exists. Investor-State arbitration tribunals have consistently applied this 'double requirement'.[426] Earlier in this chapter, I observed the basic requirements necessary for State practice to be considered relevant in the process of creating customary norms.[427] Thus, the practice needs to be uniform, consistent, extensive and representative for a rule of custom to emerge.

---

[420] See, Chapter 5, Section 5.3.
[421] See also, Sourgens, 'Law's Laboratory', p. 192, comparing the position taken by writers supporting this proposition to the one they have typically adopted in other contexts and concluding that 'Their own invocation of the new customary theory in the current, changed climate thus seems at best opportunistic and at worst, hypocritical'. For him, 'The claim that IIAs would create new custom is not without irony. Champions of IIAs as custom typically deny that UN General Assembly resolutions purporting to limit the scope of international law with regard to the rights of aliens, especially with regard to natural resource investments, created custom that relies on the traditional definition of custom'.
[422] The expression 'return' of custom is borrowed from d'Aspremont, 'International Customary Investment Law', pp. 19–20.
[423] W. Salacuse, 'The Treatification of International Investment Law?', *Law & Bus. Rev. Am.* 13 (2007), p. 155.
[424] d'Aspremont, 'International Customary Investment Law', p. 20.
[425] See, Chapter 1, Section 1.3.   [426] See, Chapter 1, Section 1.3.2.
[427] See, Chapter 1, Section 1.2.

It can be argued that States' practice of signing BITs is representative. Thus, as pointed out by one writer, 'today nearly all countries in the world have entered into at least one BIT', which is more than those which have 'joined the WTO or have adhered to most human rights conventions'.[428] Developed as well as developing States from all continents, political ideologies and religions have also entered into BITs.[429] It has been argued that 'today's investment regime approaches universal participation'.[430] One passage from the *Mondev* award suggests that due to the variety of States that have adopted BITs, the 'representative' criterion has been fulfilled.[431]

While the 'representativeness' condition may be considered to be fulfilled, this is not the case for the other requirements of State practice. Thus, the undeniable reality is that BITs are very diverse both in their content and scope. When considered together, these treaties are certainly not uniform or consistent enough to constitute the basis for any global rule of customary international law. This is indeed the position taken by the majority of writers.[432] This basic position is well explained by Sornarajah in the following passage:

[428] Alvarez, 'A Bit on Custom', p. 49.

[429] Al Faruque, 'Creating Customary International Law', p. 293; Alvarez, 'A Bit on Custom', p. 49.

[430] Alvarez, 'A Bit on Custom', p. 49. See, however: Carreau and Juillard, *Droit international économique*, p. 469, arguing (in 1998) that one should be careful about such representiveness given the fact that many States still refuse to sign BITs.

[431] *Mondev v. United States*, Award, 2 October 2002, para. 117 ('Investment treaties run between North and South, and East and West, and between States in these spheres *inter se*. On a remarkably widespread basis, States have repeatedly obliged themselves to accord foreign investment such treatment. In the Tribunal's view, such a body of concordant practice will necessarily have influenced the content of rules governing the treatment of foreign investment in current international law').

[432] Al Faruque, 'Creating Customary International Law', p. 301 ('despite the generality of practice with regard to principles, BITs do not create customary international law because the inconsistency in the detailed rules of BITs is pervasive'), p. 310 ('although there is a fair degree of uniformity of principles, wide inconsistency in detailed rules pervade the BITs, which greatly diminish their potential to give rise to precise rule on particular issues and therefore, impede the possibility of creating customary international law by BITs'); Kishoiyian, 'The Utility of Bilateral Investment Treaties', p. 372 ('there is not sufficient consistency in the terms of the investment treaties to find in them support for any definite principle of customary international law'); Congyan, 'International Investment Treaties and the Formation', pp. 664–665 ('The effect of international investment treaties in the formation of CIL rules should not be overestimated (...) There are some important differences among various BITs and thus the requirement of general practice is arguably hard to be met'), but adding at p. 666 ('the contents of the recently concluded international investment treaties become much more similar and actually there are many completely identical rules in them. Therefore, international investment treaties now are more likely to satisfy the material element of general

It is, of course, possible that, if there is a concordance of standards in these bilateral investment treaties, such standards on which there is consistent agreement evidenced by such treaties could become international law. For, it is well established that bilateral treaties could become international law through the fact that they evidence consistent agreement of states as much as multilateral treaties do. They are also evidence of customary practices of states. But, there is so much divergence in the standards in bilateral investment treaties that it is premature to conclude that they give rise to any significant rule of international law. Though the outer shell of bilateral investment treaties looks similar, thus contributing to the claim that they create customary international law, a deeper examination would indicate that the contents of the treaties vary so widely that each must be considered a carefully balanced accommodation reached after negotiation between the parties. These treaties are best seen as creating *lex specialis* between the parties rather than as creating customary principles of international law.[433]

This is also the position held by many authors who have undertaken the analysis of BITs to determine whether *specific* substantive rights contained in these treaties represent custom. These authors have concluded that there is no consistent State practice on any of the following issues: the definition of investment;[434] the control of the entry of investment and admission by the host State in its territory;[435] national treatment and the most favoured national treatment;[436] the standard of compensation as a result of measures of expropriation;[437] the criteria to determine the value

practice'); Toral and Schultz, 'The State, a Perpetual Respondent in Investment Arbitration?', p. 581; Jan Ole Voss, *The Impact of Investment Treaties on Contracts between Host States and Foreign Investors* (Leiden: Martinus Nijhoff, 2011), p. 56 ('The inclusion of a similar standard of protection in some bilateral investment treaties does not meet the conditions necessary for the creation of customary international law. Even if all treaties contained the same clause, which is by no means the case, this would not suffice to affirm the creation of customary international law'); Sourgens, 'Law's Laboratory', p. 191.

[433] M. Sornarajah, *International Law on Foreign Investment* (3rd ed., Cambridge: Cambridge University Press, 2010), p. 206, see also, at p. 215 ('Though the number of these treaties may be increasing, their contents indicate the adoption of a variety of standards depending on the negotiating positions of the different states').

[434] *Ibid.*, pp. 220–227.

[435] Kishoiyian, 'The Utility of Bilateral Investment Treaties', pp. 343–346; Al Faruque, 'Creating Customary International Law', p. 303.

[436] Al Faruque, 'Creating Customary International Law', pp. 304–305.

[437] *Ibid.*, pp. 305–306; Sornarajah, *The International Law on Foreign Investment*, pp. 436, 441–443; Kishoiyian, 'The Utility of Bilateral Investment Treaties', pp. 356–363. See also: Khalil, 'Treatment of Foreign Investment in Bilateral Investment Treaties', p. 352. See, however, the discussion mentioned in Chapter 2, Section 2.6.3, concluding that the

of expropriated property;[438] and the repatriation of profits.[439] Another area where a lack of consistency of State practice has been observed by scholars regards dispute settlement mechanisms and, in particular, the issues of amicable negotiations, the applicable procedural rules to the conduct of arbitration, the applicable law governing the dispute and the requirement of the exhaustion of local remedies before resorting to arbitration.[440] It should be noted, however, that other writers have adopted the opposite position.[441] Thus, while Alvarez admits that '[d]espite commonalities in general principle, these treaties remain bilateral agreements with textual variations that reflect differences in states' model negotiating texts and differences in relative bargaining leverage',[442] he also seems to undermine the importance of these differences.[443]

The present author has examined elsewhere the question surrounding the legal protection offered to corporations and shareholders under BITs and concluded that there were some important inconsistencies with respect to how BITs specifically define what an 'investor' is and the fundamental issue of the nationality of corporations.[444] Some treaties

overwhelming majority of modern BITs specifically refer to 'prompt adequate and effective' compensation (the Hull formula).

[438] Al Faruque, 'Creating Customary International Law', p. 306. See, however, discussion mentioned in Chapter 2, Section 2.6.3.

[439] *Ibid.*, at p. 306; Kishoiyian, 'The Utility of Bilateral Investment Treaties', pp. 353–354.

[440] Al Faruque, 'Creating Customary International Law', pp. 307–310; Sornarajah, *The International Law on Foreign Investment*, p. 250; Kishoiyian, 'The Utility of Bilateral Investment Treaties', pp. 363–372.

[441] See, Hindelang, 'Bilateral Investment Treaties', p. 799 '[S]ufficient consistency in regards to the following principles can be evidenced today: the host State is under the obligation to treat foreign investors fairly; an expropriation must be for public purposes and accompanied by something like just, or adequate, compensation; disputes between foreign investors and host States should be subject to impartial adjudication or arbitration; and international customary law is applicable to the relationship between the host State and the foreign investors'.

[442] Alvarez, 'A Bit on Custom', p. 24.

[443] *Ibid.*, p. 44: 'That BITs and FTAs differ in *some* of their content does not tell us what their effects are with respect to those provisions which are identical or similar, such as their generally common reliance on FET, "full" or "constant protection and security," or residual references to "international law"' (emphasis in the original). He also notes that these differences do not 'tell much about the tendency for those interpreting them, especially arbitrators, to attempt to find common general principles underlying many of the treaties' guarantees (...)'.

[444] P. Dumberry, 'The Legal Standing of Shareholders before Arbitral Tribunals: Has Any Rule of Customary International Law Crystallised?', *Michigan State JIL* 18 (2010) pp. 353–374. See also: Gazzini, 'The Role of Customary International Law', p. 709; Rudolf Dolzer and Margrete Stevens, *Bilateral Investment Treaties* (Martinus Nijhoff, 1995), p. 34 ff; Kishoiyian, 'The Utility of Bilateral Investment Treaties', pp. 346–353.

require that a corporation not only be incorporated in a State party, but that its effective management (such as its headquarters) also be located there.[445] Other treaties further require that the corporation be controlled by nationals of the State of incorporation or have substantial business activities in that State.[446] At the other extreme, some BITs that the Netherlands have entered into extend protection to legal entities not even incorporated in the country, provided that Dutch nationals control them.[447] In sum, the scope and extent of legal protection offered to corporations and shareholders under BITs are not consistent enough to constitute the basis for any customary rule.

Moreover, there is also a lack of consistency between the content of the BITs signed by States *individually*.[448] In other words, the content of BITs signed by one State often varies depending on the identity of the other party to the instrument.[449]

The second basic requirement of custom is States' *opinio juris*. As will be further discussed in detail,[450] there is certainly no evidence of any *opinio juris* by States entering into BITs.[451]

3.3.3.2.2.4 States reject the proposition that BITs represent custom States have explicitly rejected the proposition that customary law is coterminous with BITs. This is clearly the case in the context of NAFTA arbitration. For instance, the *Mondev* Tribunal explained that all three NAFTA parties rejected the *Pope & Talbot* Tribunal's[452] reasoning that BITs are equal to custom:

> In their post-hearing submissions, all three NAFTA Parties challenged holdings of the Tribunal in *Pope & Talbot* which find that the content of

---

[445] Several examples are discussed in: Anthony C. Sinclair, 'The Substance of Nationality Requirements in Investment Treaty Arbitration', *ICSID Rev.* 20(2) (2005), p. 374 ff. He specifically refers to the UK.–Philippines BIT and the Italy–Libya BIT.

[446] For instance, the United States Model BIT (2004) and the Canadian Model BIT (2004).

[447] For instance, the Netherlands–Bulgaria BIT, discussed in: Sinclair, 'The Substance of Nationality Requirements', p. 368.

[448] Al Faruque, 'Creating Customary International Law', p. 302.

[449] See, my own analysis of Canadian BITs: Dumberry, 'The Legal Standing of Shareholders before Arbitral Tribunals'.

[450] See, Chapter 4, Section 4.2.3.

[451] Al Faruque, 'Creating Customary International Law', p. 310; McLachlan, 'Investment Treaties and General International Law', p. 393; Congyan, 'International Investment Treaties and the Formation', para. 14.

[452] *Pope & Talbot Inc.* v. *Canada*, Award in Respect of Damages, 31 May 2002.

contemporary international law reflects the concordant provisions of many hundreds of bilateral investment treaties. In particular, attention was drawn to what those three States saw as a failure of the *Pope & Talbot* Tribunal to consider a necessary element of the establishment of a rule of customary international law, namely *opinio juris*. These States appear to question whether the parties to the very large numbers of bilateral investment treaties have acted out of a sense of legal obligation when they include provisions in those treaties such as that for "fair and equitable" treatment of foreign investment.[453]

A similar position was taken by Mexico (as a third party to the proceedings) in the *Loewen* case:

> Mexico is particularly concerned about the suggestion that the fact that the mere existence of some 1800 BITs in the world means that [sic] somehow that the corpus of these treaties creates customary international law obligations. The fact that States may agree to the same or similar obligations through different treaties involving different parties, or even the same obligations through multilateral treaties is not sufficient on its own to build customary international law.[454]
>
> [I]t is impossible to infer from the existence of a large number of BITs alone that any particular provision therein represents a rule of customary international law merely by reason of its commonality.[455]

The same position was also adopted by the United States and Canada in the *Loewen* case[456], the *Glamis* case[457] and the more recent *Chemtura* case.[458]

---

[453] *Mondev* v. *United States*, Award, 2 October 2002, para. 110. See also, at para. 106 (referring to the US position that the *Pope & Talbot* Tribunal had 'erred in its automatic equation of customary international law with the content of BITs, without regard to any question of *opinio juris*').

[454] *Loewen* v. *United States*, 'Mexico's Article 1128 Submission Concerning Loewen Corporate Restructuring', 2 July 2002, paras. 39–40.

[455] *Ibid.*, para. 39.

[456] *Loewen* v. *United States*, 'U.S. Response to Canada and Mexico's Article 1128 Submissions', 19 July 2002, p. 3 ('no rule of customary international law relevant to this NAFTA proceeding is established by the various bilateral investment agreements between States not parties to the NAFTA'); *Ibid.*, 'Canada's Article 1128 Submission on Jurisdiction Concerning Loewen Corporate Restructuring', 27 June 2002, para. 18 ('Even amongst the BITs, no consistent practice can be found. The variation of terms, and specifically the differences in the scope and nature of access to international arbitration makes it impossible to find a consistent practice. Without such a consistent practice there can be no customary norm'), see also, at paras. 25–26.

[457] *Glamis Gold Ltd* v. *United States*, 'United States' Rejoinder Memorial', 15 March 2007, p. 142 ff.

[458] *Chemtura Corporation* v. *Canada*, 'Canada's Counter-Memorial', 20 October 2008, paras. 269–273.

To the best of the present author's knowledge, no State has ever endorsed the theory that BITs are equal to custom.

3.3.3.2.2.5 Conclusion In sum, while the *Mondev* Tribunal[459] is right in stating that contemporary investment law has been 'reshaped' by these numerous BITs,[460] it remains that the proposition advanced by some writers that these thousands of BITs when *taken together* now represent the 'new' custom in this field must be rejected.

Interestingly, some writers now speak of the emergence of a 'common law of investment protection, with a substantially shared understanding of its general tenets'.[461] For McLachlan *et al.*, 'the very iterative process of the formulation and conclusion of investment treaties, and the vindication of the rights contained in these treaties in arbitration, is producing a set of general international principles about the meaning of the common substantive clauses, and indeed the larger operation of the system of investment arbitration'.[462] This 'common law of investment protection' is, of course, *not* the same as custom per se.

It is clear, as noted by the *Mondev* Tribunal, that 'such a body of concordant practice [in BITs] will necessarily have influenced the content of rules governing the treatment of foreign investment in current international law'.[463] Thus, Alvarez explains that many developing States have undertaken reforms of their own investment regimes in view of *future* BIT negotiations.[464] As a result of such reforms, he believes that 'some of the treatment that investors are entitled to receive under investment treaties is increasingly the kind of treatment that all entrepreneurs are at least formally entitled to under national laws and practices'.[465] For him, such relevant State practice 'supports Lowenfeld's principal conclusion, namely that truly global investment law exists and that it

---

[459] *Mondev v. United States*, Award, 2 October 2002, para. 125.

[460] Gazzini, 'The Role of Customary International Law', p. 703. *Contra*: Subedi, *International Investment Law*, pp. 142–143, arguing that the rules of custom have not changed since the 1962 General Assembly *Resolution on Permanent Sovereignty over Natural Resources*.

[461] McLachlan *et al.*, *International Investment Arbitration: Substantive Principles*, pp. 18–21. *Contra*: M.C. Porterfield, 'An International Common Law of Investor Rights?', *U. Pa. J. Int'l Econ. L.*, 27 (2006), p. 79.

[462] McLachlan, *et al.*, *International Investment Arbitration*, p. 20.

[463] *Mondev v. United States*, Award, 2 October 2002, para. 117.

[464] Alvarez, 'A Bit on Custom', pp. 52–53, referring to 'investor-protective reforms in many states' laws, even when they preceded BIT ratifications, [which] were undertaken in anticipation of the assumption of relevant international commitments'.

[465] *Ibid.*, p. 57.

increasingly resembles the substantive protections accorded under BITs and FTAs'.[466] One can indeed agree with the affirmation that the influence of the basic investment protections found in BITs has been clearly felt *outside* the treaty framework of those States parties to BITs. It seems clear that the existence of substantive obligations contained in BITs has had an influence on the types of investment protection found in *domestic laws*. The other question is whether or not these developments have had an *influence* on *custom* in international investment law.[467] In my opinion, the impact of BITs on customary international law in this field has been twofold.[468]

First, some of the standards of protection systematically contained in BITs have certainly contributed to the *consolidation* of *already existing* rules of custom in international investment law.[469] In the *Generation Ukraine* case, the Tribunal noted that '[i]t is plain that several of the BIT standards, and the prohibition against expropriation in particular, are simply a conventional codification of standards that have long existed in customary international law'.[470] As previously mentioned,[471] there seems to be little doubt over the fact that the obligation to provide 'appropriate' compensation for expropriation (in certain circumstances) survived the contestation led by Newly Independent States in the 1960s and 1970s. The principle was generally recognized as a rule of custom in the 1990s when the phenomenon of 'treatification' became prevalent. Modern BITs (the great majority of them containing the same conditions for lawful expropriation[472]) have thus consolidated the customary status of this principle.

Second, as previously mentioned,[473] there is no doubt that the content of a similarly drafted provision found in numerous BITs can transform into a customary rule. In my view, the FET obligation found in the vast majority of modern BITs should not be considered as a customary rule.[474] A number of scholars and other authorities have argued that the principle of *full* compensation (the Hull formula), which is found in

---

[466] *Ibid.*, pp. 56–57.
[467] McLachlan, *et al., International Investment Arbitration*, p. 20 (asking the question: 'to what extent can it be said that this common treaty practice itself contributes to the development of customary international law?').
[468] Gazzini, 'The Role of Customary International Law', p. 703.   [469] *Ibid.*, pp. 703, 714.
[470] *Generation Ukraine Inc. v. Ukraine*, ICSID Case No. ARB/00/9, Final Award, 16 September 2003, para. 11.3.
[471] See, Chapter 2, Section 2.2.2.   [472] See, discussion in Chapter 2, Section 2.6.3.
[473] See, discussion in Chapter 3, Section 3.3.3.2.1.
[474] See, discussion in Chapter 3, Section 3.3.3.2.1.3.

the overwhelming majority of modern BITs, has indeed acquired a customary status.[475] Whether or not this is the case remains a controversial question. What is clear, however, is that any such status would be a relatively recent phenomenon. In the 1980s, the Hull formula had been declared by almost everyone as no longer representing custom.[476] One possibility is therefore that the adoption of the Hull formula in almost all post-1990s BITs has somehow had the effect of 'resurrecting' the principle of full compensation and turning it into a rule of custom.

Yet, as previously mentioned, any such transformation of a treaty-based norm into custom would require the demonstration of two things. First, it would need to be shown that the practice of a large number of representative States *parties* to BITs have uniformly and consistently included the Hull formula in their BITs.[477] This is most likely the case.[478] Thus, as mentioned previously,[479] my own survey of 479 BITs from 28 representative countries from all continents (including both developing and developed States) shows that the overwhelming majority (452 treaties) specifically refer to 'prompt adequate and effective' compensation.[480] Second, it would also need to be shown that States have uniformly and consistently adopted the Hull formula in their *own* practice *outside treaties*.[481] For instance, it would be necessary to demonstrate that these States are including the Hull formula in their own domestic legislations or in their contracts with investors.

While this question is beyond the scope of this book, it is important to note that some writers believe this is *not* the case.[482] For instance, Salacuse noted that the most recent version of the *Restatement (Third) of*

---

[475] See, discussion in Chapter 2, Section 2.6.3.

[476] See, discussion in Chapter 2, Section 2.2.3.

[477] See, discussion in Chapter 3, Section 3.3.3.2.1.2.

[478] OECD, '"Indirect Expropriation" and The "Right To Regulate" in International Investment Law', Working Papers on International Investment, no. 2004/4, (2004), p. 2.

[479] See, discussion in Chapter 2, Section 2.6.3.

[480] P. Dumberry, *Rules of Customary International Law in the Field of International Investment Law*.

[481] See, discussion in Chapter 3, Section 3.3.3.2.1.2.

[482] Sornarajah, *The International Law on Foreign Investment*, pp. 451, 479–481; Salacuse, *The Law of Investment Treaties*, p. 58 ('Generally speaking, almost all of the nations in the world today would claim to recognize the principle that a state which has expropriated the property of a foreign investor has the obligation to pay compensation to that investor. However, all nations do not agree on the appropriate standard of compensation for expropriation or on its application in specific cases'). See also: Parra, 'Principles Governing Foreign Investment', p. 442, examining the national legislations of fifty-one developing countries (in 1992) and concluding that States use different criteria, but none of them refer to the Hull formula.

the Foreign Relations Law of the United States, unlike its predecessor, does not use the phrase 'prompt, adequate, and effective compensation', but instead refers to the term 'just compensation'.[483] As mentioned previously,[484] the present author has recently examined 165 different domestic laws on foreign investment from some 160 States.[485] A large number of these laws do not contain any provision dealing with expropriation (some of them in fact contain no provision on investment protection at all). Out of the one hundred laws that do contain provisions on expropriation, only thirty of them refer explicitly to 'prompt, adequate and effective' or full compensation. Another fifty laws refer instead to the concepts of just, fair, adequate or appropriate compensation. The other laws either refer simply to compensation in general terms or they make a *renvoi* to international or domestic law.

In sum, the question as to whether or not the Hull formula of full compensation found in numerous modern BITs has transformed into a customary rule remains open.

3.3.4   Statements by States

This section explores a second common source of evidence of State practice that is relevant to the formation of custom: statements by States. First, I will examine the different types of statements that are relevant in the context of general international law (Section 3.3.4.1). Second, my focus will turn to investor-State arbitration, where a number of different kinds of statements are considered as evidence of State practice by States themselves and by tribunals (Section 3.3.4.2).

3.3.4.1   Statements under international law

In simple terms, so-called 'verbal acts' or statements made by State representatives are the opposite of 'physical acts'.[486] It is what the State *says* in contrast with what the State actually *does.* This is the reason why a number of scholars consider that mere statements or assertions do *not* evidence any State 'practice' for the purpose of custom creation. In the first section, I will examine the question of whether or not statements

---

[483] Salacuse, *The Law of Investment Treaties,* p. 60, referring to: *Restatement of the Law Third,* para. 712.

[484] See, discussion in Chapter 2, Section 2.6.3.

[485] P. Dumberry, *Rules of Customary International Law in the Field of International Investment Law;* P. Dumberry, 'The Practice of States as Evidence of Custom'.

[486] See, discussion in Chapter 3, Section 3.3.2.

should be considered as evidence of State practice (Section 3.3.4.1.1). The second section will examine the question of the relative weight which should be given to statements depending on the circumstances (Section 3.3.4.1.2). Finally, I will offer readers a basic typology of many different types of statements that are relevant in general international law (Section 3.3.4.1.3).

3.3.4.1.1 Are statements evidence of State practice?   It must be established from the outset whether statements can even be considered as evidence of State practice for the purpose of custom formation. As summarized by two authors, different views have been taken on this question:

> There are differing views on what counts as State practice. Two broad approaches may be distinguished, which are not necessarily irreconcilable: a strict (or narrow) approach, which has regard only to what States actually do (physical acts), arguably in their international relations alone; and a more flexible approach that looks to a wider range of materials —-what States say, what they do, and what they say about what they do —-while having regard to all the relevant circumstances to determine their true significance.[487]

For a number of scholars, statements do not constitute evidence of State practice.[488] This is, for instance, the position taken by Wolfke.[489] Similarly, Thirlway is also of the view that 'the substance of the practice required is that States have done, or abstained from doing, certain things in the international field',[490] and, accordingly, 'the mere assertion *in abstracto* of the existence of a legal right or legal rule is not an act of State practice'.[491] One dissenting opinion of an ICJ judge seems to support (to some extent) such a position.[492] D'Aspremont has also recently

---

[487] Wood and Sender, 'State Practice', para. 6.

[488] D'Amato, *The Concept of Custom in International Law*, p. 88.

[489] Wolfke, *Custom in Present International Law*, p. 42 ('customs arise from acts of conduct and not from promises of such acts. True, repeated verbal acts are also acts of conduct in their broad meaning and can give rise to international customs, but only to customs of making such declarations, etc., and not to customs of the conduct described in the content of the verbal acts').

[490] Thirlway, *International Customary Law and Codification*, p. 58.

[491] *Ibid.*, adding that statements can nevertheless be 'relied on as supplementary evidence both of State practice and of the existence of the opinio juris'.

[492] *Fisheries case (United Kingdom v. Norway)*, ICJ Rep. 1951, p. 191, Dissenting Opinion of Judge Read: '[Customary international law] cannot be established by citing cases where coastal States have made extensive claims, but have not maintained their claims by the actual assertion of sovereignty over trespassing foreign ships ... The only convincing

been critical of the tendency amongst scholars to 'discover' practice where none really exists:

> International lawyers have been forced to resort to all new sorts of nets and traps to hunt and capture practice where there was none. The stratagems and ploys which are being used to "discover" practice are numerous and well-known. It suffices to mention a few of them. The most common of which is to turn a declarative process into a constitutive one. This is the idea that what is said about a given behaviour is constitutive of that behaviour. A clear example of this is the argument that declarations by states about what they do or do not do are themselves constitutive of practice. The possible evidence of a behaviour thus becomes the behaviour itself. Another trick is to discover behavioural practice in interpretive practice. According to this approach, what is said about an existing rule feeds into the behavioural practice supporting the customary rule. This means, for instance, that qualifications made by certain international actors of a given situation (e.g. the Security Council acting in the framework of Chapter VII) generate behavioural practice for the sake of the customary law applicable to that situation.[493]

The obvious reason why writers typically reject the evidentiary nature of statements is that they are sometimes dissociated from, or unaccompanied by, actual State actions.[494] In other words, these statements sometimes bear no 'relationship to what states actually believe or do'.[495] Thus, for the ILA, those who deny that verbal acts count as practice 'seem to be motivated (whether expressly or not) by the consideration that "talk is cheap", and that to make a statement is not the same as arresting a ship'.[496]

evidence of State practice is to be found in seizures, where the coastal State asserts its sovereignty over the waters in question by arresting a foreign ship and by maintaining its position in the course of diplomatic negotiation and international arbitration'.

[493] Jean d'Aspremont, 'Customary International Law as a Dance Floor: Part II'.

[494] D'Amato, *The Concept of Custom in International Law*, pp. 88–89 ('a state has not done anything when it makes a claim; until it takes enforcement action, the claim has little value as a prediction of what the state will actually do'); A. D'Amato, 'What "Counts" as Law?', in Nicholas Greenwood Onuf (ed.), *Law-Making in the Global Community* (Carolina Academic Press, 1982), p. 97.

[495] Andrew T. Guzman, 'Saving Customary International Law', *Michigan JIL* 27 (2006), p. 152 ('there is no certainty that these statements bear any relationship to what states actually believe or do. Statements made by governments and their representatives serve a variety of purposes, are often made strategically, and will often not reflect the reality of practice. Torture is the clearest example. There is no shortage of agreements and statements condemning torture, yet its use by states is commonplace. To declare, based on statements, that state practice is inconsistent with torture is simply a fiction').

[496] ILA, Final Report, 2000, p. 13. Along the same line, Villiger, *Customary International Law and Treaties*, pp. 18–19, referring to the position of a member of the US Judge Advocate's Office affirming that 'State practice on humanitarian law and the laws of

For the majority of scholars,[497] the ILA,[498] and the ILC,[499] statements count as evidence of State practice. Thus, as noted by one writer, it would be 'artificial to try to distinguish between what a State does and what it says' because certain 'acts of state behaviour, such as recognition of another state, do not need a physical act'.[500] It would indeed be incongruous not to consider a statement to be as fundamental as that of State recognition as State practice for the simple reason that it does not involve any concrete physical action. In any event, the *consequences* of State recognition are real enough for *both* States involved. As the Supreme Court of Canada noted, 'the viability of a would-be state in the international community depends, as a practical matter, upon recognition by other states'.[501] Moreover, while the act of recognition may be a 'mere' statement, it remains that it is generally followed by real physical acts such as the reciprocal opening of embassies and consulates. Byers explains another reason for rejecting the distinction between what States say and do:

> One reason for their opposition is that, in so far as this approach concerns the change of customary rules, it would seem to require violations of

warfare is the practice of the battlefield; it is the members of the army who make practice. You do not want to pay too much attention to the official statements made in the nice relaxed atmosphere of New York or Geneva' (the quote is originally found in: A. Cassese and J.H.H. Weiler [eds.], *Change and Stability in International Law-Making* [De Gruyter, 1988], p. 24).

[497] Villiger, *Customary International Law and Treaties*, pp. 19–20; Akehurst, 'Custom as a Source of International Law', p. 53; R. Müllerson, 'On the Nature and Scope of Customary International Law', *Austrian RIEL*, 2 (1997), pp. 341, 342; K. Skubiszewski, 'Elements of Custom and the Hague Court', *ZaöRV*, 31 (1971), pp. 810, 812; Baxter, 'Multilateral Treaties as Evidence of Customary International Law', pp. 275, 300; ILA, 'Sources of International Investment Law', report by M. Hirsch, ILA Study Group on the Role of Soft Law Instruments in International Investment Law (2011), p. 10; Gazzini, 'The Role of Customary International Law', p. 692; Wood and Sender, 'State Practice', para. 6; Shaw, *International Law*, pp. 82–83; Crawford, *Brownlie's Principles of Public International Law*, p. 24; Mendelson, 'The Formation of Customary International Law', pp. 205–206; Baxter, 'Treaties and Custom', p. 37; Guzman, 'Saving Customary International Law', p. 152; Dinstein, 'The Interaction between Customary International Law and Treaties', p. 275.

[498] ILA, Final Report, 2000, pp. 14, 15.

[499] ILC, First Report, 2013, p. 20; ILC, Second Report, 2014, p. 19, Draft Conclusion 7(1) of the ILC 'Proposed draft conclusions on the identification of customary international law' ('Practice may take a wide range of forms. It includes both physical and verbal actions'); ILC, Draft Conclusions, 2015, conclusion no. 6(1).

[500] Akehurst, 'Custom as a Source of International Law', p. 3. See also: Kammerhofer, 'Uncertainty in the Formal Sources of International Law', p. 526.

[501] *Reference re Secession of Quebec* [1998] 2 S.C.R. 217; *I.L.M.*, 37 (1998), p. 1342, para. 142.

customary international law. In short, acts in opposition to existing rules constitute violations of those rules, whereas statements in opposition do not. Consequently, this approach is, in Akehurst's words, 'hardly one to be recommended by anyone who wishes to strengthen the rule of law in international relations'. It leaves little room for diplomacy and peaceful persuasion, and, perhaps most importantly, marginalises less powerful States in the process of customary international law.[502]

In any event, States *themselves* consider statements as constitutive of such practice.[503] This is also the position adopted by international tribunals.[504] A good example is the ICJ's position in the *Nuclear Tests* case.[505] In fact, this case has shown that a State's unilateral declaration may, under certain circumstances, create legally binding obligations.[506]

Finally, it should be added that for a number of writers these statements should not count as State practice, but rather as proof of their *opinio juris*.[507] I will address the problem of so-called double-counting in Chapter 4.[508]

---

[502] Byers, *Custom, Power and the Power of Rules*, p. 134. See also: ILC, Second Report, 2014, p. 19.

[503] ILA, Final Report, 2000, p. 14; Villiger, *Customary International Law and Treaties*, pp. 19–21; Henckaerts and Doswald-Beck, *Customary International Humanitarian Law*, p. xxxviii.

[504] ILA, Final Report, 2000, p. 14, stating that 'the practice of international tribunals is replete with examples of verbal acts being treated as examples of practice', and referring to several cases.

[505] *Nuclear Tests Case (Australia & New Zealand v. France)*, ICJ Rep. 1974, p. 457, para. 49 ('There can be no doubt, in view of [the President of the Republic's] functions, that his public communications or statements, oral or written, as Head of State, are in international relations acts of the French State').

[506] This question was examined in: *CEMEX Caracas Investments B.V. and CEMEX Caracas II Investments B.V. v. Venezuela*, ICSID Case No. ARB/08/15, Decision on Jurisdiction, 30 December 2010, paras. 80–89.

[507] Roberts, 'Traditional and Modern Approaches to Customary International Law', p. 758 (for whom statements 'represent *opinio juris* because they are statements about the legality of action, rather than examples of that action [i.e. State practice]'). See also: D'Amato, *The Concept of Custom in International Law*, p. 88 ('a claim is not an act. . . . claims themselves, although they may *articulate* a legal norm, cannot constitute the material component of custom'); Wolfke, *Custom in Present International Law*, p. 43 ('The unquestionably possible role of verbal acts in the formation of international custom is the source of additional confusion in doctrine, because it mixes up the basic practice – the material element of custom – with various practices consisting, inter alia also of verbal acts, which, depending on their content and other circumstances, can constitute direct or indirect evidence of subjective element of custom, that is, the acceptance of the basic practice as law').

[508] See, Chapter 4, Section 4.1.5.2.

3.3.4.1.2   The relative weight to be given to statements depends on the circumstances For the ILA, there is no 'inherent reason' why 'verbal acts', which are a more common form of State practice than 'physical conduct', should not count as practice whilst physical acts should.[509] In fact, the ILA states that the distinction between 'just talk' and 'real action' 'goes more to the *weight* to be attributed to the conduct rather than to any inherent *inability* of verbal acts to contribute to the formation of customary rules'.[510] Put differently, while certain verbal acts should be considered as evidence of State practice, *depending on the circumstances*, they may not have the same *weight* as other physical acts in the formation of custom. As noted by the ILC Special Rapporteur, 'words cannot always be taken at face value'.[511] For instance, 'statements that amount to mere posturing – irreconcilable with the actual conduct of the interlocutor – need not be taken too seriously' insofar as 'custom cannot be founded on affectations'.[512] Yet, sometimes the opposite is true. In some circumstances, verbal acts can have more weight than physical acts for the purpose of custom creation. For instance, Wood explains that 'if a State acts unlawfully but nevertheless seeks to justify what it has done (or omitted to do) with legal argument, the justification is itself an element of State practice, and may even have more legal significance (in terms of preserving or reinforcing the law) than the action itself'.[513]

Similarly, not all statements should be treated equally in terms of the extent to which they truly represent State practice. Thus, the actual weight to be given to a statement will depend on 'who is making the statement, when, where and in what set of circumstances'.[514] Mendelson, for instance, explains that 'statements of some junior diplomat or technician, not a lawyer and quite possibly without any understanding of law

---

[509]   ILA, Final Report, 2000, p. 14.
[510]   *Ibid.*, p. 13 (emphasis in the original). See also: Akehurst, 'Custom as a Source of International Law', p. 3; ILC, Second Report, 2014, p. 19.
[511]   ILC, Second Report, 2014, p. 20.
[512]   Dinstein, 'The Interaction between Customary International Law and Treaties', p. 276, see also, at p. 275 ('State practice cannot be confined exclusively to statements detached from conduct').
[513]   Wood and Sender, 'State Practice', para. 6.
[514]   Dinstein, 'The Interaction between Customary International Law and Treaties', p. 278, adding: '[w]here statements are concerned, unlike conduct, they have to be enunciated by senior and authoritative spokesmen, competent to articulate the views of the State. Paramount examples are statements issued formally by the President, the Prime Minister, the Minister of Foreign Affairs, and plenipotentiary diplomatic agents'.

or proper instructions, in an obscure committee, clearly should not be accorded much weight', whereas 'a formal statement of position by a head of State or Government, or a formal diplomatic communication at the highest level, plainly must be taken seriously'.[515] In this context, it is worth recalling the ICJ's *dictum* as to whom in a government has the formal authority to make unilateral undertakings that would be binding on a State: 'it is a well-established rule of international law that the Head of State, the Head of Government and the Minister for Foreign Affairs are deemed to represent the State merely by virtue of exercising their functions, including for the performance, on behalf of the said State, of unilateral acts having the force of international commitments'.[516] The Court also added that 'with increasing frequency in modern international relations other persons representing a State in specific fields may be authorized by that State to bind it by their statements in respect of matters falling within their purview' and that '[t]his may be true, for example, of holders of technical ministerial portfolios exercising powers in their field of competence in the area of foreign relations, and even of certain officials'.[517]

3.3.4.1.3 Typology of different statements

This section examines the different *types* of statements that can be considered as evidence of State practice.[518] The other question of *where* to find such statements will not be examined here.[519] The ILA provides the following list of relevant statements:

> Diplomatic statements (including protests), policy statements, press releases, official manuals (e.g. on military law), instructions to armed forces, comments by governments on draft treaties, legislation, decisions of national courts and executive authorities, pleadings before

---

[515] Mendelson, 'The Formation of Customary International Law', p. 205.

[516] *Armed Activities on the Territory of the Congo (New Application: 2002) (Democratic Republic of the Congo v. Rwanda)*, Judgment, ICJ Rep. 2006, para. 46.

[517] *Ibid.*, para. 47.

[518] ILC, Second Report, 2014, p. 22, providing several case law examples for different types of statements.

[519] Suffice it to say that statements evidencing State practice can be found in a great variety of sources including (not exhaustively): official manuals dealing with legal questions (such as manuals of military law, and codes or guidelines of various kinds), historical records and archives, newspapers, etc. One very useful source are the different digests of the legal practice of States, such as, for instance, the Digest of United States Practice in International Law, the British and Foreign State Papers, etc. Another useful source are the annual reviews of State practice found in many law journals and yearbooks. This question is examined in: Wood and Sender, 'State Practice', paras. 21 ff.

international tribunals, statements in international organizations and the resolutions these bodies adopt – all of which are frequently cited as examples of State practice – are all forms of speech-act.[520]

In the following paragraphs, I will briefly examine five different types of statements that count as relevant State practice for the creation of customary rules. The practice of the executive, legislative and judiciary branches of government, as well as statements in the context of international organizations, will be examined in the following sections.[521] It should be noted at the outset that in some circumstances these statements could also evidence a State's *opinio juris* (this question will be examined in the next chapter[522]).[523]

The first type of statement recognized by scholars that counts as relevant State practice are diplomatic statements or correspondences,[524] which includes diplomatic protests.[525] The ICJ has relied upon said correspondence.[526]

The second type is government policy statements on matters of international relations.[527] One famous example of such a statement is the 'Tate letter', signalling a shift in US policy from its support to the so-called 'absolute' theory of sovereign immunity to the 'relative' theory.[528]

---

[520] ILA, Final Report, 2000, p. 14.   [521] See, Chapter 3, Sections 3.3.5. and 3.3.6.

[522] See, Chapter 4, Section 4.1.5.2.

[523] ILC, Second Report, 2014, p. 52; Hirsch, 'Sources of International Investment Law', p. 10.

[524] Ferrari-Bravo, 'Méthodes de recherche de la coutume internationale', p. 262 (providing a detailed analysis of the different types of documents considered as relevant diplomatic correspondence); Crawford, *Brownlie's Principles of Public International Law*, p. 24; Shaw, *International Law*, pp. 82–83; Mendelson, 'The Formation of Customary International Law', p. 204; D'Amato, *The Concept of Custom in International Law*, p. 86; Malanczuk, *Akehurst's Modern Introduction to International Law*, pp. 39–40; Gazzini, 'The Role of Customary International Law', p. 692; Congyan, 'International Investment Treaties and the Formation', p. 661; Tudor, *The Fair and Equitable Treatment Standard*, p. 71; Mendelson, 'The Formation of Customary International Law', p. 204; ILC, Second Report, 2014, p. 22.

[525] ILC, Second Report, 2014, p. 22; Gazzini, 'The Role of Customary International Law', p. 692.

[526] *Rights of Nationals of the United States of America in Morocco (France v. U.S.)*, ICJ Rep. 1952, p. 200.

[527] Crawford, *Brownlie's Principles of Public International Law*, p. 24; Mendelson, 'The Formation of Customary International Law', p. 204; Tudor, *The Fair and Equitable Treatment Standard*, p. 77; ILA, Final Report, 2000, p. 14; Shaw, *International Law*, pp. 82–83; ILC, Second Report, 2014, p. 22; Gazzini, 'The Role of Customary International Law', p. 692.

[528] Letter sent by the US State Department's Acting Legal Adviser, Mr. Jack B. Tate, to the American Acting Attorney-General, in: *State Dept. Bull.* 26 (1952), p. 984; *AJIL* 47

These public statements can be made to the domestic legislature,[529] at a press conference,[530] to newspapers, radio or television,[531] or via press releases and communiqués.[532]

The third type are official statements made during multilateral conferences[533] or before organs of international organizations.[534] In the ICJ *Jurisdictional Immunities of the State* case, the Court stated that 'State practice of particular significance' is to be found in, *inter alia*, 'statements made by States, first in the course of the extensive study of the subject by the International Law Commission and then in the context of the adoption of the United Nations Convention'.[535] Such statements vary and can take the form of votes, interpretative declarations, reservations,[536] as well as written comments or observations on draft texts,[537] such as the work of the ILC.[538] One recent example is certain States' reactions[539] to the 2005 study of the ICRC on customary rules in international

(1953), p. 93 (referred to in Ferrari-Bravo, 'Méthodes de recherche de la coutume internationale', pp. 271–273, also mentioning a number of other examples).

[529] Mendelson, 'The Formation of Customary International Law', p. 204; ILC, Second Report, 2014, p. 22.

[530] Mendelson, 'The Formation of Customary International Law', pp. 205–206; Malanczuk, *Akehurst's Modern Introduction to International Law*, pp. 39–40.

[531] Ferrari-Bravo, 'Méthodes de recherche de la coutume internationale', pp. 266–268.

[532] Crawford, *Brownlie's Principles of Public International Law*, p. 24; Mendelson, 'The Formation of Customary International Law', p. 204; ILA, Final Report, 2000, p. 14; Henckaerts and Doswald-Beck, *Customary International Humanitarian Law*, p. xxxviii (considering military communiqués during war as evidence of State practice).

[533] Ferrari-Bravo, 'Méthodes de recherche de la coutume internationale', pp. 289–296; Gazzini, 'The Role of Customary International Law', p. 692.

[534] Gazzini, 'The Role of Customary International Law', p. 692; Henckaerts and Doswald-Beck, *Customary International Humanitarian Law*, p. Xxxviii; ILA Report, 2000, pp. 3, 13; Mendelson, 'The Formation of Customary International Law', p. 204; Crawford, *Brownlie's Principles of Public International Law*, p. 24; Ferrari-Bravo, 'Méthodes de recherche de la coutume internationale', pp. 262–264, 265, 275–277; Villiger, *Customary International Law and Treaties*, p. 23; Malanczuk, *Akehurst's Modern Introduction to International Law*, pp. 39–40; Paparinskis, *The International Minimum Standard*, p. 16; Wood and Sender, 'State Practice', para. 18.

[535] *Jurisdictional Immunities of the State (Germany v. Italy)*, ICJ Rep. 2012, para. 55.

[536] Villiger, *Customary International Law and Treaties*, pp. 23–25.

[537] *Ibid.*, p. 23; Shaw, *International Law*, pp. 82–83; ILA Report, 2000, p. 14; Henckaerts and Doswald-Beck, *Customary International Humanitarian Law*, p. Xxxviii.

[538] Crawford, *Brownlie's Principles of Public International Law*, p. 24; Mendelson, 'The Formation of Customary International Law', p. 204; ILC, First Report, 2013, p. 20; Wood and Sender, 'State Practice', para. 18.

[539] See, for instance: 'Statement at the Meeting of National Committees on International Humanitarian Law of Commonwealth States', UK Legal Adviser of the Foreign and Commonwealth Office, 20 July 2005, *British YIL*, 76 (2005), pp. 694–695; 'Updated European Union Guidelines on Promoting Compliance with International

humanitarian law.[540] The position taken by States in the context of international organizations will be further discussed.[541]

The fourth type are statements found in official manuals on legal questions (e.g. manuals of military law[542]).[543] While a number of writers believe that the opinions of official legal advisers should also count as evidence of relevant State practice,[544] others think this should only be the case when the State's position is congruent with the legal advice.[545] Some writers hold this view because legal opinions do not necessarily represent a State's view or policy.[546] Others are also reluctant to recognize internal memoranda or governmental legal advisers' confidential opinions as forms of State practice because they do not satisfy the 'public' requirement of practice.[547]

A fifth type of statement, which is generally considered as a form of State practice, are pleadings by States involved in international litigation.[548] In the ICJ *Jurisdictional Immunities of the State* case, the Court

---

Humanitarian Law' (2009/C 303/06), sect. 7; Bellinger and Haynes, 'A US Government Response', pp. 443, 444.

[540] Henckaerts and Doswald-Beck, *Customary International Humanitarian Law*.

[541] See, Chapter 3, Section 3.3.5.1.

[542] *Prosecutor v. Tadić*, ICTY Case No. IT-94-1, Decision on the Defence Motion for Interlocutory Appeal on Jurisdiction (Appeals Chamber), 2 October 1995, para. 99. See, however, the remarks made by the United States in: Bellinger and Haynes, 'A US Government Response', p. 445 ('The initial U.S. review of the State practice volumes suggests that the Study places too much emphasis on written materials, such as military manuals and other guidelines published by States, as opposed to actual operational practice by States during armed conflict. Although manuals may provide important indications of State behavior and opinio juris, they cannot be a replacement for a meaningful assessment of operational State practice in connection with actual military operations').

[543] Crawford, *Brownlie's Principles of Public International Law*, p. 24; ILA Report, 2000, p. 14; Henckaerts and Doswald-Beck, *Customary International Humanitarian Law*, p. Xxxviii; Dinstein, 'The Interaction between Customary International Law and Treaties' p. 272; ILC, Second Report, 2014, p. 24.

[544] Crawford, *Brownlie's Principles of Public International Law*, p. 24; Mendelson, 'The Formation of Customary International Law', p. 204; Ferrari-Bravo, 'Méthodes de recherche de la coutume internationale', pp. 270–271; Henckaerts and Doswald-Beck, *Customary International Humanitarian Law*, p. xxxviii; Malanczuk, *Akehurst's Modern Introduction to International Law*, pp. 39–40; Shaw, *International Law*, pp. 82–83.

[545] Ferrari-Bravo, 'Méthodes de recherche de la coutume internationale', pp. 270–271.

[546] ILC, Second Report, 2014, p. 24, referring to: *Red Sea Islands (Eritrea/Yemen)*, Award, 9 October 1998, para. 94.

[547] ILA, Final Report, 2000, p. 15.

[548] A.E. Roberts, 'Power and Persuasion in Investment Treaty International: the Dual Role of States', *AJIL* 104 (2010), pp. 218, 219; Mendelson, 'The Formation of Customary International Law', p. 204; Crawford, *Brownlie's Principles of Public International Law*,

stated that 'State practice of particular significance is to be found' in, *inter alia*, 'the claims to immunity advanced by States before foreign courts'.[549] The importance of pleadings in investment arbitration will be discussed below.[550]

Finally, reference should be made to the comprehensive typology of statements elaborated by Dinstein. He divides them in the following three categories:

> The first category of statements is that of assertions made in connection with the previous, present or prospective conduct of the State issuing the statement. Principal specimens are:
>
> (a) We are always at liberty to do x, if we so desire.
> (b) We concede that the general rule of customary international law is y, but our conduct z is congruent with an exception to the rule.
> (c) We do not do a, inasmuch as we do not acknowledge a rule of customary international law allowing such conduct.
> (d) We shall stop doing b (either for a prescribed period of time or indefinitely).
> (e) We shall not do c unless certain conditions are met.
> (f) We shall do d, but only if specific forms are maintained.
> (g) We shall allow e to be done by others, although we are not obligated to do so.
>
> The second type of statements is that of denials and caveats concerning conduct taken or policy pursued by the State issuing them. Prime illustrations are:
>
> (a) Denial that conduct x was in breach of customary international law.
> (b) Denial that conduct y took place as alleged by another State.
> (c) Denial that conduct z was carried out intentionally.
> (d) A "disclaimer": even though conduct a did take place, it should not be viewed as a legal precedent (e.g., payment was made ex gratia).
>
> The third rubric of statements is that of protests and other responses (negative or positive) relating to the conduct of foreign States. Key examples are:

---

p. 315; ILA Report, 2000, p. 14; Henckaerts and Doswald-Beck, *Customary International Humanitarian Law*, p. xxxviii; ILC, Second Report, 2014, p. 22; Paparinskis, *The International Minimum Standard*, p. 16.

[549] *Jurisdictional Immunities of the State (Germany v. Italy)*, ICJ Rep. 2012, para. 55.

[550] See, Chapter 3, Section 3.3.4.2.2.

(a) A classical protest: State A is not at liberty to do x under customary international law.

(b) An endorsement: State B is at liberty to do y under customary international law.

(c) A caveat: conduct z can be carried out by State C only in a particular way and in no other.

(d) An interim position: although conduct a is unlawful, we shall not challenge it until a satisfactory new legal regime is agreed upon.[551]

3.3.4.2 Statements in investor-State arbitration

After examining the different types of statements that are relevant in the context of general international law, I will now specifically focus on statements in investor-State arbitration.

A number of investment tribunals have acknowledged that statements by States can be considered as evidence of State practice. For instance, the *Glamis* Tribunal stated that 'the evidence of such "concordant practice" undertaken out of a sense of legal obligation is exhibited in very few authoritative sources', including government statements.[552] The *Cargill* Tribunal also mentioned that 'the statements of States can—with care—serve as evidence of the content of custom'.[553] The Tribunal also added that in the context of NAFTA Chapter 11 arbitration proceedings, said statements could be found when States act as respondents as well as when they are non-disputing parties and decide to file so-called Article 1128 submissions (this specific type of statement will be further discussed[554]). [555]

This last remark by the *Cargill* Tribunal is important. The types of statements that are considered as important sources of State practice in the field of investment arbitration are *not exactly the same* as those in general international law. In the next sections, I will examine the

---

[551] Dinstein, 'The Interaction between Customary International Law and Treaties', pp. 279–281, providing concrete examples for each situation in footnotes.

[552] *Glamis Gold Ltd* v. *United States*, Award, 14 May 2009, para. 603. See, Margaret Clare Ryan, 'Glamis Gold, Ltd. v. The United States and the Fair and Equitable Treatment Standard', *McGill LJ* 56(4) (2011), pp. 952–953, for a critical analysis of the reasoning of the Tribunal on this point.

[553] *Cargill, Inc.* v. *Mexico*, ICSID Case No. ARB(AF)/05/02, Award, 18 September 2009, para. 275.

[554] See, Chapter 3, Section 3.3.4.2.3.

[555] *Cargill, Inc.* v. *Mexico*, Award, 18 September 2009, para. 275.

following types of statements by States that can be considered as elements of State practice in the context of investor-State arbitration[556]:

- State pleadings in arbitration proceedings (Section 3.3.4.2.2);
- Interventions by non-disputing treaty parties during arbitration proceedings (Section 3.3.4.2.3);
- Official statements made by parties to a treaty (Section 3.3.4.2.4);
- Joint statements by States parties to a treaty on matters of interpretation (Section 3.3.4.2.5); and
- Model BITs adopted by States (Section 3.3.4.2.6).

Before doing so, I will first briefly examine a number of other types of statements (mentioned in the previous section) that are considered as evidence of State practice under general international law, but that are less relevant in the specific context of investor-State arbitration (Section 3.3.4.2.1).

3.3.4.2.1 **Introductory remarks: some types of statements that are important in international law are less relevant in investor-State arbitration** The first type of statement that is important in general international law, but is much less relevant in the field of investor-State arbitration is State official manuals.[557] Official legal advisers' opinions on investor-State arbitration issues are also rarely available. One example frequently cited by writers,[558] as well as by parties in arbitral proceedings,[559] is the 1979 statement made by the Swiss Ministry of Foreign

---

[556] This list is similar to the one found in Roberts, 'Power and Persuasion in Investment Treaty International', p. 194. She mentions (at p. 194) the possibility for States parties to treaties to take an active role in interpreting such treaties, which would 'generat[e] state practice that tribunals could take into account when interpreting investment treaties'. She further provides a number of examples of such relevant State practice on matters of treaty interpretation: 'by modifying its model bilateral investment treaty (BIT), formulating pleadings as a respondent, intervening in arbitrations as a nondisputing party, issuing public statements about its understanding of particular provisions, and reaching joint interpretations with the other treaty parties, including through bodies like the FTC' (*Ibid.*).

[557] One example is found in: Pac Rim Cayman *LLC* v. El Salvador, ICSID Case No. ARB/09/12, Decision on the Respondent's Jurisdictional Objections, 1 June 2012, para. 4.29, where El Salvador refers to the 'US Department of State Foreign Affairs Manual, Volume 7 – Consular Services, Part 671, Assistance to Citizens Involved in Commercial, Investment and Other Business Related Disputes Abroad ("FAM")' as one relevant element of the United States' practice.

[558] See, for instance, Newcombe and Paradell, *Law and Practice of Investment Treaties*, p. 268.

[559] *Bureau Veritas, Inspection, Valuation, Assessment and Control, BIVAC BV* v. *Paraguay*, ICSID Case No. ARB/07/9, Further Decision on Objections to Jurisdiction, 9 October 2012, para. 152 (position of Paraguay).

Affairs to the effect that FET clauses found in Swiss BITs incorporate the minimum standard of treatment (MST) under custom.[560] Also, in the context of NAFTA Article 1105 on the FET standard, the *Glamis* Tribunal referred to a legal opinion by the US Department of the Interior as evidence of State practice for which, under international law, the US could be held accountable.[561] It should be noted, however, that expert opinions filed by *individuals* in arbitration proceedings are clearly not evidence of *State* practice (even if such opinions are prepared for States and paid for by them based on their instructions).[562]

Examples of diplomatic statements or correspondence are also rarely available in investor-State arbitration.[563] The most famous example of such correspondence is the exchange of letters between the US Secretary of State, Mr. Cordell Hull, and his Mexican counterpart. This was in response to Mexico's nationalization of US companies in 1936. In

[560] Mémoire, JAAC 1979, fasc. 43/IV, no. 113, in : L. Caflisch, 'La pratique suisse en matière de droit international public', *ASDI* 36 (1980), p. 178 ('On se réfère ainsi au principe classique du droit des gens selon lequel les États doivent mettre les étrangers se trouvant sur leur territoire et leurs biens au bénéfice du "standard minimum" international, c'est-à-dire leur accorder un minimum de droits personnels, procéduraux et économiques'). It has recently been argued by M. Schmid, 'Switzerland', in C. Brown (ed.), *Commentaries on Selected Model Investment Treaties* (Oxford: Oxford University Press, 2013), pp. 669–672, that this opinion in fact no longer reflects the actual practice of Swiss BITs under which FET clauses are considered as being an autonomous standard of treatment detached from the minimum standard under custom.

[561] *Glamis Gold Ltd* v. *United States*, Award, 14 May 2009. The case involved a Canadian company's proposal to develop the 'Imperial Project', a gold mining operation located on US federal lands in California. The approval of the Imperial Project was withdrawn based on a legal opinion of the US Department of the Interior (the 'M-Opinion'). The Tribunal framed the issue concerning this legal opinion as follows: 'whether a lengthy, reasoned legal opinion violates customary international law because it changes, in an arguably dramatic way, a previous law or prior legal interpretation upon which an investor has based its reasonable, investment-backed expectations' (para. 761). The Tribunal concluded that the M-Opinion was not 'arbitrary', that it did not exhibit 'a manifest lack of reasons', and did not demonstrate 'blatant unfairness or evident discrimination' (paras. 762–765). The reasoning of the Tribunal indicates that a government changing its past regulatory practice based on a legal opinion is not arbitrary unless this opinion 'exhibit[s] a manifest lack of reasons' (para. 759) or unless these changes specifically target an investor (paras. 542, 689, 763–765, 793–794).

[562] On the question of the interpretative value of expert opinions, see, *Mihaly International Corporation* v. *Sri Lanka*, ICSID Case No. ARB/00/2, Award, 15 March 2002, para. 58 (suggesting that they should not be considered as scholarly works under Art. 38(1)(d)) of the ICJ Statute).

[563] See, *Pope & Talbot Inc.* v. *Canada*, Award in Respect of Damages, 31 May 2002, para. 62, fn 53, referring to the position of counsel for Canada stating that 'customary international law is based on the practice of states or diplomatic correspondence'.

the correspondence, the former articulated what would become known as the 'Hull formula' on compensation.[564] Another more recent example of an exchange of letters between States on matters of treaty interpretation is found in the *Ecuador* v. *United States* case.[565] Some references to such correspondence also sometimes appear in the news.[566]

Policy statements by States on matters concerning international investment law are more frequent. Suffice it to mention a few recent examples of such statements. One example is the decision by a number of States (Ecuador,[567] Venezuela,[568] and Bolivia[569]) to denounce the ICSID Convention. In recent years a number of States (South Africa,[570] and Indonesia[571]) have also publicly stated that they would terminate some of their BITs. Some States (Canada in the past,[572] and more recently Australia[573]) have also made public statements that they would no longer

---

[564] See, discussion in Chapter 2, Section 2.1.2.

[565] *Ecuador* v. *United States*, PCA Case No. 2012–5, 'Memorial of Respondent United States of America on Objections to Jurisdiction', 25 April 2012, pp. 10–11.

[566] See, for instance, letter (dated 7 September 2012) sent by South Africa's Minister of International Relations to Belgium's Ambassador in Pretoria denouncing the South Africa-Belgium/Luxembourg BIT (mentioned in: IISD, 'South Africa begins withdrawing from EU-member BITs', 30 October 2012). See also: press release issued in 2014 by the Netherlands Embassy in Indonesia stating that it had been informed by Indonesia of its decision to terminate the BIT between the two States as well as a number of other BITs (Netherlands Embassy in Jakarta, Indonesia, 'Termination Bilateral Investment Treaty', http://indonesia.nlembassy.org/organization/departments/economic-affairs/termination-bilateral-investment-treaty.html).

[567] ICSID Press Release, 'Ecuador Submits a Notice Under Article 71 of the ICSID Convention', 9 July 2009.

[568] ICSID Press Release, 'Venezuela Submits a Notice Under Article 71 of the ICSID Convention', 26 January 2012.

[569] ICSID News Release, 'Bolivia Submits a Notice under Article 71 of the ICSID Convention', 16 May 2007.

[570] South Africa has terminated its BIT with Belgium-Luxembourg in 2012 and in 2013 gave notice of the termination of others BITs. See: UNCTAD, 'World Investment Report' (2014), p. 114. See also: Xavier Carim, 'Lessons from South Africa's BIT Review', *Columbia FDI Perspectives No. 109*, 25 November 2013, Vale Colum. Ctr. on Sustainable Int'l Investment.

[571] The Netherlands Embassy in Jakarta, Indonesia, 'Termination Bilateral Investment Treaty'.

[572] In the context of the then on-going negotiation to create the Free Trade Area of the Americas ('FTAA'), the International Trade Minister of Canada publicly stated at the end of 2000 that he would not sign any agreement that would include provisions akin to those contained within NAFTA Chapter 11, in: House of Commons Debates, 23 October 2003, p. 8673 (referred to in: *Canadian YIL* 42 (2004), pp. 513–574).

[573] Australia, 'Gillard Government Trade Policy Statement: Trading Our Way to More Jobs and Prosperity', Dep't of Foreign Aff. & Trade, 14 April 2011. Australia has, however, since then apparently abandoned that policy and signed a FTA with Korea (2013), which

enter into BITs containing an investor-State dispute settlement mechanism. The same position has also been publicly expressed by a number of States' officials in the context of on-going negotiation of the *Trans-Pacific Partnership* (TPP) and the EU–Canada *Comprehensive Economic and Trade Agreement* (CETA, signed in 2014). Finally, in the past, officials from Argentina have stated that before executing any arbitral awards in favour of claimants, it would request its own Supreme Court to assess their legality under Argentinian law.[574]

3.3.4.2.2 State pleadings in arbitration proceedings Pleadings in investor-State arbitration proceedings are rarely publicly available. There are a few exceptions, including proceedings conducted under NAFTA Chapter 11[575] and the recent Dominican Republic – Central America – United States Free Trade Agreement ('DR-CAFTA').[576] Otherwise, awards will typically only contain partial description of the arguments advanced by the parties in their respective pleadings. The rarity of publicly available State pleadings is highly problematic in the context of this book's examination of State practice.[577] This means that disproportionate weight is given to the State practice of the few parties to those agreements where pleadings are publicly available.[578] In other words, a lot of attention is given to the practice of NAFTA parties, for the simple reason that such practice has been readily available for some 20 years.

Yet, it should be added that relevant pleadings by States in the context of investor-State arbitration are *not* limited to only those made before

---

includes an ISDS mechanism (see: www.dfat.gov.au/fta/kafta/downloads/fact-sheet-isds.pdf).

[574] See, discussion, for instance, in *CMS Gas Transmission Company* v. *Argentina*, ICSID Case No. ARB/01/8 (Annulment Proceeding), Decision on the Argentine Republic's Request for a Continued Stay of Enforcement of the Award (Rule 54 of the ICSID Arbitration Rules), 1 September 2006, para. 18 ff. The Annulment Committee asked Argentina to submit a written statement on the matter. Argentina responded that 'in accordance with its obligations under the ICSID Convention, it will recognize the award rendered by the arbitral tribunal as binding and will enforce the pecuniary obligations imposed by that award within its territories, in the event that annulment is not granted' (para. 47).

[575] See, NAFTA Free Trade Commission, 'Notes of Interpretation of Certain Chapter 11 Provisions', 31 July 2001.

[576] CAFTA, Article 10.21.

[577] It should be recalled here that only pleadings *of States* matter in the context of this book, see, discussion in Chapter 3, Section 3.1.1.

[578] Paparinskis, *The International Minimum Standard*, p. 145.

arbitral tribunals. Relevant pleadings can also be found in the context of judicial review proceedings before the domestic court of the country where the arbitration took place, as well as in the context of proceedings before a national court to enforce an award.[579]

In the present section, I will first examine the importance of pleadings as evidence of State practice as well as the relative weight that they should be given depending on the circumstances (Section 3.3.4.2.2.1). I will then illustrate these principles with a few examples of how tribunals have concretely interpreted said pleadings (Section 3.3.4.2.2.2).

3.3.4.2.2.1 The relative weight to be given to pleadings depends on the circumstances As previously mentioned,[580] scholars recognize pleadings as a form of State practice relevant for the creation of custom. As acknowledged by both the *Glamis* and *Cargill* tribunals,[581] the same is true for pleadings by States involved in investment arbitration. For Paparinskis, pleadings are in fact the 'clearest example of State practice'.[582] This is because pleadings provide a unique opportunity for a State to explain what it believes to be the law on a given issue.[583] Pleadings represent the view of the State because its content often needs to be approved by several State departments or ministries.[584] The importance of pleadings as an illustration of

---

[579] The question is further discussed below in Chapter 3, Section 3.3.6.3.2.

[580] See, Chapter 3, Section 3.3.4.1.

[581] *Glamis Gold Ltd* v. *United States*, Award, 14 May 2009, para. 603; *Cargill, Inc.* v. *Mexico*, Award, 18 September 2009, para. 275.

[582] Paparinskis, *The International Minimum Standard*, p. 16.

[583] ILC, First Report, 2013, p. 20 ('[t]he attitude of States to the formation and evidence of customary international law may be seen in their pleadings before international courts and tribunals'); *Railroad Development Corporation (RDC)* v. *Guatemala*, ICSID Case No. ARB/07/23, Award, 29 June 2012, para. 217 ('The Tribunal notes further that, as such, arbitral awards do not constitute State practice, but it is also true that parties in international proceedings use them *in their pleadings* in support of their arguments of what the law is on a specific issue. There is ample evidence of such practice in these proceedings. It is an efficient manner for a party in a judicial process to *show what it believes to be the law.* (. . .)', emphasis added).

[584] J. Crawford, A. Pellet and C. Redgwell, 'Anglo-American and Continental Traditions in Advocacy before International Courts and Tribunals', *Cambridge J Intl Comp L* 2 (2013), p. 724, Crawford stating ('what you say in the International Court is read by the agent and approved by the agent, and it is as such a representative view of the state'), see also, Pellet's comment. For a description of the process in the United States: see: Barton Legum, 'The Difficulties of Conciliation in Investment Treaty Cases: A Comment on Professor Jack C. Coe's 'Toward a Complementary Use of Conciliation in Investor-State Disputes: A Preliminary Sketch,''' *Mealey's Int'l Arb. Rep.* (2006), p. 23.

State practice is also clear because any such statement has an impact that goes beyond the instant dispute between the parties. Thus, as noted by one author, 'government counsel (...) needs not only to identify the winning argument, but also to ensure, through detailed discussions with his or her colleagues in other interested agencies, that that argument properly balances the interests' of that government in view of 'hypothetical cases that might arise in the future'.[585]

Yet, one has to be careful when considering pleadings as representing a State's position on a given point of law. Thus, as noted by the ILC Special Rapporteur Wood, it is important to remember that States 'are in advocacy mode' when they make their position known in pleadings.[586] For this reason, Crawford qualifies pleadings as State practice *sub modo*.[587] This is precisely the reason why tribunals have sometimes refused to rely on State pleadings by the respondent State regarding the meaning of a treaty provision in the context of *on-going* arbitration proceedings.[588] As noted by two writers, in the context of treaty interpretation, 'such statements are likely to be perceived as self-serving and as determined by the desire to influence the tribunal's decision in favour of the state offering the interpretation'.[589] The point is well-explained by Sir Franklin Berman in his dissenting opinion in *Industria Nacional de Alimentos*:

---

[585] Barton Legum, 'Representing States – A US Perspective', *Arbitration & ADR* 6 (2001), pp. 46, 47. See also: Jeremy K. Sharpe, 'Representing a Respondent State in Investment Arbitration', in: Chiara Giorgetti (ed.), *Litigation International Investment Disputes* (Leiden; Boston: Brill Nijhoff, 2014), p. 42.

[586] ILC, First Report, 2013, p. 20.

[587] Crawford, Pellet and Redgwell, 'Anglo-American and Continental Traditions', p. 724, Crawford stating 'But it is state practice *sub modo*, because it is not free of the environment in which it occurs. The Court has to decide and the state has a compelling interest to present the best case, irrespective of what it really thinks. There may be a discrepancy between the actual view of the state on some particular issue and the view that you tell the state they will have to argue if they are going to have any chance of winning the case. That obviously has to be factored in. The stream does not rise above the source and the advocate does not rise above the court, so I think it is state practice *sub modo*').

[588] *Gas Natural SDG S.A. v. Argentina*, ICSID Case No. ARB/03/10, Decision on Preliminary Questions on Jurisdiction, 17 June 2005, para. 47 (fn no. 12).

[589] Schreuer and Dolzer, *Principles of International Investment Law*, p. 34. See also: Roberts, 'Power and Persuasion in Investment Treaty International', p. 218 ('When states submit pleadings, they are wearing their respondent hats more clearly than at any other time. The legitimate concern arises that they might be adopting expedient interpretations to avoid liability in particular cases rather than considered interpretations that they would wish to have general application'); Paparinskis, *The International Minimum Standard* (introduction to the paperback edition), p. lii ('since one of parties to the investment treaty arbitration will have been a stranger to the treaty negotiation, and the other party's

Every case of the interpretation of a BIT by an ICSID Tribunal shares this unusual feature, namely that the Tribunal has to find the meaning of a bilateral instrument, one of the Parties to which (the Respondent) will be a party before the Tribunal, while the other Treaty Party by definition will not. Or, to put the matter the other way round, one of the parties to the arbitration before the Tribunal (but not the other) will have been a stranger to the treaty negotiation (see paragraph 70 of the Committee's Decision). That circumstance surely imposes a particular duty of caution on the Tribunal: it can clearly not discount assertions put forward in argument by the Respondent as to the intentions behind the BIT and its negotiation (since that is authentic information which may be of importance), but it must at the same time treat them with all due caution, in the interests of its overriding duty to treat the parties to the arbitration on a basis of complete equality (since it is also possible that assertions by the Respondent may be incomplete, misleading or even self-serving). In other words, it must be very rarely indeed that an ICSID Tribunal, confronted with a disputed issue of interpretation of a BIT, will accept at its face value the assertions of the Respondent as to its meaning without some sufficient objective evidence to back them up.[590]

But, as mentioned by Roberts, the fact that such pleadings are self-interested does not render them irrelevant per se.[591] In fact, while pleadings should be considered as a form of State practice, the actual *weight* that should be given to them will depend on the context.[592]

On matters of *treaty interpretation*, substantial weight should be given to pleadings showing a State's uniform and consistent position.[593] For instance, substantial weight should be given to the pleadings of NAFTA Parties that have unanimously and consistently supported the conclusion that under NAFTA Article 1105 foreign investors must be accorded a FET standard under 'international law', which is a reference to the MST under customary international law.[594] The same reasoning should apply to assess the relevance of pleadings as evidence of a State's practice. Thus,

assertions may be incomplete, misleading, or even self-serving, it must be rare that a statement by a State about the meaning of its obligations is accepted at face value').

[590] *Industria Nacional de Alimentos, S.A. and Indalsa Perú, S.A. v. Peru*, ICSID Case No. ARB/03/4, Annulment Proceeding, 5 September 2007, Dissenting Opinion of Sir Franklin Berman, para. 9 (the case is also known as *Empresas Lucchetti, S.A. and Lucchetti Peru, S.A. v. Peru*, ICSID Case No. ARB/03/4).

[591] Roberts, 'Power and Persuasion in Investment Treaty International', pp. 218–219. See also: Ole Kristian Fauchald, 'The Legal Reasoning of ICSID Tribunals – An Empirical Analysis', *EJIL*, 19 (2008), p. 347.

[592] Roberts, *ibid.*; Fauchald, *ibid.*.; Paparinskis, *The International Minimum Standard* (introduction to new paperback edition), p. lii.

[593] Roberts, *ibid.*; Fauchald, *ibid.*

[594] Dumberry, *The Fair and Equitable Treatment Standard*, p. 47 ff.

as previously mentioned,[595] one of the basic requirements for State practice to be considered relevant in the process of the creation of customary norms is 'internal uniformity'. Thus, a State must have had the *same* attitude in its relation with other States (almost) every time it had the occasion. In terms of the impact on the creation of customary rules, greater weight should clearly be given to a State's uniform and consistent pleadings. On the contrary, limited weight should be given to statements in pleadings that are isolated and not representative of the State's general view. Such would be the case if a statement is in conflict with other evidence of State practice, showing a different position than the one systematically taken by a State in the past (these distinctions are discussed further in the next section).

   The next section examines how investment tribunals have assessed the importance of pleadings and the weight that they should be given as evidence of State practice.

3.3.4.2.2.2 *Arbitral awards examining pleadings* Apart from two general statements by the *Glamis* and *Cargill* tribunals recognizing pleadings as evidence of State practice, very few tribunals have actually examined the question of the weight which such statements should concretely be given in different circumstances.[596] The *Enron* case, at different phases of its proceedings, provides one rare illustration of the distinctions identified in the previous section.

   First, the post-award annulment phase of the *Enron* case illustrates the proposition that, as a matter of principle, State pleadings should be regarded as relevant evidence of State practice. The Annulment Committee explained that the claimant 'requested that the provisional stay of enforcement of the Award pursuant to Article 52(5) of the ICSID Convention be lifted, or alternatively, that if the Committee continues the stay, it be conditioned on Argentina's providing financial security'.[597] One of the grounds invoked by the claimant was the fact that 'senior executive and judicial officers and the Attorney General have stated that

---

[595] See, discussion in Chapter 3, Section 3.2.1.

[596] *Glamis Gold Ltd* v. *United States*, Award, 14 May 2009, para. 603 ('The evidence of such "concordant practice" undertaken out of a sense of legal obligation is exhibited in very few authoritative sources: treaty ratification language, statements of governments, treaty practice [e.g., Model BITs], and sometimes pleadings'); *Cargill, Inc.* v. *Mexico*, Award, 18 September 2009, para. 275.

[597] *Enron Corporation and Ponderosa Assets, L.P.* v. *Argentina*, ICSID Case No. ARB/01/3, Decision on the Argentine Republic's Request for a Continued Stay of Enforcement of the Award (Rule 54 of the ICSID Arbitration Rules), 7 October 2008, para. 14.

Argentina will not comply voluntarily with ICSID awards, but will challenge them before the International Court of Justice or before the Argentine courts'.[598] The Tribunal, however, did not rely on said statements since the same position had in fact been taken by Argentina's Attorney-General at the hearing.[599] The Tribunal's reasoning suggests that substantial weight should be given to what the Attorney-General said in the context of pleadings.[600] In any event, it should be given more weight than media reports referring to other statements made by 'senior executive and judicial officers' of Argentina. Most importantly for the purpose of the present book, the Tribunal indicated that the Attorney-General was 'speaking with the authority of the Argentine Republic at the hearing'.[601] In other words, the Tribunal considered said pleadings to be Argentina's *official position* on the matter.

Second, the merits phase of the *Enron* case also illustrates (to some extent) the other proposition (mentioned in the previous section) that relative weight should be given to pleadings depending on the circumstances. In the award, the Tribunal reiterated the position it took in its earlier decision on jurisdiction that the US claimants had *ius standi* to claim in their own rights because they were protected investors under the US-Argentina BIT. The Tribunal then examined new arguments submitted by Argentina, including its reference to the United States' position (the home State of the investors) in the NAFTA *Mondev* and *Thunderbird* cases that 'shareholders cannot assert claims under the NAFTA for damages suffered by the company in which they own

[598] *Ibid.*
[599] *Ibid.*, para. 85: 'The position stated by the *Procurador del Tesoro de la Nación* (Attorney-General), *speaking with the authority of the Argentine Republic at the hearing* of the stay application, appears to be that in the event that the award is not annulled Argentina would not comply with the award forthwith, but would instead look to the Claimants to bring proceedings for the enforcement of the Award under the provisions of Argentine law that give effect to Article 54 of the ICSID Convention' (emphasis added). The Committee held that such a position was 'in apparent non-compliance with Argentina's international law treaty obligations owed to the United States under Article VII(6) of the BIT and under Article 53(1) of the ICSID Convention' (*Ibid.*).
[600] *Ibid.*, para. 92: 'In any event, the Committee notes Argentina's submissions that under Argentine law, only the President, the Minister for Foreign Affairs or the Attorney-General may make statements that are binding on Argentina, and that media reports of statements of officials are frequently inaccurate. The Committee finds that *Argentina has expressed its position to the Committee through its duly authorised representatives* [i.e. the Attorney General in pleadings], and that in the present case the Committee has no need to resort to media reports in order to ascertain Argentina's intentions' (emphasis added).
[601] *Ibid.*, para. 85.

shares'.[602] The Tribunal then mentioned a recent decision of the US Supreme Court (in the context of the Foreign Sovereign Immunities Act) and indicated that this decision 'should probably have more weight for the purpose of the United States' views on indirect ownership than that expressed in arbitrations by counsel for that government'.[603]

The Tribunal seemed to be quite reluctant in giving any weight to the respondent State's pleadings in the context of arbitration proceedings in *other* cases. The Tribunal did not explicitly explain why, but it is presumably because of its self-interested character. In any event, the reasoning of the Tribunal seems to suggest that said pleadings should be accorded less value than a domestic judicial decision's findings. The Tribunal, however, does not explain whether this should be the case in general or why it should be so in this specific instance. In any event, it seems that the Tribunal rejected the US pleadings for an entirely unrelated (and more controversial) reason (i.e. because the pleadings were from the *home* State of the investor).[604] The Tribunal's reasoning, suggesting that the position of the home State should not be taken into account when it is contrary to the interest of one of its investors, has been criticized by scholars.[605]

---

[602] *Enron Corporation and Ponderosa Assets, L.P.* v. *Argentina*, Decision on Jurisdiction (Ancillary Claim), 2 August 2004, paras. 34, 36.

[603] *Ibid.*, para. 36.

[604] *Ibid.* In its previous award on jurisdiction (*Enron* v. *Argentina*, Decision on Jurisdiction, 14 January 2004, para. 48), the Tribunal made the following comment: 'The parties in this case have also discussed the meaning and extent of the Mondev case where, as indicated by the Argentine Republic, the United States held the view that shareholders cannot claim for injury to a corporation and can claim only for direct injuries suffered in their capacity as shareholders. The Claimants have argued that what matters is the conclusion of the tribunal in that case, which dismissed the United States' arguments and upheld the claimant's standing. *The Tribunal must note in this connection that what the State of nationality of the investor might argue in a given case to which it is a party cannot be held against the rights of the investor in a separate case to which the investor is a party.* This is precisely the merit of the ICSID Convention in that it overcame the deficiencies of diplomatic protection where the investor was subject to whatever political or legal determination the State of nationality would make in respect of its claim' (emphasis added). In its subsequent award (*Enron* v. *Argentina*, Decision on Jurisdiction (Ancillary Claim), 2 August 2004, para. 37), the Tribunal also noted that 'the greatest innovation of ICSID and other systems directed at the protection of foreign investments is precisely that the rights of the investors are not any longer subject to the political and other considerations by their governments, as was the case under the old system of diplomatic protection, often resulting in an interference with those rights. Investors may today claim independently from the view of their governments'.

[605] This question is discussed in: Roberts, 'Power and Persuasion in Investment Treaty International', p. 218.

Finally, it should be added that in a number of awards, tribunals have referred to the position taken by the respondent State in its pleadings in the context of *other* arbitration proceedings. This suggests that these tribunals viewed said pleadings as relevant practice of that State (at least in the context of treaty interpretation).[606]

3.3.4.2.3 Interventions by non-disputing treaty parties during arbitration proceedings
This section deals with a second type of statement that is different from the pleadings of the respondent State: the intervention (in the form of pleadings) by *another* State that is party to the treaty, but *not* as a respondent in the proceedings.[607] It should be noted at the outset that this section does not deal with the questions surrounding the fact that recently tribunals have allowed *non-State* third parties (such as NGOs) to submit *amicus curie* briefs.

BITs rarely deal with the possibility of interventions by non-disputing treaty parties during arbitration proceedings.[608] The most famous example of said possibility is in the context of two *multilateral* treaties: NAFTA and the DR-CAFTA. Article 1128 of NAFTA thus allows non-disputing Parties to intervene in arbitration proceedings by filing written submissions concerning questions that pertain to treaty interpretation. NAFTA Parties have filed so-called 'Article 1128 submissions' on numerous occasions. According to one recent survey conducted by a Canadian NGO,[609] as of October 2010, sixty-six publicly known claims had been filed by investors under NAFTA Chapter 11 since 1994. According to one estimate, at least sixty-four Article 1128 submissions have been filed in

---

[606] See, *inter alia: Bayindir Insaat Turizm Ticaret Ve Sanayi A.S. v. Pakistan*, ICSID Case No. ARB/03/29, Decision on Jurisdiction, 10 November 2005, para. 129; *Sempra Energy International v. Argentina*, Decision on Objections to Jurisdiction, 11 May 2005, para. 132; *Methanex Corporation v. United States*, UNCITRAL, Partial Award, 7 August 2002, para. 145.

[607] Another form of intervention that is very rare in practice is that of a State which is not acting as respondent in the proceedings, is not the home State of the claimant investor, nor even a State party to the treaty under which the proceedings have been commenced. One rare example of such an intervention is a letter (dated 1 May 2008) submitted by the United States to the *ad hoc* Annulment Committee in the case of *Siemens A.G. v. Argentina*, ICSID Case No. ARB/02/8 (involving a claim by a German investor under the Germany–Argentina BIT), whereby it gave its interpretation of several provisions of the ICSID Convention. Argentina replied to this letter by its own submission (dated 2 June 2008).

[608] Some examples of treaties dealing with the issue include: New Zealand–China FTA, Art. 155; EU–Canada Comprehensive and Economic Trade Agreement (CETA), Art. X.35.

[609] Canadian Center for Policy Alternatives, 'NAFTA Chapter 11 Investor-States Disputes' (2010).

these proceedings.[610] The DR-CAFTA is another treaty allowing such interventions by non-disputing treaty parties.[611] In recent years, a number of States have filed such statements with CAFTA tribunals on matters regarding treaty interpretation.[612]

It should be added that interventions by non-disputing treaty parties are not limited to arbitration proceedings. They can also be found in the context of domestic courts cases dealing with investment arbitration issues. For instance (as further discussed[613]), a number of setting aside proceedings were started in the domestic courts of a NAFTA Party that was not involved as the respondent State in the arbitral proceedings.[614] In some of those cases, the State where the setting aside proceedings took place intervened and explained to the court what its position was. For instance, this is what happened in the *Metalclad* case involving a claim filed before the Superior Court of British Columbia by the respondent State in the arbitration proceedings (Mexico) against the claimant.[615] In that case, Canada intervened by submitting its official position on a

---

[610] Wolfgang Alschner, 'The Return of the Home State and the Rise of 'Embedded' Investor-State Arbitration', in S. Lalani and R. Polanco (eds.), *The Role of the State in Investor-State Arbitration* (Leiden; Boston: Martinus Nijhoff/Brill, 2014), p. 198.

[611] DR-CAFTA, Article 10.20.2.

[612] See, *inter alia: Railroad Development Corporation (RDC)* v. *Guatemala*, Award, 29 June 2012, paras. 207, 208 ('Submission of the Republic of El Salvador as a Non-Disputing Party under CAFTA Article 10.20.2', 1 January 2012; 'Escrito de Parte no-Contendiente de la Republica de Honduras', 1 January 2012; 'Submission of the United States of America', 31 January 2012); *Commerce Group Corp. and San Sebastian Gold Mines, Inc.* v. *El Salvador*, ICSID Case No. ARB/09/17 ('Non-Disputing Party Submission of the Republic of Costa Rica', 20 October 2010); *Pac Rim Cayman LLC* v. *El Salvador*, ICSID Case No. ARB/09/12 ('Submission of the United States of America', 20 May 2011); *TECO Guatemala Holdings, LLC* v. *Guatemala*, ICSID Case No. ARB/10/23 ('Escrito de Parte no-Contendiente de la Republica de Honduras', undated; 'Submission of the Dominican Republic as a Non-Disputing Party', 5 October 2012; 'Non-Disputing Party Submission of the Republic of El Salvador', 5 October 2012; 'Submission by the United States', 23 November 2012); *Spence International Investments et al.* v. *Costa Rica*, UNCITRAL (ICSID Case No. UNCT/13/2) ('Non-Disputing Party Submission by the United States', 17 April 2015; 'Non-Disputing Party Submission by El Salvador', 17 April 2015).

[613] See, Chapter 3, Section 3.3.6.3.2.

[614] *International Thunderbird Gaming Corporation* v. *United Mexican States*, 473 F. Supp. 2d 80; 2007 U.S. Dist. LEXIS 10070 (D.C. Dist. Ct.): *International Thunderbird Gaming Corporation* v. *United Mexican States*, 255 Fed. Appx.531; 2007 U.S. App. LEXIS 26720 (U.S. Court of Appeals for the DC Circuit); *Mexico* v. *Karpa*, [2003] O.T.C. 1070 (Ont. SCJ); *United Mexican States* v. *Karpa*, [2005] O.J. No. 16 (Ont. CA); *Mexico* v. *Metalclad Corp.*, [2001] B.C.J. No. 950 (BCSC); *United Mexican States* v. *Cargill, Inc.*, [2011] O.J. No. 4320 (Ont. CA).

[615] *Mexico* v. *Metalclad Corp.*, [2001] B.C.J. No. 950 (BCSC).

number of treaty interpretation issues. Such a submission is clearly a relevant example of Canada's practice for custom creation purposes.

In this section, I will first examine the importance of non-disputing treaty parties' interventions during arbitration proceedings as evidence of State practice, as well as the relative weight which they should be given depending on the circumstances (Section 3.3.4.2.3.1). I will then illustrate these principles with a few examples of investor-State awards dealing with said interventions (Section 3.3.4.2.3.2).

3.3.4.2.3.1 *The relative weight to be given to such interventions depends on the circumstances*   An intervention of a non-disputing treaty party during arbitration proceedings is undoubtedly an example of a statement by a State that should be considered as evidence of State practice.[616] This is because while intervening a State has the opportunity to present to a tribunal its own position on the law on a given issue. Similarly to pleadings,[617] these interventions represent important evidence of a State's view because several State departments or ministries often approve its content and because its impact goes beyond the present dispute between the parties.

In fact, such statements are generally considered as a more 'reliable' source of practice than pleadings by respondent States.[618] This is because, as noted by one writer, 'intervening States are not attempting to avoid liability in that case and are more likely to limit their observations to general interpretive points'.[619] While it is true that these interventions are not as self-interested as pleadings by respondent States, it remains that they are not entirely 'neutral' either. I will explain why in the following paragraphs.

In the context of *bilateral* treaties, the non-disputing party is inevitably the *home* State of the investor. On the one hand, one could normally expect the intervening home State to align its position with its national involved as claimant in the arbitration proceedings. The protection of foreign investors and their investments is, after all, the very reason why States sign BITs in the first place. Yet, on the other hand, there are other reasons that may explain why the home State can adopt in the

---

[616]   A Roberts, 'Power and Persuasion in Investment Treaty International', p. 219.

[617]   See, the analysis above in Chapter 3, Section 3.3.4.2.2.1.

[618]   Andrea K. Bjorklund, 'NAFTA's Contributions to Investor-State Dispute Settlement', in M. Bungenberg, J. Griebel, S. Hobe and A. Reinisch (eds.), *International Investment Law: A Handbook* (Munich et al.: C.H. Beck, Hart, Nomos, 2015), p. 268.

[619]   Roberts, 'Power and Persuasion in Investment Treaty International', p. 219.

proceedings a position similar to that of the respondent State. This is because the home State may very well be acting as the respondent State in pending (or future) arbitration proceedings under the same BIT.[620] The home State may eventually regret having taken any pro-investor position on matters of treaty interpretation. Yet, as noted by Roberts, avoiding future liability cannot be the *only* concern of the home State. If it were, that State should simply withdraw from that treaty.[621] Ultimately, the content and scope of a non-disputing State's intervention is a balancing act that must take into account these different (and sometimes conflicting) interests.[622]

In the context of *multilateral* treaties, the non-disputing party intervening can either be the home State of the investor or any other State party to the treaty (other than the respondent State). At first glance, in the context of multilateral treaties, the position of the non-disputing party seems to be more neutral than that of an intervening party under a bilateral treaty. Thus, in this case the intervening party is neither the home State of the investor nor the respondent. However, the NAFTA experience has shown otherwise. In their 'Article 1128 submissions', intervening NAFTA States have generally adopted restrictive interpretations regarding investor's rights and have aligned their positions with that of the respondent State.[623] This is because intervening States are likely to be respondents in other pending (and future) cases involving similar legal issues. This is the reason why the *Cargill* Tribunal stated that statements by States, including Article 1128 submissions, 'can – with care – serve as evidence of the content of custom'. The Tribunal noted, however, that 'the weight of these [Article 1128 submissions] statements needs to be assessed in light of their position as respondents at the time of the statement'.[624] In other words, the *Cargill* Tribunal properly acknowledged that an intervening State's position in *one* case is likely to be influenced by the fact that the same State may also be (at the same time or in the future) the respondent in *other* cases under the same treaty.

To summarize, while non-disputing party interventions are clearly not as motivated by self-interest as pleadings by respondent States, it remains that they are not completely 'uninterested' either. For this reason, it is submitted that the weight that should be given to statements made by non-disputing

---

[620] *Ibid.*, pp. 219–220. See also: Bjorklund, 'NAFTA's Contributions to Investor-State Dispute Settlement', p. 267.

[621] Roberts, *Ibid.*, p. 220.   [622] *Ibid.*

[623] On this point, see: Ryan, 'Glamis Gold, Ltd. v. The United States', p. 951.

[624] *Cargill, Inc.* v. *Mexico*, Award, 18 September 2009, para. 275.

treaty parties will depend on a number of circumstances, including their nature and the context in which they were made. Similarly to pleadings,[625] greater weight should be given to statements that are consistent with the position taken by a State in past proceedings or in other fora.[626] The so-called internal uniformity[627] is one of the basic requirements for State practice to be considered relevant in the process of creating customary norms. Moreover, for the purpose of custom creation, the weight that should be given to a specific statement made by a non-disputing party must take into account the extent to which the position taken is self-interested. Less weight should obviously be given to interventions that are made to avoid liability in other pending cases where the same State is acting as the respondent. In other words, not all interventions by non-disputing parties should be considered equally as evidence of State practice.

The following section will explore several examples of investor-State awards involving interventions by non-disputing treaty parties.

3.3.4.2.3.2 Arbitral awards examining such interventions As previously mentioned, NAFTA Article 1128 allows non-disputing Parties to intervene in arbitration proceedings by filing written submissions concerning questions pertaining to treaty interpretation. In the context of NAFTA, the debate has not been about whether said submissions represent a form of State practice or not. The controversy has instead been focused on whether Article 1128 submissions constitute a 'subsequent practice' or a 'subsequent agreement' between the parties pursuant to Article 31(3) of the *Vienna Convention on the Law of Treaties*. Yet, NAFTA tribunals have consistently relied on Article 1128 submissions as valuable and authoritative sources of information regarding Parties' positions on various matters. For instance, the *ADM* Tribunal noted that '[t]he position of the NAFTA Parties in their intervention in other Chapter Eleven proceedings –pursuant to Article 1128 of the NAFTA– reveals indeed the Member States' view (...)'.[628] The *Canadian Cattlemen* Tribunal took the same position.[629] Both tribunals have clearly

[625] See, the analysis above in Chapter 3, Section 3.3.4.2.2.1.
[626] Roberts, 'Power and Persuasion in Investment Treaty International', p. 219.
[627] See, discussion in Chapter 3, Section 3.2.1.
[628] *Archer Daniels Midland Company and Tate & Lyle Ingredients Americas, Inc. v. Mexico*, ICSID Case No. ARB(AF)/04/5, Award, 21 November 2007, para. 176.
[629] *The Canadian Cattlemen for Fair Trade v. United States*, UNCITRAL, Award on Jurisdiction, 28 January 2008 [hereinafter *Canadian Cattlemen v. United States*], para.

considered Article 1128 submissions as relevant evidence of a State's practice because they represent that State's view on questions of law. In the *Methanex* case, both Canada and Mexico[630] agreed with the position adopted by the United States (the respondent) that Article 1128 submissions by non-disputing NAFTA Parties constituted a 'subsequent practice' pursuant to Article 31(3)(b) of the *Vienna Convention*.[631] In other words, all NAFTA Parties have considered such interventions as evidence of State practice.

The *Canadian Cattleman* Tribunal also held that Article 1128 submissions should be considered as 'subsequent practice' for the purposes of Article 31(3)(b) of the *Vienna Convention* to the extent that they are 'concordant, common, and consistent' in supporting the same interpretation.[632] In my view, significant weight should be given to the different statements made by NAFTA Parties in their interventions under Article 1128 regarding the interpretation to be given to the FET standard. This is because *all* Article 1128 submissions (made *before* the FTC issued its Note of Interpretation of July 2001) were 'concordant, common, and consistent' in supporting the *same interpretation* of the FET standard under Article 1105.[633] As noted by one scholar, 'where interventions by all of the other treaty parties support interpretations by the respondent state, this subsequent practice constitutes good evidence of an agreement on interpretation and thus should be given considerable weight'.[634] The same is true for custom creation. Thus, significant weight should be given to NAFTA Parties' positions in their respective Article 1128 submissions because these interventions represent their own uniform and consistent practice.

As previously mentioned, BITs rarely deal with the possibility of a non-disputing treaty party's intervention (i.e. the home State of the investor). It has been argued that the right to intervene implicitly exists, even when the BIT is silent on the issue.[635] There are in fact a number of

168, fn. 16: 'the Mexican government position is clear by virtue of its submission in this case under Article 1128 and by virtue of its submissions in the *Bayview* case'.
[630] *Methanex v. United States*, 'Canada's Second Article 1128 Submission', 30 April 2001, paras. 8, 37; *Ibid.*, 'Mexico's Article 1128 Submission', 30 April 2001, paras. 1, 3.
[631] *Ibid.*, 'US Memorial on Jurisdiction and Admissibility', 13 November 2000, p. 13.
[632] *Canadian Cattlemen v. United States*, Award on Jurisdiction, 28 January 2008, paras. 188, 189.
[633] The question is examined in detail in: Dumberry, *The Fair and Equitable Treatment Standard*, p. 80 ff.
[634] Roberts, 'Power and Persuasion in Investment Treaty International', p. 219.
[635] *Ibid.*, p. 220.

cases where home States have intervened in arbitration proceedings.[636] The following paragraphs briefly examine a few of these proceedings to illustrate the nature of said interventions.

SGS v. Pakistan is a famous case where such an intervention by a home State occurred.[637] In this case, the Tribunal gave a controversial interpretation to a BIT clause that was at the heart of a dispute between a Swiss investor and Pakistan. The question was whether Article 11 of the Pakistan–Switzerland BIT automatically made the breaches of contract become breaches of the treaty. After the award was rendered, Switzerland complained to the ICSID Secretariat that the Tribunal had failed to seek its own interpretation of the clause before reaching its conclusion. The letter was defending the position that the investor had adopted in the proceedings.[638] The letter is an undeniable example of Switzerland's practice regarding its own interpretation of the BIT that would have to be taken into account by any future tribunal constituted under the Pakistan–Switzerland BIT.

There are a few examples of awards where the tribunal invited the home State of the investor to provide observations concerning matters of treaty interpretation. One example is the case of Eureko B.V. v. Slovak Republic,[639] in which Slovakia argued that as a result of its accession to the EU in May 2004, the 1992 Netherlands–Czechoslovakia BIT had been terminated and, therefore, the Tribunal lacked jurisdiction to hear the dispute.[640] The Tribunal invited the home State of the investor (the Netherlands) to provide observations regarding these questions.[641]

---

[636] In one recent case, The Renco Group, Inc. v. Peru, ICSID Case No. UNCT/13/1, Procedural Order No. 2, 31 July 2014, the Tribunal has invited the Parties (a US investor and Peru) to invite the United States to comment on a provision of the US-Peru BIT.

[637] SGS Société Générale de Surveillance S.A. v. Pakistan, ICSID Case No. ARB/01/13, Award on Jurisdiction, 6 August 2003.

[638] 'Note' attached to the letter of the Swiss Secretariat for Economic Affairs to the ICSID Deputy Secretary-General, 1 October 2003, in Mealey's: Int'l Arb. Rep. 19 (2004), p. E3: '[T]he Swiss authorities are wondering why the Tribunal has not found it necessary to enquire about their view on the meaning of Article 11 [the umbrella clause] in spite of the fact that the Tribunal attributed considerable importance to the intent of the Contracting Parties in drafting this Article and indeed put this question to one of the Contracting Parties (Pakistan) (. . .) [T]he Swiss authorities are alarmed about the very narrow interpretation given to the meaning of Article 11 by the Tribunal, which not only runs counter to the intention of Switzerland when concluding the Treaty but is quite evidently neither supported by the meaning of similar articles in BITs concluded by other countries nor by academic comments on such provisions'.

[639] Eureko B.V. v. Slovak Republic, UNCITRAL, PCA Case No. 2008-13, Award on Jurisdiction, Arbitrability and Suspension, 26 October 2010.

[640] Ibid., para. 9.   [641] Ibid., paras. 154–155.

The Netherlands was of the view that the BIT was still in force between the parties.[642] The Tribunal agreed. One passage from the award suggests that the Tribunal considered the intervention as relevant evidence of State practice (at least in the context of treaty interpretation).[643]

The same is true for the *Aguas de Tunari* case where the Tribunal sought the position of the home State of the investor (the Netherlands) regarding some matters of interpretation of the Netherlands–Bolivia BIT.[644] Ultimately, however, the Tribunal gave little weight to the Netherlands' different answers because of inconsistency and lack of clarity.[645] The Tribunal concluded that for this reason the Netherlands' answers should not be considered as 'subsequent practice' establishing an agreement by the parties on matters of treaty interpretation.[646] In my view, limited weight should be given to these statements when interpreting the Netherlands' practice because they lack the 'internal' uniformity that is required for the creation of any customary rule.[647] In other words, these statements are an example of the type of interventions made by a non-disputing treaty party that should have a limited weight as relevant State practice for the purpose of custom creation.

---

[642] *Ibid.*, para. 156. See also, at para. 161.

[643] *Ibid.*, para. 217: 'The Tribunal has considered carefully the submissions made by the Parties, as well as the observations of the Government of the Netherlands and of the European Commission, all of which were helpful and for all of which the Tribunal thanks their respective authors'.

[644] *Aguas del Tunari SA* v. *Bolivia*, Decision on Respondent's Objections to Jurisdiction, 21 October 2005, para. 49. See, para. 258, referring to a letter dated 1 October 2004 sent by the Tribunal to the Legal Advisor of the Foreign Ministry of the Netherlands indicating that 'given that the Government of the Netherlands is not a party or otherwise present in this arbitration, the Tribunal concludes that information from the Government of the Netherlands would assist the work of the Tribunal'.

[645] *Ibid.*, para. 263. The case is further examined in Chapter 3, Section 3.3.4.2.4.2.

[646] *Ibid.*, para. 262: 'The Tribunal first observes that the document attached to Mr. Lammers' [Legal Advisor to the Foreign Ministry of the Netherlands] letter contained only comments of a general nature that possibly may be relevant to the task of confirming an interpretation under Article 32 ('supplementary means of interpretation') of the Vienna Convention on the Law of Treaties. It does not provide the Tribunal, however, with any information of the type suggested by Article 31 of the Vienna Convention on the Law of Treaties as being possibly relevant and upon which a general interpretative position may be based. The Tribunal has made no use of this document in arriving at its decision. Second, the Tribunal observes that Mr. Lammers in his reply cover letter states that the answers given by the Dutch government to this series of parliamentary questions were based on information from the press which at the time that the answers were given 'may not necessarily have been correct'.

[647] On this concept, see the analysis above in Chapter 3, Section 3.2.1.

To summarize, the reasoning of these tribunals supports the proposition put forward in the previous section that interventions by non-disputing treaty parties during arbitration proceedings are a form of statements by States which can be considered, depending on the context and the circumstances, as relevant evidence of State practice for custom creation.

3.3.4.2.4 Official statements made by parties to a treaty As previously mentioned,[648] scholars generally recognize that public statements by a government on policy matters are a form of State practice. The two previous sections have examined different forms of statements made by States in the context of arbitration proceedings (State pleadings and interventions by non-disputing treaty parties). This section will examine other types of statements made by States *outside* the context of specific litigation. The most common form of said statements are those made by a government before its own domestic legislature when implementing an investment treaty under domestic law.[649]

I will first examine the relevance of these official statements as evidence of State practice and the relative weight that should be given to them depending on the circumstances (Section 3.3.4.2.4.1). I will then examine how tribunals have concretely interpreted these statements (Section 3.3.4.2.4.2).

3.3.4.2.4.1 The relative weight to be given to official statements depends on the circumstances A statement made by a government before its own domestic legislature when implementing an investment treaty under domestic law should be considered, as a matter of principle, as evidence of State practice.[650] It can also be considered as a manifestation of that

---

[648] See, Chapter 3, Section 3.3.4.1.1.

[649] See, for instance, the statements made by the government of Switzerland (Conseil fédéral) to the parliament regarding recent BITs. See, for instance : 'Message concernant les accords de promotion et de protection réciproque des investissements avec la Serbie-et-Monténégro, le Guyana, l'Azerbaïdjan, l'Arabie saoudite et la Colombie du 22 septembre 2006', *Feuille Fédérale Suisse* 2006, p. 8023; 'Message concernant les accords de promotion et de protection réciproque des investissements avec le Kenya et la Syrie', 16 January 2008, *Feuille Fédérale Suisse* 2008, p. 903. The documents are available at this page of the website of the Swiss government: www.admin.ch/bundesrecht/00568/index .html?lang=fr.

[650] McLachlan, 'Investment Treaties and General International Law', p. 372 ('The transmittal statements by which domestic approval for such treaties is sought by the signatory States, to which reference is sometimes made, are merely unilateral statement and not *travaux préparatoires*. They are therefore more likely to be relevant as evidence of State practice for the purposes of a customary rule, than as to the meaning of a treaty text'); Newcombe and Paradell, *Law and Practice of Investment Treaties*, p. 268; J.C. Thomas,

State's *opinio juris*.[651] It is one of the few opportunities available for a State to explain what it believes to be the law on a given issue. These statements therefore represent an authentic description of a State's interpretation of a treaty text.[652] Substantial weight should be given to these statements because they are made at the time of the implementation of the treaty (i.e. *before* any dispute has arisen as to the proper meaning of the text). In other words, these statements are not an *a posteriori* interpretation necessarily influenced by on-going arbitration proceedings.[653] In that sense, these statements are less self-interested, and therefore more reliable, than other forms of statements made by States in the context of arbitration proceedings (State pleadings and interventions by non-disputing treaty parties[654]).

The actual weight to be given to these official statements, however, will depend on the context in which they were made. Thus, *not all* statements made by a government before its own domestic legislature should be considered as evidence of *relevant* State practice. This point is illustrated by the reasoning adopted by several tribunals in a number of awards (examined in the next section).

'Reflections on Article 1105 of NAFTA: History, State Practice and the Influence of Commentators', *ICSID Rev.* 17(1) (2002), p. 50.

[651] ILC, Second Report, 2014, pp. 52–53. The question of *opinio juris* will be examined in Chapter 4.

[652] See, *Millicom International Operations B.V.* and *Sentel GSM SA v. Senegal,* ICSID Case No. ARB/08/20, Decision on Jurisdiction, 16 July 2012, para. 72, referring to the *travaux préparatoires* and an 'Explanatory Memorandum' in the context of the adoption of a BIT as the 'understanding of the rule by the Kingdom of the Netherlands' on a matter of treaty interpretation, and adding that '[n]othing prohibits the Arbitral Tribunal from relying on [these documents] in order to confirm how this text was actually understood by one of the Contracting Parties'.

[653] Roberts, 'Power and Persuasion in Investment Treaty International', pp. 220–221, examining the question of whether or not such statements can be considered as 'subsequent practice' pursuant to Article 31(3)(b) of the *Vienna Convention*: 'subsequent practice is not limited to pleadings or interventions in investment disputes but can include other public statements by the treaty parties. Such statements have the advantage of being general in their application and not tied to the facts of specific disputes. A state could include a place for such statements on its Website, perhaps where it lists its investment treaties, or appropriate statements could be recorded in the state's yearbook of international law. (...) While the statements of one state alone will not create an agreement on interpretation, they may be persuasive when the other treaty parties agree with, or acquiesce in, these interpretations'. The question is examined in: *Canadian Cattlemen v. United States,* Award on Jurisdiction, 28 January 2008, paras. 182, 188–189.

[654] See, the analysis in Chapter 3, Sections 3.3.4.2.2 and 3.3.4.2.3.

3.3.4.2.4.2 Arbitral awards examining such statements In the context of NAFTA, tribunals have had the opportunity to examine the scope and meaning of official statements of Canada[655] and the United States'[656] for the implementation of the agreement in 1994.[657] They have also examined the procedure followed in the United States involving a 'Letter of Submittal' sent by the US State Department to the US President requesting US Senate approval of a BIT.[658] Writers generally consider these specific statements as evidence of State practice.[659] Some States have taken the same view.[660] The *Mondev* Tribunal specifically examined the 'Canadian Statement on Implementation of the NAFTA' and two US letters of submittal.[661] The Tribunal concluded that such 'explanations given by a signatory government to its own legislature in the course of ratification or implementation of a treaty' could 'certainly shed light on the purposes and approaches taken to the treaty, and thus can evidence *opinio juris*'.[662] In other words, for the Tribunal these statements are evidence of State practice. The question as to whether these statements are, in fact, evidence of State practice or *opinio juris, or both*, will be further discussed.[663]

At least one other non-NAFTA tribunal has also concluded that the United States' letters of submittal were evidence of State practice.[664] The

---

[655] Department of External Affairs, NAFTA, 'Canadian Statement on Implementation', *Canada Gazette*, 1 January 1994, p. 68.

[656] United States Statement on Administrative Action, November 1993, p. 141.

[657] See, the analysis in: Dumberry, *The Fair and Equitable Treatment Standard*, p. 47 ff.

[658] The procedure is briefly mentioned in: *Oil Platforms (Islamic Republic of Iran v. United States)*, Preliminary Objection, Judgment, ICJ Rep. 1996, p. 803, para. 29. See also, *CMS Gas Transmission Company v. Argentina*, ICSID Case No. ARB/01/8, Award, 12 May 2005, para. 362, referring to a 'letter of submission of the Treaty to Congress in Argentina'.

[659] Newcombe and Paradell, *Law and Practice of Investment Treaties*, p. 268; Thomas, 'Reflections on Article 1105 of NAFTA', p. 50, footnote 98; Fauchald, 'The Legal Reasoning of ICSID Tribunals', p. 347; Roberts, 'Power and Persuasion in Investment Treaty International', p. 222.

[660] *Loewen v. United States*, 'Rejoinder of the United States', 27 August 2001, p. 146; *Ibid.*, 'Post-Hearing Submission of Respondent United States of America on *Pope & Talbot*', 8 July 2002, p. 11; *ADF Group Inc. v. United States*, 'U.S. Rejoinder on Competence and Liability', 29 January 2002, pp. 40–41.

[661] *Mondev v. United States*, Award, 2 October 2002, para. 111 (referring to the letters sent in the context of the implementation of the US–Ecuador BIT (1993) and the US–Albania BIT (1995).

[662] *Ibid.* [663] See, Chapter 4, Section 4.1.5.2.

[664] It should be added that US letters of submittal are also referred to by other tribunals: *H&H Enterprises Investments, Inc. v. Egypt*, ICSID Case No. ARB 09/15, Decision on Respondent's Objections to Jurisdiction, 5 June 2012, paras. 46, 49, 52–56; *CMS Gas*

Generation Ukraine Tribunal described the letter as 'an article-by-article commentary to the [US–Ukraine] BIT'[665] and as the 'official and contemporaneous US interpretation' of the provisions contained in this instrument.[666] Yet, the Tribunal also added that the letter could not be considered as an element of State practice of the *other party* to a BIT.[667] On the contrary, in the *Global Trading* case, also involving the US–Ukraine BIT, the Tribunal expressed 'doubts' as to 'whether the letter represents a necessary item of interpretative material'.[668]

The *HICEE B.V.* v. *Slovak Republic* case also illustrates the fact that a statement made by a government before its own domestic legislature should be considered, as a matter of principle, as evidence of State practice. In this case, the Tribunal referred to the Dutch government's 'Explanatory Notes' in the process of its domestic ratification of the 1992 Netherlands–Czechoslovakia BIT.[669] In this case, the most important part of the Notes was the explanation of Czechoslovakia's position surrounding the fact that the treaty does not cover Dutch companies' investments that have subsidiaries incorporated in Czechoslovakia.[670] The Tribunal first explained the general nature of the Explanatory Notes:

> [I]s by no means uncommon for a party to a dispute settlement process involving treaty interpretation to support its case by invoking the terms in which the treaty was submitted internally for approval; it typically involves a statement of some kind by the executive power to the legislature as to how the terms of the treaty should be interpreted and its effect understood. What that amounts to, normally, is the invocation by a State of its own contemporaneous interpretation of a treaty text when a dispute over that text comes before a tribunal later on.[671]

Transmission Company v. *Argentina*, Decision on Objections to Jurisdiction, 17 July 2003, para. 82. These tribunals do not discuss, however, whether the letters can be considered as evidence of State practice.

[665] *Generation Ukraine Inc.* v. *Ukraine*, Final Award, 16 September 2003, para. 15.4.

[666] *Ibid.*, para. 15.6.   [667] *Ibid.*, para. 15.4.

[668] *Global Trading Resource Corp. and Globex International, Inc.* v. *Ukraine*, ICSID Case No. ARB/09/11, Award, 23 November 2010, paras. 48–51, referring to the Message from the President of the United States, 27 September 1994, p. VII. In any event, the Tribunal decided (at para. 51) that it did not have to examine specifically 'how the letter might properly be categorized within the framework for interpretation given in Articles 31 and 32 of the Vienna Convention on the Law of Treaties' because it concluded that it was not necessary to go beyond the text of the BIT.

[669] *HICEE B.V.* v. *Slovak Republic*, UNCITRAL, PCA Case No. 2009–11, 23 May 2011, paras. 37, 114.

[670] *Ibid.*, para. 126.   [671] *Ibid.*, para. 127.

The Tribunal explained, however, to what extent the Notes in this case were of a completely different nature insofar as it exposed the positions of *both* the Netherlands and Czechoslovakia as to the scope of investments covered by the BIT.[672] The Tribunal's reasoning shows that it gave, as a matter of principle, substantial weight to the Notes. This is because the content of the Notes represents an official statement by the Netherlands as to what *it* believes to be the proper interpretation to be given to a treaty provision: 'the Explanatory Notes are a formal, public document that engages the honesty and good faith of the Dutch Minister, and the tribunal does not believe that it is its place to call that into question, even implicitly'.[673] One reason why the Tribunal gave the Notes such an authoritative value is the fact that the Netherlands would have never adopted in State-to-State litigation, a position different from the one exposed in the Notes:

> Let us suppose, as a hypothesis, that the same question of interpretation of the Agreement was in dispute between the Contracting Parties themselves, and that that dispute was in litigation. (...) Had the matter gone to inter-State arbitration (or indeed to the International Court of Justice) it is surely inconceivable that the Netherlands would have wished to adopt a position in the litigation materially different from its formal public position at the time of ratification; or (in the unlikely contrary event) that the court or tribunal would have permitted it to do so. As the Latin maxim has it: nemo audietur venire contra factum suum.[674]

In other words, the Tribunal clearly considered the Notes as evidence *of the Netherlands'* practice. The other question discussed by the Tribunal was whether or not the Notes could also be considered as representing the practice *of Czechoslovakia* (and Slovakia as one of the two successor States to the former federation).

The Tribunal first mentioned that, as a matter of principle, it 'cannot accept that a Dutch investor is a more authentic exponent of

---

[672] *Ibid.*: 'By contrast, what marks the present situation out as different is the following: first, that the negotiating State [Netherlands] is not setting down its own interpretation but the intentions of its negotiating partner [Czechoslovakia]; second, that this is not a bare statement but one backed by reasons; third, that there follows an express confirmation that the other Party's intentions were agreed to, and why; fourth, that the Notes conclude with a precise indication of the recipe for avoiding the exclusionary effect of the restriction that was accepted into the treaty text. The final difference, which the Tribunal considers to be of some considerable significance, is that in this case the declaration is being invoked not by the declarant State itself, but from the opposite side of the treaty nexus'.

[673] *Ibid.*, para. 129.   [674] *Ibid.*, para. 137.

Czechoslovak views and intentions in the negotiation than the Government with which Czechoslovakia was negotiating'.[675] Thus, 'when the passage in question says that Czechoslovakia wanted to exclude subsidiaries "from the scope of this Agreement", it must be taken to mean what it says'.[676] Yet, the Tribunal added that 'what was said in the Explanatory Notes called for some substantiation or corroboration, if possible' given the fact that the document mentions that 'Czechoslovakia asked in negotiation for something that the Netherlands agreed to'.[677] Accordingly, the Tribunal required both States to produce any documents regarding the negotiation of this provision. Based on the documents it received, the Tribunal concluded, however, that it 'ha[d] nothing before it to illuminate or otherwise substantiate the basis on which the Dutch foreign Minister drew up his submission to Parliament on Article 1'.[678] The Tribunal therefore concluded that 'it must treat the Explanatory Notes as having an essentially unilateral character, not a joint one'.[679] In other words, the Tribunal viewed the Notes only as representing the Netherlands' *own* interpretation of what *it believed* to be Czechoslovakia's position. The Notes could therefore not be interpreted as representing Czechoslovakia's own State practice.[680]

I will examine in the following paragraphs three cases illustrating that the actual weight that should be given to a statement made by a government before its own domestic legislature actually depends on the circumstances surrounding such declaration.

The first case is *Aguas de Tunari* v. *Bolivia*.[681] The Tribunal mentioned that 'the Dutch government submitted an Explanatory Note to its Parliament after the [Netherlands-Bolivia] BIT was negotiated',[682] but it concluded that 'this sparse negotiating history'

---

[675] *Ibid.*, para. 128.   [676] *Ibid.*   [677] *Ibid.*, para. 130.   [678] *Ibid.*, para. 131.
[679] *Ibid.*, para. 132.
[680] The Tribunal also concluded that the Notes could not be considered as an 'agreement' between the Parties under Articles 31 and 32 of the *Vienna Convention*. Yet, it also added that this did not mean that the Notes should be disregarded altogether as the claimant suggested. This is essentially because both the respondent State (Slovakia) and the home State of the investor (the Netherlands) ultimately concurred as to the proper scope of Article 1, which was captured in the Notes. For this reason, the Tribunal concluded that the Dutch Explanatory Notes 'given their terms and content, taken together with the viewpoint adopted in these proceedings by Slovakia, constitute valid supplementary material [under Article 32 of the Vienna Convention] which the Tribunal may, and in the circumstances must, take into account in dealing with the question before it' (para. 136).
[681] *Aguas del Tunari SA* v. *Bolivia*, Decision on Respondent's Objections to Jurisdiction, 21 October 2005, para. 251.
[682] *Ibid.*, paras. 271–272.

'offer[ed] little additional insight into the meaning of the aspects of the BIT at issue, neither particularly confirming nor contradicting [its own] interpretation'.[683] This case is also significant because different ministries of the government of the Netherlands made a number of statements to the Dutch Parliament.[684] Bolivia relied on these statements to support its own interpretation of the BIT and its conclusion that both Parties to the BIT had (allegedly) agreed that the Tribunal did not possess jurisdiction over the dispute in question.[685]

The first two statements are questions asked in writing by a member of the Parliament (Mr Van Bommel) to the State Secretary for Economic Affairs and the Minister for Development Cooperation as to whether 'certain corporations could invoke the Dutch-Bolivian BIT in the specific dispute addressed by this Tribunal'.[686] The Minister never quite answered the question and instead mentioned that it was up to the 'discretion of the arbitration tribunal to which a dispute has been submitted'.[687] A group of members of Parliament subsequently asked another question on the same matter to the Minister of Housing, Spatial Planning and Environment, the Minister for Development Cooperation and the State Secretary for Economic Affairs.[688] The Minister replied in writing that the Government had recently responded to the question previously asked by Mr Van Bommel that 'the investment treaty is not applicable to this particular case'.[689] Yet, the government had never said this in its two previous answers. The Tribunal correctly observed that 'the third reply from The Netherlands government is inconsistent with the first two replies and appears to refer incorrectly to the latter'.[690] It concluded that 'as a result, little can be concluded from the three written replies of The Netherlands government'[691] and that they could not be considered as an agreement between the Netherlands and Bolivia or a subsequent practice between them on matters of interpretation.[692] Based on the fact that 'further limited information as to the basis for the written replies of The Netherlands could assist the Tribunal in its work', the Tribunal (as previously mentioned[693]) wrote a letter to the Legal Advisor of the Foreign Ministry of the Netherlands asking several specific questions.[694]

---

[683] *Ibid.*, para. 274. [684] *Ibid.*, para. 251. [685] *Ibid.* [686] *Ibid.*, para. 253. [687] *Ibid.*
[688] *Ibid.*, para. 255. [689] *Ibid.* [690] *Ibid.*, para. 257. [691] *Ibid.*
[692] *Ibid.*, paras. 251, 257.
[693] See, the analysis of this aspect of the case examined in Chapter 3, Section 3.3.4.2.3.2.
[694] *Aguas del Tunari*, para. 258.

This case demonstrates that the weight given to statements made in parliament about matters of treaty interpretation depends on the circumstances. In this case, the statements were factually incorrect and contradictory. The Tribunal rightly concluded that they should consequently be given no weight at all on what the official position of the Netherlands was on the issue of the Tribunal's jurisdiction over the dispute.[695] Little weight should also be given to such contradictory statements as evidence of the practice of the Netherlands for custom creation purposes. Thus, these statements do not fulfil the basic requirements of 'internal uniformity'.[696]

The second case is *Vladimir Berschader and Moïse Berschander* v. *Russian Federation*, which involved Belgian nationals who claimed compensation for breach of the 1992 Belgium/Luxembourg–U.S.S.R. BIT.[697] The claimant wanted to use the MFN clause in the BIT to take advantage of more favourable arbitration clauses found in other BITs signed by Russia in the late 1990s that cover disputes concerning the occurrence of an act of expropriation. The arbitration clause in the 1992 BIT limited the Tribunal's jurisdiction only to disputes concerning the amount (or mode) of compensation to be paid and did not cover the other question of whether or not an act of expropriation had actually occurred in the first place.[698] The Tribunal explained that the ordinary meaning of the 1992 BIT was 'quite clear' insofar as only disputes concerning the amount of compensation could be subject to arbitration, not those concerning whether or not an act of expropriation actually occurred.[699] The claimant invoked an explanatory statement made by the Belgian Minister of Foreign Affairs before the Belgian Parliament in connection with the ratification of the Treaty.[700] In the statement, the Minister declared that the Soviet delegation in the negotiations had accepted arbitration 'in all areas covered by Article 5', which would include the preliminary question of whether or not any expropriation occurred.[701] The Tribunal, however, gave little weight to this statement: 'the Tribunal finds the

---

[695] In any event, had the statements been considered of any value, the Tribunal would have had to take into account the important fact that they had not been made at the time of the implementation of the BIT, but in 2002, that is, *after* the claimant had already initiated the arbitration proceedings. The existence of this pending controversial dispute (involving the right to water) could have naturally influenced the government's view on matters of treaty interpretation.

[696] See, discussion above in Chapter 3, Section 3.2.1.

[697] *Vladimir Berschader and Moïse Berschander* v. *Russian Federation*, SCC Case No. 080/2004, Award, 21 April 2006.

[698] *Ibid.*, paras. 151 ff.   [699] *Ibid.*, paras. 152, 153.   [700] *Ibid.*, para. 158.   [701] *Ibid.*

language of the Treaty to be quite clear' adding that 'such language could not possibly lend itself to the interpretation suggested in the explanatory statement'.[702] This case suggests that little weight should be given to an ambiguous statement made before parliament when it is irreconcilable with a clear text that is adopted by *both* parties. Only the latter practice should be considered relevant in the context of custom creation.

The third case, *Gruslin v. Malaysia*, does not involve a statement made before a parliament. In this case, the Tribunal referred to a *note verbale* by Belgium's Embassy in Malaysia that was sent to Malaysia's Ministry of Foreign Affairs seeking clarification about the use of the term 'approved project' under the 1979 Intergovernmental Agreement (IGA) between Malaysia and the Belgo-Luxemburg Economic Union.[703] Malaysia responded with its own *note verbale* addressed to Belgium's Embassy. The Tribunal first noted that 'this exchange does not effect a direct amendment to the terms of the IGA'.[704] The Tribunal nevertheless noted that 'at this peak level of intercourse between states' the exchanges of letters 'must be regarded as an enduring and authoritative engagement expressing to the Belgo-Luxemburg Union the manner in which the respondent regards and applies the terms of the IGA with regard to investments made in its territory by nationals of the Belgo-Luxemburg Union'.[705] In other words, for the Tribunal Malaysia's *note verbale* was considered to be an authoritative statement regarding how that State interpreted the agreement. The Tribunal therefore considered, as a matter of principle, that the *note* was evidence of Malaysia's practice. Yet, the Tribunal concluded that the *note* 'remains a statement that engenders rather than resolves uncertainty as to the application' of certain provisions of the agreement.[706] This was in fact the position defended by Malaysia in the proceedings. Ultimately, the *Note* was 'a source of confusion rather than clarity with respect to the application of the terms the IGA to an investment made in Malaysia by a national of the Belgo-Luxemburg Union'.[707] To summarize, having considered all the relevant

---

[702] *Ibid.*

[703] *Philippe Gruslin v. Malaysia*, ICSID Case No. ARB/99/3, Award, 27 November 2000, para. 23.1.

[704] *Ibid.*, para. 23.4.   [705] *Ibid.*

[706] *Ibid.*, para. 23.12. The Tribunal added: 'Somewhat reluctantly the Tribunal is moved to accept the position pressed by the Respondent's counsel (. . .) that the Respondent has not produced an interpretation of the exchange constituted by the *Note Verbale* which is secure "in absolute or abstract terms"' (at para. 23.13).

[707] *Ibid.*, para. 23.16. Malaysia also referred to 'records of interview with Malaysian officials involved in the negotiations of the IGA' as well as a 'Memorandum from the Ministry of

circumstances, the Tribunal decided not to give any weight to a document, which should have normally been considered as State practice.

Finally, reference should be made to a number of other cases where tribunals have briefly mentioned statements made by States (outside the context of arbitration proceedings) without, however, examining their status as evidence of State practice:

- *CMS*: the Tribunal referred to a 'discussion of these [US BITs] in the U.S. Congress', but concluded that little weigh should be given to these discussions given the fact that they 'allow for a variety of interpretation';[708]
- *Yukos*: The Tribunal referred to the Explanatory Note submitted by the Russian Government to the parliament which 'confirmed' its conclusion on the interpretation of Article 26 of the ECT;[709] Russia also referred to a 2006 statement made by the United Kingdom's Secretary of State for Foreign and Commonwealth Affairs to support its interpretation of Article 45(1) of the ECT;[710]
- *ConocoPhillips*: The Tribunal referred to a letter from the Netherlands' Minister for Foreign Affairs to the Dutch Parliament as well as an Explanatory Statement of the Venezuelan government to the Venezuelan Congress regarding a matter of treaty interpretation;[711]
- *Planet Mining*: The Tribunal referred to the 'National Interest Analyses (NIAs) prepared by the Australian Government in connection with BITs discussed in the Australian Parliament';[712]

Trade and Industry of Malaysia to the Attorney-General's Chambers'. The Tribunal noted, however, that resorting to such 'extrinsic materials' 'for the purpose of colouring the meaning of the particular terms of the IGA' was of 'limited utility' (para. 21.4).

[708] *CMS Gas Transmission Company* v. *Argentina*, Award, 12 May 2005, para. 369. See also, the reference to 'a letter of submission of the Treaty to Congress in Argentina' (at para. 362).

[709] *Yukos Universal Limited (Isle of Man)* v. *Russian Federation*, UNCITRAL, PCA Case No. AA 227, Interim Award on Jurisdiction and Admissibility, 30 November 2009, para. 374: 'The Tribunal's conclusions are confirmed by the representations of the Government of the Russian Federation in the Explanatory Note which it submitted to the State Duma of the Federal Assembly of the Russian Federation when the ECT was submitted for ratification'. See also: *Veteran Petroleum Limited (Cyprus)* v. *Russian Federation*, UNCITRAL, PCA Case No. AA 228, Interim Award on Jurisdiction and Admissibility, 30 November 2009.

[710] *Hulley Enterprises Ltd* v. *Russian Federation*, UNCITRAL, PCA Case No AA 226, Interim Award on Jurisdiction and Admissibility, 30 November 2009, para. 294, referring to House of Commons Hansard Written Answers, pt. 3, Column 1045 W et seq.

[711] *ConocoPhillips Petrozuata B.V., ConocoPhillips Hamaca B.V. and ConocoPhillips Gulf of Paria B.V.* v. *Venezuela*, ICSID Case No. ARB/07/30, Decision on Jurisdiction and the Merits, 3 September 2013, para. 294.

[712] *Churchill Mining PLC and Planet Mining Pty Ltd* v. *Indonesia*, ICSID Case No. ARB/12/14 and 12/40, Decision on Jurisdiction, 24 February 2014, para. 136.

- *Total*: The Tribunal referred to an official statement made by the representative of the Government of Argentina to Argentina's Congress in relation to the ratification of two BITs;[713]
- *Czech Republic* v. *European Media Ventures SA* (setting aside proceedings before the United Kingdom High Court of Justice):[714] The Czech Republic referred to some documents to support its own interpretation of the Czechoslovakia-Belgium/Luxembourg BIT: an 'Explanatory Statement' in the Belgian parliamentary record, and record of the Federal Assembly of the Czech and Slovak Federative Assembly.[715] The High Court noted that these documents were equivocal and, for interpretation purposes, of little value;[716]
- *Aguas del Tunari*: The Tribunal referred to a 'Note on Investment Protection Agreement' published by the Netherlands' Ministry of Economic Affairs on its website as 'one Dutch government source' describing the goal of BITs.[717]

3.3.4.2.5 Joint statements by parties to a treaty on matters of interpretation

A number of recent BITs include clauses whereby the parties can submit a joint interpretation of treaty provisions to a tribunal.[718] This is, for instance, the case for the Canadian[719] and the US Model BITs.[720] This is also the case for many recent FTAs and BITs signed by Canada,[721]

---

[713] *Total S.A.* v. *Argentina*, ICSID Case No. ARB/04/01, Decision on Liability, 27 December 2010, para. 116.

[714] *Czech Republic* v. *European Media Ventures SA*, setting aside proceeding of the Tribunal's Award on Jurisdiction dated 15 May 2007, UK High Court of Justice, Queen's Bench Division, Commercial Court, Justice Simon, 5 December 2007, 2007 EWHC 2851 (Comm).

[715] *Ibid.*, para. 27.   [716] *Ibid.*, para. 31.

[717] *Aguas del Tunari SA* v. *Bolivia*, Decision on Respondent's Objections to Jurisdiction, 21 October 2005, para. 294.

[718] See, M. Ewing-Chow and J.J. Losari, 'Which is to be the Master?: Extra-Arbitral Interpretative Procedures for IIAs' in: A. Joubin-Bret and Jean E. Kalicki (eds.), *Reform of Investor-State Dispute Settlement: In Search of A Roadmap* (TDM Special issue, 2014), p. 8, referring to many treaties.

[719] Canada Model BIT (2004), art. 40(2), 51.   [720] US Model BIT 2012, Art. 30(3).

[721] See, for instance: FTA between Canada and the States of the European Free Trade Association (Iceland, Liechtenstein, Norway and Switzerland) (2009), Art. 28; Canada–Colombia FTA (2011), Art. 832; Canada–Chile FTA (1997), Art. N-01; Canada–Israel FTA (1997), Art. 8.2; Canada–Czech Republic BIT (2009), Article X(6); Canada–Peru BIT (2007), Art. 50; Canada–Peru FTA (2009), Art. 837; Canada–Jordan BIT (2009), Art. 40; Canada–Jordan FTA (2012), Art. 13-1. See also: EU–Canada Comprehensive and Economic Trade Agreement (CETA), signed in 2014, Art. X.27(2).

the United States[722] and Mexico.[723] A number of other BITs and trade agreements include the same mechanism.[724]

Certain treaties not only provide the possibility for the parties to issue joint statements, but also establish 'Free Trade Commissions', comprised of representatives of each party, which have the power to issue binding decisions on matters of treaty interpretation. This is the case under the CAFTA,[725] where the Commission has issued a number of 'decisions' in recent years.[726] The most famous example of this mechanism is, of course, the NAFTA Free Trade Commission (FTC).[727] In July 2001, it issued its 'Notes of Interpretation of Certain Chapter 11 Provisions' regarding two topics: confidentiality and public access to documents in Chapter 11 arbitration proceedings and the MST under Article 1105 (hereinafter referred to as 'the Notes').[728] The present author has examined elsewhere the specific context in which the NAFTA FTC Note was issued and how tribunals have interpreted it.[729]

---

[722] See, for instance: US–Australia FTA (2005), Arts. 21.1, 21.2(e); US–Chile FTA (2004), Art. 21.1; US–Colombia FTA (2012), Art. 20.1; US–Singapore FTA (2004), Art. 20.1; US–Korea FTA (2012), Art. 22.2; US–Morocco FTA (2006), Art. 19.2; US–Oman FTA (2009), Art. 19.1; US–Panama Trade Promotion Agreement (2011), Art. 19.2; US–Peru Trade Promotion Agreement (2009), Art. 20.1; US–Rwanda BIT (2008), Art. 30(3); US–Uruguay BIT (2006), Art. 30(3). The United States has also exchanged diplomatic notes with eight countries (Bulgaria, Czech Republic, Estonia, Latvia, Lithuania, Romania, Poland, and the Slovak Republic) when they joined the EU seeking to clarify specific aspects of the treaties and to ensure their consistency with EU law and that they remain in force.

[723] See, for instance: Japan–Mexico Treaty on Strengthening of the Economic Partnership (2005), Art. 165; Mexico–European Free Trade Association FTA (2001), Art. 70; Mexico–European Union FTA (2000), Art. 47; Mexico–Israel FTA (2000), Art. 10–01.

[724] See, for instance: Dominican Republic–US–Central American FTA (2006 to 2009); Belgium/Luxembourg–Cyprus BIT (1999); ASEAN–Australia–New Zealand FTA (AANZFTA) (2010), Chap. 11, Art. 27 (2)(3); ASEAN Comprehensive Investment Agreement (ACIA) (2012), art. 40(3).

[725] Articles 19.1.3(c), 10.22(3).

[726] The decisions can be found at this page: www.ustr.gov/trade-agreements/free-trade-agreements/cafta-dr-dominican-republic-central-america-fta/final-text.

[727] The Commission is composed of one 'cabinet level representatives' from each NAFTA Party (Art. 2001). The decisions are binding (Art. 1131(2)). All relevant FTC documents can be found at this page: www.international.gc.ca/trade-agreements-accords-commerciaux/agr-acc/nafta-alena/celeb2.aspx?lang=eng.

[728] Free Trade Commission, Notes of Interpretation, 31 July 2001.

[729] Dumberry, *The Fair and Equitable Treatment Standard*, p. 66 ff. See also: P. Dumberry, 'Moving the Goal Post! How Some NAFTA Tribunals have Challenged the FTC Note of Interpretation on the Fair and Equitable Treatment Standard under NAFTA Article 1105', *W. Arb & Med Rev* 8 (2014).

I will first examine the weight that should be given to such statements (Section 3.3.4.2.5.1), which will be followed by an analysis of how tribunals have interpreted them (Section 3.3.4.2.5.2).

3.3.4.2.5.1 The relative weight to be given to joint statements depends on the circumstances A joint statement by two States (or more) on matters of treaty interpretation should be considered as evidence of these States' practice.[730] A joint interpretation of this sort can also be considered as a manifestation of a State's *opinio juris*.[731] A common interpretation agreed upon by *all parties* to a treaty should have the greatest possible weight on matters of treaty interpretation.[732] It should be considered as a 'subsequent agreement between the parties' on the interpretation of a treaty pursuant to Article 31(3)a of the *Vienna Convention*. The existence of the agreement itself is more important than its form.[733]

However, as previously mentioned (in sections dealing with pleadings[734] and interventions by non-disputing treaty parties during arbitration proceedings[735]), the actual weight that should be given to any such joint interpretation as evidence of these States' practice will depend on a number of circumstances, including the context in which it was made. In accordance with the basic requirement of 'internal uniformity',[736] greater evidentiary weight should be given to a joint interpretation that is consistent with the position these States have taken in the past. A joint interpretation should normally be considered as a more 'reliable' source of practice than self-interested pleadings by the respondent State. Yet, joint interpretations are to some extent similar to interventions by non-

---

[730] Roberts, 'Power and Persuasion in Investment Treaty International', p. 194.

[731] ILC, Second Report, 2014, p. 53 (referring to 'joint declaration of States through an official document'). The question of *opinio juris* will be examined in Chapter 4.

[732] Roberts, 'Power and Persuasion in Investment Treaty International', p. 196: 'If the principals [i.e. the States parties to a BIT] disagree on interpretation, tribunals will have wide interpretive discretion [;] If they agree, tribunals' zone of discretion will be reduced and the principals' capacity to direct tribunals will be enlarged'.

[733] Roberts, 'Power and Persuasion in Investment Treaty International', p. 199: 'A subsequent agreement turns on the fact of an agreement between the treaty parties, not its form. The agreement need not be in binding or treaty form but must demonstrate that the parties intended their understanding to constitute an agreed basis for interpretation. Such agreements may be more or less formal, ranging from a jointly signed document to a series of acts or communications from which an agreement can be inferred. The more informal the basis, the greater the overlap with subsequent practice'. See also: *Methanex v. United States*, Award, 3 August 2005, pt. II, ch. B, para. 20.

[734] Chapter 3, Section 3.3.4.2.2.1.   [735] Chapter 3, Section 3.3.4.2.3.1.

[736] See, discussion in Chapter 3, Section 3.2.1.

disputing treaty parties during arbitration proceedings insofar as they
may not always be entirely 'neutral'. One important issue is the timing of
the joint interpretation in relation to any arbitration proceeding. Thus, to
what extent the position adopted by these States in a joint interpretation
is essentially self-interested and aimed at avoiding liability in pending
cases where they act as respondents. In other words, not every joint
interpretation should be given the same weight as evidence of State
practice. Joint interpretations that are clearly self-interested should be
given limited weight for custom creation purposes.

3.3.4.2.5.2   Arbitral awards examining such statements   The question
of the weight that should be given to joint statements has been controversial in the context of the 2001 NAFTA FTC Notes of interpretation.[737]
NAFTA Parties were concerned that the controversial findings of three
awards (*Metalclad*,[738] *S.D. Myers*[739] and *Pope & Talbot*[740]), which gave a
broad interpretation to Article 1105, would somehow set a trend that
would be followed by future tribunals. Thus, several other high profile
NAFTA arbitration cases were then pending (*UPS, Loewen, Mondev,
Methanex, ADF,* and *Waste Management*) in which the scope of Article
1105 had already been hotly debated between the parties. For one writer,
the NAFTA Parties have used the FTC interpretation 'as the vehicle to
pre-empt further losses'.[741] The Notes has therefore been considered by
some writers as an opportunistic method put in place in order to avoid
liability in on-going arbitration cases where NAFTA Parties were acting
as respondents.[742] In other words, the Parties were accused of acting as
both party and judge in the proceedings. According to Schreuer, '[i]t is
obvious that a mechanism whereby a party to a dispute is able to
influence the outcome of judicial proceedings, by issuing official

---

[737] The question is examined in: Dumberry, *The Fair and Equitable Treatment Standard*, p. 65 ff.

[738] *Metalclad Corporation v. Mexico*, ICSID Case No. ARB(AF)/97/1, Award, 30 August 2000, paras. 70, 76.

[739] *S.D. Myers Inc. v. Canada*, UNCITRAL, First Partial Award, 13 November 2000, para. 266.

[740] *Pope and Talbot Inc. v. Canada*, UNCITRAL, Award on the Merits of Phase II, 10 April 2001.

[741] Charles H. Brower II, 'Why the FTC Notes of Interpretation Constitute a Partial Amendment of NAFTA Article 1105', *Virginia JIL* 46 (2006), pp. 347, 352–353, 356. See also: Laird, 'Betrayal, Shock and Outrage', p. 53.

[742] Charles H. Brower II, 'Structure, Legitimacy, and NAFTA's Investment Chapter', *Vand. J. Transnat'l L.* 36 (2003), p. 81.

interpretation to the detriment of the other party, is incompatible with principles of a fair procedure and is hence undesirable'.[743] This is a sound criticism. Kaufmann-Kohler recently explained why some aspects of the Notes may be considered as contrary to due process.[744] For all of these reasons, a number of writers have argued that the Note should have been binding only on *future* tribunals, not on on-going arbitration disputes.[745]

Apart from NAFTA tribunals, very few awards have examined the question of the weight that should be given to joint interpretations. One rare example concerns the 1998 *Framework Agreement on the ASEAN Investment Area* that was signed by the Member States of the ASEAN.[746] In the *Yaung Chi Oo* case, the Tribunal referred to a 'Joint Press Release of the Inaugural Meeting of the ASEAN Investment Council of 8 October 1998' as 'clearly an authoritative statement made by relevant ministers of ASEAN Member States, including the Myanmar Minister of Industry, as to their intentions at the time of the conclusion of the Agreement'.[747] The Tribunal, therefore, considered this joint press release as representing the practice of Myanmar (the respondent in the proceedings).

Finally, reference should be made to a number of other cases where tribunals have briefly mentioned joint statements without, however,

---

[743] C. Schreuer, 'Diversity and Harmonization of Treaty Interpretation in Investment Arbitration', in M. Fitzmaurice, O. Elias and P. Merkouris (eds.), *Treaty Interpretation and the Vienna Convention on the Law of Treaties: 30 Years On* (Leiden: Martinus Nijhoff, 2010), p. 148.

[744] Gabrielle Kaufmann-Kohler, 'Interpretive Powers of the NAFTA Free Trade Commission – Necessary Safety Valve or Infringement of the Rule of Law?', in Frédéric Bachand (ed.), *Fifteen Years of NAFTA Chapter 11 Arbitration* (New York: JurisNet, 2011), p. 192: 'The difficulty here lies in the two hats worn by the respondent State. That State is at the same time a litigant and a member of the FTC. As a member of the FTC, it contributes to the content of the interpretation. As a litigant, it will benefit from the interpretation if the latter influences the outcome in its favor. This appears to be contrary to due process, specifically contrary to the principle of independence and impartiality of justice, which includes the principle that no one can be the judge of its own cause. It can also be argued that such an interpretation breaches the principle of equal treatment of the parties and the opportunity to be heard of the other party'.

[745] Charles Brower II, 'Investor-State Disputes Under NAFTA: The Empire Strikes Back', *Colum J. Transnat'l L.* 40 (2001–2002), pp. 43, 56; Bjorklund, 'NAFTA's Contributions to Investor-State Dispute Settlement', pp. 265–266.

[746] The Association of South-East Asian Nations (ASEAN) is composed of Brunei Darussalam, Indonesia, Laos, Malaysia, Myanmar, the Philippines, Singapore, Thailand and Vietnam.

[747] *Yaung Chi Oo Trading Pte. Ltd.* v. *Myanmar*, ASEAN I.D. Case No. ARB/01/1, Award, 31 March 2003, para. 74.

discussing whether or not they could be considered as evidence of State practice:

- In *National Grid* v. *Argentina*, which involved a claimant from the United Kingdom, the Tribunal referred to an exchange of diplomatic notes between Argentina and Panama containing an 'interpretative declaration' of the MFN clause of their 1996 BIT to the effect that the 'clause does not extend to dispute resolution clauses, and that this has always been their intention;'[748]
- In *Yukos*, the Tribunal referred to a 1994 joint statement issued by the EU Council, the EU Commission and the EU Member States, which Russia considered as an example of State practice.[749] The Tribunal did not discuss this issue and concluded that, in any event, little weight should be given to this document which in fact supported the claimant's position;
- In *Sanum*, Laos started set-aside proceedings in Singapore courts against the Tribunal's award, which upheld jurisdiction over the claim of a Macanese investor.[750] Laos mentioned an exchange of letters between Laos and China (after the award had been rendered) confirming the parties' shared view (which had been agreed on in a meeting in December 2013) that the Laos–China BIT was never intended to extend to the territory of Macao;
- Following the Tribunal's issuance of its Partial Award in *CME* v. *Czech Republic*, the Czech Republic used the mechanism under Article 9 of the Czech Republic–Netherlands BIT to call for consultations with the Netherlands on the proper interpretation regarding the applicable law clause found in the BIT.[751] The parties reached a 'common position' on the interpretation of the BIT and signed and exchanged Agreed Minutes (dated 1 July 2002).[752] The *CME* Tribunal did not discuss

---

[748] *National Grid plc* v. *Argentina*, UNCITRAL, Award on Jurisdiction, 20 June 2000, para. 85. The notes are also mentioned in: *Daimler Financial Services AG* v. *Argentina*, ICSID Case No. ARB/05/1, Award, 22 August 2012, para. 272, see also: Dissenting Opinion of Judge Charles N. Brower, 15 August 2012, para. 29.

[749] *Hulley Enterprises Ltd* v. *Russian Federation*, Interim Award on Jurisdiction and Admissibility, 30 November 2009, paras. 325–327. See also: *Yukos Universal Limited* v. *Russian Federation*, Interim Award on Jurisdiction and Admissibility, 30 November 2009; *Veteran Petroleum Limited* v. *Russian Federation*, Interim Award on Jurisdiction and Admissibility, 30 November 2009.

[750] *Sanum Investments Limited* v. *Laos*, UNCITRAL, PCA Case No. 2013-13, Award on Jurisdiction, 13 December 2013.

[751] *CME Czech Republic B.V.* v. *Czech Republic*, Award, 14 March 2003, para. 88.

[752] *Ibid.*, para. 89.

the authoritative nature of this common position, but it did take it into account as a confirmation of its own analysis.[753] The same Agreed Minutes were also referred to by the Tribunal in the *HICEE B.V.* v. *Slovak Republic* case,[754] but it concluded that they were of 'little assistance' in the instant case;[755]

- The *Ecuador* v. *United States* case is a good illustration of a failed attempt by the parties to a BIT to issue a joint interpretation.[756]

3.3.4.2.6 Model BITs adopted by States   A number of States have published so-called Model BITs as framework agreements for the negotiation of future BITs.[757] The United States was the first country to put together such a document.[758] According to one estimate, more than thirty States have now adopted Model BITs.[759] They have been developed in order to provide a template for treaty negotiations.[760] BITs are often negotiated on the basis of one (or two) model(s) adopted by States.[761]

---

[753] *Ibid.*, paras. 400, 437, 505.

[754] *HICEE B.V.* v. *Slovak Republic*, PCA Case No. 2009-11, Partial Award, 23 May 2011, paras. 37, 39, 122, 125.

[755] *Ibid.*, para. 125. Thus, the case involved the Slovak Republic as the respondent State (not the Czech Republic). In any event, the Minutes did not address issues relevant to the instant case. See also: *Eastern Sugar BV* v. *Czech Republic*, UNCITRAL, Partial Award and Partial Dissenting Opinion, 27 March 2007, paras. 194–197, referring to the Agreed Minutes.

[756] *Ecuador* v. *United States*, PCA Case No. 2012-5, see, the description of events in: 'Memorial of Respondent United States of America on Objections to Jurisdiction', 25 April 2012, pp. 3, 10–11, 41–44.

[757] Mark Kantor, 'Little Has Changed in the New US Model Bilateral Investment Treaty', *ICSID Rev.* 27(2) (2012), p. 338. For the texts of model BITs used by China, France, Germany, the UK and the United States, see Schreuer and Dolzer, *Principles of International Investment Law*, pp. 360–429.

[758] K. Vandevelde, *U.S. International Investment Agreements* (New York: Oxford University Press, 2009), pp. 30–64; Mark A. Clodfelter, 'The Adaptation of States to the Changing World of Investment Protection through Model BITs', *ICSID Rev.*, 24 (2009), p. 166.

[759] Clodfelter, 'The Adaptation of States to the Changing World', p. 167.

[760] As explained by Canada's Ministry of Foreign Affairs, 'The new model serves as a template for Canada in discussions with investment partners on bilateral investment rules. As a template, the provisions contained therein remain subject to negotiation and further refinement by negotiating parties. Thus, although all FIPAs can be expected to follow this approach, it is highly unlikely that any two agreements will be identical' (available at www.international.gc.ca/trade-agreements-accords-commerciaux/agr-acc/fipa-apie/fipa-apie.aspx).

[761] Chester Brown, 'Introduction, The Development and Importance of the Model Bilateral Investment Treaty', in C. Brown (ed.), *Commentaries on Selected Model Investment Treaties* (Oxford: Oxford University Press, 2013), p. 10; Kantor, 'Little Has Changed in the New US Model Bilateral Investment Treaty', p. 338.

There are, of course, many advantages in negotiating BITs on the basis of such a model.[762] There is also another important reason why States have increasingly adopted Model BITs in recent years: they reflect 'a new consciousness about the nature of the obligations that BITs entail and the risks that they pose'.[763]

What is the legal status of these Model BITs? Clearly, they are *not* international treaties since they are not signed and ratified by States. Initially, one could consider Model BITs as simply negotiation material. Doing so, however, would underestimate their relevance. Scholars generally recognize that Model BITs can be considered as 'subsequent practice' for the purpose of Article 31(3)(b) of the *Vienna Convention* on treaty interpretation.[764] Yet, it is important to remember that under that provision the subsequent practice of the parties needs to be 'in the application of the treaty'. For example, the 2004 US Model BIT was *not* drafted specifically 'in the application' of NAFTA (which entered into force 10 years before in 1994). It was conceived as a model for the drafting of *future* BITs. In other words, the 2004 US Model BIT cannot be considered as a 'subsequent practice' for the purposes of specifically interpreting NAFTA under Article 31(3)(b) of the *Vienna*

---

[762] Clodfelter, 'The Adaptation of States to the Changing World', p. 167 ('Certainly model BITs are helpful for any government intent on pursuing negotiations with multiple partners, since having a model treaty avoids the need to develop new language for each negotiation. Moreover, adherence to a model assures consistency and coherence from negotiation to negotiation, and has the added advantage of strengthening the negotiators' ability to resist concessions on the ground of needing uniform treatment of negotiating partners').

[763] *Ibid.*, p. 168 ('this new consciousness is also a direct response to decisions of arbitration tribunals that have revealed new dimensions to the risks inherent in the earlier generations of BITs. As experience has mounted, States have now had an opportunity to understand how the substantive provisions of those earlier BITs could be interpreted or misinterpreted, how and in what circumstances the procedures of investor-State arbitration would be implemented, and the uses to which BIT arbitration would be put. If the provisions of the new model BITs are any guide, these States have not been thrilled with what they have seen happening. Indeed, the extensive process that led to the 2004 U.S. model BIT was triggered by the first claim ever to be brought against the United States. Being sued for the first time compelled the U.S. to come to grips with the fact that the obligations contained in its investment treaties run both ways, and that their broad wording could result in the quite unanticipated consequence of significant awards against it. This should not have been a surprise, of course, but it was. This realization was compounded by a series of decisions emanating first from NAFTA tribunals, and later from ICSID tribunals under other treaties, holding States to obligations that they had never previously considered to exist').

[764] Roberts, 'Power and Persuasion in Investment Treaty International', p. 221.

Convention. Yet, as will be discussed in the following paragraphs, there is no doubt about the interpretative value of Model BITs.

In any event, Model BITs clearly represent a form of statements by States evidencing their practice in international relations.[765] This is *a fortiori* the case when a State explains the content of its Model BIT in an official commentary. Norway has thus published such a commentary for the 2007 and 2015 draft versions of its Model BIT.[766] Thus, their content is typically the result of long and extensive deliberation that sometimes involves several State departments or ministries.[767] For the *Glamis* Tribunal, 'treaty practice (e.g. Model BITs)' is indeed one of the 'few authoritative sources' demonstrating a 'concordant practice undertaken out of a sense of legal obligation'.[768] The *Accession* Tribunal's reasoning also suggests that Model BITs are examples of State practice.[769] This is also how States themselves have considered Model BITs in the context of arbitration proceedings.[770]

---

[765] Fauchald, 'The Legal Reasoning of ICSID Tribunals', p. 347; McLachlan, 'Investment Treaties and General International Law', p. 394; Roberts, 'Power and Persuasion in Investment Treaty International', pp. 194, 221–222.

[766] See, Norway, 'Comments on the Model for Future Investment Agreements' (2007), available at: www.italaw.com/sites/default/files/archive/ita1029.pdf; 'Comments on the Individual Provisions of the Model Agreement' (2015), available at: www.regjeringen .no/contentassets/e47326b61f424d4c9c3d470896492623/comments-on-the-model-for-future-investment-agreements-english-translation.pdf.

[767] For an overview of the US Model BIT review process involving different actors, see: Kantor, 'Little Has Changed in the New US Model Bilateral Investment Treaty', pp. 338–339.

[768] *Glamis Gold Ltd* v. *United States*, Award, 14 May 2009, para. 603.

[769] *Accession Mezzanine Capital L.P. and Danubius Kereskedöház Vagyonkezelö Zrt.* v. *Hungary*, ICSID Case No. ARB/12/3, Decision on Respondent's Objection under Arbitration Rule 41(5), 16 January 2013, para. 69: 'Given the absence of definitions of expropriation in BITs, the normal practice for investment tribunals is to focus on expropriation within the framework of international law standards, *meaning state practice*, treaties and judicial interpretations of "expropriation" in the cases. As one example, the 2012 U.S. model BIT, at Annex B, states the "shared understanding" of the parties that expropriation (Article 6(1)) "is intended to reflect customary international law concerning the obligation of States with respect to expropriation."' (emphasis added).

[770] For instance, a number of States have argued that the position taken by the United States on the scope of the FET standard under NAFTA Article 1105 is reflected in its Model BIT, which includes a detailed provision linking the standard to the minimum standard of treatment under custom. One example is *Bureau Veritas, Inspection, Valuation, Assessment and Control, BIVAC BV* v. *Paraguay*, Further Decision on Objections to Jurisdiction, 9 October 2012, para. 152, where Paraguay argued (specifically referring to the 2004 US Model BIT) that 'States, including NAFTA parties such as United States and Canada, and non NAFTA parties such as Switzerland have generally adopted the customary international law minimum standard of FET in bilateral treaties'.

One reason why substantial weight should be given to Model BITs is because they are *not* made in the context of specific arbitration proceedings. In that sense, they are more reliable than State pleadings or interventions by non-disputing treaty parties during proceedings.[771] As noted by one writer, 'these clarifications and explanations [contained in Model BITs] fairly evidence a state's general understanding of treaty terms and cannot be dismissed as opportunistic attempts to avoid liability in a particular case'.[772] While it is true that Model BITs should not be perceived as self-serving as other types of statements, it remains that a State's 'general understanding of treaty terms' is certainly not a completely disinterested and purely 'objective' assessment either. Model BITs exist to protect one State's *interests*.

A Model BIT's content is influenced by past or on-going arbitration proceedings in which a State has acted, or is acting, as the respondent.[773] To provide a simple illustration, the Model BITs adopted by the United States and Canada (both in 2004) include new languages, which makes it clear that the treatment to be given to foreign investors in accordance with 'international law' under the FET clause refers to the MST *under customary international law*.[774] The Models go so far as to explicitly define what custom means. These changes were clearly adopted to *refute* some of NAFTA tribunals' expanding interpretation of the FET clause (Article 1105), most notably the *Pope & Talbot* Tribunal, and to *incorporate* the clarifications made in the FTC Notes of Interpretation of 2001.[775]

---

[771] See, the analysis in Chapter 3, Sections 3.3.4.2.2. and 3.3.4.2.3.

[772] Roberts, 'Power and Persuasion in Investment Treaty International', p. 221.

[773] The website of Canada's Ministry of Foreign Affairs thus explained that 'in 2003, Canada updated its FIPA model to reflect, and incorporate the results of, its growing experience with the implementation and operation of the investment chapter of the NAFTA' (available at: www.international.gc.ca/trade-agreements-accords-commerciaux/agr-acc/fipa-apie/fipa-apie.aspx). See also: Caplan and Sharpe, 'United States', in C. Brown (ed.), *Commentaries on Selected Model Investment Treaties* (Oxford: Oxford University Press, 2013), p. 756; C. Lévesque and A. Newcombe, 'Commentary on the Canadian Model Foreign Promotion and Protection Agreement', in *Ibid.*, pp. 78–80; K.J. Vandelvelde, 'Model Bilateral Investment Treaties: the Way Forward', *Sw. J. Int'l L.* 18 (2011), p. 309.

[774] Kenneth Vandevelde, 'A Comparison of the 2004 and 1994 US Model BITs', *Yb Int'l Invest. L. & Pol.* 1 (2008–2009), p. 291.

[775] Céline Lévesque, 'Influences on the Canadian Model FIPA and US Model BIT: NAFTA Chapter 11 and Beyond', *Canadian YIL* 44 (2006), p. 255 ff; Vandevelde, 'A Comparison of the 2004 and 1994 US Model BITs', p. 291; Roberts, 'Power and Persuasion in Investment Treaty International', p. 222 ('The United States, for example, besides arguing for certain interpretations before tribunals as a respondent or an intervener, modifies its model BIT to confirm or reject specific jurisprudence, which helps to

In the 2004 US Model BIT, the use of phrases such as 'for greater certainty' (Art. 5(2)) and 'the Parties confirm their shared understanding' (Annex A) highlights the desire for such clarification.[776] Recent Model BITs are increasingly more protective of the host State's right to regulate by limiting investors' rights under these instruments.[777] Alvarez calls this recent phenomenon the 'Return of the State'.[778]

There is another reason why substantial weight should be given to Model BITs. While Model BITs are firmly grounded on protecting a State's interests, it remains that it is a *well-balanced* interest. When interpreting NAFTA Article 1105 (the FET standard), the *Cargill* Tribunal 'observe[d]' that 'the United States maintains a similar position as to the customary international law standard of fair and equitable treatment in its model bilateral investment treaty, a situation in which it is at least equally possible that the United States would be in the position of either respondent or the state of nationality of the claiming investor'.[779] This last observation raises an important point. A Model BIT represents a *balanced position* between, on the one hand, providing the greatest possible level of substantive and procedural rights to foreign investors doing business abroad while, on the other hand, ensuring that said rights are not excessive and ultimately to a State's detriment when acting as a respondent in arbitration proceedings. In the words of Douglas, 'a model BIT represents the set of norms that the relevant state holds out to be both reasonable and acceptable as a legal basis for the protection of foreign investment *in its own economy*'.[780] Thus, the commentary to the Norway Model BIT explains that it 'is a complete

crystallize certain *de facto* precedents and stall or prevent the formation of others'); Caplan and Sharpe, 'United States', p. 756; Clodfelter, 'The Adaptation of States to the Changing World', p. 170.

[776] Lévesque, 'Influences on the Canadian Model FIPA and US Model BIT' p. 255 ff. The same observation can be made regarding the US Model BIT explaining to future tribunals that '[e]xcept in rare circumstances, non-discriminatory regulatory actions by a Party that are designed and applied to protect legitimate public welfare objectives, such as public health, safety, and the environment, do not constitute indirect expropriations' (2004 U.S. Model BIT, Annex B, art. 4(b)).

[777] J.E. Alvarez, 'The Return of the State', *Minnesota JIL*, 20 (2011), p. 235 ff.   [778] *Ibid.*

[779] *Cargill, Inc.* v. *Mexico*, Award, 18 September 2009, para. 275.

[780] Z. Douglas, 'The Hybrid Foundations of Investment Treaty Arbitration', *British YIL* 74(1) (2003), p. 159, emphasis added (he notes, however, that in the context of his article 'These model BITs are not relied upon by the present writer as an evidentiary component for the formation of customary international law, but instead as a representative sample of the types of treaty provisions that feature in the approximately 2,000 BITs in existence'). See also: McLachlan *et al.*, *International Investment Arbitration*, p. 20, for whom Model BITs 'indicate the standards which those States find acceptable'.

proposal for the text of all provisions that [Norway] consider[s] should be included in investment agreements'.[781] A good illustration is the press release issued by the US government when it published its revised 2012 Model BIT explaining that it 'continues to provide strong investor protections and preserve the government's ability to regulate in the public interest'.[782] Model BITs, therefore, provide some valuable insight as to what a State believes a 'perfectly' balanced BIT should look like (in an ideal world) in terms of protecting the rights of its own nationals abroad while preserving its own interest at home. In that sense, Model BITs represent a rather 'neutral picture' of what a State believes to be the law on a given matter. This is another reason why Model BITs should be considered as a reliable source of State practice.

States have used Model BITs in arbitration proceedings to demonstrate to tribunals what their basic position was on different matters of treaty interpretation. As observed by Roberts, 'an updated model BIT may also be relevant to the interpretation of investment treaties based on previous model BITs or ones with slightly different language'.[783] In other words, the 2012 US Model BIT will be used by the United States, in the context of *contemporary* arbitration proceedings (and future ones) *involving pre-2012 BITs*, to demonstrate what its position has always been on a given subject. One example is the position taken by the United States in the *Glamis* case regarding allegations of expropriation. The United States stated that 'except in rare circumstances, nondiscriminatory regulations enacted for a public purpose will not be deemed expropriatory' and specifically referred to the 2004 US Model BIT, which mentions the same language.[784] It should be noted that the 1994 NAFTA provision on expropriation (Article 1110) does *not* contain such language. Nevertheless, the United States argued that the specific *new* language adopted in its Model BIT 10 years *later* reflects what its position had been all along. The United States adopted the same argument regarding Article 1105.[785] Some tribunals seem to

---

[781] See, Norway, 'Comments on the Model for Future Investment Agreements' (2007), p. 5.

[782] 'United States Concludes Review of Model Bilateral Investment Treaty', joint statement issued by the US Department of State and the Office of the United States Trade Representative, 20 April 2012, available at: www.state.gov/r/pa/prs/ps/2012/04/188198.htm.

[783] Roberts, 'Power and Persuasion in Investment Treaty International', p. 221; Kantor, 'Little Has Changed in the New US Model Bilateral Investment Treaty', p. 338.

[784] *Glamis Gold Ltd* v. *United States*, 'US Rejoinder', 15 March 2007, p. 109.

[785] *Ibid.*, p. 142, indicating that 'only a handful of such investment treaties can be said to provide any guidance' as to the meaning of the FET clause and referring in a footnote to the 2004 US Model BIT, art. 5(2).

have accepted such reasoning.[786] Moreover, it has been argued that 'the influence of model BITs in shaping investment treaty jurisprudence will be enhanced' whenever a State 'takes a proactive approach to updating and explaining its model, including by adopting revisions to endorse or reject important developments in case law'.[787]

Finally, it should be added that a Model BIT is not limited to being an interpretation tool of *that* State's past and future BITs. It will also influence *other* States on how to draft their own BITs (and Model BITs).[788] A number of tribunals have also referred to the US Model BIT to support their own interpretations in cases involving US investors as claimants.[789]

3.3.5 Activities within international organizations

This section examines a third source of evidence of State practice: the activities of States within international organizations. Writers typically refer to these activities as evidence of State practice. A good example is Crawford who refers to 'the practice of international organs, and resolutions relating to legal questions in the UN organs, notably the General

---

[786] *Lemire v. Ukraine*, ICSID No. ARB/06/18, Decision on Jurisdiction and Liability, 21 January 2010, see the Dissenting Opinion of Voss at para. 143: 'The 2004 US Model BIT shows the reaction of the United States to the post-BIT expansion of the FET standard—explicit assimilation of the standard to the scope of the international law minimum standard. A similar response had already before (in 2001) been given by the NAFTA Free Trade Commission to the first wave of claims based on the FET standard. The United States is the most prominent Member State of NAFTA so that the Commission's position was at least indicative of the US position at that time. *The hypothetical position of the United States at the conclusion of the BIT (1996) must be inferred from its actual position assumed when it became aware of the issue and reconfirmed subsequently.* It further goes without saying that Ukraine would have shared the US position in point once aware of the issue. As the capital-importing Party to the BIT it was especially interested in containing its potential liability under international law. As "reasonable persons of the same kind as the parties" (Article 4.1(2) of the UNIDROIT Principles), the common intention of the Parties to the BIT – United States and Ukraine – must therefore be interpreted to the effect that they would have assimilated the FET standard with the international law minimum standard if they had anticipated the proliferation of claims under FET' (emphasis added).

[787] Roberts, 'Power and Persuasion in Investment Treaty International', p. 222.

[788] Vandelvelde, 'Model Bilateral Investment Treaties', p. 312.

[789] See, for instance, *Pan American Energy LLC and BP Argentina Exploration Company v. Argentina*, ICSID Case No. ARB/03/13, Decision on Preliminary Objections, 27 July 2006, para. 108. See also: Roberts, 'Power and Persuasion in Investment Treaty International', p. 222, referring to other examples.

Assembly'.[790] In the following paragraphs, I will make the fundamental distinction between two different phenomena:

- The conduct *of a State* within an international organization, which can be evidence of the practice of *that* State (Section 3.3.5.1); and
- The practice of *international organizations themselves*, which can constitute evidence of the existence of a customary rule or contribute to the formation of new customary rules (Section 3.3.5.2).[791]

In both sections, I will examine the few existing examples of State practice in the context of the work of international organizations that are relevant to investor-State arbitration.

3.3.5.1   State conduct within international organizations can be evidence of State practice

Two important points should be highlighted at the outset. First, a resolution adopted by an organ of an international organization represents the practice of *that* international organization. Thus, the text of the resolution does *not* represent the practice of the States that are members of the organization.[792] This is clearly the case for UN General Assembly resolutions, which are non-binding.[793] Second, the conduct *of a State* (such as voting, statements, etc.) in the context of the adoption of a resolution by an organ of an international organization can be evidence of *that* State's

[790] Crawford, *Brownlie's Principles of Public International Law*, p. 24.
[791] ILC, Third Report, 2015, p. 48.
[792] ILA, Final Report, 2000, p. 19; Wood and Sender, 'State Practice', para. 20.
[793] One controversial question remains: whether this is also the case for UN Security Council decisions (and those resolutions passed under Chapter 7 of the UN Charter) which are legally binding on all UN members. Some writers have argued that these binding decisions and resolutions can be considered as evidence of State practice, see, Weisburd, 'Customary International Law', p. 51 ('Since Security Council decisions are legally binding on all UN members, Council resolutions would appear to be a very important type of state practice'). See also: *Prosecutor v. Tadić*, ICTY Case No. IT-94-1, Decision on the Defence Motion for Interlocutory Appeal on Jurisdiction (ICTY Appeals Chamber), 2 October 1995, para. 133, stating that 'certain resolutions unanimously adopted by the Security Council' were of 'great relevance to the formation of opinio juris to the effect that violations of general international humanitarian law governing internal armed conflict entail the criminal responsibility of those committing or ordering those violations'. On this question, see: O. Corten, 'La participation du Conseil de sécurité à l'élaboration, à la crystallisation ou à la consolidation de règles coutumières', *RBDI* (2004), pp. 552–567. See also: ILC, Third Report, 2015, p. 31, referring to Security Council resolution 2125 (2013) on Somalia, para. 13, where the Security Council underscored that 'this resolution shall not be considered as establishing customary international law' (see also: Security Council resolution 1838 (2008), para. 8).

practice.[794] The ICJ has recognized this distinction in the *Jurisdictional Immunities of the State* case.[795] This is also the position taken by the vast majority of writers.[796] Thus, as pointed out by Mendelson, 'in voting for or against a resolution which has something to say about international law – and not all do – States are engaging in a form of State practice and/ or are manifesting their subjective attitude (consent or belief) about the rule in question'.[797] The ILA differentiates that form of *State* practice from the other practice of international organizations:

> Organs of international organizations, and notably the UN General Assembly, also from time to time adopt resolutions containing statements about customary international law. *Formally*, since the decision is

[794] ILC, Third Report, 2015, p. 49.

[795] *Jurisdictional Immunities of the State (Germany v. Italy)*, ICJ Rep. 2012, para. 55, mentioning that 'State practice of particular significance is to be found' in, *inter alia*, 'statements made by States (. . .) in the context of the adoption of the United Nations Convention'. See also: *Fisheries Jurisdiction Case (United Kingdom v. Iceland)*, ICJ Rep. 1974, p. 26; *Barcelona Traction, Light and Power Company, Limited, (Belgium v. Spain)*, Judgment, ICJ Rep. 1970, pp. 302–303, Separate Opinion of Judge Ammoun ('I would observe, in addition, that the positions taken up by the delegates of States in international organizations and conferences, and in particular in the United Nations, naturally form part of State practice . . . it cannot be denied, with regard to the resolutions which emerge therefrom, or better, with regard to the votes expressed therein in the name of States, that these amount to precedents contributing to the formation of custom').

[796] Tudor, *The Fair and Equitable Treatment Standard*, p. 71; Wolfke, *Custom in Present International Law*, p. 79; Shaw, *International Law*, pp. 82–83; Henckaerts and Doswald-Beck, *Customary International Humanitarian Law*, p. xxxviii; A.E. Roberts, 'Traditional and Modern Approaches to Customary International Law: A Reconciliation', *AJIL* 95(4) (2001), p. 774; ILA Report, 2000, p. 70; Byers, *Custom, Power and the Power of Rules*, p. 42; Ferrari-Bravo, 'Méthodes de recherche de la coutume internationale', pp. 298–299; ILC, Second Report, 2014, pp. 25–26; R. Higgins, *The Development of International Law Through the Political Organs of the United Nations* (London: Oxford University Press, 1963), p. 2; I. Brownlie, *The Rule of Law in International Affairs: International Law at the Fiftieth Anniversary of the United Nations* (The Hague: Martinus Nijhoff, 1998), pp. 19–20; I. MacGibbon, 'General Assembly Resolutions: Custom, Practice and Mistaken Identity', in B. Cheng (ed.), *International Law: Teaching and Practice* (London: Stevens and Sons, 1982), pp. 10, 19; Wood and Sender, 'State Practice', para. 18. *Contra*: Wolfke, *Custom in Present International Law*, p. 84 ('[resolutions] do not of themselves constitute any evidence of acceptance of a practice as law by the member-states, considering that they are formally opinions of the organization and not of its members', see also: 'Individual positive votes cast by the members do not necessarily represent the actual acceptance as law of the conduct only verbally postulated in the content of the recommendation, since the motive for such votes may be various').

[797] Mendelson, 'The Formation of Customary International Law', p. 201. See also: K. Skubiszewski, 'Resolutions of the UN General Assembly and Evidence of Custom', in *Essays in Honor of Roberto Ago* (vol. 1, Milan: Giuffré, 1987), p. 560, referring to the position adopted by a number of writers on the issue.

recorded as a resolution of (the organ of the) organization, its adoption is a piece of practice *by the organization*; and some writers treat it in this way. However, in the context of the formation of customary international law, it is probably best regarded as a series of verbal acts by the individual member States participating in that organ. If so, it would add little or nothing to the weight of such practice *by the member States themselves* to treat the resolution itself (as distinct from voting for it) as a *further* piece of practice, this time on the part of the organization.[798]

What are the concrete examples of *State* practice within international organizations?[799] They include different types of statements made by States in the adoption of resolutions, such as voting[800] explanations given to justify such votes,[801] as well as exchanges of diplomatic correspondence. It should be noted, however, that some writers are reluctant to consider voting at the UN General Assembly as evidence of State practice. For Schwebel, States 'typically vote in response to political not legal considerations' and 'they do not conceive of themselves as creating or changing international law'.[802] In fact, he believes that States 'often

[798] ILA, Final Report, 2000, p. 19 (emphasis in the original). See also: Mendelson, 'The Formation of Customary International Law', p. 201.

[799] On this question, see G. Cahin, *La coutume internationale et les organisations internationales: l'incidence de la dimension institutionnelle sur le processus coutumier* (Paris: Pedone, 2001), p. 29 ff.

[800] Henckaerts and Doswald-Beck, *Customary International Humanitarian Law*, pp. xxxviii–xlii; Mendelson, 'The Formation of Customary International Law', p. 204; Obed Y. Asamoah, 'The Legal Significance of the Declarations of the General Assembly of the United Nations', *ICLQ* 16(4) (1967), p. 54; Higgins, *The Development of International Law*, p. 2.

[801] Henckaerts and Doswald-Beck, *Customary International Humanitarian Law*, p. xxxviii–xlii; Villiger, *Customary International Law and Treaties*, p. 23; ILA, Final Report, 2000, p. 58. *Contra*: Wolfke, *Custom in Present International Law*, p. 84.

[802] Stephen M. Schwebel, 'The Effect of Resolutions of the U.N. General Assembly on Customary International Law', *ASIL Proc.*, 73 (1979), p. 302. See also: Charney, 'International Agreements and the Development of Customary International Law', p. 993: 'As a consequence, the traditional rules for determining whether there is a rule of customary international law seek to make the most accurate appraisal of states' positions. This is why it is important to consider the actual behavior of states in real situations. Statements of officials faced with real situations have been very significant. Information on states' views derived from abstract situations has provided less authoritative information on their true positions. While resolutions of international organizations, such as those of the United Nations General Assembly, have become accepted evidence to support rules of international law there is much debate over their utility. The debate arises because resolutions are likely to represent highly politicized positions of state representatives divorced from the reality of international life. Even when a resolution is utilized as evidence of international law care should be taken to determine the specific nature of the resolution and the facts surrounding its adoption'.

don't meaningfully support what a resolution says and they almost always do not mean that the resolution is law'.[803] In any event, caution is required since the General Assembly 'is a political organ in which it is often far from clear that [States'] acts carry juridical significance'.[804]

Voting and statements made by States regarding said resolutions can also evidence their *opinio juris*.[805] This is the conclusion reached by ICJ in the *Nicaragua* case.[806] This controversial question will be discussed in more detail in the next chapter.[807] In the context of the United Nations, State practice also includes States' declarations accepting the ICJ's jurisdiction, States' pleadings before the ICJ, declarations at the General Assembly and so on.[808]

There are very few investor-State arbitration examples of situations where the position taken by a State in the context of the work of an international organization has been invoked as evidence of State practice. One instance is the *Bureau Veritas v. Paraguay* case where Paraguay invoked its own membership in the Group of 77 and, specifically, the 1964 'Joint Declaration of the Seventy-Seven Developing Countries Made at the Conclusion of the U.N. Conference on Trade and Development' in support of its position that it had always intended for the FET standard to refer to the MST.[809] Another relevant example, which will be discussed in the next section, concerns the 1967 OECD *Draft Convention on the Protection of Foreign Property*.[810]

3.3.5.2 The practice of international organizations and the formation of customary rules

There is consensus to the effect that 'resolutions adopted by States within international organizations and at international conferences may, in certain circumstances, have a role in the formation and identification of

---

[803] Schwebel, *Ibid.*
[804] ILC, Third Report, 2015, p. 33. See also: M.D. Öberg, 'The Legal Effects of Resolutions of the UN Security Council and General Assembly in the Jurisprudence of the ICJ', *EJIL* 16 (2006), pp. 879, 902.
[805] ILC, Second Report, 2014, p. 57; Wood and Sender, 'State Practice', para. 18.
[806] *Military and Paramilitary Activities in and around Nicaragua*, ICJ Rep. 1986, pp. 99–100, 101 ('This *opinio juris* may, though with all due caution, be deduced from, *inter alia*, the attitude of the Parties and the attitude of States towards certain General Assembly resolutions').
[807] See, Chapter 4, Section 4.1.5.2.   [808] Cahin, *La coutume internationale*, p. 30 ff.
[809] *Bureau Veritas, Inspection, Valuation, Assessment and Control, BIVAC BV v. Paraguay*, Further Decision on Objections to Jurisdiction, 9 October 2012, para. 152.
[810] OECD, *Draft Convention on the Protection of Foreign Property*, Art. 1 cmt.

customary international law'.[811] As noted by the ILC Special Rapporteur, 'such resolutions are accorded considerable importance' in terms of the identification of customary rules.[812] In fact, Alvarez speaks of a new form of custom ('codified custom'), which is largely the product of international organizations' lawmaking through resolutions.[813] For him, 'neither judges nor diplomats appear to have the patience to comb through laborious diplomatic exchanges to discover whether custom exists' and therefore resolutions passed at international organizations 'provided shortcuts to finding custom'.[814]

Yet, it should be recalled that resolutions adopted by international organizations are generally considered as evidence of their *own practice*, and not that of member States.[815] But such resolutions are nevertheless relevant for the identification of customary rules because they 'reflect the views expressed and the votes cast by States within them, and may thus constitute State practice or evidence of *opinio juris*'.[816] The work of these organizations may also 'serve to catalyse' by 'prompt[ing] reactions by States, which may count as practice or attest to their legal opinions'.[817]

It should be added that the vast majority of resolutions adopted by organs of international organizations are *non-binding*.[818] These resolutions, therefore, *do not* impose any *formal legal* obligations on member States.[819] As such, UN General Assembly resolutions 'do not *ipso facto*

[811] ILC, Third Report, 2015, p. 31, see also at pp. 46–54.

[812] *Ibid*. See also, Draft Conclusion 7(4) of the ILC 'Proposed draft conclusions on the identification of customary international law': 'The acts (including inaction) of international organizations may also serve as practice'.

[813] José E. Alvarez, *International Organizations as Law-Makers* (Oxford: Oxford University Press, 2005), p. 592.

[814] *Ibid*. See, however, the cautious approach adopted by R. Higgins, *Problems and Process: International Law and How We Use It* (Oxford: Clarendon Press, 1994), p. 28: '[O]ne must take care not to use General Assembly resolutions as a short cut to ascertaining international practice in its entirety on a matter — practice in the larger world arena is still the relevant canvas, although UN resolutions are part of the picture. Resolutions cannot be a substitute for ascertaining custom: this task will continue to require that other evidences of state practice be examined alongside those collective acts evidenced in General Assembly resolutions'.

[815] Cahin, *La coutume internationale*, p. 51 ff. See, ILC, Third Report, 2015, p. 52, indicating that 'the practice of international organizations relating to the international conduct of the organization or international organizations generally may, as such, serve as relevant practice for purposes of formation and identification of customary international law'.

[816] ILC, Third Report, 2015, p. 51.   [817] *Ibid*.

[818] One notable exception is, of course, resolutions adopted by the UN Security Council.

[819] Meyer, 'Codifying Custom', p. 1061; Mendelson, 'The Formation of Customary International Law', p. 360.

create new rules of customary law'.[820] Yet, as noted by two writers, 'the value accorded to any particular resolution depends on its content, its degree of acceptance and the consistency of State practice outside it'.[821] The ICJ has recognized that General Assembly resolutions 'can, in certain circumstances, provide evidence important for establishing the existence of a rule or the emergence of an *opinio juris*'.[822] This is an important point. A resolution does not (and cannot) *in itself* 'create' custom;[823] it can only provide *evidence* of State practice necessary for the identification of custom. Draft conclusion 12 of the ILC's work on the identification of customary rules reads as follows:

1. A resolution adopted by an international organization or at an inter-governmental conference cannot, of itself, create a rule of customary international law.
2. A resolution adopted by an international organization or at an inter-governmental conference may provide evidence for establishing the existence and content of a rule of customary international law, or contribute to its development.
3. A provision in a resolution adopted by an international organization or at an intergovernmental conference may reflect a rule of customary international law if it is established that the provision corresponds to a general practice that is accepted as law (*opinio juris*). [824]

These two distinct phenomena will be examined in the next paragraphs.

First, a General Assembly resolution can, in some circumstances, be considered as evidence of already *existing* customary law *per se*.[825] In these situations, 'the resolution reflects, but does not actually constitute, the customary rule which remains binding upon States *qua* customary

---

[820] ILA, Final Report, 2000, pp. 55, 60–61.
[821] Henckaerts and Doswald-Beck, *Customary International Humanitarian Law*, pp. xxxviii–xlii.
[822] *Legality of the Threat or Use of Nuclear Weapons*, advisory opinion, ICJ Rep.1996, p. 254, para. 70.
[823] Nguyen *et al., Droit International Public*, pp. 357–358; ILC, Third Report, 2015, p. 32 ('such resolutions cannot in and of themselves create customary international law, they "may sometimes have normative value" in providing').
[824] ILC, Draft Conclusions, 2015, conclusion no. 12.
[825] Chittharanjan Felix Amerasinghe, *Principles of the Institutional Law of International Organizations* (2nd edn., Cambridge: Cambridge University Press, 2005), p. 190. See, discussion in: Alvarez, *International Organizations as Law-Makers*, pp. 259–260; ILC, Third Report, 2015, p. 31.

law'.[826] As noted by the ILA, when a resolution 'expressly or impliedly' asserts the existence of a customary rule, it constitutes a 'rebuttable evidence that such is the case'.[827] Whether or not any resolution represents custom will have to be carefully assessed.[828] In any event, such a phenomenon will only occur in 'very exceptional circumstances'.[829]

One illustration of this phenomenon can be found in the 1977 *Texaco* case. In this case, the sole arbitrator examined the *Resolution on Permanent Sovereignty over Natural Resources*[830] adopted in 1962 at the UN General Assembly by a large majority of representative States (including both developed and developing States) and concluded that it represented custom *at the time*.[831] The arbitrator rejected, however, the customary status of the 1974 resolution adopted by the UN General Assembly (the *Charter of Economic Rights and Duties of States*[832]), which had been

---

[826] Villiger, *Customary International Law and Treaties*, p. 125.

[827] ILA, Final Report, 2000, pp. 57–58: 'Normally, a resolution expressly or impliedly declaring the law creates only a *rebuttable* presumption that the law is indeed as declared. The first reason is that the assertion is not opposable against those who voted against it, those who were not present or those who were not even Members of the UN. Secondly, even in the case of those who voted in favour of the resolution, one must examine more closely the precise language of the resolution and the circumstances of its adoption before one can be sure that the rule in question has been accepted by those States' (emphasis in the original). See also: Gazzini, 'The Role of Customary International Law', p. 693; Skubiszewski, 'Resolutions of the UN General Assembly', p. 519; Schachter, 'International Law in Theory and Practice', p. 90.

[828] ILC, Third Report, 2015, p. 36.

[829] ILA, Final Report, 2000, p. 59, explaining (at p. 61) what are these 'exceptional circumstances': 'Resolutions accepted unanimously or almost unanimously, and which evince a clear intention on the part of their supporters to lay down a rule of international law, are capable, very exceptionally, of creating general customary law by the mere fact of their adoption'. The Report also added that 'in the event of a lack of unanimity, a failure to include all representative groups of States will prevent the creation of a general rule of customary international law' and that 'even if all representative groups are included, individual dissenting States enjoy the benefit of the persistent objector rule'.

[830] G.A. Res. 1803 (XVII), 14 December 1962.

[831] *Texaco Overseas Petroleum Co. & California Asiatic Oil Co. v. Libyan Arab Republic* [hereinafter referred to as *Texaco v. Libya*], Award, 19 January 1977, *I.L.M.* 17 (1978), para. 87: 'En fonction des conditions de vote précédemment évoquées et traduisant une *opinio juris communis*, la résolution 1803 (XVII) paraît au tribunal de céans refléter *l'état du droit coutumier existant en la matière*. En effet, à partir du vote d'une résolution constatant *l'existence d'une règle coutumière*, les Etats expriment clairement leur opinion. L'acquiescement en l'espèce d'une majorité d'Etats appartenant aux différents groupes représentatifs indique sans ambiguïté la reconnaissance universelle des règles incorporées, à savoir, en ce qui concerne les nationalisations et l'indemnisation, l'utilisation des règles en vigueur dans l'Etat nationalisant, mais cela en conformité avec le droit international' (emphasis added).

[832] G.A. Res. 3281 (XXIX), 12 December 1974.

openly rejected by Western States.[833] The *Aminoil* Tribunal reached the same conclusion a few years later.[834]

Second, General Assembly resolutions can also have a significant influence on the *formation* and *development* of customary rules.[835] They can indeed be 'starting points for the possible development of customary law in the event that State practice happens to lock on to these proclamations'.[836] As acknowledged by the ILA, General Assembly resolutions can 'constitute an historic ("material") source of new customary rules'.[837] They can 'in appropriate cases themselves constitute part of the process of formation of new rules of customary international law',[838] and also 'help to crystallize emerging customary law'.[839] Caution is required in order to assess whether this is indeed the case.[840] As noted by the ICJ, '[I]t is necessary to look at its content and the conditions of its adoption; it is also necessary to see whether an *opinio juris* exists as to its normative character'.[841]

Yet, it must be emphasized that custom 'need[s] to be accompanied by "real" practice before a customary rule could be said to arise'.[842] As explained by Mendelson, the resolution 'is simply providing an impetus which may (but will not inevitably) lead to the creation of law by other States acting in the "traditional" manner creating conventional or customary rules through their actual conduct'.[843] This is indeed the conclusion reached by the Institut de Droit: 'Principles and rules proclaimed in a Resolution may influence State practice, or initiate a new practice that constitutes an ingredient of new customary law. A Resolution may contribute to the consolidation of State practice, or to the formation of the *opinio juris communis*'.[844]

[833] *Texaco v. Libya*, Award, 19 January 1977, para. 87.
[834] *Government of the State of Kuwait v. American Independent Oil Company (Aminoil)*, Award, 24 March 1982, *JDI* (1982), p. 893, para. 90.
[835] Gazzini, 'The Role of Customary International Law', p. 693; Wood and Sender, 'State Practice', para. 19; ILC, Third Report, 2015, pp. 31, 37.
[836] Simma and Alston, 'The Sources of Human Rights Law', pp. 89–90.
[837] ILA, Final Report, 2000, p. 59. See also: Mendelson, 'The Formation of Customary International Law', p. 361.
[838] ILA, *Ibid.*
[839] *Ibid.*, p. 55. See also: Mendelson, 'The Formation of Customary International Law', pp. 361–362.
[840] ILC, Third Report, 2015, pp. 33–35.
[841] *Legality of the Threat or Use of Nuclear Weapons*, ICJ Rep. 1996, p. 255, para. 70.
[842] Mendelson, 'The Formation of Customary International Law', p. 373. See also: ILC, Third Report, 2015, pp. 38–39.
[843] *Ibid.*, p. 361.
[844] Institut de Droit International, 'The Elaboration of General Multilateral Conventions And of Non-contractual Instruments Having a Normative Function or Objective',

In investor-State arbitration, parties[845] and tribunals[846] often refer to the 1967 OECD *Draft Convention on the Protection of Foreign Property*[847] on matters of treaty interpretation. Specifically, the document is invoked by States[848] and scholars[849] to support their view that Western States incorporated the concept of the FET standard in their BITs to simply reflect the MST under custom.[850] This is because the Drafting Committee mentioned that the term FET refers to 'the standard set by international law for the treatment due by each State with regard to the property of foreign nationals' and that 'the standard required conforms in effect to the minimum standard which forms part of customary international law'.[851] Scholars have, however, rejected the claim that the *Draft Convention* was the starting point to the subsequent development of the FET standard as a rule of custom.[852] Yet, there is no doubt that the

Session of Cairo, 1987, conclusion 22, in *Tableau des résolutions adoptées (1957–1991)* (Paris: Pedone, 1992).
[845] *Ioannis Kardassopoulos v. Georgia*, ICSID Case No. ARB/05/18, Award, 3 March 2010, para. 378, referring to the position of Georgia ('Respondent submits that the Commentary to the OECD *Draft Convention on the Protection of Foreign Property*, although not binding for the interpretation of Article 13(1)(c) of the ECT, is of some assistance'), see also, para. 394.
[846] *Eureko B.V. v. Poland*, Partial Award, 19 August 2005, para. 251; *Saluka Investments B.V. v. Czech Republic*, UNCITRAL, Partial Award, 17 March 2006, para. 259; *Ioannis Kardassopoulos v. Georgia*, Award, 3 March 2010, para. 378.
[847] OECD, *Draft Convention on the Protection of Foreign Property*, Art. 1 cmt.
[848] *Pope & Talbot Inc. v. Canada*, Award on the Merits (Phase 2), 10 April 2001, para. 112, referring to the position of the United States. See also: *Bureau Veritas, Inspection, Valuation, Assessment and Control, BIVAC BV v. Paraguay*, Further Decision on Objections to Jurisdiction, 9 October 2012, para. 152, where Paraguay argued that the Netherlands (home State of the investor) had always intended the FET standard to refer to the international minimum standard and referring specifically to the document 'as evidence' to the Netherlands' 'membership in the OECD and voting in favour of adopting the Draft Convention'.
[849] Vasciannie, 'The Fair and Equitable Treatment Standard', pp. 112–113; UNCTAD, 'Fair and Equitable Treatment', 2012, p. 8; OECD, 'Fair and Equitable Treatment Standard in International Investment Law', p. 4.
[850] See, the analysis of Newcombe and Paradell, *Law and Practice of Investment Treaties*, p. 268; Thomas, 'Reflections on Article 1105 of NAFTA', pp. 44, 47; Carreau and Juillard, *Droit international économique*, p. 454.
[851] OECD, *Draft Convention on the Protection of Foreign Property*.
[852] Vasciannie, 'The Fair and Equitable Treatment Standard', p. 155: 'The OECD Draft, having been prepared with some degree of State scrutiny, provides a possible point around which a customary rule in favour of the fair and equitable standard could have developed. For at least three reasons, however, it is difficult to argue that this process has taken place. First, the OECD Draft cannot be said to have represented a substantial cross-section of State interests on the issue, for, in essence, only developed, capital-exporting States contributed to the document. Secondly, there is no evidence that, at the

document must be considered as evidence of the practice of each OECD Member State on the meaning of the FET standard. The OECD itself noted in a 2004 report that the document 'represented the collective view and dominant trend of OECD countries on investment issues'.[853] Scholars also frequently cite this document as an element of these States' practice.[854]

3.3.6   Internal national practice of States

This section examines one last manifestation of State practice: the internal national practice of States. The ILA noted in its Report that '[t]he practice of the executive, legislative and judicial organs of the State is to be considered, according to the circumstances, as State practice'.[855] The ILC also came to the same conclusion in its Draft Conclusions.[856]

In the following paragraphs, I will provide a more in-depth analysis of the conduct of the executive (Section 3.3.6.1), the legislative (Section 3.3.6.2) and the judiciary branches of government (Section 3.3.6.3). In these sections, I will investigate the internal practice of States under both general international law as well as in the specific context of investor-State arbitration proceedings.

multilateral level, developing countries have accepted the OECD Draft; indeed, although it is difficult to identify pronouncements by developing countries against fair and equitable treatment, express support for the standard as a rule of customary law is also lacking. This points to an absence of *opinio juris* among a substantial number of States in favour of regarding the OECD Draft as enshrining the standard in customary law. And, thirdly, the OECD document did not, with the passage of time, evolve from the status of a draft treaty to that of a binding instrument: its status as a draft, in circumstances where it was open to developed countries to bring the treaty into force by their ratifications, suggests that even these countries would not regard the OECD text as reflecting customary law in its entirety'.

[853] OECD, *Fair and Equitable Treatment Standard*, p. 4.

[854] Newcombe and Paradell, *Law and Practice of Investment Treaties*, p. 269; Thomas, 'Reflections on Article 1105 of NAFTA', p. 48 ff; Dumberry, *The Fair and Equitable Treatment Standard*, p. 32; Paparinskis, *The International Minimum Standard*, p. 162; Vasciannie, 'The Fair and Equitable Treatment Standard', p. 139 (adding that the Convention 'may be said to provide evidence of the *opinio juris* of several OECD member States on the point').

[855] ILA, Final Report, 2000, p. 17. See also: Henckaerts and Doswald-Beck, *Customary International Humanitarian Law*, p. xxxviii; Dinstein, 'The Interaction between Customary International Law and Treaties', p. 272; Gazzini, 'The Role of Customary International Law', p. 692; Wood and Sender, 'State Practice', para. 9.

[856] ILC, Second Report, 2014, Draft Conclusion 6; ILC, Draft Conclusions, 2015, conclusion no. 5 ('State practice consists of conduct of the State, whether in the exercise of its executive, legislative, judicial or other functions').

3.3.6.1   Executive

What first counts as State practice is the conduct and actions/omissions of the executive branch of government.[857] The ILA Report noted that 'the actions of the whole of the executive, and not just the foreign ministry, should count'.[858] This is indeed the case in the context of investor-State arbitration where a variety of governmental conduct adopted by different actors can give rise, for instance, to claims of arbitrary conduct or expropriation in violation of treaty obligations. The ILC considers the following conduct of the executive branch as State practice:

> These may include executive orders and decrees, and other "administrative measures", as well as official statements by government such as declarations, proclamations, government statements before parliament, positions expressed by States before national or international courts and tribunals (including in *amicus curiae* briefs of States), and statements on the international plane.[859]

The following sections will examine two other sources of evidence of State practice: the conduct of the legislative and judiciary branches of government.

3.3.6.2   Legislative

It is generally recognized that acts of the legislative branch of government are manifestations of State practice which can potentially play a fundamental role in the emergence of customary rules.[860] A number of

---

[857] Henckaerts and Doswald-Beck, *Customary International Humanitarian Law*, p. xxxviii (referring specifically, in the context of humanitarian law, to orders or instructions given to the armed forces, such as Rules of Engagement); ILA, Final Report, 2000, p. 14; Shaw, *International Law*, pp. 82–83; Tudor, *The Fair and Equitable Treatment Standard*, p. 77; Crawford, *Brownlie's Principles of Public International Law*, p. 24; Mendelson, 'The Formation of Customary International Law', p. 204; J.A. Barberis, 'Réflexions sur la coutume internationale', *AFDI*, 36 (1990), p. 31; Dinstein, 'The Interaction between Customary International Law and Treaties', p. 272; Gazzini, 'The Role of Customary International Law', p. 692.

[858] ILA, Final Report, 2000, p. 17. See also: Mendelson, 'The Formation of Customary International Law', p. 198.

[859] ILC, Second Report, 2014, p. 22.

[860] Crawford, *Brownlie's Principles of Public International Law*, p. 24; Mendelson, 'The Formation of Customary International Law', p. 204; Hirsch, 'Sources of International Investment Law', p. 10; Malanczuk, *Akehurst's Modern Introduction to International Law*, pp. 39–40; Shaw, *International Law*, pp. 82–83; Henckaerts and Doswald-Beck, *Customary International Humanitarian Law*, p. xxxviii; Arthur W. Rovine (ed.), *1973 Digest of the United States Practice in International Law* (Washington DC, US Department of State, Office of the Legal Adviser, 1974) (referred to in Guzman,

international tribunals have recognized that phenomenon, including the
ICJ,[861] the Special Court for Sierra Leone,[862] and the Special Tribunal for
Lebanon.[863] This is because the legislative branch is an organ of the State.
As stated by the PCIJ in the *Certain German Interests in Polish Upper
Silesia* case, from the standpoint of international law, 'municipal laws are
merely facts which express the will and constitute the activities of
States'.[864] What is important for the purposes of this book is that the
PCIJ recognized that acts of the legislative branch are considered as those
of the State. In other words, the role of municipal law in the context of
investment arbitration is certainly not limited to that of a 'mere fact'.
Thus, as will be further discussed,[865] it is not uncommon for tribunals to
apply domestic law (along with international law) in investor-State disputes.[866] Also, as noted by one writer, domestic laws are an 'important
formal source of foreign investment law' insofar as a number of

'Saving Customary International Law', p. 126); Dinstein, 'The Interaction between
Customary International Law and Treaties', p. 273; ILC, 'Report of the International
Law Commission on the work of its thirty-second session', 5 May to 25 July 1980, UN
doc. A/35/10, *Yearbook ILC* (1980), vol. II (Part Two), p. 152 ('national legislation
constitutes an important element in the overall concept of State practice. It is clearly a
convenient measure and affords a decisive indication as to the substantive content of the
law, and as to the actual practice of States'); ILC, Second Report, 2014, p. 23 (providing
many case law examples); ILC, Draft Conclusions, 2015, conclusion no. 6(3); Gazzini,
'The Role of Customary International Law', p. 692.
[861] *Nottebohm case (Liechtenstein v. Guatemala) (Second Phase)*, Judgment, ICJ Rep. 1955,
p. 22; *Case Concerning the Arrest Warrant of 11 April 2000 (Democratic Republic of the
Congo v. Belgium)*, Judgment, ICJ Rep. 2002, p. 24, where the Court stated that it had
'carefully examined State practice, including national legislation (. . .)'.
[862] Special Court for Sierra Leone, *Prosecutor v. Norman*, SCSL-2004-14-AR72(E), 31 May
2004, p. 13, para. 17, where the Court referred to a number of States having legislations
that prohibit child recruitment to determine whether the prohibition on child recruitment to armed forces had crystallized into customary international law.
[863] ILC, First Report, 2013, p. 34, referring to the following case: Case No. STL-11-01/I,
Interlocutory Decision on the Applicable Law: Terrorism, Conspiracy, Homicide,
Perpetration, Cumulative Charging (Appeals Chamber), 16 February 2011, para. 85,
mentioning, *inter alia*, 'the legislative and judicial practice of States' as evidence for 'the
formation of a general *opinio juris* in the international community, accompanied by a
practice consistent with such *opinio*, to the effect that a customary rule of international
law regarding the international crime of terrorism, at least *in time of peace*, has indeed
emerged', see also, at para. 87.
[864] *Certain German Interests in Polish Upper Silesia (Germany v. Poland)*, (Merits) (1926)
PCIJ, ser. A No.7, p. 19.
[865] See, discussion in Chapter 5, Section 5.2.3.
[866] This is the case when a BIT or a State contract refers to the domestic law of the host State
as the applicable law to solve a dispute.

important issues (nationality of investors, the existence of an investment, its legality, etc.[867]) are governed by domestic law.[868]

The legislative branch's acts or conduct are considered as relevant evidence of State practice for the creation of new customary rules based on the assumption that their content actually reflects that State's position on a given issue. It should be recalled (as previously mentioned[869]) that 'internal uniformity' is one of the basic requirements for the practice of States to be considered as relevant in the process of custom creation. Such 'internal uniformity' would require not only that one State (almost) always adopts the same position, but also that all branches of government take a consistent approach on a given issue. This, however, is not always the case. There will be instances where the executive branch will adopt a position different from that of the parliament. As noted by two writers, 'the text of the legislation is not necessarily the whole picture: what matters more is how legislation is interpreted and applied in practice'.[870] In other words, for the purposes of custom formation, limited weight should be given to domestic legislation that is not applied by the State, or that is contradicted by the executive branch's acts. As noted by Dinstein, 'Human rights legislation that is disregarded by the executive branch, and amounts to "little more than window-dressing", cannot be relied upon "as significant evidence of practice" of the affected State for purposes of custom-making'.[871]

How does legislation influence the development of custom? It is well recognized that '[t]he national law of a state or a group of states cannot only serve as a model to other states, but it can also initiate international practice, and thus lead to the formation of an international custom'.[872] Thus, other States can gradually adopt the domestic legislation of one (or a few) State(s) and a custom rule may eventually emerge in the event that such representative practice is both uniform and consistent.[873] Scholars refer to a limited number of historical examples illustrating this

[867] See, the analysis in: Newcombe and Paradell, *Law and Practice of Investment Treaties*, p. 92 ff.

[868] Florian Grisel, 'The Sources of Foreign Investment Law', in: Z. Douglas, J. Pauwelyn and J.E. Viñuales (eds.), *The Foundations of International Investment Law: Bringing Theory into Practice* (Oxford: Oxford University Press, 2014), p. 224.

[869] See, discussion in Chapter 3, Section 3.2.1.

[870] Wood and Sender, 'State Practice', para. 14.

[871] Dinstein, 'The Interaction between Customary International Law and Treaties', p. 274, quoting from: Schachter, 'International Law in Theory and Practice', p. 335.

[872] Wolfke, *Custom in Present International Law*, p. 77.

[873] Gazzini, 'The Role of Customary International Law', p. 692.

phenomenon, including British navigation regulations which were subsequently accepted and adopted by all maritime States and are now considered as custom.[874]

What are the relevant examples of acts of the legislative branch evidencing State practice? They include States' constitutions and laws.[875] In some circumstances, the parliamentary practice can also be considered as evidence of State practice.[876] This is the case, for instance, for States where the parliament plays a meaningful role in international relations.[877] Another example is where a parliamentary organ exists independently of the executive branch of government,[878] such as in States with a pluralist democratic system.[879] Yet, there seems to be no support for the more radical view that only the national laws of democratic States should count as evidence of State practice.[880]

In the context of investment arbitration, one clear example of relevant State practice is the domestic legislation of a State on the standards of

---

[874] Wolfke, *Custom in Present International Law*, p. 77; Shaw, *International Law*, pp. 82–83 ('In the Scotia case decided by the US Supreme Court in 1871, a British ship had sunk an American vessel on the high seas. The Court held that British navigational procedures established by an Act of Parliament formed the basis of the relevant international custom since other states had legislated in virtually identical terms').

[875] ILA, Final Report, 2000 p. 17; Mendelson, 'The Formation of Customary International Law', p. 199.

[876] Ferrari-Bravo, 'Méthodes de recherche de la coutume internationale', pp. 277–278, indicating that evidence of relevant parliamentary practice may be found, for instance, in the summary of parliamentary debates, in the adoption of a resolution by members of parliament, and by declarations of government policy. See also: Dinstein, 'The Interaction between Customary International Law and Treaties', p. 277; Mendelson, 'The Formation of Customary International Law', p. 204; Malanczuk, *Akehurst's Modern Introduction to International Law*, pp. 39–40. See, however, Ferrari-Bravo, *Ibid.*, p. 282, for whom legislation has greater weight than parliamentary practice. Thus, 'un acte de législation dans un domaine relevant du droit international représente le degré le plus élevé de la pratique de l'Etat dont il émane' (p. 280). This is because, 'elle représente la prise de position de l'Etat tout entier, tandis que la pratique parlementaire reste, même lorsqu'elle se manifeste à l'occasion du processus de formation d'un acte législatif, l'expression du dialogue entre les forces politiques présentes à l'intérieur du pays et représentées au parlement' (*Ibid.*). He also explains that parliamentary practice is often driven by internal political concerns and that therefore, 'le degré de fiabilité de la pratique parlementaire (à part les actes de législation) est moins élevé que celui de la pratique diplomatique au sens strict du mot' (p. 279).

[877] ILA, Final Report, 2000, p. 18.

[878] Ferrari-Bravo, 'Méthodes de recherche de la coutume internationale', pp. 277–278.

[879] *Ibid.*; ILA, Final Report, 2000, p. 18.

[880] Lepard, *Customary International Law*, p. 176 ('national laws that are adopted by democratically elected legislatures and that are the product of vigorous consultation and debate should be given greater weight than those that are adopted by bodies not chosen though free elections or that are not the outcome of open discussion').

protection existing for both domestic and foreign investors.[881] These laws include, for instance, codes of investments and all regulations concerning foreign investments. This is the conclusion reached by Porterfield on the importance of domestic legislation regarding the prohibition of expropriation under international law:

> Thus for nations such as the United States that explicitly link their standard of treatment of foreign investors to their domestic standards of protection for property rights, it seems reasonable to conclude that domestic law regarding expropriation constitutes state practice for the purposes of identifying expropriation standards under CIL. Even for nations where there is no explicit linkage between their treatment of foreign and domestic investors, domestic expropriation standards are presumably at least relevant to identifying state practice with regard to foreign investors, absent any evidence that it is the state's practice to provide foreign investors with a higher standard of protection.[882]

There are very few examples of awards dealing with the question of the authoritative value of domestic legislations as State practice for the formation of custom.[883] The *UPS* award provides one rare concrete example. The Tribunal examined the alleged existence of a 'customary international law rule requiring the prohibiting or regulating of anticompetitive behaviour'.[884] It first noted that 'in their submissions, Canada, Mexico and the United States call attention, in terms of state practice, to studies of national competition laws'.[885] The Tribunal then examined the content of different competition laws that States had adopted. It found that many States did not have any competition laws ('only 13 out of the 34 Western Hemisphere nations and about 80 of the WTO members [did]') and that, in any event, the content of these laws differed.[886] The Tribunal concluded that there is an 'absence of current general obligations as indicated by

---

[881] Porterfield, 'State Practice and the (Purported) Obligation', p. 161.   [882] *Ibid.*, p. 188.

[883] One illustration is found in: *Apotex Holdings Inc & Apotex Inc. v. United States*, ICSID Case No. ARB(AF)/12/1, Award, 25 August 2014, para. 9.27, where the Tribunal refers to 'the state practice available to the Tribunal in the specific context presented here, namely the regulation of imported drug products, [which] weighs heavily against the assertion that the claimed protections are required by customary international law'. Another less relevant example is *ADF Group Inc. v. United States*, Award, 9 January 2003, para. 188, where the Tribunal concluded that a US measure adopted in its legislation dealing with domestic content and performance requirements in governmental procurement was common to all NAFTA Parties (as well as many other States) and that such legislation could therefore not 'be characterized as idiosyncratic or aberrant and arbitrary'.

[884] *UPS v. Canada*, Award on Jurisdiction, 22 November 2002, para. 85.   [885] *Ibid.*

[886] *Ibid.* ('national legislation, for instance that of the three NAFTA Parties, differs markedly, reflecting their unique economic, social and political environment').

state practice in national legislation.[887] These passages show that the Tribunal, as well as all three NAFTA States, clearly considered domestic legislation as relevant State practice for establishing the existence of custom. In any event, the Tribunal stated that 'there is no indication in any material before the Tribunal that any of that legislation was enacted out of a sense of general international legal obligation'.[888] It therefore concluded that there was 'no rule of customary international law prohibiting or regulating anticompetitive behaviour'.[889]

3.3.6.3   Judiciary

The present section examines the role of domestic courts' decisions in the formation of custom, first under general international law (Section 3.3.6.3.1) and then specifically in the context of investor-State arbitration (Section 3.3.6.3.2).

3.3.6.3.1   International law   As noted by Roberts, 'domestic court decisions are unique within the international law doctrine of sources because of their ability to wear two hats, representing: (1) practice of the forum State, which may be relevant to the determination of custom and the interpretation of treaties (law creation); and (2) a subsidiary means of determining international law, capable of stating international norms with more authority than attends the practice of a single State (law enforcement)'.[890] The present section only examines the *first* of these two hats.

---

[887] *Ibid.*, para. 88 (emphasis added).   [888] *Ibid.*, para. 85.   [889] *Ibid.*, para. 92.
[890] A.E. Roberts, 'Comparative International Law? The Role of National Courts in Creating and Enforcing International Law', *ICLQ* 60 (2011), p. 59, see also, at pp. 62, 63 ('This duality of national court decisions—representing evidence of State practice and a subsidiary means of determining international law—is unique in the doctrine of sources. Other practice by States, such as executive statements, military manuals and diplomatic correspondence, provide evidence of State practice only. Judicial decisions of international courts provide a subsidiary means of determining international law only. National court decisions alone have the potential to wear both hats and thus their value is often considered to be mixed'). See also: ILC, Third Report, 2015, p. 41. See also: ILC, Draft Conclusions, 2015, conclusions nos. 6(2) and 13(2) ('Regard may be had, as appropriate, to decisions of national courts concerning the existence and content of rules of customary international law, as a subsidiary means for the determination of such rules'); A. Gattini, 'Le rôle du juge international et du juge national et la coutume internationale', in D. Alland *et al.* (eds.), *Unité et diversité du droit international: écrits en l'honneur du professeur Pierre-Marie Dupuy* (Leiden: Martinus Nijhoff, 2014), pp. 253–273.

As a matter of principle, decisions of domestic courts should be regarded as manifestations of State practice. Amongst modern scholars there is near unanimity on this point.[891] Only orthodox positivist theorists have in the past denied any direct law-creating effect to national court decisions.[892] A number of international tribunals, including the Special Tribunal for Lebanon,[893] have explicitly recognized judicial decisions as a form of State practice.[894] This is also the ICJ's position.[895] For instance, in the *Arrest Warrant* case, the ICJ stated that it had 'carefully examined State practice, including (. . ..) those decisions of national higher courts, such as the House of Lords or the French Court of Cassation'.[896] In the

---

[891] Wuerth, 'National Court Decisions and *Opinio Juris*'; ILA, Final Report, 2000, p. 17; Ferrari-Bravo, 'Méthodes de recherche de la coutume internationale', pp. 283–284; Akehurst, 'Custom as a Source of International Law', pp. 39–40; Shaw, *International Law*, pp. 82–83; Henckaerts and Doswald-Beck, *Customary International Humanitarian Law*, p. xxxviii; Jia, 'The Relations between Treaties and Custom', p. 102; Gazzini, 'The Role of Customary International Law', p. 692; ILC, First Report, 2013, p. 37; ILC, Second Report, 2014, p. 23; ILC, Draft Conclusions, 2015, conclusion no. 6(3); ILA, 'Preliminary Report, Principles on the Engagement of Domestic Courts with International Law', report by A. Tzanakopoulos, ILA Study Group: Principles on the Engagement of Domestic Courts with International Law, para. 5; Malanczuk, *Akehurst's Modern Introduction to International Law*, pp. 39–40; ILA Report, 2000, p. 14, 18; Barberis, 'Réflexions sur la coutume internationale', p. 32; Dinstein, 'The Interaction between Customary International Law and Treaties', pp. 273, 315–316; Lepard, *Customary International Law*, p. 177 ff; H. Lauterpacht, 'Decisions of Municipal Courts as a Source of International Law', *British YIL*, 10 (1929), pp. 65, 84–85; Crawford, *Brownlie's Principles of Public International Law*, pp. 24, 41 (noting that decisions of national tribunals provide 'indirect evidence of the practice of the state of the forum on the question involved'); Sir Robert Y. Jennings and Sir Arthur Watts (eds.), *Oppenheim's International Law* (9th edn., London: Longman, 1992, vol. 1), p. 41; Philip Moremen, 'National Court Decisions as State Practice: A Transnational Judicial Dialogue?', *North Carolina JIL & Comm Reg* 32 (2006), pp. 263, 265–266; André Nollkaemper, 'The Role of Domestic Courts in the Case Law of the International Court of Justice', *Chinese JIL* 5 (2006), pp. 301, 303–304; Roberts, 'Comparative International Law?', p. 62; Wood and Sender, 'State Practice', para. 15.

[892] See, discussion in: Moremen, 'National Court Decisions as State Practice', pp. 275 ff, 278.

[893] Case No. STL-11-01/I, Interlocutory Decision on the Applicable Law: Terrorism, Conspiracy, Homicide, Perpetration, Cumulative Charging (Appeals Chamber), 16 February 2011, para. 85.

[894] See, ILC, Second Report, 2014, p. 23, providing several examples of cases. It should be added that *domestic* courts' decisions sometimes also explicitly refer to the national court decisions of other States as evidence of State practice. This is, for instance, the case in the United States. See, Moremen, 'National Court Decisions as State Practice', p. 285, citing a number of cases.

[895] Yet, as noted by Nollkaemper, 'The Role of Domestic Courts', p. 304, such references to domestic court decisions by the Court remain exceptional.

[896] *Case Concerning the Arrest Warrant of 11 April 2000 (Democratic Republic of the Congo v. Belgium)*, Judgment, ICJ Rep. 2002, p. 24.

Jurisdictional Immunities of the State case, the Court also stated that 'State practice in the form of judicial decisions supports the proposition that State immunity for *acta jure imperii* continues to extend to civil proceedings for acts occasioning death, personal injury or damage to property committed by the armed forces and other organs of a State in the conduct of armed conflict, even if the relevant acts take place on the territory of the forum State'.[897] In the same case, the Court also held that the 'jurisprudence of a number of national courts' demonstrated States' *opinio juris* on the matter.[898] A number of writers also consider that national court decisions can evidence a State's *opinio juris* (a point that will be further discussed[899]).[900]

One reason why municipal court decisions are considered as evidence of State practice is simply because the judiciary branch is one of the State's organs.[901] Some have drawn an analogy with the doctrine of State responsibility whereby a State is responsible for the internationally unlawful acts (or omissions) committed by its organs, including the judiciary branch.[902] There is, however, no direct link between these two issues.[903] Another reason for considering domestic court decisions as

---

[897] *Jurisdictional Immunities of the State (Germany v. Italy)*, ICJ Rep. 2012, para. 77. See also, at paras. 83–85 (referring to decisions of municipal courts as examples of State practice). See, discussion in: Ingrid Wuerth, 'International Law in Domestic Courts and *the Jurisdictional Immunities of the State Case*', *Melbourne JIL* 13 (2012), p. 819; Nollkaemper, 'The Role of Domestic Courts', pp. 301, 303–304.

[898] *Jurisdictional Immunities of the State, Ibid.*, para. 77 ('That practice is accompanied by *opinio juris*, as demonstrated by the positions taken by States and the jurisprudence of a number of national courts which have made clear that they considered that customary international law required immunity'). The question is examined in: Wuerth, 'National Court Decisions and *Opinio Juris*'.

[899] See, Chapter 4, Section 4.1.5.2.

[900] H. Lauterpacht, 'Decisions of Municipal Courts as a Source of International Law', pp. 84–85; Wuerth, 'National Court Decisions and *Opinio Juris*', pp. 1–2; Wolfke, *Custom in Present International Law*, p. 74; Lepard, *Customary International Law*, p. 179; Moremen, 'National Court Decisions as State Practice', pp. 273–274; Jennings and Watts, *Oppenheim's International Law*, p. 26; Roberts, 'Comparative International Law?', p. 62; Tzanakopoulus, 'Preliminary Report', para. 5; ILC, Second Report, 2014, p. 54 ('The jurisprudence of national courts clearly embodies a sense of legal obligation (. . .) Only when such judgments apply the rule in question in a way which demonstrates, mostly by way of its reasoning, that it is accepted as required under customary international law, could they be relevant as evidence of "acceptance as law"').

[901] Nollkaemper, 'The Role of Domestic Courts', pp. 301, 303; Gazzini, 'The Role of Customary International Law', p. 692.

[902] Arts. 5 and 6, ILC, *Draft Articles on Responsibility of States*.

[903] ILA Report, 2000, p. 17; Moremen, 'National Court Decisions as State Practice', p. 281 ('While there is an appealing symmetry to the analogy to state responsibility, the analogy is merely persuasive, not conclusive. One can question the application of state

evidence of State practice is because in many States, national courts share
the law-making function with the executive and the legislature on matters of foreign affairs.[904] The best example of the role played by domestic
courts in the development of customary norms is in the context of State
immunity:

> The general rule of international law regarding State immunity has devel-
> oped principally from the judicial practice of States. Municipal courts
> have been primarily responsible for the growth and progressive develop-
> ment of a body of customary rules governing the relations of nations in
> this particular connection.[905]

A number of writers have also highlighted the fact that the development
of the principle prohibiting expropriation without compensation has
been largely influenced by United States case-law.[906]

Another reason for considering municipal courts' decisions as evidence of State practice is that they 'often constitute evidence of acceptance of a given practice or norm by the state to which the court
belongs'.[907] Thus, sometimes what a domestic court says on a matter of
international law represents the State's view on the issue. Yet, this is the
very reason why one must carefully assess how much weight is given to
said decisions.[908] As pointed out by the ILC Special Rapporteur, 'domestic judges are not necessarily experts or even trained in public international law; and domestic courts may be influenced by their own State's

responsibility to the formation of international custom. Just because a state is responsible
for the wrongful acts of its organs, that does not necessarily and logically lead to the
conclusion that the acts of any state organ should constitute state practice. The doctrines
of state responsibility and state practice are not directly related, and there is no reason
why a result in one area should control in the other').

[904] Moremen, 'National Court Decisions as State Practice', p. 279.
[905] ILC, 'Report of the International Law Commission on the work of its thirty-second
session', (1980), p. 143. The ILC refers to a number of domestic court cases. The Report
concludes, at p. 147, that 'the rule of State immunity, which was formulated in the early
nineteenth century and was widely accepted in common law countries as well as in a
large number of civil law countries in Europe in that century, was later adopted as a
general rule of customary international law solidly rooted in the current practice of
States'. See also, at p. 149.
[906] Porterfield, 'State Practice and the (Purported) Obligation', p. 174 ff; Sornarajah, *The
International Law on Foreign Investment*, pp. 353–355; K.J. Vandevelde, *Bilateral
Investment Treaties: History, Policy and Interpretation* (Oxford: Oxford University
Press, 2010), pp. 279–280.
[907] Wolfke, *Custom in Present International Law*, p. 74.
[908] Crawford, *Brownlie's Principles of Public International Law*, p. 41 ('the value of these
decisions varies considerably, and individual decisions may present a narrow, parochial
outlook or rest on an inadequate use of sources'); ILC, Second Report, 2014, p. 24.

view of whether or not a particular rule of customary international law exists, and are anyway likely to (and perhaps should) adopt a cautious approach to developing the law'.[909] In a survey of US cases, one writer has concluded that courts are likely to follow the guidance of the executive branch when issues that relate to customary law are involved.[910] In its work on State immunities, the ILC explained how domestic courts' decisions can be influenced by the executive branch:

> It is not uncommon that, in litigation involving foreign States or Governments, the executive branch of the Government of a certain State may have a more or less active role to play or may intervene or participate, at one stage or another, in legal proceedings before the court. (...) Therefore a decision which, on the face of it, is purely judicial, may have been influenced by political considerations emanating from the territorial Government or its political branch, because the matter may have the potential tendency to affect adversely the conduct of foreign affairs, or the Government may run the risk of political embarrassment in international relations as well as in the internal political arena. (...) Since the judiciary, in principle as well as in practice, is generally independent of the executive in matters of adjudication, it appears that the courts are not always bound to follow the lead of the executive in every case. If the executive suggests that immunity should be accorded, the courts are likely to follow suit, although not in every conceivable instance.[911]

In any event, the proposition that a domestic court decision always represents that State's view on matters of international law is only valid for *certain* States, not all of them.[912] It may be a valid proposition for undemocratic States where there is no real separation of powers between the judiciary and the executive branches. For instance, one can legitimately assume that the position of the courts of, say, Zimbabwe represents their government's views. Yet, for democratic States it is difficult to simply *assume* that a court decision on matters of international law will *necessarily* represent the position of that State. For this reason, even if, as a matter of principle, domestic courts' decisions should be considered as evidence of State practice for the creation of customary rules, the *actual weight* to be

---

[909] ILC, First Report, 2013, p. 37. See also: Wolfke, *Custom in Present International Law*, p. 75 ('the role played by judicial organs in the formation of customary international law should be reduced to a necessary minimum').

[910] Phillip R. Trimble, 'A Revisionist View of Customary International Law', *UCLA L. Rev.* 33 (1986), pp. 684–687, adding that there were few cases where the court applied customary international law when the executive branch had not expressed an opinion.

[911] ILC, 'Report of the International Law Commission on the work of its thirty-second session', (1980), p. 150.

[912] Wood and Sender, 'State Practice', para. 15.

given to such decisions will depend on a number of factors and circumstances. In other words, *not all* judicial decisions should be given the same weight as evidence of State practice for the creation of customary rules. For a start, 'higher' courts' decisions should be given more weight than those of 'lower' courts.[913] Also, a case that has been reversed on a particular point is 'no longer likely to be considered as practice'.[914]

One interesting question that has divided scholars is the weight that should be given to a domestic court decision whenever it *contradicts* the government's position on matters of international law. For some, contradictory domestic court decisions should simply not count as relevant State practice and the position of the executive branch should always prevail.[915] For others, the very existence of this conflict may have an overall 'neutralizing' effect on the general weight to be given to that State's practice. Thus, it has been suggested that a State's internally conflicting views (between the executive and the judiciary branches) may simply render such practice irrelevant for custom creation purposes. For the ILA, 'the internal uniformity or consistency which is needed for a State's practice to count towards the formation of a customary rule may anyway be prejudiced'.[916] This also seems to be the position adopted by the ILC Special Rapporteur Wood, for whom 'State's practice should be "taken as a whole"' (i.e. 'account has to be taken of all available practice of a particular State')' and adding that '[w]here a State speaks in several voices, its practice is ambivalent, and such conflict may well weaken the weight to be given to the practice concerned'.[917]

For others, *both* the executive and the judiciary branches' positions should count as State practice.[918] Thus, the question is not so much one

---

[913] Roberts, 'Comparative International Law?', p. 62; Lepard, *Customary International Law*, p. 177; ILC, Second Report, 2014, p. 24.
[914] ILC, Second Report, 2014, p. 24; Wood and Sender, 'State Practice', para. 15.
[915] Tzanakopoulos, 'Preliminary Report', para. 7: '[I]t is only when decisions of domestic courts are *not* rejected by the State's executive that they constitute State practice or that they can be taken to express the State's *opinio juris*, so that they are capable of contributing towards the formation or development of customary law'.
[916] ILA, Final Report, 2000, p. 18. *Contra*: Wuerth, 'National Court Decisions and *Opinio Juris*', pp. 6–7.
[917] ILC, Second Report, 2014, p. 33. See also, ILC, Draft Conclusions, 2015, conclusion no. 7: ('1. Account is to be taken of all available practice of a particular State, which is to be assessed as a whole; 2. Where the practice of a particular State varies, the weight to be given to that practice may be reduced').
[918] Wuerth, 'International Law in Domestic Courts', pp. 9–10 ('state practice ought not be limited to one state practice attributed to each state, for this fails to capture in important ways what state practice actually is').

of *admissibility*, but rather a question of determining whether the position of the executive or the judiciary branches should be given more *weight* as evidencing State practice.[919] This is a sound approach. It has been argued that the executive's position should naturally prevail over the judiciary's: 'since it is the executive which has primary responsibility for the conduct of foreign relations, that organ's formal position ought usually to be accorded more weight than conflicting positions of the legislature or the national courts'.[920] In other words, as put by Mendelson, 'it is not that the [position taken by national courts] does not count as State practice, but that it does not normally count as much – does not weigh as heavily – as an act of the Government'.[921] Other writers have rejected this argument that is typically invoked for supporting executive primacy.[922] For them, priority should be given to the branch which is in control over the question as a matter of domestic law.[923] Thus, one example often referred to by writers[924] is the United States, where the determination of issues related to sovereign immunity is assigned exclusively to the judiciary branch by statute. These writers point out, however, that in practical terms this 'may frequently lead to favoring the executive'.[925]

In sum, while the position taken by a domestic court should normally count as relevant evidence of State practice, this will not always be the case. Thus, the position of the executive on matters of international law will normally *weigh more heavily* than that of its courts whenever their positions differ.

3.3.6.3.2 Investor-State arbitration
Generally, domestic courts rarely deal with matters involving investment law.[926] Unsurprisingly,

---

[919] Mendelson, 'The Formation of Customary International Law', p. 200.

[920] ILA, Final Report, 2000, p. 18.

[921] Mendelson, 'The Formation of Customary International Law', p. 200.

[922] Wuerth, 'National Court Decisions and *Opinio Juris*', p. 2 ff.

[923] Nollkaemper, 'National Courts and the International Rule of Law', p. 270; Roberts, 'Comparative International Law?', p. 62 ('[w]here inconsistencies emerge, the conflicting practice must be weighed, considering factors such as which branch of government has authority over the matter'); Wuerth, 'National Court Decisions and *Opinio Juris*', p. 5; Lepard, *Customary International Law*, p. 173.

[924] Moremen, 'National Court Decisions as State Practice', p. 293.

[925] Wuerth, 'National Court Decisions and *Opinio Juris*', p. 5, adding that 'but at other times it may favor courts or legislatures'. She explains both the advantages and the inconvenience of this approach.

[926] A number of relevant domestic courts' decisions can be found at this page: http://italaw .com/awards/other-proceedings. One exceptional situation is anti-suit injunctions issued

the present author has found no investor-State arbitration award concretely examining the role played by domestic courts' decisions in the
formation of customary rules. The only (somewhat) relevant case that I
have found is the *Enron* case (annulment phase). As previously mentioned,[927] the claimant requested that the provisional stay of enforcement
of an award be lifted (or if stayed, that it be conditional to Argentina
providing financial security). One of the arguments put forward was that
'a recent Argentine Supreme Court decision supports the doctrine that
Argentine Courts may review and vacate ICSID awards'.[928] The claimant
also indicated that 'this case was invoked by domestic courts as grounds
for ordering the suspension of the arbitration proceedings in the
National Grid case'.[929] The Committee noted that this case (and the
National Grid case) did not involve 'arbitrations under the ICSID
Convention' and the circumstances of this case were 'not indicative of
Argentina's intentions with respect to awards rendered against it in
proceedings under the ICSID Convention'.[930] In other words, the
Tribunal did not give much weight to this decision as representing
Argentina's position on matters of enforcement of ICSID awards. One
reason why this court decision was given little weight was because
Argentina's Attorney General argued at the hearing that Argentine courts
could review and vacate ICSID awards.[931] The Tribunal therefore indi-
cated that the Attorney General was 'speaking with the authority of the
Argentine Republic at the hearing'.[932] In other words, the Tribunal

---

by domestic courts of the respondent State in an ICSID case. See, *Société Générale de
Surveillance S.A. (SGS) v. Pakistan*, ICSID Case No. ARB/01/13, decision of the Supreme
Court of Pakistan of 3 July 2002 (in: *Arb. Int.*, 19 (2003), p. 182), Procedural Order No. 2,
16 October 2002 (in: *ICSID Rev.*, 18(1) (2003), p. 301).

[927] See, Chapter 3, Section 3.3.4.2.2.2.

[928] *Enron Corporation and Ponderosa Assets, L.P. v. Argentina*, Decision on the Argentine
Republic's Request for a Continued Stay of Enforcement of the Award (Rule 54 of the
ICSID Arbitration Rules), 7 October 2008, para. 14, referring to: Corte Suprema de
Justicia, June 1, 2004, *Cartellone c. Hidronor*, Fallos 327–1881.

[929] *Ibid.*, para. 93.　　　[930] *Ibid.*

[931] *Ibid.*, para. 85: 'The position stated by the *Procurador del Tesoro de la Nación* (Attorney-
General), speaking with the authority of the Argentine Republic at the hearing of the stay
application, appears to be that in the event that the award is not annulled Argentina
would not comply with the Award forthwith, but would instead look to the Claimants to
bring proceedings for the enforcement of the Award under the provisions of Argentine
law that give effect to Article 54 of the ICSID Convention'. The Committee held that such
a position was 'in apparent non-compliance with Argentina's international law treaty
obligations owed to the United States under Article VII(6) of the BIT and under Article
53(1) of the ICSID Convention'.

[932] *Ibid.*, para. 85.

considered said pleadings to be Argentina's *official position* on the matter. It therefore gave limited weight to the domestic court decision.

One situation where domestic court decisions can play a role in international investment law is in the context of the enforcement of awards where proceedings are always started by the investor in the courts of a country *other* than the Respondent State (which has not respected the award).[933] As a matter of principle, in said context the decision of a domestic court of State A can be considered as evidencing the practice of that State on matters of State immunity. In other words, what a domestic court of State A says on a fundamental issue of State immunity involving an international arbitration award is likely to represent State A's view on the matter. Another situation where domestic courts' decisions can potentially play an important role in international investment law is in the context of judicial review proceedings. These proceedings can be started before the domestic courts of the country where the arbitration took place (for instance, under the UNCITRAL Arbitration Rules[934] and the ICSID Additional Facility Rules[935]). As a matter of principle, nothing should prevent such a decision from being considered as evidence of State practice. Yet, there are situations where this is not the case. The following paragraph will examine one situation where only *limited weight* should be given to a domestic court decision in the context of setting aside proceedings.

In a number of NAFTA cases, setting aside litigation was brought before the courts of the *respondent State* in the arbitration proceedings. A good example is the *SD Myers* v. *Canada* case in which Canada (the respondent State in the arbitration proceedings) commenced a setting aside procedure before the Federal Court of Canada.[936] In this context,

---

[933] *Enron Corporation and Ponderosa Assets, L.P. v. Argentina*, ICSID Case No. ARB/01/3, Decision on the Application for Annulment of the Argentine Republic, 30 July 2010, para. 70: 'According to material provided by the Claimants, only four ICSID cases have reached the stage of enforcement before local courts, and in each of these cases the courts were those of a third State, rather than the courts of the State against which the award had been rendered. Argentina has not sought to contradict this information. The Committee has not been pointed to any case in which an award creditor has brought proceedings for recognition and enforcement of an award in the legal system of the State against which the award was given'.

[934] These Arbitration Rules were approved by the United Nations General Assembly on 15 December 1976, U.N. GAOR, 31st Session, Supp. No. 17, at 46, Ch. V, Sec. C, UN Doc. A/31/17, 1976.

[935] ICSID Additional Facility for the Administration of Conciliation, Arbitration and Fact-Finding Proceedings, created in 1978.

[936] *Canada (Attorney General)* v. *SD Myers*, [2004] F.C.J. No. 29 (Fed. Ct.).

the decision of a Canadian domestic court should not be considered as the most valuable source of evidence of Canada's practice in the event that it were to contradict the position of the Canadian government. This is simply because Canada's actual position on matters of international law is being represented by its *own pleadings* as the claimant in the setting aside proceedings. This is a specific situation where a domestic court decision should be given little value when assessing Canada's practice.[937] The same limited weight should also be given to the decision of an US court in the *Loewen* case where the United States (the respondent State in the arbitration proceedings) commenced setting aside proceedings before its own courts.[938] Similarly, a number of other setting aside proceedings were started in the domestic courts of a NAFTA Party that was *not* involved as the respondent State in the arbitration proceedings.[939] Thus, in four cases, Mexico, the respondent State in the arbitration proceedings, started setting aside proceedings before US courts (*Thunderbird*[940]) and Canadian courts (*Feldman,*[941] *Metalclad*[942] and *Cargill*[943]).[944] In some of these cases, the State where the setting aside proceedings took place intervened in the proceedings. This was, for

[937] Another example is the case of *Council of Canadians et al.* v. *Attorney General of Canada*, Ontario Court of Appeal, judgment of 30 November 2006, para. 2, where the Court held that government of Canada had not breached its own constitution when it entered into NAFTA. This is also a situation where the actual practice of Canada is clearly reflected in its own pleadings before the Court rather than in the Court's decision. The same issue arose in the *Hupacasath First Nation* v. *Canada (Minister of Foreign Affairs)* case where the claimant (a Native Aboriginal group in Canada) challenged the legality of the Canada–China BIT in the Federal Court of Canada.

[938] *Loewen* v. *United States*, 2005 U.S. Dist. LEXIS 44999 (DC Dist. Ct.). See also *Canfor Corporation* v. *United States*, where the claimant started set aside proceedings before a US Court against the United States: United States District Court for the District of Columbia, Civil Action No. 07–1905 (RMC), 14 August 2008.

[939] Another similar situation arose where the United States intervened (filing an *amicus* brief) in the setting aside proceedings in the case of *BG Group* v. *Argentina* before different US courts, including the US Supreme Court: 'Brief of Amicus Curiae the United States in Support of Vacatur and Remand', 3 September 2013, 'Brief for the United States as Amicus Curiae', 10 May 2013.

[940] *International Thunderbird Gaming Corporation* v. *Mexico*, 473 F. Supp. 2d 80; 2007 U.S. Dist. LEXIS 10070 (D.C. Dist. Ct.): *International Thunderbird Gaming Corporation* v. *Mexico*, 255 Fed. Appx. 531; 2007 U.S. App. LEXIS 26720 (U.S. Court of Appeals for the DC Circuit).

[941] *Mexico* v. *Karpa*, [2003] O.T.C. 1070 (Ont. SCJ); *Mexico* v. *Karpa*, [2005] O.J. No. 16 (ONCA).

[942] *Mexico* v. *Metalclad Corp.*, [2001] B.C.J. No. 950 (BCSC).

[943] *Mexico* v. *Cargill, Inc.*, [2011] O.J. No. 4320 (Ont. CA).

[944] In *Bayview Irrigation District et al.* v. *Mexico*, ICSID Case No. ARB(AF)/05/1, the claimant started setting aside proceedings before a Canadian court: *Bayview Irrigation*

instance, the situation in the *Metalclad* case, where Canada explained its official position on the case as well as on other treaty interpretation matters to the British Columbia court.[945] This is clearly a situation where Canada's actual practice is found in the submission it filed with the Court.[946]

3.4   Investment arbitration arbitral awards

Under Article 38 of the ICJ Statute, 'judicial decisions' are considered along with the 'writings of eminent publicists' as a 'subsidiary means for the determination of rules of law'.[947] As such, judicial decisions and arbitral awards are not *formal* sources of international law.[948] Unlike treaties, custom and general principles of law, judicial decisions are not means for the *creation* of the law.[949] According to Pellet, they are 'documentary "sources" indicating where the [ICJ] can find evidence of the existence of the rules it is bound to apply by virtue of the three other sub-paragraphs [i.e. treaties, custom and general principles of law]'.[950] This is also the conclusion reached by the *Methanex* Tribunal.[951] Yet, as Alvarez notes, awards 'are more than just' a *subsidiary* source of law:

District et al. v. *Mexico*, Reasons for Judgment, J. Allen, Superior Court of Justice, 5 May 2008.

[945]   *Mexico* v. *Metalclad*, Supreme Court of British Columbia, Canada, 'Outline of Argument of Intervenor Attorney General of Canada', 16 February 2001, para. 2.

[946]   The same conclusion applies to the cases of *Mexico* v. *Karpa*, [2003] O.T.C. 1070 (Ont. SCJ) and *United Mexican States* v. *Cargill, Inc.*, [2011] O.J. No. 4320 (Ont. CA), both involving decisions of Canadian courts where Canada also intervened in the proceedings. It should be added that in the *Cargill* case the United States also intervened before Ontario's Court of Appeal.

[947]   Gilbert Guillaume, 'Can Arbitral Awards Constitute a Source of International Law under Article 38 of the ICJ Statute?', in Y. Banifatemi (ed.), *Precedent in International Arbitration* (Huntington: Juris Publishing, 2008), p. 105.

[948]   Lauterpacht, *The Development of International Law by the International Court* (London: Stevens and Sons, 1958), pp. 20–21. *Contra*: Alvarez, 'A Bit on Custom', pp. 45–46.

[949]   E. de Brabandere, 'Judicial and Arbitral Decisions as a Source of Rights and Obligations', in T. Gazzini and E. de Brabandere (eds.), *International Investment Law: The Sources of Rights and Obligations* (Leiden; Boston: Martinus Nijhoff, 2012), p. 248. See also: ILC, Draft Conclusions, 2015, conclusion no. 13(1): 'Decisions of international courts and tribunals, in particular of the International Court of Justice, concerning the existence and content of rules of customary international law are a subsidiary means for the determination of such rules'.

[950]   A. Pellet, 'Article 38', in A. Zimmermann *et al.* (eds.), *The Statute of the International Court of Justice: A Commentary* (2nd edn., Oxford: Oxford University Press, 2012), p. 784.

[951]   *Methanex Corporation* v. *United States*, Partial Award, 7 August 2002, para. 141.

In today's world, states—and not merely fellow investor-state arbitrators—accord considerable more deference to the relevant decisions of supra-national dispute settlement bodies than they do to a law review article. (. . .) Arbitral decisions, like other decisions reached by respected international adjudicative bodies, have acquired such an influence on international law because they are frequently better than the few alternative places we have to look for guidance with respect to what the law is. (. . .) They are also more likely to offer useful "neutral" guidance for law interpreters than diplomatic actions by self-interested states. (. . .) it is scarcely surprising if those charged with resolving disputes turn to how others have resolved comparable disputes. The well-crafted arbitral decision, like well-crafted judicial decisions issued by any court, national or international, is intended to persuade both the disputants that have entrusted their case to third-party adjudication and the wider community to which the third party adjudicators owe their legitimacy.[952]

Roberts refers to the 'lawmaking' function of arbitral tribunals through States' delegation of interpretative powers.[953] She further explains how an 'interpretive dialogue' between States that are party to treaties and arbitral tribunals with 'shared interpretative powers' works:

States, as treaty parties, would take an active role in interpreting their investment treaties, generating state practice that tribunals could take into account when interpreting investment treaties. A state could do so in numerous ways, such as by modifying its model bilateral investment treaty (BIT), formulating pleadings as a respondent, intervening in arbitrations as a nondisputing party, issuing public statements about its understanding of particular provisions, and reaching joint interpretations with the other treaty parties, including through bodies like the FTC. (. . .) This dialogue is ongoing. The generation of state practice should influence the interpretations issued by tribunals, but their awards are also likely to have an impact on the subsequent views and practices of the treaty parties, especially when they are persuasively reasoned, as tribunal awards affect the political status quo and resulting expectations. After a tribunal has issued an award, the treaty parties should examine its reasoning and determine whether they accept or reject particular interpretations. They should then find ways to make their views known as a matter of state practice to help influence the next case in the series. The result should be an interactive and iterative development of investment treaty law.[954]

---

[952] Alvarez, 'A Bit on Custom', pp. 45–46. See also: Alvarez, 'The Public International Law Regime Governing International Investment', p. 484 ('There is also increasing recognition that another group of non-State actors, namely party-appointed investor-State arbitrators, have joined other international adjudicators as *de facto* law-makers').
[953] Roberts, 'Power and Persuasion in Investment Treaty International', pp. 189–190.
[954] *Ibid.*, p. 194.

What is clear is that under Article 59 of the ICJ Statute, the decisions of the ICJ have no 'binding force except between the parties'. There is no doctrine of *stare decisis* under international law.[955] The same is true for international investment law. Thus, ICSID Article 53(1) provides that '[t]he award shall be binding *on the parties*', and, therefore, not on *other* parties. But in view of the fact that investment tribunals are increasingly relying on the decisions of other investment tribunals when settling disputes, the question of the binding nature of these awards has become one of the most controversial question currently being debated by scholars. This question is outside the scope of this book. It is sufficient to say that the prevailing view remains that awards have no binding effect on *ad hoc* investment tribunals that are independent from each other. Increasingly, scholars,[956] and some tribunals,[957] are nevertheless referring to the existence of a *de facto* practice of precedents in investment arbitration. But, as noted by one writer, 'the massive use of precedents by investment tribunals in their reasoning is not the equivalent of the development of a rule of binding precedents'.[958] Clearly, tribunals have no *obligation* to follow precedents. However, the conclusion that awards are not formally a source of obligation should not undermine their practical importance. Thus, this *de facto* practice of precedents has had an impact on the development and harmonization of investment arbitration.[959] In doctrine, some writers now speak of the emergence of a 'common law of investment protection, with a substantially shared understanding of its general tenets'.[960] Some writers have in fact argued

---

[955] The question is examined in: de Brabandere, 'Judicial and Arbitral Decisions as a Source of Rights and Obligations', pp. 253 ff., 286; ILC, Third Report, 2015, p. 43.

[956] McLachlan, *et al., International Investment Arbitration*, p. 18; Hirsch, 'Sources of International Investment Law', p. 20; d'Aspremont, 'International Customary Investment Law', p. 43; Grisel, 'The Sources of Foreign Investment Law', p. 225 (examining the process through which the rule allowing the award of compound interests in investment disputes has emerged and arguing that 'precedent (broadly defined as the emergence of legal norms through judicial accretion) is the material source of foreign investment law, namely the process through which norms of foreign investment law emerge', see also at pp. 234–235). See also: de Brabandere, 'Judicial and Arbitral Decisions as a Source of Rights and Obligations', p. 257.

[957] *Suez, Sociedad General de Aguas de Barcelona, S.A.*and*Vivendi Universal, S.A.* v. *Argentina*, ICSID Case No. ARB/03/19, Decision on Liability, 30 July 2010, para. 189.

[958] de Brabandere, 'Judicial and Arbitral Decisions as a Source of Rights and Obligations', p. 286.

[959] *Ibid.*, pp. 266 ff., 287; Roberts, 'Power and Persuasion in Investment Treaty International', p. 189.

[960] McLachlan, *et al., International Investment Arbitration*, pp. 18–21. See also: Sourgens, 'Law's Laboratory', p. 79.

that 'reference to precedent increasingly replaces customary international law as a source of a multilateral order in the absence of a multilateral treaty'.[961] Similarly, according to McLachlan, 'the result is a
convergence, on these issues, between treaty practice and custom, in
which the modern understanding of the content of the customary right
is being elaborated primarily through the treaty jurisprudence', adding
that 'indeed, an application of the classic test for the formation of a rule of
custom in this area would have little meaning, given the paucity of any
State practice outside the treaties' reach'.[962] Once again, these issues are
beyond the scope of this book.

The present section examines a much narrower issue: whether arbitral
awards can be considered as evidence of *State* practice for the formation
of custom. Although some writers (rather ambiguously) seem to be
listing international judicial decisions and awards as examples of State
practice,[963] it is clear that this is *not* the case.[964] The reason is simple:
decisions and awards 'emanate from tribunals that are created or
appointed by but act independently from States'.[965] It is simply wrong
to suggest that since 'the authority of international courts and tribunals to
settle a dispute between States derives from agreement of the States
involved, judgments of such courts and tribunals may be seen, indirectly,
as manifestations of the practice of the States that have agreed to confer
on them such authority and the mandate to apply international – including customary – law'.[966] It does not matter that tribunals get their
jurisdiction over disputes based on States' agreements.[967] Awards are
the product of *tribunals, not States*. For this reason, awards simply cannot

[961] Stephan W. Schill, 'From Sources to Discourse: Investment Treaty Jurisprudence as the New Custom?', in *Is There an Evolving Customary International Law on Investment?* (London: BIICL, 2011), p. 2.

[962] McLachlan, 'Investment Treaties and General International Law', p. 394.

[963] Malanczuk, *Akehurst's Modern Introduction to International Law*, pp. 39–40; Shaw, *International Law*, pp. 82–83; Barberis, 'Réflexions sur la coutume internationale', p. 34 ('Le droit coutumier peut également être créé par le biais des décisions des tribunaux internationaux').

[964] Henckaerts and Doswald-Beck, *Customary International Humanitarian Law*, p. Xxxviii; Mendelson, 'The Formation of Customary International Law', p. 202; ILC, Second Report, 2014, p. 31.

[965] Gazzini, 'The Role of Customary International Law', pp. 692–693.

[966] Treves, 'Customary International Law', para. 53.

[967] ILA Report, 2000, p. 18 ('Although international courts and tribunals ultimately derive their authority from States, it is not appropriate to regard their decisions as a form of State practice').

be considered as evidence of *State practice*.[968] Similarly, what matters is the *opinio juris* of States, not that of arbitrators.[969]

In the current debate regarding the lack of consistency of arbitral awards (an issue not addressed in this book) it has been argued that if tribunals were to follow the precedents of previous tribunals a 'customary' rule of *jurisprudence constante* could eventually emerge.[970] Yet, however desirable the existence of a theory of precedents may be, it cannot be considered as a 'rule' of customary international law for the simple reason that it would be based on the practice of *tribunals*, and not that of States.

However, this being said, one should *not* conclude that awards are *irrelevant* to the development of custom. Thus, as previously mentioned,[971] judges sometimes *confirm* the existence of customary rules.[972] For Shahabuddeen, an award 'may recognise the existence of a

---

[968] Lauterpacht, *The Development of International Law*, pp. 20–21 ('[d]ecisions of international courts (...) are not direct evidence of the practice of States or of what States conceive to be the law'); Mohamed Shahabuddeen, *Precedent in the World Court* (Cambridge: Cambridge University Press, 1997), p. 71 ('It is difficult to regard a decision of the Court [or an international tribunal] as being in itself an expression of State practice ... A decision made by it is an expression not of the practice of the litigating States, but of the judicial view taken of the relations between them on the basis of legal principles which must necessarily exclude any customary law which has not yet crystallised'); Porterfield, 'State Practice and the (Purported) Obligation', p. 193; Henckaerts and Doswald-Beck, *Customary International Humanitarian Law*, p. xxxviii; Alberto Alvarez-Jimenez, 'Methods for the Identification of Customary International Law in the International Court of Justice's Jurisprudence: 2000–2009', *ICLQ*, 60 (2011), p. 709; Wolfke, *Custom in Present International Law*, p. 170; Lepard, *Customary International Law*, p. 184; Stephen M. Schwebel, 'Is Neer far from Fair and Equitable?', *Arb. Int'l* 27(4) (2011), p. 557.

[969] See, however the comment by Hirsch, 'Sources of International Investment Law', p. 10 ('A sense of obligation [i.e., whether a certain behavior is considered as legally obligatory or not] may be manifested by various means, including states' declarations, resolutions of international organizations, international treaties and decisions of international tribunals') suggesting that the *opinio juris* of States can be manifested by awards.

[970] Gabrielle Kaufmann-Kohler, 'Arbitral Precedent: Dream, Necessity or Excuse?', *Arb. Int'l*, 23 (2007), p. 377: 'Another approach to foster consistency may be for arbitral tribunals systemically to rely on the rules applied in a consistent line of cases and to depart from them only for very compelling reasons. This would actually be a *stare decisis* doctrine applied not to a single decision, but to a line of cases, or a *jurisprudence constante*. With time, this practice could even develop into customary international law. It would imply not only a well established practice but also an *opinio juris*, namely, *the belief among states, investors and arbitrators* that, in the absence of compelling reasons to do otherwise, a tribunal must follow the solution arising from a consistent line of earlier cases' (emphasis added).

[971] See, discussion in Chapter 1, Section 1.5.1.

[972] Gazzini, 'The Role of Customary International Law', pp. 692–693.

new customary law and in that limited sense it may no doubt be regarded *as the final stage of development*, but, *by itself, it cannot create one*'.[973] In other words, while awards do not have an effect in the creation of a new rule of custom, they may nevertheless have an important role by subsequently *recognizing* that the rule has crystallized into custom. An award can therefore be considered as evidence of the existence of a rule of custom.[974] For Crawford, 'the judgments of the International Court and other international tribunals have a role in the recognition and authentication of rules of customary international law'.[975] In fact, as previously mentioned,[976] the actual role of a tribunal goes beyond merely 'revealing' or confirming the existence of any given norm of custom. A statement by a tribunal on whether or not a rule exists may have a significant influence on the *very development* of said rule.[977] In that sense, awards 'have a formative effect on custom by crystallizing emerging rules';[978] they are a 'powerful custom-making factor'.[979] In a recent Memorandum, the ILC Secretariat made the following observations about how, in the past, the Commission has concretely used court decisions to identify custom:

- 'The commission has, on some occasions, relied upon decisions of international courts or tribunals as authoritatively expressing the status of a rule of customary international law';[980]

---

[973] Shahabuddeen, *Precedent in the World Court*, p. 71 (emphasis added).

[974] *Restatement of the Law Third*, para. 102 rep. note 1 ('[T]he "judicial decisions and the teachings of the most highly qualified publicists of the various nations," mentioned in Article 38(1) (d) of the Statute of the Court . . . are not sources in the same sense because they are not ways in which law is made or accepted, but opinion evidence as to whether some rule has in fact become or been accepted as international law'); Porterfield, 'State Practice and the (Purported) Obligation', p. 193; Wolfke, *Custom in Present International Law*, p. 145.

[975] Crawford, *Brownlie's Principles of Public International Law*, p. 19; Paparinskis, *The International Minimum Standard*, p. 17 ('judgements (. . .) may authoritatively and accurately reflect the content of rules of international law, representing one of the storehouses from which the content of rules can be extracted').

[976] See, discussion in Chapter 1, Section 1.5.2.

[977] Pellet, 'Article 38', p. 789 ('[T]here is no doubt that, in reality, the international jurisprudence and, primarily, the case law of the Court has been a powerful tool of consolidation and of evolution of international law').

[978] Roberts, 'Traditional and Modern Approaches to Customary International Law', p. 775. See also: Hirsch, 'Sources of International Investment Law', p. 18 ('international courts [and remarkably the ICJ] take part in the law-making process and significantly influence the development of international law').

[979] Wolfke, *Custom in Present International Law*, p. 170.

[980] ILC, Memorandum, 2013, p. 25.

- 'The commission has often relied upon judicial pronouncements as a consideration in support of the existence or non-existence of a rule of customary international law';[981]
- 'At times, the Commission has also relied upon decisions of international courts or tribunals, including arbitral awards, as secondary sources for the purpose of identifying relevant State practice'.[982]

A number of investment tribunals have addressed the question of whether or not awards should be considered as evidence of State practice. Thus, NAFTA tribunals have all concluded, as the *Merrill & Ring* Tribunal did, that 'judicial decisions, while not a source of the law in themselves, are a fundamental tool for the interpretation of the law and have contributed to its clarification and development'.[983] NAFTA Parties have also consistently taken this position.[984] Similarly, while the *Glamis* Tribunal stated that awards 'do not constitute State practice and thus cannot create or prove customary international law',[985] it added that awards can also 'serve as illustrations of customary international law if they involve an examination of customary international law'.[986] The same conclusion was reached by the *Cargill* ruling, which stated that awards 'do not create customary international law but rather, at most, reflect customary international law'.[987] The Tribunal added that 'the evidentiary weight to be afforded [to awards] is greater if the conclusions therein are supported by evidence and analysis of custom'.[988] In fact, the only support for the proposition that arbitral awards can be considered as an element of State practice is found in Wälde's separate opinion in the *Thunderbird* case. He asserted that an 'authoritative jurisprudence' (i.e., 'a consistent line of reasoning [by

[981] *Ibid.*   [982] *Ibid.*, p. 26.
[983] *Merrill & Ring Forestry L.P.* v. *Canada*, UNCITRAL, Award, 31 March 2010, para. 188, see also, at para. 206 ('judicial decisions, as a subsidiary means for the determination of the rules of law, are not lightly to be dismissed').
[984] *Glamis Gold Ltd* v. *United States*, Award, 14 May 2009, para. 543 (referring to the US position: 'international tribunals do not create customary international law. Only nations create customary international law'), para. 554 ('Customary international law cannot be proven, alleges Respondent, by decisions of international tribunals, as they do not constitute State practice'), see also, at para. 605; *Merrill & Ring Forestry L.P.* v. *Canada*, UNCITRAL, Award, 31 March 2010, para. 169 (referring to the position of Canada: 'arbitral awards are not customary international law and this, Canada believes, is not the meaning the Investor assigns to ADF'), see also, at para. 195.
[985] *Glamis, Ibid.*, para. 605.
[986] *Ibid.* See also, at para. 603 where the Tribunal does not list 'arbitral decisions' amongst the potential 'authoritative sources' of State practice which can demonstrate the existence of a rule of custom.
[987] *Cargill, Inc.* v. *Mexico*, Award, 18 September 2009, para. 277.   [988] *Ibid.*, para. 277.

arbitral tribunals] developing a principle and a particular interpretation of specific treaty obligations'[989]) may 'acquire the character of customary international law and must be respected'.[990]

Tribunals outside NAFTA have also adopted the prevailing view that awards do not constitute evidence of State practice. In the *Railroad* case,[991] this position was adopted by Guatemala (the respondent State)[992] and by two non-disputing treaty parties to these proceedings (El Salvador[993] and the United States) who filed submissions to the Tribunal.[994] The Tribunal agreed that 'as such, arbitral awards do not constitute State practice'.[995] It also added that 'parties in international proceedings use [arbitral awards] in their pleadings in support of their arguments of what the law is on a specific issue' and that it was 'an efficient manner for a party in a judicial process to show what it believes to be the law'.[996] In other words, it is not the award *itself* that should be considered as State practice, but rather the State *pleadings* that refer to the reasoning of an arbitral tribunal.[997]

Finally, it is important to take note of certain ambiguous passages found in a few awards that refer to 'State practice' without actually looking at the

---

[989] *International Thunderbird Gaming Corporation* v. *Mexico*, UNCITRAL, Separate Opinion of Thomas Wälde, 1 December 2005, para. 16.

[990] *Ibid.*

[991] *Railroad Development Corporation (RDC)* v. *Guatemala*, Award, 29 June 2012.

[992] *Ibid.*, paras. 160, 192, 203.

[993] *Ibid.*, para. 159 ('International awards are relevant to the determination of the appropriate interpretation under CAFTA, but only if and to the extent they actually examine State practice resulting from a sense of legal obligation'). See also: *Spence International Investments et al.* v. *Costa Rica*, UNCITRAL (ICSID Case No. UNCT/13/2), Non-disputing party submission by El Salvador, 17 April 2015, para. 6 ('while decisions of arbitral tribunals that discuss State practice might be useful as evidence of the State practice they discuss, arbitral decisions can never substitute for State practice as the *source* of customary international law').

[994] *Railroad Development Corporation (RDC)* v. *Guatemala*, Award, 29 June 2012, paras. 208, 207. In *Bureau Veritas, Inspection, Valuation, Assessment and Control, BIVAC BV* v. *Paraguay*, Further Decision on Objections to Jurisdiction, 9 October 2012, para. 156, the Tribunal referred to the position of Paraguay as follows: 'The Respondent considers that the Claimant's position relies on evidence from scholars and arbitrators, but it is only States that can create customary international law by means of State practice and *opinio juris*. Thus, whether or not scholars and arbitrators had the intention to set out a general standard is irrelevant to the question of the existence of such a standard'.

[995] *Railroad Development Corporation (RDC)* v. *Guatemala*, Award, 29 June 2012, para. 217.

[996] *Ibid.*

[997] The question of State pleadings in arbitration proceedings has been discussed above, see Chapter 3, Section 3.3.4.2.2.

practice of States, but instead at that of tribunals.[998] Other tribunals' reasonings also seem to suggest that awards are an element of customary international law along with State practice. For instance, the Tribunal in *ADF* noted that 'any general requirement to accord "fair and equitable treatment" must be disciplined by being based upon State practice *and judicial or arbitral case law* or other sources of customary *or general international law*'.[999] Parties in NAFTA proceedings have debated what kind of interpretation should be given to this ambiguous passage.[1000]

---

[998] See, *CMS Gas Transmission Company* v. *Argentina*, ICSID Case No. ARB/01/8, Decision on Objections to Jurisdiction, 17 July 2003, para. 47: 'State practice further supports the meaning of this changing scenario. Besides accepting the protection of shareholders and other forms of participation in corporations and partnerships, the concept of limiting it to majority or controlling participations has given way to a lower threshold in this respect. Minority and non-controlling participations have thus been included in the protection granted or have been admitted to claim in their own right. Contemporary practice relating to lump-sum agreements, the decisions of the Iran-United States Tribunal and the rules and decisions of the United Nations Compensation Commission, among other examples, evidence increasing flexibility in the handling of international claims'. See also: *Daimler Financial Services AG* v. *Argentine Republic*, ICSID Case No. ARB/05/1, Award, 22 August 2012, para. 268, where at the end of the following paragraph the reasoning seems to suggest that the Tribunal refers to the *opinio juris* of arbitrators: 'A brief look at the ways in which various investor-State tribunals and States have since resolved the question proves that neither the arbitral community nor more importantly (as public international law is not made primarily by arbitrators) common state practice has yet reached a consensus whereby an MFN clause's reference to "treatment in the territory of the host State" may nowadays be understood as covering the international settlement of disputes. To-date, at least nine known investor-State arbitral panels have found that a particular BIT's MFN clause could be used to modify its international dispute resolution provisions while another ten have reached the opposite result. Eminent arbitrators have come down on opposite sides of the debate, sometimes with respect to the very same treaty – including the Treaty presently under consideration. This relatively even split shows that there is as yet no established *opinio juris*'.

[999] *ADF Group Inc.* v. *United States*, Award, 9 January 2003, para. 184 (emphasis added). A similar passage is also found in: *Total S.A.* v. *Argentina*, Decision on Liability, 27 December 2010, para. 107 'Since this standard is inherently flexible, it is difficult, if not impossible, "to anticipate in the abstract the range of possible types of infringements upon the investor's legal position". *Its application in a given case must take into account relevant State practice and judicial or arbitral case law* as well as the text of the BIT and other sources of customary or general international law' (emphasis added).

[1000] See, *Merrill & Ring Forestry L.P.* v. *Canada*, Award, 31 March 2010, para. 169; *Ibid.*, 'Investor's Reply', 15 December 2008, paras. 308–309; *Ibid.*, 'Canada's Counter-Memorial', 13 May 2008, para. 470; *Ibid.*, 'Canada's Rejoinder', 27 March 2009, paras. 160, 161. See also: *Chemtura Corporation* v. *Canada*, 'Canada's Counter-Memorial', 20 October 2008, para. 744; *Glamis Gold Ltd* v. *United States*, Award, 14 May 2009, paras. 543, 554.

4

Opinio juris

Introduction

As mentioned in Chapter 3, under Article 38(1)b of the Statute of the International Court of Justice (ICJ), the formation of a rule of 'international custom' requires 'general practice' by States for it to be 'accepted as law'.[1] This fourth chapter examines the second requirement that must be demonstrated in order to prove the existence of a customary rule: a State's *opinio juris*.

The definition, the nature and the function of the *opinio juris* requirement raise some of the most controversial questions in international law. According to Thirlway, this question 'has probably caused more academic controversy than all the actual contested claims made by States on the basis of alleged custom, put together'.[2] The ILA has also noted that 'in the real world of diplomacy', these questions regarding the subjective element in customary international law 'may be less problematic than in the groves of Academe'.[3] The present author does not intend to examine the different and contradictory theories put forward by scholars surrounding the somewhat 'mysterious' subjective requirement of *opinio juris*. Moreover, I do not claim to have my own theory on the matter. As explained by ILC Special Rapporteur Wood, the 'theoretical torment which may accompany' the controversial question of the *opinio juris* requirement 'in the books has rarely impeded its application in practice'.[4]

---

[1] Art. 38, Statute of the I.C.J., reprinted in International Court of Justice, Charter of the United Nations, Statute and Rules of Court and other Documents 61 (No. 4 1978).
[2] H.W.A. Thirlway, *International Customary Law and Codification* (Leiden: Sijthoff, 1972), p. 47.
[3] International Law Association, 'Statement of Principles Applicable to the Formation of General Customary International Law', Final Report of the Committee on the Formation of Customary Law, Conference Report London (2000), p. 33 [hereinafter ILA, Final Report, 2000], p. 30.
[4] International Law Commission, 'Second Report on Identification of Customary International Law', by Michael Wood, Special Rapporteur, Sixty-sixth session, Geneva, 5

This is especially true in the context of investor-State arbitration disputes where the *opinio juris* requirement has only played a minimal role. For this reason, the goal of this chapter is twofold. I will first explain the nature and function of the *opinio juris* requirement under international law (Section 4.1). The second section will examine how the *opinio juris* requirement has been interpreted by scholars and effectively applied by tribunals in investor-State arbitration (Section 4.2).

4.1   *Opinio juris* under international law

This first section will examine the nature and function of the *opinio juris* requirement under international law. I will begin by observing that while *opinio juris* is a well-recognized requirement, it nevertheless remains difficult to assess in practical terms (Section 4.1.1). I will then briefly examine some of the controversial questions that have been debated by scholars, including whether or not this requirement is relevant to demonstrate the existence of customary norms (Section 4.1.2). Another theoretical question explored in this section is the so-called chronological paradox regarding how custom rules emerge (Section 4.1.3). I will then explain why it is necessary to demonstrate *opinio juris* in order for a customary rule to emerge (Section 4.1.4). The following section will analyse the different manifestations of *opinio juris,* including the possibility that it may be demonstrated by State practice (Section 4.1.5). In this context, one controversial question will be specifically examined: whether some forms of State conduct (such as statements) can be considered as evidence of *both* the practice of a State and its *opinio juris* (the so-called problem of double-counting).

4.1.1   *A well-recognized requirement but nevertheless difficult to assess*

As mentioned previously, Article 38 of the ICJ Statute uses the terms 'international custom, as evidence of a general practice accepted as law'. It is required that State practice must not only be considered general, uniform and consistent during a certain period of time,[5] but also recognized by these States as 'accepted as law', that is, *obligatory.*[6] This second

May-6 June and 7 July-8 August 2014, UN doc. A/CN.4/672, p. 47 [hereinafter referred to as ILC, Second Report, 2014].
[5] See Chapter 3, Sections 3.2.1 to 3.2.3.
[6] *North Sea Continental Shelf Cases (Federal Republic of Germany* v. *Denmark / Federal Republic of Germany* v. *Netherlands),* ICJ Rep. 1969, p. 44, para. 77.

requirement is generally referred to as the *opinio juris* of States. In other words, it is the fact that they adopt a consistent practice out of a belief or a conviction of their legal obligation to do so.[7] To continue using the colourful house analogy mentioned previously,[8] it 'is the cement of communal *opinio juris* that, when poured over the bricks of general State practice, turns [rules] into an edifice of custom'.[9] What is essential is the *opinio juris of States,* and not that of non-States actors.[10] Moreover, as noted by one author, 'acceptance as law is generally to be sought with respect to the interested States, both those who carry out the practice in question and those in a position to respond to it'.[11]

While the origin of the term *opinio juris* is subject to some controversy,[12] the requirement is well recognized in international law. The ICJ

---

[7] It should be added that a number of writers use a different terminology than *opinio juris* and also apply different conceptual frameworks. For instance, A. D'Amato, *The Concept of Custom in International Law* (Ithaca: Cornell University Press, 1971), pp. 74–87 (see also: A. D'Amato, 'Customary International Law: A Reformulation', *International Legal Theory* (1998), pp. 1–6) uses the concept of 'articulations' of a rule of international law. This approach has been rejected by most writers. For Maurice H. Mendelson, 'The Formation of Customary International Law', *Rec. des cours* 192 (1985), the problem with D'Amato's theory of 'articulations' is the fact that anyone can 'articulate' such a new rule, including scholars: 'It seems, therefore, that if a solitary professor in some obscure "ivory tower" (more likely today to be made of recycled aluminium) manages to get some eccentric idea published in a "leading journal", and decades later some State act is performed which would be consistent with the professor's rule, although the officials concerned in reality had no knowledge of the professor or his writings, this is enough to create a customary rule' (p. 267). See also, the critical analysis of Thirlway, *International Customary Law and Codification*, pp. 49–54. D'Amato's terminology has recently been endorsed by Anthea E. Roberts, 'Traditional and Modern Approaches to Customary International Law: A Reconciliation', *AJIL* 95 (2001), pp. 757–758, for whom State practice (actions) 'can form custom only if accompanied by an articulation of the legality of the action' and *opinio juris* 'concerns statements of belief rather than actual beliefs'.

[8] See, Chapter 1, Section 1.2.2.

[9] Y. Dinstein, 'The Interaction between Customary International Law and Treaties', *Rec. des cours* 322 (2006), p. 296, referring to B. Conforti, 'Cours général de droit international public', *Rec. des cours* 212 (1988), p. 65.

[10] See, discussion in Chapter 3, Section 3.1. See also: B. Lepard, *Customary International Law: A New Theory with Practical Applications* (Cambridge: Cambridge University Press, 2010), p. 186.

[11] ILC, Second Report, 2014, p. 44 (adding that 'In the modern reality of multiple multi-lateral fora such inquiry into what some refer to as "individual *opinio juris*" may be complemented or assisted by a search for "coordinated or general *opinio juris*", that is, acceptance of a certain practice as law (or otherwise) by a general consensus of States'). See: *Military and Paramilitary Activities in and against Nicaragua (Nicaragua v. United States),* Merits, Judgment, ICJ Rep. 1986, p. 109.

[12] Mendelson, 'The Formation of Customary International Law', p. 268; Curtis A. Bradley, 'The Chronological Paradox, State Preferences, and *Opinio Juris*', paper presented at the

has consistently held that evidence of States' *opinio juris* is required in order for a customary norm to emerge. As explained by the Court in the *North Sea Continental Shelf* cases:

> Not only must the acts concerned amount to a settled practice, but they must also be such, or be carried out in such a way, as to be evidence of a belief that this practice is rendered obligatory by the evidence of a rule of law requiring it. The need for such a belief, i.e. the existence of a subjective element, is implicit in the very notion of the *opinio juris sive necessitates*.[13]

States *themselves* have also expressly recognized that custom requires both State practice and *opinio juris*. This is, for instance, the case in the context of international humanitarian law.[14] The necessity of this subjective requirement has also been acknowledged by numerous States in the context of the work of the ILC[15] and in their pleadings before the ICJ,[16] as well as by a number of domestic courts.[17] The work of the ILC also recognizes this subjective requirement.[18]

Although the *opinio juris* requirement is widely recognized, it is nonetheless problematic in many respects. This is because States rarely explain their intention and the reasons for acting in one way or another. They

---

conference 'The Role of *Opinio Juris* in Customary International Law', Duke-Geneva Institute in Transnational Law, Geneva, 2013, p. 2 ff; David J. Bederman, *Custom as a Source of Law* (New York: Cambridge University Press, 2010), p. 173.

[13] *North Sea Continental Shelf Cases*, ICJ Rep. 1969, p. 44, para. 77.

[14] J.B. Bellinger and W.J. Haynes, 'A US Government Response to the International Committee of the Red Cross Study on Customary International Humanitarian Law', *Int Rev Red Cross* 89 (866) (2007), p. 444 ('There is general agreement that customary international law develops from a general and consistent practice of States followed by them out of a sense of legal obligation, or opinio juris'); United Kingdom, 'Legal Adviser of the Foreign and Commonwealth Office, statement at the Meeting of National Committees on International Humanitarian Law of Commonwealth States, Nairobi, 20 July 2005', *British YIL* 76 (2005), pp. 694–695; 'Updated European Union Guidelines on promoting compliance with international humanitarian law', 2009/C 303/06), section 7.

[15] See, the references in: ILC, Second Report, 2014, pp. 9–10.

[16] See, the references in: *Ibid.*   [17] See, the references in: *Ibid.*

[18] International Law Commission, 'Formation and Evidence of Customary International Law, Elements in the Previous Work of the ILC that Could be Particularly Relevant to the Topic', Memorandum by the Secretariat, Sixty-fifth session Geneva, 5 May-7 June and 8 July-9 August 2013, UN doc. A/CN.4/659, p. 17 [ILC, Memorandum, 2013]. See also: ILC, Second Report, 2014, p. 65; International Law Commission, 'Text of the Draft Conclusions Provisionally adopted by the Drafting Committee, Sixty-seventh session, Geneva, 4 May-5 June and 6 July-7 August 2014, 14 July 2015, A/CN.4/L.869 [hereinafter referred to as ILC, Draft Conclusions, 2015], conclusion no. 9(1): 'The requirement, as an element of customary international law, that the general practice be accepted as law (*opinio juris*) means that the practice in question must be undertaken with a sense of legal right or obligation'.

seldom expressly clarify whether or not they believe that they are acting out of a sense of obligation.[19] As noted by Judge Tanaka in his dissenting opinion in the *North Sea Continental Shelf* cases, '[t]his factor, relating to internal motivation and being of a psychological nature, cannot be ascertained very easily, particularly when diverse legislative and executive organs of a government participate in an internal process of decision making in respect of ratification or other State acts'.[20] In the words of one writer, 'we cannot know what States believe' since they are institutions and 'they do not have minds of their own'.[21] It is true that a State is composed of different branches of government involving many individuals (who may all have different views).[22] However, it has been suggested that to identify *opinio juris* as a 'psychological' element is misguided because it 'is more a question of the *positions* taken by the organs of States about international law, in their internal processes and in their interaction with other States, than of their *beliefs*'.[23]

These uncertainties have led writers to offer different explanations regarding the nature and function of *opinio juris*. These theories will be examined in the next section. This analysis will be critical since, as further discussed,[24] a number of scholars have developed alternative theories on *opinio juris* in the field of investment arbitration.

[19] R. Baxter, 'Treaties and Custom', *Rec. des cours* 129 (1970), p. 68 ('The hard fact is that States more often than not do not refer to or exhibit any sense of legal obligation in their own conduct. Mention of "obligation" and "duty" is more often to be found in statements about what other States should do than in a State's assertions about what it itself is doing'). See also: P. Guggenheim, 'Les deux éléments de la coutume en droit international', in *La technique et les principes du droit public. Etudes en l'honneur de Georges Scelle* (Paris: LGDJ, 1950), pp. 275–284; P. Haggenmacher, 'La doctrine des deux éléments du droit coutumier dans la pratique de la Cour internationale', *RGDIP*, 90 (1986), p. 10; L. Ferrari-Bravo, 'Méthodes de recherche de la coutume internationale dans la pratique des États', *Rec. des cours* 192 (1985), p. 253.

[20] *North Sea Continental Shelf Cases*, ICJ Rep. 1969, Dissenting Opinion of Judge Tanaka, p. 176.

[21] Mendelson, 'The Formation of Customary International Law', p. 269. See also: A. D'Amato, 'Custom and Treaty: A Response to Professor Weisburd', *Vand. J. Transnat'l L.*, 21 (1988), p. 471; B. Cheng, 'Custom: The Future of General State Practice In a Divided World', in R.St.J. Macdonald and D.M. Johnston (eds.), *The Structure and Process of International Law: Essays in Legal Philosophy Doctrine and Theory* (The Hague: Martinus Nijhoff, 1983), pp. 513, 530.

[22] ILA, Final Report, 2000, p. 33.

[23] Mendelson, 'The Formation of Customary International Law', p. 269 (emphasis in the original), referring to the work of M. Virally, 'The Sources of International Law', in M. Sorensen (ed.), *Manual of Public International Law* (London et al.: Macmillan, 1968), pp. 133–134.

[24] See, discussion in Chapter 4, Section 4.2.3.3.

4.1.2   Scholarly battle on the relevance of opinio juris

The nature and function of the *opinio juris* requirement is one of the most controversial questions in international law.[25] According to Stern, there is a basic dichotomy between *opinio juris* 'assentiment' and *opinio juris* 'sentiment'.[26] According to the 'objectivists' point of view, *opinio* is the 'expression of a collective conscience of the international community, as the *feeling of being bound by a rule which is imposed out of necessity*'.[27] For them, what is essential is the 'general will' of States, that is, the acceptance of a practice as law 'by the international community at large, rather than the acceptance by each state individually'.[28] *Opinio* therefore stands for the *belief* by States that a certain conduct is obligatory. On the contrary, volontarist scholars define *opinio juris* as a State's *consent* to the development of a binding customary rule.

The debate amongst scholars is also, in its essence, about whether or not it is in fact *necessary* to demonstrate *opinio juris* in order to prove the existence of any customary rule.

At one end of the spectrum, a number of classic scholars have in the past argued that it was in fact *not necessary* to specifically demonstrate States' *opinio juris* for a customary rule to emerge.[29] One comprehensive

---

[25] The different views of writers are examined in: Karol Wolfke, *Custom in Present International Law* (2nd edn., Dordrecht: Nijhoff, 1993), pp. 44–51.

[26] Brigitte Stern, 'Custom at the Heart of International Law', *Duke J Comp & IL* 11 (2001), p. 95. See also: C. Dahlman, 'The Function of opinio juris in Customary International Law', *Nordic JIL* (2012), pp. 330–331: 'Basically, scholars are divided in two main branches. One branch where *opinio juris* stands for some kind of *belief* and one branch where it stands for *acceptance*. According to the belief theory, *opinio juris* is the belief that the practice in question is a norm of international law. A state "recognises" the legal right to act in accordance with the practice as a matter of fact. According to the acceptance-theory *opinio juris* means consent. That a state "recognises" a practice as law means that it approves that all states have a legal right to act in accordance with the practice. These are obviously two very different things. It is one thing to take notice of a practice, and a completely different thing to agree to that practice', emphasis in the original.

[27] Stern, 'Custom at the Heart of International Law', p. 96 (emphasis in the original).

[28] Stephen C. Neff, 'Opinio Juris: Three Concepts Chasing a Label', paper presented at the conference 'The Role of *Opinio Juris* in Customary International Law', Duke-Geneva Institute in Transnational Law, Geneva, 2013, p. 8. For Jörg Kammerhofer, 'Customary International Law Needs both *Opinio* and *Usus*', paper presented at *Ibid.*, p. 5, 'the subjective element needs contain an act of will in order for customary international law to be able to exist as positive norms' and norm results from the 'collective will' of States.

[29] See *inter alia*: H. Kelsen, 'Théorie du droit international coutumier', *Revue internationale de la théorie du droit* (1939), p. 253 ff; H. Kelsen, *Principles of International Law* (2nd edn., New York: Holt, Rinehart and Winston, 1966), p. 450 ('in practice it appears that the opinio juris is commonly inferred from the constancy and uniformity of state conduct. But to the extent that it is so inferred, it is this conduct and not the state of mind that is

illustration of this point of view can be found by examining the position of Mendelson and that of the 2000 ILA Report on the formation of custom (in which Mendelson acted as Chairman of the ILA Committee).[30] The ILA Report does not specifically refer to the subjective element of *opinio juris* in its 'working definition' of custom (defined as a rule 'created and sustained by the constant and uniform practice of States (. . .) in circumstances which give rise to a legitimate expectation of similar conduct in the future').[31] The Report's basic position is that 'it is not *usually* necessary to demonstrate the existence of the subjective element before a customary rule can be said to have come into being. There are, however, circumstances where it is necessary'.[32] According to the ILA, when State practice is uniform, consistent, extensive and representative, *in general* 'it is not necessary to prove the existence of an *opinio juris*' because such belief 'may often be present, or it may be possible to infer it; but it is not a requirement that its existence be demonstrated'.[33] In other words, 'the more the practice, the less the need for the subjective element'.[34] The Report nevertheless adds that there are 'exceptional

---

decisive'); L. Kopelmanas, 'A Custom as Means of the Creation of the International Law', *British YIL* 18 (1937), pp. 127, 139, 140, 148; Guggenheim, 'Les deux éléments de la coutume en droit international', pp. 275–282. It should be added, however, that both Kelsen and Guggenheim have apparently (see, the analysis of J.A. Barberis, 'Nouvelles questions concernant la personnalité juridique internationale', *Rec. des cours* 179 [1983-I], p. 27) changed their views in subsequent writings: H. Kelsen, *Principles of International Law* (New York: Holt, Rinehart and Winston, 1952), p. 307; H. Kelsen, 'Théorie du droit in ternational public', *Rec. des cours* 84 (1953-III), p. 123; P. Guggenheim, *Traité de Droit international public* (2nd edn., Geneva: Librairie Georg, 1967), pp. 103–105.

[30] ILA, Final Report, 2000.

[31] *Ibid.*, p. 8. See also: Mendelson, 'The Formation of Customary International Law', p. 188.

[32] ILA, Final Report, 2000, p. 10 (emphasis in the original).

[33] *Ibid.*, p. 31. See also: Mendelson, 'The Formation of Customary International Law', p. 285 ('I would submit that it is unnecessary, either in theory or (particularly) in practice, to establish the presence either of *opinio juris* or of consent, in most cases'), see also, pp. 196, 286–289; R. Müllerson, 'The Interplay of Objective and Subjective Elements in Customary Law', in K. Wellens (ed.), *International law: Theory and Practice: Essays in Honour of Eric Suy* (The Hague: Nijhoff, 1998), pp. 161–164.

[34] ILA, Final Report, 2000, p. 41. The Report states that there are 'numerous examples where the ICJ has simply referred to the constant and uniform practice of States, without any reference to the subjective element', citing *Fisheries case (United Kingdom v. Norway)*, Judgment, ICJ Rep. 1951, p. 128; *Nottebohm case (Second Phase)*, ICJ Rep. 1955, p. 23; *Barcelona Traction, Light and Power Company, Limited, (Belgium v. Spain)*, Judgment, ICJ Rep. 1970, p. 42, para. 700; *Continental Shelf (Libya v. Malta) case,* Judgment, ICJ Rep. 1985, p. 33, para. 34. See also: Mendelson, 'The Formation of Customary International Law', p. 289: 'where there is a well-established practice, the Court and other international tribunals, not to mention States themselves, tend to conclude that there is a customary rule without looking for proof of *opinio juris* (or any other subjective element), whether

cases'[35] where *opinio juris* does matter. Thus, whenever a State's *opinio juris* is *present*, this will be 'sufficient to establish the existence of a customary rule binding on the State(s) in question'.[36] Conversely, proof of the *absence* of any *opinio juris* by a State 'can prevent that conduct from contributing to the formation of a rule of customary law'[37] which 'may mean that such a rule has not come into existence'.[38] In my view, and as will be further discussed,[39] *opinio juris* is *necessary* and must be demonstrated *in all cases*.

At the other end of the spectrum, the 'historical school of thought', which developed in the nineteenth century, maintains that 'opinio juris is the primary and fundamental component of customary law, with practice serving the subsidiary and superficial role of merely providing evidence of what opinio juris comprises'.[40] In fact, according to some writers *opinio juris* is the *only* constituent element of custom. Cheng, the most famous supporter of this view, developed the concept of 'instant custom', which could arise from a single UN General Assembly Resolution.[41]

In between these two extreme positions is the one adopted by Kirgis, who has put forward the 'sliding scale' theory, According to him, on the one hand, 'very frequent, consistent state practice establishes a customary rule without much (or any) affirmative showing of an *opinio juris*' and, on the other hand, 'a clearly demonstrated *opinio juris* establishes a customary rule without much (or any) affirmative action showing that governments are consistently behaving in accordance with the asserted rule'.[42] Kirgis further explains how to determine whether one is dealing with the former or latter situation: Where a rule is considered 'reasonable' because

individual or general, at any rate overtly. They have simply relied on the practice. The cases are indeed legion in which these bodies have baldly asserted that such and– such is the rule, without explicit reference to *either* of the famous two elements. If the rule in question is well established, the tribunal may (but may not) point out that it is accepted by States generally. But normally there is no real investigation into the subjectivities of States, either generally or individually'.

[35] ILA, Final Report, 2000, p. 31.   [36] *Ibid.*, pp. 31, 33.   [37] *Ibid.*, p. 34.
[38] *Ibid.*, p. 31 (emphasis in the original).   [39] See, Chapter 4, Section 4.1.4.
[40] Neff, 'Opinio Juris: Three Concepts Chasing a Label', p. 4.
[41] B. Cheng, 'United Resolutions on Outer Space: Instant International Customary Law?', *Indian JIL* (1965), p. 36; B. Cheng, 'The Future of General State Practice in a Divided World', in R. St J Macdonald and D.M. Johnston (eds.), *The Structure and Process of International Law* (The Hague: Martinus Nijhoff, 1983), pp. 513, 531–532.
[42] F.L. Kirgis, 'Custom on a Sliding Scale', *AJIL* 81 (1987), p. 149. See also, the position adopted by the ILA, Final Report, 2000, p. 40, for whom 'a substantial manifestation of acceptance (consent or belief) by States that a customary rule exists may compensate for a relative lack of practice, and vice versa'.

it prohibits unacceptable State behaviour, then only *opinio juris* will be sufficient to establish the existence of the customary rule (and *vice versa*).[43]

Leppard has recently developed a similar theory whereby 'a customary international law norm arises when states generally believe that it is desirable now or in the future to have an authoritative legal principle rule prescribing, permitting, or prohibiting certain conduct'.[44] According to him, 'this belief constitutes *opinio juris*, and it is sufficient to create a customary law norm'.[45] Leppard does not, however, discard State practice altogether.[46] He has developed 'criteria for determining the weight to give state practice as evidence of *opinio juris* in the case of different types of norms'.[47] For instance, on the one hand, he believes that

---

[43] Kirgis, 'Custom on a Sliding Scale', p. 149: 'Exactly how much state practice will substitute for an affirmative showing of an *opinio juris,* and how clear a showing will substitute for consistent behaviour, depends on the activity in question and on the reasonableness of the asserted customary rules. (...) The more destabilizing or morally distasteful the activity - for example, the offensive use of force or the deprivation of fundamental human rights - the more readily international decision makers will substitute one element for the other, provided that the asserted restrictive rule seems reasonable. The converse, of course, will be true as well. If the activity is not so destructive of widely accepted human values, or if the asserted rule seems unreasonable under the circumstances, the decision maker is likely to be more exacting in finding the necessary elements for the rule. A reasonable rule is always more likely to be found reflective of the state practice and/or the *opinio juris* than is an unreasonable (for example, a highly restrictive or inflexible) rule'. A similar position has been adopted by John Tasioulas, 'Custom and Consent', paper presented at the conference 'The Role of *Opinio Juris* in Customary International Law', Duke-Geneva Institute in Transnational Law, Geneva, 2013, p. 4: 'customary norms can come into being even in the absence of general state practice, or at the extreme in the teeth of even considerable countervailing practice. This is because the need for state practice can be traded off against high levels of *opinio juris*, especially if there is a strong moral case for the norm in question. That case must be constructed around those values that are especially important for the legitimacy of international law, such as peaceful co-existence, human rights, environmental protection, etc.' See also: J. Tasioulas, 'In Defence of Relative Normativity: Communitarian Values and the Nicaragua Case', *OJLS* 16 (1996) p. 85; J. Tasioulas, 'Customary International Law and the Quest for Global Justice', in A. Perreau-Saussine and J.B. Murphy (eds.), *The Nature of Customary Law: Philosophical, Historical and Legal Perspectives* (Cambridge: Cambridge University Press, 2007), p. 30.

[44] Lepard, *Customary International Law*, pp. 8, 97–98.

[45] *Ibid.*, adding that 'it is not necessary in every case to satisfy a separate "consistent state practice" requirement'.

[46] Brian D. Lepard, 'The Necessity of *opinio juris* in the Formation of Customary International Law', paper presented at the conference 'The Role of *Opinio Juris* in Customary International Law', Duke-Geneva Institute in Transnational Law, Geneva, 2013, p. 9 ('Can a customary norm be created alone by *opinio juris* (as redefined), without any state practice? In theory, that is possible, but highly unlikely. The absence of any corroborating state practice would in fact be evidence that states do not believe the norm ought to be the law').

[47] *Ibid.*, p. 9.

more evidence of uniform State practice is needed to establish *opinio juris* in the case of international trade norms since 'the absence of consistent state practice would defeat the coordinating purpose of the norm'. However, with regard to the case of human rights norms, 'any observance of the norm, despite widespread contrary practice, would further the purpose of the norm'.[48]

As further discussed,[49] the better view (adopted by the vast majority of scholars) is that customary law simply cannot be created by mere *opinio juris*, without any State practice backing such a belief.[50] As noted by one writer, these alternative theories have 'received virtually no support in the practice of States or in the case-law'[51] (with the possible exception of a few decisions of international tribunals in the specific field of the laws of war[52]). Therefore, as explained by one writer, 'deducing modern custom purely from *opinio juris* can create utopian laws that cannot regulate reality'.[53] Put differently, *opinio juris* without State practice is 'nothing more than rhetoric'.[54]

In any event, the (strictly doctrinal) controversy about whether or not the *opinio juris* requirement is *necessary* to demonstrate the existence of custom is in a way a *faux débat*. This is the case if one considers that certain State conduct (statements, including, for instance, pleadings and voting resolutions at the UN General Assembly) may constitute evidence of *both* a State's practice and its *opinio juris*. This controversial question

---

[48] *Ibid.*, p. 10.   [49] See, Chapter 4, Section 4.1.4.

[50] Mark E. Villiger, *Customary International law and Treaties: A Manual on the Theory and Practice of the Interrelation of Sources* (2nd edn., The Hague: Kluwer, 1997), p. 288 ('The legal belief of States, however firm, cannot per se create a rule, and material State practice will be needed to confirm the opinio juris and to substantiate the generality of application'); Thirlway, *International Customary Law and Codification*, p. 56; Kammerhofer, 'Customary International Law Needs both *Opinio* and *Usus*', p. 6.

[51] Mendelson, 'The Formation of Customary International Law', p. 372; Wolfke, *Custom in Present International Law*, pp. 40–41.

[52] Thus, as mentioned previously (see, Chapter 1, Section 1.1), a number of decisions of the International Tribunal for the Former Yugoslavia have found custom to exist mainly based on *opinio juris*, without requiring evidence of substantive State practice. See, the analysis in: International Law Commission, 'First Report on Formation and Evidence of Customary International Law', by Michael Wood, Special Rapporteur, Sixty-fifth session, Geneva, 6 May-7 June and 8 July-9 August 2013, UN doc. A/CN.4/663, 17 May 2013, p. 20 [hereinafter referred to as ILC, First Report, 2013], p. 29 ff.

[53] Roberts, 'Traditional and Modern Approaches to Customary International Law', p. 757. See also: Niels Peterson, 'Customary Law without Custom? Rules, Principles, and the Role of State Practice in International Norm Creation', *American University ILR* 23 (2008), p. 301.

[54] Dinstein, 'The Interaction between Customary International Law and Treaties', p. 294.

of 'double counting' will be examined in a later section.[55] Another doctrinal controversy (beyond the scope of this book) is the 'temporal' aspect of the two elements: which one should precede the other. Traditionally, it has been argued that the practice of States should come first. Yet, as noted by the ILC Special Rapporteur, 'it is possible that an acceptance that something ought to be the law (nascent *opinio juris*) may develop first, and then give rise to practice that embodies it so as to produce a rule of customary international law'.[56]

4.1.3 The chronological paradox... and one possible solution

One reason why a number of writers have had a tendency of downplaying the importance of the *opinio juris* requirement is their desire to solve the problem of the inherent circularity of customary international law, or what is often referred to as the 'chronological paradox'.[57] The problem, which has been identified by many scholars in the past,[58] can be summarized as follows:

> The belief-theory says that in order for a norm to become a part of customary international law, the norm must be generally practiced among states because states believe that the norm is valid international law. This gives the impression that, in order for a norm to become a part of international law, it must already be a part of international law. For the norm to come into existence, it must already exist.[59]

As mentioned previously, custom results from the practice of States in their international relations and their *belief* that such practice is *required*

---

[55] See, Chapter 4, Section 4.1.5.2.

[56] International Law Commission, 'Third Report on Identification of Customary International Law', by Michael Wood, Special Rapporteur, Sixty-seventh session, Geneva, 4 May-5 June and 6 July-7 August 2014, A/CN.4/682 [hereinafter referred to as ILC, Third Report, 2015], p. 7. See also: Nguyen Quoc Dinh, Patrick Dallier, Mathias Forteau and Alain Pellet, *Droit International Public* (8th edn., Paris: LGDJ, 2007), p. 362.

[57] M. Byers, *Custom, Power and the Power of Rules: International Relations and Customary International Law* (Cambridge: Cambridge University Press, 1999), pp. 130–141 (1999); See also: Olufemi Elias, 'The Nature of the Subjective Element in Customary International Law', *ICLQ* 44 (1995), p. 504; Raphael M. Walden, 'The Subjective Element in the Formation of Customary International Law', *Israel L.Rev.* 12 (1977), p. 363; Michael J. Glennon, 'How International Rules Die', *GEO. L.J.*, 93 (2005), pp. 939, 957.

[58] Kelsen, 'Théorie du droit coutumier', p. 253; M. Akehurst, 'Custom as a Source of International Law', *British YIL* 47 (1974–1975), p. 32; M. Sørensen, 'Principes de droit international public', *Rec. des cours* 101 (1960-III), p. 50.

[59] Dahlman, 'The Function of opinio juris in Customary International Law', p. 332.

by law. However, requiring *opinio juris* in the *earlier* stage of the development of a customary rule is clearly based on a legal fiction. By definition, the first occurrence of a certain behaviour (well before it eventually crystallizes as custom) must necessarily have been *contrary* to the prevailing norm of conduct at the time. How can a State that conducts itself in a certain way for the *first time* believe that it has a *legal obligation* to act in such a way? In other words, 'if state practice do not become binding as [custom] until the states involved act out of a sense of legal obligation, how do the states develop that sense of legal obligation in the first place?'[60] This raises the following issue: even though a State 'actively engaged in the *creation* of a new customary rule may well wish or accept that the practice in question will give rise to a legal rule', it remains 'logically impossible for [that State] to have an *opinio juris* in the literal and traditional sense, that is, a belief that the practice is *already* legally permissible or obligatory'.[61] Therefore, it is simply impossible for any new customary rule to emerge if all States are required to believe *at all times* that they are acting in accordance with the law.[62]

One possible solution to solve this paradox would be to say that the first few States that have adopted such conduct for the *first time* were simply *mistaken* in believing that they were under any legal obligation to do so.[63] While some writers have argued that such an 'honest mistake' can be considered as a belief necessary for creating custom,[64] others have argued that this approach is 'unsatisfactory because it is inconceivable that an entire legal process . . . could be based on a persistent misconception'.[65] In any event, as noted by one writer, the mistaken explanation is

---

[60] Bradley, 'The Chronological Paradox', p. 4. See also: D'Amato, *The Concept of Custom in International Law*, pp. 73–74.

[61] ILA, Final Report, 2000, p. 33 (emphasis in the original).

[62] Byers, *Custom, Power and the Power of Rules*, pp. 130–131.

[63] Bradley, 'The Chronological Paradox', p. 5; Dahlman, 'The Function of opinio juris in Customary International Law', p. 332.

[64] Jörg Kammerhofer, 'Uncertainty in the Formal Sources of International Law: Customary International Law and Some of Its Problems', *EJIL* 15(3) (2004), pp. 535–536, arguing that 'if a state believes some norm to be valid customary international law, it has no means of knowing whether this belief is true. States are not in a position to know whether the proposed norm they are championing has actually become law. The "mistake" is no longer clear nor "necessary" and the constitutive function of the states' beliefs comes to the fore'.

[65] Byers, *Custom, Power and the Power of Rules*, p. 131. See also: Bradley, 'The Chronological Paradox', p. 5; Dahlman, 'The Function of opinio juris in Customary International Law', p. 332 ('This idea is blatantly absurd. It means that customary law can only be created through mistakes. If the idea is taken seriously, states are unable to create customary law intentionally').

'plainly improbable' in most situations.[66] To take one famous example, the Truman Proclamation of September 1945, where the United States laid claim to 'the natural resources of the subsoil and sea bed of the continental shelf' adjacent to its coasts, was clearly not a mistake: 'Being fully cognizant of what it was doing, the United States did not proceed on the wrong assumption that the claim rested on the footing of existing law: there was only an American will or desire that this would eventually turn out to be the law'.[67] To solve this paradox, other writers have held that 'what is involved may be, not a belief that the practice is *already* legally binding, but a claim that it *ought* to be legally binding'.[68] The obvious problem with this approach is that it seems to be describing *something other* than the concept of *opinio juris*, which requires a State's actual *belief* that a legal obligation *already exists*, not what a State *wishes* the law *should be*.[69] Moreover, this approach 'does not adequately explain why states comply with customary rules when the practice is *mature*'.[70]

One reasonable solution to this problem of circularity is found in Tasioulas' concept of a 'disjunctive account'. Here, *opinio juris* can be assessed differently at specific moments in the cycle of the formation of custom.[71] This position was adopted by Judge Lachs in his dissenting opinion in the *North Sea Continental Shelf* cases.[72] The ILA Report also refers to scholars' 'failure to distinguish between different stages in the life of a customary rule'.[73] The Report states that '[o]nce a customary rule

---

[66] Mendelson, 'The Formation of Customary International Law', p. 279.

[67] Dinstein, 'The Interaction between Customary International Law and Treaties', p. 296. In the *North Sea Continental Shelf Cases*, ICJ Rep. 1969, pp. 32–33, the ICJ noted that the Truman Proclamation 'soon came to be regarded as the starting point of the positive law on the subject'. See also: Maurice Mendelson, 'Does Customary International Law Require *Opinio Juris?*', paper presented at the conference 'The Role of *Opinio Juris* in Customary International Law', Duke-Geneva Institute in Transnational Law, Geneva, 2013, p. 3.

[68] Walden, 'The Subjective Element in the Formation of Customary International Law', p. 358 (emphasis in the original); Lepard, 'The Necessity of *opinio juris* in the Formation of Customary International Law', p. 7; Lepard, *Customary International Law*, pp. 112–212 (examining the position of other writers).

[69] Mendelson, 'The Formation of Customary International Law', p. 281.

[70] Mendelson, 'Does Customary International Law Require *Opinio Juris?*', p. 3 (emphasis in the original).

[71] J. Tasioulas, '*Opinio Juris* and the Genesis of Custom: A Solution to the 'Paradox'', *Australian YIL*, 26 (2007), p. 202.

[72] *North Sea Continental Shelf Cases*, ICJ Rep. 1969, Dissenting Opinion of Judge Lachs, p. 231.

[73] ILA, Final Report, 2000, p. 7. See also: Villiger, *Customary International law and Treaties*, pp. 53–54; Wolfke, *Custom in Present International Law*, pp. 53–54; James Crawford, 'The Identification and Development of Customary International Law', ILA British Branch Conference (2014), p. 12 ('There seem to be two stages to *opinio juris* in the context of

has become established, States will naturally have a belief in its existence: but this does not *necessarily* prove that the subjective element needs to be present during the *formation* of the rule'.[74] This is simply because 'those who initiate a new practice which is inconsistent with the previous law (...) cannot realistically be said to have a belief in its legality'.[75] In other words, it is *unnecessary* to prove *opinio juris* in the early stages of the *formation* of a customary rule because such belief *does not* exist.[76] This does not mean, however, that the subjective element is *altogether irrelevant* to custom, but simply that it plays different roles at two distinct phases in the formation of customary rules.[77]

4.1.4   The reasons why it is necessary to demonstrate opinio juris

The present author, similar to the vast majority of scholars,[78] believes that both State practice and *opinio juris* must be demonstrated *in all cases*. As summarized by one writer, 'the reason why both elements can be seen to be necessary is that without *usus* it would not be customary and without *opinio* it would not be law'.[79] There are two basic reasons why it is necessary to demonstrate the subjective element of custom.

First, demonstrating the *opinio juris* of a State is essential to distinguish between, on the one hand, real international law *obligations* and, on the other hand, conduct that is merely based on other *non-legal* motivations.[80] According to Byers, *opinio juris* 'enables States to distinguish

change in the law or the development of new law where there was none before. First, there must be a practical judgment made by an individual state or some other actor. I call this a "proto-legal" move. Second, there must be a legal judgment that customary international law has changed, which must be made on a much broader basis than by an individual state').
[74] ILA, Final Report, 2000, p. 7 (emphasis in the original).   [75] *Ibid.*, p. 31.
[76] Mendelson, 'The Formation of Customary International Law', pp. 279, 284–285. See also: Kammerhofer, 'Uncertainty in the Formal Sources of International Law', p. 534.
[77] Villiger, *Customary International law and Treaties*, pp. 54–55; Wolfke, *Custom in Present International Law*, p. 61.
[78] For a long list of writers, see ILC, First Report, 2013, p. 45 ff. See also: ILC, Draft Conclusions, 2015, conclusion no. 3(2).
[79] Kammerhofer, 'Customary International Law Needs both *Opinio* and *Usus*', p. 2. See also: Wolfke, *Custom in Present International Law*, pp. 40–41 ('without practice (*consuetudo*), customary international law would obviously be a misnomer, since practice constitutes precisely the main *differentia specifica* of that kind of international law. On the other hand, without the subjective element of acceptance of the practice as law the difference between international custom and simple regularity of conduct (*usus*) or other non-legal rules of conduct would disappear').
[80] Villiger, *Customary International law and Treaties*, p. 48; Thirlway, *International Customary Law and Codification*, pp. 48, 53–56; Wolfke, *Custom in Present*

between legally relevant and legally irrelevant State practice' for the creation of custom.[81] Thus, a clear distinction needs to be made between a State's conduct regarding the 'recognition or acceptance of, or belief in, the existence of a legal rule' and other considerations such as 'courtesy, political expediency, will or compromise, precautionary measures, expressions of intent and aspirations or preferences'.[82] This essential distinction has been recognized by the ICJ[83] and by a number of ICJ judges in their individual opinions.[84] While downplaying the importance of *opinio juris*,[85] the ILA Report nevertheless recognized that '[i]t is for the purpose of distinguishing practices which generate customary rules from those that do not that *opinio juris* is most useful'.[86] According to the ILA, acts of comity practised in international relations fall outside customary law when they are performed by states who do not believe that they are legally obliged by a rule.[87] Other types of conduct that do not contribute toward establishing a rule of customary law include a State's action, accompanied by a disclaimer outlining that it is not acting under any obligation.[88] Moreover (as further discussed in a later section[89]), the practice of States 'motivated (solely) by the need to comply with treaty (or

---

International Law, pp. 40–41; Mendelson, 'The Formation of Customary International Law', pp. 245–246, 272; Crawford, 'The Identification and Development of Customary International Law', p. 7; *Case Concerning Right of Passage over Indian Territory, (Portugal v. India) (Merits)*, ICJ Rep. 1960, p. 120 (Dissenting Opinion of Judge Chagla); Abdullah Al Faruque, 'Creating Customary International Law through Bilateral Investment Treaties: a Critical Appraisal', *Indian J Int'l* 44 (2004), p. 297; Nguyen *et al.*, *Droit International Public*, p. 361. See also: ILC, Second Report, 2014, pp. 42, 65; See also: ILC, Draft Conclusions, 2015, conclusion no. 10(2): 'A general practice that is accepted as law (*opinio juris*) is to be distinguished from mere usage or habit'.

[81] Byers, *Custom, Power and the Power of Rules*, p. 148.

[82] ILC, Memorandum, 2013, p. 19.

[83] *Colombian-Peruvian Asylum Case*, Judgment, ICJ Rep. 1950, pp. 285, 286; *North Sea Continental Shelf Cases*, ICJ Rep. 1969, p. 44, para. 77.

[84] See, the list in: ILC, Second Report, 2014, pp. 42–43.

[85] See, the analysis in Chapter 4, Section 4.1.2.   [86] ILA, Final Report, 2000, p. 34.

[87] *Ibid.*, p. 35, giving the example of sending condolences on the death of a head of State and stating that 'it is generally *believed* in the international community that they do not give rise to legal obligations (a sort of *opinio non juris*), or – to put it differently - no-one *claims* performance of these duties as a matter of legal right' (emphasis in the original).

[88] *Ibid.*, p. 36. This is the case when a State makes a compensatory payment *ex gratia* or without prejudice. The ILA also adds that 'Some conduct is too ambiguous to be treated, without more, as constituting a precedent capable of contributing to the formation of a customary rule. In such cases, the conduct will only count if there is positive evidence that the State or States concerned intended, understood or accepted that a customary rule could result from, or lay behind, the conduct in question'.

[89] See, Chapter 4, Section 4.2.2.1.

some other extra-customary) obligations', does not demonstrate the existence of an *opinio juris*.[90] In contrast, the practice of States that are *not party* to a treaty, but nevertheless act in conformity with a treaty norm may (depending on circumstances examined later[91]) constitute *opinio juris*.[92]

While some writers have expressed the view that such a distinction between legal obligation and mere courtesy is unnecessary,[93] the ICJ in the *North Sea Continental Shelf* cases upheld that it is in fact essential:

> The States concerned must therefore feel that they are conforming to what amounts to a legal obligation. The frequency, or even habitual character of the acts is not in itself enough. There are many international acts, e.g., in the field of ceremonial and protocol, which are performed almost invariably, but which are motivated only by considerations of courtesy, convenience or tradition, and not by any sense of legal duty.[94]

Second, demonstrating *opinio juris* is necessary in explaining how the accumulation of uniform and consistent State practice can 'transform' into a legal rule *binding* on all States.[95] As noted by the ICJ in the *North Sea Continental Shelf* cases, 'acting, or agreeing to act in a certain way, does not itself demonstrate anything of a juridical nature'.[96] It is indeed fundamental to be able to explain how something that States *often and typically do* becomes something that they *feel they have to do* under

---

[90] ILC, Second Report, 2014, p. 43. See: *North Sea Continental Shelf Cases*, ICJ Rep. 1969, p. 43, para. 76. See also, the individual opinions of a number of ICJ judges cited in ILC, *Ibid*.

[91] See, Chapter 4, Section 4.2.2.1.   [92] ILC, Second Report, 2014, pp. 43–44.

[93] Baxter, 'Treaties and Custom', p. 69, for whom 'these acts, motivated as they are by "considerations of courtesy, convenience or tradition", bear on their face the stamp that they are not attributable to any obligation imposed by international law'. See also: Mendelson, 'Does Customary International Law Require *Opinio Juris*?', p. 5, for whom 'relations of inter-state courtesy are simply taken for granted as being outside the sphere of legal regulation, and the concept of [*opinio juris*] is a rather unwieldy and unnecessary tool to express this obvious truth'. He adds, 'we are regularly told that [*opinio juris*] (. . .) is what tells us that the widespread practice of governments sending letters of condolence when a head of state dies is not legally binding. But surely, only an idiot would think that it was'.

[94] *North Sea Continental Shelf Cases*, ICJ Rep. 1969, p. 44, para. 77.

[95] Villiger, *Customary International law and Treaties*, p. 49; Wolfke, *Custom in Present International Law*, p. 44 ('whereas practice constitutes what might be described as merely the raw material of custom, only the element of acceptance as law gives it the mark of law'), p. 161; Roberts, 'Traditional and Modern Approaches to Customary International Law', p. 776; Lepard, 'The Necessity of *opinio juris* in the Formation of Customary International Law', p. 7.

[96] *North Sea Continental Shelf Cases*, ICJ Rep. 1969, p. 44, para. 76.

international law.[97] In the words of Dinstein, *opinio juris* 'underpins the transition of State practice from the normal to the normative'.[98] It should be noted, however, that some writers have argued that this explanation of the binding force of custom is actually unnecessary.[99] In my view, in consideration of the current decentralized international legal order, characterized by the lack of a supranational entity above States, one can only conclude that a given conduct is obligatory for States when they actually believe *themselves* that this is the case.[100]

In any event, the *opinio juris* requirement is clearly necessary to distinguish between different kinds of omissions: those that count as relevant State practice in the formation of rules of custom and those that do not. As mentioned previously,[101] the fact that a State does *nothing* for no particular reason cannot be compared to the situation where a State abstains from acting based on its belief that it has an obligation to do so under the law.[102] Only the latter kind of omission or abstention can count as evidence of State practice that is relevant in the formation of custom. Such a distinction can only be made by taking into account a State's *opinio juris*. In other words, one can only determine whether or

[97] ILC, Third Report, 2015, p. 6 ('the very practice alleged to be prescribed by customary international law could usually not attest in itself to its acceptance as law'); M.N. Shaw, *International Law*, (7th edn., Cambridge: Cambridge University Press, 2014), p. 53 ('[t]he bare fact that such things are done does not mean that they have to be done').

[98] Dinstein, 'The Interaction between Customary International Law and Treaties', p. 294. See also: ILC, Second Report, 2014, p. 41.

[99] Mendelson, 'The Formation of Customary International Law', p. 246: 'If there *is* a rule saying that legal obligations arise from (certain types of) State practice, for practical purposes, that may well be all that we need to know. To take an analogy: if you know that there is a rule saying that treaties are binding, what you need to find out is whether the document you have before you is indeed a treaty, and whether any of the exclusionary rules which determine when treaties are *not* binding apply to the facts of your case. You do *not* need to speculate on the reason why the rule that treaties are binding is itself a binding legal rule: that belongs more to the more recondite realms of legal theory' (emphasis in the original). See also, at p. 279. This line of reasoning begs the fundamental and preliminary question of how to know when a rule exists and is indeed binding on States. This is where (at least in the context of the process of the formation of rules of international law) *opinio juris* matters.

[100] The phenomenon of the transformation of mere usages into customary rules is well-explained by J.A. Barberis, 'Réflexions sur la coutume internationale', *AFDI*, 36 (1990), p. 29.

[101] See, Chapter 3, Section 3.3.1.2.

[102] Kammerhofer, 'Uncertainty in the Formal Sources of International Law', p. 529; Dinstein, 'The Interaction between Customary International Law and Treaties', p. 298 ('There is a difference between an abstention from certain measures because of a sense that they are barred by international law and a similar abstention on the ground of discretion or sheer expediency').

not a State has abstained for any particular reason when assessing that State's actual belief on what the law is. This is the conclusion reached by the PCIJ in the *Lotus* case.[103] Similarly, in the *Nuclear Weapons* Advisory Opinion, the ICJ had to interpret one kind of abstention: the fact that nuclear weapons had not been used by States since 1945.[104] The Court concluded that 'the members of the international community are profoundly divided on the matter of whether non-recourse to nuclear weapons over the past 50 years constitutes the expression of an *opinio juris*'.[105] In other words, the fact that States had not used nuclear weapons since 1945 could not be explained by their actual belief that they were under any obligation to abstain from doing so under international law.

4.1.5   *Manifestations of* opinio juris

The reasoning of the ICJ in the *North Sea Continental Shelf* cases suggests that a Court must *first* examine whether any practice of States exists that is general, uniform and consistent. If this is the case, the Court should *then* determine whether States have the belief that this practice is obligatory under the law. In the *Nicaragua* case, the ICJ, however, adopted the *opposite* order by assessing first the *opinio juris* of States, that is, the fact that they *believe* that a given conduct is *obligatory* under international law. The Court also mentioned that it 'must satisfy itself that the existence of the rule in the opinio juris of States is *confirmed by practice*'.[106] The sequence of order (first *opinio juris*, then State practice[107]) is clear from the following two extracts taken from the judgment:

---

[103] *The Case of the S.S. 'Lotus'*, 1927 PCIJ Series A, No. 10, at 28: '[e]ven if the rarity of the judicial decisions to be found among the reported cases were sufficient to prove in point of fact the circumstance alleged by the Agent for the French Government, it would merely show that States had often, in practice, abstained from instituting criminal proceedings, and not that they recognized themselves as being obliged to do so, for only if such abstention were based on their *being conscious of having a duty to abstain* would it be possible to speak of an international custom' (emphasis added). In this case, the Court concluded that States had reasons to abstain from instituting criminal proceedings other than simply based on a legal duty to do so.

[104] *Legality of the Threat or Use of Nuclear Weapons*, Advisory Opinion, ICJ Rep. 1996, p. 254, para. 66.

[105] *Ibid.*, para. 67.

[106] *Military and Paramilitary Activities in and around Nicaragua, (Nicaragua v. United States)*, Merits, Judgment, ICJ Rep. 1986, para. 184 (emphasis added).

[107] O. Schachter, 'New Custom: Power, Opinio Juris and Contrary Practice', in J. Makarczyk (ed.), *Theory of International Law at the Threshold of the 21st Century: Essays in Honour of Krzysztof Skubieszewski* (The Hague: Kluwer Law International, 1996), pp. 531–532.

> The principle of non-intervention involves the right of every sovereign State to conduct its affairs without outside interference. (. . .) Expressions of an *opinio juris* regarding the existence of the principle of non-intervention in customary international law are numerous and not difficult to find. (. . .) The existence in the *opinio juris* of States of the principle of non-intervention *is backed by established and substantial practice* (. . .).[108]
>
> [I]n the present case, apart from the treaty commitments binding the Parties to the rules in question, there are various instances of their having expressed recognition of the validity thereof as customary international law in other ways. It is therefore *in the light of this 'subjective element'* (. . .) *that the Court has to appraise the relevant practice*.[109]

But how does a State's *opinio juris* manifest itself? There are two straightforward situations:

- On the one hand, when a State makes an express statement to the effect that it believes that a given rule is obligatory *qua* customary international law, this is undeniable and first hand proof of the existence of that State's *opinio juris*;
- On the other hand, when a State clearly indicates that a certain conduct is *not* obligatory and should not be considered as a rule of customary international law, this is evidence of the absence of any *opinio juris* for that State.[110]

In these two situations, such express assertions can take many forms.[111] In his Second Report, ILC Special Rapporteur Wood stated that:

> such assertions by States of rights or obligations under (customary) international law (or lack thereof) could, *inter alia*, take the form of an official statement by a government or a minister of that government, claims and legal briefs before court and tribunals, transmittal statements by which governments introduce draft legislation in parliament, a joint declaration of States through an official document, or statements made in

---

[108] *Military and Paramilitary Activities in and around Nicaragua*, ICJ Rep. 1986, para. 202 (emphasis added).

[109] *Ibid.*, para. 185 (emphasis added). See also, at para. 206 where the court states that 'it has to consider whether there might be indications of a *practice illustrative of belief* in a kind of general right for States to intervene, directly or indirectly, with or without armed force, in support of an internal opposition in another State (. . .)' (emphasis added).

[110] ILC, Second Report, 2014, p. 52.

[111] ILC, Second Report, 2014, p. 66, Draft Conclusion no. 11(1) of the ILC 'Proposed draft conclusions on the identification of customary international law' ('Evidence of acceptance of a general practice as law may take a wide range of forms. These may vary according to the nature of the rule and the circumstances in which the rule falls to be applied'); ILC, Draft Conclusions, 2015, conclusion no. 10(1).

multilateral conferences such as codification conventions or debates in the United Nations.[112]

The more difficult task is identifying concrete manifestations of a State's *opinio juris* when that State *does not expressly* take a position on the issue. This is the reason why some scholars have argued that '[f]or a typical custom it suffices that the acceptance of the practice as law should be presumed upon all circumstances of the case in question, above all on the attitude, hence conduct, of the accepting states to be bound by the customary rule'.[113] In other words, for them a State's *opinio juris* can be *presumed* in certain circumstances. The next section examines where to look for such *opinio juris*.

4.1.5.1   *Opinio juris* can be demonstrated by State practice

Since a State's belief in the obligatory nature of a given conduct is rarely measurable, its *opinio juris* will often have to be discovered by examining some form of State practice.[114] Therefore, the behaviour of States is often characterized as the sole guide in determining what they believe to be the law.[115] In other words, the only way to determine what a State *thinks* about the existence of any given norm is often to look at what that State actually *does* in practice. Alvarez explains the reasons for relying on State practice:

> Another, more complex response is to recognize that in the real world, evidence of *opinio juris* is usually drawn from the actual, practice of states, at least where those practices would otherwise be difficult to explain, and that it is the rare case where distinct or explicit evidence of the subject intentions behind a state's actions is available apart from what can be inferred from the state's actions. Indeed, most have assumed that evidence of *opinio juris* usually needs to be gleaned from state practice itself (. . .).[116]

---

[112] *Ibid.*, pp. 52–53.   [113] Wolfke, *Custom in Present International Law,* p. 44.

[114] Villiger, *Customary International law and Treaties,* pp. 50–51; Wolfke, *Custom in Present International Law,* pp. 44–45; Alexandra Diehl, *The Core Standard of International Investment Protection: Fair and Equitable Treatment* (Alphen aan den Rijn: Wolters Kluwer, 2012), p. 129.

[115] Kammerhofer, 'Uncertainty in the Formal Sources of International Law', p. 527, see also, at p. 525 ('In a sense, all that states can do or omit to do can be classified as "State practice", because their behaviour is what they do (the "objective element") and it is also our only guide as to what they want, or "believe", to be the law').

[116] Jose E. Alvarez, 'A Bit on Custom', *N.Y.U. J. Int'l L. & Pol.* 42 (2009–2010), pp. 57–59. See also: Steffen Hindelang, 'Bilateral Investment Treaties, Custom and a Healthy Investment Climate – The Question of whether BITs Influence Customary International Law Revisited', *J. World Invest. & Trade,* 5 (2004), pp. 792–793.

The ICJ in the *North Sea Continental Shelf* cases recognized that the practice of States could show evidence of their *opinio juris*. The Court thus referred to the importance of 'a settled practice' that is 'carried out in such a way, as to be evidence of a belief that this practice is rendered obligatory by the existence of a rule of law requiring it'.[117] The ILC Special Rapporteur took the same position: 'In practice, acceptance as law has indeed been indicated by or inferred from a variety of relevant conduct undertaken by States'.[118]

Some writers argue that the demonstration of a general, uniform and consistent State practice during a sufficiently long period of time *establishes a presumption* that States believe they are under an obligation to adopt such conduct.[119] This seems to be the position adopted by the ICJ in the *Gulf of Maine* case. The Court here referred to a 'set of customary rules whose presence in the opinio juris of States can *be tested by induction* based on the analysis of a sufficiently extensive and convincing practice, and not by deduction from preconceived ideas'.[120] The ILC Special Rapporteur, however, has contested the existence of any such presumption.[121] The obvious problem with accepting such a presumption is that it would mean that the subjective element is simply *irrelevant*.[122] This is contrary to the ICJ Statute requiring evidence of this subjective element.

---

[117] *North Sea Continental Shelf Cases*, ICJ Rep. 1969, para. 77.

[118] ILC, Second Report, 2014, p. 50. See also: Nguyen *et al.*, *Droit International Public*, p. 366.

[119] Wolfke, *Custom in Present International Law*, p. 62 ('In most cases the element of acceptance (. . .) is fulfilled tacitly, only by means of a presumption based upon various kinds of active or passive reactions to the practice by the interested states'); Kirgis, 'Custom on a Sliding Scale', p. 149 ('On the sliding scale, very frequent, consistent state practice establishes a customary rule without much (or any) affirmative showing of an *opinio juris*, so long as it is not negated by evidence of a non-normative intent. As the frequency and consistency of the practice decline in any series of cases, a stronger showing of *opinio juris* is required').

[120] *Delimitation of the Maritime Boundary in the Gulf of Maine Area (Canada v. United States)*, Judgment, ICJ Rep. 1984, para. 111 (emphasis added).

[121] ILC, Second Report, 2014, p. 51: 'although some have suggested that a large number of concordant acts, or the fact that such cases have been occurring over a considerable period of time, may suffice to establish the existence of *opinio juris*, this is not so. While these facts may indeed *give rise to* the acceptance of the practice as law, they do not embody such acceptance in and of themselves', emphasis in the original. See also: ILC, Draft Conclusions, 2015, conclusion no. 3(2).

[122] Crawford, 'The Identification and Development of Customary International Law', p. 8, noting about the passage in the ICJ *Gulf of Maine* case, mentioned above, that 'this *dictum* may be considered tautological' and that 'the Court in this case seems to have

In my view, the better approach is to require that the two elements of State practice and *opinio juris* be identified *separately* by a court or a tribunal.[123] Some writers have argued that the two elements are in fact inseparable.[124] Yet, the better view is the one adopted by the ILC Special Rapporteur in the draft conclusion: 'Each element is to be separately ascertained. This requires an assessment of evidence for each element'.[125] An *independent* assessment of the existence of *opinio juris* therefore remains essential.

Others, however, have taken a different view. For instance, the ILA has stated that 'the more the practice, the *less the need* for the subjective element'.[126] Similarly, the International Committee of the Red Cross ('ICRC') study on custom in the field of humanitarian law held that '[w]hen there is sufficiently dense practice, an opinio juris is generally contained within that practice and, as a result, it is *not usually necessary* to demonstrate separately the existence of an opinio juris'.[127] In my view, even when the practice is consistent and uniform, it is still *necessary* to demonstrate *opinio juris*.[128] But, clearly that task is much *easier* in situations where there is overwhelming uniform and consistent State

---

conflated the subjective and objective element: what is the point of requiring the second element if it can be inferred from the first?'.

[123] ILC, Second Report, 2004, p. 50; ILC, Third Report, 2004, p. 5; ILC, Draft Conclusions, 2015, conclusion no. 3(4).

[124] Stern, 'Custom at the Heart of International Law', p. 92 ('the two "constitutive elements" of custom are not two juxtaposed entities, but rather only two aspects of the same phenomenon: a certain action which is subjectively executed or perceived in a certain fashion'). See also: Pierre-Marie Dupuy & Yann Kerbrat, *Droit international public* (12th edn., Paris: Dalloz, 2014), p. 368, speaking of 'l'interdépendance manifeste sinon même de l'union inextricable entre l'un et l'autre' adding also that 'la coutume est l'expression d'une opinio juris manifestée dans et par une pratique. Elle ne résulte pas de l'adjonction des deux éléments, mais de la révélation d'un par l'autre'); G.M. Danilenko, *Law-Making in the International Community* (Martinus Nijhoff Publishers, 1993), pp. 81–82; R. Müllerson, 'On the Nature and Scope of Customary International Law', *Austrian RIEL* 2 (1997), pp. 341, 344–347.

[125] ILC, Draft Conclusions, 2015, conclusion no. 3(2).

[126] ILA Report, 2000, p. 41 (emphasis added).

[127] Jean-Marie Henckaerts and Louise Doswald-Beck (eds.), *Customary International Humanitarian Law* (Cambridge: Cambridge University Press, 2005, vol. I), p. xl (emphasis added).

[128] This is, for instance, the position adopted by the United States in response to the ICRC Study, *Ibid.*: 'Although the same action may serve as evidence both of State practice and opinio juris', the United States does 'not agree that opinio juris simply can be inferred from practice', adding that 'both elements instead must be assessed separately in order to determine the presence of a norm of customary international law' (Bellinger and Haynes, 'A US Government Response to the International Committee of the Red Cross Study on Customary International Humanitarian Law', p. 446).

practice. This is the case if one recognizes that certain manifestations of State practice can evidence *both* the practice of a State and its *opinio juris* (a question further discussed in this chapter[129]). Nevertheless, it still needs to be demonstrated that a State's practice is not merely based on courtesy and usage.[130]

This question raises the next issue of the type of State practice that is relevant to demonstrate a State's *opinio juris* in situations where no express affirmation of such a belief exists. In a recent Memorandum, the ILC Secretariat mentioned that the Commission had 'relied upon a variety of materials in assessing the subjective element for the purpose of identifying a rule of customary international law', and listed the following elements:

> [P]ositions of States before international organizations (including written comments and responses to questionnaires) or international conferences; pronouncements by municipal courts; statements before international courts and tribunals; stipulations in arbitration agreements; diplomatic practice and notes; a State's actual conduct (as opposed to its stated positions); a State's treaty practice; multilateral treaty practice; as well as a variety of international instruments.[131]

The ILC Special Rapporteur Wood also provides the following non-exhaustive list of the 'kind of materials where the subjective element may be found': Intergovernmental (diplomatic) correspondence, the jurisprudence of national courts, the opinions of government legal advisers, official publications in fields of international law, internal memoranda by State officials, treaties and resolutions of deliberative organs of international organizations.[132] However, *not all* manifestations of State

---

[129] See, Chapter 4, Section 4.1.5.2.

[130] Dinstein, 'The Interaction between Customary International Law and Treaties', p. 297. See, however, the position adopted by other writers: Baxter, 'Treaties and Custom', p. 69 ('there is much to commend the view that *opinio juris* is presumptively present unless evidence can be adduced that a State was acting from other than a sense of legal obligation'); H. Lauterpacht, *The Development of International Law by the International Court* (London: Stevens and Sons, 1958), p. 380 ('It would appear that the accurate principle on the subject consists in regarding all uniform conduct of Governments [. . .] as evidencing the opinio necessitates juris except when it is shown that the conduct in question was not accompanied by such attention').

[131] ILC, Memorandum, 2013, pp. 21–22.

[132] ILC, Second Report, 2014, p. 53. See also: ILC, Draft Conclusions, 2015, conclusion no. 10(2): 'Forms of evidence of acceptance as law (*opinio juris*) include, but are not limited to: public statements made on behalf of States; official publications; government legal opinions; diplomatic correspondence; decisions of national courts; treaty provisions; and conduct in connection with resolutions adopted by an international organization or at an intergovernmental conference'.

practice can show evidence of that State's *opinio juris*. According to Kammerhofer, 'the passage of a ship has no "content", but is simply the passage of a ship' that indicates nothing about that State's belief concerning the legality of such acts. In such a case, the *opinio juris* needs to be found *elsewhere*, rather than merely looking at the conduct.[133]

The following paragraphs will provide concrete illustrations of where the ICJ has found evidence of a State's *opinio juris*. In its advisory opinion on the *Legality of the Threat or Use of Nuclear Weapons*, the Court stressed that UN General Assembly resolutions can provide evidence of the *opinio juris* of States:

> General Assembly resolutions, even if they are not binding, may sometimes have normative value. They can, in certain circumstances, provide evidence important for establishing the existence of a rule or the emergence of an *opinio juris*. To establish whether this is true of a given General Assembly resolution, it is necessary to look at its content and the conditions of its adoption; it is also necessary to see whether an *opinio juris* exists as to its normative character. Or a series of resolutions may show the gradual evolution of the *opinio juris* required for the establishment of a new rule.[134]

The Court also indicated that 'the adoption each year by the General Assembly, by a large majority, of resolutions (...) requesting the member States to conclude a convention prohibiting the use of nuclear weapons in any circumstance, reveals the desire of a very large section of the international community to take, by a specific and express prohibition of the use of nuclear weapons, a significant step forward along the road to complete nuclear disarmament'.[135] The Court qualified that series of resolutions as a 'nascent' *opinio juris* on the matter.[136]

In the *Nicaragua* case, the ICJ indicated that the *opinio juris* of States concerning the binding legal obligation to refrain from the use of force 'may, though with all due caution, be deduced from, *inter alia,* the attitude of the Parties and the attitude of States towards certain General Assembly resolutions'.[137] The Court came to the conclusion that the

---

[133] Kammerhofer, 'Uncertainty in the Formal Sources of International Law', p. 528: 'A state acts in its international relations. All these actions and omissions are neutral - they are no indication that the state wishes this behaviour to be prescribed. The passage of ships through a strait is a behavioural regularity, nothing more. These regularities of behaviour constitute the material element and can only be employed for customary law-making if the will or belief on the part of the subjects of law - the subjective element - is added'.

[134] *Legality of the Threat or Use of Nuclear Weapons*, Advisory Opinion, ICJ Rep. 1996, pp. 254–255, para. 70.

[135] *Ibid.*, para. 73.   [136] *Ibid.*

[137] *Military and Paramilitary Activities in and around Nicaragua*, ICJ Rep. 1986, para. 188.

principle of non-intervention (i.e. 'the right of every sovereign State to conduct its affairs without outside interference'[138]) was part of customary international law despite the fact that 'examples of trespass against this principle are not infrequent'.[139] For the Court, 'expressions of an *opinio juris* regarding the existence of the principle of non-intervention in customary international law [were] numerous and not difficult to find', adding that the existence of such *opinio* was 'backed by established and substantial practice'.[140] The Court then listed amongst these elements of State practice a number of General Assembly resolutions,[141] the United States reservation and ratification of treaties,[142] and the Final Act of the Conference on Security and Co-operation in Europe.[143] The Court's decision, however, has been criticized for focusing on *opinio juris* (favouring the existence of the principle of non-intervention) while discarding relevant State practice, which was in fact not at all supporting such principle.[144] The next section specifically examines another ground of complaint often raised by writers about this ICJ case: the problem of so-called double-counting.

4.1.5.2   The problem of 'double-counting'

Mendelson has criticized the reasoning of the Court in the *Nicaragua* case on the ground that the vote by a State in favour of a (non-binding) UN General Assembly resolution cannot represent its *opinio juris*.[145] According to him, this would amount to 'double-counting', that is, interpreting the resolution as evidence of *both* State practice and *opinio juris*:

> And even if we grant, for the sake of argument, that the resolutions represented the *opinio juris*, where then is the practice which, the Court seemed to be saying, is an independent element? If we say that the resolutions constitute verbal practice, then we are guilty of double-counting them – both as the objective and as the subjective elements. (. . .) It might be responded that all that is needed is for the act of practice to be *accompanied* by *opinio juris*; so that what is required is not two completely separate elements, but both combined; however, to count the act of voting

---

[138] *Ibid.*, para. 202.   [139] *Ibid.*   [140] *Ibid.*   [141] *Ibid.*, paras. 202–204.
[142] *Ibid.*, para. 204.   [143] *Ibid.*
[144] Mendelson, 'The Formation of Customary International Law', p. 230.
[145] *Ibid.*, pp. 379–380. The position of Mendelson seems to be somehow contradictory since elsewhere he states that 'In voting for or against a resolution which has something to say about international law - and not all do - States are engaging in a form of State practice *and/or* are manifesting their subjective attitude (consent or belief) about the rule in question' (p. 201, emphasis added).

for the resolution as practice still looks rather like pulling oneself up by one's own bootstraps.[146]

Mendelson offers the same reasoning regarding statements by State officials:

> Verbal acts, then, can constitute a form of practice. But their *content* can be an expression of the subjective element - will or belief. For instance, if a government representative gives a press conference, he or she is both performing an act (of speech) and also, through its substance, communicating his Government's position on a particular legal question. Whether we classify a particular verbal act as an instance of the subjective or of the objective element may depend on circumstances, but it probably does not matter much which category we put it into. What must, however, be avoided is counting the same act as an instance of *both* the subjective and the objective element. If one adheres to the "mainstream" view that it is necessary for both elements to be present, and in particular for the subjective element to be accompanied by "real" practice, this must necessarily preclude treating a statement as both an act and a manifestation of belief (or will).[147]

In the present author's view, there are *no valid reasons* why so-called double-counting should be avoided at all cost.[148] As acknowledged by the

---

[146] *Ibid.*, p. 381. See also: Wolfke, *Custom in Present International Law*, p. 84 ('Individual positive votes cast by the members do not necessarily represent the actual acceptance as law of the conduct only verbally postulated in the content of the recommendation, since the motive for such votes may be various').

[147] Mendelson, 'The Formation of Customary International Law', pp. 206–207 (emphasis in the original). Similarly, Wolfke, *Custom in Present International Law*, p. 42, denies that verbal acts can be evidence of State practice for this reason: 'the origin of misunderstanding caused by considering [e.g.] verbal acts as custom-creating practice lies in confounding such practice with its evidence or with the evidence of acceptance of the practice as law'.

[148] The position adopted by the ILC, Second Report, 2014, seems contradictory when one compares these two separate affirmations: (1) 'Some practice may thus in itself be evidence of *opinio juris*, or, in other words, be relevant both in establishing the necessary practice and its "acceptance as law" ' (p. 50) and (2) '"Acceptance as law" should thus generally not be evidenced by the very practice alleged to be prescribed by customary international law. This provides, moreover, that the same conduct should not serve in a particular case as evidence of both practice and acceptance of that practice as law' (p. 52). In fact, in the Second Report (see, Draft Conclusion no. 11(4)), the ILC endorsed double-counting: 'The fact that an act (including inaction) by a State establishes practice for the purpose of identifying a rule of customary international law does not preclude the same act from being evidence that the practice in question is accepted as law'. But in the Third Report, 2015, p. 6, the Rapporteur took a clear position against double-counting: 'When seeking to identify the existence of a rule of customary international law, evidence of the relevant practice should therefore generally not serve as evidence of *opinio juris* as well:

ILA Report (the Committee was chaired by Mendelson), 'it is in fact often difficult or even impossible to disentangle the two elements'. The same assessment has been made by the ILC Special Rapporteur[149] and the ICRC study.[150]

A good illustration is found where a State is voting in favour of a UN General Assembly or making a declaration in the context of its adoption. Such conduct is clearly a form of State practice.[151] Nevertheless, the *content* of what the State is voting about may, depending on the circumstances, *simultaneously* reflect its belief that a given conduct is obligatory. Many writers believe that UN General Assembly resolutions can therefore be evidence of States' *opinio juris*.[152] This is, indeed, the position taken by the ICJ in *Legality of the Threat or Use of Nuclear Weapons*.[153] In other words, while the fact that a State *says something* constitutes an

---

such "double counting" (repeat referencing) is to be avoided'. The ILC, Draft Conclusions, 2015, does not include any reference to this issue.

[149] ILC, Second Report, 2014, p. 13.

[150] Henckaerts and Doswald-Beck, *Customary International Humanitarian Law,* p. xl: 'it proved very difficult and largely theoretical to strictly separate elements of practice and legal conviction. More often than not, one and the same act reflects both practice and legal conviction'.

[151] Villiger, *Customary International law and Treaties,* p. 23; Obed Y. Asamoah, 'The Legal Significance of the Declarations of the General Assembly of the United Nations', *ICLQ* 16(4) (1967), p. 54.

[152] Villiger, *Customary International law and Treaties,* p. 51, p. 24 ('An individual State casting its vote for or against a draft rule could be expressing its approval or disapproval of the rule, and would thus be giving some indication as to its legal conviction'), p. 49 ('a vote cast in favour of that rule, offers more conclusive evidence of a State's opinio than a vote upon, or an in discriminate statement as to the customary nature of a whole convention with dozens or hundreds of articles and as many, or more, rules'); Lepard, *Customary International Law,* pp. 180, 222; Byers, *Custom, Power and the Power of Rules,* p. 134; Jan Klabbers, *An Introduction to International Institutional Law* (2nd edn., Cambridge: Cambridge University Press, 2009), p. 188; H.G. Schermers and Niels M. Blokker, *International Institutional Law: Unity Within Diversity* (4th edn., Boston; Leiden: Martinus Nijhoff, 2003), p. 782; Chittharanjan Felix Amerasinghe, *Principles of the Institutional Law of International Organizations* (2nd edn., Cambridge: Cambridge University Press, 2005), pp. 189–190; José E. Alvarez, *International Organizations As Law-Makers* (Oxford: Oxford University Press, 2005), p. 260; ILC, Second Report, 2014, p. 57 ('Opinio juris may be deduced from the attitudes of States vis-à-vis such non-binding texts that purport, explicitly or implicitly, to declare the existing law, as may be expressed by both voting (in favour, against or abstaining) on the resolution, by joining a consensus, or by statements made in connection with the resolution'); A. Pellet, 'Article 38', in A. Zimmermann *et al.* (eds.), *The Statute of the International Court of Justice: A Commentary* (2nd edn., Oxford: Oxford University Press, 2012), p. 825.

[153] *Legality of the Threat or Use of Nuclear Weapons,* Advisory Opinion, ICJ Rep. 1996. pp. 254–255, para. 70.

element of State *practice*, the *content* of what the State is *actually saying* can also represent its *opinio juris*. This position is largely supported by scholars.[154]

It should be added, however, that there is clearly *no presumption* that a State's *opinio juris* can *always* be deduced from mere voting in favour of a UN General Assembly resolution. As pointed out by Schachter, 'it is far from clear that voting for a law-declaring resolution is in itself conclusive evidence of a belief that the resolution expresses a legal rule'.[155] One needs to actually find some expression of a State's belief in the obligatory nature of a certain practice. Thus, 'not all General Assembly resolutions have the effect of expressing communal *opinio juris*'.[156] Whether any such collective *opinio juris* exists will depend on a variety of factors,[157]

[154] Villiger, *Customary International law and Treaties*, p. 23 ('Verbal statements have the usual functions of State practice in respect of a customary rule. They may confirm a pre-existing customary rule and/or constitute instances of practice contributing towards a new rule. Thereby, they may disclose, or circumscribe the normative substance of a customary rule, or define it. (. . .) Finally, the statements may reveal their opinio juris with respect to a customary rule'); Amerasinghe, *Principles of the Institutional Law of International Organizations*, p. 190 ('The same resolution may contain both the objective and subjective elements of custom – practice and opinio juris. Just as certainly a single act of a State may be practice accompanied by the belief that that practice is required by law, resolutions adopted in a particular case might also be practice accompanied by opinio juris, and there seems no logical reason why declaratory resolutions may not also combine the two elements'); Kammerhofer, 'Uncertainty in the Formal Sources of International Law', p. 528; Andrew T. Guzman, 'Saving Customary International Law', *Michigan JIL* 27 (2006), p. 146; E. Jiménez de Aréchaga, 'General Course in Public International Law', *Rec. des cours* 159 (1978), p. 24; M. Bos, 'The Identification of Custom in International Law', *German YIL*, 25 (1982), pp. 9, 30; Müllerson, 'On the Nature and Scope of Customary International Law', p. 344; Diehl, *The Core Standard of International Investment Protection*, p. 128; S. Zamora, 'Is there Customary International Economic Law?', *German YIL* 32 (1989), p. 20.
[155] Oscar Schachter, 'Entangled Treaty and Custom', in Yoram Dinstein (ed.), *International Law at a Time of Perplexity: Essays in Honour of Shabtai Rosenne* (Martinus Nijhoff, 1989), p. 730; S. Rosenne, *Practice and Methods of International Law* (London, Oceana Publ., 1984), p 112 ('As often as not a vote is an indication of a political desideratum and not a statement of belief that that the law actually requires such a vote or contains any element of *opinio juris sive necessitatis*. . . or that the resolution is a statement of law').
[156] Dinstein, 'The Interaction between Customary International Law and Treaties', p. 304.
[157] See, *Legality of the Threat or Use of Nuclear Weapons*, Advisory Opinion, ICJ Rep. 1996, pp. 254–255, para. 70 ('The Court notes that General Assembly resolutions, even if they are not binding, may sometimes have normative value. They can, in certain circumstances, provide evidence important for establishing the existence of a rule or the emergence of an opinio juris. To establish whether this is true of a given General Assembly resolution, it is necessary to look at its content and the conditions of its adoption; it is also necessary to see whether an opinio juris exists as to its normative character').

including the conditions of the adoption of a resolution and whether it was adopted unanimously.[158] Another relevant factor is the content of the resolution and whether the language used points to a general rule of law.[159] Another important aspect, mentioned by the ICJ in the *Nicaragua* case,[160] is the attitude of States that may subsequently endorse a rule contained in a resolution and even gradually consider it as mandatory.[161]

Coming back to the problem of 'double-counting', the ICJ has recently implicitly recognized its legitimacy in the *Jurisdictional Immunities of the State* case. Thus, the Court first stated that 'State practice of particular significance [was] to be found' in, *inter alia*, 'the claims to immunity advanced by States before foreign courts'.[162] In other words, the practice of State A claiming immunity before the domestic court of State B is found in the statements (in the form of pleadings) made by State A. As for *opinio juris,* the Court said that it was, *inter alia*, 'reflected in particular in the assertion by States claiming immunity that international law accords them a right to such immunity from the jurisdiction of other States'.[163]

---

[158] Dinstein, 'The Interaction between Customary International Law and Treaties', p. 305; Lepard, *Customary International Law*, pp. 213–214; Michael P. Scharf, *Customary International Law in Times of Fundamental Change: Recognizing Grotian Moments* (Cambridge: Cambridge University Press, 2013), p. 55; ILC, Second Report, 2014, p. 58 ('While an investigation into the language and specific circumstances of adopting a given resolution is indeed indispensable, it may be suggested that in general, where "substantial numbers of negative votes and abstentions" by States are to be found, a generally held *opinio juris* as to the normative character of the resolution is missing; in other words, such resolution would "fall short of establishing the existence of an *opinio juris*". Similarly, a resolution adopted unanimously (or by an overwhelming and representative majority) may be evidence of a generally held legal conviction'). See, however, Stephen M. Schwebel, 'The Effect of Resolutions of the U.N. General Assembly on Customary International Law', *ASIL Proc.*, 73 (1979), p. 308 ('States often don't meaningfully support what a resolution says and they almost always do not mean that the resolution is law. This may be as true or truer in the case of unanimously adopted resolutions as in the case of majority-adopted resolutions. It may be truer still of resolutions adopted by consensus').

[159] Dinstein, 'The Interaction between Customary International Law and Treaties', p. 306; Lepard, *Customary International Law*, p. 212. In *Military and Paramilitary Activities in and around Nicaragua*, ICJ Rep. 1986, para. 193, the ICJ noted that 'the wording of certain General Assembly declarations adopted by States demonstrates their recognition of the principle of the prohibition of force as definitely a matter of customary law'.

[160] *Military and Paramilitary Activities in and around Nicaragua*, ICJ Rep. 1986, para. 188.

[161] Dinstein, 'The Interaction between Customary International Law and Treaties', pp. 306–307; Lepard, *Customary International Law*, p. 209.

[162] *Jurisdictional Immunities of the State (Germany v. Italy)*, ICJ Rep. 2012, para. 55.

[163] *Ibid*. See also, at para. 77 ('*opinio juris*, as demonstrated by the positions taken by States and the jurisprudence of a number of national courts which have made clear that they considered that customary international law required immunity').

Thus, the *opinio juris* of State A is to be found in the legal reasoning and arguments it adopts in claiming the existence of a *right* under custom. A number of writers, as well as the ILC,[164] believe that pleadings can sometimes be considered as an expression of *opinio juris*.[165] However, in this situation *both* the practice and the *opinio juris* come from the *same unique source*, namely the pleadings of State A before a foreign court.

In consideration of the foregoing, interpreting a statement as evidence of *both* State practice and *opinio juris* is not really 'double-counting'; it is in fact counting two different things.[166] As stated by one writer, 'State practice and *opinio iuris* may be categorically different things, but we may look for proof of either element in the same place'.[167]

Having examined the contours of the *opinio juris* requirement in general international law, the next section turns to the specific analysis of the concept in the field of investor-State arbitration.

4.2 *Opinio juris* in investor-State arbitration

This second section examines how the *opinio juris* requirement has been applied by tribunals in investor-State arbitration as well as the different interpretations of the concept given by scholars (Section 4.2.1). I will then specifically analyse the role which the *opinio juris* requirement should play regarding one controversial question which has already been explored in Chapter 3[168]: Can the content of a similarly-drafted *provision* found in numerous BITs transform into a customary rule? (Section 4.2.2). I will use the example of the FET standard to illustrate the role of *opinio juris* in such a transformation. Another controversial proposition which has been debated in doctrine is the claim that the content of *all BITs taken together* should be considered as representing

---

[164] ILC, First Report, 2013, p. 20 ('In such pleadings, States regularly adopt the two-element approach, arguing both on State practice and *opinio juris*'); ILC, Second Report, 2014, p. 52.

[165] J. Crawford, A. Pellet and C. Redgwell, 'Anglo-American and Continental Traditions in Advocacy before International Courts and Tribunals', *Cambridge J Intl Comp L* 2 (2013), p. 724, Pellet stating ('I think it is very interesting to use the pleadings before the ICJ or elsewhere to establish *opinio juris*. *Opinio juris* is something terrible to be proven, but I think it is good evidence of *opinio juris*; so it is not only practice but maybe even more *opinio juris*'); ILA, 'Sources of International Investment Law', report by M. Hirsch, ILA Study Group on the Role of Soft Law Instruments in International Investment Law (2011), p. 11.

[166] Wolfke, *Custom in Present International Law*, pp. 44–45.

[167] Kammerhofer, 'Customary International Law Needs both *Opinio* and *Usus*', p. 3.

[168] See, Chapter 3, Section 3.3.3.2.1.

the 'new' custom in investment arbitration.[169] One issue arising out of this claim is whether or not States entering into BITs do so out of any sense of legal obligation under international law (Section 4.2.3). I will examine the positions of scholars on this controversial question. Specifically, I will focus on a number of different theories that have been put forward by some of them in recent years to explain the (alleged) presence of States' *opinio juris* when signing BITs. Finally, I will critically examine some of the theories developed by scholars rejecting the necessity to specifically demonstrate *opinio juris* in investment arbitration.

4.2.1   The practice of arbitral tribunals and the position of States

As mentioned in Chapter 1,[170] the few investor-State arbitration tribunals that have defined the concept of customary international law have all referred to the necessity of demonstrating the double requirement of State practice and *opinio juris*.[171] A number of tribunals have used expressions other than *opinio juris* (or 'accepted as law' mentioned at Article 38 (1)b of the ICJ Statute) such as the requirement that States have 'a sense of legal obligation',[172] that they be 'aware that it is obligatory',[173] or that they have an 'understanding that the practice is required by law'.[174] While tribunals do mention *opinio juris*, it remains that they almost never examine such requirement in detail. This is certainly because, as pointed out by the *Glamis* Tribunal, '[a]lthough one can readily identify the practice of States, it is usually very difficult to determine the intent

---

[169] See, Chapter 3, Section 3.3.3.2.2.   [170] See, Chapter 1, Section 1.3.2.

[171] *Daimler Financial Services AG* v. *Argentina*, ICSID Case No. ARB/05/1, Award, 22 August 2012, paras. 622, 310; *Glamis Gold Ltd* v. *United States*, UNCITRAL, Award, 14 May 2009, para. 602; *MCI Power Group LC and New Turbine Incorporated* v. *Ecuador*, ICSID Case No. ARB/03/6, Award, 26 July 2007, para. 369; *Mobil Investments Canada Inc. & Murphy Oil Corporation* v. *Canada*, ICSID Case No. ARB(AF)/07/4, Decision on Liability and on Principles of Quantum, 22 May 2012, para. 127 [*Mobil* v. *Canada*]; *El Paso Energy International Co.* v. *Argentina*, ICSID Case No. ARB/03/15, Award, 31 October 2011, para. 622; *Apotex Holdings Inc & Apotex Inc.* v. *United States*, ICSID Case No. ARB(AF)/12/1, Award, 25 August 2014, paras. 99.16, 99.25.

[172] *Cambodia Power Company* v. *Cambodia and Electricité du Cambodge LLC*, ICSID Case No. ARB/09/18, Decision on Jurisdiction, 22 March 2011, para. 333; *Railroad Development Corporation (RDC)* v. *Guatemala*, ICSID Case No. ARB/07/23, Award, 29 June 2012, para. 216; *Glamis Gold Ltd* v. *United States*, Award, 14 May 2009, para. 603.

[173] *MCI Power Group LC and New Turbine Incorporated* v. *Ecuador*, Award, 26 July 2007, para. 369.

[174] *United Parcel Service of America Inc.* v. *Canada*, UNCITRAL, Award on Jurisdiction, 22 November 2002 [hereinafter *UPS* v. *Canada*], para. 84.

behind those actions'.[175] A few exceptions include the *Mondev* Tribunal that acknowledged that the so-called letters of submittal by which the US government introduces draft legislation in Congress[176] should be considered as a manifestation of that State's *opinio juris*.[177] Another example is the *Camuzzi* Tribunal, which recognized the phenomenon of 'double counting' insofar as a treaty can be a manifestation of both State practice and *opinio juris*.[178] The *Merrill & Ring* Tribunal also held that consistent and uniform practice by States could be considered as representing their *opinio juris* (a point further discussed in this chapter).[179]

Another important point worth mentioning is that States involved in arbitration disputes have often recognized that custom requires both State practice and *opinio juris*.[180] For instance, the *Mondev* Tribunal

---

[175] *Glamis Gold Ltd* v. *United States*, Award, 14 May 2009, para. 603. The Tribunal added that '[l]ooking to a claimant to ascertain custom requires it to ascertain such intent, a complicated and particularly difficult task'.

[176] These statements have been examined at Chapter 3, Section 3.3.4.2.4.2.

[177] *Mondev International Ltd.* v. *United States*, ICSID Case No. ARB(AF)/99/2, Award, 2 October 2002, para. 111 [*Mondev* v. *United States*] ('Whether or not explanations given by a signatory government to its own legislature in the course of ratification or implementation of a treaty can constitute part of the *travaux preparatoires* of the treaty for purposes of its interpretation, they can certainly shed light on the purposes and approaches taken to the treaty, and thus can evidence *opinio juris*').

[178] *Camuzzi International S.A.* v. *Argentina*, ICSID Case No. ARB/03/2, Decision on Jurisdiction, 11 May 2005, para. 144 ('there is no obstacle in international law to the expression of the will of States through treaties being at the same time an expression of practice and of the *opinio juris* necessary for the birth of a customary rule if the conditions for it are met'), See also, the same quote in: *Sempra Energy International* v. *Argentina*, ICSID Case No. ARB/02/16, Decision on Objections to Jurisdiction, 11 May 2005, para. 156.

[179] *Merrill & Ring Forestry L.P.* v. *Canada*, UNCITRAL, Award, 31 March 2010, para. 210.

[180] *ADF Group Inc.* v. *United States*, ICSID Case No. ARB(AF)/00/1, Award, 6 January 2003, para. 112 (referring to the position of the United States: 'The Pope and Talbot Tribunal did not examine the mass of existing BITs to determine whether those treaties represent concordant state practice and whether they constitute evidence of the opinio juris constituent of customary international law'); *Ibid.*, 'Mexico's Second Article 1128 Submission', 27 July 2002; *Railroad Development Corporation (RDC)* v. *Guatemala*, Award, 29 June 2012, para. 207 (referring to the position of the United States and El Salvador); *Glamis Gold Ltd* v. *United States*, Award, 14 May 2009, para. 567 (referring to the position of the United States); *Ibid.*, 'US Rejoinder', 15 March 2007, p. 141; *Mobil* v. *Canada*, Decision on Liability and on Principles of Quantum, 22 May 2012, paras. 123, 131 (referring to the position of Canada), see also, at paras. 131–132; *Chemtura Corporation* v. *Canada*, UNCITRAL, Award, 2 August 2010, para. 114 (referring to the position of Canada); *Loewen Group, Inc. and Raymond L. Loewen* v. *United States* [*Loewen* v. *United States*], 'Second Submission of Canada pursuant to NAFTA Article 1128', 27 June 2002, paras. 12, 19, 23; *Mondev* v. *United States*, Award, 2 October 2002, para. 110 (referring to the US position); *TECO Guatemala Holdings, LLC* v. *Guatemala*, ICSID Case No. ARB/10/23,

explained that all three NAFTA Parties rejected the *Pope & Talbot* Tribunal's reasoning that BITs are equal to custom without mentioning the *opinio juris* requirement.[181] In the context of the *Loewen* case, NAFTA Parties also expressed the same criticisms of the *Pope & Talbot* award's lack of reasoning on that requirement.[182] As mentioned in Chapter 1,[183] States have not only recognized the *opinio juris* requirement in their own pleadings in investor-State arbitration proceedings, but also, more recently, in their BITs. Thus, the US Model BIT (and a number of other investment treaties entered by the United States) contains an explicit reference to the 'shared understanding' of the parties that custom 'results from a general and consistent practice of States that they follow from a sense of legal obligation'.[184] The same terms are found in the Dominican Republic–Central America–United States FTA (CAFTA-DR).[185] Moreover, the Canada–China BIT also expressly refers to this double requirement of custom as 'evidenced by general State practice accepted as law'.[186]

Award, 19 December 2013, paras. 361, 366 (referring to the position Guatemala); *Ibid.*, 'Submission of the United States', 23 November 2012, para. 4; *Merrill & Ring Forestry L.P.* v. *Canada*, Award, 31 March 2010, para. 169 (referring to the position of Canada); *Spence International Investments et al.* v. *Costa Rica*, UNCITRAL (ICSID Case No. UNCT/13/2), Non-Disputing Party Submission by the United States, 17 April 2015, paras. 15–16, see also, Non-Disputing Party Submission by El Salvador, 17 April 2015, para. 6.

[181] *Mondev* v. *United States*, Award, 2 October 2002, para. 110.

[182] *Loewen* v. *United States*, 'Mexico's Article 1128 Submission Concerning Loewen Corporate Restructuring', 2 July 2002, paras. 39–40 ('The [Pope] Tribunal did not refer to the essential additional requirement of *opinio juris*. In Mexico's respectful view, the *Pope & Talbot* Tribunal's failure to observe basic principles of treaty interpretation and its treatment of proving the existence of a customary international law rule does not commend its Awards to this Tribunal. Its Awards have been wrongly decided and should be disregarded'); *Ibid.*, 'Canada's Article 1128 Submission on Jurisdiction Concerning Loewen Corporate Restructuring', 27 June 2002, paras. 18, 25–26 ('the *Pope & Talbot* Tribunal referred to no *opinio juris* surrounding these agreements and appeared unaware that such a sense of legal obligation is required before a customary norm can be found. The *Pope & Talbot* Tribunal failed to establish the fundamental preconditions to the creation of customary obligations had been met. Therefore, Canada submits that the *Pope and Talbot* Tribunal's conclusions with respect to the status of BITs as crystallizations of customary law should not be followed').

[183] See, Chapter 1, Section 1.3.2.

[184] US Model BIT (2012), Annex A; US–Rwanda BIT (2008), Annex A; US–Uruguay BIT (2005), Annex A; US–Chile FTA (2004), Annex 10-A; US–Singapore FTA (2004), Arts. 15.5 and 15.6 (with a letter exchange between the two countries, dated 6 May 2013, using the same expression to define custom).

[185] CAFTA-DR, Annex 10-b.

[186] Canada–China BIT (2014), Art. 4. The China-Mexico BIT (2008) also refers to the two elements without using the word 'custom'.

The vast majority of authors who have specifically examined the issue of custom in the field of international investment law have recognized the necessity to evidence both practice and *opinio juris*.[187] A number of them have also acknowledged that the requirement of *opinio juris* can be problematic to satisfy in practice.[188] The existence of such a requirement is recognized even by those few writers that have offered alternative theories on *how* such *opinio juris* can be demonstrated (a point further examined in this chapter).[189]

The next section examines specifically the role that the *opinio juris* requirement should play regarding one controversial question, which has already been explored in Chapter 3.

4.2.2   The role played by opinio juris *in the transformation of treaty-based norms into custom*

In Chapter 3, I examined in detail the question of whether or not the content of the same provision contained in a series of BITs can in time transform into a rule of custom and therefore become binding for *all*

---

[187] Cai Congyan, 'International Investment Treaties and the Formation, Application and Transformation of Customary International Law Rules', *Chinese JIL* 7 (2008), p. 661; Andrew T. Guzman, 'Why LDCs Sign Treaties That Hurt Them: Explaining the Popularity of Bilateral Investment Treaties', *Virginia JIL* 38(4) (1998), pp. 685–686; Al Faruque, 'Creating Customary International Law', pp. 297, 310; Tarcisio Gazzini, 'The Role of Customary International Law in the Field of Foreign Investment', *J. World Invest. & Trade*, 8 (2007), p. 694; Jan Ole Voss, *The Impact of Investment Treaties on Contracts between Host States and Foreign Investors* (Leiden: Martinus Nijhoff, 2011), p. 56; Kishoiyian, 'The Utility of Bilateral Investment Treaties', *Northwestern J. Int'l L. & Bus* 14(2) (1993), p. 336; C. McLachlan, 'Investment Treaties and General International Law', *ICLQ* 57 (2008), p. 393; M. Sornarajah, *The International Law on Foreign Investment* (2nd edn., Cambridge: Cambridge University Press, 2004), p. 204; Hindelang, 'Bilateral Investment Treaties', pp. 792–793; Hirsch, 'Sources of International Investment Law', p. 10; J. Harrison, 'The International Law Commission and the Development of International Investment Law', *Geo. Wash. Int'l L. Rev*, 45 (2013), p. 433; Stephen Vasciannie, 'The Fair and Equitable Treatment Standard in International Investment Law and Practice', *British YIL* 70 (1999), pp. 157–160; Jeswald W. Salacuse, *The Law of Investment Treaties* (Oxford: Oxford University Press, 2010), pp. 45–46.

[188] Congyan, 'International Investment Treaties and the Formation', p. 663; Voss, *The Impact of Investment Treaties on Contracts*, p. 56; Gazzini, 'The Role of Customary International Law', p. 703; Guzman, 'Why LDCs Sign Treaties That Hurt Them', p. 661; R. Kläger, *Fair and Equitable Treatment in International Investment Law* (Cambridge: Cambridge University Press, 2011), p. 268.

[189] See, for instance, Ionna Tudor, *The Fair and Equitable Treatment Standard in International Foreign Investment Law* (Oxford: Oxford University Press, 2008), p. 72, 126 ff.

States, including those that have not entered into BITs containing such a clause (and those that have not signed any BITs at all).[190] Scholars generally agree that the transformation of a treaty-based norm into a customary rule is possible.[191] However, for any such transformation to occur, the following two conditions must be met:

- First, it must be shown that a large number of States have entered into numerous BITs that contain the *same provision* (or very similarly-drafted clauses). In other words, the practice of States *parties* to BITs must be uniform, consistent and representative[192];
- Second, it must be shown, more generally, that States (including those who are *not party* to these BITs) have also adopted in their *own* practice (outside treaties) the type of conduct prescribed in these instruments. Such practice outside treaties must also be uniform, consistent, and representative for a provision contained in BITs to crystallize into custom.[193]

It is only once these two conditions have been met that the question of States' *opinio juris* will matter. Having examined the question from the angle of State practice in Chapter 3, I will now consider in the next two sections the role that *opinio juris* should play in this transformation of a treaty-based norm into a customary rule. I will use the example of the FET standard as a concrete illustration.

4.2.2.1   Which States' *opinio juris* matters and what needs to be demonstrated

The *opinio juris* of two different groups of States matters.

First (using again the FET clause as an illustration), it must be shown that States believe that they have an FET obligation towards investors outside the treaty framework. For instance, it would have to be demonstrated that States *not parties* to BITs (or those parties to BITs not containing any FET clause) believe that they have an obligation under international law to provide FET protection to foreign investors *despite* having no formal *treaty* obligation to do so.[194] Manifestations of any such belief by third parties will in practice be difficult to find.[195] One obvious place to look for this type of conviction will be in any kind of statements made by States. Such statements could, for instance, be found in the context of a State's domestic law or in a State

---

[190] See Chapter 3, Section 3.3.3.2.1.   [191] See, discussion in Chapter 3, Section 3.3.3.2.1.1.
[192] See, discussion in Chapter 3, Section 3.3.3.2.1.2.   [193] *Ibid.*
[194] ILC, Second Report, 2014, p. 55.
[195] Hindelang, 'Bilateral Investment Treaties', p. 794.

contract. Another possibility would be pleadings in proceedings before domestic courts or before any international tribunal. *Opinio juris* could also be found in judgments of domestic courts.

Second, the *opinio juris* of States *parties* to BITs also matters. It is important to note that 'textual repetition by itself is no guarantee of the emergence of the required *opinio juris*'.[196] Thus, according to the ILC Special Rapporteur, treaties '*may potentially* demonstrate the existence of "acceptance as law"'.[197] However, one has to adopt a cautious approach.[198] Wood specifically commented on the question of 'whether the repetition of a similar or identical provisions in a large number of bilateral treaties, may be of evidence of "acceptance as law"'.[199] According to him, 'the provision (and the treaty in which it is incorporated) would need to be analyzed in their context and in the light of the circumstances surrounding their adoption'.[200] Weiler came to the same conclusion in his analysis of whether the FET standard can be considered as a customary norm:

> It would seem that the most appropriate approach to determining whether a standard such as FET can be regarded as custom today would be to examine the treaty text, any available *travaux preparatoires*, and any notes or commentaries attached to it for any signs that the drafters thought they were codifying, reaffirming or including CIL by references with their work. Just because a standard has been repeated hundreds upon hundreds of times, in similar treaties, should not mean that any of the scores of parties to them ever considered any of the standards contained in them to be owed, by them, to all, as a matter of CIL. Indeed, one could assume that, given the *lex specialis* nature of enforcement contained within each regime, an opposite conclusion would be appropriate.[201]

Regarding the general context, Wood specifically referred to '[t]he multiplicity of treaties' as 'a double-edged weapon'.[202] He quoted the ICJ

---

[196] Dinstein, 'The Interaction between Customary International Law and Treaties', p. 300.

[197] ILC, Second Report, 2014, p. 54 (emphasis added). See also: Hirsch, 'Sources of International Investment Law', p. 10; Kishoiyian, 'The Utility of Bilateral Investment Treaties in the Formulation of Customary International Law', p. 337.

[198] Wolfke, *Custom in Present International Law*, p. 70 ('even more doubtful is the possible role of treaties as element of acceptance of a practice as law or at least as evidence of that element').

[199] ILC, Second Report, 2014, p. 56.   [200] *Ibid.*

[201] Todd Weiler, *The Interpretation of International Investment Law: Equality, Discrimination, and Minimum Standards of Treatment in Historical Context* (Leiden: Martinus Nijhoff Publishers, 2013), p. 236.

[202] ILC, Second Report, 2014, pp. 56–57, quoting from *Barcelona Traction, Light and Power Company, Limited, (Belgium* v. *Spain)*, Judgment, ICJ Rep. 1970, pp. 3, 306 (Separate Opinion of Judge Ammoun).

Diallo case[203] to the effect that a great number of treaties do not necessarily prove the existence of any customary rule and that it can sometimes demonstrate the exact opposite. Wood also referred to the ILA Report's conclusion that no presumption of a succession of similar treaty provisions gives rise to a new rule of customary law exists.[204] Villiger provides the following three reasons for *not* automatically deducing a State's belief that it acted out of a sense of obligation from the mere fact of having signed a treaty:

> Although the acceptance of a convention may, perhaps, indicate a familiarity with the rules therein, its significance as State practice, namely as an expression of *opinio juris*, is lessened for three reasons. First, States may enter into a convention for opposing reasons. Second, acceptance of a convention would involve recognition of dozens of articles with an indeterminate number of rules contained therein. Third *opinio juris* includes the conviction that a conduct is *customary* law. Now, ratification and accession are means by which a State expresses its "consent to be bound by a treaty" (Article 11 of the 1969 Vienna Convention on the Law of Treaties). Surely, a State which is ratifying a treaty is, at that stage, concerned first of all with its contractual obligations and not with any conviction vis-à-vis a customary rule. (. . .) It would appear then that for the signature or the ratification of a convention, or the subsequent practice of the parties, to have any significance for the formation of customary law, the *opinio juris* would have to be demonstrated *beyond the mere contractual obligation.*[205]

In the context of a BIT between States A and B containing an FET clause, both States are providing the FET standard of protection to the investors of the other party simply because they are under a treaty obligation to do so. *A priori*, this has nothing to do with custom.[206] The ILC Special Rapporteur also affirms this point: 'when the parties to a treaty act in fulfilment of their conventional obligations, this does not generally demonstrate the existence

---

[203] *Ahmadou Sadio Diallo, (Republic of Guinea v. Democratic Republic of the Congo),* Preliminary Objections, Judgment, ICJ Rep. 2007, pp. 582, 615 ('The fact invoked by Guinea that various international agreements, such as agreements for the promotion and protection of foreign investments and the Washington Convention, have established special legal regimes governing investment protection, or that provisions in this regard are commonly included in contracts entered into directly between States and foreign investors, is not sufficient to show that there has been a change in the customary rules of diplomatic protection; it could equally show the contrary').

[204] ILA, Final Report, 2000, p. 47.

[205] Villiger, *Customary International law and Treaties,* pp. 26–27 (emphasis in the original).

[206] Dinstein, 'The Interaction between Customary International Law and Treaties', p. 299 ('consent to be bound by a treaty does not *per se* indicate that the State concerned necessarily believes that the text is concordant with custom').

of an *opinio juris*.[207] As explained by the ICJ in the *Nicaragua* case, 'the shared view of the Parties as to the content of what they regard as the rule is not enough' to demonstrate the existence of a customary rule.[208] Thus, as noted by ILC Special Rapporteur Wood, 'for a treaty to serve as evidence of *opinio juris*' States 'must be shown to regard the rule(s) enumerated in the treaty as binding on them as rules of law regardless of the treaty'.[209]

In the context of the FET standard, it must be demonstrated that both States A and B believe that they have an *obligation* under international law to provide FET protection to each other's investors *notwithstanding* the fact that such protection is set out in the BIT.[210] This issue raises a fundamental question. *Why* did States start to include FET clauses in their BITs in the first place? As mentioned in Chapter 3,[211] Western States started including such a reference in their BITs in the 1960s and 1970s because of the ambiguities surrounding the concept of the minimum standard of treatment (MST) and the fact that developing States rejected the existence of such standard.[212] In this context, as noted by one writer, 'it would be difficult to posit that there was consensus between developed and developing countries that the [FET] standard had passed into customary law: there may have been some degree of uniformity and consistency in practice in the decade preceding discussions on the New International Economic Order, but one would be hard-pressed to identify supportive *opinio juris*, particularly on the part of developing States'.[213] The situation is not different today: 'developing countries

---

[207] ILC, Second Report, 2014, p. 43, citing a number of individual opinions of ICJ judges. See also: *North Sea Continental Shelf Cases,* ICJ Rep. 1969, p. 43, para. 76.

[208] *Military and Paramilitary Activities in and around Nicaragua,* ICJ Rep. 1986, para. 184 ('Where two States agree to incorporate a particular rule in a treaty, their agreement suffices to make that rule a legal one, binding upon them; but in the field of customary international law, the shared view of the Parties as to the content of what they regard as the rule is not enough. The Court must satisfy itself that the existence of the rule in the opinio juris of States is confirmed by practice').

[209] ILC, Second Report, 2014, p. 55. See also: Diehl, *The Core Standard of International Investment Protection*, p. 129.

[210] Al Faruque, 'Creating Customary International Law', p. 300; R. Dolzer 'New Foundations of the Law of Expropriation of Alien Property', *AJIL* (1981), p. 566, for whom it needs to be shown that 'the states concluding the treaties felt themselves legally obligated to regulate their relationship in the way they phrased the treaty'.

[211] See, Chapter 3, Section 3.2.4.

[212] Weiler, *The Interpretation of International Investment Law*, pp. 199, 211–212, 216, 227, 239–240; Vasciannie, 'The Fair and Equitable Treatment Standard', pp. 157–158; Patrick Dumberry, *The Fair and Equitable Treatment Standard: A Guide to NAFTA Case Law on Article 1105* (Alphen aan den Rijn: Wolters Kluwer, 2013), p. 31 ff.

[213] Vasciannie, 'The Fair and Equitable Treatment Standard', pp. 157–158.

have still not clearly indicated acceptance of the notion that they are obliged, as a matter of international law, to offer investors fair and equitable treatment'.[214] The same is true for developed States. In other words, there is no indication in treaty texts (or even in *travaux preparatoires* or anywhere else) establishing that States include FET clauses in their BITs out of a sense of conviction that this is the type of protection they *must* accord to foreign investors under international law. While the present author has found elsewhere a number of BITs containing provisions that plainly explain that the treaty obligation exists under custom (they are examined in the next section) none was found regarding the FET clause.

   In sum, I have found no indicia showing that States believe that they have an *obligation* under international law to provide FET protection to foreign investors.[215] They include such clauses in their BITs 'as a means of facilitating investment in their respective countries'.[216] In other words, they include FET clauses because they believe that this is in their best interest. Thus, on the one hand, the inclusion of such a clause may result in attracting foreign investors. On the other hand, such a clause provides proper legal protection to these States' own investors doing business abroad.

4.2.2.2   Examples of where to find States' *opinio juris*

So where can evidence of *opinio juris* by treaty parties be found *outside* the treaty itself? One relatively straightforward situation is in a treaty that is *declaratory* of customary international law.[217] States parties' acceptance of the declaratory nature of the treaty may serve as clear evidence of their *opinio juris*.[218] However, as mentioned

---

[214] *Ibid.*, p. 158. See also his comment (at p. 161) that *opinio juris* must be found 'among a significant cross-section of countries, having special regard to the different perspectives which have been traditionally presented by both capital-exporting and importing States, as well as the views of countries with economies in transition'.

[215] Vasciannie, 'The Fair and Equitable Treatment Standard', pp. 160–164; Kläger, *Fair and Equitable Treatment*, pp. 267–268; Marcela Klein Bronfman, 'Fair and Equitable Treatment: An Evolving Standard', *Max Planck Yrbk. UNL*, 10 (2006), pp. 670–671. This issue is discussed further in Chapter 4, Section 4.2.3.3.1.

[216] Hussein Haeri, 'A Tale of Two Standards: 'Fair and Equitable Treatment' and the Minimum Standard in International Law', *Arb. Int'l*, 27 (2011), p. 43.

[217] ILC, Second Report, 2014, p. 55.

[218] *Ibid.*, p. 55. See also: Weiler, *The Interpretation of International Investment Law*, pp. 236–237: 'On the other hand, if an explicit statement has been made – either in the treaty text or in an accompanying official document – that one or more of the standards found in the treaty is considered by that State to be universally binding upon it, that would be a

above,[219] the content of BITs cannot be considered as globally 'declaratory' of customary international law. In this context, it is arguably more difficult to find evidence of any *opinio juris* of a State party to a BIT when considering the binding nature of an obligation (*notwithstanding* the fact that such protection is set out in the BIT). This point is well-explained by Baxter:

> What weight is in principle to be accorded to such evidence must also turn on how positivistic a view of the law is entertained by the user of it. A strict application of the requirement of *opinio juris* may lead to the rejection of those agreements that fail to reflect any sense of legal obligation. But there will still remain cases in which either the text of the treaty or the history of its negotiation will plainly indicate that it was concluded out of a sense of legal obligation.[220]

Baxter's last point is important. While the text of a BIT itself will very rarely contain any indication of a State's belief that a provision is obligatory under international law,[221] one cannot exclude such possibility. The next paragraphs will examine a number of concrete existing examples of BIT provisions where such *opinio* can be found. I will also examine other examples of where to find States' *opinio juris*.

The present author has found a number of BITs containing a provision that plainly explains that the treaty obligation exists under custom. Such a clause is found in the most recent US Model BIT, the Dominican Republic–Central America–United States FTA,[222] as well as in a number of BITs entered into by the United States with other States.[223] These

very good reason to conclude that these parties meant what they said about the applicable standard's status as custom'); Hindelang, 'Bilateral Investment Treaties', p. 794 ('If each State, or each treaty subsequently concluded, stipulates that the States acted with an *opinio juris*, then the generation or existence of a rule of customary law identical with the treaty rule is beyond doubt').

[219] See, discussion in Chapter 3, Section 3.3.3.2.2.

[220] Baxter, 'Treaties and Custom', p. 80.

[221] J.I. Charney, 'International Agreements and the Development of Customary International Law', *Washington L.R.*, 61 (1986), p. 991 ('If, however, an isolated rule contained within an agreement can form the basis upon which customary law is established, then one must assume that the negotiation and acceptance of the agreement as a whole can be relied upon to provide the elements of customary law. This would be difficult. For example, it is not clear how such proof can support the conclusion that there has been acceptance or opinio juris with respect to a rule that is isolated from the context of the agreement as a whole').

[222] Dominican Republic–Central America–United States Free Trade Agreement, Annex 10-C.

[223] US–Rwanda BIT (2008), Annex A; US–Uruguay BIT (2005), Annex A; US–Chile FTA (2004), Annex 10-A; US–Singapore FTA (2004), Arts. 15.5 and 15.6 (with a letter

treaties indicate that it is the 'shared understanding' of the parties that the clause on expropriation 'is intended to reflect customary international law concerning the obligation of States with respect to expropriation'.[224] Such an explicit clause is evidence of States parties' belief in the customary nature of the prohibition of expropriation (as formulated in the BIT).

There are a few other examples of such an explicit clause in the context of the FET standard. The Protocol to the 2005 Australia–Mexico BIT explains that the FET clause 'prescribes the customary international law standard of treatment of aliens as the MST to be afforded to investments of Investors of another Contracting Party'.[225] In other words, these States recognize the customary nature of the MST. The same affirmation is found in a number of other BITs,[226] including several BITs entered into by Mexico[227] and by Canada,[228] as well as recent FTAs entered into by the United States.[229] While other treaties do not explicitly refer to the customary nature of the MST, the language that is used strongly suggests that the parties believe this is the case.[230]

exchange between the two countries, dated 6 May 2013, using the same expression to define custom).

[224] US Model BIT (2004). [225] Australia–Mexico BIT (2005), Art. 4.

[226] See, *inter alia*: Japan–Laos BIT (2008), art. 5; Colombia's Model BIT (2008), art. 3; China–Peru FTA (2009), art. 132.

[227] Czech Republic–Mexico BIT (2002), art. 2 protocol; Iceland–Mexico BIT (2005), art. 3, protocol; India–Mexico BIT (2007), art. 5; United Kingdom–Mexico BIT (2006), art. 3; Trinidad and Tobago–Mexico BIT (2006), Art. 5; China–Mexico BIT (2008), art. 5.

[228] Canada–Czech Republic BIT (2009), Art. 3; Canada–Jordan BIT (2009), art. 5; Canada–Latvia BIT (2009), art. 5; Canada–Peru BIT (2006), art. 5; Canada–Romania BIT (2009), art. 2; Canada–Slovakia BIT (2010), art. 3.

[229] See, Andrew P. Tuck, 'The "Fair And Equitable Treatment" Standard Pursuant to the Investment Provisions of the U.S. Free Trade Agreements with Peru, Colombia and Panama', *L. & Bus. Rev. Am.* 16 (2010), p. 385. Explicit references to custom are also found in recent FTAs entered into by the United States with Australia (2004), Central America (CAFTA, 2004), Chile (2003), Morocco (2004) and Singapore (2003, see the side letter of 6 May 2003). See also: US Model BIT (2004), Annex 1; US–Uruguay BIT (2005), art. 5(2), Annex A.

[230] Agreement Establishing the ASEAN–Australia–New Zealand Free Trade Area (2009), Chp. 11, Art. 6 ('1. Each Party shall accord to covered investments fair and equitable treatment and full protection and security. 2. For greater certainty (. . .) the concepts of "fair and equitable treatment" and "full protection and security" do not require treatment in addition to or beyond that which is required under customary international law, and do not create additional substantive rights'). See also: Malaysia–New Zealand FTA (2009), art. 10.10(2) (c); Belgium/Luxembourg Economic Union–Peru BIT (2005), art 3(1); China–Mexico BIT (2008).

Apart from these few clear examples found in BITs, concrete manifestations of a State's *opinio juris* are rare. Such indication could, for instance, be found in statements by States, including pleadings, declarations and so on. For example, in the context of NAFTA Article 1105 (the FET clause), the United States,[231] Canada[232] and Mexico[233] have explicitly recognized in their pleadings the customary nature of the MST.

The present author has found a number of other concrete examples of where to find *opinio juris*. One example can be found in the context of the procedure (already mentioned in the previous chapter[234]) used in the United States where a 'Letter of Submittal' (or 'Transmittal') is sent by the US State Department to the US President, requesting approval of any BIT by the US Senate. For instance, the Letter of Transmittal for the 1997 US–Azerbaijan BIT indicates that the provision on expropriation 'incorporates into the Treaty customary international law standards for expropriation'. The same reference is found in several other letters.[235] This is a clear example of a statement by a State affirming its *opinio juris* regarding the customary nature of a treaty provision. Another similar example is the explanation found in these letters regarding the FET clause, which typically states that the host State 'shall in no case accord treatment less favorable than that required by international law'. A number of these letters explain that this provision 'sets out a minimum standard of treatment based on standards found in customary international law' and that '[t]he general reference to international law also implicitly incorporates other fundamental rules of customary international law regarding the treatment of foreign investment'.[236] Such a reference is

---

[231] *Glamis Gold Ltd* v. *United States*, 'US Rejoinder', 15 March 2007, pp. 6, 139–140 ('there is no dispute between the parties that Article 1105 prescribes the customary international law minimum standard of treatment'); *ADF Group Inc.* v. *United States*, Award, 9 January 2003, para. 110, citing 'Post-Hearing Submission of Respondent United States of America on Article 1105(1) and *Pope & Talbot*', 27 June 2002, p. 2.

[232] See, for instance, *Merrill & Ring Forestry L.P.* v. *Canada*, 'Canada's Rejoinder', 27 March 2009, paras. 149–150, 166 ff; *Methanex Corporation* v. *United States*, UNCITRAL, 'Canada's Second 1128 Submission', 30 April 2001, para. 26 ('Canada agrees with the disputing parties that NAFTA Article 1105 incorporates the international minimum standard of treatment recognized by customary international law').

[233] *Methanex Corporation* v. *United States*, 'Mexico's Article 1128 Submission', 15 May 2001, para. 9.

[234] See, Chapter 3, Section 3.3.4.2.4.2.

[235] Letters regarding *inter alia* the following BITs: US–Bahrain BIT (1999); US–Bolivia BIT (1998); US–El Salvador BIT (1999); US–Honduras BIT (1995); US–Jordan BIT (1997); US–Lithuania BIT (1998); US–Mozambique BIT (1998); US–Croatia BIT (1996).

[236] See, the letters regarding the following BITs: US–Azerbaijan BIT (1997); US–Bahrain BIT (1999); US–Bolivia BIT (1998); US–El Salvador BIT (1999); US–Honduras BIT

an explicit acknowledgment by the United States of its own *opinio juris* regarding the customary nature of the MST. The same is true for Canada's 1994 'Statement on Implementation' of NAFTA, which explains that the FET obligation under Article 1105 constitutes a reference to the MST under customary international law.[237]

4.2.3   Do States have any opinio juris when they sign BITs?

As mentioned in the previous chapter,[238] one of the most controversial issues currently debated in academia is whether the thousands of BITs *taken together* represent the 'new' custom in the field of investment law. I have already provided several reasons why this proposition should be rejected.[239] As mentioned in Chapter 3, one of the main weaknesses of the proposition that BITs are equal to custom is its basic failure to meet the first requirement of the definition of customary international law.[240] BITs are very diverse in their content and scope. Taken together, these treaties are certainly not consistent enough to constitute the basis of any rule of customary international law. However, that does not mean that no customary rules exist in the field of investment law. Chapter 2 has shown the existence of at least two such rules.[241]

Having examined the first requirement of State practice, the next sections will now analyse *opinio juris*. Specifically, I will examine whether there is any evidence of *opinio juris* by States when signing BITs. I will look at the arguments advanced by scholars on this controversial

(1995); US–Jordan BIT (1997); US–Lithuania BIT (1998); US–Mozambique BIT (1998). A number of letters only contain the first sentence ('This paragraph sets out a minimum standard of treatment based on customary international law'), see: US–Albania BIT (1995); US–Armenia BIT (1992); US–Ecuador BIT (1993); US–Estonia BIT (1994); US–Jamaica BIT (1994); US–Kazakhstan BIT (1992); US–Kyrgyzstan BIT (1993); US–Latvia BIT (1995); US–Moldova BIT (1993); US–Mongolia BIT (1994); US-Trinidad and Tobago BIT (1994); US–Ukraine BIT (1994). Very similar wording is used in other letters, see: US–Georgia BIT (1994); US–Croatia BIT (1996).

[237] Department of External Affairs, NAFTA, Canadian Statement on Implementation, *Canada Gazette*, 1 January 1994, p. 68, at p. 149 ('Article 1105, which provides for treatment in accordance with international law, is intended to assure a minimum standard of treatment of investments of NAFTA investors. National treatment provides a relative standard of treatment while this article provides for a minimum absolute standard of treatment, based on long-standing principles of customary international law').

[238] See, Chapter 3, Section 3.3.3.2.2.   [239] See Chapter 3, Section 3.3.3.2.2.2.
[240] See Chapter 3, Section 3.3.3.2.2.3.   [241] See, Chapter 2, Section 2.6.

question and the reasons they generally invoke for rejecting this proposition (Sections 4.2.3.1 and 4.2.3.2). I will also focus on a number of different theories which have been put forward by other writers in recent years to explain the (alleged) presence of States' *opinio juris* when signing BITs (Section 4.2.3.3).

4.2.3.1 States sign BITs to protect their own interests, not out of any sense of obligation

According to the *UPS* Tribunal, '[w]hile BITs are large in number, their coverage is limited (. . .) and in terms of *opinio juris* there is no indication that they reflect a general sense of obligation'.[242] The Tribunal does not further explain precisely why no *opinio juris* exists. It simply notes that the failure of efforts to establish a multilateral agreement on investment (MAI) in the 1990s 'provides further evidence of that lack of a sense of obligation'.[243]

In the next paragraphs, I will examine the circumstances and the reasons why States have signed BITs. I will show that they do so solely based on their (perceived) economic interests. They do not sign BITs out of any sense of conviction that this is what they *must* do under international law.[244] This is indeed the position that States (at least in the NAFTA context) have *themselves* adopted.[245]

As explained by one writer, 'a BIT between a developed and a developing country is founded on a grand bargain: a *promise* of protection of capital in return for the *prospect* of more capital in the future'.[246] Thus, '[t]he most common explanation to the BIT puzzle is that developing countries sign BITs as a means to *promote* foreign investment and to increase the amount of capital and associated technology flowing to their

---

[242] *UPS* v. *Canada*, Award on Jurisdiction, 22 November 2002, para. 97.   [243] *Ibid.*

[244] Al Faruque, 'Creating Customary International Law', p. 310; McLachlan, 'Investment Treaties and General International Law', p. 393; Congyan, 'International Investment Treaties and the Formation', para. 14.

[245] *Mondev* v. *United States*, Award, 2 October 2002, para. 110, explaining that all three NAFTA Parties have rejected the *Pope & Talbot* Tribunal's reasoning omitting to mention the *opinio juris* requirement and adding that 'These States appear to question whether the parties to the very large numbers of bilateral investment treaties have acted out of a sense of legal obligation when they include provisions in those treaties such as that for "fair and equitable" treatment of foreign investment'.

[246] J.W. Salacuse, 'The Treatification of International Investment Law: a Victory of Form Over Life? A Crossroads Crossed?', *TDM* 3(3) (2006), p. 7 (emphasis in the original).

territories'.[247] As explained in Chapter 2,[248] Guzman provides another
explanation as to why developing countries that had long rejected the so-
called Hull formula on compensation for expropriation have nevertheless
signed hundreds of BITs containing provisions with similar language.[249]
According to him, these States sign BITs to have 'an advantage in the
competition for foreign investment'.[250] Most importantly, for the purpose of the present book, Guzman believes that it is 'simply not possible
to explain the paradoxical behaviour of [less developed countries] toward
foreign investment based on a view that BITs reflect *opinio juris*'.[251]
According to Guzman, these BITs 'do not reflect a sense of legal obligation but are rather the result of countries using the international tools at
their disposal to pursue their economic interests'.[252]

Guzman is right in claiming that economic interests primarily moti-
vate States to enter into BITs. These treaties are indeed the result of trade-
offs and mutual concessions between States.[253] Their content depends on
the political and economic bargaining power of each party to the

---

[247] *Ibid.* (emphasis in the original), providing four other reasons why developing States sign
BITs: relationship-building, economic liberalization, domestic investment encouragement, to improve governance and to strengthen the rule of law.

[248] See, discussion in Chapter 2, Section 2.3.3.

[249] Guzman, 'Why LDCs Sign Treaties That Hurt Them', p. 640.   [250] *Ibid.*, p. 687.

[251] *Ibid.* See also: Al Faruque, 'Creating Customary International Law', p. 313. *Contra*:
Alvarez, 'A Bit on Custom', p. 41 ('While Guzman is correct that most BITs do not
affirm, in so many words, their intent to codify or progressively develop the general law,
many of them do the next best thing: they expressly include the protections extended by
customary law and make these subject to investor-state dispute settlement. Guzman is
therefore wrong to suggest that the content of BITs does not suggest an intent to affirm
customary law').

[252] Guzman, 'Why LDCs Sign Treaties That Hurt Them', p. 687. See also, p. 643 ('because
BITs are signed by developing countries in pursuit of their economic self-interest rather
than out of sense of legal obligation, these treaties do not support a rule of customary
international law that incorporates the Hull Rule'). For a critical analysis, see: Hindelang,
'Bilateral Investment Treaties', p. 799 ff.

[253] Kishoiyian, 'The Utility of Bilateral Investment Treaties', pp. 372, 333 ('Each treaty is
bound to be different from the other as each depends on the internal political order and
the economic aspirations of each developing country. A country may concede far
reaching rights to another on account of the quids it receives in return for such
concessions. Each treaty then stands on its feet as formulating a particular legal order
shared by only two countries and it reflects a compromise of the particular interests of
the parties. As such, they do not give rise to any international consensus capable of
creating a structure for the protection of foreign investment'); Al Faruque, 'Creating
Customary International Law', p. 316 ('BITs create a special legal regime as each BIT is in
real sense and isolated bargain, which seeks to accommodate economic interests of
contracting parties'); D. Carreau and P. Juillard, *Droit international économique* (Paris:
LGDJ, 1998), p. 469.

negotiations.[254] BITs are therefore the result of a compromise between conflicting interests. While it is true that economic interests are not the only reasons why developing States sign BITs,[255] what is clear is that they do not do so based on any perceived legal obligation. Many writers have come to the same conclusion.[256] On the contrary, Alvarez is of the view that 'the "original intent" behind the signing of BITs is, as time passes, increasingly irrelevant' to determine *opinio juris*.[257]

4.2.3.2   Other reasons given by scholars to explain States' lack of *opinio juris*

States' self-interest is not the only explanation offered by scholars to elucidate why they sign BITs. This section will examine a number of other arguments that have been put forward by scholars to reject the existence of any *opinio juris* by States when signing BITs.

---

[254] O. Schachter, 'International Law in Theory and Practice: General Course in Public International Law', *Rec. des cours* 178 (1982), p. 303; Kishoiyian, 'The Utility of Bilateral Investment Treaties', p. 333.

[255] Alvarez, 'A Bit on Custom', p. 41 ff, indicating a number of other reasons.

[256] Carreau and Juilliard, *Droit international économique,* p. 469; Courtney C. Kirkman, 'Fair and Equitable Treatment: Methanex v. United States and the Narrowing Scope of NAFTA Article 1105', *Law & Pol'y Int'l Bus.,* 34 (2002–2003), p. 385; Vasciannie, 'The Fair and Equitable Treatment Standard', pp. 158–161; Klein Bronfman, 'Fair and Equitable Treatment', pp. 670–671; Sornarajah, *The International Law on Foreign Investment,* p. 206; Alexander Orakhelashvili, 'The Normative Basis of "Fair and Equitable Treatment": General International Law on Foreign Investment?', *Archiv des Völkerrechts* 1 (2008), p. 77; A. Newcombe and L. Paradell, *Law and Practice of Investment Treaties: Standards of Treatment* (Alphen aan den Rijn: Kluwer, 2009), pp. 270–271; Peter T. Muchlinski, *Multinational Enterprises & the Law* (2nd edn., Oxford: Oxford University Press, 2007), p. 701; Manu Sanan, 'International Investment Law; Questions Riddling an Answer', *Trade, law and Development,* 2(1) (2010), p. 14; Haeri, 'A Tale of Two Standards', p. 43; Congyan, 'International Investment Treaties and the Formation', p. 665. A different position is adopted by a few writers: Thomas Wälde, *Nouveaux horizons pour le droit international des investissements dans le contexte de la mondialisation de l'économie* (Paris: Pedone, 2004), p. 44 ('Le fait que les pays en voie de développement ou en transition espèrent accroître l'attirance de leurs conditions d'investissement en concluant un traité bilatéral d'investissement n'est pas nécessairement un argument contre la présupposition de l'*opinio juris* qui accompagne de telles signatures, c. à. d. l'idée qu'ils s'engagent à respecter des règles qui sont de toute façon les règles en vigueur dans les nations civilisées'); Charles Leben, 'L'évolution du droit international des investissements' *Journal CEPMLP,* 7(12) (2000).

[257] Alvarez, 'A Bit on Custom', p. 44, adding 'whether or not LDCs or others entered into BITs out of greed, altruism, or other "internal" political considerations tells us nothing about the current state of custom or general principles of law'.

One common theme amongst writers is the so-called unequal and uneven bargaining strength of the parties in BIT negotiation. According to some writers, this feature effectively prevents developing States from entering into these instruments with any sense of legal obligation. For instance, Al Faruque argues that the 'unequal bargaining strength especially manifested in BITs between developed and developing countries, diminishes the developing country's autonomy to give consent to BIT considerably'.[258] Congyan adopts the same position where he states that 'one should be cautious in identifying the *opinio juris* from treaties' because many BITs 'are brought out in the absence of free will of the contracting parties'.[259] According to him, 'the appropriate justification to deny the existence of *opinio juris* from some developing countries in BIT is that in many cases these countries conclude BITs (. . .) as the result of undue pressure from developed countries (. . .)'.[260]

Another closely related argument invoked by other writers is the fact that 'developing countries may well accept bilateral investment treaties out of perceived necessity'.[261] As a result, Vasciannie believes that 'it would be artificial to argue, in the absence of other supporting evidence,

[258] Al Faruque, 'Creating Customary International Law', pp. 310, 315. See also: Bronfman, 'Fair and Equitable Treatment', p. 671.

[259] Congyan, 'International Investment Treaties and the Formation', p. 663.

[260] *Ibid.*, p. 665. In this regard, he notes that despite the 'huge disparities of power' in such negotiation, it remains that the foundation of multilateral treaties is more equitable than BITs: 'As to the issue whether multilateral treaties and bilateral treaties have different implications in the formation of *opinio juris*, my answer is YES. (. . .) That is to say, there are often huge disparities of power both in the negotiation of multilateral treaties and bilateral treaties: in the negotiation of multilateral treaties, the "multilateral game mechanism" engaged in by all negotiating States makes it possible to redress to a large extent such disparities of power between pairs of negotiating States; on the contrary, in the negotiation of bilateral treaties, "bilateral game mechanism" engaged in by only two negotiating States in many cases leads to direct confrontation between the two States, the result of which is either the breakdown of negotiation or the success of negotiation at the expense of the interest of one party. Thus, the foundation of multilateral treaties is more equitable than that of bilateral treaties. It is this perception that makes it necessary for one to be extremely cautious to assert the existence of *opinio juris*' (p. 663). See also: Bronfman, 'Fair and Equitable Treatment', pp. 670–671 ('There is a lack of opinio juris by developing countries that have accepted the inclusion of the standard more for political or economical reasons that may be imposed by developed countries than on the basis of conviction. (. . .) Moreover, an unequal bargaining power may contribute to this').

[261] Vasciannie, 'The Fair and Equitable Treatment Standard', p. 159, adding that 'for the most part, the contents of modern bilateral investment treaties are largely determined by developed countries, and developing countries have the option of accepting developed country proposals with limited modifications, or of rejecting the treaties in their entirety'.

that [developing countries] accept particular provisions in these treaties as rules of customary law'.[262] According to him, even in the context of BITs entered into *between* developing countries, it would have to be shown that they have included an FET clause out of a sense of obligation.[263] Finally, according to other writers, a lack of *opinio juris* arises from the fact that BITs often serve political and ideological purposes for some developed States, such as, for instance, the promotion of capitalism, liberalism and democracy.[264]

While it is true that BITs have historically been signed between developed and developing States, the general panorama has drastically changed since then. Developing States are increasingly concluding treaties with each other. In 2008, 'South–South' BITs represented 26% of the total number of BITs.[265] Empirical studies show that the content of these 'South–South' BITs is *not* significantly different from the other treaties entered into by developing States with developed States.[266] Accordingly, as noted by one writer, 'it is untenable to describe the network of BITs and FTAs as an enterprise that excludes the Global South as willing participants[;] whatever it once was, investment law is not *now* a set of one-sided tools for the imposition of Western power'.[267]

While the unequal nature of the negotiations between *some* (but not all) treaty partners is undeniable,[268] it remains that sovereign States

---

[262] *Ibid.*   [263] *Ibid.*

[264] Al Faruque, 'Creating Customary International Law', p. 315, referring to the BIT program of the United States in Eastern Europe and ex-USSR and also indicating that 'developing countries sometimes use BIT to pursue a variety of economic nationalist and populist policies prompted by special political consideration'. See also: Congyan, 'International Investment Treaties and the Formation', p. 665: 'the appropriate justification to deny the existence of *opinio juris* from some developing countries in BIT is that in many cases these countries conclude BITs (...) as a result of their aspiration for international legitimacy during economic or political transformation' (adding, however, that this argument is no longer valid when a developing State becomes capital exporting).

[265] UNCTAD, 'Recent Developments in International Investment Agreements (2007–June 2008)', *IIA Monitor* 2 (2008), p. 3. The Report does not include as 'developing States' countries from 'South-East Europe' and the 'Commonwealth of Independent States'.

[266] C. Schreuer and R. Dolzer, *Principles of International Investment Law* (Oxford: Oxford University Press, 2008), p. 16. One study (UNCTAD, 'South-South Cooperation in International Investment Arrangements', UNCTAD Series on International Investment Policies for Development [2005], p. 45) concluded that '[t]o a large part, South-South IIAs [international Investment Agreements] are similar to North-South IIAs'.

[267] Alvarez, 'A Bit on Custom', p. 51 (emphasis in the original). See also: José E. Alvarez, 'The Contemporary International Investment Regime: An "Empire of Law" or the "Law of Empire"?', *Alabama L.Rev.* 60 (2009), p. 943.

[268] Sornarajah, *The International Law on Foreign Investment*, pp. 218–219.

cannot (at least in modern days) be forced into signing BITs without their express consent. The present author is unaware of any documented case where a State has been literally *forced* by another to sign a BIT.[269] While it is true that political and economic pressure can sometimes play an important role in a State's decision to sign a BIT with another, Alvarez notes that 'international law does not affirm that treaties are void or voidable if one of the treaty parties succumbed to economic pressure'.[270] Ultimately, even the reluctant State will decide to sign a BIT because it believes (rightly or wrongly) that it has an interest in doing so. Therefore, as Baxter has argued, the unequal nature of the parties involved in treaty negotiation should not *per se* be an obstacle from discovering *opinio juris*.[271]

In my view, States' self-interest remains the best explanation as to why they sign BITs. That interest may be political, economic, ideological and so on, but ultimately, States do not sign BITs out of any belief or conviction that they are under an obligation to do so under international law.

4.2.3.3   Alternative theories put forward by scholars in support of the claim that States have an *opinio juris* when signing BITs

As explained in the last two sections, States clearly do not show evidence of any *opinio juris* when they sign BITs. However, in recent years, a number of scholars have put forward alternative theories, aimed at explaining that States are in fact acting out of a belief or conviction that they have an obligation to sign BITs. The present section will examine these different theories that have been put forward by writers. According to some scholars, *opinio juris* can simply be deduced from the fact that a large number of States have adopted close to three thousand BITs containing similar provisions (Section 4.2.3.3.1). Moreover, other writers argue that States' *opinio juris* exists simply

---

[269] Sornarajah, *Ibid.*, p. 208 ('It is unlikely that, if any doctrine of unequal treaties does exist outside the field of coercion, it could be applied to the situation of BITs. BITs are voluntary, and there is no element of coercion involved in their making').

[270] Alvarez, 'A Bit on Custom', p. 38.

[271] Baxter, 'Treaties and Custom', p. 89 ('If one were to seek absolute equality of bargaining power and the complete absence of inducements or pressures, very few settlements of international disputes or arrangements of matters of mutual concern could be taken as evidence of customary international law. And proof of the complete equality of the two States involved in each episode would make intolerably cumbersome the establishment of "a general practice accepted as law"').

because the protection of foreign investments in BITs is in the best interests of all States (Section 4.2.3.3.2).

4.2.3.3.1 States' *opinio juris* is embodied in their practice   One of the most comprehensive alternative approaches to *opinio juris* has been developed by Tudor in her book on the FET standard. I have already specifically addressed her claim that the FET standard is a norm of customary international law.[272] This section only focuses on her position regarding *opinio juris*.

Tudor first explains that the ICJ has been hesitant in some cases concerning the role of this subjective requirement[273] and that a number of classic authors have rejected the relevance of demonstrating *opinio juris*.[274] She rejects the two-element theory, requiring both State practice and *opinio juris*, which she qualifies as 'rigid'.[275] Quoting the work of Jennings,[276] she concludes that these different arguments 'underline that in a modern society, governed by fast tools of communication and by continuous contacts among States, constant and uniform state practice is sufficient to form a custom'.[277] According to her, 'opinio juris may thus have, in effect, become obsolete for the formation of custom in many areas of law', including investment arbitration.[278] It is true that, as mentioned by Mendelson, 'one of the results of this huge increase in the quantity of international interaction is a vast proliferation of the opportunities for international law-making in all senses of that term'.[279] In other words, as a result of the rapid increase in the speed of communications, there is clearly more opportunities for State practice to develop very quickly.[280] Not only do States have more opportunity to

---

[272] See, Chapter 3, Section 3.2.4.
[273] Tudor, *The Fair and Equitable Treatment Standard*, p. 73.   [274] *Ibid.*, p. 80.
[275] *Ibid.*
[276] Robert Y. Jennings, 'What is International Law and How do We Tell When We see It', *ASDI* 37 (1981) ('perhaps it is time to face squarely the fact that the orthodox tests of custom – practice and *opinio juris* – is often not only inadequate but even irrelevant for the identification of much new law today').
[277] Tudor, *The Fair and Equitable Treatment Standard*, p. 81.   [278] *Ibid.*, p. 82.
[279] Mendelson, 'The Formation of Customary International Law', p. 349. See also, Wolfke, *Custom in Present International Law*, p. 59, but also noting, at p. 60 that '[n]ot only can the requirement of practice be fulfilled faster but, for the same reasons, also quantitatively is less practice needed nowadays than in the past'.
[280] Mendelson, 'The Formation of Customary International Law', p. 349 ('The velocity of modern life means that a quick response is often required, and the increase in the occasions for interaction means that the requisite quantity of precedents can sometimes develop remarkably quickly').

adopt specific conducts and actions and to make statements on a variety of issues, but other States will also be able to quickly analyse and respond to such statements and conduct. Yet, even in light of these undeniable recent developments, it does not logically follow that *opinio juris* has suddenly become irrelevant.

According to Tudor, 'the inclusion of the FET clause in a large majority of BITs suggests that the FET standard became somewhat unavoidable in the international law of foreign investments' and 'stands for the States' belief that this principle is one of the fundamental concepts applicable to investment law relations'.[281] Tudor's main reason for rejecting the need to show *opinio* is because this subjective element is 'embodied in the State practice under consideration'[282]:

> it is argued that the idea of justice that is embodied both in the concept of 'fairness' and in the one of 'equity' directly encapsulates opinio juris within state practice. In the case of the fair and equitable treatment standard, the existing constant and uniform state practice may suffice to demonstrate the customary character of FET, without the necessity to examine the existence of an opinio juris. Should uniform state practice be established in front of a tribunal, it should fall upon the State party to rebut the presumption that it had not displayed the commensurate conviction when it embarked upon past practice.[283]

She further explains her affirmation that 'the idea of justice' 'encapsulates *opinio juris* within state practice' as follows:

> The existence of inherent elements of fairness and equity in a great number of national legal systems indicates a subjective intention of the States to respect these elements also at the international level, especially if domestic law makes specific references to international law in this regard. The States' motivation to respect fairness and equitableness and repeat this behaviour is motivated by the States' conviction of being legally bound by them. It would be difficult to argue that a system of law does not respect fairness and equitableness or that States do not feel a legal obligation to respect these two concepts.[284]

Tudor's theory seems to be based on two interconnected propositions that are well-captured in this extract: 'this [constant and uniform] state practice together with the demonstration that opinio juris in the context of FET is firstly, not relevant, and secondly, even if it were relevant, is

---

[281] Tudor, *The Fair and Equitable Treatment Standard*, p. 77.   [282] *Ibid.*, p. 83.

[283] *Ibid.*, p. 80.

[284] *Ibid.*, pp. 82–83. The (almost) exact same passage is also found in: Diehl, *The Core Standard of International Investment Protection*, p. 143.

embodied in the manifestation of the practice, were sufficient to qualify the FET as a customary norm'.[285] These two propositions will now be examined.

First, let's examine Tudor's argument that constant and uniform State practice is sufficient on its own to demonstrate the existence of a rule of custom, without the necessity to show any *opinio juris*. It is true that the ICJ in the *North Sea Continental Shelf* cases recognized that the practice of States could show evidence of their *opinio juris*. It is also true that the task of finding *opinio juris* is relatively easier in situations where there is an overwhelming, uniform and consistent State practice.[286] Nevertheless, the two elements must still be *separately* identified.[287] The burden of proof to demonstrate *opinio juris* rests on the party alleging the existence of any such custom.[288] It is wrong to affirm that when faced with uniform State practice, the burden of proof simply shifts. Tudor seems to suggest that a State would somehow have to prove that it *did not* enter a BIT out of a sense of obligation. There is simply no support for Tudor's reverse burden of proof theory.

As mentioned earlier in this book,[289] *in theory,* nothing prevents treaty-based norms contained in BITs from transforming into customary rules. Yet, this can only be achieved when two conditions are met.[290] Tudor's analysis only focuses on one of these conditions. She only refers to the practice of States *parties* to BITs, which she claims is constant and uniform (an affirmation controversial in and of itself, which is rejected by the present author[291]). She does not mention that any customary rule based on treaty practice needs to be confirmed by the actual concordant practice of States *outside the treaty framework*. In other words, Tudor should have shown, for instance, that States *not party* to BITs (or States parties to BITs *not* containing any FET clause) are adopting the FET standard in their *own* practice and offering such protection to foreign investors. She also fails to examine these States' *opinio juris.*[292] These important shortcomings undermine her analysis.

Tudor's second controversial proposition is that the required States' *opinio juris* is 'embodied' in the practice of States ratifying BITs, which include the FET standard. According to her, at the heart of the FET standard of protection lies the concept of 'fairness' and 'equity', which are said to be 'part of any liberal system of justice' and found in 'a great

---

[285] Tudor, *The Fair and Equitable Treatment Standard*, p. 233.
[286] See, Chapter 4, Section 4.1.5.1.   [287] *Ibid.*   [288] See, Chapter 1, Section 1.4.
[289] See, Chapter 3, Section 3.3.3.2.1.   [290] See Chapter 3, Section 3.3.3.2.1.2.
[291] See, discussion in Chapter 3, Section 3.2.4.   [292] *Ibid.*

number of national legal systems'.[293] This would apparently demonstrate States' belief that they have a legal obligation to provide the same level of protection to their BITs partners' investors. However, Tudor does not provide any evidence supporting her assertion that numerous domestic legal systems contain concepts similar to that of the FET standard. While affirming that 'most developed and developing countries do recognise in their domestic laws that FET is to be applied to foreign investment',[294] she also admits to not having undertaken the actual comparative analysis of domestic legislation.[295] The present author examined 165 foreign investment laws adopted by States and found that only ten contain an FET clause.[296] Moreover, Tudor fails to provide any evidence supporting her assertion that liberal democracies somehow believe they have an *obligation* to offer FET protection to foreign investors based on the fair way they treat their own nationals.

In sum, Tudor's claim that States' *opinio juris* is embodied in their practice of ratifying BITs containing FET clauses does not fulfil the strict conditions under which a treaty-based rule can transform into customary international law. Ultimately, States simply have no *opinio juris* when signing BITs containing FET causes.[297]

Alvarez developed a similar theory to that of Tudor's. He first provides two arguments suggesting that States' *opinio juris* can actually be easily identified. First, he states that 'one easy response to the contention that investment treaties lack the requisite *opinio juris* relevant to *making* CIL [customary international law] is merely to point out the extent to which BITs or FTAs simply rely on *existing* CIL'.[298] Yet, while BITs are increasingly referring to the concept of custom, it remains that even today only a minority of them do so. Second, Alvarez adds that 'if one agrees that, contrary to Guzman's contentions, the *opinio juris* establishing basic propositions of international investment law (as with respect to the international minimum standard or the general proposition that compensation after an expropriation is regulated by international and not only national law) was left undisturbed by the Assembly's NIEO efforts,

---

[293] Tudor, *The Fair and Equitable Treatment Standard*, pp. 82–83.   [294] *Ibid.*, p. 104.
[295] *Ibid.*
[296] See, discussion in Chapter 3, Section 3.3.3.2.1.3. See also: P. Dumberry, 'The Practice of States as Evidence of Custom: An Analysis of Fair and Equitable Treatment Standard Clauses in States' Foreign Investment Laws', McGill Journal of Dispute Resolution (forthcoming, 2016).
[297] Bronfman, 'Fair and Equitable Treatment', pp. 670–672; Haeri, 'A Tale of Two Standards', p. 43.
[298] Alvarez, 'A Bit on Custom', p. 57 (emphasis in the original).

the network of subsequent BITs and FTAs affirming such rules only provides additional evidence of *opinio juris* and hardly detracts from it'.[299] But even if one agrees with him, this would prove the *opinio juris* of States regarding *only two provisions* found in BITs (the MST and the general prohibition against expropriation without compensation). Moreover, my own survey of BITs,[300] as well as that of Tudor,[301] has shown that only a small minority of FET clauses actually contain language explicitly linking the standard with the MST under custom. Ultimately, Alvarez is careful *not* to embrace the proposition that *taken together* these more than 2,500 BITs represent the new custom and insists on limiting his observations to 'some rights' contained in BITs.[302]

In any event, Alvarez's main argument is that 'in the real world, evidence of *opinio juris* is usually drawn from the actual practice of states'.[303] Thus, he believes that:

> the fact that states are choosing or are compelled by external circumstances (from the force of the market to the injunctions of the IMF) to take national and international actions to encourage and protect free capital flows, and that these actions are affirmed by both their national and international legal commitments (as under BITs), provides, in itself, evidence of both state practice and *opinio juris*.[304]

In the present author's view, however, the mere fact, as acknowledged by Alvarez himself, that States are *choosing* (or are *compelled* by exterior forces) to adopt BITs or national laws protecting foreign investment shows that they do not *believe* that they have an *obligation* under international law to do so. As mentioned previously, they sign these BITs to protect their own interests. Alvarez also adds another argument: 'We ought to presume that when states routinely acquiesce in arbitration decisions that conclude they owe damages for the violation of a BIT and a customary international legal obligation that such acquiescence

---

[299] *Ibid.*
[300] P. Dumberry, *Rules of Customary International Law in the Field of International Investment Law*, SSHRC Research Project (2012–2014).
[301] Tudor, *The Fair and Equitable Treatment Standard*, p. 25.
[302] Alvarez, 'A Bit on Custom', pp. 59–60: 'This is *not* an argument that the complex number of actions that states undertake pursuant to or that are attributed to the "Washington Consensus" are, in their entirety, CIL or supported by *opinio juris*. It is a contention, however, that as Lowenfeld suggests, *some* rights now affirmed in BITs and FTAs have this quality' (emphasis in the original).
[303] *Ibid.*, pp. 57–58.   [304] *Ibid.*, p. 59.

itself constitutes evidence of *opinio juris*'.[305] However, in my opinion, the mere fact that a State agrees to pay compensation in accordance with a BIT only shows its belief that it has an obligation to do so *under that treaty*. Nothing can be said to demonstrate that it has a sense of obligation to *sign that BIT* in the first place.

To summarize, while strong evidence of consistent and uniform practice by a representative group of States can facilitate finding States' *opinio juris*, such investigation must nevertheless be undertaken separately. This is also the case when the same clause is found in numerous treaties. It still must be shown that both parties and non-parties to these instruments *believe* that they have the *obligation* to provide such protection to investors *outside* the treaty framework. These are basic requirements that have not been taken into account by a number of writers. Surprisingly, the *Merrill & Ring* Tribunal also held that consistent State practice could be considered as representing these States' *opinio juris*:

> A requirement that aliens be treated fairly and equitably in relation to business, trade and investment is the outcome of this changing reality and as such it has become sufficiently part of widespread and consistent practice so as to demonstrate that it is reflected today in customary international law as opinio juris.[306]

The next section will examine another argument put forward by some scholars claiming that States have an *opinio juris* when signing BITs.

4.2.3.3.2 States' *opinio juris* exists because it represents their general interests

Some scholars who argue that States have an *opinio juris* when signing BITs refer to the so-called common interests of States. At the heart of this approach is the proposition that customary international law must conform to a fundamental interest of States.[307] This is no doubt true since, as noted by one writer, 'otherwise States would not have originally engaged in such practice in the first place'.[308] Judge Tanaka in his dissenting opinion in the *North Sea Continental Shelf* cases noted that States' *opinio juris* should be found

---

[305] *Ibid.* This position is endorsed by Weiler, *The Interpretation of International Investment Law*, p. 237.

[306] *Merrill & Ring Forestry L.P. v. Canada*, Award, 31 March 2010, para. 210.

[307] See, Kläger, *Fair and Equitable Treatment in International Investment Law*, p. 268, indicating a number of writers supporting this position and citing, *inter alia*, K. Doehring, 'Gewohnheitsrecht aus Verträgen', *ZaöRV*, 36 (1976), p. 93.

[308] Villiger, *Customary International Law and Treaties*, p. 61.

in the 'necessity felt in the international community' for the creation of a customary rule.[309]

Based on this conception of custom, a number of writers have argued that *opinio juris* means something other than a practice recognized by States as 'accepted as law'. For instance, according to Lepard, *opinio juris* can be defined 'as a requirement that states generally believe that it is *desirable* now or in the near future to have an authoritative legal principle or rule prescribing, permitting, or prohibiting certain state conduct'.[310] According to these writers, *opinio juris* is proven by the mere fact that a State believes that its conduct is in its best *interest*. Some writers have applied this proposition in the field of investor-State arbitration. Hindelang's position is as follows:

> Having established that the existence of custom derived from a treaty rule or a set of similar treaty rules is never assumed but must be specifically proven, it is necessary to turn attention to the question of what conditions must be met in order to prove the existence of such a rule. It has been suggested that in order to examine whether a succession of treaty rules provides evidence of custom or is mere *quid pro quo,* one has to look at the "interests of States" in a rule of customary international law because customary international law cannot be generated against the "interest of States". In order to establish the "interest of States", one would have to ask whether States would be willing to give up their own interests for the benefit of the "common interests of States".[311]

---

[309] *North Sea Continental Shelf Cases,* ICJ Rep. 1969, Dissident Opinion of Judge Tanaka, p. 176: 'This factor, relating to internal motivation and being of a psychological nature, cannot be ascertained very easily, particularly when diverse legislative and executive organs of a government participate in an internal process of decision making in respect of ratification or other State acts. There is no other way than to ascertain the existence of *opinio juris* from the fact of the external existence of a certain custom and *its necessity felt in the international community,* rather than to seek evidence as to the subjective motives for each example of State practice, which is something which is impossible of achievement' (emphasis added).

[310] Lepard, *Customary International Law,* pp. 98–99 (emphasis added), see also, at p. 11 (arguing that 'a norm ought to be considered customary law if states generally believe that is desirable, now or in the near future, to institute the norm as legally binding on the global community of states, and if it comports with certain fundamental ethical principles in contemporary international law anchored in the principle of unity in diversity').

[311] Hindelang, 'Bilateral Investment Treaties', pp. 795–796, referring to K. Doehring, *Volkerrecht* (2nd edn., Heidelberg: Müller, 2004), margin no. 317 ff. See also, a similar argument developed by Congyan, 'International Investment Treaties and the Formation', p. 661, quoting from Antonio Cassese, *International Law* (2nd edn. Oxford: Oxford University Press, 2005), p. 156.

Hindelang argues that since all States have (apparently) a 'common interest' in establishing basic principles on the protection of foreign investments such existing protections should consequently be considered as a rule of customary international law. However, it would constitute a rule of custom without the need to specifically demonstrate any *opinio juris* by States. This is because the subjective element is (apparently) found in these thousands of BITs:

> [T]he states have left us today with a network of more than 2,300 BITs – a broad statement that almost the whole community of States views foreign investment favourably and its protection by international law not only desirable but necessary. Can this, however, also be viewed as a statement in favour of common principles embodied in customary international law? The answer is almost certainly yes.[312]
>
> [t]here is a real 'interest of States' in a set of basic principles on foreign investment in customary international law. Sovereignty must step back. Due to the fact that it is not possible to see any convincing 'interest' in the preservation of sovereignty, but a real interest in a set of basic principles on foreign investment embodied in custom, *opinio juris* can be derived in the case of BITs. Thus, it is clear that BITs definitely have an influence on customary international law in regards to the establishment of principles on foreign investment.[313]

The affirmation that 'it is not possible to see any convincing "interest" in the preservation of sovereignty' is (at best) a controversial proposition.[314] The most comprehensive version of this 'common interests' approach has been put forward by Diehl in her recent book. She concludes that the FET standard is a customary rule based on the uniformity of State practice found in BITs. According to her, *opinio juris* may be established by looking at, *inter alia*, bilateral and multilateral investment treaties.[315] She first acknowledges that 'an inquiry into the subjective motivations of the States parties to the BITs needs to be conducted'.[316] She further notes that 'it has been suggested [referring to the work of Doehring] that in order to examine whether a succession of treaty rules provides such evidence, one has to look at the "interests of states" in a rule of customary international law because customary international law cannot be

---

[312] Hindelang, 'Bilateral Investment Treaties', p. 806.   [313] *Ibid.*, p. 808.

[314] See also: *Ibid.*, p. 796, where he states 'it seems that nowadays State sovereignty is no longer the core value of the international community'.

[315] Diehl, *The Core Standard of International Investment Protection*, p. 129.

[316] *Ibid.*, p. 138.

generated against the "interests of states".[317] In her view, the mere fact that States have 'a real interest in a customary FET standard' is enough to show that they have an *opinio juris* to that effect, and that, consequently, such a customary rule exists:

> It is consequently submitted that States have a real interest in a set of basic principles on foreign investment in customary international law. Since FET is the core standard in the law of foreign investment, States especially have a real interest in a customary FET standard. Hence, the element of opinio iuris is present. In light to the over-arching interest in a healthy investment climate described above, a reliable legal framework, fostered by a set of principles in customary international law and de-escalating potential conflicts in an area of overlapping treaties and sovereignties is in the interest of the community of States. It is even in the interests of developing States, as they would be able to present themselves as more reliable partners: In the absence of treaty protection, the FET of investments would be guaranteed pursuant to customary international law.[318]

In my view, scholars advancing this theory of 'common interest' are using a conception of *opinio juris* that is completely disconnected from the basic understanding of the principle under international law. This view of *opinio juris* makes the concept completely meaningless. It is difficult to envisage a situation where States would have adopted, over a long period of time, a uniform, consistent and representative conduct that would *not* be in their global interest. In any event, while it may be true that all States have a global 'interest' in the existence of a set of basic principles on foreign investment, this has nothing to do with custom. For there to be customary rules binding on all States, international law requires *something other* than mere States' 'interest'. It requires that States adopt such a practice out of a sense of *legal obligation*, not merely because it is in their best interests. Mendelson rightly affirmed that it is 'important to reiterate that an alleged rule is not law just because it is (alleged to be) socially necessary'.[319]

---

[317] *Ibid.* It should be noted that this is an (almost) verbatim quote from the work of Hindelang, 'Bilateral Investment Treaties', p. 796 (without any reference to his article).

[318] *Ibid.*, p. 145. See also, at p. 178 ('Those who doubt that the element of opinio juris is present should consider the following: In light of the over-arching interest in a healthy investment climate described above, a liable legal framework, fostered by a set of principles in customary international law and de-escalating potential conflicts in an area of overlapping treaties and sovereignties, is in the interest of the community of States').

[319] Mendelson, 'The Formation of Customary International Law', p. 271.

In my opinion, supporters of the 'common interest' approach should be frank and either admit that their aim is to simply dump *opinio juris* altogether or acknowledge that they have adopted a novel conception of *opinio juris* that is completely detached from its original meaning under international law. For instance, the latter option was clearly chosen by Lowenfeld, where he admitted that his conclusion that BITs are equal to custom[320] 'may be inconsistent with the traditional definition of customary law', but added 'I am suggesting, at least tentatively, that the undertaking of legal obligations by a large group of states, even from a mixture of motives, has resulted in something like customary law' and that 'perhaps' the traditional definition of custom 'is wrong, or at least in this area, incomplete'.[321]

---

[320] See, discussion in Chapter 3, Section 3.3.3.2.2.1.

[321] Andreas F. Lowenfeld, 'Investment Agreements and International Law', 42 *Colum. J. Transnat'l L.* 123 (2003), p. 124.

5

The fundamental importance of customary rules in international investment law

Introduction

As mentioned in the Introduction of this book,[1] customary rules of international investment law remain of fundamental importance even in light of the present proliferation of BITs.[2] The three reasons traditionally invoked why custom remains important in contemporary international law have been succinctly summarized by ILC Special Rapporteur Wood as follows:

> Even in fields where there are widely accepted "codification" conventions, the rules of customary international law continue to govern questions not regulated by the conventions and continue to apply in relations with and between non-parties. Rules of customary international law may also fill possible lacunae in treaties, and assist in their interpretation.[3]

The present chapter will begin by examining in detail these three 'traditional' reasons (Section 5.1).[4] I will also explain another reason why arbitral tribunals should *always* take into account relevant rules of customary international law (Section 5.2). This is because 'international law' is the applicable law in an overwhelming majority of arbitration disputes. Even when this is not the case, international law must play an important role. Any tribunal having to apply international law will necessarily have to take into account relevant customary norms.

The present chapter will demonstrate, however, that custom is no *panacea* in the field of international investment law. The existence of a

---

[1] See, Introduction.

[2] Tarcisio Gazzini, 'The Role of Customary International Law in the Field of Foreign Investment', *J. World Invest. & Trade*, 8 (2007), p. 691.

[3] International Law Commission, 'First Report on Formation and Evidence of Customary International Law', by Michael Wood, Special Rapporteur, Sixty-fifth session, Geneva, 6 May-7 June and 8 July-9 August 2013, UN doc. A/CN.4/663, 17 May 2013, p. 20 [hereinafter referred to as ILC, First Report, 2013], p. 15.

[4] These issues are examined in detail by Gazzini, 'The Role of Customary International Law', p. 691.

few rules of custom[5] cannot solve all problems facing foreign investors. In particular, custom does not provide them access to international arbitration. The host State must consent to arbitration. Individuals and corporations lack any *automatic jus standi* before international tribunals in the absence of specific State consent. No customary rule has emerged that provides investors with a procedural 'right' to bring arbitration claims against the State where they make their investments. This question is further examined in Section 5.3.

Finally, I will examine the controversial theory of the 'persistent objector'. While everyone agrees that a rule of customary international law is binding upon all States, scholars continue to debate another controversial question: whether a State should be permitted not to be bound by such a rule in the event that it objected to it in the early stage of its formation and does so consistently thereafter. In Section 5.4, I will examine the concrete application of the theory in the field of investor-State arbitration. Here, I will argue that the concept of persistent objector should *not* be used by an arbitral tribunal in investor-State arbitration proceedings to prevent the application of a rule of customary law.

5.1 Traditional reasons for the remaining importance of custom

This first section examines the three traditional reasons given by scholars to explain the important role played by custom in contemporary international law despite the proliferation of treaties. The first reason is that custom is the applicable legal regime of protection in the absence of any BIT (Section 5.1.1). Second, custom is, of course, also important in the many instances where BITs make explicit reference to the concept (Section 5.1.2). Third, custom plays a gap-filling role whenever a treaty, a contract or domestic legislation is silent on a given issue (Section 5.1.3).

5.1.1 *Custom is the applicable legal regime in the absence of any BIT*

However numerous BITs have become, they still do not cover the whole spectrum of possible bilateral treaty relationships between States. According to one writer, BITs in fact only cover some 13% of the total bilateral

---

[5] See, discussion in Chapter 2, Section 2.6.

relationship between States worldwide.[6] For instance, as of 2014, Canada had signed BITs (called 'FIPAs' in Canada) with twenty-seven States,[7] one multilateral treaty with two other States (NAFTA), four free trade agreements (containing investment protections) with individual States and one with the European Free Trade Association (EFTA) (comprising four States).[8] In total, Canada has entered into instruments providing for investor-State arbitration with fewer than forty States. Since a BIT is only binding on the parties to the treaty and not on third parties,[9] the limited worldwide geographical scope of BITs necessarily results in gaps in the legal protection of foreign investments.[10] Therefore, a foreign investor originating from a State that has not entered into a BIT with the State where the investment is made will not be given the legal protection which would have otherwise been typically offered under such a treaty.

According to the Canadian government, all instruments mentioned in the previous paragraph 'provide protection for 56.7% of the known stock of outward direct investment of Canadian businesses at the end of 2012'.[11] In other words, the Canadian investment treaties framework covers only half of the investments made abroad by Canadian investors.[12] Those Canadian investors not covered by investment treaties will still get some legal protection under contracts or under the domestic legislations of the countries where they have made their investments. They will also benefit from existing customary rules in the field of international investment law. Thus, custom applies to *all States*, including those which have not entered into any BITs. Customary rules can therefore be invoked by *any foreign investor* irrespective of whether its State of origin has entered

---

[6] Gazzini, 'The Role of Customary International Law', p. 691.

[7] The treaties can be found at this page: www.international.gc.ca/trade-agreements-accords-commerciaux/agr-acc/fipa-apie/index.aspx?lang=eng.

[8] Canada also signed in 2014 an FTA ('Comprehensive and Economic Trade Agreement', CETA) with the member States of the European Union (EU), but at the time of writing the instrument had not yet entered into force.

[9] *Vienna Convention on the Law of Treaties*, signed in 1969 and entered into force on 27 January 1980, UNTS 1155 (1969), p. 331, Art. 34.

[10] R. Dolzer and C. Schreuer, *Principles of International Investment Law* (Oxford: Oxford University Press, 2008), p. 17; ILA, 'Sources of International Investment Law', report by M. Hirsch, ILA Study Group on the Role of Soft Law Instruments in International Investment Law (2011), pp. 7–8.

[11] Canada's Ministry of Foreign Affairs, available at www.international.gc.ca/trade-agree ments-accords-commerciaux/agr-acc/fipa-apie/fipa-purpose.aspx?lang=en.

[12] The picture will, of course, be completely different once the CETA with the EU has entered into force and as a result of the ongoing negotiation of a *Trans-Pacific Partnership* (TPP) with many States.

into a BIT with the country where it makes its investment. Custom is therefore the applicable legal regime in the absence of any BIT. This is the first reason why the determination of the content of customary rules remains so fundamental. Even in light of the proliferation of BITs, these rules continue to play an important role in investment protection.

5.1.2   Many BITs make explicit reference to custom

In this section, I will observe the continuing relevance of custom in three closely related situations: when a BIT makes explicit reference to the application of 'customary international law', when one of the parties to a treaty argues in pleadings that one provision must be interpreted taking into account custom, and, finally, when a treaty requires interpreting treaty provisions in accordance with customary international law. These three points will be examined separately in the next paragraphs.

One fundamental reason for the remaining importance of custom is that several BITs make explicit reference to the application of 'customary international law'.[13] Yet, it should be highlighted that an explicit reference to custom is found in only a small *minority* of investment treaties. An arbitral tribunal must necessarily determine the content of a customary rule when faced with such a specific provision. For example, one provision found in the recent Canada–Peru BIT indicates that the standard of treatment to be accorded to an investor is that existing under 'customary international law'.[14]

Such a direct reference to custom is sometimes found in fair and equitable treatment (FET) standard clauses. This is a rather new phenomenon. Since there have been varied and conflicting interpretations on the scope and content of the FET standard, a number of States have started to explicitly specify in their BITs that the standard is not only

---

[13]   The issue is discussed in: Dolzer and Schreuer, *Principles of International Investment Law*, p. 16; C. McLachlan, 'Investment Treaties and General International Law', *ICLQ* 57 (2008), p. 399; Ole Kristian Fauchald, 'The Legal Reasoning of ICSID Tribunals — An Empirical Analysis', *EJIL* 19 (2008), p. 309; C. McLachlan, L. Shore and M. Weiniger, *International Investment Arbitration: Substantive Principles* (Oxford: Oxford University Press, 2007), pp. 16–17; J. Harrison, 'The International Law Commission and the Development of International Investment Law', *Geo. Wash. Int'l L. Rev*, 45 (2013), pp. 432, 437; Hirsch, 'Sources of International Investment Law', p. 8.

[14]   Article 5(1) of the Canada–Peru BIT provides that 'each party shall accord to covered investments treatment *in accordance with the customary international law minimum standard of treatment of aliens*, including fair and equitable treatment and full protection and security' (emphasis added).

linked to 'international law', but that it is in fact a reference to the minimum standard of treatment (MST) under *customary* international law.[15] The clearest example of such a reaction is that of NAFTA Parties regarding Article 1105.[16] Under this provision, NAFTA Parties must accord a 'fair and equitable treatment' under 'international law' to foreign investors. Under the aegis of the Free Trade Commission (FTC), NAFTA Parties responded to three controversial awards that had been rendered in 2000 (*Metalclad*,[17] *S.D. Myers*[18] and *Pope & Talbot*[19]) on the scope and meaning of Article 1105 by issuing in 2001 its 'Notes of Interpretation of Certain Chapter 11 Provisions'. The Notes clarified, *inter alia*, that 'Article 1105(1) prescribes the customary international law minimum standard of treatment of aliens as the minimum standard of treatment to be afforded to investments of investors of another Party' and that the concept of FET does 'not require treatment in addition to or beyond that which is required by the customary international law minimum standard of treatment of aliens'. As mentioned by one writer, after the FTC Notes, all NAFTA arbitral decisions regarding the FET standard were '*necessarily* efforts to interpret and apply customary law'.[20] NAFTA Parties have repeatedly argued in their pleadings the customary nature of the MST applicable under Article 1105.[21]

It should be noted that the United States and Canada have subsequently followed this path in their respective Model BITs (both adopted in 2004). For instance, Article 5(1) of the US Model BIT provides that '[e]ach Party shall accord to covered investments treatment in accordance with *customary* international law, including fair and equitable treatment and full protection and security'.[22] Article 5(2) further states that:

---

[15] UNCTAD, 'Fair and Equitable Treatment', UNCTAD Series on Issues in International Investment Agreements II, United Nations (2012), p. 29.

[16] Patrick Dumberry, *The Fair and Equitable Treatment Standard: A Guide to NAFTA Case Law on Article 1105* (Alphen aan den Rijn: Wolters Kluwer, 2013).

[17] *Metalclad Corporation* v. *Mexico*, ICSID Case No. ARB(AF)/97/1, Award, 30 August 2000, paras. 70, 76.

[18] *S.D. Myers Inc.* v. *Canada*, UNCITRAL, First Partial Award, 13 November 2000, para. 266.

[19] *Pope and Talbot Inc.* v. *Canada*, UNCITRAL, Award on the Merits of Phase II, 10 April 2001.

[20] Jose E. Alvarez, 'A Bit on Custom', *N.Y.U. J. Int'l L. & Pol.* 42 (2009–2010), pp. 34–35 (emphasis in the original).

[21] See, for instance, *ADF Group Inc.* v. *United States*, ICSID Case No. ARB(AF)/00/1, Award, 6 January 2003, para. 112 (referring to the position of the United States); *Glamis Gold Ltd* v. *United States*, UNCITRAL, Award, 14 May 2009, para. 543 (referring to the position of the United States).

[22] US Model BIT (2004) (emphasis added). See, Gilbert Gagné and Jean-Frédéric Morin, 'The Evolving American Policy on Investment Protection: Evidence from Recent FTAs and the 2004 Model BIT', *J. Int'l Econ. L.* 9 (2006), p. 357.

> For greater certainty, paragraph 1 prescribes the customary interna-
> tional law minimum standard of treatment of aliens as the minimum
> standard of treatment to be afforded to covered investments. The con-
> cepts of 'fair and equitable treatment' and 'full protection and security'
> do not require treatment in addition to or beyond that which is required
> by that standard, and do not create additional substantive rights . . .[23]

Canada and the United States have adopted such language to refute the
expanding interpretation applied by some NAFTA tribunals, most notably the *Pope & Talbot* Tribunal, and to incorporate the clarification made
in the NAFTA FTC Notes of 2001.[24] The two BITs entered into by the
United States after 2004 with Uruguay and Rwanda also contain the same
clause referring specifically to the MST under custom.[25] Recent FTAs
entered into by the United States also contain the same FET clause.[26] The
same is true for recent BITs (and FTAs) entered into by Canada[27] as well
as a number of BITs entered into by Mexico.[28]

While such specific language is clearly the result of the NAFTA
experience, the phenomenon is not limited to the North American
context.[29] In fact, several other treaties entered into by other States also

---

[23] US Model BIT (2004).

[24] Céline Lévesque, 'Influences on the Canadian Model FIPA and US Model BIT: NAFTA
Chapter 11 and Beyond', *Canadian YIL* 44 (2006), p. 255; Kenneth Vandevelde,
'A Comparison of the 2004 and 1994 US Model BITs', *Yb Int'l Invest. L. & Pol.* 1 (2008–
2009), p. 291; C. Lévesque and A. Newcombe, 'Commentary on the Canadian Model
Foreign Promotion and Protection Agreement', in C. Brown (ed.), *Commentaries on
Selected Model Investment Treaties* (Oxford: Oxford University Press, 2013), pp. 78–80.

[25] US–Uruguay BIT (2006), Art. 5(1)(2); US–Rwanda BIT (2012), Art. 5(1)(2).

[26] *See*, Andrew P. Tuck, 'The "Fair And Equitable Treatment" Standard Pursuant to the
Investment Provisions of the U.S. Free Trade Agreements with Peru, Colombia and
Panama', *L. & Bus. Rev. Am.* 16 (2010), p. 385. See, FTAs entered into by the United
States with Australia (2004), Central America (CAFTA, 2004), Chile (2003), Morocco
(2004) and Singapore (2003, see the side letter of 6 May 2003).

[27] See, Canada–Czech Republic BIT (2009), Art. 3; Canada–Jordan BIT (2009), Art. 5;
Canada–Latvia BIT (2009), Art. 5; Canada–Peru BIT (2007), Art. 5; Canada–Romania
BIT (2009), Art. 2; Canada–Slovakia BIT (2010), Art. 3.

[28] Australia–Mexico BIT (2005), Protocol, clause 1 indicating that: Article 4 on FET 'pre-
scribes the customary international law standard of treatment of aliens as the minimum
standard of treatment to be afforded to investments of Investors of another Contracting
Party'. Similarly-drafted clauses are also found in: Czech Republic–Mexico BIT (2002),
Protocol; Iceland–Mexico BIT (2005); India–Mexico BIT (2007), art. 5; Trinidad and
Tobago–Mexico BIT (2006), art. 5; United Kingdom–Mexico BIT (2006), art. 3.

[29] UNCTAD, 'Fair and Equitable Treatment', p. 25, referring to the Agreement Establishing
the ASEAN–Australia–New Zealand Free Trade Area (2009), the Japan–Philippines FTA
(2006), the China–Peru FTA (2009), the Malaysia–New Zealand FTA (2009), and the
India–Korea Comprehensive Economic Partnership Agreement (2009).

contain similar language referring to custom.[30] For instance, Guatemala recently argued that the FET clause found in the CAFTA (which contains the same language as the US Model BIT) 'requires only the minimum standard of treatment under customary international law and does not create additional substantive rights'.[31]

The goal of such clauses is clearly to limit the scope of the FET obligation.[32] Interestingly enough, in the recent EU–Canada *Comprehensive Economic and Trade Agreement* (CETA), signed in 2014, the Parties tried to achieve the same goal (limiting the scope of the FET clause) by including a specific enumeration of the different situations involving a breach of the FET obligation, *without* specifically referring to the term 'customary international law'.[33] In fact, the list of situations mentioned in the provision basically encapsulates the NAFTA case law on the FET standard (Article 1105), which is *explicitly* linked to the MST under custom.[34] In other words, the absence of the term 'custom' cannot in any way be considered a sign that the Parties avoided the use of the expression altogether. On the contrary, the provision is in fact a *reflection*

---

[30] For instance, the Belgium/Luxembourg–Peru BIT (2005), art. 3: 'All investments made by investors of one Contracting Party shall enjoy a fair and equitable treatment in the territory of the other Contracting Party, in accordance with customary international law'. See also: Korea–Singapore FTA (2006), Art. 10.5; Chile–Australia FTA (2009), Art. 10.5; Japan–Laos BIT (2008), Art. 5; Japan–Brunei (2007), Art. 59 (see 'Note'). The Colombian Model BIT (2008) contains a similar provision indicating that 'Each Contracting Party shall accord fair and equitable treatment in accordance with customary international law' and adding that the FET concept does 'not require additional treatment to that required under the minimum standard of treatment of aliens in accordance with the standard of customary international law'. See also, the position adopted by Norway in its commentary to its 2015 Model BIT, 'Comments on the Individual Provisions of the Model Agreement' (2015), p. 8 ('The right of investors to fair and equitable treatment and full protection and security is based on the international minimum standard under customary international law, which specifies the minimum threshold for the treatment of foreign nationals').

[31] *Railroad Development Corporation (RDC)* v. *Guatemala*, ICSID case No. ARB/07/23, Award, 29 June 2012, para. 159. The same position was adopted by El Salvador (*Ibid.*, paras. 207–209) and Honduras (*Ibid.*, paras. 207, 211), both filing submissions as non-disputing States parties during the proceedings.

[32] UNCTAD, 'Fair and Equitable Treatment', p. 28.

[33] Art. X.9. CETA consolidated Text, available at: www.international.gc.ca/trade-agreements-accords-commerciaux/agr-acc/ceta-aecg/text-texte/toc-tdm.aspx. See also: Nathalie Bernasconi-Osterwalder and Howard Mann, 'A Response to the European Commission's December 2013 Document "Investment Provisions in the EU-Canada Free Trade Agreement (CETA)",' *IISD* (2014), p. 5, discussing the following draft documents: 'Draft CETA Investment Chapter' (21 November 2013); 'Draft CETA Investor-to-State Dispute Settlement' (4 February 2014) (these texts are available at: www.tradejustice.ca/leakeddocs/).

[34] See, the analysis in: Dumberry, *The Fair and Equitable Treatment Standard.*

of the customary principle of the MST (at least in the context of NAFTA Article 1105).[35]

One related noteworthy issue is the fact that the recent BIT signed by Canada and China uses the term 'international law' instead of the phrase 'customary international law minimum standard of treatment of aliens', which is commonly used in other BITs. Only the most recent China BITs have started using the term 'international law', while still avoiding using the term 'custom' for political reasons. These treaties apparently never mention the word 'custom', because China is of the view that these principles have been developed by Western States without China's participation.[36] It is noteworthy to mention, however, that the FET clause in the Canada–China BIT expressly refers to the two elements of the definition of custom ('evidenced by general State practice accepted as law').[37] Another example is the China–New Zealand FTA, which uses the expression 'commonly accepted rules of international law'.[38] A (not exhaustive) survey has also found (at least) one China BIT (with Peru) using the expression 'customary international law'.[39]

Finally, it should be added that there are some BIT clauses on the prohibition of expropriation which also refer specifically to custom.[40]

---

[35] It is also noteworthy that in a previous draft, the parties had included a specific paragraph indicating that the FET protection could also cover other treatment than those specifically enumerated if they were 'contrary to the fair and equitable treatment obligation recognized in the general practice of States accepted as law'. This clause essentially acknowledged the evolving nature of the FET standard. It allowed for the content of the FET clause to change over time and to cover new situations which may become contrary to custom in the future. This provision was not kept in the final text. The final provision (Art. X.9(al.3)) only mentions that 'The Parties shall regularly, or upon request of a Party, review the content of the obligation to provide fair and equitable treatment. The Committee on Services and Investment may develop recommendations in this regard and submit them to the Trade Committee for decision'.

[36] See, discussion in: W. Shan and N. Gallaguer, 'China', in C. Brown (ed.), *Commentaries on Selected Model Investment Treaties* (Oxford: Oxford University Press, 2013), p. 159.

[37] Canada–China (2014), Art. 4. See also: China–Mexico BIT (2008) referring to 'international law minimum standard of treatment of aliens' without using the term 'customary', but nevertheless mentioning the two elements of the definition.

[38] China–New Zealand FTA (2008), art. 143.   [39] China–Peru FTA (2009), art. 132.

[40] See, Article 10.7.1 of the Dominican Republic–Central America–United States Free Trade Agreement (CAFTA-DR) with Annex 10-C further providing that its rule on expropriation in this provision 'is intended to reflect customary international law concerning the obligation of States with respect to expropriation'. The same reference is found in the US Model BIT (see, paragraph 1 of Annex B). This reference has been criticized by Stephen Schwebel, 'The United States 2004 Model Bilateral Investment Treaty: An Exercise in the Regressive Development of International Law', *TDM* 3(1) (2006), p. 5 ('That is a remarkable proviso, since it is incontestable that the content of customary international law on expropriation is

In sum, the continuing relevance of custom is undeniable in situations where the BITs expressly refer to the concept and where a tribunal must therefore apply such rules. While the number of investment treaties expressly referring to custom is rapidly increasing, it remains that such reference is still only found in a small *minority* of treaties.

There is a second closely-related reason for the remaining importance of custom in contemporary international investment law. The majority of BITs include so-called autonomous or stand-alone FET clauses where the standard of treatment is *not* linked to 'international law' or the MST under custom.[41] In other words, these FET clauses contain no reference to custom. In a number of arbitration proceedings the respondent States parties to these treaties have, however, argued in their pleadings that such 'autonomous' FET clauses should nevertheless be interpreted as a reference to the MST under custom. The following paragraphs provide a number of (not exhaustive) examples.

In particular, several South American countries have expressed the position that an autonomous FET clause is in fact a reference to the MST under customary international law. For instance, Argentina has repeatedly argued that the concept of FET 'does not establish an autonomous and independent standard[,] but rather coincides with the minimum standard' under custom.[42] In fact, Argentina took that position regardless of the actual FET clause at hand: in the context of an 'autonomous' FET clause,[43] when the clause is expressly linked to international law,[44] and in cases of so-called 'no less' FET clauses where the standard is *not*

---

contentious. The authors of this provision do not seem to have borne in mind the holding of the Supreme Court of the United States in *Banco Nacional de Cuba v. Sabbatino*: "There are few if any issues in international law today on which opinion seems to be so divided as the limitations on a state's power to expropriate the property of aliens'").

[41] P. Dumberry, *Rules of Customary International Law in the Field of International Investment Law*, SSHRC Research Project, (2012–2014). See, discussion in Chapter 3, Section 3.2.4.2.

[42] *EDF International SA and ors v. Argentina*, ICSID Case No. ARB/03/23, Final Award, 11 June 2012, para. 343.

[43] See, for instance, the position taken by Argentina regarding the FET clause found in the UK–Argentina BIT in these cases: *BG Group plc v. Argentina*, UNCITRAL, Final Award, 24 December 2007, paras. 284, 290; *National Grid PLC v. Argentina*, UNCITRAL, Award, 3 November 2008, para. 161. See also: *Metalpar S.A. and Buen Aire S.A. v. Argentina*, ICSID Case No. ARB/03/5, Award on the Merits, 6 June 2008, para. 117 (Chile-Argentina BIT); *Siemens AG v. Argentina*, ICSID Case No. ARB/02/8, Award and Separate Opinion, 17 January 2007, paras. 289–292 (Germany–Argentina BIT).

[44] See, for instance, the position taken by Argentina regarding the FET clauses found in the France–Argentina BIT (Article 3: 'Each of the Contracting Parties undertakes to grant, within its territory and its maritime area, fair and equitable treatment according to the

directly linked to the level of treatment existing under international law, but where international law sets a *floor* below which State actions are considered illegal.[45] Ecuador also argued (in the context of a 'no less' FET clause) that the 'function' of the FET clause 'is to incorporate the customary international law minimum standard of treatment, not to create new standards binding upon the treaty parties'.[46] Paraguay[47] and Costa Rica[48] have also adopted the same position.

principles of international law to investments made by investors of the other Party, and to do it in such a way that the exercise of the right thus recognized is not obstructed de jure or de facto') in, *inter alia*, these cases: *Compañía de Aguas del Aconquija SA and Vivendi Universal SA* v. *Argentina*, ICSID Case No. ARB/97/3, Award, 20 August 2007, paras. 5.2.2., 6.6.2.; *EDF International SA and ors* v. *Argentina*, ICSID Case No. ARB/03/23, Final Award, 11 June 2012, para. 343; *SAUR International SA* v. *Argentina*, ICSID Case No. ARB/04/4, Decision on jurisdiction and liability, 6 June 2012, para. 472; *Total SA* v. *Argentina*, ICSID Case No. ARB/04/1, Decision on Liability, 27 December 2010, para. 125.

[45] See, for instance, the position taken by Argentina regarding the FET clause found in the US–Argentina BIT (Article II(2)(a): 'Investment shall at all times be accorded fair and equitable treatment, shall enjoy full protection and security and shall in no case be accorded treatment less than that required by international law') in, *inter alia*, the following cases: *Azurix Corp* v. *Argentina*, ICSID Case No. ARB/01/12, Award, 14 July 2006, paras. 332–333; *CMS Gas Transmission Company* v. *Argentina*, ICSID Case No. ARB/01/8, Award, 25 April 2005, paras. 270–271, 282; *Continental Casualty Company* v. *Argentina*, ICSID Case No. ARB/03/9, Award, 5 September 2008, paras. 56, 248, 253; *El Paso Energy International Company* v. *Argentina*, ICSID Case No. ARB/03/15, Award, 31 October 2011, para. 329; *Enron Corporation and Ponderosa Assets, LP* v. *Argentina*, ICSID Case No. ARB/01/3, Award, 22 May 2007, para. 253; *LG&E Energy Corp., LG&E Capital Corp. and LG&E International Inc.* v. *Argentina*, ICSID Case No. ARB/02/1, Decision on Liability, 3 October 2006, para. 113; *Sempra Energy International* v. *Argentina*, ICSID Case No. ARB/02/16, Award, 28 September 2007, paras. 292, 294.

[46] *Chevron Corporation and Texaco Petroleum Corporation* v. *Ecuador*, UNCITRAL, Partial Award on Merits, 30 March 2010, para. 227 (US–Ecuador BIT). See also, the position adopted by Ecuador in the following cases also involving the US–Ecuador BIT: *Ulysseas, Inc* v. *Ecuador*, UNCITRAL, Final Award, 12 June 2012, paras. 206–207 (the FET clause 'does not establish a higher standard than the customary international law minimum standard of treatment'); *MCI Power Group LC and New Turbine Inc* v. *Ecuador*, ICSID Case No. ARB/03/6, Award, 31 July 2007, para. 250; *Duke Energy Electroquil Partners and Electroquil SA* v. *Ecuador*, ICSID Case No. ARB/04/19, Award, 18 August 2008, para. 331 ('the duty to grant fair and equitable treatment under the BIT cannot be extended beyond what customary international law provides with respect to foreign investment').

[47] *Bureau Veritas, Inspection, Valuation, Assessment and Control, BIVAC BV* v. *Paraguay*, ICSID Case no ARB/07/9, Further Decision on Objections to Jurisdiction, 9 October 2012, paras. 105, 152–153 (arguing that the 'FET clause in the BIT incorporates the international minimum standard under customary international law', interpreting the Netherlands–Paraguay BIT containing a stand-alone FET clause).

[48] *Unglaube and Unglaube* v. *Costa Rica*, ICSID Case Nos. ARB/08/1 and ARB/09/20, Award, 16 May 2012, para. 242 (interpreting the Germany–Costa Rica BIT containing a stand-alone FET clause).

A number of States outside the Americas (for instance, the Czech Republic[49] and Tanzania[50]) have also argued, similar to Georgia in *Kardassopoulos,* that 'the FET standard is an objective standard synonymous with customary international law'.[51] The same position was also adopted by two respondent States (Kazakhstan and Pakistan) in two cases where the BITs did not even contain any FET clause. In both cases, the claimants relied on the MFN clause in these treaties to allege breaches of the FET obligation contained in other BITs entered into by the respondent States.[52]

In sum, these examples show that States have argued that the FET standard of protection should be interpreted in accordance with the MST existing *under custom* even when the BIT does not refer at all to the concept of custom. In my view, these examples provide a clear illustration of the continuing relevance of custom in contemporary investment arbitration.[53] The relevance of custom is also apparent given the reasoning of several tribunals that have interpreted a stand-alone FET clause,[54] or a 'no less' FET clause,[55] as an implicit reference to international law.

[49] *Saluka Investments BV* v. *Czech Republic,* UNCITRAL, Partial Award, 17 March 2006, para. 289 (interpreting the Netherlands-Czech Republic BIT containing a stand-alone FET clause).

[50] *Biwater Gauff (Tanzania) Ltd* v. *Tanzania,* ICSID Case No. ARB/05/22, Award and Concurring and Dissenting Opinion, 24 July 2008, para. 587 (interpreting the UK–Tanzania BIT containing a stand-alone FET clause).

[51] *Kardassopoulos* v. *Georgia and joined case,* ICSID Case Nos. ARB/05/18 and ARB/07/15, Award, 3 March 2010, paras. 409, 417 (interpreting the Georgia–Greece and Georgia–Israel BITs, both stand-alone FET clauses).

[52] *Rumeli Telekom AS and Telsim Mobil Telekomikasyon Hizmetleri AS* v. *Kazakhstan,* ICSID Case no ARB/05/16, Award, 29 July 2008, para. 611 (interpreting the Kazakhstan–Turkey BIT); *Bayindir Insaat Turizm Ticaret ve Sanayi A Ş* v. *Pakistan,* ICSID Case No. ARB/03/29, Award, 27 August 2009, paras. 164, 173 (interpreting the Turkey–Pakistan BIT). These awards are examined in: P. Dumberry, 'The Importation of the Fair and Equitable Treatment Standard Through MFN Clauses: An Empirical Study of BITs', ICSID Rev. (forthcoming, 2016).

[53] The same is true for much rarer cases where respondent States have, on the contrary, argued that the FET clause provides for a *lower* level of protection than that of the MST under custom. It should be noted the rather awkward position adopted by Mongolia in *Paushok and ors* v. *Mongolia,* UNCITRAL, Award on Jurisdiction and Liability, 28 April 2011, arguing that 'the lack of reference to customary international law' in the stand-alone FET clause contained in the Russia–Mongolia BIT was 'indicative of the very limited scope of the protections granted, which protections [were] *below* the customary international law standard' (paras. 272, 403, emphasis added). Mongolia also 'contest[ed] that the minimum international standard of treatment is part of customary international law' (para. 277).

[54] *See,* for instance, *Siemens AG* v. *Argentina,* ICSID No. ARB/02/8, Award, 17 January 2007, para. 291; *El Paso Energy International Company* v. *Argentina,* ICSID Case no ARB/03/15, Award, 31 October 2011, paras. 335–337.

[55] *Occidental Exploration and Production Co* v. *Ecuador,* LCIA Case No. UN3467, Award, 1 July 2004, paras. 188–190; *Lauder* v. *Czech Republic,* UNCITRAL, Final Award, 3

Finally, the importance of custom is also undeniable when a tribunal is required to *interpret* treaty provisions in accordance with customary international law.[56] A good example is the applicable law provision found in the EU–Canada CETA, which provides that '[a] Tribunal established under this Chapter shall render its decision consistent with this Agreement as interpreted in accordance with the Vienna Convention on the Law of Treaties, and other *rules and principles of international law applicable between the Parties*'.[57] Surely, rules of customary international law are 'applicable' between EU Member States and Canada.

There is another related situation where a tribunal would have to take into account the content of custom. Many BITs entered into by the Netherlands provide for the application of custom whenever it leads to a more favourable treatment than the one existing under the treaty.[58] This specific feature is also contained in the Model BIT adopted by India,[59] as well as in several BITs entered into by Switzerland.[60] In *Saipem*, the Tribunal indicated that pursuant to a similar clause found in the Italy–Bangladesh BIT, it would 'also apply general international law where it may provide a more favourable solution than the one arising from the BIT'.[61] This is clearly a situation where a tribunal would have to apply customary rules.

September 2001, para. 292; *Alex Genin, Eastern Credit Limited, Inc. and A.S. Baltoil Genin v. Estonia*, Award, 25 June 2001, para. 367.

[56] For instance, Korea–Singapore FTA (2006), art. 20.2(5): 'The Parties and the arbitral panel appointed under this Chapter shall interpret and apply the provisions of this Agreement in the light of the objectives of this Agreement and in accordance with customary rules of public international law'.

[57] EU–Canada CETA, Art. X.27(1), emphasis added.

[58] For instance, Art. 3(5) of the Netherlands–Czech Rep. BIT: 'If the provisions of law of either Contracting Party or *obligations under international law existing at present or established hereafter* between the Contracting Parties in addition to the present Agreement contain rules, whether general or specific, entitling investments by investors of the other Contracting Party to a treatment more favourable than is provided for by the present Agreement, such rules shall to the extent that they are more favourable prevail over the present Agreement' (emphasis added).

[59] India Model BIT, Art. 13.

[60] See, *inter alia*, the BITs entered into with Venezuela (1994, art. 11), Tanzania, (2006, art. 11), Namibia (2000, art. 8.1), India (2000, art. 12), Mozambique (2004, art. 11), Serbia (2011, art. 10), Philippines (1999, art. 10), Oman (2005, art. 10.1), Mongolia, (1999, art. 10,1), Mauritius (1978, art. 11(1), Libya (2004, art. 10), Jordan (2001, art. 11), Guatemala (2005), art. 10, United Arab Emirates (1999, art. 11), Lebanon (2001, art. 9) (the list is not exhaustive).

[61] *Saipem v. Bangladesh*, ICSID Case No. ARB/05/07, Award, 30 June 2009, para. 99. The relevant clause in the Italy–Bangladesh BIT reads as follows: 'Whenever any issue is governed both by this Agreement and by another International Agreement to which both

The US Model BIT provides another example of a State claiming the application of custom despite the *absence* of any reference to the concept in the instrument. The 1987 US Model BIT contained a 'no less' type of FET clause referring to 'international law' (but *not* to custom).[62] The exact same FET clause was adopted in thirteen of the BITs signed by the United States in the 1990s. In a statement made by the US State Department to the Senate, the 'no less' FET clause contained in the 1992 US Model BIT (the same clause as in the 1987 Model BIT) was described as setting 'a minimum standard of treatment based on customary international law'.[63] The same position was also taken in five so-called Letters of Submittal sent by the US State Department to the US President in 1993, requesting approval of BITs by the US Senate. These 'Letters of Submittal' describe the 'no less' FET clause contained in the treaties as a guarantee that investments shall be granted FET 'in accordance with international law' and that 'this paragraph sets out a minimum standard of treatment based on customary international law'.[64] After 1994, all 'Letters of Submittal' sent by the U.S. State Department systematically contain the same phrase stating that the term international law constitutes a reference to the MST under custom.[65] The letters are examples of the importance given to custom by States even when the term is not found in the treaty.

In sum, this section has shown that the concept of custom is increasingly referred to by States in investment treaties (even if it remains that

---

the Contracting Parties are parties, or whenever it is governed otherwise by general international law, the most favourable provisions, case by case, shall be applied to the Contracting Parties and to their investors'.

[62] The 1987 Draft Treaty Between the United States and ____ Concerning the Reciprocal Encouragement and Protection of Investments (hereinafter the '1987 Model BIT'): '[i]nvestment shall at all times be accorded fair and equitable treatment, shall enjoy full protection and security and shall in no case be accorded treatment less than that required by international law'.

[63] Description of the United States Model Bilateral Investment Treaty (BIT) – February 1992, Submitted by the State Department, 30 July 1992, in: Hearing before the Committee on the Foreign Relations, United States Senate, 102nd Congress, Second Session, 4 Aug. 1992, S. HRG. 102–795, p. 62, quoted in: Andrew Newcombe and Luis Paradell, *Law and Practice of Investment Treaties: Standards of Treatment* (Kluwer, 2009), p. 269.

[64] US–Kazakhstan BIT (1994), Letter of Submittal, 4 September 1993; US–Armenia BIT (1996), Letter of Submittal, 27 August 1993; US–Kyrgyzstan BIT (1994), Letter of Submittal, 7 September 1993; US–Moldova BIT (1994), Letter of Submittal, 25 August 1993; US–Ecuador BIT (1997), Letter of Submittal, 7 September 1993.

[65] The letters can be found at this page of the website of the Office of the United States Trade Representative: http://tcc.export.gov/Trade_Agreements/Bilateral_Investment_Treaties/index.asp.

today such a reference is still only found in a small *minority* of treaties). This new phenomenon clearly demonstrates the continuing importance and relevance of custom in contemporary international investment law.

5.1.3   Custom plays a gap-filling role

This section will examine two closely related questions:

- What happens when there is a contradiction between a rule found in custom and a treaty rule?
- What happens when a BIT is silent on a particular legal issue?

Tribunals rarely address the issues arising out of the interaction between custom and investment treaties. For instance, what happens when there is a contradiction between a rule found in custom and a treaty rule? According to one writer:

> Under international law, generally, treaty and custom have equal weight, and inconsistencies are regulated by three interrelated principles: (i) *lex specialis derogat generali* - a specific rule prevails over a general one; (ii) *lex posterior derogate priori* - a later rule prevails over a prior one; (iii) respecting the parties' intentions - where the parties intended to replace a rule deriving from one source of international law with another rule included in another source of law (e.g., replacing a customary rule with a treaty rule), the rule preferred by the parties will prevail.[66]

In the *ADM* case, the Tribunal stated that the substantive obligations contained in a multilateral investment treaty (Section A of NAFTA Chapter 11) 'offers a form of *lex specialis* to supplement the under-developed standards of customary international law relating to the treatment of aliens and property'.[67] Based on this *lex specialis* position, a number of tribunals have affirmed that treaty obligations prevail over

---

[66] Hirsch, 'Sources of International Investment Law', pp. 25–26, referring to: International Law Commission, 'Conclusions of the work of the Study Group on the Fragmentation of International Law: Difficulties arising from the Diversification and Expansion of International Law', adopted by the ILC at its Fifty-eighth session, in 2006, and submitted to the General Assembly as a part of the Commission's report covering the work of that session (UN doc. A/61/10, para. 251), in: *ILC Yearbook, 2006*, vol. II (2), conclusions no. 5, 10 and 24.

[67] *Archer Daniels Midland Company and Tate & Lyle Ingredients Americas, Inc.* v. *Mexico,* ICSID Case No. ARB (AF)/04/5, Award, 21 November 2007, para. 117 [hereinafter *ADM* v. *Mexico*].

rules of customary international law.[68] While this is normally the case,[69] there are some rather exceptional situations where another solution should prevail.[70] For instance, there are some treaties (mentioned in the previous section) which expressly indicate that the investor should be entitled to receive any better treatment existing under international law, which includes custom.[71]

Another exception is *jus cogens* norms, i.e. the rules having a peremptory character.[72] These peremptory norms include the prohibitions of aggression, genocide, slavery, racial discrimination, crimes against humanity and torture, and the right to self-determination.[73] The Parties cannot derogate in treaties (or contracts) from these norms.[74] A few investor-State arbitration tribunals have stated that they have a duty to apply such norms.[75] Moreover, while international law (as it now stands) does not impose any *direct* legal obligations on

---

[68] *ADC Affiliate Ltd & ADC & ADMC Management Ltd* v. *Hungary*, ICSID Case No. ARB /03/16, Award, 2 October 2006 [hereinafter *ADC* v. *Hungary*], para. 481 ('there is general authority for the view that a BIT can be considered as a *lex specialis* whose provisions will prevail over rules of customary international law'); *AES Corp.* v. *Argentina*, ICSID Case No. ARB /02/17, Decision on Jurisdiction, 26 April 2005, para. 23 (referring to the *specialia generalibus derogant* rule whereby 'treaty obligations prevail over rules of customary international law under the condition that the latter are not of a peremptory character'); *Enron Corporation and Ponderosa Assets, LP* v. *Argentina*, ICSID Case No. ARB/01/3, Award, 15 May 2007, para. 334 ('The expert opinion of Dean Slaughter and Professor Burke-White expresses the view that the treaty regime is different and separate from customary law as it is *lex specialis*. This is no doubt correct in terms that a treaty regime specifically dealing with a given matter will prevail over more general rules of customary law. Had this been the case here the Tribunal would have started out its considerations on the basis of the Treaty provision and would have resorted to the Articles on State Responsibility only as a supplementary means. But the problem is that the Treaty itself did not deal with these elements').

[69] Gazzini, 'The Role of Customary International Law', p. 698. [70] *Ibid.*

[71] See, for instance, Art. 3(5) of the Netherlands–Czech Rep. BIT.

[72] Art. 53 of the *Vienna Convention on the Law of Treaties* defines rules of *jus cogens* as follows: 'For the purposes of the present Convention, a peremptory norm of general international law is a norm accepted and recognized by the international community of States as a whole as a norm from which no derogation is permitted and which can be modified only by a subsequent norm of general international law having the same character'.

[73] ILC, 'Report of the ILC on the Work of its Fifty-Third Session', Official Records of the General Assembly, Fifty-sixth session, Supplement No. 10 (UN doc. A/56/10), chp. IV. E.2, p. 208.

[74] ILC, 'Conclusions of the Work of the Study Group', paras. 10, 32, 33, 40 and 41.

[75] *Methanex Corporation* v. *United States*, UNCITRAL, Award, 3 August 2005, Part IV, Chap. C, p. 11, para. 24 ('as a matter of international constitutional law a tribunal has an independent duty to apply imperative principles of law or jus cogens and not to give effect to parties' choices of law that are inconsistent with such principles').

corporations,[76] one notable exception is clearly *jus cogens* norms for which corporations can be held directly accountable.[77] According to the UN Special Representative Ruggie, 'under customary international law, emerging practice and expert opinion increasingly do suggest that corporations may be held liable for committing, or for complicity in, the most heinous human rights violations amounting to international crimes, including genocide, slavery, human trafficking, forced labour, torture and some crimes against humanity'.[78] In fact, several authors[79] (including myself[80]), as well as UNCTAD,[81] have argued that a tribunal should find a claim submitted by an investor which has committed *jus cogens* violations to be inadmissible. Support for this proposition is found in the reasoning of the *Phoenix Action* Tribunal.[82]

---

[76] David Kinley and Junko Tadaki, 'From Talk to Walk: The Emergence of Human Rights Responsibilities for Corporations at International Law', *Virginia JIL* 44(4) (2004), p. 135; Clara Reiner and Christoph Schreuer, 'Human Rights and International Investment Arbitration', in P.M. Dupuy, F. Francioni and E.U. Petersmann (eds.), *Human Rights in International Investment Law and Arbitration* (Oxford: Oxford University Press, 2009), pp. 86–87; Howard Mann, 'International Investment Agreements, Business and Human Rights: Key Issues and Opportunities', IISD, (2008) p. 9; Adefolake Adeyeye, 'Corporate Responsibility in International Law: Which Way to go?', *Singapore YB Int'L* 11 (2007), p. 148; Luke Eric Peterson, 'Human Rights and Bilateral investment Treaties. Mapping the Role of Human Rights Law within Investor-State Arbitration', Rights and Democracy, International Centre for Human Rights and Democratic Development (2009), p. 15.

[77] Carlos M. Vazquez, 'Direct vs. Indirect Obligations of Corporations Under International Law', *Colum. J. Transnat'l L.* 43 (2005), p. 927; Lahra Liberti, 'Investissements et droits de l'homme', in P. Kahn and T. Wälde (eds.), *New Aspects of International Investment Law* (Hague Academy of International Law, Leiden: Nijhoff, 2007), p. 836.

[78] 'Interim Report of the Special Representative of the Secretary-General of the United Nations on the Issue of Human Rights and Transnational Corporations and Other Business Enterprises', John Ruggie, U.N. Doc. E/CN.4/2006/97, 22 February 2006, para. 61.

[79] Luke E. Peterson and Kevin Gray, 'International Human Rights in Bilateral Investment Treaties and Investment Treaty Arbitration', Working Paper for the Swiss Ministry for Foreign Affairs (2003), p. 18 (referring to 'certain egregious human rights violations'); Liberti, 'Investissements et droits de l'homme', pp. 830–831 (speaking of 'graves violations des droits de l'homme'), see also at p. 840.

[80] P. Dumberry and G. Dumas-Aubin, 'When and How Allegations of Human Rights Violations can be Raised in Investor-State Arbitration', *J. World Invest. & Trade*, 13(3) (2012), p. 366. See also: P. Dumberry and G. Dumas-Aubin, 'The Doctrine of "Clean Hands" and the Inadmissibility of Claims by Investors Breaching International Human Rights Law', in Ursula Kriebaum (ed.), *Aligning Human Rights and Investment Protection*, 10(1) (*TDM Special Issue* 2013).

[81] UNCTAD, 'Selected Recent Developments in IIA Arbitration and Human Rights', *IIA Monitor* No. 2 (2009) p. 15.

[82] *Phoenix Action, Ltd.* v. *Czech Republic*, ICSID Case No. ARB/06/5, Award, 15 April 2009, para. 78: 'It is evident to the Tribunal that the same holds true in international investment law and that the ICSID Convention's jurisdictional requirements – as well as those of the

Another related question arises from situations when a BIT is silent on a particular legal issue. Scholars agree that solving this issue will involve using customary international law.[83] Custom therefore operates in a residual way. This is the conclusion reached by the ILC Report on fragmentation. The Report concluded that one of the applications of the principle of 'systemic integration' (mentioned at Article 31 (3)(c) of the *Vienna Convention on the Law of Treaties*[84]) is that '[t]he parties are taken to refer to customary international law and general principles of law for all questions which the treaty does not itself resolve in express terms'.[85] The Report further adds that customary international law is 'of particular relevance to the interpretation of a treaty under Article 31 (3)(c) especially where (...) the treaty rule is unclear or open-textured'.[86] The gap-filling role played by customary international law demonstrates its remaining importance in this age of 'treatification'.[87]

> BIT – cannot be read and interpreted in isolation from public international law, and its general principles. To take an extreme example, nobody would suggest that ICSID protection should be granted to investments made in violation of the most fundamental rules of protection of human rights, like investments made in pursuance of torture or genocide or in support of slavery or trafficking of human organs'.

[83] Dolzer and Schreuer, *Principles of International Investment Law*, p. 17; McLachlan, 'Investment Treaties and General International Law', p. 400; Gazzini, 'The Role of Customary International Law', p. 711; Cai Congyan, 'International Investment Treaties and the Formation, Application and Transformation of Customary International Law Rules', *Chinese JIL* 7 (2008), para. 32; Fauchald, 'The Legal Reasoning of ICSID Tribunals', p. 309; Hirsch, 'Sources of International Investment Law', pp. 7–8; Florian Grisel, 'The Sources of Foreign Investment Law', in Z. Douglas, J. Pauwelyn and J.E. Viñuales (eds.), *The Foundations of International Investment Law: Bringing Theory into Practice* (Oxford: Oxford University Press, 2014), p. 222; Jean d'Aspremont, 'International Customary Investment Law: Story of a Paradox', in T. Gazzini and E. de Brabandere (eds.), *International Investment Law: The Sources of Rights and Obligations* (Leiden; Boston: Martinus Nijhoff, 2012), p. 27; A. Ruzza 'Expropriation and Nationalization', in Rüdiger Wolfrum (ed.), *Max Planck Encyclopedia of Public International Law* (Oxford: Oxford University Press, vol. 9, 2013), para. 32; UNCTAD, 'Expropriation', UNCTAD Series on Issues in International Investment Agreements II (2012), p. 5 ('Today virtually all bilateral investment treaties (BITs) contain an expropriation provision. Customary international law also contains rules on the expropriation of foreign owned property and continues to supplement IIAs on those issues where the latter leave gaps or require interpretation').

[84] This provision requires the interpreter of a treaty to take into account 'any relevant rules of international law applicable in relations between the parties'.

[85] ILC, Study Group on the Fragmentation of International Law (2006), para. 251.

[86] *Ibid.*, para. 20(a).

[87] Y. Dinstein, 'The Interaction between Customary International Law and Treaties', *Rec. des cours* 322 (2006), p. 394.

Several tribunals have resorted to using custom to fill gaps.[88] For instance, when faced with a BIT which 'did not deal with the legal elements necessary for the legitimate invocation of a state of necessity', the *Sempra* Tribunal held that 'rules governing such questions will thus be found under customary law'.[89] The same conclusion was reached by the *ADM* Tribunal.[90] Similarly, the *ADC* Tribunal concluded that since the BIT did not 'contain any *lex specialis* rules' governing 'the issue of the standard for assessing damages in the case of an unlawful expropriation', it was 'required to apply the default standard contained in customary international law in the present case'.[91]

5.2   Arbitral tribunals always have to take into account custom to resolve disputes

The previous section has examined the three traditional reasons generally invoked by scholars to explain the continuing relevance of custom in contemporary international law. This section will investigate another reason showing the importance of custom in investor-State arbitration. International law is the applicable law in the overwhelming majority of arbitration disputes. In fact, I will argue in this section that international law should play an important role in *all* investor-State arbitration cases. In this context, any tribunal applying international law will *necessarily*

---

[88] *Saipem v. Bangladesh*, Award, 30 June 2009, para. 99 ('Since Saipem's claim is based on Article 5 of the BIT [on expropriation], the Tribunal will primarily apply the BIT as the applicable rule of international law. The Tribunal will also apply the general rules of international law that may be applicable, *either because an issue of international law is not directly dealt with in the BIT* or, if necessary, to interpret the BIT', emphasis added); *Asian Agricultural Products Ltd (AAPL) v. Sri Lanka*, ICSID Case No. ARB/87/3, Award, 27 June 1990, para. 22 (referring to the 'supplementary role of the recourse - regarding certain issues-to general customary international law').

[89] *Sempra Energy International v. Argentina*, ICSID Case No. ARB/02/16, Award, 28 September 2007, para. 378. See also, *Loewen Group, Inc. and Raymond L. Loewen v. United States*, ICSID Case No. ARB(AF)/98/3, Award, 26 June 2003, para. 226: 'There is no language in those articles [NAFTA Articles 1116 and 1117], or anywhere else in the treaty, which deals with the question of whether nationality must continue to the time of resolution of the claim. It is that silence in the Treaty that requires the application of customary international law to resolve the question of the need for continuous national identity'.

[90] *ADM v. Mexico*, Award, 21 November 2007, para. 110: 'Chapter 11 of the NAFTA constitutes *lex specialis* in respect to its express content, but customary international law continues to govern all matters not covered by Chapter 11'.

[91] *ADC v. Hungary*, Award, 2 October 2006, para. 483. See also, *ADM v. Mexico*, Award, 21 November 2007, para. 122.

have to take into account relevant rules of 'customary international law'. In any event, there are good reasons to argue (at least in the context of State contracts and BITs) that customary rules should apply to all investment disputes *independently* of the question of the choice of law made by the parties.

In the following sections, I will examine the question of the application of international law (and custom) by tribunals through the different ways arbitration claims can be introduced by foreign investors: proceedings under the terms of a State contract (Section 5.2.1), under the host State's domestic law (Section 5.2.2) and under an investment treaty (Section 5.2.3).

5.2.1 Arbitration under a State contract

As explained by the present author elsewhere,[92] a State contract is a binding legal instrument entered into between a foreign investor and a State.[93] These contracts typically contain, *inter alia*, an applicable law clause. The applicable law clause establishes the substantive law that will be applied by a tribunal to resolve a dispute between the parties to the contract, should ever one arise. The decision regarding the choice of a substantive applicable law is likely to be contentious. For instance, in contract negotiations between a foreign private party and a State, the State will often insist on the application of its own domestic law, while the other party will generally propose non-national rules such as, *inter alia*, international law or general principles of law.

The cornerstone principle here is party autonomy, which leaves the parties with the freedom to choose the law applicable to the contract.[94] A number of options are possible.[95] The first, and most obvious, choice is the law of the host State of the investment. This is, in fact, the option that

---

[92] Patrick Dumberry, 'International Investment Contracts', in Gazzini and de Brabandere (eds.), *International Investment Law: The Sources of Rights and Obligations*, p. 223 ff.

[93] UNCTAD, 'State Contracts', UNCTAD Series on Issues in International Investment Agreements (2004), p. 4; Jan Ole Voss, *The Impact of Investment Treaties on Contracts between Host States and Foreign Investors* (Leiden: Martinus Nijhoff, 2010), pp. 15–16.

[94] Institut de Droit international, 'The Proper Law of the Contract in Agreements between a State and a Foreign Private Person', art. 2, in *Tableau des résolutions adoptées (1957–1991)* (Paris: Pedone, 1992), p. 333: 'The parties may in particular choose as the proper law of the contract either one or several domestic legal systems or the principles common to such systems, or the general principles of law, or the principles applied in international economic relations, or international law, or a combination of these sources of law'.

[95] See, discussion in: Dumberry, 'International Investment Contracts', p. 223 ff.; P. Dumberry and J. Stone, 'International Law, Whether You Like It or Not: An Analysis of Arbitral Tribunal Practice Regarding the Applicable Law in Deciding State Contracts Disputes

is by far the most prevalent in State contracts.[96] While the application of international law to State contracts is one of the most contentious issues in doctrine, it remains that very few contracts provide for the application of international law *only*.[97]

The question surrounding the applicable law for State contracts takes on a whole new dimension when the parties decide to submit their disputes to arbitration under the ICSID Convention. In doing so, they agree to have any issue regarding the substantive law to be applied to the contract decided in accordance with Article 42 of the ICSID Convention. In other words, regardless of which law(s) is chosen by the parties in their contract, a tribunal constituted under the ICSID Convention will have to apply that choice in accordance with Article 42.[98] This provision gives precedence to the choice of the parties (the first sentence), but also establishes a framework for determining the applicable law in the absence of an agreement to that effect (the second sentence).

The present author has examined elsewhere the recent practice of ICSID tribunals in the specific context of State contracts distinguishing between situations where the parties *have* chosen the law applicable and those where the parties *have not*.[99] Most scholars now agree that international law should apply to disputes in a corrective or complementary manner under the first sentence of Article 42(1), regardless of party choice.[100] My conclusion is that the application of international law is

---

under the ICSID Convention in the Twenty First Century', *Yb Int'l Invest. L. & Pol.* 5 (2012–2013), pp. 477–516.

[96] Ch. Leben, 'La théorie du contrat d'État et l'évolution du droit international des investissements', *Rec. des cours* 302 (2003), p. 266; Jean-Michel Jacquet, 'Contrat d'État', *Jurisclasseur Droit international*, fasc. 565, 11/98 (Paris: Dalloz, 1998), paras. 57–58; Ahmed S. El-Kosheri and Tarek F. Riad, 'The Law Governing a New Generation of Petroleum Agreements: Changes in the Arbitration Process', *ICSID Rev.* 1 (1986), p. 266; George R. Delaume, 'The Proper Law of State Contracts Revisited', *ICSID Rev.* 12 (1997), p. 24.

[97] Leben, 'La théorie du contrat d'État', pp. 278–279; Voss, *The Impact of Investment Treaties on Contracts*, p. 46.

[98] Article 42(1) establishes the substantive law to be applied to investment disputes over which an ICSID arbitral tribunal has jurisdiction: 'The Tribunal shall decide a dispute in accordance with such rules of law as may be agreed by the parties. In the absence of such agreement, the Tribunal shall apply the law of the Contracting State party to the dispute (including its rules on the conflict of laws) and such rules of international law as may be applicable.'

[99] Dumberry and Stone, 'International Law, Whether You Like It or Not', p. 507.

[100] Christoph H. Schreuer, Loretta Malintoppi, August Reinisch and Anthony Sinclair, *The ICSID Convention; A Commentary* (2nd edn., Cambridge: Cambridge University Press, 2009), p. 585 'The complete exclusion of standards of international law as a consequence

necessary under the first sentence of Article 42(1) in the following situations: when the application of the law chosen by the parties results in an outcome that is unjust or in violation of international law and when the law chosen by the parties contains a *lacuna.*[101]

When the parties have *not* chosen the applicable law to the contract, Article 42(1) (second sentence) calls for the application of a combination of the host country's law and international law. According to ICSID tribunals, however, this provision is seen as giving supremacy to international law over domestic law. This is shown in the classic case *Klöckner* v. *Cameroon*, where the *ad hoc* Annulment Committee held that international law has 'a dual role, that is, *complementary* (in the case of a '*lacuna*' in the law of the State), or *corrective*, should the State's law not conform on all points to the principles of international law'.[102] Older cases (*Amco Asia Corp.* v. *Indonesia I*[103]) as well as more recent ICSID awards have endorsed the corrective and supplementary functions of international law.[104] This is also the prevailing view in doctrine.[105]

Some authors see no reason to limit international law to a simply corrective or supplemental role under the second sentence of

of an agreed choice of law pointing towards a domestic legal system would indeed lead to some extraordinary consequences. It would mean that an ICSID tribunal would have to uphold discriminatory and arbitrary action by the host country, breaches of its undertakings which are evidently in bad faith or amount to a denial of justice as long as they conform to the applicable domestic law, which is most likely going to be that of the host country. It would mean that a foreign investor, simply by assenting to a choice of law, could sign away the minimum standards for the protection of aliens and their property developed in customary international law. Such a solution would hardly be in accordance with one of the goals of the Convention, namely " ... promoting an atmosphere of mutual confidence and thus stimulating a larger flow of private international capital into those countries which wish to attract it." (...) In a similar vein, the prospect of awards which are in disregard of international law would be difficult to reconcile with the general obligation to recognize and enforce awards under Art. 54(1) of the Convention'. See also: Leben, 'La théorie du contrat d'État', pp. 283–288; Elihu Lauterpacht, 'The World Bank Convention on the Settlement of International Investment Disputes', *Recueil d'Etudes de Droit International en Hommage à Paul Guggenheim* (Geneva: Tribune, 1968), pp. 658–660.

[101] Dumberry and Stone, 'International Law, Whether You Like It or Not', p. 506 ff.

[102] *Klöckner Industrie-Anlagen GmbH and Ors.* v. *Cameroon and Société Camerounaise des Engrais*, ICSID Case No. ARB/81/2, Decision of ad hoc Committee on Claimant's Application for Annulment, 3 May 1985, p. 122, para. 69 (emphasis in the original).

[103] *Amco Asia Corporation and Ors.* v. *Indonesia*, ICSID Case No. ARB/81/1, Decision of ad hoc Committee on the Application for Annulment, 16 May 1986, p. 509.

[104] See, the analysis in: Dumberry and Stone, 'International Law, Whether You Like It or Not'.

[105] Schreuer *et al., The ICSID Convention: A Commentary*, p. 626.

Article 42(1). They suggest, for instance, that there is 'room for a third view of the role of international law (...) that of a truly independent body of substantive rules which may be applied by itself, and not through the filter of the law of the host country'.[106] The claimant in *Duke* v. *Peru* argued for the 'triple role' played by international law whereby investors would be granted 'certain independent and autonomous rights' and 'notably the right to a minimum standard of treatment under customary international law and general principles of law'.[107] According to the *Duke* Tribunal, this issue centred on the question of whether or not Article 42(1) entitles a claimant 'to bring independent and autonomous claims based on recognized sources of international law, namely customary international law and general principles of law?'[108] The Tribunal accepted, as a matter of principle, the notion of a 'third' role to be played by international law, beyond its basic corrective and supplementary functions.[109]

To summarize, recent case-law concerning Article 42 of the ICSID Convention shows two things: (1) international law *may* be applicable even in cases where the parties *have* chosen a *different* law to settle their disputes and (2) international law should *always* apply when the parties have *not* chosen the applicable law. The practical implications of these findings are important. A tribunal applying international law in these circumstances will *necessarily* have to take into account relevant rules of 'customary international law'.[110] This is because custom is one of the main sources of international law.[111] As noted by the *Pope & Talbot* Tribunal, 'international law is a broader concept than customary international law, which is only one of its components'.[112]

The other question is whether rules of customary international law should be applicable *even* in situations where international law *does not* apply to the dispute? This would be the case, for instance, in the context of an *ad hoc* arbitration where the parties to a contract have expressly chosen the domestic law of the host State. Normally, the tribunal should apply that law. An ICSID tribunal should also normally apply domestic law under Article 42 of the Convention when such law has been expressly

---

[106] Emmanuel Gaillard and Yas Banifatemi, 'The Meaning of "and" in Article 42(1), Second Sentence of the Washington Convention: The Role of International Law in the ICSID Choice of Law Process', *ICSID Rev.* 18 (2003), p. 381.

[107] *Duke Energy International Peru Investments No. 1, Ltd.* v. *Peru*, ICSID Case No. ARB/03/28, Award, 18 August 2008, para. 147.

[108] *Ibid.*, para. 159.   [109] *Ibid.*, para. 161.

[110] Schreuer *et al.*, *The ICSID Convention: A Commentary*, p. 606.

[111] ICJ Statute, Art. 38.

[112] *Pope & Talbot Inc.* v. *Canada*, UNCITRAL, Award on Damages, 31 May 2002, para. 46.

chosen by the parties in a State contract (and when that law does *not* contain any *lacuna,* or when its concrete application does *not* result in an unjust outcome or a violation of international law). In the event that such domestic law does *not* incorporate general international law, the question arises as to whether a tribunal should *also* apply relevant customary rules in these circumstances.

In my view, *as a matter of principle,* relevant rules of custom should apply to *all cases,* even those situations mentioned in the previous paragraph where a tribunal should normally apply domestic law (and not international law) to settle the dispute. The reason is simple. Customary international law applies to *all* States and such protection can therefore be invoked by *any* foreign investor in the context of arbitration proceedings. Schreuer notably observes that 'the mandatory rules of international law, which provides an international minimum standard of protection for aliens, exists independently of any choice of law made for a specific transaction'.[113] Therefore, the application of rules of customary international law should be deemed an entirely *different* question than that of the applicable law to a dispute:

> International law does not thereby become the law applicable to the contract. The transaction remains governed by the domestic legal system chosen by the parties. However, this choice is checked by the application of a number of mandatory international rules such as the prohibition of denial of justice, the discriminatory taking of property of the arbitrary repudiation of contractual undertaking.[114]

To summarize, customary rules should apply to all investment disputes under State contracts *independently* of the question of any choice of law made by the parties in their contract.

This position was adopted by the Tribunal in the *Cambodia Power Company* case, which involved three contracts between different entities including the claimant (a Cambodian company incorporated and existing under the laws of Cambodia, but owned by a US corporation) and the respondents (the State of Cambodia and Électricité du Cambodge, a Cambodian State-owned company).[115] The Tribunal first endorsed Schreuer's position (mentioned previously) that 'customary international

---

[113] Schreuer *et al., The ICSID Convention: A Commentary,* p. 587. See also: A.F.M. Maniruzzaman, 'State Contracts in Contemporary International Law: Monist versus Dualist Controversies', *EJIL* 12 (2001), p. 323.

[114] Schreuer *et al., The ICSID Convention: A Commentary,* p. 587.

[115] *Cambodia Power Company* v. *Cambodia and Électricité du Cambodge LLC,* ICSID Case No. ARB/09/18, Decision on Jurisdiction, 22 March 2011.

law exists and may be applied independently of any choice of law'.[116] The Tribunal also added that:

> Customary international law is inevitably relevant in the context of foreign investment (and ICSID arbitration), given that it comprises a body of norms that establish minimum standards of protection in this field. It is simply unrealistic to assume that the parties to a foreign investment contract such as those in question here would have intended to exclude such inherent protection by simply choosing an applicable national law.[117]

5.2.2   Arbitration under the host State's law

An arbitral tribunal may have jurisdiction over a dispute based on the consent to arbitration given by the host State in its own domestic law. The domestic investment law may, for instance, accept in advance arbitration under the ICSID Convention.[118] In this section, I will examine the question of which law(s) should be applied by an arbitral tribunal. Two situations must be distinguished: when the domestic investment law explicitly mentions the applicable law to be applied by a tribunal and when it does not.

First, domestic investment laws rarely contain any specific indication as to the law which should be applied by an arbitral tribunal.[119] When they do, they normally refer to the law of the host State.[120] In that situation, a tribunal should apply that law. This is because 'acceptance by the investor of the offer to consent to jurisdiction would include the acceptance of the clause on applicable law leading to an agreed choice of law'.[121] That does not mean, however, that international law is altogether irrelevant. For instance, international law is incorporated into the domestic law of many States. When this is the case, international law can be relied upon by the parties and applied by an ICSID tribunal.[122]

---

[116] *Ibid.*, para. 332.   [117] *Ibid.* para. 334.

[118] See, David Caron, 'The Interpretation of National Foreign Investment Laws as Unilateral Acts under International Law', in Mahnoush Arsanjani *et al.* (eds.), *Looking to the Future: Essays on International Law in Honor of W. Michael Reisman* (Leiden: Martinus Nijhoff, 2010), pp. 649–674, p. 655, indicating that the question of whether or not an unilateral act by the host State contains an actual *consent* to ICSID arbitration is a question to be determined in accordance with international law.

[119] Schreuer *et al.*, *The ICSID Convention: A Commentary*, p. 570.

[120] *Ibid.*, p. 570, giving the example of the Madagascar Investment Code, 1989, providing for the application of the law of Madagascar in the case of ICSID arbitration.

[121] *Ibid.*, p. 570.   [122] *Ibid.*, p. 582.

What about the situation where international law is *not* incorporated into domestic law? It seems that the reasoning mentioned in the previous section on State contracts[123] should also apply with respect to the host State's investment law. According to Schreuer, 'the practice of ICSID tribunals, the overwhelming weight of writers and important policy considerations all indicate that there is at least some place for international law even in the presence of an agreement on choice of law which does not incorporate it'.[124] In other words, international law (including, by definition, customary rules) is relevant *even* when the host State's investment law explicitly mentions that the applicable law is that State's law.

Second, when the domestic investment law is silent on the question of the applicable law, an ICSID tribunal (under the second sentence of Article 42) should apply *both* the host State's law and the rules of international law. It is generally recognized that 'the mere fact that [the tribunal's] jurisdiction is based on a provision of the host State's law' cannot be taken as a choice of the host State's law'.[125] A good example of this is demonstrated in *SPP* v. *Arab Republic of Egypt*, which involves an investor starting proceedings based on Egyptian Law.[126] The Tribunal upheld jurisdiction based on the consent given to arbitration by Egypt in its law.[127] In its award of 1992,[128] the Tribunal emphasized the role to be played by international law *even* if it were to accept Egypt's argument that the parties had implicitly chosen Egyptian law:

> Even accepting the Respondent's view that the Parties have implicitly agreed to apply Egyptian law, such an agreement cannot entirely exclude the direct applicability of international law in certain situations. The law of the [Arab Republic of Egypt], like all municipal legal systems, is not complete or exhaustive, and where a *lacuna* occurs it cannot be said that there is agreement as to the application of a rule of law which, *ex hypothesi*, does not exist. In such case, it must be said that there is 'absence of agreement' and, consequently, the second sentence of Article 42(1) would come into play.[129]

In the Tribunal's view, 'when municipal law contains a *lacuna*, or international law is violated by the exclusive application of municipal law, the

[123] See, discussion in Chapter 5, Section 5.2.1.
[124] Schreuer *et al.*, *The ICSID Convention: A Commentary*, p. 570. *Ibid.*, p. 583.
[125] *Ibid.*, p. 570.
[126] *Southern Pacific Properties (Middle East) Limited, Southern Pacific Properties Limited v. Egypt*, ICSID Case No. ARB/84/3, Decision on Jurisdiction, 27 November 1985, pp. 16–39.
[127] *Ibid.*, para. 70.
[128] *Southern Pacific Properties (Middle East) Ltd. v. Egypt*, ICSID Case No. ARB/84/3, Award, 20 May 1992.
[129] *Ibid.*, para. 80.

Tribunal is bound in accordance with Article 42 of the Washington Convention to apply directly the relevant principles and rules of international law'.[130] In other words, international law always plays a complementary and corrective role.

A somewhat different interpretation seems (at first) to have been adopted by the *Tradex Hellas* Tribunal. In its decision on jurisdiction, the Tribunal determined that it only had jurisdiction on the basis of the Albanian law on foreign investments (which is silent on the applicable law).[131] The Tribunal clearly took the view that it had to apply *that law* to the merits of the dispute and was in fact 'prevented from examining the claim on any other possible legal basis such as any other of the various investment laws issued in Albania, the Bilateral Investment Treaty between Albania and Greece, as well as other sources of international law'.[132] Nevertheless, the Tribunal added that it would 'make use of sources of international law insofar as that seems appropriate for the interpretation of terms used in the 1993 Law, such as "expropriation"'.[133] Later in the award, the Tribunal made reference to relevant rules of international law to interpret this principle.[134] The Tribunal's reasoning suggests that it would have applied relevant principles of international law had Albania's law on expropriation contained any *lacunae* or had it been inappropriate to solve the dispute. In other words, ultimately the award does not deny the complementary and corrective role that international law should play.

To summarize, international law has an important role to play whenever a tribunal decides a dispute submitted by an investor based on the host State's domestic law. This is the case in both situations when the domestic law explicitly mentions that the host State's law is the applicable law and when the domestic law is silent on the issue. As mentioned in the previous section,[135] a tribunal applying international law in these circumstances will have to take into account relevant rules of customary international law.

5.2.3   *Arbitration under an investment treaty*

BITs sometimes contain choice of law clauses indicating the law applicable to settle disputes under the instrument. Whenever an investor starts arbitration proceedings under a BIT, it agrees to comply with the dispute

---

[130] *Ibid.*, paras. 83–84.
[131] *Tradex Hellas S.A.* v. *Albania*, ICSID Case No. ARB/94/2, Decision on Jurisdiction, 24 December 1996.
[132] *Tradex Hellas S.A.* v. *Albania*, ICSID Case No. ARB/94/2, Award, 29 April 1999, para. 69.
[133] *Ibid.*   [134] *Ibid.*, para. 135.   [135] See, discussion in Chapter 5, Section 5.2.1.

settlement mechanism contained in the arbitration agreement, including the law applicable to the dispute. In other words, the applicable law mentioned in the BIT is 'deemed to be chosen directly by the parties to the arbitration'.[136] Many tribunals have adopted this position.[137] BITs offer a great variety of different choice of law clauses.[138] Some BITs refer to international law only. The most common type of clause, however, calls for the application of a variety of legal sources.[139] In fact, the majority of such clauses refer to four sources of law: '(1) the IIA itself; (2) the municipal law of the host state; (3) the provisions of any investment agreement or contract relating to the investment; and (4) general principles of international law'.[140] Whenever the parties refer to 'applicable rules of international law' (for instance at NAFTA Article 1131) or language such as 'other rules and principles of international law applicable between the Parties' (such as under CETA Article X.27), this should be considered as an implicit reference to, *inter alia*, custom.

In the absence of a choice of law clause in the BIT, the question of the applicable law must be determined by the arbitral tribunal in accordance with the rules under which the proceeding is conducted.[141] All tribunals have applied international law.[142] The reason is simple: The issue of the liability of the host State can only be governed by international law.[143]

---

[136] See, the analysis of case law by these writers: Y. Banifatemi, 'The Law Applicable in Investment Treaty Arbitration', in Katia Yannaca-Small (ed.), *Arbitration Under International Investment Agreements: A Guide to the Key Issues* (Oxford: Oxford University Press, 2010), p. 194; Dolzer and Schreuer, *Principles of International Investment Law*, p. 266; O. Spiermann, 'Applicable Law', in: P. Muchlinski, F. Ortino and C. Schreuer (eds.), *The Oxford Handbook of International Investment Law* (Oxford: Oxford University Press, 2008), p. 107.

[137] *Antoine Goetz et al.* v. *Burundi*, ICSID Case No. ARB/95/3, Award, 10 February 1999, para. 94.

[138] See, the analysis of 6 different options in: Andrew Newcombe and Luis Paradell, *Law and Practice of Investment Treaties: Standards of Treatment* (Kluwer, 2009), p. 79 ff.

[139] Newcombe and Paradell, *Law and Practice of Investment Treaties*, p. 79. See, the analysis of Banifatemi, 'The Law Applicable in Investment Treaty Arbitration', p. 197.

[140] Newcombe and Paradell, *Law and Practice of Investment Treaties*, p. 79, referring to the example of the choice of law clause contained in the Argentina–UK BIT (1990).

[141] Article 42(1) of the ICSID Convention. See also: UNCITRAL Arbitral Rules (2010), Article 35.

[142] Spiermann, 'Applicable Law', p. 107; Antonio Parra, 'Applicable Law in Investor-State Arbitration', in: Arthur Rovine (ed.), *Contemporary Issues in International Arbitration and Mediation* (Leiden: Brill, 2008), p. 6.

[143] Newcombe and Paradell, *Law and Practice of Investment Treaties*, pp. 98–99: 'The principal matter in an IIA dispute, the issue of the liability of the host state for measures that breach the IIA, is a matter for international law, not domestic law. Although domestic law is relevant at the first stage of analysis (to determine the existence and

This is the conclusion reached by the ICSID *ad hoc* Annulment Committee in the *Vivendi* case.[144] Another reason, mentioned by the *MTD* Tribunal,[145] is that BITs are treaties, which according to the *Vienna Convention on the Law of Treaties*, are governed by international law.[146] It is interesting to note that tribunals have come to this conclusion using different paths. Two different approaches will be briefly examined in the next paragraphs.

First, a number of tribunals have considered that because an arbitration proceeding is commenced under a BIT, it can be considered as an agreement between the parties for applying both the provisions of the BIT and international law.[147] For instance, in the *ADC* case, the Tribunal held that the disputing parties had 'consented to the applicability of the provisions of the [BIT]' and that such 'consent must also be deemed to comprise a choice for general international law, including customary international law, if and to the extent that it comes into play for interpreting and applying the provisions of the [BIT]'.[148] Another example is found in the *MTD* case where the Tribunal declared that '[t]his being a

scope of the investment, any governmental guarantees and commitments regarding the investment, and host state measures), these issues then need to be analyzed through the lens of international law. At this second stage of analysis the IIA regime and international law take over – the host state conduct must be assessed against the standards of protection in the IIA, and international law'; Banifatemi, 'The Law Applicable in Investment Treaty Arbitration', p. 210 ('irrespective of whether or not an investment treaty refers to international law as the law applicable to the merits of the dispute, international law will always be the law governing the interpretation and the application of the treaty providing the basis for the arbitration, to the extent that what is at stake, in investment treaty arbitration, is the international responsibility of a State'); Parra, 'Applicable Law in Investor-State Arbitration', p. 6.

[144] *Compañiá de Aguas del Aconquija S.A. and Vivendi Universal S.A.* v. *Argentina*, ICSID Case No. ARB/97/3 (formerly *Compañía de Aguas del Aconquija, S.A. and Compagnie Générale des Eaux* v. *Argentina*), Decision on Annulment, 3 July 2002, para. 102.

[145] *MTD Equity Sdn. Bhd. and MTD Chile S.A.* v. *Chile*, ICSID Case No. ARB/01/7, Award, 25 May 2004, para. 86, see also, at para. 87 ('At this point, the Tribunal will limit itself to note that, for purposes of Article 42(1) of the Convention, the parties have agreed to this arbitration under the BIT. This instrument being a treaty, the agreement to arbitrate under the BIT requires the Tribunal to apply international law'). See also: *Phoenix Action Ltd.* v. *the Czech Republic*, Award, 14 April 2009, para. 78 ('It is evident to the Tribunal that the same holds true in international investment law and that the ICSID Convention's jurisdictional requirements – as well as those of the BIT – cannot be read and interpreted in isolation from public international law, and its general principles').

[146] Newcombe and Paradell, *Law and Practice of Investment Treaties*, p. 99.

[147] *AAPL* v. *Sri Lanka*, Award, 27 June 1990, paras. 19–20.

[148] *ADC* v. *Hungary*, Award, 2 October 2006, para. 290.

dispute under a BIT, the parties have agreed that the merits of the dispute will be decided in accordance with international law'.[149]

Second, in other cases where tribunals have found no agreement between the parties as to the applicable law, they have applied the second sentence of Article 42(1) of the ICSID Convention whereby a tribunal must apply the law of the host State *and* international law. In such situations, all tribunals have applied the provisions of the underlying treaties, general international law rules and, in some circumstances, the law of the host State concerned.[150]

These two different paths used by tribunals ultimately come to the *same* conclusion of the application of international law. This situation is well-summarized by Parra as follows:

> It could be said that little seems to turn in the ICSID Convention BIT cases on whether the applicable rules of law are seen as being derived from the provision of the first or the provision of the second sentence of Article 42(1). Under either alternative, the result, broadly speaking, has been that the applicable rules of law have been those of the investment treaty and general international law, with host State law rules also having a role.[151]

In sum, in the event that the BIT does *not* contain a choice of law clause, international law plays a decisive and controlling role.[152] Therefore, when a tribunal is applying international law in these circumstances, it will *necessarily* have to take into account relevant rules of customary international law.[153] For instance, according to the *LG&E* Tribunal, 'applying the rules of international law is to be understood as comprising the general international law, including customary international law, to

---

[149] *MTD Equity Sdn. Bhd. and MTD Chile S.A. v. Chile*, Award, 25 May 2004, para. 86. See also: *Azurix Corp. v. Argentina*, ICSID Case No. ARB/01/12, Award, 14 July 2006, para. 67.

[150] Parra, 'Applicable Law', pp. 6, 11–13. See also: *Saipem v. Bangladesh*, Award, 30 June 2009, para. 99 ('Since Saipem's claim is based on Article 5 of the BIT [on expropriation], the Tribunal will primarily apply the BIT as the applicable rule of international law. The Tribunal will also apply the general rules of international law that may be applicable, either because an issue of international law is not directly dealt with in the BIT or, *if necessary, to interpret the BIT*' (emphasis added). See also, at para. 100 ('Moreover, pursuant to Article 42(1) of the ICSID Convention, national Bangladeshi law may also come into play in the present arbitration, in particular when Article 5 of the BIT itself refers to national law').

[151] Parra, 'Applicable Law', p. 13.

[152] Schreuer *et al*, *The ICSID Convention: A Commentary*, p. 578.

[153] Congyan, 'International Investment Treaties and the Formation', p. 671.

be used as an instrument for the interpretation of the [BIT]'.[154] It is important to note as well that domestic law also plays a limited role.[155] For instance, the question of the *very existence* of an 'investment' made in the host State remains a domestic law issue.[156]

In any event, in my view there is another reason why custom should always find application in the context of ICSID arbitration proceedings started under a BIT.

As mentioned previously, ICSID tribunals have to apply Article 42 of the Convention whereby the parties to a BIT are free to choose the applicable law. If the BIT is silent on the issue, the tribunal must apply 'such rules of international law as may be applicable'. What are these applicable rules? The meaning of this expression was clarified in *Waste Management I*, where the Tribunal had to interpret NAFTA Article 1131, which provided for similar terms ('A Tribunal established under this Section shall decide the issues in dispute in accordance with this Agreement and applicable rules of international law'). The Tribunal came to the conclusion that 'applicable rules of international law' included the rules of treaty interpretation contained in the *Vienna Convention on the Law of Treaties*.[157] In fact, even if the parties to a

---

[154] *LG&E Energy Corp., LG&E Capital Corp., and LG&E International, Inc.* v. *Argentina*, ICSID Case No. ARB/02/1, Decision on Liability, 3 October 2006, para. 89. See also: *ADC* v. *Hungary*, Award, 2 October 2006, para. 290.

[155] Spiermann, 'Applicable Law', pp. 107, 110; *MTD Equity Sdn Bhd and MTD Chile SA* v. *Chile*, Decision on Annulment, 16 February 2007, paras. 61 and 72 ('As noted above, the *lex causae* in this case based on a breach of the BIT is international law. However it will often be necessary for BIT tribunals to apply the law of the host State, and this necessity is reinforced for ICSID tribunals by Article 42(1) of the ICSID Convention. Whether the applicable law here derived from the first or second sentence of Article 42(1) does not matter: the Tribunal should have applied Chilean law to those questions which were necessary for its determination and of which Chilean law was the governing law. At the same time, the *implications* of some issue of Chilean law for a claim under the BIT were for international law to determine. In short, both laws were relevant'); *Wena Hotels Ltd.* v. *Egypt*, ICSID Case No. ARB/98/4, Decision on Application for Annulment, 5 February 2002, para. 40 ('What is clear is that the sense and meaning of the negotiations leading to the second sentence of Article 42(1) allowed for both legal orders to have a role. The law of the host State can indeed be applied in conjunction with international law if this is justified. So too international law can be applied by itself if the appropriate rule is found in this other ambit').

[156] Newcombe and Paradell, *Law and Practice of Investment Treaties*, p. 92 ff, providing other examples where domestic law is relevant.

[157] *Waste Management, Inc.* v. *Mexico*, ICSID Case No. ARB(AF)/98/2, Award, 2 June 2000, para. 9. See also: *Methanex Corporation* v. *United States*, UNCITRAL, Partial Award, 7 August 2002, para. 100; *Phoenix Action, Ltd.* v. *Czech Republic*, Award, 15 April 2009, para. 75 ('It is not disputed that the interpretation of the ICSID Convention and of the

BIT decide to choose *domestic* law as the applicable law to solve disputes, this 'choice will not operate to exclude the application of international law rules on treaty interpretation in interpreting the ICSID Convention'.[158] This is because Articles 31 and 32 of the *Vienna Convention on the Law of Treaties* are generally recognized as rules of customary international law on matters of treaty interpretation.[159] Many arbitral tribunals have come to the same conclusion.[160] Thus, tribunals consistently apply the *Vienna Convention* when interpreting BITs 'either because both State parties [to the BIT] are signatories to the [Convention] or because the rules of interpretation it provides represent customary international law'.[161]

Articles 31 and 32 of the *Vienna Convention on the Law of Treaties* will therefore govern questions regarding the interpretation of BITs.[162] Under Article 31(3)(c) of the *Vienna Convention*, a tribunal should take into account, together with the context of the treaty, 'any relevant rules of international law applicable in the relations between the parties'. These 'rules of international law' certainly include rules of customary international law.[163] In other words, through the application of the

---

BIT is governed by international law, including the customary principles of interpretation embodied in the Vienna Convention on the Law of Treaties and the general principles of international law'). See also, the analysis of Schreuer *et al.*, *The ICSID Convention: A Commentary*, pp. 604–605.

[158] J. Romesh Weeramantry, *Treaty Interpretation in Investment Arbitration* (Oxford: Oxford University Press, 2012), p. 14.

[159] *Ibid.*, pp. 6, 24 ff, providing several references to ICJ cases.

[160] *Ibid.*, p. 28 ff, providing several examples.

[161] McLachlan *et al.*, *International Investment Arbitration*, p. 66.

[162] Weeramantry, *Treaty Interpretation in Investment Arbitration*, p. 14; *Eureko B.V. v. Poland*, UNCITRAL, Partial Award and Dissenting Opinion, 19 August 2005, para. 247 ('This Tribunal is interpreting and applying a Treaty, a bilateral investment treaty (. . .). The authoritative codification of the law of treaties is the Vienna Convention on the Law of Treaties, a treaty in force among the very great majority of the States of the world community'); *Aguas del Tunari, S.A. v. Bolivia*, ICSID Case No. ARB/02/3, Decision on Respondent's Objections to Jurisdiction, 21 October 2005, paras. 478–479; *Chevron Corporation (USA) and Texaco Petroleum Company (USA) v. Ecuador*, UNCITRAL, PCA Case No. 34877, Interim Award, 1 December 2008, para. 118.

[163] This is the position of these writers: McLachlan, 'Investment Treaties and General International Law', p. 290; Panagiotis Merkouris, *Article 31(3)(c) of the VCLT and the Principle of Systemic Integration*, PhD. Thesis, Queen Mary University of London (2010), p. 186 ff.; M. Paparinskis, 'Sources of Law and Arbitral Interpretations of *Pari Materia* Investment Protection Rules', in O. K. Fauchald and A. Nollkaemper (eds.), *The Practice of International and National Courts and the (De-)Fragmentation of International Law* (Oxford; Portland: Hart Publ., 2012), pp. 87–115; Martins Paparinskis, *The International Minimum Standard and Fair and Equitable Treatment* (Oxford: Oxford University Press, 2013), p. 155; Gazzini, 'The Role of Customary International Law', p. 710;

principle of systemic integration set out at Article 31(3)(c) of the *Vienna Convention,* a tribunal deciding a dispute under a BIT will necessarily have to take into account relevant customary rules.[164]

Ultimately, it is safe to conclude that customary rules should apply to all investment disputes under a BIT *independently* of the question of the choice of law made by the parties in the instrument.

Finally, it should be added that the question of the application of international law by a tribunal should not be confused with that of the scope of its jurisdiction over a given dispute. Thus, there may be rare situations where, depending on the BIT's breadth of the investor-State dispute settlement clause, a claim alleging breaches of the MST could fall outside the tribunal's jurisdiction if it is unrelated to any allegation of breach of the BIT itself.[165] But even when the scope of the tribunal's jurisdiction is limited under such a narrow clause, it will still have (for the reasons set out in the previous paragraph) to decide the dispute under international law (including customary rules). In the *Chevron* case, the Tribunal had to decide whether the claimants could bring their claims for 'failure to provide a remedy and the denial of justice under customary international law' within the purview of a BIT clause which conferred

---

P. Sands, 'Treaty, Custom and the Cross-fertilization of International Law', *Yale Human Rights & Dev. Law Journal*, 88 (1998), p. 95; Harrison, 'The International Law Commission', pp. 432–433; Martins Paparinskis, 'Investment Treaty Interpretation and Customary Investment Law: Preliminary Remarks', in Chester Brown and Kate Miles (eds.), *Evolution in Investment Treaty Law and Arbitration* (Oxford: Oxford University Press, 2011), p. 70.

[164] This is the conclusion reached by the Tribunal in *Saluka Investments B.V. v. Czech Republic*, UNCITRAL, Partial Award, 17 March 2006, para. 254: 'In interpreting a treaty, account has to be taken of "any relevant rules of international law applicable in the relations between the parties" – a requirement which the International Court of Justice ("ICJ") has held includes relevant rules of general customary international law'.

[165] On this point, *see*: UNCTAD, 'Fair and Equitable Treatment': 'The question is whether an investor would be able to enforce the minimum standard of treatment of aliens through an IIA's investor-State dispute settlement (ISDS) mechanism. This will depend on the breadth of the treaty's ISDS clause. For instance, the ISDS clause in the India Singapore Comprehensive Economic Cooperation Agreement applies only to disputes "concerning an alleged breach of an obligation of the former under this Chapter" (Article 6.21); therefore, given the absence of the FET clause in the treaty, claims alleging breaches of the minimum standard of treatment of aliens will fall outside the tribunal's jurisdiction. In contrast, the New Zealand-Thailand Closer Economic Partnership Agreement's arbitration clause encompasses all disputes "with respect to a covered investment" (Article 9.16) – there is no requirement that relevant claims arise from a violation of the Agreement itself. Such a clause is broad enough to include, among others, claims of violation of the minimum standard of treatment of aliens under customary international law'.

jurisdiction over disputes 'arising out of or relating to ... an investment agreement'.[166] The Tribunal came to the conclusion that this provision did confer 'jurisdiction over customary international law claims' since the clause was 'not limited to causes of action based on the treaty' and that such language was 'broad enough to allow [it] to hear a denial of justice claim relating to the Concession Agreements'.[167]

In any event, the question is beyond the scope of this book. As further discussed in the next section, the question of the existence of customary rules and their application by tribunals is an entirely different question than that of access to arbitration.

5.3 The limits of custom: no access to international arbitration without the host State's consent

In the previous section, I have argued that arbitral tribunals should *always* take into account relevant rules of customary international law. Yet, this is only a valid proposition when a tribunal has jurisdiction over a dispute. The existence of customary rules should not be confused with the different question of a tribunal's *jurisdiction* over a claim filed by an investor.

International arbitration is based on the principle of consent.[168] The *Palma* Tribunal insisted on this fundamental requirement of consent *even* in the context of the proliferation of BITs which typically allow investors to submit claims to arbitration.[169] For instance, in the case of arbitration under the ICSID Convention, the consent of the parties (the investor and the host State of the investment) is required in order to have their dispute settled by an arbitral tribunal established under the Convention. The simple fact that the host State of the investment has ratified the Convention does not, on its own, constitute that State's

[166] *Chevron Corporation (USA) and Texaco Petroleum Company (USA) v. Ecuador*, Interim Award, 1 December 2008, paras. 203–209.
[167] *Ibid.*, para. 209.
[168] O. Diallo, *Le consentement des parties à l'arbitrage international* (Paris: PUF, 2010).
[169] *Plama Consortium Ltd. v. Bulgaria*, ICSID Case No. ARB/03/24, Decision on Jurisdiction, 8 February 2005, para. 198: 'With the advent of bilateral and multilateral investment treaties since the 1980s (today estimated to be more than 1,500), the traditional diplomatic protection mechanism by home states for their nationals investing abroad has been largely replaced by direct access by investors to arbitration against host states. Nowadays, arbitration is the generally accepted avenue for resolving disputes between investors and states. Yet, that phenomenon does not take away the basic prerequisite for arbitration: an agreement of the parties to arbitrate'.

consent to the Centre's jurisdiction over a dispute. A more specific type of consent is required. Such consent may be found either (i) in a direct agreement between the investor and the host State,[170] (ii) in a provision of the domestic legislation of the host State, or (iii) in a provision of an investment treaty. In the case of domestic legislations and treaties, the consent of the host State is typically offered unilaterally and generally to *any* investor that can meet the requirements of the law or the treaty.[171] These situations can give rise to what is called 'arbitration without privity',[172] that is, where an arbitral tribunal can have jurisdiction over a dispute even when there is no direct contractual link between the State and the foreign investor. Finally, for all three situations mentioned, an investor must also 'accept' the offer of arbitration.[173]

In the event that none of these three forms of State consent are met, an investor will *not* have access to international arbitration.[174] This lack of consent cannot be bypassed by a claimant investor using the MFN clause contained in another BIT entered into by the respondent State. As stated by Stern in her 'Concurring and Dissenting Opinion' in the *Impregilo* case, a 'MFN clause cannot enlarge the scope of the basic treaty's right to international arbitration, it cannot be used to grant access to international arbitration when this is not possible under the conditions provided for in the basic treaty'.[175] When no access to arbitration exists, the

---

[170] In the case of a direct agreement (a contract), the consent is mutual from the start and is usually targeted to a specific investment.

[171] Thus, a BIT typically contains a dispute resolution mechanism whereby each State consents (in *advance*) to ICSID arbitration for claims that are submitted by nationals of the other State party to the treaty and that satisfy the requirements of the treaty (nationality, definition of investment, etc.). The consent to arbitration is offered by the host State to potentially *all foreign investors* of the other party to the treaty investing in the host State.

[172] J. Paulsson, 'Arbitration Without Privity', *ICSID Rev.* 10 (1995), p. 232.

[173] By starting ICSID proceedings, the investor accepts the host State's offer and is deemed to have consented to ICSID arbitration.

[174] In such a situation, a foreign investor will normally be entitled to commence legal proceedings before the domestic courts of the State where it has made its investment. One interesting question, which will not be examined in this book, is to what extent domestic courts can apply rules of customary international law. On this question, see: A. Nollkaemper, *National Courts and the International Rule of Law* (Oxford: Oxford University Press, 2011).

[175] *Impregilo S.p.A.* v. *Argentina*, ICSID Case No. ARB/07/17, Award, 21 June 2001, Concurring and Dissenting Opinion of Professor Brigitte Stern, para. 47 ('I contend that an MFN clause can only concern the rights that an investor can enjoy, it cannot modify the fundamental conditions for the enjoyment of such rights, in other words, the insuperable conditions of access to the rights granted in the BIT'). See also, at para. 80.

inherent legal protections offered to foreign investors under custom will remain rather theoretical on the international plane. The existence of customary rules does not 'magically' grant access to arbitration for investors when none exists. As recently enunciated by the ICJ in *Armed Activities on the Territory of the Congo (New Application: 2002)*, the existence of a customary norm and the rule of consent to jurisdiction are two *different* questions. This is the case *even when* the rule is considered as *jus cogens* and has an *erga omnes* character.[176]

The rest of this section examines the controversial question of whether or not a rule of customary international law provides *all* foreign investors with a procedural right to bring arbitration claims against *any* State where they make an investment *despite* the absence of any actual consent to arbitration being given by the host State. One passage from the *CMS* v. *Argentina* case mentions that investor-State arbitration, which first developed as a *lex speciali,* had now, in fact, become a *general* rule.[177] However, in the subsequent case of *Camuzzi* v. *Argentina,* another tribunal (with Vicuña acting as president just like in the *CMS* case) clarified the meaning of this ambiguous passage contained in the *CMS* award and explained that no rule of custom had emerged giving investors access to arbitration.[178]

---

[176] *Armed Activities on the Territory of the Congo (New Application: 2002) (Democratic Republic of the Congo v. Rwanda),* Jurisdiction of the Court and Admissibility of the Application, Judgment, 3 February 2006, ICJ Rep. 2006, para. 64.

[177] *CMS Gas Transmission Company v. Argentina,* ICSID Case No. ARB/01/8, Decision of the Tribunal on Objections to Jurisdiction, 17 July 2003, para. 48: 'The Tribunal therefore finds no bar in current international law to the concept of allowing claims by shareholders independently from those of the corporation concerned, not even if those shareholders are minority or non-controlling shareholders. Although it is true, as argued by the Republic of Argentina, that this is mostly the result of *lex specialis* and specific treaty arrangements that have so allowed, the fact is that *lex specialis in this respect is so prevalent that it can now be considered the general rule,* certainly in respect of foreign investments and increasingly in respect of other matters. To the extent that customary international law or generally the traditional law of international claims might have followed a different approach—a proposition that is open to debate—then that approach can be considered the exception' (emphasis added).

[178] *Camuzzi International S.A. v. Argentina,* ICSID Case No. ARB/03/2, Decision on Jurisdiction, 11 May 2005, para. 145: 'In CMS, the tribunal held that the system of treaties on protection gives rise to a lex specialis which "can now be considered the general rule, certainly in respect of foreign investments and international claims . . . ." *However, this does not necessarily mean that it refers to the emergence of a customary rule.* The general rule is evidenced by the fact that practically all disputes relating to foreign investments are today submitted to arbitration by resorting to the mechanisms of that lex specialis, as expressed by means of bilateral or multilateral treaties or other agreements. Only in very exceptional instances do the affected parties resort to diplomatic protection;

Some writers, however, have argued otherwise.[179] For instance, Laird is of the view that 'with the recent exponential development and growth of international investment treaties and related jurisprudence since the ELSI case, a reasonable argument can be now made that we have reached that tipping point at which a general rule of international law, as evidenced in state practice motivated by *opinio juris*, can be said to have emerged with respect to *shareholders' rights to bring claims*'.[180] According to him, 'a strong argument can now be made that *sufficient consistency* does exist in investment instruments and related jurisprudence, and that this particular area of international law has evolved to reflect a *new and consistent* state of international custom'.[181] The same position also seems to have been adopted by Lowenfeld, for whom the 'understanding . . . that disputes between foreign investors and host State should be subjected to impartial adjudication or arbitration [is] a *general principle*[] and do[es] not depend on the wording or indeed the *existence of any given treaty*'.[182]

As noted by Audit and Forteau, the existence of such a rule would have to be considered as no less than a 'genuine revolution' of international

---

the latter cannot then be considered the general rule in the system of international law presently governing the matter, but as a residual mechanism available when the affected individual has no direct channel to claim on its own right' (emphasis added).

[179] The question is framed as follows by Mathias Audit and Mathias Forteau, 'Investment Arbitration without BIT: Toward a Foreign Investment Customary Based Arbitration?', *J. Int'l Arb.* 29(5) (2012), pp. 581–604, p. 586: 'One can therefore legitimately ask whether this practice has given rise to a new customary international rule according to which, in the field of foreign investment law, any State would be considered as consenting to arbitration before international tribunals in cases of disputes with any foreign investor, even if the defendant State did not expressly consent to arbitration through the adoption of a legal instrument such as a BIT or a domestic law. In other words, is there now a customary right for any foreign investor to enter into international arbitration against States in the specific field of foreign investments?'.

[180] Ian A. Laird, 'A Community of Destiny: The Barcelona Traction Case and the Development of Shareholder Rights to Bring Investment Claims', in Todd Weiler (ed.), *International Investment Law and Arbitration: Leading Cases from the ICSID, NAFTA, Bilateral Treaties and Customary International Law* (London: Cameron May, 2005), p. 86 (emphasis added).

[181] *Ibid.*, p. 96 (emphasis added). See also: Steffen Hindelang, 'Bilateral Investment Treaties, Custom and a Healthy Investment Climate – The Question of whether BITs Influence Customary International Law Revisited' *J. World Invest. & Trade*, 5 (2004), p. 799, for whom 'sufficient consistency in regards to the following principles can be evidenced today: (. . .) disputes between foreign investors and host States should be subject to impartial adjudication or arbitration'.

[182] Andeas F. Lowenfeld, *International Economic Law* (2nd edn., Oxford: Oxford University Press, 2008), p. 586 (emphasis added).

law.[183] They believe, however, that 'the revolution is perhaps nothing more than an evolution'[184] and that there are many reasons for supporting the emergence of such a new norm. They support the establishment of a custom rule whereby the *specific* consent required under the ICSID Convention would no longer be necessary for investors to have access to international arbitration.[185] Lowenfeld adopted a similar position: an investor should have access to arbitration even in the absence of a BIT between the home State of that investor and the host State, provided that the latter is party to the ICSID Convention or has consented to arbitration under any set of rules of an organized body (such as ICSID or UNCITRAL).[186] Audit and Forteau ultimately contend, however, that any such 'right to international arbitration' rule 'remains doubtful, even if it can be considered to some extent as being *in statu nascendi*'.[187]

As explained elsewhere,[188] the present author would maintain that no rule of customary international law on the legal standing of foreign investors before arbitral tribunals has crystallized.[189] This is the case for four reasons.

First, investor-State arbitration clauses found in BITs are not consistent and uniform enough to consider that any customary rule has

---

[183] Audit and Forteau, 'Investment Arbitration without BIT', p. 587.   [184] *Ibid.*, p. 587.

[185] *Ibid.*, p. 599, further explaining that 'It would not be possible, for example, for a customary rule to grant jurisdiction to ICSID for a dispute between State A and a legal person indirectly controlled by a national of State B concerning an expropriation allegedly involving the violation of the BIT between State A and State B if State A is not a party to ICSID Convention (. . .). But a more modest customary rule could perfectly well be constructed, which would work as follows. The only thing the rule would disable would be the requirement of a specific State consent. On the other hand, it would not deactivate the other jurisdictional requirements. According to this rule, States would agree that any *available* international judicial mean of settlement (ICSID, for instance, provided that it has jurisdiction according to its own rules) could be activated by the investor without requiring an additional consent by the defendant State'.

[186] Andreas F. Lowenfeld, 'Investment Agreements and International Law', *Columbia JTL* 42 (2003), p. 129. See also: E. Chalamish, 'Future of Bilateral Investment Treaties: A De Facto Multilateral Agreement', *Brook. J. Int'l L.* 34 (2008–2009), p. 342.

[187] Audit and Forteau, 'Investment Arbitration without BIT', pp. 591, 598 ('But in light of the above, it remains true that it is quite disputable that BIT practice currently reflects the *opinio juris* of the states that, as a matter of positive international law, there exists a customary right to international arbitration that any investor could activate against any State').

[188] P. Dumberry, 'The Legal Standing of Shareholders Before Arbitral Tribunals: Has any Rule of Customary International Law Crystallised?', *Michigan State JIL* 18 (2010), pp. 353–374.

[189] *Ibid.* See also: d'Aspremont, 'International Customary Investment Law', p. 35 ('As is especially exemplified by the claim that customary international law prescribes legal standing for shareholders before international tribunals, international investment lawyers do not balk at attributing customary status to standards which are of architectural, institutional or technical nature, i.e. those standards whose existence is dependent on there being a system').

emerged. While it is true that most recent BITs and multilateral conventions on foreign investments include provisions on the settlement of investor-State disputes, this is not the case for a number of older agreements[190] as well as for a few recent ones.[191] In any event, these numerous investment treaties only cover some 13% of the total potential bilateral relationships between States worldwide.[192] In other words, it is more often than not that a corporation making an investment in another country will not benefit from an investor-State arbitration mechanism and will have simply no direct access to international arbitration under an investment treaty.[193]

In any event, it is important to add that the actual content of investor-State arbitration clauses varies.[194] For instance, in terms of the venue of arbitration, many clauses refer to ICSID arbitration or UNCITRAL or other institutions (or give the option to choose from one of those). Moreover, there are some important inconsistencies between these clauses with respect to how they specifically define what an 'investor' is and the issue of the nationality of corporations.[195] This is important because nationality is the gateway to legal protection under an

---

[190] See, for instance: Agreement Between the Federated Republic of Germany and the Federation of Malaysia Concerning the Promotion and Reciprocal Protection of Investments, 22 December 1960, providing only for a State-to-State dispute settlement mechanism.

[191] See, for instance: Australia–US FTA.

[192] Gazzini, 'The Role of Customary International Law', p. 691.

[193] Audit and Forteau, 'Investment Arbitration without BIT', p. 595.

[194] Abdullah Al Faruque, 'Creating Customary International Law through Bilateral Investment Treaties: a Critical Appraisal', *Indian J Int'l* 44 (2004), pp. 307–310; M. Sornarajah, *The International Law on Foreign Investment* (2nd edn., Cambridge: Cambridge University Press, 2004), p. 250; Bernard Kishoiyian, 'The Utility of Bilateral Investment Treaties in the Formulation of Customary International Law', *Northwestern J. Int'l L. & Bus* 14(2) (1993), p. 362 ff, 368 ('The foregoing examination of various BITs demonstrates that though the settlement of investment disputes through arbitration is accepted in BITs, the mere reference to it in the treaties should not be made the basis of an assessment that arbitration has come to be accepted as the method of settling investment disputes or that there is an obligation to refer such disputes to international arbitration so that they may be settled in accordance with a supranational body of legal principles or what is now commonly known as *lex mercantoria*. The diversity of the clauses does not admit the making of such claims. However, it is plausible to claim that on the basis of these treaties, the trend is towards the acceptance of international arbitration, particularly arbitration by ICSID of foreign investment disputes').

[195] Gazzini, 'The Role of Customary International Law', p. 709; Kishoiyian, 'The Utility of Bilateral Investment Treaties' pp. 346–353. See, discussion in Chapter 3, Section 3.3.3.2.2.3.

investment treaty.[196] One OECD study concluded that 'there is no single test used by all investment treaties to define the link required between a legal person seeking protection under the treaty and the contracting state under whose treaty the investor asks for protection'.[197] Another study on BITs entered into by countries in the Americas also highlighted the great inconsistency in the definitions of corporate nationality.[198] In fact, completely different approaches are sometimes adopted by the *same country* depending on the treaty.[199]

Second, there is no evidence of any *opinio juris* by States about the existence of any such an alleged procedural right to arbitration. Thus, nothing about such a belief can logically be deduced from the mere fact that a State has signed many BITs that contain an investor-State arbitration mechanism. There is simply no evidence suggesting that States parties to BITs provide access to arbitration to foreign investors out of any sense of legal obligation. They do so based on their self-interest depending on which State is sitting on the other side of the negotiation table. For instance, Australia recently explained that it would consider whether to include Investor-State Dispute Settlement provisions in its FTAs 'on a case-by-case basis'.[200] Australia thus decided not to include such a clause in its FTA with the United States. It, however, included one

[196] Anthony C. Sinclair, 'The Substance of Nationality Requirements in Investment Treaty Arbitration', *ICSID Rev.* 20 (2005), p. 357; Pia Acconci, 'Determining the Internationally Relevant Link between a State and a Corporate Investor, Recent Trends Concerning the Application of the 'Genuine Link' Test', *J. World Invest. & Trade* 5 (2004), p. 139.

[197] OECD, 'International Investment Law: Understanding Concepts and Tracking Innovations' (2008), pp. 18–19, further explaining that 'Bilateral investment treaties have essentially relied on the following tests for determining the nationality of legal persons: i) the place of constitution in accordance with the law in force in the country; ii) the place of incorporation or where the registered office is; iii) the country of the seat, i.e. where the place of administration is; and iv) less frequently, the country of control. Most investment treaties use a combination of the tests for nationality of legal persons so that a company must satisfy two or more of them in order to be covered. The most common approach is a combination of the place of incorporation or constitution and seat, although the combination of incorporation or constitution and control and also of all three tests is also found'.

[198] Lawrence Jahoon Lee, 'Barcelona Traction in the 21st Century: Revisiting its Customary and Policy Underpinnings 35 Years Later', *Stanford JIL* 42 (2006), pp. 272–273 (out of forty BITs examined, the author found no less than five different definitions of 'investor').

[199] Kishoiyian, 'The Utility of Bilateral Investment Treaties', p. 352. A good illustration is Canada's position concerning holding corporations and direct/indirect investments. This question is discussed in: Dumberry, 'The Legal Standing of Shareholders Before Arbitral Tribunals', p. 365 ff.

[200] Australia's Ministry of Foreign Affairs, available at www.dfat.gov.au/fta/isds-faq.html (further explaining that Australia has ISDS provisions in four FTAs and twenty-one BITs).

in its recent FTA with South Korea. Moreover, there is clearly no evidence that States that are *not* parties to BITs actually believe that they *must* (under international law) provide access to international arbitration to *all* foreign investors.[201]

Third, the unlikelihood of the emergence of any rule of customary international law on the legal right of investors to bring claims to international arbitration is clear when one considers the *practical* consequences of recognizing the existence of such a rule. If such a 'rule' were to exist, it could be invoked by *any foreign investor* irrespective of whether or not its State of origin has entered into a BIT with the country where it made its investment. In practical terms, this would mean that *any* investor investing *anywhere* in the world could rely on such a 'rule' for legal protection and have access to international arbitration to settle a dispute with the host State. In other words, access to arbitration would exist *despite* the absence of consent by the host State. Yet, the question remains as to *how* a claimant investor could practically start arbitration proceedings in this context. For instance, how would the arbitral tribunal be established? Which tribunal would have jurisdiction over such a claim? Could domestic courts (and if so which ones?) appoint such a tribunal? (and if so, under which circumstances?).[202]

Fourth, in any event, recognizing the existence of such a rule would be contrary to one of the most fundamental tenets of international law. At the heart of international law lies the principle that corporations (just like individuals) lack any *automatic jus standi* before international tribunals to contest a violation of international law.[203] As mentioned previously, their standing to submit claims against States directly before international judicial bodies does not exist without the *consent* of the State against which a claim is submitted.[204] In other words, foreign investors do not have direct access to international tribunals in the

---

[201] The same conclusion is reached by Audit and Forteau, 'Investment Arbitration without BIT', p. 595: 'if France, for instance, has not concluded a BIT with ninety States, it would seem rather surprising to suggest that it must be considered as having offered a right to international arbitration to any foreign investor having the nationality of those States on the basis of customary international law'.

[202] These questions are discussed in: Audit and Forteau, 'Investment Arbitration without BIT', p. 599 ff.

[203] R.J. Zedalis, 'Claims by Individuals in International Economic Law: NAFTA Developments', *American Rev. Int'l Arb.* 7(2) (1996), p. 115; F. Francioni, 'Access to Justice, Denial of Justice and International Investment Law', *EJIL* 20(3) (2009), p. 731.

[204] E. de Brabandere, *Investment Treaty Arbitration as Public International Law: Procedural Aspects and Implications* (Cambridge: Cambridge University Press, 2014), p. 23.

absence of a specific instrument providing for such access. The point is well explained by Stern in her Concurring and Dissenting Opinion in the 2011 *Impregilo* case:

> It is of utmost importance not to forget that no participant in the international community, be it a State, an international organization, a physical or a legal person, has an inherent right of access to a jurisdictional recourse. Just as a State cannot sue another State, unless there is a specific consent to that effect, ... in the same manner, in the framework of BITs, investors are not capable of intervening on the international level against States for the recognition of their rights, unless States grant them such a right under conditions that they determine.[205]

In contemporary international law, the procedural capacity of individuals (and corporations) to submit claims against States directly before international judicial bodies remains the *exception* and not the rule.[206] This is the case even though an increasingly important number of tribunals and courts do provide for such direct access for individuals.[207]

In sum, for all these reasons, almost all scholars agree that access to international adjudication (existing under modern BITs) has not crystallized into a rule of customary international law.[208] This is indeed one of the 'limits' of custom. The existence of substantive rules of custom is unhelpful to an investor when the host State has not consented to arbitration or when a tribunal lacks jurisdiction over a given dispute.

---

[205] *Impregilo S.p.A. v. Argentina*, ICSID Case No.ARB/07/17, Award, 21 June 2001, Concurring and Dissenting Opinion of Brigitte Stern, para. 53.

[206] Rudolf Dolzer and Margrete Stevens, *Bilateral Investment Treaties* (Martinus Nijhoff, 1995), p. 119; Ian Brownlie, *Principles of Public International Law* (Oxford: Oxford University Press, 1998), p. 585.

[207] For a number of examples, see Dumberry, 'The Legal Standing of Shareholders Before Arbitral Tribunals', p. 370.

[208] Kishoiyian, 'The Utility of Bilateral Investment Treaties' p. 368; McLachlan *et al.*, *International Investment Arbitration*, pp. 11, 17; Gazzini, 'The Role of Customary International Law', pp. 707–710; Stephen M. Schwebel, 'Investor-State Disputes and the Development of International Law: The Influence of Bilateral Investment Treaties on Customary International Law', *ASIL Proc.*, 98 (2004), p. 30 ('In view of the treaty-specific nature of grants of international adjudication, and the presumption that States are not amenable to international adjudication unless they consent to it, it would not be tenable to suggest that BIT provisions that afford arbitral recourse have themselves found their way into the body of customary international law').

5.4   Can a State claim the status of persistent objector?

As mentioned in Chapter 2,[209] it is undeniable that there are some rules of customary law that exist today in the field of international investment law. In his classic book, Professor Sornarajah argues, to the contrary, that 'it would be difficult to show that there was free consent on the part of all the developing states to the creation of any customary international law' in international investment law.[210] In any event, he believes that even 'if there was such customary international law, many developing States would regard themselves as persistent objectors who were not bound by the customary law'.[211]

A rule that has *already* crystallized into customary law is binding upon *all* States of the international community. Therefore, a State is not allowed to opt out unilaterally.[212] The ICJ has clearly stated that customary rules 'by their very nature, must have equal force for all members of the international community, and cannot therefore be the subject of any right of unilateral exclusion exercisable at will by any one of them in its favour'.[213] One controversial question, however, is whether a State should nevertheless be allowed *not* to be bound by a rule of customary law because it objected to this rule in the early stage of its formation and actively, unambiguously and persistently maintained such an objection thereafter.[214] This is the much-debated theory of the 'persistent objector'.

---

[209]   See, Chapter 2, Section 2.6.

[210]   Sornarajah, *The International Law on Foreign Investment*, p. 213. He, however, admits at p. 89, that there are 'few' rules of custom in the field of international investment law.

[211]   *Ibid.* Elsewhere the author also argues (at p. 151) that 'it is difficult to establish that state responsibility for economic injuries to alien investors was recognised as a principle of customary international law. Latin American states as well as African and Asian States must be taken to be persistent objectors to the formation of such customary international law'. See also: M. Sornarajah, 'Power and Justice in Foreign Investment Arbitration', *J. Int'l Arb.*, 14(3) (1997), p. 118; Stephen Vasciannie, 'The Fair and Equitable Treatment Standard in International Investment Law and Practice', *British YIL*, 70 (1999), p. 99, fn. 305.

[212]   Michael Akehurst, 'Custom as a Source of International Law', *British YIL*, (1974–1975), pp. 24–26. Some writers have challenged that point in recent years: Curtis A. Bradley and G. Mitu Gulati, 'Withdrawing from International Custom', *Yale LJ*, 120 (2010), p. 201. For a rebuttal, see: Anthea Roberts, 'Who Killed Article 38(1)(b)? A Reply to Bradley and Gulati', *Duke J Comp & IL*, 21 (2010), p. 173.

[213]   *North Sea Continental Shelf Cases (Federal Republic of Germany v. Denmark / Federal Republic of Germany v. Netherlands)*, ICJ Rep. 1969, p. 38.

[214]   G. Fitzmaurice, 'The Law and Procedure of the International Court of Justice, 1951–54: General Principles and Sources of Law', *British YIL* (1953), p. 26; International Law Association, 'Statement of Principles Applicable to the Formation of General Customary International Law', Final Report of the Committee on the Formation of Customary Law,

It should be stressed at this juncture that the only direct potential effect of a State's timely objection to the formation of a new customary rule is for *that State* to be not bound by that rule. Its opposition would not, however, prevent the rule from eventually crystallizing into customary law and, thus, being recognized as general international law amongst all *other* States.[215] Yet, this distinction is not always easy to make in reality.[216]

This section will critically examine the concept of persistent objector in the context of international investment law.[217] The first section will analyse the basic definition of the concept of persistent objector and its conditions of application in general international law (Section 5.4.1). In the second section, I will examine the application of the theory to investor-State arbitration proceedings and the recent cases where the argument was raised (Section 5.4.2). In my view, there are three reasons why the concept of persistent objector should *not* be successfully used in investor-State arbitration proceedings to prevent the application of a rule of customary law by an arbitral tribunal.

5.4.1 The concept of persistent objector in international law

It is important to briefly explain the origin of the concept of the persistent objector. As mentioned in Chapter 2,[218] in the 1960s and 1970s Newly Independent States emerging from colonialism represented the majority of States at the United Nations and began using such status to advance their interests through resolutions and declarations at the General Assembly.[219] They held the view that such resolutions would constitute

Conference Report London (2000), p. 27 [hereinafter ILA, Final Report, 2000]; David A. Colson, 'How Persistent Must the Persistent Objector be', *Washington L.R.*, 61 (1986), pp. 965–969.

[215] Akehurst, 'Custom as a Source of International Law', pp. 26–27.
[216] For instance, the persistent objection of a small but particularly dynamic and/or powerful group of States to a new rule may in fact prevent the rule from crystallizing into customary law. See, US pleadings before the ICJ arguing that its opposition blocked the development of a customary norm preventing the threat and the use of nuclear weapons: *Legality of the Threat or Use of Nuclear Weapons*, Advisory Opinion, ICJ Rep. 1996.
[217] This section is a modified and updated version of an article previously published: P. Dumberry, 'The Last Citadel! Can a State Claim the Status of Persistent Objector to Prevent the Application of a Rule of Customary International Law in Investor-State Arbitration?', *Leiden JIL* 23(2) (2010), pp. 379–400.
[218] See, Chapter 2, Section 2.2.1.
[219] M. Byers, *Custom, Power and the Power of Rules: International Relations and Customary International Law* (Cambridge: Cambridge University Press, 1999), p. 41.

new customary rules, thus replacing the old existing rules, to which they had not participated and which they believed were contrary to their own interests. These arguments were rejected at the time by Western States. They feared that their influence on the evolution and the formulation of international law rules was eroding as a result of these important changes.[220] In one landmark article, Professor Weil explained the 'danger' arising from some of the characteristics of contemporary law-making of these customary rules:

> The classic theory of custom depends on a delicate, indeed, precarious, equilibrium between two opposite concerns: on the one hand, to permit customary rules to emerge without demanding the individual consent of every state; on the other hand, to permit individual States to escape being bound by any rule they do not recognise as such. (...) it is this opportunity for each individual State to opt out of a customary rule that constitutes the acid test of custom's voluntarist nature. (...) It is this equilibrium that is threatened today. For the past several years, the degree of generality required of a practice, to enable it to serve as the basis of a customary rule, has been steadily diminished, while, on the contrary, the binding character of such a rule once formed is being conceived of as increasingly general in scope. The result is a danger of imposing more and more customary rules on more and more States, even against their clearly expressed will.[221]

It is in this context that the American Law Institute published in 1987 its third edition of its *Restatement of the Law, The Foreign Relations Law of the United States*.[222] The *Restatement* introduced for the first time the concept of persistent objector: 'a state that indicates its dissent from a practice while the law is still in the process of development is not bound by that rule of law even after it matures'.[223] This change has been attributed to the fact that the authors of the *Restatement* 'very clearly perceived that the international legal order had undergone profound changes' in the last decades since its last edition in 1965.[224] Stein

---

[220] T.L. Stein, 'The Approach of the Different Drummer: The Principle of the Persistent Objector in International Law', *Harvard ILJ* (1985), p. 466.

[221] P. Weil, 'Toward Relative Normativity in International Law', *AJIL* 77 (1983), pp. 433–434.

[222] American Law Institute, *Restatement of the Law Third: the Foreign Relations Law of the United States*, vol 1, ch 1, St Paul, 1987. While not an official document of the US Government, the influence of the *Restatement* should not be underestimated.

[223] *Ibid.*, para. 102, no. 26.

[224] Stein, 'The Approach of the Different Drummer', p. 470. He examines in detail the work of the Institute.

explained the United States' newly found interest in the concept of persistent objector as follows:

> [I]n this structure, new, generally applicable international law can be made through the adoption of multilateral treaties and be 'evidenced' by the resolutions of international organisations. It is a structure from which the United States must have an escape hatch since it cannot always control the process resulting in treaty texts or resolutions.[225]
>
> [The United States] should find in the persistent objector principle a doctrinal basis for freeing themselves from the results of multilateral processes that are seen as subject to the domination of a hostile majority.[226]

The concept of persistent objector, which had already been recognized by some authors in the past,[227] was now suddenly embraced by the United States as a result of this new uncomfortable minority position.[228] One writer has eloquently described the persistent objector theory as 'the Western counter-reformation to this revolution'.[229]

Supporters of the concept's legitimacy argue that it is 'firmly established in the orthodox doctrine on the sources of international law'.[230] This is in fact the prevailing position in doctrine,[231] and is also the

---

[225] *Ibid.*, p. 472.   [226] *Ibid.*, p. 468.

[227] For instance, these writers supported the concept: Akehurst, 'Custom as a Source of International Law', pp. 23–31; H. Waldock, 'General Course on Public International Law' *Rec. des cours* 106 (1962), pp. 49–52; G. Fitzmaurice, 'The General Principles of International Law', *Rec. des cours* 92 (1957), p. 101. However, A. D'Amato, *The Concept of Custom in International Law* (Ithaca: Cornell University Press, 1971), p. 21, already opposed the concept.

[228] P.-M. Dupuy, 'A propos de l'opposabilité de la coutume générale: enquête brève sur l'objecteur persistant', in *Mélanges Michel Virally* (Paris: Pédone, 1991), p. 269; Weil, 'Toward Relative Normativity in International Law', p. 196.

[229] J. Patrick Kelly, 'The Twilight of Customary International Law', *Virginia JIL*, 40 (2000), pp. 513–514. See also: Olivier Barsalou, 'La doctrine de l'objecteur persistant en droit international', *RQDI*, 19(1) (2006), p. 4.

[230] Stein, 'The Approach of the Different Drummer', p. 463.

[231] Fitzmaurice, 'The General Principles of International Law', pp. 21–26; Louis Henkin, 'International Law: Politics, Values and Function: General Course on Public International Law', *Rec. des cours* 216 (1989-IV), pp. 53–58; Prosper Weil, 'Le droit international en quête de son identité, Cours général de droit international public', *Rec. des cours* 237 (1992-VI), pp. 189–201; Akehurst, 'Custom as a Source of International Law', pp. 23–27; Philippe Cahier, 'Changement et continuité du droit international: Cours général de droit international public', *Rec. des cours* 195 (1985-VI), pp. 231–237; Oscar Schachter, 'International Law in Theory and Practice: General Course in Public International Law', *Rec. des cours* 178 (1982-V), pp. 36–39; Maurice H. Mendelson, 'The Formation of Customary International Law', *Rec. des cours* 272 (1998), pp. 228–233; Brock J. McClane, 'How Late in the Emergence of a Norm of Customary International Law May a Persistent Objector Object?', *I.L.S.A. J.I.L.*, 13 (1989), p. 6.

position adopted by the ILA in its 2000 Report on custom[232] and by ILC Special Rapporteur Wood in his Third Report.[233] Several leading scholars, however, have criticized the concept of persistent objector.[234] The debate amongst writers has been described as a 'theological war of principles'.[235]

The present author has critically examined elsewhere the controversial theory of the 'persistent objector'.[236] I have argued that there is only weak judicial recognition of the theory of persistent objector and that there is very limited actual State practice supporting it. I have also taken the view that the theory is logically incoherent and that its application is inconsistent.

5.4.2   The application of the concept of persistent objector in the context of international investment law

This section examines the concept of persistent objector in the specific context of international investment law. Apart from one article published by the present author on the question,[237] the question of the role of the concept of persistent objector in this field of law is almost never addressed by scholars.[238]

---

[232] ILA, Final Report, 2000, p. 27 ('[i]f whilst a practice is developing into a rule of general law, a State persistently and openly dissents from the rule, it will not be bound by it').

[233] ILC, Third Report, 2015, pp. 59–67. See also: International Law Commission, 'Text of the Draft Conclusions Provisionally adopted by the Drafting Committee, Sixty-seventh session, Geneva, 4 May-5 June and 6 July-7 August 2014, 14 July 2015, A/CN.4/L.869 [hereinafter referred to as ILC, Draft Conclusions, 2015], conclusion no. 15: '1. Where a State has objected to a rule of customary international law while that rule was in the process of formation, the rule is not opposable to the State concerned for so long as it maintains its objection. 2. The objection must be clearly expressed, made known to other States, and maintained persistently'.

[234] Christian Tomuschat, 'Obligations Arising for States Without or Against Their Will', Recueil des cours 241 (1993-IV), pp. 284–290; Jonathan Charney, 'The Persistent Objector Rule and the Development of Customary International Law', British YIL 56 (1985); Dupuy, 'A propos de l'opposabilité de la coutume générale'; Benedetto Conforti, 'Cours général de droit international public', Rec. des cours 212 (1988-V), pp. 74–77; Georges Abi-Saab, 'Cours général de droit international public', Rec. des cours 207 (1987-VII), pp. 180–182; D'Amato, The Concept of Custom in International Law; Barsalou, 'La doctrine de l'objecteur persistant en droit international public', p. 4; Kelly, 'The Twilight of Customary International Law', p. 508 ff.

[235] Tomuschat, 'Obligations Arising for States Without or Against Their Will', p. 285.

[236] P. Dumberry, 'Incoherent and Ineffective: The Concept of Persistent Objector Revisited', ICLQ 59 (2010), pp. 779–802.

[237] Dumberry, 'The Last Citadel'.

[238] The question is examined by Sornarajah, The International Law on Foreign Investment, pp. 213, 151. A few other writers have briefly mentioned the concept. Their limited

First, I will briefly examine a few recent investor-State arbitration cases where the persistent objector argument was raised (Section 5.4.2.1). Second, I will submit three reasons why, in my view, the concept of persistent objector should *not* be used by an arbitral tribunal in investor-State arbitration proceedings to prevent the application of a rule of customary law (Section 5.4.2.2).

5.4.2.1 Arbitration cases where the argument was raised

To the best of my knowledge, the persistent objector argument was first raised in arbitration proceedings in the case of *BG Group* v. *Argentina*.[239] BG Group Plc (BG), a UK company that was an indirect shareholder in the Argentinian gas distributor MetroGAS S.A., commenced arbitration proceedings alleging that measures taken by Argentina in the context of the financial crisis of 1999–2002, including derogation from an earlier-agreed tariff, were contrary to the UK–Argentina BIT. As a defence, Argentina invoked the state of necessity doctrine to exclude its international responsibility under both the BIT and customary international law, as codified in Article 25 of the International Law Commission (ILC)'s *Articles on State Responsibility*.[240] The claimant objected to this argument on the ground that the ILC Articles were a 'non-binding codification of customary international law' and that its Article 25 had no application in bilateral relations involving the United Kingdom and Argentina.[241] The claimant also argued that the United Kingdom had been 'formally opposed to the inclusion by the ILC of a provision on "necessity"' and was, therefore, a 'persistent objector' to any such alleged principle of

reasoning suggests that they believe that a State could invoke the status of persistent objector in investment arbitration: Al Faruque, 'Creating Customary International Law through Bilateral Investment Treaties', pp. 295–296; R. Dolzer, 'New Foundations of the Law of Expropriation of Alien Property', *AJIL* (1981), p. 571; Roland Kläger, *Fair and Equitable Treatment in International Investment Law* (Cambridge: Cambridge University Press, 2011), p. 265 (mentioning that if the FET standard were to be considered as custom this would impose an obligation upon all States, but adding, in a footnote, that 'this is, of course, only true for states that are not qualified as persistent objectors to the norm in question'); Vasciannie, 'The Fair and Equitable Treatment Standard', p. 153 (indicating that custom rules apply to all States, but adding 'This, of course, is based on the assumption that the State in question has not been a persistent dissenter with respect to the putative rule; on persistent dissent').

[239] *BG Group Plc* v. *Argentina*, UNCITRAL, Award, 24 December 2007.
[240] *Titles and Texts of the Draft Articles on Responsibility of States for Internationally Wrongful Acts Adopted by the Drafting Committee on Second Reading*, 26 July 2001, U.N. Doc. A/CN.4/L.602/Rev.1.ILC.
[241] *BG Group Plc* v. *Argentina*, UNCITRAL, Award, 24 December 2007, para. 400.

necessity under custom'.[242] The Tribunal simply noted in a footnote that it was 'dismissing BG's allegation that the UK has always been a persistent objector'[243], without further discussing the concept.[244]

The defence of the persistent objector was also raised by the United States in the *Grand River* case.[245] The claimants, three individual members of Native American tribes and their Canadian company, were seeking compensation in a dispute related to the regulation of tobacco products in the United States. In their claim of breach of the FET clause (NAFTA Article 1105), the claimants made reference to an 'emerging' customary international law norm specifically applicable to indigenous peoples, requiring States to 'pro-actively consult' with 'First Nations investors' before taking regulatory action that could substantially affect their interests.[246] In its award, the Tribunal refers more generally to the argument raised by the claimants to the effect that it should take into account a number of 'customary law rules affecting indigenous peoples'[247]:

> The Claimants also invoked several propositions they viewed as reflecting customary international law. These included "an evolving norm of customary international law, [embodying] the duty of States to respect and protect the rights and interests of First Nations across borders, in good faith," a customary rule requiring States "to honor obligations undertaken with respect to First Nations," an obligation "to respect the rights of indigenous peoples to occupy and enjoy their traditional territories," and a principle of "constant promotion and protection for First Nations members" in respect of traditional commercial activities carried on in their territories across borders. The Claimants also invoked the jurisprudence of the Inter-American Court of Human Rights in contending that

---

[242] *Ibid.*   [243] *Ibid.*, footnote 328.

[244] The Tribunal thus held that Argentina could not invoke the doctrine of necessity under customary international law to excuse its liability under the UK–Argentina BIT because the Treaty contains no express provision on the matter. It also stated that even if it were to apply Article 25 of the ILC Articles, Argentina would not have met the restrictive conditions for its application. The Tribunal ultimately held that Argentina had breached the FET requirement under Article 2.2 of the Treaty and ordered it to pay more than US$185 million plus interest in compensation. Argentina challenged the final award before the International Court of Arbitration of the International Chamber of Commerce (ICC). The ICC Court dismissed the challenge.

[245] *Grand River Enterprises Six Nations, Ltd., et al. v. United States*, UNCITRAL, Award, 12 January 2011.

[246] *Ibid.*, Claimant's Memorial, 10 July 2008, paras. 184–192, 213–214.

[247] *Grand River Enterprises Six Nations, Ltd., et al. v. United States*, Award, 12 January 2011, para. 66.

their interests should be assessed in harmony with the communal property rights of indigenous peoples.[248]

The United States flatly denied the existence of any such customary norms.[249] It also explained that 'the minimum standard of treatment cannot be construed to include particular protections for certain classes of aliens and not for others'.[250] Specifically, the United States rejected the claimants' argument that customary international law imposes an obligation to consult indigenous investors.[251] In any event, the United States also argued that it could not be bound by such a 'rule' based on its persistent objection to it:

> Even if Claimants had established the existence of such an "emerging" norm, the United States clearly and consistently has articulated its view that the UN Indigenous Declaration and its provision requiring consultation prior to the adoption of legislation does not reflect customary international law. Given that "in principle, a [S]tate that indicates its dissent from a practice while the law is still in the process of development is not bound by that rule even after it matures," the United States cannot be bound by any consultation requirements contained in the UN Indigenous Declaration.[252]

The United States further explained that the principle of persistent objector is one 'which States and scholars regard as central to the legitimacy of an international legal order governed by rules of customary international law'.[253] The Tribunal did not, however, specifically address the persistent objector argument. The Tribunal also remained neutral on the question of whether any rule of customary international law requiring States to consult indigenous peoples on policies affecting them exists.[254] It added that 'in any event, any obligations requiring

[248] *Ibid.*, para. 67.
[249] *Ibid.*, 'Counter-Memorial of the United States', 22 December 2008, pp. 127–128. This is also the position of Canada as explained in its Article 1128 submission, 19 January 2009.
[250] *Ibid.*, 'Counter-Memorial of the United States', 22 December 2008, p. 134.
[251] *Grand River Enterprises Six Nations, Ltd., et al.* v. *United States*, Award, 12 January 2011, para. 200.
[252] *Ibid.*, 'Counter-Memorial of the United States', 22 December 2008, pp. 128–129 (quoting from *Restatement of the Law Third*, § 102 (d), Reporters' no. 2.
[253] *Ibid.*, p. 129, footnote 466.
[254] *Grand River Enterprises Six Nations, Ltd., et al.* v. *United States*, Award, 12 January 2011, para. 210: 'It may well be, as the Claimants urged, that there does exist a principle of customary international law requiring governmental authorities to consult indigenous peoples on governmental policies or actions significantly affecting them. One member of the Tribunal has written that there is such a customary rule. Moreover, a recent study by a committee of several international law experts assembled under the auspices of the

consultation run between the state and indigenous peoples as such, that is, as collectivities bound in community'.[255] Such obligations could not oblige 'consultations with individual investors', such as the claimants.[256] In any event, it seems that the Tribunal is rejecting the idea that a customary norm could apply to one group of indigenous investors and not to *all* foreign investors.[257]

Only one tribunal seems to have accepted the legitimacy of the concept of persistent objector in investor-State arbitration. This was in *Daimler v. Argentina*, where the majority of the Tribunal noted that 'consent is therefore the cornerstone of all international treaty commitments'.[258] In a footnote, the Tribunal made the following statement regarding the role of consent in the specific context of the development of rules of customary international law:

> Even in the case of customary international law, it can be argued that consent, or at least the consent of a majority of the world's states, underlies all of the norms reflected in customary international law. Without such consent (as demonstrated by the combination of a sufficiently broad, lasting and consistent state practice and supported by *opinio juris*), those norms would not have evolved into customary law in the first place. The Dissenting Opinion correctly points out that the consent

International Law Association, after an exhaustive survey of relevant state and international practice, found a wide range of customary international law norms concerning indigenous peoples, including "the right to be consulted with respect to any project that may affect them." As pointed out by the Claimants, the duty of states to consult with indigenous peoples is featured in the UN Declaration of the Rights of Indigenous Peoples, particularly in its Article 19 as well as in several other articles. In its Counter-Memorial the Respondent maintained in sweeping terms that the Declaration does not represent customary international law, as did Canada in its non-disputing party submission. However, when questioned by the Tribunal on this point at the hearing, the Respondents' counsel stated that some parts of the Declaration could reflect fundamental human rights principles and emerging customary law'.

[255] *Ibid.*, para. 211.

[256] *Ibid.*, para. 211. See also, at para. 213 ('the possible existence of a customary rule calling for expanded consultation between governments and indigenous peoples does not assist Arthur Montour as an individual investor').

[257] *Ibid.*, para. 213: 'Even if one were to indulge a supposition that a customary rule required consultations directly with an individual First Nations investor under the circumstances of this case, it would be difficult to construe such a rule as part of the customary minimum standard of protection that must be accorded to every foreign investment pursuant to Article 1105. The notion of specialized procedural rights protecting some investors, but not others, cannot readily be reconciled with the idea of a minimum customary standard of treatment due to all investments'.

[258] *Daimler Financial Services AG* v. *Argentina*, ICSID Case No. ARB/05/1, Award, 22 August 2012, para. 168.

underlying customary international law is of an implied and not express nature. It stresses that "established rules of customary international law can bind States that never granted, explicitly or otherwise, consent to individual acts of the type that gave rise to the principles in question." (Dissenting Opinion of Charles N. Brower at note 8). Yet *the existence of the persistent objector doctrine* – which allows states not in agreement with an evolving customary norm to avoid becoming legally bound by it – *demonstrates that consent is nevertheless fundamental to customary international law.* The only major exception to the foundational nature of state consent within public international law arises in the context of peremptory norms, among which a state's submission to the jurisdiction of an international arbitral tribunal cannot be counted.[259]

In his dissenting opinion, Brower also endorsed the reasoning of the Tribunal on the concept of the persistent objector.[260] In the following section, I will explain why, in my view, a tribunal should reject the concept.

5.4.2.2 Reasons for rejecting the application of the concept in arbitration proceedings

Apart from the above-mentioned shortcomings of the concept of persistent objector,[261] there are also other fundamental reasons specific to international investment law that explain why such an argument should be rejected by arbitral tribunals. The starting point of the analysis is the 'test' adopted by Professor Schachter to determine when the status of persistent objector may be permissible:

---

[259] *Ibid.*, footnote 310 (emphasis added).

[260] *Ibid.*, Dissenting Opinion of Charles N. Brower, para. 3, footnote 8: 'The Award's focus on "affirmative evidence" appears to be in tension with the Award's observation in note 310 [...] This statement is accurate insofar as "consent" underlies the individual State acts that, given their sufficiently broad and lasting recurrence (State practice), combined with evidence of the acting States' view that their actions are based on existing obligations (*opinio juris*), give rise to customary international law. Ordinarily, however, an individual State need not "consent" to the establishment of customary international law itself; that "consent" is inferred via the combination of State practice and *opinio juris* [referring to Malcolm M. Shaw, *International Law*, 5th ed., 2003, 70–72]. Thus, established rules of customary international law can bind States that never granted, explicitly or otherwise, consent to individual acts of the type that gave rise to the principles in question. Those States' consent to be bound is presumed. As the Award points out in note 310, a non-consenting State is obliged then to give "affirmative evidence" of its non-consent via the "persistent objector doctrine"'.

[261] See, Dumberry, 'Incoherent and Ineffective: The Concept of Persistent Objector Revisited'.

It would be germane to consider a variety of factors including the circumstances of adoption of the new principles, the reasons for its importance to the generality of States, the grounds for dissent, and the relevant position of the dissenting States. The degree to which new customary rules may be imposed on recalcitrant States will depend, and should depend, on the whole set of relevant circumstances.[262]

These three criteria will now be briefly examined.

The first criterion is the circumstances surrounding the adoption of rules of customary law in the field of investment law. It has been argued by some writers that the so-called 'rules' of customary law have been imposed on developing States that have consistently rejected them.[263] One eminent arbitrator, Jan Paulsson, admits that 'it may be true that in the beginning of this century, and until the 1950s, arbitrations conducted by various international tribunals or commissions evidenced bias against developing countries'.[264] Still today, it is undeniable that the 'apparent equality as stated in the BIT can be overshadowed by parties' actual bargaining power, which is inherently unequal'.[265] There is, indeed, an asymmetry in BITs entered into between developing and developed States.[266] Moreover, developing countries will sometimes lack expertise

---

[262] Schachter, 'International Law in Theory and Practice', pp. 37–38.

[263] Sornarajah, *The International Law on Foreign Investment*, pp. 92–93; Sornarajah, 'Power and Justice in Foreign Investment Arbitration', pp. 103–104, 139–140.

[264] Jan Paulsson, 'Third-World Participation in International Investment Arbitration', *ICSID Rev.* 2 (1987), p. 21. See also, Virtus Chitoo Igbokwe, 'Developing Countries and the Law Applicable to International Arbitration of Oil Investment Disputes. Has the Last Word been Said?', *J. Int'l Arb.*, 14(1) (1997), pp. 100–101: 'With the dismantling of the colonial edifice across Asia and Africa in the latter part of the twentieth century and the development of international norms against the use of force, the use of gun-boat diplomacy to settle international investment disputes was no longer acceptable. International arbitration was thus conceived by Western European nations in response to the need to provide some other form of protection for international investment contracts. (...) Thus, since international arbitration was conceived as an investment protection measure, its early rules were tailored towards the attainment of that objective. The resource sectors of the economy of developing countries were tied up by a series of unequal contracts such as the traditional concession agreements. International arbitration played the primary role of bolstering up this regime in favour of the foreign investor'.

[265] Al Faruque, 'Creating Customary International Law through Bilateral Investment Treaties', p. 314.

[266] J.W. Salacuse, 'Towards a Global Treaty on Foreign Investment: The Search for a Grand Bargain', in: N. Horn and S. Kröll (eds.), *Arbitrating Foreign Investment Disputes. Procedural and Substantive Legal Aspects* (The Hague: Kluwer Law International, 2004), p. 70: 'A bilateral investment treaty purports to create a symmetrical relationship between the two contracting states for it provides that the nationals and companies of *either* party to the treaty may invest under the same conditions and be treated in the same

in international investment law and may have to conduct treaty negotiations on the basis of the existing model agreements of their negotiating partners.[267]

This reality, however, does not necessarily mean that the types of legal protection that exist for foreign investors under customary law are biased against developing States. While these rules may be 'Western' *in origin*, it can no longer be argued that they are strictly 'Western' *in nature*. For instance, developing States have long rejected the 'Hull formula', which was supported by developed States and affirmed that the host State must pay 'prompt, adequate and effective' compensation in the event of an expropriation.[268] As mentioned in Chapter 2,[269] in recent years, however, developing States have signed hundreds of BITs with provisions containing the 'Hull formula'. In any event, one would normally expect that customary rules on expropriation which have allegedly been 'imposed' by the West, would *not* find their way in recent BITs entered into between developing States *themselves*. As mentioned in Chapter 4,[270] 'South–South' BITs, now representing 26% of the total number of BITs,[271] are *not* significantly different from other BITs entered into by developing States with developed States.[272] Most importantly, the UNCTAD Report does not mention any differences concerning the core sets of legal

way in the territory of the other. In reality, of course, in a BIT between an industrialized country and a developing nation, an asymmetry exists between the parties since one state (the industrialized country) will be the source and the other state (the developing country) the recipient of that capital' (emphasis in the original). See also: Gus van Harten, *Investment Treaty Arbitration and Public Law* (Oxford: Oxford University Press, 2007), p. 41.

[267] UNCTAD, 'Bilateral Investment Treaties 1995–2006: Trends in Investment Rulemaking' (2007), p. 144. Prof. José E. Alvarez provides the following explanation: 'For many, a BIT relationship is hardly a voluntary, uncoerced transaction. They [US BIT partners] feel that they must enter into the arrangement, or that they would be foolish not to ... [But] the truth is to date the U.S. model BIT has been regarded as, generally-speaking, a "take it or leave it" proposition ... A BIT negotiation is not a discussion between sovereign equals. It is more like an intensive training seminar conducted by the United States, on U.S. terms, on what it would take to comply with the U.S. drafts' (quoted in: Gennady Pilch, 'The Development and Expansion of Bilateral Investment Treaties', *ASIL Proc.*, 96 (1992), pp. 552–553).

[268] See, discussion in Chapter 2, Sections 2.2 and 2.2.3.   [269] See Chapter 2, Section 2.6.3.

[270] See, discussion in Chapter 4, Section 4.2.3.2.

[271] UNCTAD, 'Recent Developments in International Investment Agreements (2007–June 2008)', IIA Monitor No. 2, (2008), p. 3.

[272] Dolzer and Schreuer, *Principles of International Investment Law*, p. 16; UNCTAD, 'South-South Cooperation in International Investment Arrangements', UNCTAD Series on International Investment Policies for Development (2005), p. 45.

protections existing under customary international law (such as the prohibition against expropriation).[273]

In sum, the circumstances of the adoption of the few customary rules existing in international investment law[274] do not demonstrate any inherent bias against developing States. Since these rules represent universally recognized values and are not biased against developing States, there is no reason why these States (or, as a matter of principle, any State) should be allowed to opt out unilaterally from them.

The second criterion to be examined is the reasons for the importance of these customary rules to States. As already examined in Chapter 2,[275] there are only a few rules applicable in investor-State arbitration which are said to have crystallized to the rank of customary law. These rules play an important role in investor-State arbitration. Custom is thus the residual legal regime applicable between a foreign investor and the host State, in the absence of any BIT.[276] Custom also plays a gap-filling role.[277] To allow a State to benefit from the status of persistent objector would mean, in practical terms, that there would simply be no minimum standard existing for the protection of foreign investors in that country. It would also mean that a State could expropriate foreign property without having to provide any compensation in return. The coherence of the system of international investment law requires that a set of basic legal protections applies to any foreign investors *at all times*. It also requires that *all States* have the same basic obligations. These features of the field of investment arbitration strongly militate against allowing any State the status of persistent objector in order to opt out from such basic requirements.

The third criterion to be examined is the grounds for dissent, which could be invoked by a State seeking the status of persistent objector. It has been argued that 'when a rule is developed in response to certain States' behaviour, their claim to persistent objection is weakened' since 'the application of the doctrine in this way does not benefit the "international community" and is, thus difficult to justify'.[278] There is, indeed, quite a

---

[273] UNCTAD, 'South-South Cooperation', *Ibid.*, p. 45.

[274] See, discussion in Chapter 2, Sections 2.3.3 and 2.6.   [275] *Ibid.*

[276] See, discussion in Chapter 5, Section 5.1.1.

[277] See, discussion in Chapter 5, Section 5.1.3.

[278] Camilla G. Guldahl, 'The Role of Persistent Objection in International Humanitarian Law', *Nordic JIL*, 77 (2008), p. 84. Stein, 'The Approach of the Different Drummer', p. 479, seems to be arguing that a State cannot claim the status of persistent objector whenever a customary rule emerged specifically to counter the practice of that particular State.

significant difference between one State's objection (such as the United Kingdom) to the extension of the territorial sea from three to twelve nautical miles and another State's objection to provide proper compensation to a foreign investor for its expropriated property. In the former case, a State adopts the *less favourable* regime of fishing rights within only three nautical miles from its coast, while all other States extend their fishing rights to twelve nautical miles. In other words, this is a situation where a less favourable regime is *self-imposed*. In the case of expropriation, however, the host State's dissenting position is solely for its own benefit and to the *detriment* of foreign nationals of other States that have adopted more stringent rules. In one situation (fishing rights), the objecting State suffers from all the disadvantages of upholding its dissenting position without any of the advantages enjoyed by all other States. In the other situation (expropriation), the objecting State is the only beneficiary as a result of its dissenting actions. In this example, the dissenting action of the expropriator State is clearly more damaging to the general interests of the international community than that of another State's *self-imposed* restriction on its *own* fishing rights.

In my view, a dissenting State would have to raise some significantly compelling reasons to convince an arbitral tribunal to not apply such a basic principle as the requirement for the host State to provide foreign investors with the MST under custom. Moreover, one can hardly think of any reasons persuasive enough to prevent the application of such an essential legal protection as the prohibition of expropriation without any appropriate compensation in return. This would *a fortiori* be the case in the event that the objector were to argue that while it has no obligation to provide certain very basic legal protections to foreign investors, it nevertheless believes that its *own* investors doing business abroad should be entitled to such protection. There is simply no reason why an arbitral tribunal should reward a 'free rider' on the entire international legal order.

General conclusion

This final chapter summarizes this book's main findings.

C.1 The remaining fundamental importance of custom in the present age of 'treatification'

The fascinating story of the two main sources of international law (custom and treaties) and their changing relative importance at different times in the evolution of international investment law has provided the perfect backdrop to the present book. Customary rules first played a predominant role. In the early twentieth century, the concept of the 'minimum standard of treatment' and the general prohibition against expropriation without compensation emerged as the two main sources of international law obligations for States.

The customary nature of these principles was met with contestation by non-Western States at different phases in the evolution of international investment law. For instance, the 1960s and 1970s were marked by serious and continuing challenges to the very existence of these two rules by a large segment of States, including those which emerged from colonialism. In the 1980s, many developing (and socialist) States believed that the absence of consensus on existing basic legal protection had in effect prevented the development and crystallization of rules of customary international law in the field of international investment law. Other (mainly developed) States held the view that while such customary rules existed, their effectiveness was limited due to the vehement opposition by a large number of States. As a result, the foundation of these two rules as the basic set of legal investment protection for investors doing business abroad was severely weakened. In any event, at the time all States could agree on the obvious fact that the few rules that were said to exist did not in fact provide any solid legal protection for investors doing business abroad.

These events marked a defining moment in the history of investment law, notably the decline of the importance of customary rules as the main source of investment protection for foreign investors.

The prevailing uncertainties surrounding the nature and scope of existing rules on investment protection led States to begin signing BITs *en masse*. This phenomenon was accentuated by the climate of the early 1990s, which was marked by globalization. At the time, a newly found consensus emerged amongst States regarding the necessity to offer better legal protection to foreign investments in order to accelerate economic development. The fact that developing States fundamentally changed their position on the benefits of foreign direct investments is a remarkable development of this era. They began to embrace BITs even though these instruments provided the very basic legal protection that they had rejected for decades. This new phenomenon of the proliferation of BITs (or 'treatification') marked a fundamental shift in the relative importance of the different sources of international law in the field of investor-State arbitration. Treaties had replaced custom as the prevalent source of investment protection.

In light of the fact that existing legal rules in the field of investment arbitration are now overwhelmingly found in bilateral and multilateral investment treaties, one might naturally question what remains of the historical importance of custom?

While the goal of this book was *not* to comprehensively analyse all existing customary rules in international investment law, I have nevertheless briefly examined the contours of two rules which are largely recognized by scholars and tribunals: the minimum standard of treatment and the general prohibition against expropriation without compensation. The very existence of those rules is a testament to the continuing importance of custom in contemporary investment arbitration. In fact, I have argued in this book that these protections are so fundamental and basic that the concept of 'persistent objector' should *not* be successfully used by any State in investor-State arbitration proceedings to prevent the application of these rules by an arbitral tribunal. This book has also shown that no rule of customary international law has emerged providing investors with any automatic procedural 'right' to bring arbitration claims against States where they make their investments. States (still) need to consent to arbitration.

One of the main themes of this book is explaining the reasons why custom remains fundamentally important to all actors involved in contemporary investor-State arbitration. As explained by the International Law Commission (ILC) Special Rapporteur Michael Wood (in the more general context of public international law), 'even in fields where there are widely accepted "codification" conventions, the rules of customary international law continue to govern questions not regulated by the conventions and continue to apply in relations with and between non-parties' and 'rules of customary international law may also fill possible lacunae in treaties, and assist in their interpretation'.[1] This conclusion applies to the field of international investment law.

Thus, while there has been a significant number of BITs signed in the past decades, they do not in fact cover the whole spectrum of possible bilateral treaty relationships between States. According to one writer, BITs only cover some 13% of the total bilateral relationship between States worldwide.[2] It is therefore safe to estimate that the majority of foreign investors doing business abroad are not covered by this investment treaty framework. On the other hand, custom applies to *all States*, including those which have not entered into any BITs. Any foreign investor, irrespective of whether its State of origin has entered into a BIT with the country where it makes its investment, can invoke customary rules. Therefore, because of its fallback nature as an applicable legal regime in the absence of any BIT, customary rules continue to play an important role in investment protection. This role will remain fundamental in the future even if States continue to enter into investment treaties.

Another reason for the remaining importance of custom is the fact that an increasing number of BITs are making explicit reference to the concept. One would assume that had custom really become an obsolete concept, States would simply stop referencing to it. Yet, this is not what is currently happening. The concept of custom has never been so 'popular' in BITs (but it remains that such specific reference to custom is still only found in a small *minority* of treaties). In any case, where a tribunal has to interpret a provision specifically referring to custom, it will necessarily have to assess questions related to the formation and identification of such norms.

---

[1] International Law Commission, 'First Report on Formation and Evidence of Customary International Law', by Michael Wood, Special Rapporteur, Sixty-fifth session, Geneva, 6 May-7 June and 8 July-9 August 2013, UN doc. A/CN.4/663, 17 May 2013, p. 20 [hereinafter referred to as ILC, First Report, 2013], p. 15.

[2] Tarcisio Gazzini, 'The Role of Customary International Law in the Field of Foreign Investment', *J. World Invest. & Trade*, 8 (2007), p. 691.

Finally, custom remains important because of the gap-filling role it plays whenever a treaty, a contract or domestic legislation is silent on a given issue. Tribunals have had to frequently apply customary rules as the ultimate reservoir of investment protection norms. They will continue to do so in the future.

In fact, I have argued in this book that the role of custom should not be limited only to such a gap-filling role. In my view, arbitral tribunals should *always* take into account relevant rules of customary international law. The main reason for this is simply because 'international law' is the applicable law in the overwhelming majority of arbitration disputes.[3] Any tribunal having to apply 'international law' will *necessarily* have to take into account relevant existing customary norms in the field of international investment law. This book has further argued that, *as a matter of principle*, relevant rules of custom should apply to *all cases*, even those situations where a tribunal should normally apply domestic law (and not international law) to settle the dispute. As noted by Schreuer, customary rules apply 'independently of any choice of law made for a specific transaction'.[4] Thus, customary rules should apply to all investment disputes *independently* of the choice of the applicable law made by the parties. This is clearly the case in the context of State contracts and BITs. Moreover, through the application of Article 31(3)(c) of the *Vienna Convention on the Law of Treaties,* a tribunal deciding a dispute under a BIT will have to take into account, together with the context of the treaty, 'any relevant rules of international law applicable in the relations between the parties'. These 'relevant rules' necessarily include existing customary rules in investment arbitration.

In sum, this book has shown the many reasons why customary rules remain fundamentally important in today's international investment law that is dominated by the proliferation of investment treaties.

C.2 The importance of the question of the formation and identification of customary rules

Considering the remaining fundamental importance of custom in contemporary investment arbitration, it is surprising that so little attention

---

[3] In fact, even when this is not the case and where domestic law applies, it remains that international law must still play an important role.

[4] Christoph H. Schreuer, Loretta Malintoppi, August Reinisch and Anthony Sinclair, *The ICSID Convention; A Commentary* (2nd edn., Cambridge: Cambridge University Press, 2009), p. 587.

has been given to the topic in the literature. In my view, three related questions should be investigated by scholars:

- How do rules of customary international law emerge in the field of investor-State arbitration?
- What are the different types of manifestations (or evidence) of State practice and *opinio juris* that are relevant in the context of the creation of customary rules in this field of law?
- Which specific standard of protection or rule should (or should not) be considered as customary international law?

This book has only fully addressed the first two questions. It focused on the question of the *formation* and the *identification* of rules of customary international law in the field of international investment law. Why is this relevant? In my view, before conducting any analysis on the question of whether any specific standard of investment protection should (or should not) be considered as a customary rule, one should necessarily ask two very basic *preliminary* questions: (1) how these customary rules are created, and (2) how they can be identified. Thus, according to ILC Special Rapporteur Wood, 'in order to determine whether a rule of customary international law exists, it is necessary to consider both the requirements for the formation of a rule of customary international law, and the types of evidence that establish the fulfilment of those requirements'.[5] This book provides the essential tools that are necessary for stakeholders to assess any claim of the existence of a customary rule. In a way, the hope of the present author is also that this book will establish the necessary theoretical foundation that will pave the way for future works on the concrete analysis of custom rules. While this book has explained the customary nature of two rules, much work remains to be undertaken regarding the actual contours of one of them. Thus, the standard of compensation for expropriation remains controversial. Further research remains to be done to determine whether or not the Hull formula can now be considered as a rule of customary law.[6] The same is true for the fair and equitable treatment (FET) standard. I have argued in this book that the standard should not be considered as a customary rule.[7] Yet, further work should be undertaken regarding the presence (or absence) of the FET standard of protection in domestic legislations. My analysis of FET protection has so far only focused on

---

[5] ILC, First Report, 2013, p. 6.
[6] See, discussion in Chapter 2, Sections 2.6.3 and 2.2.3 and Chapter 3, Section 3.3.3.2.2.5.
[7] See, discussion in Chapter 3, Sections 3.2.4. and 3.3.3.2.1.3.

one aspect of States' domestic laws (foreign investment laws).[8] I hope that the findings of the present book will be useful to other writers in their quest to further investigate customary rules in the field of investment arbitration.

While the question of the formation and the identification of rules of customary international law has been the topic of two important studies in general public international law,[9] surprisingly no wide-ranging investigation has ever been conducted in the specific area of investment arbitration. Tribunals have also rarely analysed the fundamental question of where to find concrete manifestations of State practice and *opinio juris*. One exception is the *Glamis* award.[10] Moreover, this book has shown that tribunals (with the exception of one, *UPS v Canada*[11]) have not conducted their *own* analysis regarding the existence of customary rules. They have consistently relied on the findings of the ICJ or on the reasoning of *other tribunals* when 'revealing' the customary nature of rules instead of examining on their own whether or not there was any consistent and uniform State practice and *opinio juris*. Ultimately, the inescapable conclusion is that tribunals have done a poor job at explaining the phenomenon of custom and at identifying its manifestations. This book will provide future tribunals with useful guidance regarding these fundamental questions.

C.3   Comparing custom formation and identification in investment arbitration and general international law

ILC Special Rapporteur Wood noted in his Second Report the importance of determining whether 'there are different approaches to the

---

[8] P. Dumberry, 'The Practice of States as Evidence of Custom: An Analysis of Fair and Equitable Treatment Standard Clauses in States' Foreign Investment Laws', McGill Journal of Dispute Resolution (forthcoming, 2016).

[9] International Law Association, 'Statement of Principles Applicable to the Formation of General Customary International Law', Final Report of the Committee on the Formation of Customary Law, Conference Report London (2000) [hereinafter referred to as ILA, Final Report, 2000]; ILC, First Report, 2013; International Law Commission, 'Second Report on Identification of Customary International Law', by Michael Wood, Special Rapporteur, Sixty-sixth session, Geneva, 5 May-6 June and 7 July-8 August 2014, A/CN.4/672, p. 2 [hereinafter referred to as ILC, Second Report, 2014]; International Law Commission, 'Third Report on Identification of Customary International Law', by Michael Wood, Special Rapporteur, Sixty-seventh session, Geneva, 4 May-5 June and 6 July-7 August 2014, UN doc. A/CN.4/682.

[10] *Glamis Gold Ltd* v. *United States*, UNCITRAL, Award, 14 May 2009.

[11] *United Parcel Service of America Inc.* v. *Canada*, UNCITRAL, Award on Jurisdiction, 22 November 2002.

formation and evidence of customary international law in different fields of international law' and 'to what degree, different weight may be given to different materials depending on the field in question'.[12] This book provides the answer to this question in the field of investment arbitration.

The present book has shown that there are indeed a number of noteworthy elements surrounding the formation and identification of customary international law in international investment law. The following sections will summarize my findings distinguishing between aspects that are *different* from general international law and those which are *similar*. These distinctions will first be made in the context of the formation of customary rules (Section C.3.1). The next section will examine the issue regarding the identification of customary rules (Section C.3.2).

C.3.1   The basic principles regarding the formation of customary rules in investment arbitration are not different from those applicable in general international law

Any book dealing with the sources of law in investor-State arbitration must be solidly grounded in general international law and its sources mentioned at Article 38(1) of the ICJ Statute. This is because investment arbitration is part of international law. Therefore, since custom is one of the sources of international law, it must apply to investor-State arbitration.

The fundamental tenets regarding the formation of customary rules in the sub-field of international investment law are not different from those existing under general international law. For instance, the existence of any customary rule in international investment law requires evidence of both State practice and *opinio juris*. These two requirements have in fact been recognized by States in their pleadings in arbitration proceedings. They have also been consistently applied by arbitral tribunals. Similarly, tribunals have also recognized the basic principle that it is for the party that alleges the existence of a customary rule to demonstrate that the norm has acquired such status by presenting relevant evidence of State practice and *opinio juris*. Therefore, it can be concluded that customary rules are created in the same way in both areas of law.

What about the role played by judges and arbitrators in the formation of customary rules? Clearly, judicial decisions do not *create* law and judges are *not* law-makers. Judges have indeed no *formal* role in the

---

[12] ILC, Second Report, 2014, pp. 7–8.

creation of customary rules. The role of arbitrators in investor-State arbitration is not any different. Similarly, just like international court decisions, arbitral awards cannot be considered as evidence of *State* practice for the formation of rules of custom. Awards are the product of *tribunals, not of States*. Moreover, what matters is the *opinio juris* of States, not that of arbitrators. Yet, it is undeniable that decisions and awards still play an important role in the evolution of customary rules. Not only do they play an essential role in 'revealing', confirming and clarifying the existence of such rules, but they also play a role in their development. As mentioned previously, however, tribunals have generally failed in their task of properly revealing the existence of customary rules. This phenomenon is not limited to the world of investment arbitration, as scholars have long identified similar shortcomings in the decisions of the ICJ.

This book has highlighted a number of other specific aspects regarding the formation of customary rules in the field of international investment law that are *not* different from the situation prevailing in general international law.

First, the basic requirements for the practice of States to be considered relevant for the creation of customary norms are the same. Relevant practice includes both 'positive' acts of States (i.e. their actual conduct) as well as non-ambiguous omissions and abstentions. Such practice also needs to be uniform (both 'internally' and 'collectively'), consistent, extensive and representative and must have taken place during a certain period of time. There are simply no reasons why these basic requirements should not apply in investor-State arbitration. Thus, in order for a customary rule to emerge, it needs to be demonstrated that a certain conduct or a standard of behaviour has been uniformly and consistently adopted by a large number of representative States, including developed and developing States coming from all continents. The present author is unaware of any instances where a State has argued otherwise or where a tribunal has taken a different position on the matter.

Second, the reasons why it is necessary to demonstrate the subjective element of *opinio juris* are the same in both general international law and in international investment law. First, it is essential to distinguish real international law *obligations* from the other forms of conduct that are merely based on *non-legal* motivations, such as courtesy and political expediency. Second, demonstrating *opinio juris* is also necessary to explain how the accumulation of uniform and consistent State practice can 'transform' into a legal rule *binding* on all States. In other words, it is fundamental to explain how something that States *often and typically do* becomes something they *believe they have to do* under international law. Moreover, *opinio juris* is necessary in distinguishing between different kinds of omissions: those that count as relevant State practice in the formation of rules of custom and those that do not. In my view, and in contrast to the position taken by some scholars in recent years (a point further discussed later in this chapter), there is simply no reason why States' *opinio juris* should not be demonstrated for a rule of custom to emerge in the field of investment arbitration.

In sum, this book has shown that the basic principles regarding the *formation* of customary rules in the field of investor-State arbitration are not different from those applicable in general international law. The next section examines whether the same conclusion can be reached regarding the different question of the *identification* of customary rules.

C.3.2   Some aspects regarding the identification of customary rules in investment arbitration are different from international law while others are similar

One of the central themes of this book has been the examination of the different 'manifestations' (or evidence) of State practice that are considered relevant for the creation of custom in both general international law and investor-State arbitration. We have seen that positive acts of States (i.e. the opposite of omissions) can take a variety of forms. Thus, the 'physical' conduct of a State in international relations is only one (and the most obvious) form of relevant practice for custom creation purposes. This book has examined four different categories of 'manifestations' of State practice: international treaties, statements by States, activities within international organizations and internal national practice of States.

It has been notably observed by Wood that '[w]hat we look for as State practice or what counts as sufficient State practice may vary depending on the rule (and more generally, the area of international law) concerned'.[13] One of the book's goals was precisely to discover whether the elements evidencing State practice in international investment law are *different* from those relevant in general international law. As further

---

[13] Michael Wood and Omri Sender, 'State Practice', in Rüdiger Wolfrum (ed.), *Max Planck Encyclopedia of Public International Law* (Oxford: Oxford University Press, 2013), para. 3.

explained in the next sections, the present author's conclusion is that some aspects related to the identification of customary rules are indeed different, while others are in fact similar.

C.3.2.1 The role played by treaties in the formation of customary rules is the same in both fields

In general international law, treaties can contribute to the formation of *new* rules of customary international law and they can also codify *existing* customary rules. The same is true for investment arbitration.[14] There is no doubt that, under certain specific circumstances, a series of similarly drafted provisions contained in numerous BITs can give the necessary impulse for the development of subsequent State practice in line with these provisions which will gradually crystallize into a rule of custom. In other words, there is no theoretical objection to the possibility that certain provisions found in a series of BITs can in time become binding on *all States*, including those that have not entered into BITs containing such a clause (and those that have not signed any BITs at all). That phenomenon is therefore recognized in both general international law and investment arbitration.

Yet, as observed by the ILA, '[t]here is no *presumption* that a succession of similar treaty provisions gives rise to a new customary rule with the same content'.[15] Therefore, no determination can necessarily be made on the customary status of a specific provision based on the sole fact that States have entered into numerous BITs containing the same type of clauses. Whether or not a provision contained in a BIT should be regarded as a new customary norm requires a concrete and detailed analysis taking into account a number of factors and circumstances. The first basic preliminary question to be asked is whether or not that provision can actually be a potential candidate for the transformation of a treaty-based rule into custom. In the words of the ICJ, such a provision must be of a 'fundamentally norm-creating character such as could be regarded as forming the basis of a general rule of law'.[16] Moreover, two strict conditions need to be satisfied for a treaty-based rule to transform into a rule of custom.

---

[14] It should be added that the process of codification of rules contained in *bilateral* treaties is a rare phenomenon unlikely to take place in investment arbitration.

[15] ILA, Final Report, 2000, p. 47 (emphasis added).

[16] *North Sea Continental Shelf Cases (Federal Republic of Germany* v. *Denmark / Federal Republic of Germany* v. *Netherlands)*, ICJ Rep 1969, para. 72.

First, it must be demonstrated that a large number of States have entered into many BITs that contain the *same provision* (or very similarly drafted clauses). In other words, the practice of State *parties* to BITs must be uniform, consistent and representative. The fulfilment of this consistency requirement would necessitate, for instance, that one State has *individually* consistently included the same (or very similar) clause in the different BITs it has entered into with other States. It would also require that a large number of States have *collectively* adopted amongst themselves the same clause in their BITs. Moreover, the practice of States also needs to be representative in that it includes both developing and developed States from different continents. With regard to *opinio juris*, the fact that State parties to BITs are providing foreign investors with one standard of protection contained in the treaty is not relevant for custom creation purposes. This is because these States parties are simply fulfilling their treaty obligation. As noted by ILC Special Rapporteur Wood, 'for a treaty to serve as evidence of *opinio juris*', States 'must be shown to regard the rule(s) enumerated in the treaty as binding on them as rules of law regardless of the treaty'.[17] Thus, it must be demonstrated that the parties to a BIT actually believe that they have an *obligation* under international law to provide a certain standard of protection to each other's investors *notwithstanding* the fact that such protection is set out in the instrument.

Second, it needs to be demonstrated that States (including those *not party* to these BITs) have uniformly and consistently adopted in their *own* practice *outside* the treaty the type of conduct prescribed in these instruments. Such practice could be found, for instance, in the domestic legislation of host States or in State contracts. In terms of *opinio juris*, it must be shown that these States also believe that they have an *obligation* to provide that same standard of protection to foreign investors *despite* having no formal *treaty* obligation to do so. Manifestations of any such belief by States, however, will in practice be difficult to find.

The existence of these two strict conditions largely explains why the transformation of treaty-based rules into custom is a rare phenomenon in practice. One controversial question worth considering, and one that is beyond the scope of this book, is whether the so-called Hull formula requiring 'prompt, adequate and effective' compensation for the expropriation of foreign investments should be considered as a contemporary illustration of this phenomenon. While most scholars in the 1980s declared that the Hull formula no longer represented custom, the full

---

[17] ILC, Second Report, 2014, p. 55.

compensation requirement undeniably made a great comeback a decade later. The overwhelming majority of modern BITs now specifically refer to 'prompt, adequate and effective' compensation.

In sum, it can be said that the role played by treaties in the formation and development of customary rules is overall the same in both international law and investment arbitration.

Finally, reference should be made to one aspect of the interaction between custom and treaties which is truly unique to the field of investment arbitration. One controversial issue currently being debated in academia and amongst arbitrators is related to the impact that the more than 2,500 BITs have had *globally* on the content of custom. The *Mondev* Tribunal stated that the 'body of concordant practice' found in BITs 'will necessarily have influenced the content of rules governing the treatment of foreign investment in current international law'.[18] One can indeed agree that the influence of the basic investment protections found in BITs has been clearly felt *outside* the treaty framework of those States parties to BITs. In fact, these developments have certainly had an *influence* on customary international law. For instance, some of the standards of protection systematically contained in BITs have contributed to the *consolidation* of *already existing* rules of custom in international investment law. This is certainly the case of the general prohibition against expropriation without compensation and the four conditions under which such conduct is considered to be legal. More controversially, some scholars recently have gone much further and argued that these numerous BITs should now be considered globally as representing the 'new' custom in this field. According to them, the content of modern custom in investment arbitration would somehow be the *same* as that of *all* BITs *taken together*. This book has explained in some detail why this proposition should be rejected.

C.3.2.2   States' *opinio juris* manifests itself in the same way in both fields

This book has shown that the *opinio juris* requirement has only played a minimal role in the context of investor-State arbitration disputes. While no tribunal has denied the necessity to demonstrate States' *opinio juris* for custom to emerge, they still have yet to address the issue of why this requirement exists and how such conviction manifests itself in real life. In

---

[18] *Mondev International Ltd.* v. *United States*, ICSID Case No. ARB(AF)/99/2, Award, 2 October 2002, para. 117.

contrast, this question has garnered considerable attention from scholars, some of them adopting controversial positions on the matter (a point further discussed in the next paragraphs).

One controversial issue in international law has been the question of where to find concrete examples of States' *opinio juris*. There are straightforward situations where, for instance, a State makes an express statement to the effect that it believes that a given rule is obligatory *qua* customary international law. This is undeniable and first-hand proof of the existence of that State's *opinio juris*. However, since a State's actual belief regarding the obligatory character of a given conduct is rarely assessable, its *opinio juris* will often have to be discovered by looking at some form of State practice. Therefore, in many instances, the only way to determine what a State *thinks* about the existence of any given norm is to look at what that State actually *does* in practice. Yet, there is no presumption that proof of general, uniform and consistent practice by States during a sufficiently long period of time *necessarily* demonstrates that they believe they are under an obligation to adopt such conduct. Even when faced with such uniform and consistent State practice, it is still necessary to identify *opinio juris* separately. On the other hand, it is clear that such a finding is much *easier* in cases where State practice is overwhelmingly uniform and consistent. This is because certain manifestations of State conduct (such as statements, pleadings and voting at international organizations) can evidence *both* the practice of a State and its *opinio juris*. In other words, there is no reason to avoid the so-called problem of 'double counting'.

The same basic principles also apply in the field of investor-State arbitration. This book has in fact highlighted a number of concrete examples of where to find *opinio juris*. For instance, I have referred to a number of BITs containing provisions that explicitly state that a certain treaty obligation exists under custom. I have also referred to a number of pleadings and other forms of statements (such as, for instance, United States' so-called letters of submittal) where States have explicitly recognized the customary nature of certain standards of protection. In sum, *opinio juris* is not that difficult to find once you know where to look for it.

The question of whether or not BITs can evidence a State's *opinio juris* remains controversial. I have shown in this book that States do not sign BITs out of any sense of conviction that this is what they *must* do under international law. This is indeed the position that States have themselves adopted, as well as the one supported by the majority of writers. The prevailing view in doctrine, and the one adopted by the present author, is that States sign these instruments solely based on their (perceived) economic interests. This book has rejected a number of other explanations that have been put forward by writers in recent years. It should be added, however, that the fact that States have no *opinio juris* when they sign BITs does not mean that they have no such sense of conviction regarding *specific* provisions found in BITs.

While the vast majority of authors who have specifically examined the issue of custom in the field of international investment law have recognized the necessity to demonstrate *opinio juris*, a number of them have also acknowledged that such proof can be problematic to satisfy in practice. This is the reason why some of them have put forward alternative theories on how such *opinio juris* can be evidenced. For instance, Tudor argues that 'this [constant and uniform] state practice together with the demonstration that *opinio juris* in the context of FET is firstly, not relevant, and secondly, even if it were relevant, is embodied in the manifestation of the practice, were sufficient to qualify the FET as a customary norm'.[19] In other words, not only does she believe that *opinio juris* does not have to be demonstrated, but she is also of the view that States' *opinio juris* is, at any rate, embodied in their practice of ratifying BITs containing FET clauses. The problem with such an assertion is that it is not based on any comprehensive assessment of the two abovementioned conditions under which treaty-based norms can transform into customary rules. She thus failed to show that parties to BITs actually believe that they have the obligation to provide such an FET protection to investors *outside* the treaty framework. She also does not demonstrate that States have adopted the FET standard of protection in their own practice *outside* treaties and that they have the necessary *opinio juris*. In other words, her conclusion regarding the customary nature of the FET standard does not apply the proper methodology highlighted in this book concerning the formation and identification of customary rules.

Similarly, other writers have argued in recent years that in order to fulfil the *opinio juris* requirement it simply needs to be shown that States have, in general, a common 'interest' for such standard of protection to exist. Thus, Hindelang and Diehl have argued that since all States have a 'common interest' in establishing basic principles on the protection of foreign investments, some of these existing protections should consequently be considered as rules of customary international law without the

---

[19] Ionna Tudor, *The Fair and Equitable Treatment Standard in International Foreign Investment Law* (Oxford: Oxford University Press, 2008), p. 233.

need to specifically demonstrate any *opinio juris* by States.[20] This book has argued that scholars advancing this theory of 'common interest' are using a conception of *opinio juris* that is completely disconnected with the basic understanding of the principle under international law. Thus, the creation of customary rules requires that States adopt a practice out of a sense of *legal obligation*, not merely because they believe it is in their best interests.

In sum, while strong evidence of consistent and uniform practice by a representative group of States can sometimes demonstrate their *opinio juris*, it nevertheless remains that such investigation must be *separately* undertaken. The situation is no different when the same clause is found in numerous treaties. This is a very basic international law principle, which seems to have been discarded by a number of writers in recent years. Arbitral tribunals should pay limited attention to theories that are not solidly grounded in public international law.

The next sections examine a number of manifestations evidencing State practice in international investment law which are *different* from those relevant in general international law.

C.3.2.3   The conduct of States within international organizations and the internal national practice of States only play a limited role in the creation of custom in investment arbitration

This book has explained that the conduct of a State within an international organization or the practice of international organizations themselves can constitute evidence of the existence of a customary rule or contribute to the formation of new customary rules. While these two phenomena are important sources of State practice for the purpose of custom creation in general international law, they have had almost no impact in the field of investment arbitration. I have in fact found only a very limited number of awards where the position taken by a State in the context of the work of an international organization has been invoked as evidence of State practice.

The same is true for the internal national practice of States. The ILA noted in its Report that '[t]he practice of the executive, legislative and

---

[20] Steffen Hindelang, 'Bilateral Investment Treaties, Custom and a Healthy Investment Climate – The Question of whether BITs Influence Customary International Law Revisited', *J. World Invest. & Trade*, 5 (2004), pp. 795–796, 806, 808; Alexandra Diehl, *The Core Standard of International Investment Protection: Fair and Equitable Treatment* (Wolters Kluwer, 2012), pp. 129, 138.

judicial organs of the State is to be considered, according to the circumstances, as State practice'.[21] This is based on the assumption that legislative acts actually reflect the position of that State on a given issue. This is
not always the case, however. For the purposes of custom formation,
limited weight should be given to domestic legislation that is not applied
by the State, or that is contradicted by acts of the executive branch.
Decisions of domestic courts should also be regarded as manifestations
of State practice. One reason is because sometimes what a domestic court
says on a matter of international law represents the view of that State on
the issue. However, this proposition is only valid for *certain* States, not all
of them. In general, the position of the executive branch on matters of
international law will weigh more heavily in evidencing State practice
than that of its courts whenever their positions differ.

It has been recognized by many international tribunals, scholars and
other authorities that acts of the legislative and judiciary branches of
government are manifestations of State practice that can potentially play
a fundamental role in the emergence of customary rules in international
law. Thus, the domestic legislation of one (or a few) State(s) can be
gradually adopted by other States and a custom rule may eventually
emerge in the event that such representative practice is both uniform
and consistent. The same is true for domestic courts' decisions. Thus, the
rules of international law regarding State immunity have developed in
the last century principally from the practice of a few domestic courts,
which was then subsequently adopted by the municipal courts of other
States.

In any event, in the field of investment arbitration, the domestic
legislations of States has had a much more limited role in evidencing
practice relevant for the formation of customary rules. Tribunals have
also almost never examined the question of the authoritative value of
domestic legislation as a relevant form of State practice. Similarly, domestic courts' decisions have played only a marginal role in the development
of international investment law. No award has in fact examined their role
in the formation of custom rules.

To summarize, the conduct of States within international organizations and the internal national practice of States are two examples of
situations where such manifestations of State practice have had a much
more limited role in custom creation in the field of investment arbitration
than in general international law.

---

[21] ILA, Final Report, 2000, p. 17.

C.3.2.4   The types of statements by States that matter as evidence of State practice are different in investment arbitration

Statements made by States are a form of manifestation evidencing State practice. However, while verbal acts of States should be considered, as a matter of principle, as evidence of State practice, it remains that, depending on the circumstances, they may not have the same *weight* in the formation of custom as those physical acts performed by States. In fact, this book has shown that the actual weight to be given to a statement in the formation of custom will depend not only on who is making the statement, but also on a number of other relevant circumstances as well as the context in which the statement was made. In other words, not all statements should be treated equally in terms of the extent to which they truly represent State practice.

This book provides the first analysis of the different types of statements that are relevant for the formation of customary rules in the specific area of international investment law. One important finding of this book is that the statements that are considered as evidence of State practice in this field are *not the same* as those in general international law.

The following paragraphs will summarize my findings concerning several types of statements which are considered relevant in international law but that have had only a limited impact in investment arbitration. I will also review some other types of statements which are unique to the field of investment arbitration or have a specific importance in this field of law when compared to international law, where they are less frequently used.

First, there are a number of specific types of statements which are considered as important elements of State practice under general international law but which have had only a limited impact in investment arbitration. Some illustrations of this phenomenon include diplomatic statements and correspondence. Others are statements by governments on policy issues. Opinions of legal advisers on investor-State arbitration issues are also rarely publicly available.

States, tribunals and scholars all recognize that pleadings by States in international (or even domestic) litigation are a form of State practice relevant for the creation of custom. This is because pleadings provide a unique opportunity for a State to explain what it believes to be the law on a given issue. However, such pleadings in investor-State arbitration proceedings are rarely made publicly available (with the notable exceptions of some treaties, including NAFTA and CAFTA). In any event, the actual *weight* that should be given to pleadings in investment arbitration will depend on their nature and the context in which they are made. One relevant aspect will be whether or not the content of such pleadings is consistent with the position adopted by that State in the past. Another will be whether such pleadings are self-interested and principally aimed at avoiding liability as a respondent State in on-going arbitration proceedings. In sum, while pleadings are an important source of practice in both fields of law, it remains that their impact has been much more limited in investment arbitration.

Second, some types of statements that I have examined in this book are unique to the field of investment arbitration. This is, for instance, the case of Model BITs adopted by States for the purpose of treaty negotiation. They clearly represent a form of statements made by States evidencing their practice in international relations. The authoritative nature of Model BITs as representing State practice has been recognized by States themselves as well as by a few tribunals. Their content is typically the result of long and extensive deliberations, sometimes involving several State departments or ministries. Another reason why substantial weight should be given to Model BITs is because they are *not* made in the context of specific proceedings. In that sense, they are statements which are typically more reliable and 'neutral' than State pleadings. They also represent a *balanced position* between, on the one hand, providing the greatest possible level of substantive and procedural rights to foreign investors doing business abroad, while on the other hand, ensuring that such rights are not excessive and are ultimately to a State's own detriment when acting as respondent in arbitration proceedings.

Another example of a form of statement which is rarely found in fields other than investment arbitration is the possibility offered to the parties under a number of investment treaties to submit to a tribunal a joint interpretation regarding treaty provisions. Such statements should be considered as clear evidence of the practice of these States. However, it should be added that less weight should be given for custom creation purposes to joint interpretations that are self-interested in the context of on-going arbitration proceedings.

Finally, this book has also examined a number of other types of statements which have a specific importance in this field of law when compared to general international law, where they are less frequently used.

One example of such a statement is the possibility recognized in a few instruments of an intervention (in the form of pleadings) by a non-disputing State party to a treaty (i.e. by a State party to the treaty, but not acting as respondent in the proceedings). Such interventions are examples of a statement made by a State which should be considered as evidence of its practice. They thus provide a State with a unique opportunity to explain to a tribunal its own position on legal issues. In fact, such statements are generally considered as a more 'reliable' source of practice by respondent States than pleadings because they are *a priori* less self-interested.

Another form of State practice which has been frequently referred to by arbitral tribunals are statements made by a government before its own domestic legislature when implementing an investment treaty under domestic law. Substantial weight should be given to such official statements because they represent an authentic description of a State's interpretation of a treaty text. Such statements are also not self-interested because they are made *before* any dispute has arisen as to the proper meaning to be given to the text. However, our survey of awards has shown that the actual weight that should be given to these official statements will depend on the context in which they were made as well as a number of other circumstances.

In sum, this book has shown that the types of statements by States that are relevant for custom creation purposes in the field of investment arbitration are not the same as those in general international law.

BIBLIOGRAPHY

I Case law

A. *Investor-State arbitration arbitral awards*

Accession Mezzanine Capital L.P. and Danubius Kereskedöház Vagyonkezelö Zrt. v. *Hungary*, ICSID Case No. ARB/12/3, Decision on Respondent's Objection under Arbitration Rule 41 (5), 16 January 2013.

ADC Affiliate Ltd & ADC & ADMC Management Ltd v. *Hungary*, ICSID Case No. ARB /03/16, Award, 2 October 2006.

ADF Group Inc. v. *United States*, ICSID Case No. ARB(AF)/00/1, Award, 9 January 2003.

AES Corp. v. *Argentina*, ICSID Case No. ARB/02/17, Decision on Jurisdiction, 26 April 2005.

Aguas del Tunari SA v. *Bolivia*, ICSID Case No. ARB/02/3, Decision on Respondent's Objections to Jurisdiction, 21 October 2005.

Ambiente Ufficio S.p.A. and others v. *Argentina*, ICSID Case No. ARB/08/9 (formerly *Giordano Alpi and others* v. *Argentina)*, Decision on Jurisdiction and Admissibility, 8 February 2013.

Amco Asia Corporation, Pan American Development Limited, PT Amco Indonesia v. *Indonesia*, ICSID Case No. ARB/81/1, Award, 20 November 1984.

Amco Asia Corporation and Ors. v. *Indonesia*, ICSID Case No. ARB/81/1, Decision of the ad hoc Committee on the Application for Annulment, 16 May 1986.

American Manufacturing & Trading (AMT) v. *Republic of Zaire*, ICSID Case No. ARB/93/1, Award, 21 February 1997.

Antoine Biloune (Syria) and Marine Drive Complex Ltd. (Ghana) v. *Ghana Investment Centre and the Government of Ghana*, UNCITRAL, Award on Jurisdiction and Liability, 27 October 1989.

Antoine Goetz et al. v. *Burundi*, ICSID Case No. ARB/95/3, Award, 10 February 1999.

Apotex Holdings Inc & Apotex Inc. v. *United States*, ICSID Case No. ARB(AF)/12/1, Award, 25 August 2014.

Archer Daniels Midland Company and Tate & Lyle Ingredients Americas, Inc. v. *Mexico*, ICSID Case No. ARB(AF)/04/5, Award, 21 November 2007.

Asian Agricultural Products Ltd (AAPL) v. *Sri Lanka*, ICSID Case No. ARB/87/3, Final Award, 27 June 1990.

Azurix Corp. v. *Argentina*, ICSID Case No. ARB/01/12, Award, 14 July 2006.

Bayindir Insaat Turizm Ticaret Ve Sanayi A.S. v. *Pakistan*, ICSID Case No. ARB/03/29, Decision on Jurisdiction, 10 November 2005.

Bayview Irrigation District et al. v. *Mexico*, ICSID Case No. ARB(AF)/05/1, Award, 19 June 2007.

BG Group Plc v. *Argentina*, UNCITRAL, Award, 24 December 2007.

Biwater Gauff (Tanzania) Ltd. v. *Tanzania*, ICSID Case No. ARB/05/22, Award, 24 July 2008.

Bureau Veritas, Inspection, Valuation, Assessment and Control, BIVAC BV v. *Paraguay*, ICSID Case No. ARB/07/9, Further Decision on Objections to Jurisdiction, 9 October 2012.

Cambodia Power Company v. *Cambodia and Electricité du Cambodge LLC*, ICSID Case No. ARB/09/18, Decision on Jurisdiction, 22 March 2011.

Camuzzi International S.A. v. *Argentina*, ICSID Case No. ARB/03/2, Decision on Jurisdiction, 11 May 2005.

Cargill, Inc. v. *Mexico*, ICSID Case No. ARB(AF)/05/02, Award, 18 September 2009.

The Canadian Cattlemen for Fair Trade v. *United States*, UNCITRAL, Award on Jurisdiction, 28 January 2008.

CEMEX Caracas Investments B.V. and CEMEX Caracas II Investments B.V. v. *Venezuela*, ICSID Case No. ARB/08/15, Decision on Jurisdiction, 30 December 2010.

Chemtura Corporation v. *Canada*, UNCITRAL, Award, 2 August 2010.

Chevron Corporation (USA) and Texaco Petroleum Company (USA) v. *Ecuador*, UNCITRAL, PCA Case No. 34877, Interim Award, 1 December 2008.

Chevron Corporation (USA) and Texaco Petroleum Company (USA) v. *Ecuador*, UNCITRAL, PCA Case No. 34877, Partial Award on Merits, 30 March 2010.

Churchill Mining PLC and Planet Mining Pty Ltd v. *Republic of Indonesia*, ICSID Case No. ARB/12/14 and 12/40, Decision on Jurisdiction, 24 February 2014.

CME Czech Republic B.V. v. *Czech Republic*, UNCITRAL, Award, 14 March 2003.

CMS Gas Transmission Company v. *Argentina*, ICSID Case No. ARB/01/8, Decision on Objections to Jurisdiction, 17 July 2003.

CMS Gas Transmission Company v. *Argentina*, ICSID Case No. ARB/01/8, Award, 12 May 2005.

CMS Gas Transmission Company v. *Argentina*, ICSID Case No. ARB/01/8 (Annulment Proceeding) Decision on the Argentine Republic's Request for a Continued Stay of Enforcement of the Award (Rule 54 of the ICSID Arbitration Rules), 1 September 2006.

Compañiá de Aguas del Aconquija S.A. and Vivendi Universal S.A. v. *Argentina*, ICSID Case No. ARB/97/3 (formerly *Compañía de Aguas del Aconquija, S.A.*

and Compagnie Générale des Eaux v. Argentine Republic), Decision on Annulment, 3 July 2002.

ConocoPhillips Petrozuata B.V., ConocoPhillips Hamaca B.V. and ConocoPhillips Gulf of Paria B.V. v. Venezuela, ICSID Case No. ARB/07/30, Decision on Jurisdiction and the Merits, 3 September 2013.

Daimler Financial Services AG v. Argentina, ICSID Case No ARB/05/1, Award, 22 August 2012.

Daimler Financial Services AG v. Argentina, ICSID Case No. ARB/05/1, Dissenting Opinion of Judge Charles N. Brower, 15 August 2012.

Desert Line Projects LLC v. Yemen, ICSID Case No. ARB/05/17, Award, 6 February 2008.

Duke Energy International Peru Investments No. 1, Ltd. v. Peru, ICSID Case No. ARB/03/28, Award, 18 August 2008.

Eastern Sugar BV v. Czech Republic, UNCITRAL, Partial Award and Partial Dissenting Opinion, 27 March 2007.

El Paso Energy International Co. v. Argentina, ICSID Case No. ARB/03/15, Award, 31 October 2011.

Emilio Agustín Maffezini v. Spain, ICSID Case No. ARB/97/7, Decision on Objections to Jurisdiction, 25 January 2000.

Enron Corporation and Ponderosa Assets, L.P. v. Argentina, ICSID Case No. ARB/01/3, Decision on Jurisdiction (Ancillary Claim), 2 August 2004.

Enron Corporation and Ponderosa Assets, L.P. v. Argentina, ICSID Case No. ARB/01/3, Decision on Jurisdiction, 14 January 2004.

Enron Corporation and Ponderosa Assets LP v. Argentina, ICSID Case No. ARB/01/3, Award, 15 May 2007.

Enron Corporation and Ponderosa Assets, L.P. v. Argentina, ICSID Case No. ARB/01/3, Decision on the Argentine Republic's Request for a Continued Stay of Enforcement of the Award (Rule 54 of the ICSID Arbitration Rules), 7 October 2008.

Enron Corporation and Ponderosa Assets, L.P. v. Argentine Republic, ICSID Case No. ARB/01/3, Decision on the Application for Annulment of the Argentine Republic, 30 July 2010.

Eureko B.V. v. Poland, UNCITRAL, Partial Award and Dissenting Opinion, 19 August 2005.

Eureko B.V. v. Slovak Republic, UNCITRAL, PCA Case No. 2008-13, Award on Jurisdiction, Arbitrability and Suspension, 26 October 2010.

Gas Natural SDG S.A. v. Argentina, ICSID Case No. ARB/03/10, Decision on Preliminary Questions on Jurisdiction, 17 June 2005.

Generation Ukraine, Inc. v. Ukraine, ICSID Case No. ARB/00/9, Award, 16 September 2003.

Glamis Gold Ltd v. United States, UNCITRAL, Award, 14 May 2009.

Global Trading Resource Corp. and Globex International, Inc. v. *Ukraine*, ICSID Case No. ARB/09/11, Award, 23 November 2010.

Grand River Enterprises Six Nations, Ltd., et al. v. *United States*, UNCITRAL, Award, 12 January 2011.

H&H Enterprises Investments, Inc. v. *Egypt*, ICSID Case No. ARB 09/15, Decision on Respondent's Objections to Jurisdiction, 5 June 2012.

HICEE B.V. v. *The Slovak Republic*, UNCITRAL, PCA Case No. 2009–11, Partial Award, 23 May 2011.

Hulley Enterprises Ltd v. *Russian Federation*, UNCITRAL, PCA Case No AA 226, Interim Award on Jurisdiction and Admissibility, 30 November 2009.

Impregilo S.p.A. v. *Argentina*, ICSID Case No.ARB/07/17, Award, 21 June 2001, Concurring and Dissenting Opinion of Professor Brigitte Stern.

Industria Nacional de Alimentos, S.A. and Indalsa Perú, S.A. v. *Peru*, ICSID Case No. ARB/03/4, Annulment Proceeding, 5 September 2007.

International Thunderbird Gaming Corporation v. *Mexico*, UNCITRAL, Award, 26 January 2006.

International Thunderbird Gaming Corporation v. *Mexico*, UNCITRAL, Separate Opinion of Thomas Wälde, 1 December 2005.

Ioannis Kardassopoulos v. *Georgia*, ICSID Case No. ARB/05/18, Award, 3 March 2010.

Klöckner Industrie-Anlagen GmbH and Ors. v. *Cameroon and Société Camerounaise des Engrais*, ICSID Case No. ARB/81/2, Decision of ad hoc Committee on Claimant's Application for Annulment, 3 May 1985.

Lanco International Inc. v. *Argentina*, ICSID Case No. ARB/97/6, Decision on Jurisdiction, 8 December 1998.

LG&E Energy Corp., LG&E Capital Corp., and LG&E International, Inc. v. *Argentina*, ICSID Case No. ARB/02/1, Decision on Liability, 3 October 2006.

Loewen Group, Inc. and Raymond L. Loewen v. *United States*, ICSID Case No. ARB(AF)/98/3, Award on Merits, 26 June 2003.

MCI Power Group LC and New Turbine Incorporated v. *Ecuador*, ICSID Case No. ARB/03/6, Award, 26 July 2007.

Merrill & Ring Forestry L.P. v. *Canada*, UNCITRAL, Award, 31 March 2010.

Metalclad Corporation v. *Mexico*, ICSID Case No. ARB(AF)/97/1, Award, 30 August 2000.

Methanex Corp. v. *United States*, UNCITRAL, Partial Award, 7 August 2002.

Methanex Corp. v. *United States*, UNCITRAL, Award, 3 August 2005.

Mihaly International Corporation v. *Sri Lanka*, ICSID Case No. ARB/00/2, Award, 15 March 2002.

Millicom International Operations B.V. and Sentel GSM SA v. *Senegal*, ICSID Case No. ARB/08/20, Decision on Jurisdiction, 16 July 2012.

Mobil Investments Canada Inc. & Murphy Oil Corporation v. *Canada*, ICSID Case No. ARB(AF)/07/4, Decision on Liability and on Principles of Quantum, 22 May 2012.

Mondev International Ltd. v. *United States*, ICSID Case No. ARB(AF)/99/2, Award, 2 October 2002.

MTD Equity Sdn. Bhd. and MTD Chile S.A. v. *Chile*, ICSID Case No. ARB/01/7, Award, 25 May 2004.

MTD Equity Sdn Bhd and MTD Chile SA v. *Chile*, ICSID Case No. ARB/01/7, Decision on Annulment, 16 February 2007.

National Grid plc v. *Argentina*, UNCITRAL, Award on Jurisdiction, 20 June 2000.

Noble Ventures, Inc. v. *Romania*, ICSID Case No. ARB/01/11, Award, 12 October 2005.

Pac Rim Cayman LLC v. *El Salvador*, ICSID Case No. ARB/09/12, Decision on the Respondent's Jurisdictional Objections, 1 June 2012.

Pan American Energy LLC and BP Argentina Exploration Company v. *Argentina*, ICSID Case No. ARB/03/13, Decision on Preliminary Objections, 27 July 2006.

Philippe Gruslin v. *Malaysia*, ICSID Case No. ARB/99/3, Award, 27 November 2000.

Phoenix Action, Ltd. v. *Czech Republic*, ICSID Case No. ARB/06/5, Award, 15 April 2009.

Plama Consortium Ltd. v. *Bulgaria*, ICSID Case No. ARB/03/24, Decision on Jurisdiction, 8 February 2005.

Pope & Talbot Inc. v. *Canada*, UNCITRAL, Award on Damages, 31 May 2002.

Pope & Talbot Inc. v. *Canada*, UNCITRAL, Award on the Merits (Phase 2), 10 April 2001.

Railroad Development Corporation (RDC) v. *Guatemala*, ICSID Case No. ARB/07/23, Award, 29 June 2012.

Renco Group, Inc. v. *Peru*, ICSID Case No. UNCT/13/1, Procedural Order No. 2, 31 July 2014.

Renta 4 S. V.S.A, Ahorro Corporación Emergentes F.I., Ahorro Corporación Eurofondo F.I., Rovime Inversiones SICAV S.A., Quasar de Valors SICAV S. A., Orgor de Valores SICAV S.A., GBI 9000 SICAV S.A. v. *Russian Federation*, SCC No. 24/2007, Award on Preliminary Objections, Separate Opinion of Charles N. Brower, 20 March 2009.

Rumeli Telekom AS and Telsim Mobil Telekomikasyon Hizmetleri AS v. *Kazakhstan*, ICSID Case No. ARB/05/16, Award, 29 July 2008.

S.A.R.L. Benvenuti & Bonfant v. *People's Republic of the Congo*, ICSID Case No. ARB/77/2, Award, 8 August 1980.

S.D. Myers Inc. v. *Canada*, UNCITRAL, First Partial Award, 13 November 2000.

Saipem v. *Bangladesh*, ICSID Case No. ARB/05/07, Award, 30 June 2009.

Saluka Investments B.V. v. *Czech Republic*, UNCITRAL, Partial Award, 17 March 2006.

Sanum Investments Limited v. *Laos*, UNCITRAL, PCA Case No. 2013–13, Award on Jurisdiction, 13 December 2013.

Sempra Energy International v. *Argentina*, ICSID Case No. ARB/02/16, Decision on Objections to Jurisdiction, 11 May 2005.

Sempra Energy International v. *Argentina*, ICSID Case No. ARB/02/16, Award, 28 September 2007.

Siemens A.G. v. *Argentina*, ICSID Case No. ARB/02/8, Decision on Jurisdiction, 3 August 2004.

SGS Société Générale de Surveillance S.A. v. *Pakistan*, ICSID Case No. ARB/01/13, Award on Jurisdiction, 6 August 2003.

Société Générale de Surveillance S.A. (SGS) v. *Pakistan*, ICSID Case No. ARB/01/13, Procedural Order No. 2, 16 October 2002.

Southern Pacific Properties (Middle East) Limited, Southern Pacific Properties Limited v. *Egypt*, ICSID Case No. ARB/84/3, Decision on Jurisdiction, 27 November 1985.

Southern Pacific Properties (Middle East) Ltd. v. *Egypt*, ICSID Case No. ARB/84/3, Award, 20 May 1992.

Suez, Sociedad General de Aguas de Barcelona, S. A. and Vivendi Universal, S.A. v. *Argentina*, ICSID Case No. ARB/03/19, Decision on Liability, 30 July 2010.

TECO Guatemala Holdings, LLC v. *Guatemala*, ICSID Case No. ARB/10/23, Award, 19 December 2013.

Total S.A. v. *Argentina*, ICSID Case No. ARB/04/01, Decision on Liability, 27 December 2010.

Tradex Hellas S.A. v. *Albania*, ICSID Case No. ARB/94/2, Decision on Jurisdiction, 24 December 1996.

Tradex Hellas S.A. v. *Albania*, ICSID Case No. ARB/94/2, Award, 29 April 1999.

United Parcel Service of America Inc. v. *Canada*, UNCITRAL, Award on Jurisdiction, 22 November 2002.

Veteran Petroleum Limited (Cyprus) v. *Russian Federation*, UNCITRAL, PCA Case No. AA 228, Interim Award on Jurisdiction and Admissibility, 30 November 2009.

Victor Pey Casado and President Allende Foundation v. *Chile*, ICSID Case No. ARB/98/2, Award, 8 May 2008.

Vladimir Berschader and Moïse Berschander v. *Russian Federation*, SCC Case No. 080/2004, Award, 21 April 2006.

Waguih Elie George Siag and Clorinda Vecchi v. *Egypt*, ICSID Case No. ARB/05/15, Award, 1 June 2009.

Waste Management, Inc. v. *Mexico ("Number 2")*, ICSID Case No. ARB(AF)/00/3, Award, 30 April 2004.

Waste Management, Inc. v. *Mexico*, ICSID Case No. ARB(AF)/98/2, Award, 2 June 2000.

Wena Hotels Ltd. v. *Egypt*, ICSID Case No. ARB/98/4, Award, 8 December 2000.

Wena Hotels Ltd. v. *Egypt*, ICSID Case No. ARB/98/4, Decision on Application for Annulment, 5 February 2002.

William Ralph Clayton, William Richard Clayton, Douglas Clayton, Daniel Clayton and Bilcon of Delaware, Inc. v. *Canada*, UNCITRAL, Award on Jurisdiction and Liability, 17 March 2015.

Yaung Chi Oo Trading Pte. Ltd. v. *Myanmar*, ASEAN I.D. Case No. ARB/01/1, Award, 31 March 2003.

Yukos Universal Limited (Isle of Man) v. *Russian Federation*, UNCITRAL, PCA Case No. AA 227, Interim Award on Jurisdiction and Admissibility, 30 November 2009.

B. ICJ and PCIJ cases

Ahmadou Sadio Diallo (Republic of Guinea v. *Democratic Republic of the Congo)*, Preliminary Objections, ICJ Rep. 2007.

Application of the Convention on the Prevention and Punishment of the Crime of Genocide (Croatia v. *Serbia)*, Judgment, ICJ Rep. 2015.

Armed Activities on the Territory of the Congo (New Application: 2002) *(Democratic Republic of the Congo* v. *Rwanda)*, Judgment, ICJ Rep. 2006.

Barcelona Traction, Light and Power Company, Limited (Belgium v. *Spain)*, Judgment, ICJ Rep. 1970.

Case Concerning Certain German Interests in Polish Upper Silesia (Merits), PCIJ, Series A. No. 7, at 19 (1926).

Case concerning Right of Passage over Indian Territory (Portugal v. *India), (Merits)*, ICJ Rep. 1960.

Case Concerning Right of Passage over Indian Territory (Portugal v. *India)*, Preliminary Objections, ICJ Rep. I957.

Case Concerning Rights of Nationals of the United States of America in Morocco (France. v. *U.S.)*, ICJ Rep. 1952.

Case Concerning the Arrest Warrant of 11 April 2000 (Democratic Republic of the Congo v. *Belgium)*, Judgment, ICJ Rep. 2002.

Certain German Interests in Polish Upper Silesia (Germany v. *Poland)*, (Merits) (1926) PCIJ, ser. A No.7, 19.

Colombian-Peruvian Asylum case, Judgment, ICJ Rep. 1950.

Continental Shelf (Libya v. *Malta) case*, Judgment, ICJ Rep.1985.

Continental Shelf case (Tunisia v. *Libya)*, Judgment, ICJ Rep. 1982.

Delimitation of the Maritime Boundary in the Gulf of Maine Area (Canada v. *United States)*, Judgment, ICJ Rep. 1984.

Factory at Chorzów (Indemnity), P.C.I.J. Ser. A. No. 17 (1928).

Fisheries case (United Kingdom v. *Norway)*, Judgment, ICJ Rep. 1951.

Fisheries Jurisdiction case (United Kingdom v. *Iceland)*, ICJ Rep. 1974, *Pleadings*, vol. II, (Reply submitted by the Government of the United Kingdom)

Fisheries Jurisdiction Case (United Kingdom v. *Iceland)*, Merits, ICJ Rep. 1974.

Frontier Dispute (Burkina Faso v. *Mali)*, Judgment, ICJ Rep.1986.

Gabčíkovo-Nagymaros Project (Hungary v. *Slovakia)*, Judgment, ICJ Rep. 1997.

German Settlers in Poland, PCIJ, Series B., No. 6, 19–20, 35–38 (1923).

Jurisdictional Immunities of the State (Germany v. *Italy: Greece intervening)*, Judgment, ICJ Rep. 2012.

Legality of the Threat of Use or Nuclear Weapons, Advisory Opinion, ICJ Rep. 1996.

Lotus Case (France v. *Turkey)*, PCIJ Rep Series A No 10 (1927).

Maritime Delimitation and Territorial Questions between Qatar and Bahrain, Merits, Judgment, ICJ Rep. 2001.

Military and Paramilitary Activities in and against Nicaragua (Nicaragua v. *United States)*, Merits, Judgment, ICJ Rep.1986.

North Sea Continental Shelf Cases (Federal Republic of Germany v. *Denmark / Federal Republic of Germany* v. *Netherlands)*, ICJ Rep. 1969.

Nottebohm case (Liechtenstein v. *Guatemala) (Second Phase)*, Judgment, ICJ Rep. 1955.

Nuclear Tests Case (Australia & New Zealand v. *France)*, ICJ Rep. 1974.

Oil Platforms (Islamic Republic of Iran v. *United States)*, Preliminary Objection, Judgment, ICJ Rep. 1996.

Reparations for Injuries Suffered in the Service of the United Nations, Advisory Opinion, ICJ Rep. 1947.

Sicula S.p.A. (ELSI) (US v. *Italy)*, Judgment, ICJ Rep. 1989.

South West Africa Case (Second Phase) (Ethiopia v. *South Africa, Liberia* v. *South Africa)*, ICJ Rep. 1966.

Territorial Dispute Case (Libyan Arab Jamahiriya v. *Chad)*, Judgment, ICJ Rep. 1994

C.   Other arbitral awards

Aboilard Case, (Haiti, France), 9 *UNRIAA*, 1925, p. 71.

Amoco Int'l Fin. Corp. v. *Government of the Islamic Republic of Iran*, Iran-US CT, 14 July 1987, in: 83 *ILR*, 1990.

Chevreau v. *United Kingdom*, Award, 9 June 1931, 2 *UNRIAA*, p. 1113.

George W. Cook Case, (Mexico, United States), 4 *UNRIAA*, 1927, p. 213.

George W. Hopkins v. *Mexico*, Award, 31 March 1926, 4 *UNRIAA*, IV, p. 41.

Kuwait v. *American Independent Oil Company (Aminoil)*, 21 *ILM*, 1982.

Lalanne and Ledoux Case, (France, Venezuela), 10 *UNRIAA*, 1902, p. 17.

Red Sea Islands (Eritrea/Yemen), Award, 9 October 1998.

Robert E. Brown Case, (United Kingdom, United States), 6 *UNRIAA*, 1923, p. 120.

Roberts v. *Mexico*, Award, 2 November 1926, 4 *UNRIAA*, p. 77.

Texaco Overseas Petroleum Co. & California Asiatic Oil Co. v. *Libyan Arab Republic*, Award, 19 January 1977, *17 ILM*, 1978.

USA (LF Neer) v. *Mexico*, Award, 15 October 1926, 4 *UNRIAA*, p. 60

D.   Pleadings in investor-State arbitration proceedings

ADF Group Inc. v. *United States*, ICSID No. ARB(AF)/00/1, 'Mexico's Second Article 1128 Submission', 22 July 2012.

ADF Group Inc. v. *United States*, ICSID No. ARB(AF)/00/1, 'U.S. Rejoinder on Competence and Liability', 29 January 2002.

ADF v. *United States*, ICSID No. ARB(AF)/00/1, 'US Post Hearing Submission', 27 June 2002.

Chemtura Corporation v. *Canada*, UNCITRAL, 'Canada's Counter-Memorial', 20 October 2008.

Commerce Group Corp. and San Sebastian Gold Mines, Inc. v. *El Salvador*, ICSID Case No. ARB/09/17, 'Non-Disputing Party Submission of the Republic of Costa Rica', 20 October 2010.

Glamis Gold Ltd v. *United States*, UNCITRAL, 'United States' Rejoinder Memorial', 15 March 2007.

Glamis Gold Ltd v. *United States*, UNCITRAL, 'US Counter-Memorial', 9 September 2006.

Grand River Enterprises Six Nations, Ltd., et al. v. *United States*, UNCITRAL, 'Claimant's Memorial', 10 July 2008.

Grand River Enterprises Six Nations, Ltd., et al. v. *United States*, 'Counter-Memorial of the United States', 22 December 2008.

Loewen Group, Inc. and Raymond L. Loewen v. *United States*, ICSID Case No. ARB(AF)/98/3, 'Canada's Article 1128 Submission on Jurisdiction Concerning Loewen Corporate Restructuring', 27 June 2002.

Loewen Group, Inc. and Raymond L. Loewen v. *United States*, ICSID Case No. ARB(AF)/98/3, 'Mexico's Article 1128 Submission Concerning Loewen Corporate Restructuring', 2 July 2002.

Loewen Group, Inc. and Raymond L. Loewen v. *United States*, ICSID Case No. ARB(AF)/98/3, 'Second Submission of Canada pursuant to NAFTA Article 1128', 27 June 2002.

Loewen Group, Inc. and Raymond L. Loewen v. *United States*, ICSID Case No. ARB(AF)/98/3, 'Rejoinder of the United States', 27 August 2001.

Loewen Group, Inc. and Raymond L. Loewen v. *United States*, ICSID Case No. ARB(AF)/98/3, 'U.S. Response to Canada and Mexico's Article 1128 Submissions', 19 July 2002.

Loewen Group, Inc. and Raymond L. Loewen v. *United States*, ICSID Case No. ARB(AF)/98/3, 'US Counter-Memorial', 30 March 2001.

Merrill & Ring Forestry L.P. v. *Canada*, UNCITRAL, 'Canada's Rejoinder', 27 March 2009.

Merrill & Ring Forestry L.P. v. *Canada*, UNCITRAL, 'Investor's Reply', 15 December 2008.

Merrill & Ring Forestry L.P. v. *Canada*, UNCITRAL, 'Canada's Counter-Memorial', 13 May 2008.*Methanex Corporation* v. *United States*, UNCITRAL 'Mexico's Article 1128 Submission', 15 May 2001.

Methanex Corporation v. *United States*, UNCITRAL, 'US Statement of Defense', 12 May 2004.

Methanex Corporation v. *United States*, UNCITRAL, 'Canada's Second Article 1128 Submission', 30 April 2001.

Methanex Corporation v. *United States*, UNCITRAL, 'Mexico's Article 1128 Submission', 30 April 2001.

Methanex Corporation v. *United States*, UNCITRAL, 'US Amended Statement of Defense', 5 December 2003.

Methanex Corporation v. *United States*, UNCITRAL, 'US Memorial on Jurisdiction and Admissibility', 13 November 2000.

Pac Rim Cayman LLC v. *El Salvador*, ICSID Case No. ARB/09/12, 'Submission of the United States of America', 20 May 2011.

Pope & Talbot Inc. v. *Canada*, UNCITRAL, 'Post-Hearing Submission of Respondent United States of America on *Pope & Talbot*', 8 July 2002.

Railroad Development Corporation (RDC) v. *Guatemala*, ICSID Case No. ARB/07/23, 'Submission of the United States of America', 31 January 2012.

Railroad Development Corporation (RDC) v. *Guatemala*, ICSID Case No. ARB/07/23, 'Submission of the Republic of El Salvador as a Non-Disputing Party under CAFTA Article 10.20.2', 1 January 2012.

Republic of Ecuador v. *United States of America*, PCA Case No. 2012–5, 'Memorial of Respondent United States of America on Objections to Jurisdiction', 25 April 2012.

Spence International Investments et al. v. *Costa Rica*, UNCITRAL (ICSID Case No. UNCT/13/2), 'Non-Disputing Party Submission by the United States', 17 April 2015.

Spence International Investments et al. v. *Costa Rica*, UNCITRAL (ICSID Case No. UNCT/13/2), Non-Disputing Party Submission by El Salvador, 17 April 2015.

TECO Guatemala Holdings, LLC v. *Guatemala*, ICSID Case No. ARB/10/23, 'Submission of the United States', 23 November 2012.

TECO Guatemala Holdings, LLC v. *Guatemala*, ICSID Case No. ARB/10/23, 'Escrito de Parte no-Contendiente de la Republica de Honduras', undated.

TECO Guatemala Holdings, LLC v. *Guatemala*, ICSID Case No. ARB/10/23, 'Submission of the Dominican Republic as a Non-Disputing Party', 5 October 2012.

TECO Guatemala Holdings, LLC v. *Guatemala*, ICSID Case No. ARB/10/23, 'Non-Disputing Party Submission of the Republic of El Salvador', 5 October 2012

E. Domestic court decisions

Banco National de Cuba v. *Chase Manhattan Bank*, Court of Appeals for the Second Circuit, 658 F, 2nd 875(2nd Cir. 1981).

Bayview Irrigation District et al. v. *Mexico*, Reasons for Judgment, J. Allen, Ontario Superior Court of Justice, 5 May 2008.

Canada (Attorney General v. *SD Myers*, [2004] F.C.J. No. 29 (Fed. Ct.).

Canfor Corporation v. *United States*, US District Court for the District of Columbia, Civil Action No. 07-1905 (RMC), 14 August 2008.

Council of Canadians et al. v. *Attorney General of Canada*, Ontario Court of Appeal, judgment of 30 November 2006.

Cartellone c. Hidronor, Corte Suprema de Justicia, June 1, 2004, Fallos 327–1881.

Czech Republic v. *European Media Ventures SA*, setting aside proceeding of the Tribunal's Award on Jurisdiction dated 15 May 2007, UK High Court of Justice, Queen's Bench Division, Commercial Court, Justice Simon, 5 December 2007, 2007 EWHC 2851 (Comm).

International Thunderbird Gaming Corporation v. *Mexico*, 473 F. Supp. 2d 80; 2007 U.S. Dist. LEXIS 10070 (D.C. Dist. Ct.).

International Thunderbird Gaming Corporation v. *Mexico*, 255 Fed. Appx. 531; 2007 U.S. App. LEXIS 26720 (U.S. Court of Appeals for the DC Circuit).

International Thunderbird Gaming Corporation v. *Mexico*, 2007 U.S. App. LEXIS 26720 (U.S. Court of Appeals for the DC Circuit).

Loewen v. *United States*, 2005 U.S. Dist. LEXIS 44999 (DC Dist. Ct.).

Mexico v. *Cargill, Inc.*, [2011] O.J. No. 4320 (Ont. CA).

Mexico v. *Karpa*, [2003] O.T.C. 1070 (Ont. SCJ).

Mexico v. *Karpa*, [2005] O.J. No. 16 (Ont. CA).

Mexico v. *Metalclad Corp.*, [2001] B.C.J. No. 950 (BCSC).

Mexico v. *Metalclad*, Supreme Court of British Columbia, Canada, 'Outline of Argument of Intervenor Attorney General of Canada', 16 February 2001, para. 2.

R. v. *Hape*, Supreme Court of Canada, 292, 2007 SCC 26, para. 46.

Reference re Secession of Quebec, Supreme Court of Canada, [1998] 2 S.C.R. 217; 37 I.L.M., 1998, 1342, para. 142.

United Mexican States v. *Cargill, Inc.*, [2011] O.J. No. 4320 (Ont. CA).

F.   Others

Case No. STL-11-01/I, Special Tribunal for Lebanon, Interlocutory Decision on the Applicable Law: Terrorism, Conspiracy, Homicide, Perpetration, Cumulative Charging (Appeals Chamber), 16 February 2011.

Case number 001/18-07-2007-ECCC/SC, Appeal Judgment of the Extraordinary Chambers in the Courts of Cambodia (Supreme Court Chamber), 3 February 2012.

Prosecutor v. *Delalić*, International Criminal Tribunal for the former Yugoslavia (ICTY), Case No. IT-96-21-T, Judgment (Trial Chamber), 16 November 1998.

Prosecutor v. *Kupreškić*, International Criminal Tribunal for the former Yugoslavia (ICTY), Case No. IT-95-16-T (ICTY Trial Chamber), 14 January 2000.

Prosecutor v. *Norman*, Special Court for Sierra Leone, SCSL-2004-14-AR72(E), 31 May 2004.

Prosecutor v. *Tadic*, International Criminal Tribunal for the former Yugoslavia (ICTY), ICTY Appeals Chamber, Decision on the Defence Motion for Interlocutory Appeal on Jurisdiction, 2 October 1995.

The M/V "SAIGA" (No. 2) Case (Saint Vincent and the Grenadines v. *Guinea)*, International Tribunal for the Law of the Sea, Merits, Judgment, ITLOS Case No 2, ICGJ 336 (ITLOS 1999),1st July 1999.

Rankin v. *Iran*, Award No. 326-10913-2, Iran-U.S. Claims Trib., Award, 3 November 1987, para. 30(c).

United States – Standards for Reformulated and Conventional Gasoline, WTO Appellate Body Report, WT/DS2/AB/R, adopted on 20 May 1996.

II Books

Alvarez, José E., *International Organizations as Law-Makers*, Oxford: Oxford University Press, 2005.

Amerasinghe, Chittharanjan Felix, *Principles of the Institutional Law of International Organizations*, 2nd edn., Cambridge: Cambridge University Press, 2005.

Anzilotti, Dionisio, *Cours de droit international*, Paris: Recueil Sirey, 1929.

Arajärvi, N., *The Changing Nature of Customary International Law: Methods of Interpreting the Concept of Custom in International Criminal Tribunals*, London; New York: Routledge, 2014.

Arend, A.C., *Legal Rules and International Society*, New York: Oxford University Press, 1999.

Arsanjani, Mahnoush H. *et al.* (eds.), *Looking to the Future: Essays on International Law in Honor of W. Michael Reisman*, Leiden: Martinus Nijhoff, 2011.

Bederman, David J., *Custom as a Source of Law*, New York: Cambridge University Press, 2010.

Bishop, R.D, Crawford, J. and Reisman, W.M., *Foreign Investment Disputes: Cases, Materials and Commentary*, The Hague: Kluwer Law International, 2005.

Bjorklund, Andrea K. and Reinisch, August (eds.), *International Investment Law and Soft Law*, Cheltenham: Elgar, 2012.

Borchard, Edwin, *The Diplomatic Protection of Citizens Abroad*, New York: Bank Law Publishing Co., 1915.

Boyle A. and Chinkin, C., *The Making of International Law*, Oxford: Oxford University Press, 2007.

Brierly, J.L., *The Law of Nations: An Introduction to the International Law of Peace*, 6th edn., Oxford: Clarendon Press, 1963.

Brownlie, Ian, *Principles of Public International Law*, Oxford: Clarendon Press, 1998.

Brownlie, Ian, *The Rule of Law in International Affairs: International Law at the Fiftieth Anniversary of the United Nations*, The Hague: Martinus Nijhoff, 1998.

Byers, M., *Custom, Power and the Power of Rules: International Relations and Customary International Law*, Cambridge: Cambridge University Press, 1999.

Cahin, Gérard, *La coutume internationale et les organisations internationales: l'incidence de la dimension institutionnelle sur le processus coutumier*, Paris: Pedone, 2001.

Carreau, Dominique and Juillard, Patrick, *Droit international économique*, Paris: Dalloz, 2013.

Cassese, A. and Weiler, J.H.H. (eds.), *Change and Stability in International Law-Making*, Berlin: De Gruyter, 1988.

Cassese, Antonio, *International Law*, 2nd edn., Oxford: Oxford University Press, 2005.

Clapham, Andrew, *Human Rights Obligations of Non-State Actors*, Oxford: Oxford University Press, 2006.

Cobbett, Pitt, *Leading Cases on International Law*, London: Sweet & Maxwell, 5th edn., vol. 1, 1931–1937.

Corten, O., *Métholodologie du droit international public*, Brussels: Ed. Université de Bruxelles, 2009.

Corten O. and Klein, P., *The Vienna Convention on the Law of Treaties: A Commentary*, 2nd edn., Oxford: Oxford University Press, 2011.

Crawford, James, *Brownlie's Principles of Public International Law*, 8th edn., Oxford: Oxford University Press, 2012.

Crepet Daigremont, Claire, 'Les sources du droit international des investissements', in C. Leben (ed.) *Droit international des investissements et l'arbitrage transnational*, Paris: Pedone, 2015.

D'Amato, A., *The Concept of Custom in International Law*, Ithaca: Cornell University Press, 1971.

d'Aspremont, J., *Formalism and the Sources of International Law*, Oxford: Oxford University Press, 2011.

Danilenko, G.M., *Law-Making in the International Community*, Dordrecht: Martinus Nijhoff, 1993.

de Brabandere, E., *Investment Treaty Arbitration as Public International Law: Procedural Aspects and Implications*, Cambridge: Cambridge University Press, 2014.

de Visscher, Charles, *Théories et réalités en droit international public*, Paris: Pedone, 1953.

de Visscher, Charles, *Theory and Reality in Public International Law*, Princeton: Princeton University Press, 1968.

Diallo, O., *Le consentement des parties à l'arbitrage international*, Paris: PUF, 2010.

Diehl, Alexandra, *The Core Standard of International Investment Protection: Fair and Equitable Treatment*, Alphen aan den Rijn: Wolters Kluwer, 2012.

Doehring, K., *Völkerrecht*, 2nd edn., Heidelberg: Müller, 2004.

Dolzer, Rudolf and Stevens, Margrete, *Bilateral Investment Treaties*, The Hague: Martinus Nijhoff, 1995.

Dugan, Christopher, Rubins, Noah D., Wallace, Don and Sabahi, Borzu, *Investor-State Arbitration*, New York: Oxford University Press, 2008.

Dumberry, Patrick, *The Fair and Equitable Treatment Standard: A Guide to NAFTA Case Law on Article 1105*, Alphen aan den Rijn: Wolters Kluwer, 2013.

Dupuy, Pierre-Marie, *Droit international public*, 4th edn., Paris: Dalloz, 1998.

Dupuy, Pierre-Marie and Kerbrat, Yann, *Droit international public*, 12th edn., Paris: Dalloz, 2014.

Dupuy, P-M., Francioni, F. and Petersmann, E.U. (eds.), *Human Rights in International Investment Law and Arbitration*, Oxford: Oxford University Press, 2009.

Eagleton, Clyde, *The Responsibility of States in International Law*, New York: New York University Press, 1928.

García Amador, F.V., Sohn, Louis B. and Baxter, R.R., *Recent Codification of the Law of State Responsibility for Injuries to Aliens*, Dobbs Ferry: Oceana Publ., 1974.

Gazzini, T. and de Brabandere, E. (eds.), *International Investment Law: The Sources of Rights and Obligations*, Leiden; Boston: Martinus Nijhoff, 2012.

Goldsmith, Jack L. and Posner, Eric A., *The Limits of International Law*, New York: Oxford University Press, 2005.

Guggenheim, P., *Traité de Droit international public*, 2nd edn., Geneva: Georg, 1967.

Hackworth, Green H., *Digest of International Law*, vol. 3, Washington DC: Department of State, 1942.

Henckaerts, Jean-Marie and Doswald-Beck, Louise (eds.), *Customary International Humanitarian Law*, Cambridge: Cambridge University Press, 2005, vol. I.

Higgins, Rosalyn, *The Development of International Law Through the Political Organs of the United Nations*, London: Oxford University Press, 1963.

Higgins, Rosalyn, *Problems and Process: International Law and How We Use It*, Oxford: Clarendon Press, 1994.

Jennings, R. and Watts, A., *Oppenheim's International Law*, 9th edn., London: Longman, 1996, vol. 1(1).

Johnston, D.M. and Macdonald, R. St. J. (eds.), *The Structure and Process of International Law: Essays in Legal Philosophy Doctrine and Theory*, The Hague: Martinus Nijhoff, 1983.

Kelsen, H., *Principles of International Law*, New York: Rinehart & Company, 1952.

Kelsen, H., *Principles of International Law*, 2nd edn., New York: Holt, Rinehart & Winston, 1966.

Kinnear, M., Biorklund, A. and Hannaford, J.F.G., *Investment Disputes under NAFTA: An Annotated Guide to NAFTA Chapter 11*, Alphen aan den Rijn: Kluwer Law International, 2006.

Kinsella, N. Stephan and Rubins, Noah D., *International Investment, Political Risk, and Dispute Resolution*, Dobbs Ferry: Oceana, 2005.

Klabbers, Jan, *An Introduction to International Institutional Law*, 2nd edn., Cambridge: Cambridge University Press, 2009.

Kläger, Roland, *Fair and Equitable Treatment in International Investment Law*, Cambridge: Cambridge University Press, 2011.

Kontou, Nancy, *The Termination and Revision of Treaties in the Light of New Customary International Law*, Oxford: Clarendon Press, 1995.

Lauterpacht, Elihu, *The Development of International Law by the International Court*, London: Stevens, 1958.

Laviec, Jean-Pierre, *Protection et promotion des investissements, étude de droit international économique*, Paris: PUF, 1985.

Lepard, B., *Customary International Law: A New Theory with Practical Applications*, New York: Cambridge University Press, 2010.

Lowenfeld, Andreas F., *International Economic Law*, 2nd edn., Oxford: Oxford University Press, 2008.

Malanczuk, Peter, *Akehurst's Modern Introduction to International Law*, 7th edn., London and New York: Routledge, 1997.

McLachlan, C., Shore, L. and Weiniger, M., *International Investment Arbitration: Substantive Principles*, Oxford: Oxford University Press, 2007.

Meriboute, Zidane, *La codification de la succession d'États aux traités: décolonisation, sécession, unification*, Paris: PUF, 1984.

Meron, T., *Human Rights and Humanitarian Norms as Customary Law*, Oxford: Clarendon Press, 1991.

Montt, Santiago, *State Liability in Investment Treaty Arbitration*, Oxford: Hart Publ., 2009.

Muchlinski, Peter, *Multinational Enterprises & the Law*, 2nd edn., Oxford: Oxford University Press, 2007.

Murphy, J.B. and Perreau-Saussine, A. (eds.), *The Nature of Customary Law: Philosophical, Historical and Legal Perspectives*, Cambridge: Cambridge University Press, 2007.

Newcombe, Andrew and Paradell, Luis, *Law and Practice of Investment Treaties: Standards of Treatment*, Alphen aan den Rijn: Kluwer, 2009.

Nollkaemper, A., *National Courts and the International Rule of Law*, Oxford: Oxford University Press, 2011.

O'Connell, D.P., *International Law*, London: Stevens & Sons, 1970.

Paparinskis, Martins, *The International Minimum Standard and Fair and Equitable Treatment*, Oxford: Oxford University Press, 2013.

Parry, C., *The Sources and Evidences of International Law*, Manchester: University Press & Dobbs Ferry: Oceana, 1965.

Nguyen Quoc Dinh, Patrick Dallier, Mathias Forteau and Alain Pellet, *Droit International Public*, 8th edn., Paris: LGDJ, 2007.

Reed, L., Paulsson, J. and Blackaby, N., *A Guide to ICSID Arbitration*, The Hague: Kluwer Law, 2004.

Rosenne, S., *Practice and Methods of International Law*, London: Oceana Publications, 1984.

Roth, Andreas Hans, *The Minimum Standard of International Law Applied to Aliens*, The Hague: A.W. Sijthoff, 1949.

Rovine, Arthur W. (ed.), 1973 *Digest of the United States Practice in International Law*, Washington DC, US Department of State, Office of the Legal Adviser, 1974.

Salacuse, Jeswald W., *The Law of Investment Treaties*, Oxford: Oxford University Press 2010.

Salacuse, Jeswald W., *The Three Laws of International Investment National, Contractual, and International Frameworks for Foreign Capital*, Oxford: Oxford University Press, 2013.

Scharf, Michael P., *Customary International Law in Times of Fundamental Change: Recognizing Grotian Moments*, Cambridge: Cambridge University Press, 2013.

Schermers, H.G. and Blokker, N.M., *International Institutional Law: Unity Within Diversity*, 4th edn., Boston; Leiden: Martinus Nijhoff, 2003.

Schill, S., *The Multilateralization of International Investment Law*, Cambridge: Cambridge University Press, 2009.

Schokkaert, Jan and Heckscher, Yvon, *International Investments Protection: Comparative Law Analysis of Bilateral and Multilateral Interstate Conventions, Doctrinal Texts and Arbitral Jurisprudence Concerning Foreign Investments*, Brussels: Bruylant, 2009.

Schreuer, C. and Dolzer, R., *Principles of International Investment Law*, Oxford: Oxford University Press, 2008.

Schreuer, Christoph H., Malintoppi, Loretta, Reinisch, August and Sinclair, Anthony, *The ICSID Convention; A Commentary*, 2nd edn., Cambridge: Cambridge University Press, 2009.

Schwartzenberger, G., *International Law as Applied by International Courts and Tribunals*, London: Stevens & Sons, 1949.

Schwarzenberger, G., *International Law*, vol. 1, 3rd edn. London: Stevens & Sons, 1957.

Shahabuddeen, M., *Precedent in the World Court*, Cambridge: Cambridge University Press, 1996.

Shaw, Malcolm N., *International Law*, 6th edn., Cambridge: Cambridge University Press, 2008.

Shaw, Malcolm N., *International Law*, 7th edn., Cambridge: Cambridge University Press, 2014.

Sornarajah, M., *The International Law on Foreign Investment*, 2nd edn., Cambridge: Cambridge University Press, 2004.

Sornarajah, M., *The International Law on Foreign Investment*, 3rd edn., Cambridge: Cambridge University Press, 2010.

Subedi, Surya P., *International Investment Law: Reconciling Policy and Principle*, Oxford: Hart Publ., 2008.

Thirlway, H.W.A., *International Customary Law and Codification*, Leiden: Sijthoff, 1972.

Tudor, Ioana, *The Fair and Equitable Treatment Standard in International Foreign Investment Law*, Oxford: Oxford University Press, 2008.

van Harten, Gus, *Investment Treaty Arbitration and Public Law*, Oxford: Oxford University Press, 2007.

van Hoof, G.J.H., *Rethinking the Sources of International Law*, Deventer: Kluwer, 1983.

Vandevelde, K.J., *Bilateral Investment Treaties: History, Policy and Interpretation*, Oxford: Oxford University Press, 2010.

Vandevelde, K.J., *U.S. International Investment Agreements*, New York: Oxford University Press, 2009.

Villanueva, Gabriel Cavazos, *The Fair and Equitable Treatment Standard: The Mexican Experience*, Saarbrücken: VDM Verlag, 2008.

Villiger, Mark E., *Customary International law and Treaties: A Manual on the Theory and Practice of the Interrelation of Sources*, 2nd edn., The Hague: Kluwer & Zürich: Schulthess Polygraphischer Verlag, 1997.

Voss, Jan Ole, *The Impact of Investment Treaties on Contracts between Host States and Foreign Investors*, Leiden: Martinus Nijhoff, 2011.

Wälde, Thomas, *Nouveaux horizons pour le droit international des investissements dans le contexte de la mondialisation de l'économie*, Paris: Pedone, 2004.

Wang, Dong, *China's Unequal Treaties: Narrating National History*, Lanham, MD: Lexington Books, 2005.

Weeramantry, J. Romesh, *Treaty Interpretation in Investment Arbitration*, Oxford: Oxford University Press, 2012.

Weiler, Todd, *The Interpretation of International Investment Law: Equality, Discrimination and Minimum Standards of Treatment in Historical Context*, Leiden: Martinus Nijhoff, 2013.

Wilson, Robert R., *The International Law Standard in Treaties of the United States*, Cambridge, Mass.: Harvard University Press, 1953.

Wolfke, Karol, *Custom in Present International Law*, 2nd edn., Dordrecht: Nijhoff, 1993.

III Articles

Abi-Saab, Georges, 'The Newly Independent States and the Rules of International Law: An Outline', *Howard L. J* 8 (1962), pp. 95–121.

Abi-Saab, Georges, 'La coutume dans tous ses États ou le dilemme du développement du droit international général dans un monde éclaté', in: *Le droit international à l'heure de sa codification : études en l'honneur de Roberto Ago* (Milan: Giuffrè, 1987), pp. 53–65.

Abi-Saab, Georges, 'Custom and Treaties' in A. Cassese and J.H.H. Weiler (eds.), *Change and Stability in International Law-Making* (Berlin: Walter de Gruyter, 1988).

Abs H. and Shawcross, H., 'The Proposed Convention to Protect Private Foreign Investment: A Round Table: Comment on the Draft Convention by its Authors', *J.P.L.* 9 (1960), pp. 119–124.

Acconci, P., 'Determining the Internationally Relevant Link between a State and a Corporate Investor, Recent Trends Concerning the Application of the "Genuine Link" Test', *J. World Invest. & Trade* 5 (2004), pp 139–175.

Acconci, P., 'The Requirement of Continuous Corporate Nationality and Customary International Rules on Foreign Investment: the Loewen Case', *Italian YIL* 14 (2004), pp. 195–223.

Adeyeye, Adefolake, 'Corporate Responsibility in International Law: Which Way to go?', *Singapore YB Int'L* 11 (2007), pp. 141–161.

Akehurst, M., 'Custom as a Source of International Law', *British YIL* 47 (1974–1975), pp. 1–53.

Akinsanya, A.,'International Protection of Direct Foreign Investments in the Third World', *ICLQ* 36 (1987), pp 58–75.

Al Faruque, Abdullah, 'Creating Customary International Law through Bilateral Investment Treaties: a Critical Appraisal', *Indian JIL* 44 (2004), pp. 292–318.

Alschner, Wolfgang, 'The Return of the Home State and the Rise of 'Embedded' Investor-State Arbitration', in S. Lalani and R. Polanco (eds.), *The Role of the State in Investor-State Arbitration* (Leiden; Boston: Martinus Nijhoff/Brill, 2014), pp. 192–218.

Alvarez-Jimenez, Alberto, 'Methods for the Identification of Customary International Law in the International Court of Justice's Jurisprudence: 2000–2009', *ICLQ* 60 (2011), pp. 681–712.

Alvarez, J.E., 'The Contemporary International Investment Regime: An "Empire of Law" or the "Law of Empire"?', *Alabama L. Rev.* 60 (2009), pp. 943–975.

Alvarez, J.E., 'A BIT on Custom', *N.Y.U. J. Int'l L. & Pol.* 42 (2009–2010), pp. 17–80.

Alvarez, J.E., 'The Once and Future Investment Regime' in Mahnoush Arsanjani *et al.* (eds.), *Looking to the Future: Essays on International Law in Honor of W. Michael Reisman* (Leiden: Martinus Nijhoff, 2011), pp. 607–648.

Alvarez, J.E., 'Are Corporations "Subjects" of International Law?', *Santa Clara J. Int'l L.* 9 (2011), pp. 1–36.

Alvarez, J.E., 'The Return of the State', *Minnesota JIL* 20 (2011), pp. 223–264.

Arajärvi, N., 'From State-Centricism to Where? The Formation of (Customary) International Law and Non-State Actors', *SSRN* (2010).

Asamoah, Obed Y., 'The Legal Significance of the Declarations of the General Assembly of the United Nations', *ICLQ* 16(4) (1967), pp. xviii–274.

Audit, Mathias and Forteau, Mathias, 'Investment Arbitration without BIT: Toward a Foreign Investment Customary Based Arbitration?', *J. Int'l Arb.* 29 (2012), pp. 581–604.

Baker, R.B., 'Customary International Law in the 21st Century: Old Challenges and New Debates', *EJIL* 21(1) 2010, pp. 173–204.

Banifatemi, Y., 'The Law Applicable in Investment Treaty Arbitration', in Katia Yannaca-Small (ed.), *Arbitration Under International Investment Agreements: A Guide to the Key Issues* (Oxford: Oxford University Press, 2010), pp. 191–210.

Barberis, J.A., 'Réflexions sur la coutume internationale', *AFDI* 36 (1990), pp. 9–46.

Baxter, R., 'Multilateral Treaties as Evidence of Customary International Law', *British YIL* 41 (1965–1966), pp. 275–300.

Berezowski, C., 'Les problèmes de la subjectivité internationale', in V. Ibler (ed.) *Mélanges offerts à Juraj Andrassy* (La Haye: Martinus Nijhoff Publ., 1968), pp. 31–53.

Bernasconi-Osterwalder, Nathalie and Mann, Howard, 'A Response to the European Commission's December 2013 Document "Investment Provisions in the EU-Canada Free Trade Agreement (CETA)", *'IISD* (2014), pp. 1–26.

Bethlehem, D., 'The Secret Life of International Law', *Cambridge J Intl Comp L* 23 (2012), pp. 23–36.

Bjorklund, Andrea K., 'Reconciling State Sovereignty and Investor Protection in Denial of Justice Claims', *Virginia JIL* 45 (2005), pp. 809–895.

Bjorklund, Andrea K., 'NAFTA's Contributions to Investor-State Dispute Settlement' in M. Bungenberg, J. Griebel, S. Hobe and A. Reinisch (eds.), *International Investment Law: A Handbook* (Munich: C.H. Beck, Oxford: Hart, Baden-Baden: Nomos, 2015), pp. 261–282.

Borchard, Edwin, 'The "Minimum Standard" of the Treatment of Aliens', *ASIL Proc.* 33 (1939), pp. 51–70.

Bos, M., 'The Identification of Custom in International Law', *German YIL* 25 (1982), pp. 9–53.

Bradley, Curtis A. & Gulati, Mitu, 'Withdrawing from International Custom', *Yale LJ* 120 (2010), pp. 202–275.

Bronfman, Marcela Klein, 'Fair and Equitable Treatment: An Evolving Standard', *Max Planck Yrbk. UNL* 10 (2006), pp. 609–680.

Brower II, Charles H. and Tepe, John B., 'Charter of Economic Rights and Duties of States-A Reflection or Rejection of International Law?', *Int'l Law* 9 (1975), pp. 295–318.

Brower II, Charles H., 'Investor-State Disputes Under NAFTA: The Empire Strikes Back', *Colum J. Transnat'l L.* 40 (2001–2002), pp. 43–84.

Brower II, Charles H., 'Structure, Legitimacy, and NAFTA's Investment Chapter', *Vand. J. Transnat'l L.* 36 (2003), pp. 37–94.

Brower II, Charles H., 'Why the FTC Notes of Interpretation Constitute a Partial Amendment of NAFTA Article 1105', *Va. J. Int'l L.* 46 (2006), pp. 347–363.

Brown, Chester, 'Introduction. The Development and Importance of the Model Bilateral Investment Treaty', in C. Brown (ed.), *Commentaries on Selected Model Investment Treaties* (Oxford: Oxford University Press, 2013), pp. 1–13.

Brown, Chester, 'The Evolution of the Regime of International Investment Agreements: History, Economics and Politics', in M. Bungenberg, J. Griebel, S. Hobe and A. Reinisch (eds.), *International Investment Law: A Handbook* (München: C.H. Beck, Oxford: Hart, Baden-Baden: Nomos, 2015), pp. 153–185.

Bubrowski, Helene, 'Counterclaims', in A. De Mestral and C. Lévesque (eds.), *Improving International Investment Treaties: Negotiation, Substantive Obligations and Dispute Resolution* (London: Routledge, 2013), pp. 212–229.

Caplan, Lee M. and Sharpe, Jeremy K., 'United States', in C. Brown (ed.), *Commentaries on Selected Model Investment Treaties* (Oxford: Oxford University Press, 2013), pp. 755–851.

Caron, David, 'The Interpretation of National Foreign Investment Laws as Unilateral Acts under International Law', in Mahnoush Arsanjani *et al.* (eds.), *Looking to the Future: Essays on International Law in Honor of W. Michael Reisman* (Leiden: Martinus Nijhoff, 2011), pp. 649–674.

Carreau, D., 'Investissements', in *Répertoire de droit international* (Paris: Dalloz, 1998).

Chalamish, E., 'Future of Bilateral Investment Treaties: A De Facto Multilateral Agreement', *Brook. J. Int'l L.* 34 (2008–2009), pp. 303–354.

Charney, J., 'The Persistent Objector Rule and the Development of Customary International Law', *British YIL* 56 (1985), pp. 1–24.

Charney, J., 'International Agreements and the Development of Customary International Law', *Washington L. R.* 61 (1986), pp. 971–996.

Charney, J., 'Universal International Law', *AJIL* 87 (1993), pp. 529–551.

Cheng, Bin, 'United Nations Resolutions on Outer Space: "Instant" International Customary Law?', *Indian JIL* 5 (1965), pp. 23–48.

Cheng, Bin, 'Custom: The Future of General State Practice In a Divided World', in R. St.J. Macdonald and D.M. Johnston (eds.), *The Structure and Process of*

International Law: Essays in Legal Philosophy Doctrine and Theory (The Hague: Martinus Nijhoff, 1983), pp. 513–554.

Clodfelter, Mark A., 'The Adaptation of States to the Changing World of Investment Protection through Model BITs', *ICSID Rev.* 24 (2009), pp. 165–175.

Cohen-Jonathan, G., 'La coutume locale', *AFDI* 7 (1961), pp. 119–140.

Colson, David A., 'How Persistent Must the Persistent Objector be', *Washington L. R.* 61 (1986), pp. 957–970.

Congyan, Cai, 'International Investment Treaties and the Formation, Application a Transformation of Customary International Law Rules', *Chinese JIL* 7 (2008), pp. 659–679.

Corten, O., 'La participation du Conseil de sécurité à l'élaboration, à la crystallisation ou à la consolidation de règles coutumières', *RBDI* (2004), pp. 552–567.

Crawford, J., Pellet, A. and Redgwell, C., 'Anglo-American and Continental Traditions in Advocacy before International Courts and Tribunals', *Cambridge J Intl Comp L* 2 (2013), pp. 715–737.

d'Aspremont, J., 'The Doctrinal Illusion of Heterogenity of International Lawmaking Processes', in H. Ruiz-Fabri, R. Wolfrum, and J. Gogolin (eds.), *Select Proceedings of the European Society of International Law* (Oxford: Hart, vol. 2, 2010), pp. 297–312.

d'Aspremont, J., 'International Customary Investment Law: Story of a Paradox', in T. Gazzini and E. de Brabandere (eds.), *International Investment Law: The Sources of Rights and Obligations* (Leiden: Martinus Nijhoff, 2012), pp. 5–47.

d'Aspremont, J., 'An Autonomous Regime of Identification of Customary International Humanitarian Law: Do Not Say What You Do Or Do Not Do What You Say?', in R. van Steenberghe (ed.), *Droit international humanitaire: un régime spécial de droit international?* (Brussels: Bruylant, 2013), pp. 1–26.

d'Aspremont, J., 'Inclusive Law-Making and Law-Enforcement Processes for an Exclusive International Legal System', in J. d'Aspremont (ed.), *Participants in the International Legal System: Multiple Perspectives on Non-State Actors in International Law* (London: Routledge, 2013), pp. 425–439.

d'Aspremont, J., 'Customary International Law as a Dance Floor: Part I', *EJIL Talks!*, 15 April 2014.

d'Aspremont, J., 'Customary International Law as a Dance Floor: Part II', *EJIL Talks!*, 15 April 2014.

D'Amato, Anthony, 'The Concept of Special Custom in International Law', *AJIL* 63 (1969), pp. 211–223.

D'Amato, Anthony, 'What "Counts" as Law?', in Nicholas Greenwood Onuf (ed.) *Law-Making in the Global Community* (Durham: Carolina Academic Press, 1982), pp. 83–107.

D'Amato, Anthony, 'Trashing Customary International Law', *AJIL* 81 (1987), pp. 101–105.

D'Amato, Anthony, 'Custom and Treaty: A Response to Professor Weisburd', *Vand. J. Transnat'l L.* 21 (1988), pp. 459–472.

D'Amato, Anthony, 'Customary International Law: A Reformulation', *International Legal Theory* (1998), pp. 1–6.

Dahlman, C., 'The Function of opinio juris in Customary International Law', *Nordic JIL* (2012), pp. 327–339.

de Brabandere, E., 'Judicial and Arbitral Decisions as a Source of Rights and Obligations', in: T. Gazzini and E. de Brabandere (eds), *Sources of Transnational Investment Law* (Leiden; Boston: Martinus Nijhoff, 2012), pp. 245–288.

Delaume, George R., 'The Proper Law of State Contracts Revisited', *ICSID Rev.* 12 (1997), pp. 1–28.

Denza, E. and Brooks, S., 'Investment Protection Treaties: United Kingdom Experience', *ICLQ* 36 (1987), pp. 908–923.

Dickerson, Hollin, 'Minimum Standards', *Max Planck Encyclopedia of Public International Law* (Oxford: Oxford University Press, vol. 9, 2013).

Doehring, K., 'Gewohnheitsrecht aus Verträgen', *ZaöRV* 36 (1976), pp. 77–95.

Dolzer, R., 'New Foundations of the Law of Expropriation of Alien Property', *AJIL* (1981), pp. 553–589.

Dolzer, R., 'Indirect Expropriation of Alien Property', *ICSID Rev.* (1987), pp. 41–65.

Dolzer, R., 'Fair And Equitable Treatment in International Law, Remarks', *ASIL Proc.* 100 (2006), p. 69.

Dolzer, R. and von Walter, A., 'Fair and Equitable Treatment – Lines of Jurisprudence on Customary Law', in F. Ortino (ed.), *Investment Treaty Law, Current Issues II* (London: BIICL, 2007), pp. 99–115.

Dominicé, C., 'La personnalité juridique internationale du CICR', in C. Swinarski (ed.), *Studies and Essays on International Humanitarian Law and Red Cross Principles in Honour of Jean Pictet* (The Hague: Nijhoff/Geneva: ICRC, 1984), pp. 663–673.

Dominicé, C., 'L'émergence de l'individu en droit international public', *Annales d'études internationales* 16 (1987–1988), pp. 1–16.

Douglas, Z., 'The Hybrid Foundations of Investment Treaty Arbitration', *British YIL* 74(1) (2003), pp. 151–289.

Duchesne, M.S., 'The Continuous Nationality of Claims Principle: Its Historical Development and Current Relevance to Investor-State Investment Disputes', *Geo. Wash. Int'l L. Rev.* 36 (2004), pp. 783–815.

Dumberry, P., 'L'entreprise, sujet de droit international? Retour sur la question à la lumière des développements récents du droit international des investissements', *RGDIP* 108(1) (2004), pp. 103–122.

Dumberry, P., 'Are BITs Representing the "New" Customary International Law in International Investment Law?', *Penn State ILR* 28(4) (2010), pp. 675–702.

Dumberry, P., 'Incoherent and Ineffective: The Concept of Persistent Objector Revisited', *ICLQ* 59 (2010), pp. 779–802.

Dumberry, P., 'The Last Citadel! Can a State Claim the Status of Persistent Objector to Prevent the Application of a Rule of Customary International Law in Investor-State Arbitration?', *Leiden JIL* 23(2) (2010), pp. 379–400.

Dumberry, P., 'The Legal Standing of Shareholders before Arbitral Tribunals: Has Any Rule of Customary International Law Crystallised?', *Michigan State JIL* 18 (2010), pp. 353–374.

Dumberry, P. and Labelle Eastaugh, E., 'Non-State Actors in International Investment Law: The Legal Personality of Corporations and NGOs in the Context of Investor-State Arbitration', in Jean d'Aspremont (ed.), *Participants in the International Legal System: Multiples Perspectives on Non-State Actors in International Law* (London: Routledge-Cavendish, 2011), pp. 360–371.

Dumberry, P. and Dumas-Aubin, G., 'How to Impose Human Rights Obligations on Corporations under Investment Treaties?', *Yb Int'l Invest. L. & Pol.* 4 (2011–2012), pp. 569–600.

Dumberry, P. and Dumas-Aubin, G., 'When and How Allegations of Human Rights Violations can be Raised in Investor-State Arbitration', *J. World Invest. & Trade* 13(3) (2012), pp. 349–372.

Dumberry, P., 'Corporate Investors' International Legal Personality and their Accountability for Human Rights Violations under Investment Treaties', in A. De Mestral and C. Lévesque (eds.), *Improving International Investment Agreements Negotiation, Substantive Obligations and Dispute Resolution* (London: Routledge, 2013), pp. 179–194.

Dumberry, P. 'International Investment Contracts', in T. Gazzini and E. de Brabandere (eds.), *International Investment Law: The Sources of Rights and Obligations* (Leiden: Martinus Nijhoff & Brill, 2012), pp. 215–243.

Dumberry, P. and Stone, J., 'International Law, Whether You Like It or Not: An Analysis of Arbitral Tribunal Practice Regarding the Applicable Law in Deciding State Contracts Disputes under the ICSID Convention in the Twenty First Century', *Yb Int'l Invest. L. & Pol.* 5 (2012–2013), pp. 477–516.

Dumberry, P. and Dumas-Aubin, G., 'The Doctrine of "Clean Hands" and the Inadmissibility of Claims by Investors Breaching International Human Rights Law', in Ursula Kriebaum (ed.), *Aligning Human Rights and Investment Protection*, TDM Special Issue, 10 (1) (2013).

Dumberry, P., 'Denial of Justice under NAFTA Article 1105: A Review of 20 Years of Case Law', *ASA Bull.* 32(2) (2014), pp. 145–163.

Dumberry, P., 'The Protection of Investors' Legitimate Expectations and the Fair and Equitable Treatment Standard under NAFTA Article 1105', *J. Int'l Arb.* 31(1) (2014), pp. 47–74.

Dumberry, P., 'Moving the Goal Post! How Some NAFTA Tribunals have Challenged the FTC Note of Interpretation on the Fair and Equitable Treatment Standard under NAFTA Article 1105', *W. Arb & Med Rev* 8 (2014), pp. 251–293.

Dumberry, P., 'The Prohibition Against Arbitrary Conduct and the Fair and Equitable Treatment Standard under NAFTA Article 1105', *J. World Invest. & Trade* 15 (2014), pp. 117–151.

Dumberry, P., 'The Practice of States as Evidence of Custom: An Analysis of Fair and Equitable Treatment Standard Clauses in States' Foreign Investment Laws', McGill Journal of Dispute Resolution (forthcoming, 2016).

Dumberry, P., 'Has the Fair and Equitable Treatment Standard become a Rule of Customary international Law? An Empirical Study of the Practice of States (forthcoming, 2016).

Dumberry, P., 'The Importation of the Fair and Equitable Treatment Standard Through MFN Clauses: An Empirical Study of BITs', ICSID Rev. (forthcoming, 2016).

Dumberry, P., 'Shopping for a Better Deal: The Use of MFN Clauses to Get 'Better' Fair and Equitable Treatment Protection under other treaties' (forthcoming 2016).

Dunbar, N.C.H., 'The Myth of Customary International Law', *Australian YIL* 8 (1983), pp. 1–19.

Dupuy, P.-M., 'A propos de l'opposabilité de la coutume générale: enquête brève sur l'objecteur persistant', in *Mélanges Michel Virally* (Paris: Pedone, 1991), pp. 257–272.

Dupuy, R.J., 'Coutume sage et coutume sauvage', in *Mélanges Rousseau* (Paris: Pedone, 1974), pp. 75–87.

El-Kosheri, Ahmed S. and Riad, Tarek F., 'The Law Governing a New Generation of Petroleum Agreements: Changes in the Arbitration Process', *ICSID Rev.* 1 (1986), pp. 257–288.

Elias, Olufemi, 'The Nature of the Subjective Element in Customary International Law', *ICLQ* 44 (1995), pp. 501–520.

Ewing-Chow, M. and Losari, J.J., 'Which is to be the Master?: Extra-Arbitral Interpretative Procedures for IIAs', in A. Joubin-Bret and Jean E. Kalicki (eds.), *Reform of Investor-State Dispute Settlement: In Search of A Roadmap* (TDM Special issue, 2014).

Falsafi, Alireza, 'The International Minimum Standard of Treatment of Foreign Investors' Property: A Contingent Standard', *Suffolk Transnat'l L. Rev.* 30 (2006–2007), pp. 317–363.

Fauchald, Ole Kristian, 'The Legal Reasoning of ICSID Tribunals – An Empirical Analysis', *EJIL* 19 (2008), pp. 301–364.

Fitzmaurice, G., 'The Law and Procedure of the International Court of Justice, 1951–54: General Principles and Sources of Law', *British YIL* 30 (1953), pp. 1–70.

Francioni, F., 'Access to Justice, Denial of Justice and International Investment Law', *EJIL* 20(3) (2009), pp. 729–748.

Fumagalli, Luigi, 'Evidence before the International Court of Justice: Issues of Fact and Questions of Law in the Determination of International Custom', in Nerina Boschiero *et al.* (eds.), *International Courts and the Development of International Law: Essays in Honour of Tullio Treves* (The Hague: Asser Press, 2013), pp. 137–148.

Gagné, Gilbert and Morin, Jean-Frédéric, 'The Evolving American Policy on Investment Protection: Evidence from Recent FTAs and the 2004 Model BIT', *J. Int'l Econ. L.* 9 (2006), pp. 357–382.

Gaillard, Emmanuel and Banifatemi, Yas, 'The Meaning of 'and' in Article 42 (1), Second Sentence of the Washington Convention: The Role of International Law in the ICSID Choice of Law Process', *ICSID Rev.* 18 (2003), pp. 375–411.

Gamble, John King and Ku, Charlotte, 'International Law—New Actors and New Technologies: Center Stage for NGOs?', *Law & Pol'y Int'l. Bus.* 31 (2000), pp. 221–262.

Gattini, A., 'Le rôle du juge international et du juge national et la coutume internationale', in D. Alland *et al.* (eds.), *Unité et diversité du droit international: écrits en l'honneur du professeur Pierre-Marie Dupuy* (Leiden: Martinus Nijhoff, 2014), pp. 253–273.

Gazzini, Tarcisio, 'The Role of Customary International Law in the Field of Foreign Investment', *J. World Invest. & Trade* 8 (2007), pp. 691–715.

Geiger, R.H., 'Customary International Law in the Jurisprudence of the International Court of Justice: A Critical Appraisal', in U. Fastenrath *et al.* (eds.), *From Bilateralism to Community Interest: Essays in Honour of Judge Bruno Simma* (Oxford: Oxford University Press, 2011), pp. 673–694.

Glennon, Michael J., 'How International Rules Die', *GEO. L. J.* 93 (2005), pp. 939–991.

Goldsmith, Jack L. and Posner, Eric A., 'A Theory of Customary International Law', *Chicago L. Rev.* 66 (1999), pp. 1113–1177.

Goldsmith, Jack L. and Posner, Eric A., 'Understanding the Resemblance Between Modern and Traditional Customary International Law', *Virginia JIL* 40 (2000), pp. 639–672.

Grisel, Florian, 'The Sources of Foreign Investment Law', in: Z. Douglas, J. Pauwelyn and J.E. Viñuales (eds.), *The Foundations of International Investment Law: Bringing Theory into Practice* (Oxford: Oxford University Press, 2014), pp. 213–233.

Guggenheim, P., 'Les deux éléments de la coutume en droit international', in *La technique et les principes du droit public. Etudes en l'honneur de Georges Scelle* (Paris: LGDJ, 1950), pp. 275 ff.

Guha-Roy, S-N., 'Is the Law of Responsibility of States for Injuries to Aliens A Part of Universal International Law?', *AJIL* 55 (1961), pp. 863–891.

Guillaume, Gilbert, 'Can Arbitral Awards Constitute a Source of International Law under Article 38 of the ICJ Statute?', in Y. Banifatemi (ed.), *Precedent in International Arbitration* (Huntington: Juris Publishing, 2008), pp. 105–112.

Guldahl, Camilla G., 'The Role of Persistent Objection in International Humanitarian Law', *Nordic JIL* 77 (2008), pp. 51–86.

Gunning, Isabelle R., 'Modernizing Customary International Law: The Challenge of Human Rights', *Virginia JIL* 31 (1991), pp. 211–247.

Guzman, Andrew T., 'Why LDCs Sign Treaties That Hurt Them: Explaining the Popularity of Bilateral Investment Treaties', *Va.J.Int'l L.* 38(4) (1998), pp. 639–688.

Guzman, Andrew T., 'A Compliance-Based Theory of International Law', *Cal. L. Rev.* 90 (2002), pp. 1827–1887.

Guzman, Andrew T., 'Saving Customary International Law', *Michigan JIL* 27 (2006), pp. 115–176.

Haeri, Hussein, 'A Tale of Two Standards: 'Fair and Equitable Treatment' and the Minimum Standard in International Law', *Arb. Int'l* 27 (2011), pp. 27–46.

Haggenmacher, P., 'La doctrine des deux éléments du droit coutumier dans la pratique de la Cour internationale', *RGDIP* 90 (1986), pp. 5–126.

Harrison, J., 'The International Law Commission and the Development of International Investment Law', *Geo. Wash. Int'l L. Rev*, 45 (2013), pp. 413–442.

Heiskanen, Veijo, 'Arbitrary and Unreasonable Measures', in A. Reinisch (ed.), *Standards of Investment Protection* (Oxford: Oxford University Press, 2008), pp. 87–110.

Henckaerts, J.M., 'International Humanitarian Law as Customary International Law', *Refugee Survey Quarterly* 21 (3) (2002), pp. 186–193.

Higgins, R., 'The ICJ, the ECJ, and the Integrity of International Law', *ICLQ* 52 (2003), pp. 1–20.

Hindelang, Steffen, 'Bilateral Investment Treaties, Custom and a Healthy Investment Climate – The Question of whether BITs Influence Customary International Law Revisited', *J. World Invest. & Trade* 5 (2004), pp. 789–809.

Igbokwe, Virtus Chitoo, 'Developing Countries and the Law Applicable to International Arbitration of Oil Investment Disputes Has the Last Word been Said?', *J. Int'l Arb.* 14(1) (1997), pp. 99–124.

Jacquet, Jean-Michel, 'Contrat d'État', *Jurisclasseur Droit international*, fasc. 565, 11/98 (Paris: Dalloz, 1998).

Jenks, W.C., 'Multinational Entities in the Law of Nations', in *Transnational Law in a Changing Society: Essays in Honor of Philip C. Jessup* (New York: Columbia University Press, 1972), pp. 70–83.

Jennings, R., 'What is International Law and How Do We Tell It When We See It', *ASDI* 37 (1981) (also in: *The Cambridge Tilburg Lectures*, Deventer: Kluwer, 1983, pp. 59–91).

Jia, Bing Bing, 'The Relations between Treaties and Custom', *Chinese JIL* 9(1) (2010), pp. 81–109.

Kammerhofer, J., 'Uncertainty in the Formal Sources of International Law: Customary International Law and Some of Its Problems', *EJIL* 15(3) (2004), pp. 523–553.

Kammerhofer, J., 'Law-Making by Scholarship? The Dark Side of 21st Century International Legal "Methodology"', in J. Crawford *et al.* (eds), *Selected Proceedings of the European Society of International Law* (Oxford: Hart, vol. 3, 2011), pp. 115–126.

Kammerhofer, J., 'Orthodox Generalists and Political Activists in International Legal Scholarship', in M. Happold (ed.), *International Law in a Multipolar World* (London: Routledge, 2012), pp. 138–157.

Kammerhofer, J., 'Law-making by Scholars' in Catherine Brölmann and Yannick Radi (eds.), *Research Handbook on the Theory and Practice of International Law-Making* (Cheltenham: Edward Elgar 2013).

Kantor, Mark, 'Little Has Changed in the New US Model Bilateral Investment Treaty', *ICSID Rev.* 27(2) (2012), pp. 335–378.

Kaufmann-Kohler, Gabrielle, 'Arbitral Precedent: Dream, Necessity or Excuse?', *Arb. Int'l* 23 (2007), pp. 357–378.

Kaufmann-Kohler, Gabrielle, 'Interpretive Powers of the NAFTA Free Trade Commission – Necessary Safety Valve or Infringement of the Rule of Law?', in Frédéric Bachand (ed.), *Fifteen Years of NAFTA Chapter 11 Arbitration* (New York: JurisNet, 2011), pp. 175–194.

Kaushal, Asha, 'Revisiting History: How the Past Matters for the Present Backlash Against the Foreign Investment Regime', *Harvard ILJ* 50(2) (2009), pp. 491–534.

Kelly, J. Patrick, 'The Twilight of Customary International Law', *Virginia JIL* 40 (2000), pp. 449–543.

Kelsen, H., 'Théorie du droit coutumier', *Revue internationale de la théorie du droit* (1939), pp. 253–274.

Khalil, Mohamed, 'Treatment of Foreign Investment in BITs', *ICSID Rev.* 7(2) (1992), p. 339–383.

Kill, T., 'Don't Cross the Streams: Past and Present Overstatement of Customary International Law in Connection with Conventional Fair and Equitable Treatment Obligations', *Michigan LR* 106 (2008), pp. 853–880.

Kinley, David and Tadaki, Junko, 'From Talk to Walk: The Emergence of Human Rights Responsibilities for Corporations at International Law', *Virginia J. I. L.* 44(4) (2004), pp. 931–1023.

Kirakosyan, Yeghishe, 'Finding Custom: the ICJ and the International Criminal Courts and Tribunals compared', in Larissa van den Herik and Carsten Stahn (eds.) *The Diversification and Fragmentation of International Criminal Law* (Leiden: Brill & Nijhoff, 2012), pp. 149–161.

Kirkman, Courtney C., 'Fair and Equitable Treatment: Methanex v. United States and the Narrowing Scope of NAFTA Article 1105', *Law & Pol'y Int'l Bus.* 34 (2002–2003), pp. 343–392.

Kirgis, F.L., 'Custom on a Sliding Scale', *AJIL* 81 (1987), pp. 146–151.

Kishoiyian, Bernard, 'The Utility of Bilateral Investment Treaties in the Formulation of Customary International Law', *Northwestern J. Int'l L & Bus* 14(2) (1993), pp. 327–375.

Knoll-Tudor, Ioana, 'The Fair and Equitable Treatment Standard and Human Rights Norms', in P.M. Dupuy, F. Francioni and E.U. Petersmann (eds.), *Human Rights in International Investment Law and Arbitration* (Oxford: Oxford University Press, 2009), pp. 310–343.

Kolb, R., 'Selected Problems in the Theory of Customary International Law', *Netherlands ILR* 50 (2003), pp. 119–150.

Kopelmanas, L., 'Custom as Means of the Creation of the International Law', *British YIL* 18 (1937), pp. 127–151.

Laborde, Gustavo, 'The Case for Host State Claims in Investment Arbitration', *J. Int Disp Settl* 1(1) (2010), pp. 97–122.

Laird, I., 'Betrayal, Shock and Outrage – Recent Developments in NAFTA Article 1105', in T. Weiler (ed.) *NAFTA Investment Law and Arbitration: Past Issues, Current Practice, Future Prospects* (Ardsley: Transnational Publ. 2004), pp. 49–75.

Laird, I., 'A Community of Destiny – The Barcelona Traction Case and the Development of Shareholder Rights to Bring Investment Claims', in Todd Weiler (ed.), *International Investment Law and Arbitration: Leading Cases from the ICSID, NAFTA, Bilateral Treaties and Customary International Law* (London: Cameron May, 2005), pp. 77–96.

Lauterpacht, H., 'The World Bank Convention on the Settlement of International Investment Disputes', *Recueil d'Etudes de Droit International en Hommage à Paul Guggenheim* (Geneva: Tribune, 1968), pp. 642–664.

Leben, Charles, 'L'Évolution du droit international des investissements', *Journal CEPMLP*, 7(12) (2000).

Lee, Lawrence Jahoon, 'Barcelona Traction in the 21st Century: Revisiting its Customary and Policy Underpinnings 35 Years Later', *Stanford JIL* 42 (2006), pp. 237–289.

Legum, Barton, 'Representing States – A US Perspective', *Arbitration & ADR* 6 (2001), p. 46.

Legum, Barton, 'Dallas Workshop 2001: Commentary Scene III: ICSID Proceedings in the Absence of a Bilateral Investment Treaty', *Arb. Int'l* 18(3) (2002).

Legum, Barton, 'The Difficulties of Conciliation in Investment Treaty Cases: A Comment on Professor Jack C. Coe, "Toward a Complementary Use of Conciliation in Investor-State Disputes: A Preliminary Sketch"', *Mealey's Int'l Arb. Rep.* (2006).

Lévesque, C. and Newcombe, A., 'Commentary on the Canadian Model Foreign Promotion and Protection Agreement', in C. Brown (ed.), *Commentaries on Selected Model Investment Treaties* (Oxford: Oxford University Press, 2013), pp. 53–130.

Lévesque, C. 'Influences on the Canadian Model FIPA and US Model BIT: NAFTA Chapter 11 and Beyond', *Can. YIL* 44 (2006), pp. 249–298.

Liberti, Lahra, 'Investissements et droits de l'homme', in P. Kahn and T. Wälde (eds.), *New Aspects of International Investment Law* (Hague Academy of International Law, Leiden: Nijhoff, 2007), pp. 791–852.

Lillich, R.B., 'The Growing Importance of Customary International Human Rights Law', *Ga. J. Int'l & Comp. L.* 25 (1995/6), pp. 1–30.

Lorz, Ralph Alexander, 'Protection and Security (Including the NAFTA Approach)', in M. Bungenberg, J. Griebel, S. Hobe and A. Reinisch (eds.), *International Investment Law: A Handbook* (München: C.H. Beck, Oxford: Hart, Baden-Baden: Nomos, 2015), pp. 764–789.

Lowenfeld, Andeas F., 'Investment Agreements and International Law', *Columbia JTL* 42 (2003), pp. 123–130.

MacGibbon, I., 'General Assembly Resolutions: Custom, Practice and Mistaken Identity', in B. Cheng (ed.), *International Law: Teaching and Practice* (London: Stevens & Sons, 1982), pp. 10–26.

Maniruzzaman, A.F.M., 'State Contracts in Contemporary International Law: Monist versus Dualist Controversies', *EJIL* 12 (2001), pp. 309–328.

Mann, F.A., 'British Treaties for the Promotion and Protection of Investment', *British YIL* 52 (1981), pp. 241–254.

Mann, Howard, 'International Investment Agreements, Business and Human Rights: Key Issues and Opportunities', *IISD* (2008), pp. 1–42.

Mayeda, Graham, 'Playing Fair: The Meaning of Fair and Equitable Treatment in Bilateral Investment Treaties', *J. World Trade* 41(2) (2007), pp. 273–291.

McClane, Brock J., 'How Late in the Emergence of a Norm of Customary International Law May a Persistent Objector Object?', *I.L.S.A. J.I.L.* 13 (1989), pp. 1–26.

McCorquodale, Robert, 'An Inclusive International Legal System', *Leiden JIL* 17 (2004), pp. 477–504.

McLachlan, Campbell, 'Investment Treaties and General International Law', *ICLQ* 57 (2008), pp. 361–401.

Mendelson, Maurice, 'Disentangling Treaty and Customary International Law', *ASIL Proc.* 81 (1987), pp. 157–164.

Mendelson, Maurice, 'The Subjective Element in Customary International Law',
    British YIL 66 (1996), pp. 177–208.
Mendelson, Maurice, 'The Runaway Train: the Continuous Nationality Rule from
    the Panevezys-Saldutiskis Railway Case to Loewen', in T. Weiler (ed.)
    International Investment Law and Arbitration: Leading Cases from the
    ICSID, NAFTA, Bilateral Treaties and Customary International Law
    (London: Cameron May, 2005), pp. 97–149.
Menon, K.P., 'The Legal Personality of Individuals', *Sri Lanka J. Int'l L.* 6 (1994),
    pp. 127–156.
Meron, T., 'The Continuing Role of Custom in the Formation of International
    Humanitarian Law', *AJIL* 90 (1996), pp. 238–249.
Meron, T., 'Revival of Customary Humanitarian Law', *AJIL* 99 (2005), pp.
    817–834.
Mertus, J., 'Considering Nonstate Actors in the New Millennium: Toward
    Expanded Participation in Norm Generation and Norm Application',
    International Law and Politics 32 (2000), pp. 537–566.
Meyer, T.L., 'Codifying Custom', *Univ. Pennsylvania LR* 160 (2012), pp. 995–1069.
Moremen, Philip, 'National Court Decisions as State Practice: A Transnational
    Judicial Dialogue?', *North Carolina JIL & Comm Reg* 32 (2006), pp.
    259–309.
Muchlinski, Peter T., 'Policy Issues', in Peter Muchlinski, Federico Ortino and
    Christoph Schreuer (eds.), *The Oxford Handbook of International*
    Investment Law (Oxford: Oxford University Press, 2008), pp. 3–48.
Muller, Till, 'Customary Transnational Law: Attacking the Last Resort of State
    Sovereignty Conference on Democracy and the Transnational Private
    Sector', *Ind. J. Global Legal Stud.* 15 (2008), pp. 19–47.
Müllerson, R., 'On the Nature and Scope of Customary International Law',
    Austrian RIEL 2 (1997), pp. 341–360.
Müllerson, R., 'The Interplay of Objective and Subjective Elements in Customary
    Law', in K. Wellens (ed.), *International law: Theory and Practice: Essays in*
    Honour of Eric Suy (The Hague: Nijhoff, 1998), pp. 161–178.
Nollkaemper, A., 'The Role of Domestic Courts in the Case Law of the
    International Court of Justice', *Chinese JIL* 5 (2006), pp. 269–300.
Norman, George and Trachtman, Joel, 'The Customary International Law Game',
    AJIL 99 (2005), pp. 541–580.
Nowrot, Karsten, 'Legal Consequences of Globalization: The Status of NGO's
    Under International Law', *Ind. J. Global Legal Stud.* 6 (1999), pp. 579–645.
Öberg, M.D., 'The Legal Effects ofResolutions of the UN Security Council and
    General Assembly in the Jurisprudence of the ICJ', *EJIL* 16 (2006), pp.
    879–906.
Ochoa, Christiana, 'The Individual and Customary International Law Formation',
    Virginia JIL 48 (2007), pp. 119–186.

Orakhelashvili, Alexander, 'The Position of the Individual in International Law', *Cal. W. Int'l.J.* 31 (2001), pp. 241–276.

Orakhelashvili, Alexander, 'The Normative Basis of "Fair and Equitable Treatment": General International Law on Foreign Investment?', *Archiv des Völkerrechts* 1 (2008), pp. 74–105.

Orellana, M.A., 'International Law on Investment: The Minimum Standard of Treatment (MST)', *TDM* 3 (2004).

Paparinskis, Martins, 'Investment Treaty Interpretation and Customary Investment Law: Preliminary Remarks', in Chester Brown and Kate Miles (eds.), *Evolution in Investment Treaty Law and Arbitration* (Cambridge: Cambridge UP, 2011), pp. 65–96.

Paparinskis, Martins, 'Sources of Law and Arbitral Interpretations of Pari Materia Investment Protection Rules', in: O. K. Fauchald and A. Nollkaemper (eds.), *The Practice of International and National Courts and the (De-) Fragmentation of International Law* (Oxford; Portland: Hart Publ., 2012), pp. 87–115.

Parra, Antonio R., 'Principles Governing Foreign Investment, as Reflected in National Investment Codes', *ICSID Rev.* 7 (1992), pp. 428–452.

Parra, Antonio R., 'Applicable Law in Investor-State Arbitration', in: Arthur Rovine (ed.), *Contemporary Issues in International Arbitration and Mediation* (Leiden: Brill & Nijhoff, 2008), pp. 3–12.

Paulsson, J., 'Third-World Participation in International Investment Arbitration', *ICSID Rev.* 2 (1987), pp. 19–65.

Paulsson, J. 'Arbitration Without Privity', *ICSID Rev.* 10 (1995), pp. 232–257.

Paulsson, J. and Petrochilos, G., 'Neer-ly Misled?', *ICSID Rev.* 22(2) (2007), pp. 242–257.

Paust, Jordan J., 'The Complex Nature, Sources and Evidences of Customary Human Rights', *Ga. J. Int'l & Comp. L.* 25 (1996), pp. 147–164.

Paust, Jordan J., 'Non-State Actor Participation in International Law and the Pretense of Exclusion', *Virginia JIL* 51(4) (2011), pp. 977–1004.

Pellet, Alain, 'Shaping the Future of International Law: The Role of the World Court in Law-Making', in M.H. Arsanjani *et al.* (eds.), *Looking to the Future: Essays on International Law in Honor of W. Michael Reisman* (Leiden: Martinus Nijhoff, 2011), pp. 1065–1083.

Pellet, Alain, 'Article 38', in A. Zimmermann *et al.* (eds.), *The Statute of the International Court of Justice: A Commentary* (2nd edn., Oxford: Oxford University Press, 2012), pp. 731–870.

Peterson, Niels, 'Customary Law without Custom? Rules, Principles, and the Role of State Practice in International Norm Creation', *American University ILR* 23 (2008), pp. 275–310.

Peterson, Luke Eric, 'Human Rights and Bilateral investment Treaties. Mapping the Role of Human Rights Law within Investor-State Arbitration', Rights &

Democracy, *International Centre for Human Rights and Democratic Development* (2009), pp. 1–45.

Picherack, J. Roman, 'The Expanding Scope of the Fair and Equitable Treatment Standard: Have Recent Tribunals Gone Too Far?', *J. World Invest. & Trade* 9(4) (2008), pp. 255–291.

Pilch, Gennady, 'The Development and Expansion of Bilateral Investment Treaties', *ASIL Proc.* 96 (1992).

Porterfield, M.C., 'An International Common Law of Investor Rights?', *U. Pa. J. Int'l Econ. L.* 27 (2006), pp. 79–114.

Porterfield, M.C., 'State Practice and the (Purported) Obligation under Customary International Law to Provide Compensation for Regulatory Expropriations', *North Carolina JIL & Comm Reg* 37 (2011), pp. 159–197.

Reiner, Clara and Schreuer, Christoph, 'Human Rights and International Investment Arbitration', in P.M. Dupuy, F. Francioni and E.U. Petersmann (eds.), *Human Rights in International Investment Law and Arbitration* (Oxford: Oxford University Press, 2009), pp. 82–96.

Reinisch, August, 'Legality of Expropriations', in A. Reinisch (ed.), *Standards of Investment Protection* (Oxford: Oxford University Press, 2008), pp. 171–204.

Reisman, W. Michael and Sloane, Robert D., 'Indirect Expropriation and its Valuation in the BIT Generation', *British YIL* 74 (2003), pp. 115–150.

Reuter, P., 'La personnalité juridique internationale du Comité international de la Croix-Rouge', *Studies and Essays on International Humanitarian Law and Red Cross Principles in Honour of Jean Pictet* (The Hague: Nijhoff/Geneva : ICRC, 1984), pp. 783–791.

Roach, J.A., 'Today's Customary International Law of the Sea', *Ocean Development and International Law*, 45 (2014), pp. 239–259.

Roberts, Anthea, 'Traditional and Modern Approaches to Customary International Law: A Reconciliation', *AJIL* 95 (2001), pp. 757–791.

Roberts, Anthea, 'Power and Persuasion in Investment Treaty Interpretation: The Dual Role of States', *AJIL* 104 (2010), pp. 179–225.

Roberts, Anthea, 'Who Killed Article 38(1)(b)? A Reply to Bradley and Gulati', *Duke J Comp & IL* 21 (2010), pp. 173–190.

Roberts, Anthea and Sivakumaran, Sandesh, 'Lawmaking by Nonstate Actors: Engaging Armed Groups in the Creation of International Humanitarian Law', *Yale JIL* 37 (2012), pp. 107–152.

Roberts, Anthea, 'Comparative International Law? The Role of National Courts in Creating and Enforcing International Law', *ICLQ* 60 (2011), pp. 57–92.

Roberts, Anthea, 'Custom, Public Law and the Human Rights Analogy', *EJIL Talks*, 14 August 2013.

Robinson, R., 'Expropriation in the Restatement (Revised)', *AJIL* 78 (1984), pp. 176–178.

Root, Elihu, 'The Basis of Protection to Citizens Residing Abroad', *AJIL* 4 (1910), pp. 517–528.

Rubins, N., 'Loewen v. United States: the Burial of an Investor-State Arbitration Claim', *Arb. Int.* 21 (2005), pp. 1–36.

Ruzza, Alice, 'Expropriation and Nationalization', in Rüdiger Wolfrum (ed.), *Max Planck Encyclopedia of Public International Law* (Oxford: Oxford University Press, vol. 9, 2013).

Ryan, Margaret Clare, 'Glamis Gold, Ltd. v. The United States and the Fair and Equitable Treatment Standard', *McGill LJ* 56(4) (2011), pp. 919–958.

Salacuse, Jeswald W., 'BIT by BIT: The Growth of Bilateral Investment Treaties and Their Impact on Foreign Investment in Developing Countries', *Int'l L.* 24 (1990), pp. 655–675.

Salacuse, Jeswald W., 'Towards a Global Treaty on Foreign Investment: the Search for a Grand Bargain', in N. Horn and S. Kröll (eds.), *Arbitrating Foreign Investment Disputes. Procedural and Substantive Legal Aspects* (The Hague: Kluwer International Law, 2004), pp. 51–88.

Salacuse, Jeswald W., 'The Treatification of International Investment Law: a Victory of Form Over Life? A Crossroads Crossed?', *TDM* 3(3) (2006).

Sanan, Manu, 'International Investment Law; Questions Riddling an Answer', *Trade, law and Development* 2(1) (2010), pp. 9–18.

Sands, P., 'Treaty, Custom and the Cross-fertilization of International Law', *Yale Human Rights & Dev. law journal* 88 (1998), pp. 39–60.

Schabas, W., 'Customary Law or 'Judge-Made' Law: Judicial Creativity at the UN Criminal Tribunals', in J. Doria *et al.* (eds.), *The Legal Regime of the International Criminal Court: Essays in Honour of Professor Igor Blishchenko* (Leiden: Martinus Nijhoff, 2009), pp. 77–101.

Schachter, O., 'Compensation for Expropriation', *AJIL* 78 (1986), pp. 119–130.

Schachter, O., 'Entangled Treaty and Custom', in Yoram Dinstein (ed.), *International Law at a Time of Perplexity: Essays in Honour of Shabtai Rosenne* (Drodrecht: Martinus Nijhoff, 1989), pp. 717–738.

Schachter, O., 'New Custom: Power, Opinio Juris and Contrary Practice', in J Makarczyk (ed.), *Theory of International Law at the Threshold of the 21st Century: Essays in Honour of Krzysztof Skubieszewski* (The Hague: Kluwer Law International, 1996), pp. 531–540.

Schill, Stephan W, 'Fair and Equitable Treatment as an Embodiment of the Rule of Law', in R. Hofmann and C. Tams (eds.), *The International Convention on the Settlement of Investment Disputes (ICSID): Taking Stock after 40 Years* (Baden-Baden: Nomos 2007), pp. 31–72.

Schill, S.W., book review of Tudor's book, *EJIL* 20 (2009).

Schill, Stephan W., 'From Sources to Discourse: Investment Treaty Jurisprudence as the New Custom?', in *Is There an Evolving Customary International Law on Investment?* (London: BIICL, 2011).

Schill, Stephan W., 'Multilateralization: An Ordering Paradigm for International Investment Law', in M. Bungenberg, J. Griebel, S. Hobe and A. Reinisch (eds.), *International Investment Law: A Handbook* (Munich: C.H. Beck; Oxford: Hart; Baden-Baden: Nomos, 2015), pp. 1817–1838.

Schmid, M., 'Switzerland', in C. Brown (ed.), *Commentaries on Selected Model Investment Treaties* (Oxford: Oxford University Press, 2013), pp. 651–696.

Schreuer, C., 'Diversity and Harmonization of Treaty Interpretation in Investment Arbitration', in M. Fitzmaurice, O. Elias & P. Merkouris (eds.), *Treaty Interpretation and the Vienna Convention on the Law of Treaties: 30 Years On* (Leiden: Martinus Nijhoff Publishers 2010), pp. 129–151.

Schwebel, Stephen M., 'The Story of the U. N.'s Declaration on Permanent Sovereignty over Natural Resources', *ABAJ* 49 (1963), pp. 463–496.

Schwebel, Stephen M., 'The Effect of Resolutions of the U.N. General Assembly on Customary International Law', *ASIL Proc.* 73 (1979), pp. 301–309.

Schwebel, Stephen M., 'Investor-State Disputes and the Development of International Law: The Influence of Bilateral Investment Treaties on Customary International Law', *ASIL Proc.* 98 (2004), pp. 27–30.

Schwebel, Stephen M., 'The United States 2004 Model Bilateral Investment Treaty: An Exercise in the Regressive Development of International Law', in *Global Reflections on International Law, Commerce and Dispute Resolution, Liber Amicorum in honour of Robert Briner* (Paris: ICC Pub. No. 693, 2005), pp. 815–823.

Schwebel, Stephen M., 'Is Neer far from Fair and Equitable?', *Arb. Int'l* 27(4) (2011), pp. 555–561.

Scott, G.L. and Carr, C.L., 'The International Court of Justice and the Treaty/Custom Dichotomy', *Texas ILJ* 16 (1981), pp. 347–359.

Séfériadès, S., 'Aperçu sur la coutume juridique internationale et notamment sur son fondement', *RGDIP* 43 (1936).

Shan, W. and Gallaguer, N., 'China', in C. Brown (ed.), *Commentaries on Selected Model Investment Treaties* (Oxford: Oxford University Press, 2013).

Sharpe, Jeremy K., 'Representing a Respondent State in Investment Arbitration', in Chiara Giorgetti (ed.), *Litigating International Investment Disputes: A Practitioner's Guide* (Leiden; Boston: Brill Nijhoff, 2014), pp. 41–79.

Simma, B. and Alston, P., 'The Sources of Human Rights Law: Custom, *Jus Cogens*, and General Principles', *Australian YIL* 12 (1988–1989), pp. 82–108.

Simma B. and Pulkowski, D., 'Two Worlds, but Not Apart: International Investment Law and General International Law', in M. Bungenberg, J. Griebel, S. Hobe and A. Reinisch (eds.), *International Investment Law: A Handbook* (Munich: C.H. Beck, Oxford: Hart, Baden-Baden: Nomos, 2015), pp. 361–371.

Sinclair, Anthony C., 'The Substance of Nationality Requirements in Investment Treaty Arbitration', *ICSID Rev.* 20(2) (2005), pp. 357–388.

Siwy, A., 'Investment Arbitration – Indirect Expropriation and the Legitimate Expectations of the Investor', in Christian Klausegger, Peter Klein, *et al.* (eds.), *Austrian Arbitration Yearbook* (Vienna: C.H. Beck, Stämpfli & Manz 2007), pp. 355–377.

Skubiszewski, K., 'Elements of Custom and the Hague Court', *ZaöRV* 31 (1971), pp. 810–854.

Skubiszewski, K., 'Resolutions of the UN General Assembly and Evidence of Custom' in *Essays in Honour of Roberto Ago* (vol. 1, Milan: Giuffré, 1987), pp. 503–513.

Sohn, L., 'The International Law of Human Rights: A Reply to Recent Criticisms', *Hofstra L Rev* 9 (1981), pp. 347–356.

Sohn, L., 'The Law of the Sea: Customary International Law Developments', *American University LR* 34 (1985), pp. 271–280.

Sohn, L., '"Generally Accepted" International Rules', *Washington L Rev* 61 (1986), pp. 1073–1080.

Sornarajah, M., 'Power and Justice in Foreign Investment Arbitration', *J. Int'l Arb.* 14(3) (1997), pp. 103–140.

Sornarajah, M., 'The Fair and Equitable Standard of Treatment: Whose Fairness? Whose Equity?', in Federico Ortino *et al.* (eds.), *Investment Treaty Law: Current Issues II* (London: BIICL, 2007), pp. 167–181.

Sourgens, Frédéric G., 'Law's Laboratory: Developing International Law on Investment Protection as Common Law', *Northwestern J. Int'l L & Bus* 34 (2014), pp. 181–247.

Spiermann, O., 'Applicable Law' in: P. Muchlinski, F. Ortino and C. Schreuer (ed.), *The Oxford Handbook of International Investment Law* (Oxford: Oxford University Press, 2008), pp. 1373–1390.

Steer, C., 'Non-State Actors in International Criminal Law', in J. d'Aspremont (ed.), *Participants in the International Legal System: Multiple Perspectives on Non-State Actors in International Law* (London: Routledge, 2011), pp. 295–310.

Stern, Brigitte, 'Custom at the Heart of International Law', *Duke J Comp & IL* 11 (2001), pp. 89–108.

Swaine, Edward T., 'Rational Custom', *Duke L. J.* 52 (2002), pp. 559–627.

Swart, M., 'Judicial Lawmaking at the ad hoc Tribunals: The Creative Use of the Sources of International Law and "Adventurous Interpretation"', *ZaöRV* 70 (2010), pp. 459–486.

Tams, C. and Tzanakopoulos, A., '*Barcelona Traction*: the ICJ as an Agent of Legal Development', *Leiden JIL* 23 (2010), pp. 781–800.

Tams, C., 'The Sources of International Investment Law', in T. Gazzini and E. de Brabandere (eds.), *International Investment Law: The Sources of Rights and Obligations* (Leiden: Nijhoff & Brill, 2012), pp. 320–331.

Tasioulas, J., 'In Defence of Relative Normativity: Communitarian Values and the Nicaragua Case', *OJLS* 16 (1996), pp. 85–128.

Tasioulas, J., 'Customary International Law and the Quest for Global Justice', in A. Perreau-Saussine and J.B. Murphy (eds.), *The Nature of Customary Law: Philosophical, Historical and Legal Perspectives* (Cambridge: Cambridge University Press, 2007), pp. 307–335.

Thomas, J.C., 'Fair and Equitable Treatment under NAFTA's Investment Chapter; Remarks', *ASIL Proc.* 96 (2002).

Thomas, J.C., 'Reflections on Article 1105 of NAFTA: History, State Practice and the Influence of Commentators', *ICSID Rev.* 17(1) (2002), pp. 21–101.

Tomka, Peter, 'Custom and the International Court of Justice', *Law & Prac Int'l Cts & Tribunals* 12(2) (2013), pp. 195–216.

Toral, Mehmet and Schultz, Thomas, 'The State, a Perpetual Respondent in Investment Arbitration? Some Unorthodox Considerations', in Michael Waibel, Asha Kaushal, Kyo-Hwa Liz Chung, and Claire Balchin (eds.), *The Backlash Against Investment Arbitration: Perceptions And Reality* (Alphen aan den Rijn: Kluwer Law International, 2010), pp. 577–602.

Treves, T., 'Customary International Law', in Rüdiger Wolfrum (ed.), *Max Planck Encyclopedia of Public International Law* (Oxford: Oxford University Press, vol. 9, 2012).

Trimble, Phillip R., 'A Revisionist View of Customary International Law', *UCLA L. Rev.* 33 (1986), p. 665.

Tuck, Andrew P., 'The "Fair And Equitable Treatment" Standard Pursuant to the Investment Provisions of the U.S. Free Trade Agreements with Peru, Colombia and Panama', *L. & Bus. Rev. Am.* 16 (2010), pp. 385–408.

Tucker, Edwin W., 'Has the Individual Become the Subject of International Law?', *U. Cin. L. Rev.* 34 (1965), p. 341.

Tunkin, G.I., 'Remarks on the Juridical Nature of Customary Norms of International Law', *California Law Review* 49 (1961), pp. 419–430.

Vandevelde, K.J., 'The BIT Program: A Fifteen-Year Appraisal', *ASIL Proc.* 86 (1992), pp. 532–540.

Vandevelde, K.J., 'U.S. Bilateral Investment Treaties: The Second Wave', *Michigan JIL* 14 (1993), pp. 621–704.

Vandevelde, K.J., 'A Comparison of the 2004 and 1994 US Model BITs', *Yb Int'l Invest. L. & Pol.* 1 (2008–2009), p. 283.

Vandevelde, K.J., 'Model Bilateral Investment Treaties: the Way Forward', *Sw. J. Int'l L.* 18 (2011), pp. 307–314.

Vasciannie, Stephen, 'The Fair and Equitable Treatment Standard in International Investment Law and Practice', *British YIL* 70 (1999), pp. 99–164.

Vazquez, Carlos M., 'Direct vs. Indirect Obligations of Corporations Under International Law', *Colum. J. Transnat'l L.* 43 (2005), pp. 927–959.

Verdier, Pierre-Hugues, 'Cooperative States: International Relations, State Responsibility and the Problem of Custom', *Virginia JIL* 42 (2002), pp. 839–867.

Verdier P. -H. and Voeten, E., 'Precedent, Compliance, and Change in Customary International Law: An Explanatory Theory', *AJIL* 108 (2014), pp. 389–434.

Vicuña, F. Orrego, 'Changing Approaches to the Nationality of Claims in the Context of Diplomatic Protection and International Dispute Settlement', in S. Schlemmer-Schulte and K.-Y. Tung (eds.) *Liber amicorum Ibrahim F.I. Shihata: International Finance and Development Law* (The Hague: Kluwer Law International, 2001), pp. 503–525.

Vicuña, F. Orrego, 'Customary International Law in a Global Community: Tailor Made?', *Estudios Internacionales* 148 (2005), pp. 21–38.

Virally, M., 'The Sources of International Law', in M. Sørensen (ed.), *Manual of Public International Law* (London, Melbourne, Toronto, New York: Macmillan, 1968), pp. 116–174.

Walden, Raphael M., 'The Subjective Element in the Formation of Customary International Law', *Israel L. Rev.* 12 (1977), pp. 344–364.

Weil, Prosper, 'Toward Relative Normativity in International Law', *AJIL* 77 (1983), pp. 413–432.

Weiler, T., 'NAFTA Investment Arbitration and the Growth of International Economic Law', *Bus. L. Int'l* 2 (2002), pp. 405–435.

Weiler, Todd, 'Methanex Corp. v. U. S. A:Turning the Page on NAFTA Chapter Eleven?', *J. World Invest. & Trade* 6(6) (2005), p. 903.

Weiler, T. & Laird, I., 'Standards of Treatment', in Peter Muchlinski, Federico Ortino and Christoph Schreuer (eds.), *The Oxford Handbook of International Investment Law* (Oxford: Oxford University Press, 2008), pp. 259–304.

Weiler, Todd, 'An Historical Analysis of the Function of the Minimum Standard of Treatment in International Investment Law', in Todd Weiler and Freya Baetens (eds.), *New Directions in International Economic Law: In Memoriam Thomas Wälde* (Leiden: Martinus Nijhoff, 2011).

Weisburd, Arthur Mark, 'Customary International Law: The Problem of Treaties', *Vand. J. Transnat'l L.* 21 (1988), p. 1.

Westberg, Arthur Mark, 'Compensation in Cases of Expropriation and Nationalization: Awards of the Iran-United States Claims Tribunal', *ICSID Rev.* 5 (1990), pp. 256–291.

Wisner, R. and Gallus, N., 'Nationality Requirements in Investor-State Arbitration', *J. World Invest. & Trade* 5 (2004), pp. 927–945.

Wolfke, K., 'Some Persistent Controversies Regarding Customary International Law', *NYBIL* 24 (1993), pp. 1–24.

Wood, Michael, 'Teachings of the Most Highly Qualified Publicists (Art. 38 (1)ICJ Statute)', in Rüdiger Wolfrum (ed.), *Max Planck Encyclopedia of Public International Law* (Oxford: Oxford University Press, vol. 9, 2012).

Wood, Michael and Sender, Omri, 'State Practice', in Rüdiger Wolfrum (ed.), *Max Planck Encyclopedia of Public International Law* (Oxford: Oxford University Press, 2013).

Wouters, J. and Ryngaert, C., 'Impact on the Process of the Formation of Customary International Law', in M. Kamminga & M. Scheinin (eds.), *The Impact of Human Rights Law on General International Law* (Oxford: Oxford University Press, 2009), pp. 111–131.

Wuerth, Ingrid, 'International Law in Domestic Courts and *the Jurisdictional Immunities of the State Case*', *Melbourne JIL* 13 (2012), pp. 819–837.

Yannaca-Small, Katia, 'Fair and Equitable Treatment Standard: Recent Developments', in A. Reinisch (ed.), *Standards of Investment Protection* (Oxford: Oxford University Press, 2008), pp. 111–130.

Yasuaki, O., 'Is the International Court of Justice an Emperor Without Clothes?', *International Legal Theory* 81 (2002), pp. 1–28.

Zamora, Stephen, 'Is there Customary International Economic Law?', *German YIL* 32 (1989), pp. 9–42.

Zedalis, R.J., 'Claims by Individuals in International Economic Law: NAFTA Developments', *American Rev. Int'l Arb.* 7(2) (1996), pp. 115–147.

Zemanek, K., 'What is 'State Practice' and who Makes It?' in U. Beyerlin *et al.* (eds.), *Festschrift für Rudolf Bernhardt* (Berlin: Springer-Verlag, 1995), pp. 289–306.

IV   Courses

Abi-Saab, Georges, 'Cours général de droit international public', *Rec. des cours*, 207 (1987-VII), pp. 9–463.

Alvarez, José E., 'The Public International Law Regime Governing International Investment', *Rec. des cours*, 344 (2009), pp. 193–452.

Barberis, J.A., 'Nouvelles questions concernant la personnalité juridique internationale', *Rec. des cours*, 179 (1983-I), pp. 145–304.

Baxter, R., 'Treaties and Custom', *Rec. des cours*, 129 (1970), pp. 25–106.

Bedjaoui, Mohammed, 'Problèmes récents de succession d'États dans les États nouveaux', *Rec. des cours*, 130 (1970-II), pp. 455–586.

Cahier, Philippe, 'Changement et continuité du droit international: Cours général de droit international public', *Rec. des cours*, 195 (1985-VI), pp. 9–374.

Conforti, Benedetto, 'Cours général de droit international public', *Rec. des cours*, 212 (1988-V), pp. 9–210.

Dinstein, Y., 'The Interaction between Customary International Law and Treaties', *Rec. des cours*, 322 (2006), pp. 243–428.

Dupuy, Pierre-Marie, 'L'unité de l'ordre juridique international', *Rec. des cours*, 297 (2002), pp. 9–496.

Ferrari-Bravo, L., 'Méthodes de recherche de la coutume internationale dans la pratique des États', *Rec. des cours*, 192 (1985), pp. 233–330.

Fitzmaurice, G., 'The General Principles of International Law', *Rec. des cours*, 92 (1957), pp. 1–228.

Franck, T.M., 'Fairness in the International Legal and Institutional System: General Course on Public International Law', *Rec. des cours* 240 (1993), pp. 9–498.

Henkin, L., 'International Law: Politics, Values and Function: General Course on Public International Law', *Rec. des cours*, 216 (1989), pp. 9–416.

Jennings, R., 'General Course on Principles of International Law', *Rec. des cours*, 121 (1967-II), pp. 323–606.

Jiménez de Aréchaga, E., 'General Course in Public International Law', *Rec. des cours*, 159 (1978), pp. 1–343.

Juillard, Patrick, 'L'évolution des sources du droit des investissements', *Rec. des cours*, 250 (1994), pp. 9–216.

Kelsen, H., 'Théorie du droit international public', *Rec. des cours*, 84 (1953-III), pp. 1–204.

Leben, Ch., 'La théorie du contrat d'État et l'évolution du droit international des investissements', *Rec. des cours*, 302 (2003), pp. 197–386.

Makonnen, Yilma, 'State Succession in Africa: Selected Problems', *Rec. des cours*, 200 (1986-V), pp. 93–234.

Mendelson, Maurice H., 'The Formation of Customary International Law', *Rec. des cours*, 192 (1985), pp. 155–410.

Schachter, O., 'International Law in Theory and Practice: General Course in Public International Law', *Rec. des cours*, 178 (1982), pp. 9–395.

Sørensen, M., 'Principes de droit international public', *Rec. des cours*, 101 (1960-III), pp. 1–254.

Tomuschat, C., 'Obligations Arising for States Without or Against Their Will', *Rec. des cours*, 241 (1993), pp. 195–374.

Treves, T., 'Codification du droit international et pratique des Etats dans le droit de la mer', *Rec. des cours* 223 (1990), pp. 9–302.

Waldock, H., 'General Course on Public International Law', *Rec. des cours* 106 (1962), pp. 1–252.

Weil, Prosper, 'Le droit international en quête de son identité, Cours général de droit international public', *Rec. des cours*, 237 (1992-VI), pp. 9–370.

V Treaties

A. Multilateral treaties

ASEAN Comprehensive Investment Agreement (ACIA) (2012).

Convention for the Protection of Human Rights and Fundamental Freedom, Protocol 11 of 1st Novembers 1998.

Convention on the Settlement of Investment Disputes between States and Nationals of Other States, 18 March 1965, entered into force 14 Oct. 1966, 575 *U.N.T.S.* 160; 4 *I.L.M.* 532 (1965).

Convention on the Prevention and Punishment of the Crime of Genocide, 1948, entered into force 12 Jan. 1951, 78 *U.N.T.S.* 277.

Dominican Republic-Central America-United States Free Trade Agreement (2006 to 2009).

Geneva Convention on the High Seas, 29 April 1958, entered into force 30 September 1962 450 *U.N.T.S.* 11.

Montevideo Convention on the Rights and Duties of States, 26 Dec. 1933, entered into force 26 Dec. 1934, 165 *L.N.T.S.* 19.

Multilateral Agreement on Investment: Draft Consolidated Text, DAFFE/MAI(98)7/REV1 (22 April 1998).

North American Free Trade Agreement, signed on 17 December 1992 and came into force on 1 January 1994, 1.

Statute of the I. C.J.,reprinted in International Court of Justice, Charter of the United Nations, Statute and Rules of Court and other Documents 61 (No. 4 1978).

Titles and Texts of the Draft Articles on Responsibility of States for Internationally Wrongful Acts Adopted by the Drafting Committee on Second Reading, 26 July 2001, U.N. Doc. A/CN.4/L.602/Rev.1.ILC.

Vienna Convention on Succession of States in Respect of Treaties, signed on 23 August 1978, entered into force on 6 November 1996, 1946 *U.N.T.S*, 3 *I.L. M.*, 17 (1978).

UNCITRAL Arbitral Rules, UN Doc. A/RES/31/98; 15 *I.L.M.* 701 (1976) revised in 2010.

B.   Bilateral investment treaties

Australia–Mexico BIT (2005)
Belgium/Luxembourg Economic Union–Peru BIT (2005)
Belgium/Luxembourg–Cyprus BIT (1999)
Canada Model BIT (2004)
Canada–China BIT (2014)
Canada–Czech Republic BIT (2009)
Canada–Jordan BIT (2009)
Canada–Latvia BIT (2009)
Canada–Peru BIT (2007)
Canada–Romania BIT (2009)
Canada–Slovakia BIT (2010)
China–Mexico BIT (2008)
Colombian Model BIT (2008)

Czech Republic–Mexico BIT (2002)
Iceland–Mexico BIT (2005)
India–Mexico BIT (2007)
Italy–Bangladesh BIT
Japan–Laos BIT (2008)
Netherlands–Czech Rep. BIT.
Switzerland–Venezuela BIT (1994)
Switzerland–Tanzania BIT (2006)
Switzerland–Namibia BIT (2000)
Switzerland–India BIT (2000)
Switzerland–Mozambique BIT (2004)
Switzerland–Serbia BIT (2011)
Switzerland–Philippines BIT (1999)
Switzerland–Oman BIT (2005)
Switzerland–Mongolia BIT (1999)
Switzerland–Mauritius BIT (1978)
Switzerland–Libya BIT (2004)
Switzerland–Jordan BIT (2001)
Switzerland–Guatemala BIT (2005)
Switzerland–United Arab Emirates BIT (1999)
Switzerland–Lebanon BIT (2001)
Trinidad and Tobago–Mexico BIT (2006)
United Kingdom–Mexico BIT (2006)
US Model BIT (2004)
US Model BIT (2012)
US–Albania BIT (1995)
US–Armenia BIT (1992)
US–Azerbaijan BIT (1997)
US–Bahrain BIT (1999)
US–Bolivia BIT (1998)
US–Croatia BIT (1996).
US–Ecuador BIT (1993)
US–EL Salvador BIT (1999)
US–Estonia BIT (1994)
US–Georgia BIT (1994)
US–Honduras BIT (1995)
US–Jamaica BIT (1994)
US–Jordan BIT (1997)
US–Kazakhstan BIT (1992)
US–Kyrgyzstan BIT (1993)
US–Latvia BIT (1995)
US–Lithuania BIT (1998)

US–Moldova BIT (1993)
US–Mongolia BIT (1994)
US–Mozambique BIT (1998)
US–Rwanda BIT (2008)
US–Trinidad and Tobago BIT (1994)
US–Ukraine BIT (1994)
US–Uruguay BIT (2005)

C.   Free trade agreements

Agreement Establishing the ASEAN–Australia–New Zealand Free Trade Area (2009)
ASEAN–Australia–New Zealand FTA (AANZFTA) (2010)
Canada–Chile FTA (1997)
Canada–Colombia FTA (2011)
Canada–Israel FTA (1997)
Canada–Jordan FTA (2012)
Canada–Peru FTA (2009)
Canada–European Free Trade Association FTA (2009)
Chile–Australia FTA (2009)
China–New Zealand FTA (2008)
China–Peru FTA (2009)
EU–Canada Comprehensive and Economic Trade Agreement (CETA), signed in 2014
Japan–Brunei FTA (2007)
Japan–Mexico Treaty on Strengthening of the Economic Partnership (2005)
Korea–Singapore FTA (2006)
Malaysia–New Zealand FTA (2009)
Mexico–European Free Trade Association FTA (2001)
Mexico–European Union FTA (2000)
Mexico–Israel FTA (2000)
US–Australia FTA (2005)
US–Chile FTA (2004)
US–Colombia FTA (2012)
US–Morocco FTA (2006)
US–Oman FTA (2009)
US–Singapore FTA (2004)
US–Korea FTA (2012)
US–Panama Trade Promotion Agreement (2011)
US–Peru Trade Promotion Agreement (2009)

D. Others

Canadian Model Foreign Investment Protection and Promotion Agreement (2004).
United States Model BIT (2012)

VI   Resolutions

International Law Commission, *Draft Articles on Diplomatic Protection with commentaries*, Text adopted by the ILC at its fifty-eighth session, in 2006, and submitted to the General Assembly as a part of the Commission's report covering the work of that session (UN doc. A/61/10).
Institut de Droit International, 'The Elaboration of General Multilateral Conventions and of Non-contractual Instruments Having a Normative Function or Objective', Session of Cairo, 1987, in *Tableau des résolutions adoptées (1957–1991)* (Paris: Pedone, 1992).
Institut de Droit international, Resolution on 'The Proper Law of the Contract in Agreements between a State and a Foreign Private Person', in *Tableau des résolutions adoptées (1957–1991)* (Paris: Pedone, 1992).
United Nations, General Assembly, *Declaration of Principles of International Law Concerning Friendly Relations and Cooperation Among States in Accordance with the Charter of the United Nations*, Res. 2625 (XXV), of 24 October 1970.
United Nations, General Assembly, Res. 3171, U.N. GAOR, 28th Sess., Supp. No. 30, at 52, U.N. Doc. A/9030 (1974), in *ILM* 13 (1974).
United Nations, General Assembly, Res. 3281, U.N. GAOR, 29th Sess., Supp. No. 31, at 50–55, U.N. Doc. A/9631 (1974), in *ILM* 14 (1975).
United Nations, General Assembly, Res. 1803 (XVII), 14 December 1962.
United Nations, General Assembly, Res. 1803, 14 December 1962, U.N. GAOR, 17th Sess., Supp. No. 17, at 15, U.N. Doc. A/5217 (1962), in *I.L.M.* 2 (1963).
United Nations, General Assembly, Res. 3281 (XXIX), 12 December 1974.
United Nations, Security Council resolution 2125 (2013).
United Nations, Security Council resolution 1838 (2008).

VII   Reports

American Law Institute, *Restatement of the Law Third: the Foreign Relations Law of the United States*, vol 1, ch 1, St Paul, 1987.
'Draft Convention on the International responsibility of States for injuries to Aliens', prepared for the International Law Commission by Sohn and Baxter of the Harvard Law School in 1961, in: *AJIL* 55 (1961), pp. 545, 553.

International Law Association, 'Report' by A.K. Bjorklund and A. Reinisch, ILA
    Study Group on the Role of Soft-Law Instruments in International
    Investment Law, ILA Conference, Sofia (2012).
International Law Association, 'General Public International Law and
    International Investment Law – A Research Sketch on Selected Issues', *The
    International Law Association German Branch Sub-Committee on
    Investment Law* (2009).
International Law Association, 'Sources of International Investment Law', report
    by M. Hirsch, ILA Study Group on the Role of Soft Law Instruments in
    International Investment Law (2011).
International Law Association, 'Preliminary Report, Principles on the Engagement
    of Domestic Courts with International Law', report by A. Tzanakopoulos,
    ILA Study Group: Principles on the Engagement of Domestic Courts with
    International Law.
International Law Association, 'General Public International Law and
    International Investment Law – A Research Sketch on Selected Issues', *The
    International Law Association German Branch Sub-Committee on
    Investment Law* (2009).
International Law Association, 'Statement of Principles Applicable to the
    Formation of General Customary International Law', Final Report of the
    Committee on the Formation of Customary Law, Conference Report
    London (2000).
International Law Association, 'Second Report of the Committee Non-State Actors
    in International Law: Lawmaking and Participation Rights', Committee on
    'Non State Actors' (2012).
International Law Commission, 'Interim Report of the Special Representative of
    the Secretary-General of the United Nations on the Issue of Human Rights
    and Transnational Corporations and Other Business Enterprises', John
    Ruggie, UN Doc. E/CN.4/2006/97, 22 February 2006.
International Law Commission, 'Report of the International Law Commission on
    the work of its thirty-second session' 5 May 25 July 1980, UN doc. A/35/10,
    Yearbook ILC 1980, vol. II (Part Two).
International Law Commission, 'Report of the ILC on the Work of its Fifty-Third
    Session', Official Records of the General Assembly', Fifty-sixth session,
    Supplement No. 10 (UN doc. A/56/10).
International Law Commission, 'Report of the ILC on the work of its sixty-fourth
    session', 7 May to 1 June and 2 July to 3 August 2012, UN Doc. A/67/10, 2012.
International Law Commission, 'Formation and Evidence of Customary
    International Law, Elements in the Previous Work of the ILC that Could
    be Particularly Relevant to the Topic', Memorandum by the Secretariat,
    International Law Commission Sixty-fifth session Geneva, 5 May-7 June
    and 8 July-9 August 2013, UN doc. A/CN.4/659.

International Law Commission, 'First Report on Formation and Evidence of Customary International Law', by Michael Wood, Special Rapporteur, ILC Sixty-fifth session, Geneva, 6 May-7 June and 8 July-9 August 2013, UN doc. A/CN.4/663, 17 May 2013.

International Law Commission, 'Second Report on Identification of Customary International Law', by Michael Wood, Special Rapporteur, ILC, Sixty-sixth session, Geneva, 5 May-6 June and 7 July-8 August 2014, UN doc. A/CN.4/672.

International Law Commission, 'Third Report on Identification of Customary International Law', by Michael Wood, Special Rapporteur, ILC, Sixty-seventh session, Geneva, 4 May-5 June and 6 July-7 August 2014, UN doc. A/CN.4/682.

International Law Commission, 'Text of the Draft Conclusions Provisionally adopted by the Drafting Committee, Sixty-seventh session, Geneva, 4 May-5 June and 6 July-7 August 2014, 14 July 2015, A/CN.4/L.869.

International Law Commission, 'Report of the International Law Commission on the work of its thirty-second session' 5 May 25 July 1980, UN doc. A/35/10, Yearbook ILC 1980, vol. II (Part Two).

International Law Commission, 'Conclusions of the work of the Study Group on the Fragmentation of International Law: Difficulties arising from the Diversification and Expansion of International Law', adopted by the ILC at its Fifty-eighth session, in 2006, and submitted to the General Assembly as a part of the Commission's report covering the work of that session (UN doc. A/61/10, para. 251), in: ILC Yearbook, 2006, vol. II (2).

OECD Committee on International Investment and Multinational Enterprise, Inter-Governmental Agreements Relating to Investment in Developing Countries, Doc. No. 84/14, 27 May 1984.

OECD, Draft Convention on the Protection of Foreign Property, adopted on 12 October 1967, ILM 7 (1967).

OECD, 'Fair and Equitable Treatment Standard in International Investment Law', Working Papers on International Investment Law, No. 2004/3 (2004).

OECD, 'International Investment Law: A Changing Landscape: A Companion Volume to International Investment Perspectives' (2005).

OECD, 'International Investment Law: Understanding Concepts and Tracking Innovations' (2008).

'Report of the Fourth Session of the Asian African Legal Consultative Committee', 2 Yearbook ILC (1961).

UNCTAD, 'Recent Developments in International Investment Agreements (2007–June 2008)', IIA Monitor 2 (2008).

UNCTAD, 'Selected Recent Developments in IIA Arbitration and Human Rights', IIA Monitor No. 2 (2009).

UNCTAD, 'South-South Cooperation in International Investment Arrangements', UNCTAD Series on International Investment Policies for Development (2005).

UNCTAD, 'State Contracts', UNCTAD Series on Issues in International Investment Agreements (2004).

UNCTAD, 'Bilateral Investment Treaties 1995–2006: Trends in Investment Rulemaking' (2007).

UNCTAD, 'Expropriation', UNCTAD Series on Issues in International Investment Agreements II (2012).

UNCTAD, 'Fair and Equitable Treatment', UNCTAD Series on Issues in International Investment Agreements II, United Nations (2012).

UNCTAD, 'Most-Favoured-nation Treatment', UNCTAD Series on Issues in International Investment Agreements II (2010).

UNCTAD, 'Recent Developments in International Investment Agreements (2008–June 2009)', IIA Monitor No. 3 (2009).

UNCTAD, 'Recent Developments in Investor-State Dispute Settlement' (ISDS), ILA Issue Notes No. 1 (2014).

UNCTAD, 'Recent Trends, in IIAs and ISDS', IIA Issues Note, no. 1, Feb. 2015.

UNCTAD, 'Trends in International Investment Agreements: An Overview' (1999).

UNCTAD, 'World Investment Report' (2014).

VIII   Studies/research papers/thesis/conference papers

Arajärvi, N., 'Changing Customary International Law and the Fluid Nature of Opinio Juris', paper presented at the conference 'The Role of *Opinio Juris* in Customary International Law', Duke-Geneva Institute in Transnational Law, Geneva, 2013.

Bradley, Curtis A., 'The Chronological Paradox, State Preferences, and *Opinio Juris*', paper presented at the conference 'The Role of *Opinio Juris* in Customary International Law', Duke-Geneva Institute in Transnational Law, Geneva, 2013.

Canadian Center for Policy Alternatives, 'NAFTA Chapter 11 Investor-States Disputes' (2010).

Crawford, James, 'The Identification and Development of Customary International Law', ILA British Branch Conference, 2014.

Dumberry, Patrick, *Rules of Customary International Law in the Field of International Investment Law*, SSHRC Research Project, 2012–2014.

Gulati, Mitu, 'How the Courts Find International Custom?', paper presented at the conference 'The Role of *Opinio Juris* in Customary International Law', Duke-Geneva Institute in Transnational Law, Geneva, 2013.

Kammerhofer, Jörg, 'Customary International Law Needs both *Opinio* and *Usus*', paper presented at the conference 'The Role of *Opinio Juris* in Customary International Law', Duke-Geneva Institute in Transnational Law, Geneva, 2013.

Kelly, J. Patrick, 'Opinio Juris in Historical Context', paper presented at the conference 'The Role of *Opinio Juris* in Customary International Law', Duke-Geneva Institute in Transnational Law, Geneva, 2013.

Kuprieieva, Anna, 'Regulatory Freedom and Indirect Expropriation: Seeking Compatibility with Sustainable Development In New Generation of Bilateral Investment Treaties', Master of Laws Thesis, University of Ottawa, 2015.

Lepard, Brian D., 'The Necessity of *opinio juris* in the Formation of Customary International Law', paper presented at the conference 'The Role of *Opinio Juris* in Customary International Law', Duke-Geneva Institute in Transnational Law, Geneva, 2013.

Mendelson, Maurice, 'Does Customary International Law Require *Opinio Juris?*', paper presented at the conference 'The Role of *Opinio Juris* in Customary International Law', Duke-Geneva Institute in Transnational Law, Geneva, 2013.

Merkouris, Panagiotis, *Article 31(3)(c) of the VCLT and the Principle of Systemic Integration*, PhD. thesis, Queen Mary University of London (2010).

Neff, Stephen C., 'Opinio Juris: Three Concepts Chasing a Label', paper presented at the conference 'The Role of *Opinio Juris* in Customary International Law', Duke-Geneva Institute in Transnational Law, Geneva, 2013.

Pauwelyn, J., 'Treaty Regimes and *opinio juris*', paper presented at the conference 'The Role of *Opinio Juris* in Customary International Law', Duke-Geneva Institute in Transnational Law, Geneva, 2013.

Peterson, Luke E. and Gray, Kevin, 'International Human Rights in Bilateral Investment Treaties and Investment Treaty Arbitration', Working Paper for the Swiss Ministry for Foreign Affairs (2003).

Tasioulas, John, 'Custom and Consent', paper presented at the conference 'The Role of *Opinio Juris* in Customary International Law', Duke-Geneva Institute in Transnational Law, Geneva, 2013.

Trachtman, Joel P., 'The Obsolescence of Customary International Law', SSRN Working Paper (2014).

Weisburd, Arthur Mark, 'The International Court of Justice and the Concept of State Practice', UNC Legal Studies Research Paper No. 1282684.

Wuerth, Ingrid, 'National Court Decisions and *Opinio Juris*', paper presented at the conference 'The Role of *Opinio Juris* in Customary International Law', Duke-Geneva Institute in Transnational Law, Geneva, 2013.

IX   Statements by States

Australia, 'Gillard Government Trade Policy Statement: Trading Our Way to More Jobs and Prosperity', Dep't of Foreign Aff. & Trade, 14 April 2011.

Canada, 'Statement on Implementation of NAFTA', in *Canada Gazette*, 1 January 1994.

European Union, 'Updated European Union Guidelines on Promoting Compliance with International Humanitarian Law' (2009/C 303/06), sect. 7.

NAFTA, Free Trade Commission Notes of Interpretation, 31 July 2001.

Netherlands Embassy in Indonesia, 'Termination Bilateral Investment Treaty' (2014).

Norway, 'Comments on the Model for Future Investment Agreements', 2007.

Norway, 'Comments on the Individual Provisions of the Model Agreement', 2015.

Switzerland, Mémoire, JAAC 1979, fasc. 43/IV, no. 113, in : L. Caflisch, 'La pratique suisse en matière de droit international public', *ASDI* 36 (1980), p. 178.

Switzerland, 'Message concernant les accords de promotion et de protection réciproque des investissements avec la Serbie-et-Monténégro, le Guyana, l'Azerbaïdjan, l'Arabie saoudite et la Colombie du 22 septembre 2006', *Feuille Fédérale Suisse* 2006, p. 8023.

Switzerland, 'Message concernant les accords de promotion et de protection réciproque des investissements avec le Kenya et la Syrie', 16 January 2008, *Feuille Fédérale Suisse* 2008, p. 903.

United Kingdom, 'Legal Adviser of the Foreign and Commonwealth Office, statement at the Meeting of National Committees on International Humanitarian Law of Commonwealth States, Nairobi, 20 July 2005', *British YIL* 76 (2005).

United Kingdom 'Statement at the Meeting of National Committees on International Humanitarian Law of Commonwealth States', UK Legal Adviser of the Foreign and Commonwealth Office, 20 July 2005, *British YIL*, 76 (2005) pp. 694–695.

United States, Bellinger, J.B. and Haynes, W.J., 'A US Government Response to the International Committee of the Red Cross Study on Customary International Humanitarian Law', *International Review of the Red Cross* 89 (866) (2007).

United States, 'United States Concludes Review of Model Bilateral Investment Treaty', joint statement issued by the U.S. Department of State and the Office of the United States Trade Representative, 20 April 2012.

United States Statement on Administrative Action, November 1993, p. 141.

X Others

Canadian Press, 'Canada Seeks Review of NAFTA's Chapter 11', 13 December 2000.

ICSID News Release, 'Bolivia Submits a Notice under Article 71 of the ICSID Convention', 16 May 2007. ICSID Press Release, 'Ecuador Submits a Notice Under Article 71 of the ICSID Convention', 9 July 2009.

ICSID Press Release, 'Venezuela Submits a Notice Under Article 71 of the ICSID Convention' 26 January 2012.

Letter of South Africa's Minister of International Relations to Belgium's Ambassador in Pretoria denouncing the South Africa–Belgium/Luxembourg BIT, 7 September 2012.

Letter of the United States to the *ad hoc* annulment Committee, 1 May 2008, in the case of *Siemens A.G.* v. *Argentina*, ICSID Case No. ARB/02/8

Letter of the Swiss Secretariat for Economic Affairs to the ICSID Deputy Secretary-General, 1 October 2003, in *Mealey's: Int'l Arb. Rep.* 19 (2004), p. E3.

Letter of U.S. State Department's Acting Legal Adviser, Mr. Jack B. Tate, to the American Acting Attorney-General, in: *State Dept. Bull.* 26 (1952), p. 984; *A.J.I.L.* 47 (1953), p. 93.

Twain, Mark, 'Cable from London to the Associated Press' (1897), *Bartlett's Familiar Quotations* (15th edn., 1980).

INDEX

rejection of existing rules by,
393–394
and tacit consent, 27–28
'The Newly Independent States and the
Rules of International Law'
(Georges Abi-Saab), 71n58
NGOs (non-governmental
organizations), 119
Nicaragua case. *See Military and*
Paramilitary Activities in and
Around Nicaragua
non-binding resolutions, passed by
international organisations, 262
non-disputing party interventions,
227–235, 424
and arbitral awards, 231–235
relative weight given,
229–231
uniformity in, 231
non-governmental organizations
(NGOs), 119
non-State actors, 117–128
and formation of customary rules,
118–125
international legal personality of
corporations, 125–128
'The Normative Basis of "Fair and
Equitable Treatment"'
(A. Orakhelashvili), 185n374
North American Free Trade
Agreement. *See* NAFTA
North Sea Continental Shelf Cases,
28n74, 134–135, 139, 163n244,
164–165, 167–168, 294–295,
296, 304n67, 307, 312,
347n309
'North-South' BITs, 402–403
Norway, 99n171
Norway Model BIT, 99n171, 253,
255–256, 357n30
'Notes of Interpretation of Certain
Chapter 11 Provisions' (NAFTA),
100n184, 355
Nottebohm case (Liechtenstein
v. Guatamala), 269n861
Nouveaux horizons pour le droit
international des investissements
dans le contexte de la

mondialisation de l'économie
(Thomas Wälde), 337n256
Nuclear Tests Case (Australia
& New Zealand v. France),
209n505, 205
Nuclear Weapons Advisory Opinion,
22, 309

obligations
of corporations, under international
law, 127–128
of States, under BITs, 124
'Obligations Arising for States Without
or Against Their Will'
(C. Tomuschat), 29n81
'The Obsolescence of Customary
International Law' (Joel
P. Trachtman), 89n135
official manuals on legal questions, 214,
217–218
official statements, 235–245
and arbitral awards, 237–245
made before domestic
legislature, 424
made during multilateral
conferences or before
international organisations,
213–214
relative weight given, 235–236
omissions, as State practice, 153–155
opinio juris, 12–13, 292–350
and BITs, 334–350
BITs as evidence of, 418–419
and chronological paradox, 302–305
demonstrated by State practice,
311–316
difficulties assessing, 293–296
and 'double-counting,' 316–321
and formation of custom, 417–420
importance of demonstrating,
305–309
under international law,
293–321
and investor-State arbitration, 9,
321–350, 389–390
lack of, in BITs, 196–200
manifestations of, 309–321
non-treaty sources of, 330–334

Ruggie, John, 366
Rules of Customary International Law in the Field of International Investment Law (P. Dumberry), 113n237
Ryngaert, C., 16n8

Saipem v. Bangladesh, 362, 368n88, 379n150
Salacuse, J. W., 2n6, 76n83, 78n91, 82n107, 111n226, 204n482, 204–205, 402–403n266
Saluka Investments B.V. v. Czech Republic, 382n164
Sanum case, 250
'Saving Customary International Law' (Andrew T. Guzman), 26n60, 34n110, 207n495
Schachter, Oscar, 78–79n94, 163n245, 182, 319, 401–402
Scharf, Michael P., 32n97
Schill, S. W., 65n24, 88n134, 88, 150n181, 149–150n175, 184–185n371
Schmid, M., 218n560
scholars
 on customary rules, 92–96
 on customary status of fair and equitable treatment, 140–145
 on *opinio juris*, 297–302, 337–350
 role in identification of custom, 55–59
 on transformation of rules in BITs to customary rules, 172–176
Schreuer, C., 83, 87n130, 90n143, 248–249, 370–371n100, 373, 375
Schwebel, S. M., 72, 74n76, 75n80, 83n109, 103n191, 138n109, 189, 191, 194, 260–261, 320n158, 358–359n40, 391n208
SD Myers v. Canada, 281–282
Second Report, 2014 (ILC), 120n15, 133n81, 134n88, 135n96, 158, 267n856, 275n900, 278n917, 294n11, 295n18, 306n80, 310n111, 311n112, 312n121, 317n148, 318n152, 320n158, 321n164
'Second Report of the Committee Non-State Actors' (ILA), 123n35

Sempra Energy International v. Argentina, 102n189, 368
Senegal, 146
SGS v. Pakistan, 233
Shahabuddeen, Mohamed, 287n968, 287–288
Shaw, M. N., 271n874, 308n97
Sicula S.p.A. (ELSI) (US v. Italy), 76n81
Siemens A.G. v. Argentina, 227n607
Sinclair, Anthony, 87n130, 370–371n100
Sivakumaran, Sandesh, 119–120n12
Slovakia, 233–234
Sohn, L., 162n242
Sornarajah, M., 94n157, 93–94, 104n194, 104, 107n206, 107n206, 114n245, 175n325, 178n341, 198n433, 197–198, 340n269, 392n211, 392
'The Sources of Foreign Investment Law' (Florian Grisel), 21n31, 285n956
'Sources of International Investment Law' (M. Hirsch), 48n188, 59n246, 287n969, 288n978
Sourgens, F. G., 196n421
South Africa, 219n570, 219n566
'South-South' BITs, 339, 403–404
'South-South Cooperation in International Investment Arrangements,' 339n266
Special Court for Sierra Leone, *Prosecutor v. Norman*, 269n862
'special custom,' 175–176
'specially affected' States, 135–136
Spence International Investments et al v. Costa Rica, 290n993
SPP v Arab Republic of Egypt, 375–376
standard clause, 182–188
State contracts, 124
 arbitration under, 369–374
 legal personality of corporations under, 127
State immunities, 276, 277
'Statement on Implementation of NAFTA' (Canada), 100n185, 334n237, 334

statements, under general international
    law, 12
statements by States, 205–257
    and formation of custom, 422–424
    under international law, 205–216
    in investor-State arbitration,
        216–257
    relative weight given to, 210–211
    sources of, 211n519
    types of, 211–216
State pleadings, 422–423
    and arbitral awards, 224–227
    in arbitration proceedings, 220–235
    in international litigation, 214–215
    relative weight given to, 221–224
    uniformity of, 223–224
State practice, 12, 116–291
    basic requirements of, 128–151
    defined, 118–119
    as extensive and representative,
        133–138
    of fair and equitable treatment
        clauses in BITs, 140–151
    forms of, and their relative weight,
        155–159
    informed by previous court findings,
        46n174
    internal national, 267–283
    within international organisations,
        257–267
    international treaties, 159–205
    investment arbitral awards, 283–291
    and investment arbitration, 8–9
    lack of, in BITs, 196–200
    manifestation of, 152–283
    non-State actors in, 117–128
    omissions as, 153–155
    and opinio juris, 30–38, 311–316,
        341–346
    publicity requirement for, 152–153
    as requirement for formation of
        custom, 413
    research of, 56–57
    statements by States, 205–257
    of States not party to a treaty,
        167–168, 185–186
    time duration requirement for,
        138–139

as uniform and consistent, 129–133
'State Practice and the (Purported)
    Obligation under Customary
    International Law to Provide
    Compensation for Regulatory
    Expropriations' (Matthew
    C. Porterfield), 111n227, 136n100
States
    conduct of, in international
        organisations, 12, 420–421
    double requirement approach of,
        35–38
    expropriation in domestic laws
        of, 113
    internal national practice of, 12,
        420–421
    as international legal personalities,
        125–126
    Model BITs adopted by, 251–257
    obligations of, under BITs, 124
    and opinio juris, 323–325, 346–350
    as persistent objectors, 13, 392–405
    reasons of, for entering treaties, 169,
        335–337
    rejection of BITs representing
        custom by, 200–202
    'specially affected,' 135–136
    under State contracts, 124
    statements by, 205–257
    use of previous court findings by, 47
Statute of the International Court of
    Justice (ICJ)
    Article 38(1), 18–20, 30–31, 42, 116,
        118, 283, 292
    Article 59, 285
Stein, T. L., 394–395, 404n278
Stern, B., 44n160, 297, 313n124,
    384n175, 384, 391
subsequent practice, Model BITs as,
    252–253
Supreme Court, Canada, 208
Supreme Court, US, 226
*Suwz, Sociedad General de Aguas de
    Barcelona S.A. and Vivendi
    Universal S.A. v. Argentina,*
    102n189
Switzerland, 233
'Switzerland' (M. Schmid), 218n560

CAMBRIDGE STUDIES IN INTERNATIONAL AND
COMPARATIVE LAW

Books in the series

Printed in Great Britain
by Amazon

31415274R00295